Economic, Social, and Cultural Rights

Pennsylvania Studies in Human Rights

Bert B. Lockwood, Jr., Series Editor

A complete list of books in the series is available from the publisher.

Economic, Social, and Cultural Rights

A Legal Resource Guide

Edited by Scott Leckie and Anne Gallagher

PENN

University of Pennsylvania Press

Philadelphia

Printed in the United States of America on acid-free paper

10 9 8 7 6 5 4 3 2 1

Published by
University of Pennsylvania Press
Philadelphia, Pennsylvania 19104-4112

Library of Congress Cataloging-in-Publication Data

Economic, social, and cultural rights : a legal resource guide / edited by
Scott Leckie and Anne Gallagher.
p. cm.—(Pennsylvania studies in human rights)
Includes index
ISBN-13: 978-0-8122-3916-4
ISBN-10: 0-8122-3916-4 (cloth : alk. paper)
1. Human rights—Sources. I. Leckie, Scott. II. Gallagher, Anne. III. Series
K3238 .E27 2006
341.4′8—dc22 2005045653

Contents

Foreword

Virginia B. Dandan

In my position as Chairperson of the UN Committee on Economic, Social and Cultural Rights, I have come to understand how the Covenant on Economic, Social and Cultural Rights (and other texts supporting these rights) are far from the listless and defeated documents that some commentators would like us to believe they are. The promise of the Covenant to the billions of people who cannot be said to enjoy the full spectrum of human rights, remains as much a source of hope as it was when adopted decades ago. Indeed, my faith in the Covenant and the legal, economic and social order it was designed to facilitate has only grown during my years working in the Committee.

I am convinced that countries which wish to have societies where the social, economic and cultural rights of everyone are addressed, where income and wealth distribution are equitable enough to ensure that no one goes hungry or becomes homeless and where economic, social and cultural rights are treated as seriously as civil and political rights, can use the Covenant and the norms and principles it so eloquently establishes, as the basis for a framework of national social justice.

However, for too many States and even human rights NGOs, economic, social and cultural rights have long been considered secondary to civil and political rights. While law and policy have widely recognised these rights (as evidenced by the contents of this resource guide), it remains far too easy for Governments to ignore their freely-undertaken obligations to secure these rights for those most in need. It is indeed true that much progress has been made in recent years with respect to ESC rights. However, it is equally true that despite these advances, the violations of ESC rights are still widely perceived as inevitabilities, as a "normal" state of affairs in an unfair world where goods, resources and power are divided in a grossly inequitable manner. I firmly believe that the years to come will see considerable legal progress, policy progress and even political progress with respect to ESC rights. The sheer scale of the denial of ESC rights in many parts of the world demands that such progress does indeed occur. What worries me much more than this, however, is the increasingly common view of those holding the reigns of power that the lack of enjoyment of ESC rights either has nothing to do with them or, worse yet, that it is the fault of the very people who suffer such indignities. Moves afoot in numerous cities in the world to apply criminal sanctions against homeless persons is but one example of this trend. If the movement for ESC rights is to continue to gain ground—on the ground—it must address this disturbing phenomenon with far greater resolve than it has in the past.

My work as the Chairperson of the UN Committee on Economic, Social and Cultural Rights has enabled me to witness firsthand many of the views of Government delegations concerning their responsibilities to uphold ESC rights. While the performance of some States parties was sadly inadequate, I have more often than not been struck by the clear conviction of many delegates that ESC rights are not empty promises, but are in fact something to be taken very seriously indeed. While some of these sentiments may simply be diplomatic posturing, the longer I work with the Committee the more convinced I become that many Governments would do more to respect and protect ESC rights, *if they could.* While some States continue to resolutely oppose the very nature of ESC rights (fortunately, very few in number), I am increasingly of the belief that the vast majority of States are more committed to ESC rights than many people think. What stops these States from securing rights to housing, food, health and work is not always a lack of political commitment, but rather a global economic system that is heavily stacked against ESC rights.

The past two decades have been hugely beneficial to the privileged, but for the poor and disadvantaged, the last twenty years have been deplorable. Income *inequality* has never been so massive, and the gap between what is possible in terms of ESC rights, and the actual on the ground situation of ESC rights, has equally never been as large as at present. What is needed, therefore, are renewed and vigourous efforts to integrate ESC rights into laws and policies at the national and international levels. Instead of ignoring ESC rights in the development of policy, States need to ask what the impact of a given policy will be on ESC rights, and consequently ensure that no retrogressive measures are undertaken to undermine ESC rights. States need to use ESC rights as the basis for decision-making and not treat them as an afterthought or as an irrelevant or impossible concern. I believe that if ESC rights were to take a more guiding role in the political, economic and legal spheres, the promise of ESC rights would come closer to realisation than ever before. I am confident that this legal resource guide by Scott Leckie and Anne Gallagher will be a solid contribution toward this aim.

Preface

Mary Robinson

Law is, first and foremost, a tool for change. International human rights law provides one of the most important and powerful tools for effecting positive change in the lives of individuals and communities throughout the world.

The growing recognition and acceptance of economic, social and cultural rights has been a significant achievement of the international human rights system. While these rights are still not always accorded the same status as civil and political rights, their importance in securing human welfare and justice is now widely appreciated.

Our understanding of the nature and content of economic, social, and cultural rights has increased tremendously over the past decade. Detailed legal standards have been developed at the regional and international levels. Many of these standards have been extensively supplemented by interpretive texts and other materials from United Nations human rights treaty bodies and special rapporteurs. Nongovernmental organisations and activists have also played a key role in improving our understanding of economic, social, and cultural rights and our ability to use law in securing these rights.

As High Commissioner for Human Rights I came to more fully appreciate the direct relevance of economic, social, and cultural rights to the lives of so many individuals and groups. Works such as this international legal resource guide which aim to make the law accessible to these persons and their advocates are a vital part of the battle to ensure all human rights for all.

Introduction
Why a Legal Resource Guide for Economic, Social, and Cultural Rights?

The notion of human rights has been characterized as one of the defining ideas of modern civilization. Economic, social, and cultural rights are an essential part of the human rights equation. The right to an adequate standard of living, the right to work; the right to education, and the right to health are not optional extras but are fundamentally important to human security, happiness, and fulfillment. The international community has recognized this reality and responded to it by developing a range of legal instruments designed to establish standards in this area. Taken together, these instruments provide a framework for the analysis, interpretation, and enforcement of economic, social, and cultural rights. The basic purpose of this book is to promote economic and social justice by improving accessibility to a legal framework which is still poorly understood.

The persistent neglect of economic, social, and cultural rights by states, intergovernmental bodies and nongovernmental organizations has been well documented. Despite repeated assertions that all rights are "equal, indivisible, interrelated, and interdependent," economic, social, and cultural rights, in comparison with political and civil rights, remain far behind in terms of normative development, monitoring, enforcement. and implementation. For example:

- The international human rights enforcement machinery is much stronger for civil and political rights than it is for economic, social, and cultural rights;
- Violations of civil and political rights are invariably considered more serious than even massive and systematic violations of economic, social, and cultural rights;
- International nongovernmental organisations still only rarely focus on economic, social, and cultural rights issues;
- Few international human rights lawyers have adequate knowledge of, or experience in economic, social, and cultural rights;
- At the national level, economic, social, and cultural rights are much less likely to be protected in constitutions or legislation than civil and political rights, and there are comparatively fewer governmental institutions mandated to protect and promote economic, social, and cultural rights. National courts are almost invariably reluctant to take up issues relating to economic, social, and cultural rights.

It is important to understand the reasons why economic, social, and cultural rights continue to be the poor relation of the international human rights family. Much has been written on this subject and it is generally agreed that political and ideological differences between powerful States as to the nature and effect of such rights have been an important factor in their marginalisation. A range of doctrinal and technical objections to the recognition and enforcement of economic, social, and cultural rights have also been raised. Most commonly, it is asserted that economic, social, and cultural rights are too vague to be characterized as legal obligations; that they are therefore incapable of being protected or upheld ("justiciable"); and that the obligation to guarantee economic, social, and cultural rights is impossible to achieve. These and other issues are examined in detail below.

Principal Rights and Their Primary Sources

Economic, social, and cultural rights are recognized in and protected by a large number of legal instruments. The following paragraphs provide an overview of the principal rights and their primary sources—focusing specifically on the major international and regional treaties. All instruments referred to below are included in this Resource Guide.

The Universal Declaration of Human Rights (UDHR), adopted as a resolution of the General Assembly in 1948, remains one of the original and most important sources of economic, social, and cultural rights. The UDHR specifically identifies the right to social security (Article 22); the right to work (Article 23); the right to rest and leisure (Article 24); the right to an adequate standard of living (Article 25); the right to education (Article 26); and the right to benefits of science and culture (Article 27).

The International Covenant on Economic, Social and Cultural Rights (ICESCR) is the foremost international legal source of these rights. Rights recognized in and protected by this instrument include the right to work and to favorable conditions of work (Articles 6 and 7); the right to organize and take collective labor action (Article 8); the right to social security (Article 9); the right to protection of the family including protection of mothers and children (Article 10); the right to an adequate standards of living including adequate food, clothing, and housing (Article 11); the right to enjoyment of the highest attainable standard of health (Article 12); the right to education (Article 13); and cultural rights including the right to participate in cultural life, to benefit from scientific progress and one's own scientific, literary or artistic production (Article 15).

The International Covenant on Civil and Political Rights, adopted at the same time as the ICESCR, also protects certain core economic, social, and cultural rights including the right to form and join trade unions (Article 22) and the right of ethnic, religious or linguistic minorities to enjoy their own culture, to profess and practice their own religion, and to use their own language (Article 27). The Convention on the Rights of the Child upholds the applicability of many of the rights contained in the ICESCR to children. These include the right to health (Article 24); the right to social security (Article 25); the right to an adequate standard of living (Article 27); the right to education (Article 28); and protection from economic exploitation (Article 32). Of the other major international human rights instruments, several contain provisions which are directly relevant to economic, social, and cultural rights. The Convention on Elimination of all Forms of Racial Discrimination, for example, prohibits discrimination on the basis of racial or ethnic origin with respect to a range of economic, social, and cultural rights. The Convention on the Elimination of Discrimination Against Women affirms the applicability of the full range of economic, social, and cultural rights to women. A broad range of worker-related rights has been developed under the auspices of the International Labour Organization (ILO) and enshrined in ILO Conventions and other legal instruments.

At the regional level, the African Charter on Human and Peoples' Rights protects the right to work (Article 15), the right to health (Article 16), and the right to education (Article 17). The European Social Charter protects the full range of economic, social, and cultural rights including the right to work, to favorable conditions of work, and to organize and take collective labor action (Articles 1–10); the right to health (Article 11); the right to social security, social and medical assistance, and social welfare services (Articles 12–14); and protection of especially vulnerable groups (Articles 15–17, 19). Similar protections are contained in the Protocol of San Salvador, developed within the Inter-American Human Rights system.

Understanding Economic, Social, and Cultural Rights: The Importance of Secondary Sources

One of the criticisms often leveled against economic, social, and cultural rights concerns their alleged "vagueness." While such criticisms may occasionally be politically motivated, they do address an important point. The need for specificity in terms of defining human rights is very real. It is only through understanding the content of a right that one can draw conclusions as to the nature of a State's obligations with respect to that right, the ways in which that right can be violated and the means by which it can be most effectively implemented.

In addition to the standards outlined above, there exists a wide range of secondary legal resources which provide valuable guidance on understanding the nature and implications of economic, social, and cultural rights. One of the most important sources of such information is the United Nations Committee on Economic, Social and Cultural Rights which is responsible for overseeing the implementation of the ICESCR. Through its work, the Committee has made considerable progress in developing the normative content of the key economic, social, and cultural rights; in interpreting the obligations of States Parties, and in identifying the actions that contribute to both violation and fulfillment of those obligations. Its key pronouncements (usually in the form of "general comments") are reproduced in this Guide along with General Comments of other Human Rights Treaty Bodies which are relevant to economic, social, and cultural rights.

The work of the Committee on Economic, Social and Cultural Rights has been supplemented by efforts of international legal experts and scholars to formulate detailed principles on implementation of economic, social, and cultural rights. Two of the most important documents to emerge from this work are the Limburg Principles on the

Implementation of the International Covenant on Economic, Social and Cultural Rights (1987) and the Maastricht Guidelines on Violations of Economic, Social and Cultural Rights (1997)–both included in the present compilation. The Limburg Principles delineate the general contours of possible violations of economic, social, and cultural rights and have been extensively used within national legal systems as an interpretive tool. The Maastricht Guidelines build upon the Limburg Principles by seeking to identify in detail the legal implications of acts and omissions amounting to violations of economic, social, and cultural rights.

The various United Nations Special Rapporteurs appointed by the Commission on Human Rights and its Sub-Commission have also played a significant role in promoting a common understanding of obligations and entitlements inherent in economic, social, and cultural rights. The Resource Guide includes extracts from reports of key rapporteurs including the Special Rapporteur on the Realization of Economic, Social and Cultural Rights; the Special Rapporteur on the Right to Adequate Housing; the Special Rapporteur on the Right to Education; and the Special Rapporteur on Violence Against Women.

Understanding the Legal Implications of Economic, Social, and Cultural Rights

Economic, social, and cultural rights are legally protected in binding, universally accepted treaties. Accordingly, and as explained in more detail in the following section, States are under a legal obligation to respect, protect, and fulfill these rights. There has been considerable discussion (and disagreement) as to the exact nature of State's obligations vis-à-vis implementation of economic, social, and cultural rights. Most attention on this point has been given to the ICESCR. In relation to that instrument, the primary and secondary documentation contained in the Resource Guide supports the following positions:

- States Parties are required to take "progressive action" toward fulfillment of the rights contained in the ICESCR. While this provision represents an acknowledgement that immediate fulfillment may not be possible, it does not permit postponement of positive action. States parties must be able to show that genuine efforts are being made in good faith to secure the rights set out in the Covenant. The burden of proof in such situations rests with the State and not with the individual claiming breach.
- The prohibition on discrimination in relation to economic, social, and cultural rights is of immediate effect. States parties are required to abolish any laws, policies or practices which affect the enjoyment of economic, social, and cultural rights. They are also required to take action to prevent discrimination by private persons and bodies in any field of public life.
- All States parties, irrespective of their level of economic development, are required to ensure respect for minimum subsistence rights for all. Resource scarcity does not relieve the State of these minimum obligations.
- States Parties should ensure equitable and effective use of (and access to) available

resources. Governmental priorities with regard to resource allocation should therefore be subject to scrutiny.

- Legislative measures alone are insufficient to satisfy the requirements of the ICESCR. Other measures would include providing for judicial remedies where appropriate, as well as administrative, financial, educational, and social measures.

These and other key points relating to the legal implications of economic, social and cultural rights are discussed in the following sub-sections.

Economic, social, and cultural rights and the language of violations

It is important to use the terminology of violations when referring to situations not in conformity with internationally recognized economic, social, and cultural rights. This terminology underscores the cornerstone principles of indivisibility, interdependence, and permeability of all human rights. It also serves to reinforce the central notion that all human rights can be violated and that intentional noncompliance by a State with any clearly defined obligation is a breach of the duty of that State and of the rights of any person affected by such breaches. At the same time, it is essential that the language of violations, whether as a specific label or as a general description is used cautiously. There can be many situations which are far from ideal in terms of economic and social conditions within a given State. However, this does not necessarily mean that the State in question has violated a legal obligation. To label all less-than-perfect situations as violations of human rights, even when the State concerned has acted in good faith and sought to rectify problematic dilemmas relating to social and economic policy would serve only to erode the seriousness of the term. The term "violations" should only be utilized in situations where a legal obligation exists and a corresponding failure to meet that obligation can be identified.

Progressive implementation and the question of immediate obligation

The requirement for progressive realization of economic, social, and cultural rights, as set out in the ICESCR, is occasionally taken to imply that the rights established by that instrument are to be realized only once a country reaches a certain level of economic development. However, this interpretation does not accurately reflect the clear duty, on all States Parties, irrespective of their current levels of development, to move as quickly as possible towards the realization of economic, social, and cultural rights. Any interpretation of "progressive development" which implies a right, by a State Party, to postpone efforts to ensure the enjoyment of the rights in the Covenant would be inconsistent with the clear intention of the ICESCR and therefore in conflict with basic principles of international treaty law.

It is true, of course, that many rights contained in the ICESCR can only ever be implemented progressively. The right to health, for example, is not something that a government will be able to make a reality for all persons overnight. Nevertheless, this does not detract from the requirement that a State Party begin, in good faith, to do everything within its present power to implement that and other rights. At the same time, it is evident that certain aspects of economic, social, and cultural rights *are*, in fact, capable of immediate implementation. For example, there is no reason why the nondiscrimination clause of the ICESCR should not become immediately effective. In the same way, States Parties would be considered to be under an immediate duty to refrain from actively violating economic, social, and cultural rights or withdrawing legal and other protections relating to these rights. The Committee on Economic, Social and Cultural Rights has asserted that this duty exists independently of an increase in available resources and thus recognizes that all existing resources must be devoted in the most effective way possible toward the realization of the rights enshrined in the Covenant.

In summary, and as affirmed in the Limburgh Principles (21–24), States Parties are required to move as expeditiously and effectively as possible towards the goal of realizing fully the economic, social, and cultural rights established pursuant to the Covenant. This obligation exists independent of any increase in available resources. Any "deliberately retrogressive measures" affecting these rights can only be justified by reference to the totality of the rights provided for in the Covenant and in the context of the full utilization of a state's maximum available resources.

Implementation to the maximum of available resources

Along with the progressive realization provision, the 'available resources' standard is often used to justify or excuse State failure to implement economic, social, and cultural rights. However, as recognized in the Limburg Principles (see Principles 25–28), this requirement obliges States Parties to ensure minimum subsistence rights for everyone, regardless of the level of economic development in a given country and is by no means intended as an escape clause for less developed countries. The term "available resources" applies both to domestic resources and to any international economic or technical assistance or co-operation available to a State Party. In the use of the available resources due priority should be given to the realization of rights recognized in the Covenant, considering the need to assure to everyone the satisfaction of subsistence requirements as well as the provision of essential services.

The Maastricht Guidelines further confirm that resource scarcity does not relieve States of certain minimum obligations in respect of the implementation of economic, social, and cultural rights (Guideline 10). The Committee on Economic, Social and Cultural Rights has taken a similar view in its General Comment No. 4 (see especially paragraphs 14 and 15).

Public expenditure has often been viewed as the only major "resource" which a State must use toward securing the rights found in the Covenant. As crucial as this resource is many other resources can also be devoted towards this end. Public expenditure will, however, always remain central to the realization of economic, social, and cultural rights and is therefore a logical focus of attention. The Committee on Economic, Social and Cultural Rights has implied that where there is no apparent justification for a reduction in public expenditure, the State might be considered to have violated its obligations under the Covenant.

The question of justiciability

Justiciability in this context refers to the capacity of economic, social, and cultural rights to be recognized and defended legally. Those opposed to legal recognition of economic, social, and cultural rights have argued that the relevant norms and the obligations they create are too vague to become the subject of legal argument or action. Such views have, in a sense been self-fulfilling: a belief in the non-justiciability of economic, social, and cultural rights has deterred national courts from dealing with such issues and thereby from developing the jurisprudence which facilitates judicial consideration.

While some of the legal issues surrounding the justiciability question are yet to be settled, there is a growing international acceptance of the justiciability of economic, social, and cultural rights, based particularly on the frequent consideration of these matters by national courts. The Committee on Economic, Social and Cultural Rights has asserted in its General Comment No. 3 that "Among the measures which might be considered appropriate, in addition to legislation, is the provision of judicial remedies with respect to the rights which may, in accordance with the national legal system, to be justiciable." The Committee also indicated that a number of articles within the Covenant are capable of immediate implementation, including articles 3, 7(a)(i), 8, 10(3), 13(2)(a), 13(3), 13(4), and 15(3).

While the norms found in the Covenant on Economic, Social and Cultural Rights may or may not be directly subject to a complaint procedure within domestic law, this text must still play a significant role in the application and interpretation of domestic law. At a minimum, the judicial bodies of States parties should consider international human rights law as an interpretive aid to domestic law and ensure that domestic law is interpreted and applied in a manner consistent with the provisions of international human rights instruments to which a State is bound. Judges should ensure that any decisions they issue do not result in the relevant government violating the terms of a treaty which it has ratified.

The failure of a State to provide a judicial or other remedy is certainly not solid evidence of the non-justiciable nature of a particular norm. Even within jurisdictions where justiciability is limited, it would be difficult to sustain arguments that it is primarily the nature of economic, social, and cultural rights, rather than the competence or willingness of the adjudicating body to entertain, examine, and pronounce on claims of these rights that have so often kept such demands away from judicial realms.

The central concept of nondiscrimination

As noted above, States Parties to the CESCR are obliged to immediately address issues relating to discrimination in the realization of economic, social, and cultural rights. The provisions of article 2(2) of the CESCR require States parties to ensure the provision of judicial review and other recourse procedures should discrimination occur. The grounds of discrimination mentioned in this article are not exhaustive and thus it would appear that additional forms of unfair discrimination which are intended or operate to negatively affecting the enjoyment of the rights found in the Covenant should be eliminated. According to the Limburg Principles (Principles 35–40), special measures taken for the sole purpose of securing adequate advancement of certain groups or individuals requiring such protection as may be necessary in order to ensure to such groups and individuals equal enjoyment of economic, social, and cultural rights are not considered discrimination, provided, however, that such measures do not, as a consequence, lead to the maintenance of separate rights for different groups and that such measures shall not be continued after their intended objectives have been achieved. Article 2(2) not only obliges States to desist from discriminatory behavior and to alter laws and practices which allow discrimination. It also applies to the duty of States parties to prohibit private persons and bodies (third parties) from practicing discrimination in any field of public life.

The Obligations to Protect, Respect, Promote, and Fulfill Economic, Social, and Cultural Rights

The analytical framework of "protect, respect, promote, and fulfill" is now widely used to identify specific legal obligations under international human rights law. In the present context, the obligation to *respect* rights requires the State to refrain from committing any act or omission that violates or interferes with enjoyment of economic, social, and cultural rights. The obligation to *protect* rights requires the State to take active measures aimed at preventing violations whether committed by the state or its agents or third parties (see section 6 below). The obligation to *promote* requires the State to take active steps to advocate for, encourage, and otherwise support the advancement of rights, including through ensuring that its own laws and procedures are kept under review. Finally, the obligation to *fulfill* rights requires the State to implement affirmative measures including legislative, judicial, budgetary, and administrative measures which are necessary for the full realization of economic, social, and cultural rights.

The instruments presented in this Resource Guide support the following additional observations regarding the duty of States to respect, protect, promote, and fulfill economic, social, and cultural rights.

Respecting economic, social, and cultural rights

The obligation to *respect* economic, social, and cultural rights constitutes what is essentially a negative duty on the part of the State to neither inpede nor restrict the exercise of these rights. As a consequence of this obligation, rights which are currently enjoyed cannot be arbitrarily revoked in law, principle, or practice.

Elements of the obligation to respect include

- Developing legal protections against the arbitrary deprivation of rights already in place.
- Noninterference in the free exercise of all economic, social, and culural rights.
- Refraining from the adoption of deliverately retrogressive measures which seek or result in an erosion of existing rights.
- Ensuring the full and immediate application of rights to equality of treatment and nondiscrimination.

Protecting economic, social, and cultural rights

The obligation to *protect* economic, social, and cultural rights obliges the State and its agents to prevent the violation of any individual's rights by any other person or entity. Beneficiaries of economic, social, and cultural rights must, therefore, be protected from abuse by a third party capable of infringing these rights. Where such infringements do occur, public authorities should act to preclude further deprivations as well as guaranteeing access to legal remedies for any infringement caused. Effective measures protecting persons from racial or other forms of discrimination, harassment, withdrawal of services, or other threats must also be established.

Generic elements of the protect obligation could include

- Immediate steps to ensure that ongoing violations of economic, social, and cultural rights standards by the State and its agents are, to the maximum extent, ended.
- Immediate steps to ensure that violations of economic, social, and cultural rights by third parties are prevented.
- Ensuring access to impartial legal remedies in cases of alleged violations of economic, social, and cultural rights, by both State and non-State actors.
- Active measures designed to protect all persons against racial or other forms of discrimination, harassment, and withdrawal of services.

Promoting economic, social, and cultural rights

While the duty to respect essentially implies a series of limits of State action and the duty to protect addresses the need to regulate non-State actors, the obligation to *promote* requires governments to recognize the multifaceted human rights dimensions of economic, social, and cultural rights and to take steps to ensure that no measures are taken with the intention of deliberately eroding the legal and practical status of these rights. Moreover, this implies that comprehensive legislative review should take place with a view to identifying existing legislation or policies negatively affecting the exercise of ESC rights subject to repeal. Importantly, the Committee on Economic, Social and Cultural Rights, in its General Comment No. 4 has emphasized that "policies and legislation should not be designed to benefit already advantaged social groups at the expense of others" (para. 11).

Generic elements of the obligation to promote economic, social, and cultural rights could include

- Comprehensive legislative and policy review of all laws, regulations, or other directives in order to identify negative impacts having any negatively bearing on the fulfillment of economic, social, and cultural rights.
- Legislative and policy recognition of economic, social, and cultural rights.
- Development and implementation of targeted policies, designed to ensure the full realization of economic, social, and cultural rights in the shortest possible period for all sectors of society.

- Establishment of benchmarks designed to monitor economic, social and cultural rights, including the development and application of appropriate indicators.
- Special attention, in the development of laws, strategies and programmes, to the economic and social rights of disadvantaged groups, including the elderly, children, the physically disabled, the terminally ill, HIV-positive individuals, persons with persistent medical problems, the mentally ill, victims of natural disasters, and people living in disaster-prone areas.

Fulfilling economic, social, and cultural rights

The obligation to *fulfill* economic, social, and cultural rights obliges States to take proactive and positive measures to facilitate the full enjoyment of these rights within their territory. This obligation may involve consideration of abroad range of fiscal and policy issues such as public expenditure, governmental regulation of the economy, the provision of basic public services and infrastructure, taxation, and other redistributive economic measures. The Committee on Economic, Social and Cultural rights has devoted considerable attention to the nature of the obligation to fulfill in relation to a number of specific rights. including the right to adequate food, the right to health, and the right to education.

Generic elements of the fulfill obligation could include

- The devotion of a reasonable proportion of public expenditure toward the progressive realization of economic, social, and cultural rights.
- The provision by the State of public services, including infrastructure, water, electricity, sanitation, heating, sewage, draining, roads, health care facilities, and emergency services.
- The development of targeted plans of action, with specific time-frame and financial requirements, toward the full realization of economic, social, and cultural rights.

Legal Responsibility for Violations of Economic, Social, and Cultural Rights

The violation of an international legal norm entails responsibility. To what extent can States be held responsible under international law for violations of economic, social, and cultural rights? This is not an abstract issue but one with highly practical implications. The State remains the primary actor in international law. It is the State which bears primary responsibility for implementing economic, social, and cultural rights. It is through the State that individuals may seek protection, and it is against the State that those same individuals may claim reparations or redress for violations. A breach of international law must generally be linked to a State in order for it to be justiciable at the international level. It follows that an act or omission must have some connection to the State if it is to be characterized as a human rights violation—rather than, for example, a criminal offence. In many cases, the involvement of the State in a situation involving violations of economic, social, or cultural rights will be clear. However, the issue is often complicated by the fact that those directly implicated in such violations may be non-State actors—individuals, corporations, and even intergovernmental entities.

There will of course be situations where the involvement of a State in violations of economic, social, and cultural rights is clearly apparent. However, the fact that of non-State involvement in such violations does not prevent States from being held directly and indirectly responsible under international law for the actions of others. Where human rights violations occur with official support or acquiescence then the State is held to be complicit and therefore directly responsible for the violation itself.[1] The direct involvement of the state in large scale forced evictions, for example, would be an example of conduct leading to direct state responsibility—as would public sector corruption which deprives the population of minimum subsistence rights. Another example is provided by discriminatory property ownership or inheritance laws which impoverish women. In situations where the government has allowed the violative act to take place without taking effective measures to prevent it or to punish those responsible, then the State itself is indirectly responsible for the human rights violations flowing from that private act. The question, in this latter case, is whether the State exercised due diligence in preventing and responding to the violative act.[2] Tolerance of abusive labor standards in the private sector could, for example, indirectly engage a State's responsibility for violation of the right to just and favorable conditions of work.

Can non-State entities be held legally responsible for violations of economic, social, and cultural rights? Traditional views of human rights law distinguish between public and private actors. This once widely accepted dichotomy, however, has become blurred such that private actors (often in conjunction with the State) may now be deemed liable for violations of economic, social, and cultural rights.

Intergovernmental organizations also wield considerable influence over the realization of economic, social, and cultural rights. The extent to which intergovernmental organizations (including the World Bank, the IMF, and even the UN Security Council)

1. The jurisprudence on this point is relatively recent and somewhat scant. The usual citation for the principle is the *Velásquez-Rodríguez* case, Judgement of July 29, (1988) Inter-Am. Ct.H.R. (Ser.C) No. 4, para. 182: "What is decisive is whether a violation of the rights recognized by the [Inter-American Convention on Human Rights] has occurred with the support or acquiescence of the government, or whether the State has allowed the act to take place without taking measures to prevent it or to punish those responsible." The U.S. Restatement is more cautious: "a state violates international law if, *as a matter of state policy*, it practices, encourages or condones human rights violations, including genocide and others capable of being committed by non-state actors." American Law Institute, Restatement (Third) of the Foreign Relations law of the United States (1987), para. 702 (emphasis added).

2. "An illegal act which violates human rights and which is initially not directly imputable to a state (for example, because it is the act of a private person or because the person responsible has not been identified) can lead to international responsibility of the State, not because of the act itself but because of the lack of due diligence to prevent the violation or to respond to it" (*Velásquez-Rodríguez*, para. 172). The court went on to say: "This duty to prevent includes all those means of a legal, political, administrative and cultural nature that promote the protection of human rights and ensure that any violations are considered and treated as illegal acts which, as such, may lead to punishment of those responsible and the obligation to indemnify the victim for damages" (para. 175).

can be held directly responsible for human rights violations is yet to be settled. This is an area which requires the attention of international lawyers and activists working to secure economic, social, and cultural rights.

The Maastricht Guidelines deal extensively with the issue of state responsibility for violations of economic, social, and cultural rights, including responsibility for acts of non-State entities (Guideline 18) and intergovernmental organizations (Guideline 19).

The Question of Remedies

It is widely accepted that the violation of any international legal norm gives rise to a right of remedy. Both the Universal Declaration of Human Rights (Article 8) and the Covenant on Civil and Political Rights (Article 2) guarantee that any person whose rights or freedoms are violated shall have an effective remedy. Although the Covenant on Economic, Social and Cultural Rights does not contain a similar provision, the right to a remedy is accepted as a general principle of public international law and can therefore be applied in this context without difficulty. Implementation however, remains generally weak. It is true that an increasing number of States have developed judicial and/or non-judicial remedies for violations of economic, social, and cultural rights. Some have gone even further, entrenching constitutional guarantees which act to prevent legislative acceptance of policies manifestly inconsistent with such guarantees. Overall, however, in most jurisdictions, effective remedies are only rarely provided for. Even where judicial remedies are available, courts have often proven reluctant to adjudicate on such matters.

It is not difficult to argue that those who have been victimized by severe violations of economic, social, and cultural rights are entitled to a remedy. Efforts geared to preventing abuses of economic, social, and cultural rights must emphasize the fundament of securing compensation, restitution, and reparation in the event that such rights are compromised.

A Final Note on the Structure of This Guide

This Guide is divided into two sections. Section One contains full texts or excerpts from 66 international instruments and resources. These include treaties, declarations, supplementary UN standards and resources, world conference documents, interpretive texts, and reports of UN human rights rapporteurs. Section Two contains full texts or excerpts from 12 regional instruments and resources. While the Resource Guide is not exhaustive, it has been designed to be a comprehensive collection of the key legal documents and supporting texts that would be required for any student, scholar, or practitioner of economic, social, and cultural rights.

A special feature of this Guide is the comprehensive index designed to facilitate access to all references of a given term throughout the entire book. By using this index, readers are able to identify quickly each place in which a given term (e.g., "women" or "housing") appears.

All documents appear with their original wording.

Acknowledgments

The editors are deeply appreciative of the assistance provided by many people in the lengthy preparation of this compilation. We would like to thank, in particular, Zarema Arutyunova, Bret Thiele, Corey Sherman, Liliana Luper, and Andrea Lindemann for their excellent editorial efforts and in sharing their good spirits with us. We are also grateful to Rob Lichtman for his extensive technical assistance. Special thanks also go to Virginia Dandan and Mary Robinson for their kindness in providing the Foreword and Preface of this book. We are grateful, as well, to Nancy Ent and Bert Lockwood for their kind assistance and patience and to Roy and HG for reminding us of what is truly important. Thanks most of all to the Harling and KC for the enduring support, wisdom, and infinite joy they provide.

Section One
International Instruments and Resources

A. TREATIES

Chapter 1
International Covenant on Economic, Social and Cultural Rights

Preamble

The States Parties to the present Covenant,

Considering that, in accordance with the principles proclaimed in the Charter of the United Nations, recognition of the inherent dignity and of the equal and inalienable rights of all members of the human family is the foundation of freedom, justice and peace in the world,

Recognizing that these rights derive from the inherent dignity of the human person,

Recognizing that, in accordance with the Universal Declaration of Human Rights, the ideal of free human beings enjoying freedom from fear and want can only be achieved if conditions are created whereby everyone may enjoy his economic, social and cultural rights, as well as his civil and political rights,

Considering the obligation of States under the Charter of the United Nations to promote universal respect for, and observance of, human rights and freedoms,

Realizing that the individual, having duties to other individuals and to the community to which he belongs, is under a responsibility to strive for the promotion and observance of the rights recognized in the present Covenant,

Agree upon the following articles:

Part I

Article 1

1. All peoples have the right of self-determination. By virtue of that right they freely determine their political status and freely pursue their economic, social and cultural development.

Adopted and opened for signature, ratification and accession by General Assembly resolution 2200A (XXI) of 16 December 1966, *entry into force* 3 January 1976, in accordance with Article 27.

2. All peoples may, for their own ends, freely dispose of their natural wealth and resources without prejudice to any obligations arising out of international economic co-operation, based upon the principle of mutual benefit, and international law. In no case may a people be deprived of its own means of subsistence.

3. The States Parties to the present Covenant, including those having responsibility for the administration of Non-Self-Governing and Trust Territories, shall promote the realization of the right of self-determination, and shall respect that right, in conformity with the provisions of the Charter of the United Nations.

Part II

Article 2

1. Each State Party to the present Covenant undertakes to take steps, individually and through international assistance and co-operation, especially economic and technical, to the maximum of its available resources, with a view to achieving progressively the full realization of the rights recognized in the present Covenant by all appropriate means, including particularly the adoption of legislative measures.

2. The States Parties to the present Covenant undertake to guarantee that the rights enunciated in the present Covenant will be exercised without discrimination of any kind as to race, colour, sex, language, religion, political or other opinion, national or social origin, property, birth or other status.

3. Developing countries, with due regard to human rights and their national economy, may determine to what extent they would guarantee the economic rights recognized in the present Covenant to non-nationals.

Article 3

The States Parties to the present Covenant undertake to ensure the equal right of men and women to the enjoyment of all economic, social and cultural rights set forth in the present Covenant.

Article 4

The States Parties to the present Covenant recognize that, in the enjoyment of those rights provided by the State in conformity with the present Covenant, the State may subject such rights only to such limitations as are determined by law only in so far as this may be compatible with the nature of these rights and solely for the purpose of promoting the general welfare in a democratic society.

Article 5

1. Nothing in the present Covenant may be interpreted as implying for any State, group or person any right to engage in any activity or to perform any act aimed at the destruction

of any of the rights or freedoms recognized herein, or at their limitation to a greater extent than is provided for in the present Covenant.

2. No restriction upon or derogation from any of the fundamental human rights recognized or existing in any country in virtue of law, conventions, regulations or custom shall be admitted on the pretext that the present Covenant does not recognize such rights or that it recognizes them to a lesser extent.

Part III

Article 6

1. The States Parties to the present Covenant recognize the right to work, which includes the right of everyone to the opportunity to gain his living by work which he freely chooses or accepts, and will take appropriate steps to safeguard this right.

2. The steps to be taken by a State Party to the present Covenant to achieve the full realization of this right shall include technical and vocational guidance and training programmes, policies and techniques to achieve steady economic, social and cultural development and full and productive employment under conditions safeguarding fundamental political and economic freedoms to the individual.

Article 7

The States Parties to the present Covenant recognize the right of everyone to the enjoyment of just and favourable conditions of work which ensure, in particular:

(a) Remuneration which provides all workers, as a minimum, with:

(i) Fair wages and equal remuneration for work of equal value without distinction of any kind, in particular women being guaranteed conditions of work not inferior to those enjoyed by men, with equal pay for equal work;

(ii) A decent living for themselves and their families in accordance with the provisions of the present Covenant;

(b) Safe and healthy working conditions;

(c) Equal opportunity for everyone to be promoted in his employment to an appropriate higher level, subject to no considerations other than those of seniority and competence;

(d) Rest, leisure and reasonable limitation of working hours and periodic holidays with pay, as well as remuneration for public holidays.

Article 8

1. The States Parties to the present Covenant undertake to ensure:

(a) The right of everyone to form trade unions and join the trade union of his choice, subject only to the rules of the organization concerned, for the promotion and protection of his economic and social interests. No restrictions may be placed on the exercise of this right other than those prescribed by law and which are necessary in a democratic society in the interests of national security or public order or for the protection of the rights and freedoms of others;

(b) The right of trade unions to establish national federations or confederations and the right of the latter to form or join international trade-union organizations;

(c) The right of trade unions to function freely subject to no limitations other than those prescribed by law and which are necessary in a democratic society in the interests of national security or public order or for the protection of the rights and freedoms of others;

(d) The right to strike, provided that it is exercised in conformity with the laws of the particular country.

2. This article shall not prevent the imposition of lawful restrictions on the exercise of these rights by members of the armed forces or of the police or of the administration of the State.

3. Nothing in this article shall authorize States Parties to the International Labour Organisation Convention of 1948 concerning Freedom of Association and Protection of the Right to Organize to take legislative measures which would prejudice, or apply the law in such a manner as would prejudice, the guarantees provided for in that Convention.

Article 9

The States Parties to the present Covenant recognize the right of everyone to social security, including social insurance.

Article 10

The States Parties to the present Covenant recognize that:

(a) The widest possible protection and assistance should be accorded to the family, which is the natural and fundamental group unit of society, particularly for its establishment and while it is responsible for the care and education of dependent children. Marriage must be entered into with the free consent of the intending spouses.

(b) Special protection should be accorded to mothers during a reasonable period before and after childbirth. During such period working mothers should be accorded paid leave or leave with adequate social security benefits.

(c) Special measures of protection and assistance should be taken on behalf of all children and young persons without any discrimination for reasons of parentage or other conditions. Children and young persons should be protected from economic and social exploitation. Their employment in work harmful to their morals or health or dangerous to life or likely to hamper their normal development should be punishable by law. States should also set age limits below which the paid employment of child labour should be prohibited and punishable by law.

Article 11

1. The States Parties to the present Covenant recognize the right of everyone to an adequate standard of living for himself and his family, including adequate food, clothing and housing, and to the continuous improvement of living conditions. The States Parties will take appropriate steps to ensure the realization of this right, recognizing to this effect the essential importance of international co-operation based on free consent.

2. The States Parties to the present Covenant, recognizing the fundamental right of everyone to be free from hunger, shall take, individually and through international co-operation, the measures, including specific programmes, which are needed:

(a) To improve methods of production, conservation and distribution of food by making full use of technical and scientific knowledge, by disseminating knowledge of the principles of nutrition and by developing or reforming agrarian systems in such a way as to achieve the most efficient development and utilization of natural resources;

(b) Taking into account the problems of both food-importing and food-exporting countries, to ensure an equitable distribution of world food supplies in relation to need.

Article 12

1. The States Parties to the present Covenant recognize the right of everyone to the enjoyment of the highest attainable standard of physical and mental health.

2. The steps to be taken by the States Parties to the present Covenant to achieve the full realization of this right shall include those necessary for:

(a) The provision for the reduction of the stillbirth-rate and of infant mortality and for the healthy development of the child;

(b) The improvement of all aspects of environmental and industrial hygiene;

(c) The prevention, treatment and control of epidemic, endemic, occupational and other diseases;

(d) The creation of conditions which would assure to all medical service and medical attention in the event of sickness.

Article 13

1. The States Parties to the present Covenant recognize the right of everyone to education. They agree that education shall be directed to the full development of the human personality and the sense of its dignity, and shall strengthen the respect for human rights and fundamental freedoms. They further agree that education shall enable all persons to participate effectively in a free society, promote understanding,

tolerance and friendship among all nations and all racial, ethnic or religious groups, and further the activities of the United Nations for the maintenance of peace.

2. The States Parties to the present Covenant recognize that, with a view to achieving the full realization of this right:

(a) Primary education shall be compulsory and available free to all;

(b) Secondary education in its different forms, including technical and vocational secondary education, shall be made generally available and accessible to all by every appropriate means, and in particular by the progressive introduction of free education;

(c) Higher education shall be made equally accessible to all, on the basis of capacity, by every appropriate means, and in particular by the progressive introduction of free education;

(d) Fundamental education shall be encouraged or intensified as far as possible for those persons who have not received or completed the whole period of their primary education;

(e) The development of a system of schools at all levels shall be actively pursued, an adequate fellowship system shall be established, and the material conditions of teaching staff shall be continuously improved.

3. The States Parties to the present Covenant undertake to have respect for the liberty of parents and, when applicable, legal guardians to choose for their children schools, other than those established by the public authorities, which conform to such minimum educational standards as may be laid down or approved by the State and to ensure the religious and moral education of their children in conformity with their own convictions.

4. No part of this article shall be construed so as to interfere with the liberty of individuals and bodies to establish and direct educational institutions, subject always to the observance of the principles set forth in paragraph 1 of this article and to the requirement that the education given in such institutions shall conform to such minimum standards as may be laid down by the State.

Article 14

Each State Party to the present Covenant which, at the time of becoming a Party, has not been able to secure in its metropolitan territory or other territories under its jurisdiction compulsory primary education, free of charge, undertakes, within two years, to work out and adopt a detailed plan of action for the progressive implementation, within a reasonable number of years, to be fixed in the plan, of the principle of compulsory education free of charge for all.

Article 15

1. The States Parties to the present Covenant recognize the right of everyone:

(a) To take part in cultural life;

(b) To enjoy the benefits of scientific progress and its applications;

(c) To benefit from the protection of the moral and material interests resulting from any scientific, literary or artistic production of which he is the author.

2. The steps to be taken by the States Parties to the present Covenant to achieve the full realization of this right shall include those necessary for the conservation, the development and the diffusion of science and culture.

3. The States Parties to the present Covenant undertake to respect the freedom indispensable for scientific research and creative activity.

4. The States Parties to the present Covenant recognize the benefits to be derived from the encouragement and development of international contacts and co-operation in the scientific and cultural fields.

Part IV

Article 16

1. The States Parties to the present Covenant undertake to submit in conformity with this part of the Covenant reports on the measures which they have adopted and the progress made in achieving the observance of the rights recognized herein.

2. (a) All reports shall be submitted to the Secretary-General of the United Nations, who shall transmit copies to the Economic and Social Council for consideration in accordance with the provisions of the present Covenant;

(b) The Secretary-General of the United Nations shall also transmit to the specialized agencies copies of the reports, or any relevant parts therefrom, from States Parties to the present Covenant which are also members of these specialized agencies in so far as these reports, or parts therefrom, relate to any matters which fall within the responsibilities of the said agencies in accordance with their constitutional instruments.

Article 17

1. The States Parties to the present Covenant shall furnish their reports in stages, in accordance with a programme to be established by the Economic and Social Council within one year of the entry into force of the present Covenant after consultation with the States Parties and the specialized agencies concerned.

2. Reports may indicate factors and difficulties affecting the degree of fulfilment of obligations under the present Covenant.

3. Where relevant information has previously been furnished to the United Nations or to any specialized agency by any State Party to the present Covenant, it will not be necessary to reproduce that information, but a precise reference to the information so furnished will suffice.

Article 18

Pursuant to its responsibilities under the Charter of the United Nations in the field of human rights and fundamental freedoms, the Economic and Social Council may make arrangements with the specialized agencies in respect of their reporting to it on the progress made in achieving the observance of the provisions of the present Covenant falling within the scope of their activities. These reports may include particulars of decisions and recommendations on such implementation adopted by their competent organs.

Article 19

The Economic and Social Council may transmit to the Commission on Human Rights for study and general recommendation or, as appropriate, for information the reports concerning human rights submitted by States in accordance with Articles 16 and 17, and those concerning human rights submitted by the specialized agencies in accordance with Article 18.

Article 20

The States Parties to the present Covenant and the specialized agencies concerned may submit comments to the Economic and Social Council on any general recommendation under Article 19 or reference to such general recommendation in any report of the Commission on Human Rights or any documentation referred to therein.

Article 21

The Economic and Social Council may submit from time to time to the General Assembly reports with recommendations of a general nature and a summary of the information received from the States Parties to the present Covenant and the specialized agencies on the measures taken and the progress made in achieving general observance of the rights recognized in the present Covenant.

Article 22

The Economic and Social Council may bring to the attention of other organs of the United Nations, their subsidiary organs and specialized agencies concerned with furnishing technical assistance any matters arising out of the reports referred to in this part of the present Covenant which may assist such bodies in deciding, each within its field of competence, on the advisability of international measures likely to contribute to the effective progressive implementation of the present Covenant.

Article 23

The States Parties to the present Covenant agree that international action for the achievement of the rights recognized in the present Covenant includes such methods as the conclusion of conventions, the adoption of recommendations, the furnishing of technical assistance and the holding of regional meetings and technical meetings for the purpose of consultation and study organized in conjunction with the Governments concerned.

Article 24

Nothing in the present Covenant shall be interpreted as impairing the provisions of the Charter of the United Nations and of the constitutions of the specialized agencies which define the respective responsibilities of the various organs of the United Nations and of the specialized agencies in regard to the matters dealt with in the present Covenant.

Article 25

Nothing in the present Covenant shall be interpreted as impairing the inherent right of all peoples to enjoy and utilize fully and freely their natural wealth and resources.

Part V

Article 26

1. The present Covenant is open for signature by any State Member of the United Nations or member of any of its specialized agencies, by any State Party to the Statute of the International Court of Justice, and by any other State which has been invited by the General Assembly of the United Nations to become a party to the present Covenant.

2. The present Covenant is subject to ratification. Instruments of ratification shall be deposited with the Secretary-General of the United Nations.

3. The present Covenant shall be open to accession by any State referred to in paragraph 1 of this article.

4. Accession shall be effected by the deposit of an instrument of accession with the Secretary-General of the United Nations.

5. The Secretary-General of the United Nations shall inform all States which have signed the present Covenant or acceded to it of the deposit of each instrument of ratification or accession.

Article 27

1. The present Covenant shall enter into force three months after the date of the deposit with the Secretary-General of the United Nations of the thirty-fifth instrument of ratification or instrument of accession.

2. For each State ratifying the present Covenant or acceding to it after the deposit of the thirty-fifth instrument of ratification or instrument of accession, the present Covenant shall enter into force three months after the date of the deposit of its own instrument of ratification or instrument of accession.

Article 28

The provisions of the present Covenant shall extend to all parts of federal States without any limitations or exceptions.

Article 29

1. Any State Party to the present Covenant may propose an amendment and file it with the Secretary-General of the United Nations. The Secretary-General shall thereupon communicate any proposed amendments to the States Parties to the present Covenant with a request that they notify him whether they favour a conference of States Parties for the purpose of considering and voting upon the proposals. In the event that at least one third of the States Parties favours such a conference, the Secretary-General shall convene the conference under the auspices of the United Nations. Any amendment adopted by a majority of the States Parties present and voting at the conference shall be submitted to the General Assembly of the United Nations for approval.

2. Amendments shall come into force when they have been approved by the General Assembly of the United Nations and accepted by a two-thirds majority of the States Parties to the present Covenant in accordance with their respective constitutional processes.

3. When amendments come into force they shall be binding on those States Parties which have accepted them, other States Parties still being bound by the provisions of the present Covenant and any earlier amendment which they have accepted.

Article 30

Irrespective of the notifications made under Article 26, paragraph 5, the Secretary-General of the United Nations shall inform all States referred to in paragraph 1 of the same article of the following particulars:

(a) Signatures, ratifications and accessions under Article 26;

(b) The date of the entry into force of the present Covenant under Article 27 and the date of the entry into force of any amendments under Article 29.

Article 31

1. The present Covenant, of which the Chinese, English, French, Russian and Spanish texts are equally authentic, shall be deposited in the archives of the United Nations.

2. The Secretary-General of the United Nations shall transmit certified copies of the present Covenant to all States referred to in Article 26.

Chapter 2
Convention on the Rights of the Child

Preamble

The States Parties to the present Convention,

Considering that, in accordance with the principles proclaimed in the Charter of the United Nations, recognition of the inherent dignity and of the equal and inalienable rights of all members of the human family is the foundation of freedom, justice and peace in the world,

Bearing in mind that the peoples of the United Nations have, in the Charter, reaffirmed their faith in fundamental human rights and in the dignity and worth of the human person, and have determined to promote social progress and better standards of life in larger freedom,

Recognizing that the United Nations has, in the Universal Declaration of Human Rights and in the International Covenants on Human Rights, proclaimed and agreed that everyone is entitled to all the rights and freedoms set forth therein, without distinction of any kind, such as race, colour, sex, language, religion, political or other opinion, national or social origin, property, birth or other status,

Recalling that, in the Universal Declaration of Human Rights, the United Nations has proclaimed that childhood is entitled to special care and assistance,

Convinced that the family, as the fundamental group of society and the natural environment for the growth and well-being of all its members and particularly children, should be afforded the necessary protection and assistance so that it can fully assume its responsibilities within the community,

Recognizing that the child, for the full and harmonious development of his or her personality, should grow up in a family environment, in an atmosphere of happiness, love and understanding,

Considering that the child should be fully prepared to live an individual life in society, and brought up in the spirit of the ideals proclaimed in the Charter of the United

Adopted and opened for signature, ratification and accession by General Assembly resolution 44/25 of 20 November 1989, *entry into force* 2 September 1990, in accordance with Article 49.

Nations, and in particular in the spirit of peace, dignity, tolerance, freedom, equality and solidarity,

Bearing in mind that the need to extend particular care to the child has been stated in the Geneva Declaration of the Rights of the Child of 1924 and in the Declaration of the Rights of the Child adopted by the General Assembly on 20 November 1959 and recognized in the Universal Declaration of Human Rights, in the International Covenant on Civil and Political Rights (in particular in Articles 23 and 24), in the International Covenant on Economic, Social and Cultural Rights (in particular in Article 10) and in the statutes and relevant instruments of specialized agencies and international organizations concerned with the welfare of children,

Bearing in mind that, as indicated in the Declaration of the Rights of the Child, "the child, by reason of his physical and mental immaturity, needs special safeguards and care, including appropriate legal protection, before as well as after birth,"

Recalling the provisions of the Declaration on Social and Legal Principles relating to the Protection and Welfare of Children, with Special Reference to Foster Placement and Adoption Nationally and Internationally; the United Nations Standard Minimum Rules for the Administration of Juvenile Justice (The Beijing Rules); and the Declaration on the Protection of Women and Children in Emergency and Armed Conflict,

Recognizing that, in all countries in the world, there are children living in exceptionally difficult conditions, and that such children need special consideration,

Taking due account of the importance of the traditions and cultural values of each people for the protection and harmonious development of the child,

Recognizing the importance of international co-operation for improving the living conditions of children in every country, in particular in the developing countries,

Have agreed as follows:

Part I

Article 1

For the purposes of the present Convention, a child means every human being below the age of eighteen years unless under the law applicable to the child, majority is attained earlier.

Article 2

1. States Parties shall respect and ensure the rights set forth in the present Convention to each child within their jurisdiction without discrimination of any kind, irrespective of the child's or his or her parent's or legal guardian's race, colour, sex, language, religion, political or other opinion, national, ethnic or social origin, property, disability, birth or other status.

2. States Parties shall take all appropriate measures to ensure that the child is protected against all forms of discrimination or punishment on the basis of the status, activities, expressed opinions, or beliefs of the child's parents, legal guardians, or family members.

Article 3

1. In all actions concerning children, whether undertaken by public or private social welfare institutions, courts of law, administrative authorities or legislative bodies, the best interests of the child shall be a primary consideration.

2. States Parties undertake to ensure the child such protection and care as is necessary for his or her well-being, taking into account the rights and duties of his or her parents, legal guardians, or other individuals legally responsible for him or her, and, to this end, shall take all appropriate legislative and administrative measures.

3. States Parties shall ensure that the institutions, services and facilities responsible for the care or protection of children shall conform with the standards established by competent authorities, particularly in the areas of safety, health, in the number and suitability of their staff, as well as competent supervision.

Article 4

States Parties shall undertake all appropriate legislative, administrative, and other measures for the implementation of the rights recognized in the present Convention. With regard to economic, social and cultural rights, States Parties shall undertake such measures to the maximum extent of their available resources and, where needed, within the framework of international co-operation.

Article 5

States Parties shall respect the responsibilities, rights and duties of parents or, where applicable, the members of the extended family or community as provided for by local custom, legal guardians or other persons legally responsible for the child, to provide, in a manner consistent with the evolving capacities of the child, appropriate direction and guidance in the exercise by the child of the rights recognized in the present Convention.

Article 6

1. States Parties recognize that every child has the inherent right to life.

2. States Parties shall ensure to the maximum extent possible the survival and development of the child.

Article 7

1. The child shall be registered immediately after birth and shall have the right from

birth to a name, the right to acquire a nationality and, as far as possible, the right to know and be cared for by his or her parents.

2. States Parties shall ensure the implementation of these rights in accordance with their national law and their obligations under the relevant international instruments in this field, in particular where the child would otherwise be stateless.

Article 8

1. States Parties undertake to respect the right of the child to preserve his or her identity, including nationality, name and family relations as recognized by law without unlawful interference.

2. Where a child is illegally deprived of some or all of the elements of his or her identity, States Parties shall provide appropriate assistance and protection, with a view to re-establishing speedily his or her identity.

Article 9

1. States Parties shall ensure that a child shall not be separated from his or her parents against their will, except when competent authorities subject to judicial review determine, in accordance with applicable law and procedures, that such separation is necessary for the best interests of the child. Such determination may be necessary in a particular case such as one involving abuse or neglect of the child by the parents, or one where the parents are living separately and a decision must be made as to the child's place of residence.

2. In any proceedings pursuant to paragraph 1 of the present article, all interested parties shall be given an opportunity to participate in the proceedings and make their views known.

3. States Parties shall respect the right of the child who is separated from one or both parents to maintain personal relations and direct contact with both parents on a regular basis, except if it is contrary to the child's best interests.

4. Where such separation results from any action initiated by a State Party, such as the detention, imprisonment, exile, deportation or death (including death arising from any cause while the person is in the custody of the State) of one or both parents or of the child, that State Party shall, upon request, provide the parents, the child or, if appropriate, another member of the family with the essential information concerning the whereabouts of the absent member(s) of the family unless the provision of the information would be detrimental to the well-being of the child. States Parties shall further ensure that the submission of such a request shall of itself entail no adverse consequences for the person(s) concerned.

Article 10

1. In accordance with the obligation of States Parties under Article 9, paragraph 1, applications by a child or his or her parents to enter or leave a State Party for the

purpose of family reunification shall be dealt with by States Parties in a positive, humane and expeditious manner. States Parties shall further ensure that the submission of such a request shall entail no adverse consequences for the applicants and for the members of their family.

2. A child whose parents reside in different States shall have the right to maintain on a regular basis, save in exceptional circumstances, personal relations and direct contacts with both parents. Toward that end and in accordance with the obligation of States Parties under Article 9, paragraph 1, States Parties shall respect the right of the child and his or her parents to leave any country, including their own, and to enter their own country. The right to leave any country shall be subject only to such restrictions as are prescribed by law and which are necessary to protect the national security, public order (ordre public), public health or morals or the rights and freedoms of others and are consistent with the other rights recognized in the present Convention.

Article 11

1. States Parties shall take measures to combat the illicit transfer and non-return of children abroad.

2. To this end, States Parties shall promote the conclusion of bilateral or multilateral agreements or accession to existing agreements.

Article 12

1. States Parties shall assure to the child who is capable of forming his or her own views the right to express those views freely in all matters affecting the child, the views of the child being given due weight in accordance with the age and maturity of the child.

2. For this purpose, the child shall in particular be provided the opportunity to be heard in any judicial and administrative proceedings affecting the child, either directly, or through a representative or an appropriate body, in a manner consistent with the procedural rules of national law.

Article 13

1. The child shall have the right to freedom of expression; this right shall include freedom to seek, receive and impart information and ideas of all kinds, regardless of frontiers, either orally, in writing or in print, in the form of art, or through any other media of the child's choice.

2. The exercise of this right may be subject to certain restrictions, but these shall only be such as are provided by law and are necessary:

(a) For respect of the rights or reputations of others; or

(b) For the protection of national security or of public order (ordre public), or of public health or morals.

Article 14

1. States Parties shall respect the right of the child to freedom of thought, conscience and religion.

2. States Parties shall respect the rights and duties of the parents and, when applicable, legal guardians, to provide direction to the child in the exercise of his or her right in a manner consistent with the evolving capacities of the child.

3. Freedom to manifest one's religion or beliefs may be subject only to such limitations as are prescribed by law and are necessary to protect public safety, order, health or morals, or the fundamental rights and freedoms of others.

Article 15

1. States Parties recognize the rights of the child to freedom of association and to freedom of peaceful assembly.

2. No restrictions may be placed on the exercise of these rights other than those imposed in conformity with the law and which are necessary in a democratic society in the interests of national security or public safety, public order (ordre public), the protection of public health or morals or the protection of the rights and freedoms of others.

Article 16

1. No child shall be subjected to arbitrary or unlawful interference with his or her privacy, family, home or correspondence, nor to unlawful attacks on his or her honour and reputation.

2. The child has the right to the protection of the law against such interference or attacks.

Article 17

States Parties recognize the important function performed by the mass media and shall ensure that the child has access to information and material from a diversity of national and international sources, especially those aimed at the promotion of his or her social, spiritual and moral well-being and physical and mental health. To this end, States Parties shall:

(a) Encourage the mass media to disseminate information and material of social and cultural benefit to the child and in accordance with the spirit of Article 29;

(b) Encourage international co-operation in the production, exchange and dissemination of such information and material from a diversity of cultural, national and international sources;

(c) Encourage the production and dissemination of children's books;

(d) Encourage the mass media to have particular regard to the linguistic needs of the child who belongs to a minority group or who is indigenous;

(e) Encourage the development of appropriate guidelines for the protection of the child from information and material injurious to his or her well-being, bearing in mind the provisions of Articles 13 and 18.

Article 18

1. States Parties shall use their best efforts to ensure recognition of the principle that both parents have common responsibilities for the upbringing and development of the child. Parents or, as the case may be, legal guardians, have the primary responsibility for the upbringing and development of the child. The best interests of the child will be their basic concern.

2. For the purpose of guaranteeing and promoting the rights set forth in the present Convention, States Parties shall render appropriate assistance to parents and legal guardians in the performance of their child-rearing responsibilities and shall ensure the development of institutions, facilities and services for the care of children.

3. States Parties shall take all appropriate measures to ensure that children of working parents have the right to benefit from child-care services and facilities for which they are eligible.

Article 19

1. States Parties shall take all appropriate legislative, administrative, social and educational measures to protect the child from all forms of physical or mental violence, injury or abuse, neglect or negligent treatment, maltreatment or exploitation, including sexual abuse, while in the care of parent(s), legal guardian(s) or any other person who has the care of the child.

2. Such protective measures should, as appropriate, include effective procedures for the establishment of social programmes to provide necessary support for the child and for those who have the care of the child, as well as for other forms of prevention and for identification, reporting, referral, investigation, treatment and follow-up of instances of child maltreatment described heretofore, and, as appropriate, for judicial involvement.

Article 20

1. A child temporarily or permanently deprived of his or her family environment, or in whose own best interests cannot be allowed to remain in that environment, shall be entitled to special protection and assistance provided by the State.

2. States Parties shall in accordance with their national laws ensure alternative care for such a child.

3. Such care could include, inter alia, foster placement, kafalah of Islamic law, adoption or if necessary placement in suitable institutions for the care of children. When considering solutions, due regard shall be paid to the desirability of continuity in a child's upbringing and to the child's ethnic, religious, cultural and linguistic background.

Article 21

States Parties that recognize and/or permit the system of adoption shall ensure that the best interests of the child shall be the paramount consideration and they shall:

(a) Ensure that the adoption of a child is authorized only by competent authorities who determine, in accordance with applicable law and procedures and on the basis of all pertinent and reliable information, that the adoption is permissible in view of the child's status concerning parents, relatives and legal guardians and that, if required, the persons concerned have given their informed consent to the adoption on the basis of such counselling as may be necessary;

(b) Recognize that inter-country adoption may be considered as an alternative means of child's care, if the child cannot be placed in a foster or an adoptive family or cannot in any suitable manner be cared for in the child's country of origin;

(c) Ensure that the child concerned by inter-country adoption enjoys safeguards and standards equivalent to those existing in the case of national adoption;

(d) Take all appropriate measures to ensure that, in inter-country adoption, the placement does not result in improper financial gain for those involved in it;

(e) Promote, where appropriate, the objectives of the present article by concluding bilateral or multilateral arrangements or agreements, and endeavour, within this framework, to ensure that the placement of the child in another country is carried out by competent authorities or organs.

Article 22

1. States Parties shall take appropriate measures to ensure that a child who is seeking refugee status or who is considered a refugee in accordance with applicable international or domestic law and procedures shall, whether unaccompanied or accompanied by his or her parents or by any other person, receive appropriate protection and humanitarian assistance in the enjoyment of applicable rights set forth in the present Convention and in other international human rights or humanitarian instruments to which the said States are Parties.

2. For this purpose, States Parties shall provide, as they consider appropriate, co-operation in any efforts by the United Nations and other competent intergovernmental organizations or non-governmental organizations co-operating with the United Nations to protect and assist such a child and to trace the parents or other members of the family of any refugee child in order to obtain information necessary for reunification with his or her family. In cases where no parents or other members of the family

can be found, the child shall be accorded the same protection as any other child permanently or temporarily deprived of his or her family environment for any reason, as set forth in the present Convention.

Article 23

1. States Parties recognize that a mentally or physically disabled child should enjoy a full and decent life, in conditions which ensure dignity, promote self-reliance and facilitate the child's active participation in the community.

2. States Parties recognize the right of the disabled child to special care and shall encourage and ensure the extension, subject to available resources, to the eligible child and those responsible for his or her care, of assistance for which application is made and which is appropriate to the child's condition and to the circumstances of the parents or others caring for the child.

3. Recognizing the special needs of a disabled child, assistance extended in accordance with paragraph 2 of the present article shall be provided free of charge, whenever possible, taking into account the financial resources of the parents or others caring for the child, and shall be designed to ensure that the disabled child has effective access to and receives education, training, health care services, rehabilitation services, preparation for employment and recreation opportunities in a manner conducive to the child's achieving the fullest possible social integration and individual development, including his or her cultural and spiritual development.

4. States Parties shall promote, in the spirit of international cooperation, the exchange of appropriate information in the field of preventive health care and of medical, psychological and functional treatment of disabled children, including dissemination of and access to information concerning methods of rehabilitation, education and vocational services, with the aim of enabling States Parties to improve their capabilities and skills and to widen their experience in these areas. In this regard, particular account shall be taken of the needs of developing countries.

Article 24

1. States Parties recognize the right of the child to the enjoyment of the highest attainable standard of health and to facilities for the treatment of illness and rehabilitation of health. States Parties shall strive to ensure that no child is deprived of his or her right of access to such health care services.

2. States Parties shall pursue full implementation of this right and, in particular, shall take appropriate measures:

(a) To diminish infant and child mortality;

(b) To ensure the provision of necessary medical assistance and health care to all children with emphasis on the development of primary health care;

(c) To combat disease and malnutrition, including within the framework of primary health care, through, inter alia, the application of readily available technology and through the provision of adequate nutritious foods and clean drinking-water, taking into consideration the dangers and risks of environmental pollution;

(d) To ensure appropriate pre-natal and post-natal health care for mothers;

(e) To ensure that all segments of society, in particular parents and children, are informed, have access to education and are supported in the use of basic knowledge of child health and nutrition, the advantages of breastfeeding, hygiene and environmental sanitation and the prevention of accidents;

(f) To develop preventive health care, guidance for parents and family planning education and services.

3. States Parties shall take all effective and appropriate measures with a view to abolishing traditional practices prejudicial to the health of children.

4. States Parties undertake to promote and encourage international co-operation with a view to achieving progressively the full realization of the right recognized in the present article. In this regard, particular account shall be taken of the needs of developing countries.

Article 25

States Parties recognize the right of a child who has been placed by the competent authorities for the purposes of care, protection or treatment of his or her physical or mental health, to a periodic review of the treatment provided to the child and all other circumstances relevant to his or her placement.

Article 26

1. States Parties shall recognize for every child the right to benefit from social security, including social insurance, and shall take the necessary measures to achieve the full realization of this right in accordance with their national law.

2. The benefits should, where appropriate, be granted, taking into account the resources and the circumstances of the child and persons having responsibility for the maintenance of the child, as well as any other consideration relevant to an application for benefits made by or on behalf of the child.

Article 27

1. States Parties recognize the right of every child to a standard of living adequate for the child's physical, mental, spiritual, moral and social development.

2. The parent(s) or others responsible for the child have the primary responsibility to secure, within their abilities and financial capacities, the conditions of living necessary for the child's development.

3. States Parties, in accordance with national conditions and within their means, shall take appropriate measures to assist parents and others responsible for the child to implement this right and shall in case of need provide material assistance and support programmes, particularly with regard to nutrition, clothing and housing.

4. States Parties shall take all appropriate measures to secure the recovery of maintenance for the child from the parents or other persons having financial responsibility for the child, both within the State Party and from abroad. In particular, where the person having financial responsibility for the child lives in a State different from that of the child, States Parties shall promote the accession to international agreements or the conclusion of such agreements, as well as the making of other appropriate arrangements.

Article 28

1. States Parties recognize the right of the child to education, and with a view to achieving this right progressively and on the basis of equal opportunity, they shall, in particular:

(a) Make primary education compulsory and available free to all;

(b) Encourage the development of different forms of secondary education, including general and vocational education, make them available and accessible to every child, and take appropriate measures such as the introduction of free education and offering financial assistance in case of need;

(c) Make higher education accessible to all on the basis of capacity by every appropriate means;

(d) Make educational and vocational information and guidance available and accessible to all children;

(e) Take measures to encourage regular attendance at schools and the reduction of drop-out rates.

2. States Parties shall take all appropriate measures to ensure that school discipline is administered in a manner consistent with the child's human dignity and in conformity with the present Convention.

3. States Parties shall promote and encourage international cooperation in matters relating to education, in particular with a view to contributing to the elimination of ignorance and illiteracy throughout the world and facilitating access to scientific and technical knowledge and modern teaching methods. In this regard, particular account shall be taken of the needs of developing countries.

Article 29

1. States Parties agree that the education of the child shall be directed to:

(a) The development of the child's personality, talents and mental and physical abilities to their fullest potential;

(b) The development of respect for human rights and fundamental freedoms, and for the principles enshrined in the Charter of the United Nations;

(c) The development of respect for the child's parents, his or her own cultural identity, language and values, for the national values of the country in which the child is living, the country from which he or she may originate, and for civilizations different from his or her own;

(d) The preparation of the child for responsible life in a free society, in the spirit of understanding, peace, tolerance, equality of sexes, and friendship among all peoples, ethnic, national and religious groups and persons of indigenous origin;

(e) The development of respect for the natural environment.

2. No part of the present article or Article 28 shall be construed so as to interfere with the liberty of individuals and bodies to establish and direct educational institutions, subject always to the observance of the principle set forth in paragraph 1 of the present article and to the requirements that the education given in such institutions shall conform to such minimum standards as may be laid down by the State.

Article 30

In those States in which ethnic, religious or linguistic minorities or persons of indigenous origin exist, a child belonging to such a minority or who is indigenous shall not be denied the right, in community with other members of his or her group, to enjoy his or her own culture, to profess and practise his or her own religion, or to use his or her own language.

Article 31

1. States Parties recognize the right of the child to rest and leisure, to engage in play and recreational activities appropriate to the age of the child and to participate freely in cultural life and the arts.

2. States Parties shall respect and promote the right of the child to participate fully in cultural and artistic life and shall encourage the provision of appropriate and equal opportunities for cultural, artistic, recreational and leisure activity.

Article 32

1. States Parties recognize the right of the child to be protected from economic exploitation and from performing any work that is likely to be hazardous or to interfere with the child's education, or to be harmful to the child's health or physical, mental, spiritual, moral or social development.

2. States Parties shall take legislative, administrative, social and educational measures to ensure the implementation of the present article. To this end, and having regard to the relevant provisions of other international instruments, States Parties shall in particular:

(a) Provide for a minimum age or minimum ages for admission to employment;

(b) Provide for appropriate regulation of the hours and conditions of employment;

(c) Provide for appropriate penalties or other sanctions to ensure the effective enforcement of the present article.

Article 33

States Parties shall take all appropriate measures, including legislative, administrative, social and educational measures, to protect children from the illicit use of narcotic drugs and psychotropic substances as defined in the relevant international treaties, and to prevent the use of children in the illicit production and trafficking of such substances.

Article 34

States Parties undertake to protect the child from all forms of sexual exploitation and sexual abuse. For these purposes, States Parties shall in particular take all appropriate national, bilateral and multilateral measures to prevent:

(a) The inducement or coercion of a child to engage in any unlawful sexual activity;

(b) The exploitative use of children in prostitution or other unlawful sexual practices;

(c) The exploitative use of children in pornographic performances and materials.

Article 35

States Parties shall take all appropriate national, bilateral and multilateral measures to prevent the abduction of, the sale of or traffic in children for any purpose or in any form.

Article 36

States Parties shall protect the child against all other forms of exploitation prejudicial to any aspects of the child's welfare.

Article 37

States Parties shall ensure that:

(a) No child shall be subjected to torture or other cruel, inhuman or degrading treatment or punishment. Neither capital punishment nor life imprisonment without possibility of release shall be imposed for offences committed by persons below eighteen years of age;

(b) No child shall be deprived of his or her liberty unlawfully or arbitrarily. The arrest, detention or imprisonment of a child shall be in conformity with the law and shall be used only as a measure of last resort and for the shortest appropriate period of time;

(c) Every child deprived of liberty shall be treated with humanity and respect for the inherent dignity of the human person, and in a manner which takes into account the needs of persons of his or her age. In particular, every child deprived of liberty shall be separated from adults unless it is considered in the child's best interest not to do so and shall have the right to maintain contact with his or her family through correspondence and visits, save in exceptional circumstances;

(d) Every child deprived of his or her liberty shall have the right to prompt access to legal and other appropriate assistance, as well as the right to challenge the legality of the deprivation of his or her liberty before a court or other competent, independent and impartial authority, and to a prompt decision on any such action.

Article 38

1. States Parties undertake to respect and to ensure respect for rules of international humanitarian law applicable to them in armed conflicts which are relevant to the child.

2. States Parties shall take all feasible measures to ensure that persons who have not attained the age of fifteen years do not take a direct part in hostilities.

3. States Parties shall refrain from recruiting any person who has not attained the age of fifteen years into their armed forces. In recruiting among those persons who have attained the age of fifteen years but who have not attained the age of eighteen years, States Parties shall endeavour to give priority to those who are oldest.

4. In accordance with their obligations under international humanitarian law to protect the civilian population in armed conflicts, States Parties shall take all feasible measures to ensure protection and care of children who are affected by an armed conflict.

Article 39

States Parties shall take all appropriate measures to promote physical and psychological recovery and social reintegration of a child victim of: any form of neglect, exploitation, or abuse; torture or any other form of cruel, inhuman or degrading treatment or punishment; or armed conflicts. Such recovery and reintegration shall take place in an environment which fosters the health, self-respect and dignity of the child.

Article 40

1. States Parties recognize the right of every child alleged as, accused of, or recognized as having infringed the penal law to be treated in a manner consistent with the promotion of the child's sense of dignity and worth, which reinforces the child's respect for the human rights and fundamental freedoms of others and which takes into account the child's age and the desirability of promoting the child's reintegration and the child's assuming a constructive role in society.

2. To this end, and having regard to the relevant provisions of international instruments, States Parties shall, in particular, ensure that:

(a) No child shall be alleged as, be accused of, or recognized as having infringed the penal law by reason of acts or omissions that were not prohibited by national or international law at the time they were committed;

(b) Every child alleged as or accused of having infringed the penal law has at least the following guarantees:

(i) To be presumed innocent until proven guilty according to law;

(ii) To be informed promptly and directly of the charges against him or her, and, if appropriate, through his or her parents or legal guardians, and to have legal or other appropriate assistance in the preparation and presentation of his or her defence;

(iii) To have the matter determined without delay by a competent, independent and impartial authority or judicial body in a fair hearing according to law, in the presence of legal or other appropriate assistance and, unless it is considered not to be in the best interest of the child, in particular, taking into account his or her age or situation, his or her parents or legal guardians;

(iv) Not to be compelled to give testimony or to confess guilt; to examine or have examined adverse witnesses and to obtain the participation and examination of witnesses on his or her behalf under conditions of equality;

(v) If considered to have infringed the penal law, to have this decision and any measures imposed in consequence thereof reviewed by a higher competent, independent and impartial authority or judicial body according to law;

(vi) To have the free assistance of an interpreter if the child cannot understand or speak the language used;

(vii) To have his or her privacy fully respected at all stages of the proceedings.

3. States Parties shall seek to promote the establishment of laws, procedures, authorities and institutions specifically applicable to children alleged as, accused of, or recognized as having infringed the penal law, and, in particular:

(a) The establishment of a minimum age below which children shall be presumed not to have the capacity to infringe the penal law;

(b) Whenever appropriate and desirable, measures for dealing with such children without resorting to judicial proceedings, providing that human rights and legal safeguards are fully respected.

4. A variety of dispositions, such as care, guidance and supervision orders; counselling; probation; foster care; education and vocational training programmes and other alternatives to institutional care shall be available to ensure that children are dealt with in a manner appropriate to their well-being and proportionate both to their circumstances and the offence.

Article 41

Nothing in the present Convention shall affect any provisions which are more conducive to the realization of the rights of the child and which may be contained in:

(a) The law of a State party; or

(b) International law in force for that State.

Part II

Article 42

States Parties undertake to make the principles and provisions of the Convention widely known, by appropriate and active means, to adults and children alike.

Article 43

1. For the purpose of examining the progress made by States Parties in achieving the realization of the obligations undertaken in the present Convention, there shall be established a Committee on the Rights of the Child, which shall carry out the functions hereinafter provided.

2. The Committee shall consist of ten experts of high moral standing and recognized competence in the field covered by this Convention. The members of the Committee shall be elected by States Parties from among their nationals and shall serve in their personal capacity, consideration being given to equitable geographical distribution, as well as to the principal legal systems.

3. The members of the Committee shall be elected by secret ballot from a list of persons nominated by States Parties. Each State Party may nominate one person from among its own nationals.

4. The initial election to the Committee shall be held no later than six months after the date of the entry into force of the present Convention and thereafter every second year. At least four months before the date of each election, the Secretary-General of the United Nations shall address a letter to States Parties inviting them to submit their nominations within two months. The Secretary-General shall subsequently prepare a list in alphabetical order of all persons thus nominated, indicating States Parties which have nominated them, and shall submit it to the States Parties to the present Convention.

5. The elections shall be held at meetings of States Parties convened by the Secretary-General at United Nations Headquarters. At those meetings, for which two thirds of States Parties shall constitute a quorum, the persons elected to the Committee shall be those who obtain the largest number of votes and an absolute majority of the votes of the representatives of States Parties present and voting.

6. The members of the Committee shall be elected for a term of four years. They shall be eligible for re-election if renominated. The term of five of the members elected at the first election shall expire at the end of two years; immediately after the first election, the names of these five members shall be chosen by lot by the Chairman of the meeting.

7. If a member of the Committee dies or resigns or declares that for any other cause he or she can no longer perform the duties of the Committee, the State Party which

nominated the member shall appoint another expert from among its nationals to serve for the remainder of the term, subject to the approval of the Committee.

8. The Committee shall establish its own rules of procedure.

9. The Committee shall elect its officers for a period of two years.

10. The meetings of the Committee shall normally be held at United Nations Headquarters or at any other convenient place as determined by the Committee. The Committee shall normally meet annually. The duration of the meetings of the Committee shall be determined, and reviewed, if necessary, by a meeting of the States Parties to the present Convention, subject to the approval of the General Assembly.

11. The Secretary-General of the United Nations shall provide the necessary staff and facilities for the effective performance of the functions of the Committee under the present Convention.

12. With the approval of the General Assembly, the members of the Committee established under the present Convention shall receive emoluments from United Nations resources on such terms and conditions as the Assembly may decide.

Article 44

1. States Parties undertake to submit to the Committee, through the Secretary-General of the United Nations, reports on the measures they have adopted which give effect to the rights recognized herein and on the progress made on the enjoyment of those rights:

(a) Within two years of the entry into force of the Convention for the State Party concerned;

(b) Thereafter every five years.

2. Reports made under the present article shall indicate factors and difficulties, if any, affecting the degree of fulfilment of the obligations under the present Convention. Reports shall also contain sufficient information to provide the Committee with a comprehensive understanding of the implementation of the Convention in the country concerned.

3. A State Party which has submitted a comprehensive initial report to the Committee need not, in its subsequent reports submitted in accordance with paragraph 1(b) of the present article, repeat basic information previously provided.

4. The Committee may request from States Parties further information relevant to the implementation of the Convention.

5. The Committee shall submit to the General Assembly, through the Economic and Social Council, every two years, reports on its activities.

6. States Parties shall make their reports widely available to the public in their own countries.

Article 45

In order to foster the effective implementation of the Convention and to encourage international co-operation in the field covered by the Convention:

(a) The specialized agencies, the United Nations Children's Fund, and other United Nations organs shall be entitled to be represented at the consideration of the implementation of such provisions of the present Convention as fall within the scope of their mandate. The Committee may invite the specialized agencies, the United Nations Children's Fund and other competent bodies as it may consider appropriate to provide expert advice on the implementation of the Convention in areas falling within the scope of their respective mandates. The Committee may invite the specialized agencies, the United Nations Children's Fund, and other United Nations organs to submit reports on the implementation of the Convention in areas falling within the scope of their activities;

(b) The Committee shall transmit, as it may consider appropriate, to the specialized agencies, the United Nations Children's Fund and other competent bodies, any reports from States Parties that contain a request, or indicate a need, for technical advice or assistance, along with the Committee's observations and suggestions, if any, on these requests or indications;

(c) The Committee may recommend to the General Assembly to request the Secretary-General to undertake on its behalf studies on specific issues relating to the rights of the child;

(d) The Committee may make suggestions and general recommendations based on information received pursuant to Articles 44 and 45 of the present Convention. Such suggestions and general recommendations shall be transmitted to any State Party concerned and reported to the General Assembly, together with comments, if any, from States Parties.

Part III

Article 46

The present Convention shall be open for signature by all States.

Article 47

The present Convention is subject to ratification. Instruments of ratification shall be deposited with the Secretary-General of the United Nations.

Article 48

The present Convention shall remain open for accession by any State. The instruments of accession shall be deposited with the Secretary-General of the United Nations.

Article 49

1. The present Convention shall enter into force on the thirtieth day following the date of deposit with the Secretary-General of the United Nations of the twentieth instrument of ratification or accession.

2. For each State ratifying or acceding to the Convention after the deposit of the twentieth instrument of ratification or accession, the Convention shall enter into force on the thirtieth day after the deposit by such State of its instrument of ratification or accession.

Article 50

1. Any State Party may propose an amendment and file it with the Secretary-General of the United Nations. The Secretary-General shall thereupon communicate the proposed amendment to States Parties, with a request that they indicate whether they favour a conference of States Parties for the purpose of considering and voting upon the proposals. In the event that, within four months from the date of such communication, at least one third of the States Parties favour such a conference, the Secretary-General shall convene the conference under the auspices of the United Nations. Any amendment adopted by a majority of States Parties present and voting at the conference shall be submitted to the General Assembly for approval.

2. An amendment adopted in accordance with paragraph 1 of the present article shall enter into force when it has been approved by the General Assembly of the United Nations and accepted by a two-thirds majority of States Parties.

3. When an amendment enters into force, it shall be binding on those States Parties which have accepted it, other States Parties still being bound by the provisions of the present Convention and any earlier amendments which they have accepted.

Article 51

1. The Secretary-General of the United Nations shall receive and circulate to all States the text of reservations made by States at the time of ratification or accession.

2. A reservation incompatible with the object and purpose of the present Convention shall not be permitted.

3. Reservations may be withdrawn at any time by notification to that effect addressed to the Secretary-General of the United Nations, who shall then inform all States. Such notification shall take effect on the date on which it is received by the Secretary-General.

Article 52

A State Party may denounce the present Convention by written notification to the Secretary-General of the United Nations. Denunciation becomes effective one year after the date of receipt of the notification by the Secretary-General.

Article 53

The Secretary-General of the United Nations is designated as the depositary of the present Convention.

Article 54

The original of the present Convention, of which the Arabic, Chinese, English, French, Russian and Spanish texts are equally authentic, shall be deposited with the Secretary-General of the United Nations.

IN WITNESS THEREOF the undersigned plenipotentiaries, being duly authorized thereto by their respective governments, have signed the present Convention.

Chapter 3
International Convention on the Elimination of All Forms of Racial Discrimination

Preamble

The States Parties to this Convention,

Considering that the Charter of the United Nations is based on the principles of the dignity and equality inherent in all human beings, and that all Member States have pledged themselves to take joint and separate action, in co-operation with the Organization, for the achievement of one of the purposes of the United Nations which is to promote and encourage universal respect for and observance of human rights and fundamental freedoms for all, without distinction as to race, sex, language or religion,

Considering that the Universal Declaration of Human Rights proclaims that all human beings are born free and equal in dignity and rights and that everyone is entitled to all the rights and freedoms set out therein, without distinction of any kind, in particular as to race, colour or national origin,

Considering that all human beings are equal before the law and are entitled to equal protection of the law against any discrimination and against any incitement to discrimination,

Considering that the United Nations has condemned colonialism and all practices of segregation and discrimination associated therewith, in whatever form and wherever they exist, and that the Declaration on the Granting of Independence to Colonial Countries and Peoples of 14 December 1960 (General Assembly resolution 1514 (XV)) has affirmed and solemnly proclaimed the necessity of bringing them to a speedy and unconditional end,

Considering that the United Nations Declaration on the Elimination of All Forms of Racial Discrimination of 20 November 1963 (General Assembly resolution 1904 (XVIII)) solemnly affirms the necessity of speedily eliminating racial discrimination throughout the world in all its forms and manifestations and of securing understanding of and respect for the dignity of the human person,

Adopted and opened for signature and ratification by General Assembly resolution 2106 (XX) of 21 December 1965, *entry into force* 4 January 1969, in accordance with Article 19.

Convinced that any doctrine of superiority based on racial differentiation is scientifically false, morally condemnable, socially unjust and dangerous, and that there is no justification for racial discrimination, in theory or in practice, anywhere,

Reaffirming that discrimination between human beings on the grounds of race, colour or ethnic origin is an obstacle to friendly and peaceful relations among nations and is capable of disturbing peace and security among peoples and the harmony of persons living side by side even within one and the same State,

Convinced that the existence of racial barriers is repugnant to the ideals of any human society,

Alarmed by manifestations of racial discrimination still in evidence in some areas of the world and by governmental policies based on racial superiority or hatred, such as policies of apartheid, segregation or separation,

Resolved to adopt all necessary measures for speedily eliminating racial discrimination in all its forms and manifestations, and to prevent and combat racist doctrines and practices in order to promote understanding between races and to build an international community free from all forms of racial segregation and racial discrimination,

Bearing in mind the Convention concerning Discrimination in respect of Employment and Occupation adopted by the International Labour Organisation in 1958, and the Convention against Discrimination in Education adopted by the United Nations Educational, Scientific and Cultural Organization in 1960,

Desiring to implement the principles embodied in the United Nations Declaration on the Elimination of All Forms of Racial Discrimination and to secure the earliest adoption of practical measures to that end,

Have agreed as follows:

Part I

Article I

1. In this Convention, the term "racial discrimination" shall mean any distinction, exclusion, restriction or preference based on race, colour, descent, or national or ethnic origin which has the purpose or effect of nullifying or impairing the recognition, enjoyment or exercise, on an equal footing, of human rights and fundamental freedoms in the political, economic, social, cultural or any other field of public life.

2. This Convention shall not apply to distinctions, exclusions, restrictions or preferences made by a State Party to this Convention between citizens and non-citizens.

3. Nothing in this Convention may be interpreted as affecting in any way the legal provisions of States Parties concerning nationality, citizenship or naturalization, provided that such provisions do not discriminate against any particular nationality.

4. Special measures taken for the sole purpose of securing adequate advancement of certain racial or ethnic groups or individuals requiring such protection as may be necessary

in order to ensure such groups or individuals equal enjoyment or exercise of human rights and fundamental freedoms shall not be deemed racial discrimination, provided, however, that such measures do not, as a consequence, lead to the maintenance of separate rights for different racial groups and that they shall not be continued after the objectives for which they were taken have been achieved.

Article 2

1. States Parties condemn racial discrimination and undertake to pursue by all appropriate means and without delay a policy of eliminating racial discrimination in all its forms and promoting understanding among all races, and, to this end:

(a) Each State Party undertakes to engage in no act or practice of racial discrimination against persons, groups of persons or institutions and to ensure that all public authorities and public institutions, national and local, shall act in conformity with this obligation;

(b) Each State Party undertakes not to sponsor, defend or support racial discrimination by any persons or organizations;

(c) Each State Party shall take effective measures to review governmental, national and local policies, and to amend, rescind or nullify any laws and regulations which have the effect of creating or perpetuating racial discrimination wherever it exists;

(d) Each State Party shall prohibit and bring to an end, by all appropriate means, including legislation as required by circumstances, racial discrimination by any persons, group or organization;

(e) Each State Party undertakes to encourage, where appropriate, integrationist multiracial organizations and movements and other means of eliminating barriers between races, and to discourage anything which tends to strengthen racial division.

2. States Parties shall, when the circumstances so warrant, take, in the social, economic, cultural and other fields, special and concrete measures to ensure the adequate development and protection of certain racial groups or individuals belonging to them, for the purpose of guaranteeing them the full and equal enjoyment of human rights and fundamental freedoms. These measures shall in no case entail as a consequence the maintenance of unequal or separate rights for different racial groups after the objectives for which they were taken have been achieved.

Article 3

States Parties particularly condemn racial segregation and apartheid and undertake to prevent, prohibit and eradicate all practices of this nature in territories under their jurisdiction.

Article 4

States Parties condemn all propaganda and all organizations which are based on ideas or theories of superiority of one race or group of persons of one colour or ethnic origin, or which attempt to justify or promote racial hatred and discrimination in any form, and undertake to adopt immediate and positive measures designed to eradicate all incitement to, or acts of, such discrimination and, to this end, with due regard to the principles embodied in the Universal Declaration of Human Rights and the rights expressly set forth in Article 5 of this Convention, inter alia:

(a) Shall declare an offence punishable by law all dissemination of ideas based on racial superiority or hatred, incitement to racial discrimination, as well as all acts of violence or incitement to such acts against any race or group of persons of another colour or ethnic origin, and also the provision of any assistance to racist activities, including the financing thereof;

(b) Shall declare illegal and prohibit organizations, and also organized and all other propaganda activities, which promote and incite racial discrimination, and shall recognize participation in such organizations or activities as an offence punishable by law;

(c) Shall not permit public authorities or public institutions, national or local, to promote or incite racial discrimination.

Article 5

In compliance with the fundamental obligations laid down in Article 2 of this Convention, States Parties undertake to prohibit and to eliminate racial discrimination in all its forms and to guarantee the right of everyone, without distinction as to race, colour, or national or ethnic origin, to equality before the law, notably in the enjoyment of the following rights:

(a) The right to equal treatment before the tribunals and all other organs administering justice;

(b) The right to security of person and protection by the State against violence or bodily harm, whether inflicted by government officials or by any individual group or institution;

(c) Political rights, in particular the right to participate in elections-to vote and to stand for election-on the basis of universal and equal suffrage, to take part in the Government as well as in the conduct of public affairs at any level and to have equal access to public service;

(d) Other civil rights, in particular:

(i) The right to freedom of movement and residence within the border of the State;

(ii) The right to leave any country, including one's own, and to return to one's country;

(iii) The right to nationality;

(iv) The right to marriage and choice of spouse;

(v) The right to own property alone as well as in association with others;

(vi) The right to inherit;

(vii) The right to freedom of thought, conscience and religion;

(viii) The right to freedom of opinion and expression;

(ix) The right to freedom of peaceful assembly and association;

(e) Economic, social and cultural rights, in particular:

(i) The rights to work, to free choice of employment, to just and favourable conditions of work, to protection against unemployment, to equal pay for equal work, to just and favourable remuneration;

(ii) The right to form and join trade unions;

(iii) The right to housing;

(iv) The right to public health, medical care, social security and social services;

(v) The right to education and training;

(vi) The right to equal participation in cultural activities;

(f) The right of access to any place or service intended for use by the general public, such as transport hotels, restaurants, cafes, theatres and parks.

Article 6

States Parties shall assure to everyone within their jurisdiction effective protection and remedies, through the competent national tribunals and other State institutions, against any acts of racial discrimination which violate his human rights and fundamental freedoms contrary to this Convention, as well as the right to seek from such tribunals just and adequate reparation or satisfaction for any damage suffered as a result of such discrimination.

Article 7

States Parties undertake to adopt immediate and effective measures, particularly in the fields of teaching, education, culture and information, with a view to combating prejudices which lead to racial discrimination and to promoting understanding, tolerance and friendship among nations and racial or ethnical groups, as well as to propagating the purposes and principles of the Charter of the United Nations, the Universal Declaration of Human Rights, the United Nations Declaration on the Elimination of All Forms of Racial Discrimination, and this Convention.

Part II

Article 8

1. There shall be established a Committee on the Elimination of Racial Discrimination (hereinafter referred to as the Committee) consisting of eighteen experts of high moral

standing and acknowledged impartiality elected by States Parties from among their nationals, who shall serve in their personal capacity, consideration being given to equitable geographical distribution and to the representation of the different forms of civilization as well as of the principal legal systems.

2. The members of the Committee shall be elected by secret ballot from a list of persons nominated by the States Parties. Each State Party may nominate one person from among its own nationals.

3. The initial election shall be held six months after the date of the entry into force of this Convention. At least three months before the date of each election the Secretary-General of the United Nations shall address a letter to the States Parties inviting them to submit their nominations within two months. The Secretary-General shall prepare a list in alphabetical order of all persons thus nominated, indicating the States Parties which have nominated them, and shall submit it to the States Parties.

4. Elections of the members of the Committee shall be held at a meeting of States Parties convened by the Secretary-General at United Nations Headquarters. At that meeting, for which two thirds of the States Parties shall constitute a quorum, the persons elected to the Committee shall be nominees who obtain the largest number of votes and an absolute majority of the votes of the representatives of States Parties present and voting.

5. (a) The members of the Committee shall be elected for a term of four years. However, the terms of nine of the members elected at the first election shall expire at the end of two years; immediately after the first election the names of these nine members shall be chosen by lot by the Chairman of the Committee;

(b) For the filling of casual vacancies, the State Party whose expert has ceased to function as a member of the Committee shall appoint another expert from among its nationals, subject to the approval of the Committee.

6. States Parties shall be responsible for the expenses of the members of the Committee while they are in performance of Committee duties. (amendment (see General Assembly resolution 47/111 of 16 December 1992)

Article 9

1. States Parties undertake to submit to the Secretary-General of the United Nations, for consideration by the Committee, a report on the legislative, judicial, administrative or other measures which they have adopted and which give effect to the provisions of this Convention:

(a) within one year after the entry into force of the Convention for the State concerned; and

(b) thereafter every two years and whenever the Committee so requests. The Committee may request further information from the States Parties.

2. The Committee shall report annually, through the Secretary-General, to the General Assembly of the United Nations on its activities and may make suggestions and general

recommendations based on the examination of the reports and information received from the States Parties. Such suggestions and general recommendations shall be reported to the General Assembly together with comments, if any, from States Parties.

Article 10

1. The Committee shall adopt its own rules of procedure.

2. The Committee shall elect its officers for a term of two years.

3. The secretariat of the Committee shall be provided by the Secretary-General of the United Nations.

4. The meetings of the Committee shall normally be held at United Nations Headquarters.

Article 11

1. If a State Party considers that another State Party is not giving effect to the provisions of this Convention, it may bring the matter to the attention of the Committee. The Committee shall then transmit the communication to the State Party concerned. Within three months, the receiving State shall submit to the Committee written explanations or statements clarifying the matter and the remedy, if any, that may have been taken by that State.

2. If the matter is not adjusted to the satisfaction of both parties, either by bilateral negotiations or by any other procedure open to them, within six months after the receipt by the receiving State of the initial communication, either State shall have the right to refer the matter again to the Committee by notifying the Committee and also the other State.

3. The Committee shall deal with a matter referred to it in accordance with paragraph 2 of this article after it has ascertained that all available domestic remedies have been invoked and exhausted in the case, in conformity with the generally recognized principles of international law. This shall not be the rule where the application of the remedies is unreasonably prolonged.

4. In any matter referred to it, the Committee may call upon the States Parties concerned to supply any other relevant information.

5. When any matter arising out of this article is being considered by the Committee, the States Parties concerned shall be entitled to send a representative to take part in the proceedings of the Committee, without voting rights, while the matter is under consideration.

Article 12

1. (a) After the Committee has obtained and collated all the information it deems necessary, the Chairman shall appoint an ad hoc Conciliation Commission (hereinafter

referred to as the Commission) comprising five persons who may or may not be members of the Committee. The members of the Commission shall be appointed with the unanimous consent of the parties to the dispute, and its good offices shall be made available to the States concerned with a view to an amicable solution of the matter on the basis of respect for this Convention;

(b) If the States parties to the dispute fail to reach agreement within three months on all or part of the composition of the Commission, the members of the Commission not agreed upon by the States parties to the dispute shall be elected by secret ballot by a two-thirds majority vote of the Committee from among its own members.

2. The members of the Commission shall serve in their personal capacity. They shall not be nationals of the States parties to the dispute or of a State not Party to this Convention.

3. The Commission shall elect its own Chairman and adopt its own rules of procedure.

4. The meetings of the Commission shall normally be held at United Nations Headquarters or at any other convenient place as determined by the Commission.

5. The secretariat provided in accordance with Article 10, paragraph 3, of this Convention shall also service the Commission whenever a dispute among States Parties brings the Commission into being.

6. The States parties to the dispute shall share equally all the expenses of the members of the Commission in accordance with estimates to be provided by the Secretary-General of the United Nations.

7. The Secretary-General shall be empowered to pay the expenses of the members of the Commission, if necessary, before reimbursement by the States parties to the dispute in accordance with paragraph 6 of this article.

8. The information obtained and collated by the Committee shall be made available to the Commission, and the Commission may call upon the States concerned to supply any other relevant information.

Article 13

1. When the Commission has fully considered the matter, it shall prepare and submit to the Chairman of the Committee a report embodying its findings on all questions of fact relevant to the issue between the parties and containing such recommendations as it may think proper for the amicable solution of the dispute.

2. The Chairman of the Committee shall communicate the report of the Commission to each of the States parties to the dispute. These States shall, within three months, inform the Chairman of the Committee whether or not they accept the recommendations contained in the report of the Commission.

3. After the period provided for in paragraph 2 of this article, the Chairman of the Committee shall communicate the report of the Commission and the declarations of the States Parties concerned to the other States Parties to this Convention.

Article 14

1. A State Party may at any time declare that it recognizes the competence of the Committee to receive and consider communications from individuals or groups of individuals within its jurisdiction claiming to be victims of a violation by that State Party of any of the rights set forth in this Convention. No communication shall be received by the Committee if it concerns a State Party which has not made such a declaration.

2. Any State Party which makes a declaration as provided for in paragraph 1 of this article may establish or indicate a body within its national legal order which shall be competent to receive and consider petitions from individuals and groups of individuals within its jurisdiction who claim to be victims of a violation of any of the rights set forth in this Convention and who have exhausted other available local remedies.

3. A declaration made in accordance with paragraph 1 of this article and the name of any body established or indicated in accordance with paragraph 2 of this article shall be deposited by the State Party concerned with the Secretary-General of the United Nations, who shall transmit copies thereof to the other States Parties. A declaration may be withdrawn at any time by notification to the Secretary-General, but such a withdrawal shall not affect communications pending before the Committee.

4. A register of petitions shall be kept by the body established or indicated in accordance with paragraph 2 of this article, and certified copies of the register shall be filed annually through appropriate channels with the Secretary-General on the understanding that the contents shall not be publicly disclosed.

5. In the event of failure to obtain satisfaction from the body established or indicated in accordance with paragraph 2 of this article, the petitioner shall have the right to communicate the matter to the Committee within six months.

6. (a) The Committee shall confidentially bring any communication referred to it to the attention of the State Party alleged to be violating any provision of this Convention, but the identity of the individual or groups of individuals concerned shall not be revealed without his or their express consent. The Committee shall not receive anonymous communications;

(b) Within three months, the receiving State shall submit to the Committee written explanations or statements clarifying the matter and the remedy, if any, that may have been taken by that State.

7. (a) The Committee shall consider communications in the light of all information made available to it by the State Party concerned and by the petitioner. The Committee shall not consider any communication from a petitioner unless it has ascertained that the petitioner has exhausted all available domestic remedies. However, this shall not be the rule where the application of the remedies is unreasonably prolonged;

(b) The Committee shall forward its suggestions and recommendations, if any, to the State Party concerned and to the petitioner.

8. The Committee shall include in its annual report a summary of such communications and, where appropriate, a summary of the explanations and statements of the States Parties concerned and of its own suggestions and recommendations.

9. The Committee shall be competent to exercise the functions provided for in this article only when at least ten States Parties to this Convention are bound by declarations in accordance with paragraph 1 of this article.

Article 15

1. Pending the achievement of the objectives of the Declaration on the Granting of Independence to Colonial Countries and Peoples, contained in General Assembly resolution 1514 (XV) of 14 December 1960, the provisions of this Convention shall in no way limit the right of petition granted to these peoples by other international instruments or by the United Nations and its specialized agencies.

2. (a) The Committee established under Article 8, paragraph 1, of this Convention shall receive copies of the petitions from, and submit expressions of opinion and recommendations on these petitions to, the bodies of the United Nations which deal with matters directly related to the principles and objectives of this Convention in their consideration of petitions from the inhabitants of Trust and Non-Self-Governing Territories and all other territories to which General Assembly resolution 1514 (XV) applies, relating to matters covered by this Convention which are before these bodies;

(b) The Committee shall receive from the competent bodies of the United Nations copies of the reports concerning the legislative, judicial, administrative or other measures directly related to the principles and objectives of this Convention applied by the administering Powers within the Territories mentioned in subparagraph (a) of this paragraph, and shall express opinions and make recommendations to these bodies.

3. The Committee shall include in its report to the General Assembly a summary of the petitions and reports it has received from United Nations bodies, and the expressions of opinion and recommendations of the Committee relating to the said petitions and reports.

4. The Committee shall request from the Secretary-General of the United Nations all information relevant to the objectives of this Convention and available to him regarding the Territories mentioned in paragraph 2 (a) of this article.

Article 16

The provisions of this Convention concerning the settlement of disputes or complaints shall be applied without prejudice to other procedures for settling disputes or complaints in the field of discrimination laid down in the constituent instruments of, or conventions adopted by, the United Nations and its specialized agencies, and shall not prevent the States Parties from having recourse to other procedures for settling a dispute in accordance with general or special international agreements in force between them.

Part III

Article 17

1. This Convention is open for signature by any State Member of the United Nations

or member of any of its specialized agencies, by any State Party to the Statute of the International Court of Justice, and by any other State which has been invited by the General Assembly of the United Nations to become a Party to this Convention.

2. This Convention is subject to ratification. Instruments of ratification shall be deposited with the Secretary-General of the United Nations.

Article 18

1. This Convention shall be open to accession by any State referred to in Article 17, paragraph 1, of the Convention.

2. Accession shall be effected by the deposit of an instrument of accession with the Secretary-General of the United Nations.

Article 19

1. This Convention shall enter into force on the thirtieth day after the date of the deposit with the Secretary-General of the United Nations of the twenty-seventh instrument of ratification or instrument of accession.

2. For each State ratifying this Convention or acceding to it after the deposit of the twenty-seventh instrument of ratification or instrument of accession, the Convention shall enter into force on the thirtieth day after the date of the deposit of its own instrument of ratification or instrument of accession.

Article 20

1. The Secretary-General of the United Nations shall receive and circulate to all States which are or may become Parties to this Convention reservations made by States at the time of ratification or accession. Any State which objects to the reservation shall, within a period of ninety days from the date of the said communication, notify the Secretary-General that it does not accept it.

2. A reservation incompatible with the object and purpose of this Convention shall not be permitted, nor shall a reservation the effect of which would inhibit the operation of any of the bodies established by this Convention be allowed. A reservation shall be considered incompatible or inhibitive if at least two thirds of the States Parties to this Convention object to it.

3. Reservations may be withdrawn at any time by notification to this effect addressed to the Secretary-General. Such notification shall take effect on the date on which it is received.

Article 21

A State Party may denounce this Convention by written notification to the Secretary-General of the United Nations. Denunciation shall take effect one year after the date of receipt of the notification by the Secretary General.

Article 22

Any dispute between two or more States Parties with respect to the interpretation or application of this Convention, which is not settled by negotiation or by the procedures expressly provided for in this Convention, shall, at the request of any of the parties to the dispute, be referred to the International Court of Justice for decision, unless the disputants agree to another mode of settlement.

Article 23

1. A request for the revision of this Convention may be made at any time by any State Party by means of a notification in writing addressed to the Secretary-General of the United Nations.

2. The General Assembly of the United Nations shall decide upon the steps, if any, to be taken in respect of such a request.

Article 24

The Secretary-General of the United Nations shall inform all States referred to in Article 17, paragraph 1, of this Convention of the following particulars:

(a) Signatures, ratifications and accessions under Articles 17 and 18;

(b) The date of entry into force of this Convention under Article 19;

(c) Communications and declarations received under Articles 14, 20 and 23;

(d) Denunciations under Article 21.

Article 25

1. This Convention, of which the Chinese, English, French, Russian and Spanish texts are equally authentic, shall be deposited in the archives of the United Nations.

2. The Secretary-General of the United Nations shall transmit certified copies of this Convention to all States belonging to any of the categories mentioned in Article 17, paragraph 1, of the Convention.

Chapter 4

Convention on the Elimination of All Forms of Discrimination Against Women

Preamble

The States Parties to the present Convention,

Noting that the Charter of the United Nations reaffirms faith in fundamental human rights, in the dignity and worth of the human person and in the equal rights of men and women,

Noting that the Universal Declaration of Human Rights affirms the principle of the inadmissibility of discrimination and proclaims that all human beings are born free and equal in dignity and rights and that everyone is entitled to all the rights and freedoms set forth therein, without distinction of any kind, including distinction based on sex,

Noting that the States Parties to the International Covenants on Human Rights have the obligation to ensure the equal rights of men and women to enjoy all economic, social, cultural, civil and political rights,

Considering the international conventions concluded under the auspices of the United Nations and the specialized agencies promoting equality of rights of men and women,

Noting also the resolutions, declarations and recommendations adopted by the United Nations and the specialized agencies promoting equality of rights of men and women,

Concerned, however, that despite these various instruments extensive discrimination against women continues to exist,

Recalling that discrimination against women violates the principles of equality of rights and respect for human dignity, is an obstacle to the participation of women, on equal terms with men, in the political, social, economic and cultural life of their countries, hampers the growth of the prosperity of society and the family and makes more difficult the full development of the potentialities of women in the service of their countries and of humanity,

Adopted and opened for signature, ratification and accession by General Assembly resolution 34/180 of 18 December 1979, *entry into force* 3 September 1981, in accordance with Article 27(1).

Concerned that in situations of poverty women have the least access to food, health, education, training and opportunities for employment and other needs,

Convinced that the establishment of the new international economic order based on equity and justice will contribute significantly towards the promotion of equality between men and women,

Emphasizing that the eradication of apartheid, all forms of racism, racial discrimination, colonialism, neo-colonialism, aggression, foreign occupation and domination and interference in the internal affairs of States is essential to the full enjoyment of the rights of men and women,

Affirming that the strengthening of international peace and security, the relaxation of international tension, mutual co-operation among all States irrespective of their social and economic systems, general and complete disarmament, in particular nuclear disarmament under strict and effective international control, the affirmation of the principles of justice, equality and mutual benefit in relations among countries and the realization of the right of peoples under alien and colonial domination and foreign occupation to self-determination and independence, as well as respect for national sovereignty and territorial integrity, will promote social progress and development and as a consequence will contribute to the attainment of full equality between men and women,

Convinced that the full and complete development of a country, the welfare of the world and the cause of peace require the maximum participation of women on equal terms with men in all fields,

Bearing in mind the great contribution of women to the welfare of the family and to the development of society, so far not fully recognized, the social significance of maternity and the role of both parents in the family and in the upbringing of children, and aware that the role of women in procreation should not be a basis for discrimination but that the upbringing of children requires a sharing of responsibility between men and women and society as a whole,

Aware that a change in the traditional role of men as well as the role of women in society and in the family is needed to achieve full equality between men and women,

Determined to implement the principles set forth in the Declaration on the Elimination of Discrimination against Women and, for that purpose, to adopt the measures required for the elimination of such discrimination in all its forms and manifestations,

Have agreed on the following:

Part I

Article 1

For the purposes of the present Convention, the term "discrimination against women" shall mean any distinction, exclusion or restriction made on the basis of sex which has the effect or purpose of impairing or nullifying the recognition, enjoyment or exercise by women, irrespective of their marital status, on a basis of equality of men and women, of human rights and fundamental freedoms in the political, economic, social, cultural, civil or any other field.

Article 2

States Parties condemn discrimination against women in all its forms, agree to pursue by all appropriate means and without delay a policy of eliminating discrimination against women and, to this end, undertake:

(a) To embody the principle of the equality of men and women in their national constitutions or other appropriate legislation if not yet incorporated therein and to ensure, through law and other appropriate means, the practical realization of this principle;

(b) To adopt appropriate legislative and other measures, including sanctions where appropriate, prohibiting all discrimination against women;

(c) To establish legal protection of the rights of women on an equal basis with men and to ensure through competent national tribunals and other public institutions the effective protection of women against any act of discrimination;

(d) To refrain from engaging in any act or practice of discrimination against women and to ensure that public authorities and institutions shall act in conformity with this obligation;

(e) To take all appropriate measures to eliminate discrimination against women by any person, organization or enterprise;

(f) To take all appropriate measures, including legislation, to modify or abolish existing laws, regulations, customs and practices which constitute discrimination against women;

(g) To repeal all national penal provisions which constitute discrimination against women.

Article 3

States Parties shall take in all fields, in particular in the political, social, economic and cultural fields, all appropriate measures, including legislation, to ensure the full development and advancement of women, for the purpose of guaranteeing them the exercise and enjoyment of human rights and fundamental freedoms on a basis of equality with men.

Article 4

1. Adoption by States Parties of temporary special measures aimed at accelerating de facto equality between men and women shall not be considered discrimination as

defined in the present Convention, but shall in no way entail as a consequence the maintenance of unequal or separate standards; these measures shall be discontinued when the objectives of equality of opportunity and treatment have been achieved.

2. Adoption by States Parties of special measures, including those measures contained in the present Convention, aimed at protecting maternity shall not be considered discriminatory.

Article 5

States Parties shall take all appropriate measures:

(a) To modify the social and cultural patterns of conduct of men and women, with a view to achieving the elimination of prejudices and customary and all other practices which are based on the idea of the inferiority or the superiority of either of the sexes or on stereotyped roles for men and women;

(b) To ensure that family education includes a proper understanding of maternity as a social function and the recognition of the common responsibility of men and women in the upbringing and development of their children, it being understood that the interest of the children is the primordial consideration in all cases.

Article 6

States Parties shall take all appropriate measures, including legislation, to suppress all forms of traffic in women and exploitation of prostitution of women.

Part II

Article 7

States Parties shall take all appropriate measures to eliminate discrimination against women in the political and public life of the country and, in particular, shall ensure to women, on equal terms with men, the right:

(a) To vote in all elections and public referenda and to be eligible for election to all publicly elected bodies;

(b) To participate in the formulation of government policy and the implementation thereof and to hold public office and perform all public functions at all levels of government;

(c) To participate in non-governmental organizations and associations concerned with the public and political life of the country.

Article 8

States Parties shall take all appropriate measures to ensure to women, on equal terms with men and without any discrimination, the opportunity to represent their Governments at the international level and to participate in the work of international organizations.

Article 9

1. States Parties shall grant women equal rights with men to acquire, change or retain their nationality. They shall ensure in particular that neither marriage to an alien nor change of nationality by the husband during marriage shall automatically change the nationality of the wife, render her stateless or force upon her the nationality of the husband.

2. States Parties shall grant women equal rights with men with respect to the nationality of their children.

Part III

Article 10

States Parties shall take all appropriate measures to eliminate discrimination against women in order to ensure to them equal rights with men in the field of education and in particular to ensure, on a basis of equality of men and women:

(a) The same conditions for career and vocational guidance, for access to studies and for the achievement of diplomas in educational establishments of all categories in rural as well as in urban areas; this equality shall be ensured in pre-school, general, technical, professional and higher technical education, as well as in all types of vocational training;

(b) Access to the same curricula, the same examinations, teaching staff with qualifications of the same standard and school premises and equipment of the same quality;

(c) The elimination of any stereotyped concept of the roles of men and women at all levels and in all forms of education by encouraging coeducation and other types of education which will help to achieve this aim and, in particular, by the revision of textbooks and school programmes and the adaptation of teaching methods;

(d) The same opportunities to benefit from scholarships and other study grants;

(e) The same opportunities for access to programmes of continuing education, including adult and functional literacy programmes, particulary those aimed at reducing, at the earliest possible time, any gap in education existing between men and women;

(f) The reduction of female student drop-out rates and the organization of programmes for girls and women who have left school prematurely;

(g) The same opportunities to participate actively in sports and physical education;

(h) Access to specific educational information to help to ensure the health and well-being of families, including information and advice on family planning.

Article 11

1. States Parties shall take all appropriate measures to eliminate discrimination against women in the field of employment in order to ensure, on a basis of equality of men and women, the same rights, in particular:

(a) The right to work as an inalienable right of all human beings;

(b) The right to the same employment opportunities, including the application of the same criteria for selection in matters of employment;

(c) The right to free choice of profession and employment, the right to promotion, job security and all benefits and conditions of service and the right to receive vocational training and retraining, including apprenticeships, advanced vocational training and recurrent training;

(d) The right to equal remuneration, including benefits, and to equal treatment in respect of work of equal value, as well as equality of treatment in the evaluation of the quality of work;

(e) The right to social security, particularly in cases of retirement, unemployment, sickness, invalidity and old age and other incapacity to work, as well as the right to paid leave;

(f) The right to protection of health and to safety in working conditions, including the safeguarding of the function of reproduction.

2. In order to prevent discrimination against women on the grounds of marriage or maternity and to ensure their effective right to work, States Parties shall take appropriate measures:

(a) To prohibit, subject to the imposition of sanctions, dismissal on the grounds of pregnancy or of maternity leave and discrimination in dismissals on the basis of marital status;

(b) To introduce maternity leave with pay or with comparable social benefits without loss of former employment, seniority or social allowances;

(c) To encourage the provision of the necessary supporting social services to enable parents to combine family obligations with work responsibilities and participation in public life, in particular through promoting the establishment and development of a network of child-care facilities;

(d) To provide special protection to women during pregnancy in types of work proved to be harmful to them.

3. Protective legislation relating to matters covered in this article shall be reviewed periodically in the light of scientific and technological knowledge and shall be revised, repealed or extended as necessary.

Article 12

1. States Parties shall take all appropriate measures to eliminate discrimination against women in the field of health care in order to ensure, on a basis of equality of men and women, access to health care services, including those related to family planning.

2. Notwithstanding the provisions of paragraph 1 of this article, States Parties shall ensure to women appropriate services in connection with pregnancy, confinement and

the post-natal period, granting free services where necessary, as well as adequate nutrition during pregnancy and lactation.

Article 13

States Parties shall take all appropriate measures to eliminate discrimination against women in other areas of economic and social life in order to ensure, on a basis of equality of men and women, the same rights, in particular:

(a) The right to family benefits;

(b) The right to bank loans, mortgages and other forms of financial credit;

(c) The right to participate in recreational activities, sports and all aspects of cultural life.

Article 14

1. States Parties shall take into account the particular problems faced by rural women and the significant roles which rural women play in the economic survival of their families, including their work in the non-monetized sectors of the economy, and shall take all appropriate measures to ensure the application of the provisions of the present Convention to women in rural areas.

2. States Parties shall take all appropriate measures to eliminate discrimination against women in rural areas in order to ensure, on a basis of equality of men and women, that they participate in and benefit from rural development and, in particular, shall ensure to such women the right:

(a) To participate in the elaboration and implementation of development planning at all levels;

(b) To have access to adequate health care facilities, including information, counselling and services in family planning;

(c) To benefit directly from social security programmes;

(d) To obtain all types of training and education, formal and non-formal, including that relating to functional literacy, as well as, inter alia, the benefit of all community and extension services, in order to increase their technical proficiency;

(e) To organize self-help groups and co-operatives in order to obtain equal access to economic opportunities through employment or self employment;

(f) To participate in all community activities;

(g) To have access to agricultural credit and loans, marketing facilities, appropriate technology and equal treatment in land and agrarian reform as well as in land resettlement schemes;

(h) To enjoy adequate living conditions, particularly in relation to housing, sanitation, electricity and water supply, transport and communications.

Part IV

Article 15

1. States Parties shall accord to women equality with men before the law.

2. States Parties shall accord to women, in civil matters, a legal capacity identical to that of men and the same opportunities to exercise that capacity. In particular, they shall give women equal rights to conclude contracts and to administer property and shall treat them equally in all stages of procedure in courts and tribunals.

3. States Parties agree that all contracts and all other private instruments of any kind with a legal effect which is directed at restricting the legal capacity of women shall be deemed null and void.

4. States Parties shall accord to men and women the same rights with regard to the law relating to the movement of persons and the freedom to choose their residence and domicile.

Article 16

1. States Parties shall take all appropriate measures to eliminate discrimination against women in all matters relating to marriage and family relations and in particular shall ensure, on a basis of equality of men and women:

(a) The same right to enter into marriage;

(b) The same right freely to choose a spouse and to enter into marriage only with their free and full consent;

(c) The same rights and responsibilities during marriage and at its dissolution;

(d) The same rights and responsibilities as parents, irrespective of their marital status, in matters relating to their children; in all cases the interests of the children shall be paramount;

(e) The same rights to decide freely and responsibly on the number and spacing of their children and to have access to the information, education and means to enable them to exercise these rights;

(f) The same rights and responsibilities with regard to guardianship, wardship, trusteeship and adoption of children, or similar institutions where these concepts exist in national legislation; in all cases the interests of the children shall be paramount;

(g) The same personal rights as husband and wife, including the right to choose a family name, a profession and an occupation;

(h) The same rights for both spouses in respect of the ownership, acquisition, management, administration, enjoyment and disposition of property, whether free of charge or for a valuable consideration.

2. The betrothal and the marriage of a child shall have no legal effect, and all necessary

action, including legislation, shall be taken to specify a minimum age for marriage and to make the registration of marriages in an official registry compulsory.

Part V

Article 17

1. For the purpose of considering the progress made in the implementation of the present Convention, there shall be established a Committee on the Elimination of Discrimination against Women (hereinafter referred to as the Committee) consisting, at the time of entry into force of the Convention, of eighteen and, after ratification of or accession to the Convention by the thirty-fifth State Party, of twenty-three experts of high moral standing and competence in the field covered by the Convention. The experts shall be elected by States Parties from among their nationals and shall serve in their personal capacity, consideration being given to equitable geographical distribution and to the representation of the different forms of civilization as well as the principal legal systems.

2. The members of the Committee shall be elected by secret ballot from a list of persons nominated by States Parties. Each State Party may nominate one person from among its own nationals.

3. The initial election shall be held six months after the date of the entry into force of the present Convention. At least three months before the date of each election the Secretary-General of the United Nations shall address a letter to the States Parties inviting them to submit their nominations within two months. The Secretary-General shall prepare a list in alphabetical order of all persons thus nominated, indicating the States Parties which have nominated them, and shall submit it to the States Parties.

4. Elections of the members of the Committee shall be held at a meeting of States Parties convened by the Secretary-General at United Nations Headquarters. At that meeting, for which two thirds of the States Parties shall constitute a quorum, the persons elected to the Committee shall be those nominees who obtain the largest number of votes and an absolute majority of the votes of the representatives of States Parties present and voting.

5. The members of the Committee shall be elected for a term of four years. However, the terms of nine of the members elected at the first election shall expire at the end of two years; immediately after the first election the names of these nine members shall be chosen by lot by the Chairman of the Committee.

6. The election of the five additional members of the Committee shall be held in accordance with the provisions of paragraphs 2, 3 and 4 of this article, following the thirty-fifth ratification or accession. The terms of two of the additional members elected on this occasion shall expire at the end of two years, the names of these two members having been chosen by lot by the Chairman of the Committee.

7. For the filling of casual vacancies, the State Party whose expert has ceased to function

as a member of the Committee shall appoint another expert from among its nationals, subject to the approval of the Committee.

8. The members of the Committee shall, with the approval of the General Assembly, receive emoluments from United Nations resources on such terms and conditions as the Assembly may decide, having regard to the importance of the Committee's responsibilities.

9. The Secretary-General of the United Nations shall provide the necessary staff and facilities for the effective performance of the functions of the Committee under the present Convention.

Article 18

1. States Parties undertake to submit to the Secretary-General of the United Nations, for consideration by the Committee, a report on the legislative, judicial, administrative or other measures which they have adopted to give effect to the provisions of the present Convention and on the progress made in this respect:

(a) Within one year after the entry into force for the State concerned;

(b) Thereafter at least every four years and further whenever the Committee so requests.

2. Reports may indicate factors and difficulties affecting the degree of fulfilment of obligations under the present Convention.

Article 19

1. The Committee shall adopt its own rules of procedure.

2. The Committee shall elect its officers for a term of two years.

Article 20

1. The Committee shall normally meet for a period of not more than two weeks annually in order to consider the reports submitted in accordance with Article 18 of the present Convention.

2. The meetings of the Committee shall normally be held at United Nations Headquarters or at any other convenient place as determined by the Committee.

Article 21

1. The Committee shall, through the Economic and Social Council, report annually to the General Assembly of the United Nations on its activities and may make suggestions and general recommendations based on the examination of reports and information received from the States Parties. Such suggestions and general recommendations shall be included in the report of the Committee together with comments, if any, from States Parties.

2. The Secretary-General of the United Nations shall transmit the reports of the Committee to the Commission on the Status of Women for its information.

Article 22

The specialized agencies shall be entitled to be represented at the consideration of the implementation of such provisions of the present Convention as fall within the scope of their activities. The Committee may invite the specialized agencies to submit reports on the implementation of the Convention in areas falling within the scope of their activities.

Part VI

Article 23

Nothing in the present Convention shall affect any provisions that are more conducive to the achievement of equality between men and women which may be contained:

(a) In the legislation of a State Party; or

(b) In any other international convention, treaty or agreement in force for that State.

Article 24

States Parties undertake to adopt all necessary measures at the national level aimed at achieving the full realization of the rights recognized in the present Convention.

Article 25

1. The present Convention shall be open for signature by all States.

2. The Secretary-General of the United Nations is designated as the depositary of the present Convention.

3. The present Convention is subject to ratification. Instruments of ratification shall be deposited with the Secretary-General of the United Nations.

4. The present Convention shall be open to accession by all States. Accession shall be effected by the deposit of an instrument of accession with the Secretary-General of the United Nations.

Article 26

1. A request for the revision of the present Convention may be made at any time by any State Party by means of a notification in writing addressed to the Secretary-General of the United Nations.

2. The General Assembly of the United Nations shall decide upon the steps, if any, to be taken in respect of such a request.

Article 27

1. The present Convention shall enter into force on the thirtieth day after the date of deposit with the Secretary-General of the United Nations of the twentieth instrument of ratification or accession.

2. For each State ratifying the present Convention or acceding to it after the deposit of the twentieth instrument of ratification or accession, the Convention shall enter into force on the thirtieth day after the date of the deposit of its own instrument of ratification or accession.

Article 28

1. The Secretary-General of the United Nations shall receive and circulate to all States the text of reservations made by States at the time of ratification or accession.

2. A reservation incompatible with the object and purpose of the present Convention shall not be permitted.

3. Reservations may be withdrawn at any time by notification to this effect addressed to the Secretary-General of the United Nations, who shall then inform all States thereof. Such notification shall take effect on the date on which it is received.

Article 29

1. Any dispute between two or more States Parties concerning the interpretation or application of the present Convention which is not settled by negotiation shall, at the request of one of them, be submitted to arbitration. If within six months from the date of the request for arbitration the parties are unable to agree on the organization of the arbitration, any one of those parties may refer the dispute to the International Court of Justice by request in conformity with the Statute of the Court.

2. Each State Party may at the time of signature or ratification of the present Convention or accession thereto declare that it does not consider itself bound by paragraph 1 of this article. The other States Parties shall not be bound by that paragraph with respect to any State Party which has made such a reservation.

3. Any State Party which has made a reservation in accordance with paragraph 2 of this article may at any time withdraw that reservation by notification to the Secretary-General of the United Nations.

Article 30

The present Convention, the Arabic, Chinese, English, French, Russian and Spanish texts of which are equally authentic, shall be deposited with the Secretary-General of the United Nations.

IN WITNESS WHEREOF the undersigned, duly authorized, have signed the present Convention.

Chapter 5
International Covenant on Civil and Political Rights

Preamble

The States Parties to the present Covenant,

Considering that, in accordance with the principles proclaimed in the Charter of the United Nations, recognition of the inherent dignity and of the equal and inalienable rights of all members of the human family is the foundation of freedom, justice and peace in the world,

Recognizing that these rights derive from the inherent dignity of the human person,

Recognizing that, in accordance with the Universal Declaration of Human Rights, the ideal of free human beings enjoying civil and political freedom and freedom from fear and want can only be achieved if conditions are created whereby everyone may enjoy his civil and political rights, as well as his economic, social and cultural rights,

Considering the obligation of States under the Charter of the United Nations to promote universal respect for, and observance of, human rights and freedoms,

Realizing that the individual, having duties to other individuals and to the community to which he belongs, is under a responsibility to strive for the promotion and observance of the rights recognized in the present Covenant,

Agree upon the following articles:

Part I

Article 1

1. All peoples have the right of self-determination. By virtue of that right they freely determine their political status and freely pursue their economic, social and cultural development.

Adopted and opened for signature, ratification and accession by General Assembly resolution 2200A (XXI) of 16 December 1966, *entry into force* 23 March 1976, in accordance with Article 49.

2. All peoples may, for their own ends, freely dispose of their natural wealth and resources without prejudice to any obligations arising out of international economic co-operation, based upon the principle of mutual benefit, and international law. In no case may a people be deprived of its own means of subsistence.

3. The States Parties to the present Covenant, including those having responsibility for the administration of Non-Self-Governing and Trust Territories, shall promote the realization of the right of self-determination, and shall respect that right, in conformity with the provisions of the Charter of the United Nations.

Part II

Article 2

1. Each State Party to the present Covenant undertakes to respect and to ensure to all individuals within its territory and subject to its jurisdiction the rights recognized in the present Covenant, without distinction of any kind, such as race, colour, sex, language, religion, political or other opinion, national or social origin, property, birth or other status.

2. Where not already provided for by existing legislative or other measures, each State Party to the present Covenant undertakes to take the necessary steps, in accordance with its constitutional processes and with the provisions of the present Covenant, to adopt such laws or other measures as may be necessary to give effect to the rights recognized in the present Covenant.

3. Each State Party to the present Covenant undertakes:

(a) To ensure that any person whose rights or freedoms as herein recognized are violated shall have an effective remedy, notwithstanding that the violation has been committed by persons acting in an official capacity;

(b) To ensure that any person claiming such a remedy shall have his right thereto determined by competent judicial, administrative or legislative authorities, or by any other competent authority provided for by the legal system of the State, and to develop the possibilities of judicial remedy;

(c) To ensure that the competent authorities shall enforce such remedies when granted.

Article 3

The States Parties to the present Covenant undertake to ensure the equal right of men and women to the enjoyment of all civil and political rights set forth in the present Covenant.

Article 4

1. In time of public emergency which threatens the life of the nation and the existence of which is officially proclaimed, the States Parties to the present Covenant may take

measures derogating from their obligations under the present Covenant to the extent strictly required by the exigencies of the situation, provided that such measures are not inconsistent with their other obligations under international law and do not involve discrimination solely on the ground of race, colour, sex, language, religion or social origin.

2. No derogation from Articles 6, 7, 8 (paragraphs 1 and 2), 11, 15, 16 and 18 may be made under this provision.

3. Any State Party to the present Covenant availing itself of the right of derogation shall immediately inform the other States Parties to the present Covenant, through the intermediary of the Secretary-General of the United Nations, of the provisions from which it has derogated and of the reasons by which it was actuated. A further communication shall be made, through the same intermediary, on the date on which it terminates such derogation.

Article 5

1. Nothing in the present Covenant may be interpreted as implying for any State, group or person any right to engage in any activity or perform any act aimed at the destruction of any of the rights and freedoms recognized herein or at their limitation to a greater extent than is provided for in the present Covenant.

2. There shall be no restriction upon or derogation from any of the fundamental human rights recognized or existing in any State Party to the present Covenant pursuant to law, conventions, regulations or custom on the pretext that the present Covenant does not recognize such rights or that it recognizes them to a lesser extent.

Part III

Article 6

1. Every human being has the inherent right to life. This right shall be protected by law. No one shall be arbitrarily deprived of his life.

2. In countries which have not abolished the death penalty, sentence of death may be imposed only for the most serious crimes in accordance with the law in force at the time of the commission of the crime and not contrary to the provisions of the present Covenant and to the Convention on the Prevention and Punishment of the Crime of Genocide. This penalty can only be carried out pursuant to a final judgement rendered by a competent court.

3. When deprivation of life constitutes the crime of genocide, it is understood that nothing in this article shall authorize any State Party to the present Covenant to derogate in any way from any obligation assumed under the provisions of the Convention on the Prevention and Punishment of the Crime of Genocide.

4. Anyone sentenced to death shall have the right to seek pardon or commutation of the sentence. Amnesty, pardon or commutation of the sentence of death may be granted in all cases.

5. Sentence of death shall not be imposed for crimes committed by persons below eighteen years of age and shall not be carried out on pregnant women.

6. Nothing in this article shall be invoked to delay or to prevent the abolition of capital punishment by any State Party to the present Covenant.

Article 7

No one shall be subjected to torture or to cruel, inhuman or degrading treatment or punishment. In particular, no one shall be subjected without his free consent to medical or scientific experimentation.

Article 8

1. No one shall be held in slavery; slavery and the slave-trade in all their forms shall be prohibited.

2. No one shall be held in servitude.

3. (a) No one shall be required to perform forced or compulsory labour;

(b) Paragraph 3(a) shall not be held to preclude, in countries where imprisonment with hard labour may be imposed as a punishment for a crime, the performance of hard labour in pursuance of a sentence to such punishment by a competent court;

(c) For the purpose of this paragraph the term "forced or compulsory labour" shall not include:

(i) Any work or service, not referred to in subparagraph (b), normally required of a person who is under detention in consequence of a lawful order of a court, or of a person during conditional release from such detention;

(ii) Any service of a military character and, in countries where conscientious objection is recognized, any national service required by law of conscientious objectors;

(iii) Any service exacted in cases of emergency or calamity threatening the life or well-being of the community;

(iv) Any work or service which forms part of normal civil obligations.

Article 9

1. Everyone has the right to liberty and security of person. No one shall be subjected to arbitrary arrest or detention. No one shall be deprived of his liberty except on such grounds and in accordance with such procedure as are established by law.

2. Anyone who is arrested shall be informed, at the time of arrest, of the reasons for his arrest and shall be promptly informed of any charges against him.

3. Anyone arrested or detained on a criminal charge shall be brought promptly before a judge or other officer authorized by law to exercise judicial power and shall be entitled to trial within a reasonable time or to release. It shall not be the general rule that

persons awaiting trial shall be detained in custody, but release may be subject to guarantees to appear for trial, at any other stage of the judicial proceedings, and, should occasion arise, for execution of the judgement.

4. Anyone who is deprived of his liberty by arrest or detention shall be entitled to take proceedings before a court, in order that court may decide without delay on the lawfulness of his detention and order his release if the detention is not lawful.

5. Anyone who has been the victim of unlawful arrest or detention shall have an enforceable right to compensation.

Article 10

1. All persons deprived of their liberty shall be treated with humanity and with respect for the inherent dignity of the human person.

2. (a) Accused persons shall, save in exceptional circumstances, be segregated from convicted persons and shall be subject to separate treatment appropriate to their status as unconvicted persons;

(b) Accused juvenile persons shall be separated from adults and brought as speedily as possible for adjudication.

3. The penitentiary system shall comprise treatment of prisoners the essential aim of which shall be their reformation and social rehabilitation. Juvenile offenders shall be segregated from adults and be accorded treatment appropriate to their age and legal status.

Article 11

No one shall be imprisoned merely on the ground of inability to fulfill a contractual obligation.

Article 12

1. Everyone lawfully within the territory of a State shall, within that territory, have the right to liberty of movement and freedom to choose his residence.

2. Everyone shall be free to leave any country, including his own.

3. The above-mentioned rights shall not be subject to any restrictions except those which are provided by law, are necessary to protect national security, public order (ordre public), public health or morals or the rights and freedoms of others, and are consistent with the other rights recognized in the present Covenant.

4. No one shall be arbitrarily deprived of the right to enter his own country.

Article 13

An alien lawfully in the territory of a State Party to the present Covenant may be expelled therefrom only in pursuance of a decision reached in accordance with law and shall, except where compelling reasons of national security otherwise require, be allowed to submit the reasons against his expulsion and to have his case reviewed by, and be represented for the purpose before, the competent authority or a person or persons especially designated by the competent authority.

Article 14

1. All persons shall be equal before the courts and tribunals. In the determination of any criminal charge against him, or of his rights and obligations in a suit at law, everyone shall be entitled to a fair and public hearing by a competent, independent and impartial tribunal established by law. The press and the public may be excluded from all or part of a trial for reasons of morals, public order (ordre public) or national security in a democratic society, or when the interest of the private lives of the parties so requires, or to the extent strictly necessary in the opinion of the court in special circumstances where publicity would prejudice the interests of justice; but any judgement rendered in a criminal case or in a suit at law shall be made public except where the interest of juvenile persons otherwise requires or the proceedings concern matrimonial disputes or the guardianship of children.

2. Everyone charged with a criminal offence shall have the right to be presumed innocent until proved guilty according to law.

3. In the determination of any criminal charge against him, everyone shall be entitled to the following minimum guarantees, in full equality:

(a) To be informed promptly and in detail in a language which he understands of the nature and cause of the charge against him;

(b) To have adequate time and facilities for the preparation of his defence and to communicate with counsel of his own choosing;

(c) To be tried without undue delay;

(d) To be tried in his presence, and to defend himself in person or through legal assistance of his own choosing; to be informed, if he does not have legal assistance, of this right; and to have legal assistance assigned to him, in any case where the interests of justice so require, and without payment by him in any such case if he does not have sufficient means to pay for it;

(e) To examine, or have examined, the witnesses against him and to obtain the attendance and examination of witnesses on his behalf under the same conditions as witnesses against him;

(f) To have the free assistance of an interpreter if he cannot understand or speak the language used in court;

(g) Not to be compelled to testify against himself or to confess guilt.

4. In the case of juvenile persons, the procedure shall be such as will take account of their age and the desirability of promoting their rehabilitation.

5. Everyone convicted of a crime shall have the right to his conviction and sentence being reviewed by a higher tribunal according to law.

6. When a person has by a final decision been convicted of a criminal offence and when subsequently his conviction has been reversed or he has been pardoned on the ground that a new or newly discovered fact shows conclusively that there has been a miscarriage of justice, the person who has suffered punishment as a result of such conviction shall be compensated according to law, unless it is proved that the non-disclosure of the unknown fact in time is wholly or partly attributable to him.

7. No one shall be liable to be tried or punished again for an offence for which he has already been finally convicted or acquitted in accordance with the law and penal procedure of each country.

Article 15

1. No one shall be held guilty of any criminal offence on account of any act or omission which did not constitute a criminal offence, under national or international law, at the time when it was committed. Nor shall a heavier penalty be imposed than the one that was applicable at the time when the criminal offence was committed. If, subsequent to the commission of the offence, provision is made by law for the imposition of the lighter penalty, the offender shall benefit thereby.

2. Nothing in this article shall prejudice the trial and punishment of any person for any act or omission which, at the time when it was committed, was criminal according to the general principles of law recognized by the community of nations.

Article 16

Everyone shall have the right to recognition everywhere as a person before the law.

Article 17

1. No one shall be subjected to arbitrary or unlawful interference with his privacy, family, home or correspondence, nor to unlawful attacks on his honour and reputation.

2. Everyone has the right to the protection of the law against such interference or attacks.

Article 18

1. Everyone shall have the right to freedom of thought, conscience and religion. This right shall include freedom to have or to adopt a religion or belief of his choice, and freedom, either individually or in community with others and in public or private, to manifest his religion or belief in worship, observance, practice and teaching.

2. No one shall be subject to coercion which would impair his freedom to have or to adopt a religion or belief of his choice.

3. Freedom to manifest one's religion or beliefs may be subject only to such limitations as are prescribed by law and are necessary to protect public safety, order, health, or morals or the fundamental rights and freedoms of others.

4. The States Parties to the present Covenant undertake to have respect for the liberty of parents and, when applicable, legal guardians to ensure the religious and moral education of their children in conformity with their own convictions.

Article 19

1. Everyone shall have the right to hold opinions without interference.

2. Everyone shall have the right to freedom of expression; this right shall include freedom to seek, receive and impart information and ideas of all kinds, regardless of frontiers, either orally, in writing or in print, in the form of art, or through any other media of his choice.

3. The exercise of the rights provided for in paragraph 2 of this article carries with it special duties and responsibilities. It may therefore be subject to certain restrictions, but these shall only be such as are provided by law and are necessary:

(a) For respect of the rights or reputations of others;

(b) For the protection of national security or of public order (ordre public), or of public health or morals.

Article 20

1. Any propaganda for war shall be prohibited by law.

2. Any advocacy of national, racial or religious hatred that constitutes incitement to discrimination, hostility or violence shall be prohibited by law.

Article 21

The right of peaceful assembly shall be recognized. No restrictions may be placed on the exercise of this right other than those imposed in conformity with the law and which are necessary in a democratic society in the interests of national security or public safety, public order (ordre public), the protection of public health or morals or the protection of the rights and freedoms of others.

Article 22

1. Everyone shall have the right to freedom of association with others, including the right to form and join trade unions for the protection of his interests.

2. No restrictions may be placed on the exercise of this right other than those which are prescribed by law and which are necessary in a democratic society in the interests of national security or public safety, public order (ordre public), the protection of public

health or morals or the protection of the rights and freedoms of others. This article shall not prevent the imposition of lawful restrictions on members of the armed forces and of the police in their exercise of this right.

3. Nothing in this article shall authorize States Parties to the International Labour Organisation Convention of 1948 concerning Freedom of Association and Protection of the Right to Organize to take legislative measures which would prejudice, or to apply the law in such a manner as to prejudice, the guarantees provided for in that Convention.

Article 23

1. The family is the natural and fundamental group unit of society and is entitled to protection by society and the State.

2. The right of men and women of marriageable age to marry and to found a family shall be recognized.

3. No marriage shall be entered into without the free and full consent of the intending spouses.

4. States Parties to the present Covenant shall take appropriate steps to ensure equality of rights and responsibilities of spouses as to marriage, during marriage and at its dissolution. In the case of dissolution, provision shall be made for the necessary protection of any children.

Article 24

1. Every child shall have, without any discrimination as to race, colour, sex, language, religion, national or social origin, property or birth, the right to such measures of protection as are required by his status as a minor, on the part of his family, society and the State.

2. Every child shall be registered immediately after birth and shall have a name.

3. Every child has the right to acquire a nationality.

Article 25

Every citizen shall have the right and the opportunity, without any of the distinctions mentioned in Article 2 and without unreasonable restrictions:

(a) To take part in the conduct of public affairs, directly or through freely chosen representatives;

(b) To vote and to be elected at genuine periodic elections which shall be by universal and equal suffrage and shall be held by secret ballot, guaranteeing the free expression of the will of the electors;

(c) To have access, on general terms of equality, to public service in his country.

Article 26

All persons are equal before the law and are entitled without any discrimination to the equal protection of the law. In this respect, the law shall prohibit any discrimination and guarantee to all persons equal and effective protection against discrimination on any ground such as race, colour, sex, language, religion, political or other opinion, national or social origin, property, birth or other status.

Article 27

In those States in which ethnic, religious or linguistic minorities exist, persons belonging to such minorities shall not be denied the right, in community with the other members of their group, to enjoy their own culture, to profess and practise their own religion, or to use their own language.

Part IV

Article 28

1. There shall be established a Human Rights Committee (hereafter referred to in the present Covenant as the Committee). It shall consist of eighteen members and shall carry out the functions hereinafter provided.

2. The Committee shall be composed of nationals of the States Parties to the present Covenant who shall be persons of high moral character and recognized competence in the field of human rights, consideration being given to the usefulness of the participation of some persons having legal experience.

3. The members of the Committee shall be elected and shall serve in their personal capacity.

Article 29

1 . The members of the Committee shall be elected by secret ballot from a list of persons possessing the qualifications prescribed in Article 28 and nominated for the purpose by the States Parties to the present Covenant.

2. Each State Party to the present Covenant may nominate not more than two persons. These persons shall be nationals of the nominating State.

3. A person shall be eligible for renomination.

Article 30

1. The initial election shall be held no later than six months after the date of the entry into force of the present Covenant.

2. At least four months before the date of each election to the Committee, other than an election to fill a vacancy declared in accordance with Article 34, the Secretary-General of the United Nations shall address a written invitation to the States Parties to the present Covenant to submit their nominations for membership of the Committee within three months.

3. The Secretary-General of the United Nations shall prepare a list in alphabetical order of all the persons thus nominated, with an indication of the States Parties which have nominated them, and shall submit it to the States Parties to the present Covenant no later than one month before the date of each election.

4. Elections of the members of the Committee shall be held at a meeting of the States Parties to the present Covenant convened by the Secretary-General of the United Nations at the Headquarters of the United Nations. At that meeting, for which two thirds of the States Parties to the present Covenant shall constitute a quorum, the persons elected to the Committee shall be those nominees who obtain the largest number of votes and an absolute majority of the votes of the representatives of States Parties present and voting.

Article 31

1. The Committee may not include more than one national of the same State.

2. In the election of the Committee, consideration shall be given to equitable geographical distribution of membership and to the representation of the different forms of civilization and of the principal legal systems.

Article 32

1. The members of the Committee shall be elected for a term of four years. They shall be eligible for re-election if renominated. However, the terms of nine of the members elected at the first election shall expire at the end of two years; immediately after the first election, the names of these nine members shall be chosen by lot by the Chairman of the meeting referred to in Article 30, paragraph 4.

2. Elections at the expiry of office shall be held in accordance with the preceding articles of this part of the present Covenant.

Article 33

1. If, in the unanimous opinion of the other members, a member of the Committee has ceased to carry out his functions for any cause other than absence of a temporary character, the Chairman of the Committee shall notify the Secretary-General of the United Nations, who shall then declare the seat of that member to be vacant.

2. In the event of the death or the resignation of a member of the Committee, the Chairman shall immediately notify the Secretary-General of the United Nations, who

shall declare the seat vacant from the date of death or the date on which the resignation takes effect.

Article 34

1. When a vacancy is declared in accordance with Article 33 and if the term of office of the member to be replaced does not expire within six months of the declaration of the vacancy, the Secretary-General of the United Nations shall notify each of the States Parties to the present Covenant, which may within two months submit nominations in accordance with Article 29 for the purpose of filling the vacancy.

2. The Secretary-General of the United Nations shall prepare a list in alphabetical order of the persons thus nominated and shall submit it to the States Parties to the present Covenant. The election to fill the vacancy shall then take place in accordance with the relevant provisions of this part of the present Covenant.

3. A member of the Committee elected to fill a vacancy declared in accordance with Article 33 shall hold office for the remainder of the term of the member who vacated the seat on the Committee under the provisions of that article.

Article 35

The members of the Committee shall, with the approval of the General Assembly of the United Nations, receive emoluments from United Nations resources on such terms and conditions as the General Assembly may decide, having regard to the importance of the Committee's responsibilities.

Article 36

The Secretary-General of the United Nations shall provide the necessary staff and facilities for the effective performance of the functions of the Committee under the present Covenant.

Article 37

1. The Secretary-General of the United Nations shall convene the initial meeting of the Committee at the Headquarters of the United Nations.

2. After its initial meeting, the Committee shall meet at such times as shall be provided in its rules of procedure.

3. The Committee shall normally meet at the Headquarters of the United Nations or at the United Nations Office at Geneva.

Article 38

Every member of the Committee shall, before taking up his duties, make a solemn declaration in open committee that he will perform his functions impartially and conscientiously.

Article 39

1. The Committee shall elect its officers for a term of two years. They may be re-elected.

2. The Committee shall establish its own rules of procedure, but these rules shall provide, inter alia, that:

(a) Twelve members shall constitute a quorum;

(b) Decisions of the Committee shall be made by a majority vote of the members present.

Article 40

1. The States Parties to the present Covenant undertake to submit reports on the measures they have adopted which give effect to the rights recognized herein and on the progress made in the enjoyment of those rights:

(a) Within one year of the entry into force of the present Covenant for the States Parties concerned;

(b) Thereafter whenever the Committee so requests.

2. All reports shall be submitted to the Secretary-General of the United Nations, who shall transmit them to the Committee for consideration. Reports shall indicate the factors and difficulties, if any, affecting the implementation of the present Covenant.

3. The Secretary-General of the United Nations may, after consultation with the Committee, transmit to the specialized agencies concerned copies of such parts of the reports as may fall within their field of competence.

4. The Committee shall study the reports submitted by the States Parties to the present Covenant. It shall transmit its reports, and such general comments as it may consider appropriate, to the States Parties. The Committee may also transmit to the Economic and Social Council these comments along with the copies of the reports it has received from States Parties to the present Covenant.

5. The States Parties to the present Covenant may submit to the Committee observations on any comments that may be made in accordance with paragraph 4 of this article.

Article 41

1. A State Party to the present Covenant may at any time declare under this article that it recognizes the competence of the Committee to receive and consider communications to the effect that a State Party claims that another State Party is not fulfilling its obligations under the present Covenant. Communications under this article may be received and considered only if submitted by a State Party which has made a declaration recognizing in regard to itself the competence of the Committee. No communication shall be received by the Committee if it concerns a State Party which has not made such a declaration. Communications received under this article shall be dealt with in accordance with the following procedure:

(a) If a State Party to the present Covenant considers that another State Party is not giving effect to the provisions of the present Covenant, it may, by written communication, bring the matter to the attention of that State Party. Within three months after the receipt of the communication the receiving State shall afford the State which sent the communication an explanation, or any other statement in writing clarifying the matter which should include, to the extent possible and pertinent, reference to domestic procedures and remedies taken, pending, or available in the matter;

(b) If the matter is not adjusted to the satisfaction of both States Parties concerned within six months after the receipt by the receiving State of the initial communication, either State shall have the right to refer the matter to the Committee, by notice given to the Committee and to the other State;

(c) The Committee shall deal with a matter referred to it only after it has ascertained that all available domestic remedies have been invoked and exhausted in the matter, in conformity with the generally recognized principles of international law. This shall not be the rule where the application of the remedies is unreasonably prolonged;

(d) The Committee shall hold closed meetings when examining communications under this article;

(e) Subject to the provisions of subparagraph (c), the Committee shall make available its good offices to the States Parties concerned with a view to a friendly solution of the matter on the basis of respect for human rights and fundamental freedoms as recognized in the present Covenant;

(f) In any matter referred to it, the Committee may call upon the States Parties concerned, referred to in subparagraph (b), to supply any relevant information;

(g) The States Parties concerned, referred to in subparagraph (b), shall have the right to be represented when the matter is being considered in the Committee and to make submissions orally and/or in writing;

(h) The Committee shall, within twelve months after the date of receipt of notice under subparagraph (b), submit a report:

(i) If a solution within the terms of subparagraph (e) is reached, the Committee shall confine its report to a brief statement of the facts and of the solution reached;

(ii) If a solution within the terms of subparagraph (e) is not reached, the Committee shall confine its report to a brief statement of the facts; the written submissions and record of the oral submissions made by the States Parties concerned shall be attached to the report. In every matter, the report shall be communicated to the States Parties concerned.

2. The provisions of this article shall come into force when ten States Parties to the present Covenant have made declarations under paragraph 1 of this article. Such declarations shall be deposited by the States Parties with the Secretary-General of the United Nations, who shall transmit copies thereof to the other States Parties. A declaration may be withdrawn at any time by notification to the Secretary-General. Such a withdrawal shall not prejudice the consideration of any matter which is the subject of a communication already transmitted under this article; no further communication

by any State Party shall be received after the notification of withdrawal of the declaration has been received by the Secretary-General, unless the State Party concerned has made a new declaration.

Article 42

1. (a) If a matter referred to the Committee in accordance with Article 41 is not resolved to the satisfaction of the States Parties concerned, the Committee may, with the prior consent of the States Parties concerned, appoint an ad hoc Conciliation Commission (hereinafter referred to as the Commission). The good offices of the Commission shall be made available to the States Parties concerned with a view to an amicable solution of the matter on the basis of respect for the present Covenant;

(b) The Commission shall consist of five persons acceptable to the States Parties concerned. If the States Parties concerned fail to reach agreement within three months on all or part of the composition of the Commission, the members of the Commission concerning whom no agreement has been reached shall be elected by secret ballot by a two-thirds majority vote of the Committee from among its members.

2. The members of the Commission shall serve in their personal capacity. They shall not be nationals of the States Parties concerned, or of a State not Party to the present Covenant, or of a State Party which has not made a declaration under Article 41.

3. The Commission shall elect its own Chairman and adopt its own rules of procedure.

4. The meetings of the Commission shall normally be held at the Headquarters of the United Nations or at the United Nations Office at Geneva. However, they may be held at such other convenient places as the Commission may determine in consultation with the Secretary-General of the United Nations and the States Parties concerned.

5. The secretariat provided in accordance with Article 36 shall also service the commissions appointed under this article.

6. The information received and collated by the Committee shall be made available to the Commission and the Commission may call upon the States Parties concerned to supply any other relevant information.

7. When the Commission has fully considered the matter, but in any event not later than twelve months after having been seized of the matter, it shall submit to the Chairman of the Committee a report for communication to the States Parties concerned:

(a) If the Commission is unable to complete its consideration of the matter within twelve months, it shall confine its report to a brief statement of the status of its consideration of the matter;

(b) If an amicable solution to the matter on tie basis of respect for human rights as recognized in the present Covenant is reached, the Commission shall confine its report to a brief statement of the facts and of the solution reached;

(c) If a solution within the terms of subparagraph (b) is not reached, the Commission's report shall embody its findings on all questions of fact relevant to the issues between the States Parties concerned, and its views on the possibilities of an amicable solution of the matter. This report shall also contain the written submissions and a record of the oral submissions made by the States Parties concerned;

(d) If the Commission's report is submitted under subparagraph (c), the States Parties concerned shall, within three months of the receipt of the report, notify the Chairman of the Committee whether or not they accept the contents of the report of the Commission.

8. The provisions of this article are without prejudice to the responsibilities of the Committee under Article 41.

9. The States Parties concerned shall share equally all the expenses of the members of the Commission in accordance with estimates to be provided by the Secretary-General of the United Nations.

10. The Secretary-General of the United Nations shall be empowered to pay the expenses of the members of the Commission, if necessary, before reimbursement by the States Parties concerned, in accordance with paragraph 9 of this article.

Article 43

The members of the Committee, and of the ad hoc conciliation commissions which may be appointed under Article 42, shall be entitled to the facilities, privileges and immunities of experts on mission for the United Nations as laid down in the relevant sections of the Convention on the Privileges and Immunities of the United Nations.

Article 44

The provisions for the implementation of the present Covenant shall apply without prejudice to the procedures prescribed in the field of human rights by or under the constituent instruments and the conventions of the United Nations and of the specialized agencies and shall not prevent the States Parties to the present Covenant from having recourse to other procedures for settling a dispute in accordance with general or special international agreements in force between them.

Article 45

The Committee shall submit to the General Assembly of the United Nations, through the Economic and Social Council, an annual report on its activities.

Part V

Article 46

Nothing in the present Covenant shall be interpreted as impairing the provisions of the Charter of the United Nations and of the constitutions of the specialized agencies which define the respective responsibilities of the various organs of the United Nations and of the specialized agencies in regard to the matters dealt with in the present Covenant.

Article 47

Nothing in the present Covenant shall be interpreted as impairing the inherent right of all peoples to enjoy and utilize fully and freely their natural wealth and resources.

Part VI

Article 48

1. The present Covenant is open for signature by any State Member of the United Nations or member of any of its specialized agencies, by any State Party to the Statute of the International Court of Justice, and by any other State which has been invited by the General Assembly of the United Nations to become a Party to the present Covenant.

2. The present Covenant is subject to ratification. Instruments of ratification shall be deposited with the Secretary-General of the United Nations.

3. The present Covenant shall be open to accession by any State referred to in paragraph 1 of this article.

4. Accession shall be effected by the deposit of an instrument of accession with the Secretary-General of the United Nations.

5. The Secretary-General of the United Nations shall inform all States which have signed this Covenant or acceded to it of the deposit of each instrument of ratification or accession.

Article 49

1. The present Covenant shall enter into force three months after the date of the deposit with the Secretary-General of the United Nations of the thirty-fifth instrument of ratification or instrument of accession.

2. For each State ratifying the present Covenant or acceding to it after the deposit of the thirty-fifth instrument of ratification or instrument of accession, the present Covenant shall enter into force three months after the date of the deposit of its own instrument of ratification or instrument of accession.

Article 50

The provisions of the present Covenant shall extend to all parts of federal States without any limitations or exceptions.

Article 51

1. Any State Party to the present Covenant may propose an amendment and file it with the Secretary-General of the United Nations. The Secretary-General of the United Nations shall thereupon communicate any proposed amendments to the States Parties to the present Covenant with a request that they notify him whether they favour a conference of States Parties for the purpose of considering and voting upon the proposals. In the event that at least one third of the States Parties favours such a conference, the Secretary-General shall convene the conference under the auspices of the United Nations. Any amendment adopted by a majority of the States Parties present and voting at the conference shall be submitted to the General Assembly of the United Nations for approval.

2. Amendments shall come into force when they have been approved by the General Assembly of the United Nations and accepted by a two-thirds majority of the States Parties to the present Covenant in accordance with their respective constitutional processes.

3. When amendments come into force, they shall be binding on those States Parties which have accepted them, other States Parties still being bound by the provisions of the present Covenant and any earlier amendment which they have accepted.

Article 52

Irrespective of the notifications made under Article 48, paragraph 5, the Secretary-General of the United Nations shall inform all States referred to in paragraph 1 of the same article of the following particulars:

(a) Signatures, ratifications and accessions under Article 48;

(b) The date of the entry into force of the present Covenant under Article 49 and the date of the entry into force of any amendments under Article 51.

Article 53

1. The present Covenant, of which the Chinese, English, French, Russian and Spanish texts are equally authentic, shall be deposited in the archives of the United Nations.

2. The Secretary-General of the United Nations shall transmit certified copies of the present Covenant to all States referred to in Article 48.

Chapter 6

Convention Relating to the Status of Refugees (excerpts)

Preamble

The High Contracting Parties,

Considering that the Charter of the United Nations and the Universal Declaration of Human Rights approved on 10 December 1948 by the General Assembly have affirmed the principle that human beings shall enjoy fundamental rights and freedoms without discrimination,

Considering that the United Nations has, on various occasions, manifested its profound concern for refugees and endeavoured to assure refugees the widest possible exercise of these fundamental rights and freedoms,

Considering that it is desirable to revise and consolidate previous international agreements relating to the status of refugees and to extend the scope of and the protection accorded by such instruments by means of a new agreement,

Considering that the grant of asylum may place unduly heavy burdens on certain countries, and that a satisfactory solution of a problem of which the United Nations has recognized the international scope and nature cannot therefore be achieved without international co-operation,

Expressing the wish that all States, recognizing the social and humanitarian nature of the problem of refugees, will do everything within their power to prevent this problem from becoming a cause of tension between States,

Noting that the United Nations High Commissioner for Refugees is charged with the task of supervising international conventions providing for the protection of refugees, and recognizing that the effective co-ordination of measures taken to deal with this problem will depend upon the co-operation of States with the High Commissioner,

Have agreed as follows:

Adopted 28 July 1951 by the United Nations Conference of Plenipotentiaries on the Status of Refugees and Stateless Presons convened under General Assembly resolution 429 (V) of 14 December 1950, *entry into force* 22 April 1954, in accordance with Article 43.

Chapter I: General Provisions

Article 1. Definition of the term "refugee"

A. For the purposes of the present Convention, the term "refugee" shall apply to any person who:

(1) Has been considered a refugee under the Arrangements of 12 May 1926 and 30 June 1928 or under the Conventions of 28 October 1933 and 10 February 1938, the Protocol of 14 September 1939 or the Constitution of the International Refugee Organization;

Decisions of non-eligibility taken by the International Refugee Organization during the period of its activities shall not prevent the status of refugee being accorded to persons who fulfill the conditions of paragraph 2 of this section;

(2) As a result of events occurring before 1 January 1951 and owing to well-founded fear of being persecuted for reasons of race, religion, nationality, membership of a particular social group or political opinion, is outside the country of his nationality and is unable, or owing to such fear, is unwilling to avail himself of the protection of that country; or who, not having a nationality and being outside the country of his former habitual residence as a result of such events, is unable or, owing to such fear, is unwilling to return to it. In the case of a person who has more than one nationality, the term "the country of his nationality" shall mean each of the countries of which he is a national, and a person shall not be deemed to be lacking the protection of the country of his nationality if, without any valid reason based on well-founded fear, he has not availed himself of the protection of one of the countries of which he is a national.

B. (1) For the purposes of this Convention, the words "events occurring before 1 January 1951" in Article 1, section A, shall be understood to mean either (a) "events occurring in Europe before 1 January 1951"; or (b) "events occurring in Europe or elsewhere before 1 January 1951"; and each Contracting State shall make a declaration at the time of signature, ratification or accession, specifying which of these meanings it applies for the purpose of its obligations under this Convention.

(2) Any Contracting State which has adopted alternative (a) may at any time extend its obligations by adopting alternative (b) by means of a notification addressed to the Secretary-General of the United Nations.

C. This Convention shall cease to apply to any person falling under the terms of section A if:

(1) He has voluntarily re-availed himself of the protection of the country of his nationality; or

(2) Having lost his nationality, he has voluntarily reacquired it; or

(3) He has acquired a new nationality, and enjoys the protection of the country of his new nationality; or

(4) He has voluntarily re-established himself in the country which he left or outside which he remained owing to fear of persecution; or

(5) He can no longer, because the circumstances in connection with which he has been recognized as a refugee have ceased to exist, continue to refuse to avail himself of the protection of the country of his nationality;

Provided that this paragraph shall not apply to a refugee falling under section A (1) of this article who is able to invoke compelling reasons arising out of previous persecution for refusing to avail himself of the protection of the country of nationality;

(6) Being a person who has no nationality he is, because the circumstances in connection with which he has been recognized as a refugee have ceased to exist, able to return to the country of his former habitual residence; provided that this paragraph shall not apply to a refugee falling under section A (1) of this article who is able to invoke compelling reasons arising out of previous persecution for refusing to return to the country of his former habitual residence.

D. This Convention shall not apply to persons who are at present receiving from organs or agencies of the United Nations other than the United Nations High Commissioner for Refugees protection or assistance.

When such protection or assistance has ceased for any reason, without the position of such persons being definitively settled in accordance with the relevant resolutions adopted by the General Assembly of the United Nations, these persons shall ipso facto be entitled to the benefits of this Convention.

E. This Convention shall not apply to a person who is recognized by the competent authorities of the country in which he has taken residence as having the rights and obligations which are attached to the possession of the nationality of that country.

F. The provisions of this Convention shall not apply to any person with respect to whom there are serious reasons for considering that:

(a) He has committed a crime against peace, a war crime, or a crime against humanity, as defined in the international instruments drawn up to make provision in respect of such crimes;

(b) He has committed a serious non-political crime outside the country of refuge prior to his admission to that country as a refugee;

(c) He has been guilty of acts contrary to the purposes and principles of the United Nations.

Article 2. General obligations

Every refugee has duties to the country in which he finds himself, which require in particular that he conform to its laws and regulations as well as to measures taken for the maintenance of public order.

Article 3. Non-discrimination

The Contracting States shall apply the provisions of this Convention to refugees without discrimination as to race, religion or country of origin.

Article 4. Religion

The Contracting States shall accord to refugees within their territories treatment at least as favourable as that accorded to their nationals with respect to freedom to practise their religion and freedom as regards the religious education of their children.

Article 5. Rights granted apart from this Convention

Nothing in this Convention shall be deemed to impair any rights and benefits granted by a Contracting State to refugees apart from this Convention.

Article 6. The term "in the same circumstances"

For the purposes of this Convention, the term "in the same circumstances" implies that any requirements (including requirements as to length and conditions of sojourn or residence) which the particular individual would have to fulfill for the enjoyment of the right in question, if he were not a refugee, must be fulfilled by him, with the exception of requirements which by their nature a refugee is incapable of fulfilling.

Article 7. Exemption from reciprocity

1. Except where this Convention contains more favourable provisions, a Contracting State shall accord to refugees the same treatment as is accorded to aliens generally.

2. After a period of three years residence, all refugees shall enjoy exemption from legislative reciprocity in the territory of the Contracting States.

3. Each Contracting State shall continue to accord to refugees the rights and benefits to which they were already entitled, in the absence of reciprocity, at the date of entry into force of this Convention for that State.

4. The Contracting States shall consider favourably the possibility of according to refugees, in the absence of reciprocity, rights and benefits beyond those to which they are entitled according to paragraphs 2 and 3, and to extending exemption from reciprocity to refugees who do not fulfill the conditions provided for in paragraphs 2 and 3.

5. The provisions of paragraphs 2 and 3 apply both to the rights and benefits referred to in Articles 13, 18, 19, 21 and 22 of this Convention and to rights and benefits for which this Convention does not provide.

Article 8. Exemption from exceptional measures

With regard to exceptional measures which may be taken against the person, property or interests of nationals of a foreign State, the Contracting States shall not apply such measures to a refugee who is formally a national of the said State solely on account of such nationality. Contracting States which, under their legislation, are prevented from applying the general principle expressed in this article, shall, in appropriate cases, grant exemptions in favour of such refugees.

Article 9. Provisional measures

Nothing in this Convention shall prevent a Contracting State, in time of war or other grave and exceptional circumstances, from taking provisionally measures which it considers to be essential to the national security in the case of a particular person, pending a determination by the Contracting State that that person is in fact a refugee and that the continuance of such measures is necessary in his case in the interests of national security.

Article 10. Continuity of residence

1. Where a refugee has been forcibly displaced during the Second World War and removed to the territory of a Contracting State, and is resident there, the period of such enforced sojourn shall be considered to have been lawful residence within that territory.

2. Where a refugee has been forcibly displaced during the Second World War from the territory of a Contracting State and has, prior to the date of entry into force of this Convention, returned there for the purpose of taking up residence, the period of residence before and after such enforced displacement shall be regarded as one uninterrupted period for any purposes for which uninterrupted residence is required.

Article 11. Refugee seamen

In the case of refugees regularly serving as crew members on board a ship flying the flag of a Contracting State, that State shall give sympathetic consideration to their establishment on its territory and the issue of travel documents to them or their temporary admission to its territory particularly with a view to facilitating their establishment in another country.

Chapter II: Juridical Status

Article 12. Personal status

1. The personal status of a refugee shall be governed by the law of the country of his domicile or, if he has no domicile, by the law of the country of his residence.

2. Rights previously acquired by a refugee and dependent on personal status, more particularly rights attaching to marriage, shall be respected by a Contracting State, subject to compliance, if this be necessary, with the formalities required by the law of that State, provided that the right in question is one which would have been recognized by the law of that State had he not become a refugee.

Article 13. Movable and immovable property

The Contracting States shall accord to a refugee treatment as favourable as possible and, in any event, not less favourable than that accorded to aliens generally in the same circumstances, as regards the acquisition of movable and immovable property and other rights pertaining thereto, and to leases and other contracts relating to movable and immovable property.

Article 14. Artistic rights and industrial property

In respect of the protection of industrial property, such as inventions, designs or models, trade marks, trade names, and of rights in literary, artistic and scientific works, a refugee shall be accorded in the country in which he has his habitual residence the same protection as is accorded to nationals of that country. In the territory of any other Contracting States, he shall be accorded the same protection as is accorded in that territory to nationals of the country in which he has his habitual residence.

Article 15. Right of association

As regards non-political and non-profit-making associations and trade unions the Contracting States shall accord to refugees lawfully staying in their territory the most favourable treatment accorded to nationals of a foreign country, in the same circumstances.

Article 16. Access to courts

1. A refugee shall have free access to the courts of law on the territory of all Contracting States.

2. A refugee shall enjoy in the Contracting State in which he has his habitual residence the same treatment as a national in matters pertaining to access to the courts, including legal assistance and exemption from cautio judicatum solvi.

3. A refugee shall be accorded in the matters referred to in paragraph 2 in countries other than that in which he has his habitual residence the treatment granted to a national of the country of his habitual residence.

Chapter III: Gainful Employment

Article 17. Wage-earning employment

1. The Contracting States shall accord to refugees lawfully staying in their territory the most favourable treatment accorded to nationals of a foreign country in the same circumstances, as regards the right to engage in wage-earning employment.

2. In any case, restrictive measures imposed on aliens or the employment of aliens for the protection of the national labour market shall not be applied to a refugee who was already exempt from them at the date of entry into force of this Convention for the Contracting State concerned, or who fulfills one of the following conditions:

(a) He has completed three years residence in the country;

(b) He has a spouse possessing the nationality of the country of residence. A refugee may not invoke the benefit of this provision if he has abandoned his spouse;

(c) He has one or more children possessing the nationality of the country of residence.

3. The Contracting States shall give sympathetic consideration to assimilating the rights of all refugees with regard to wage-earning employment to those of nationals, and in particular of those refugees who have entered their territory pursuant to programmes of labour recruitment or under immigration schemes.

Article 18. Self-employment

The Contracting States shall accord to a refugee lawfully in their territory treatment as favourable as possible and, in any event, not less favourable than that accorded to aliens generally in the same circumstances, as regards the right to engage on his own account in agriculture, industry, handicrafts and commerce and to establish commercial and industrial companies.

Article 19. Liberal professions

1. Each Contracting State shall accord to refugees lawfully staying in their territory who hold diplomas recognized by the competent authorities of that State, and who are desirous of practising a liberal profession, treatment as favourable as possible and, in any event, not less favourable than that accorded to aliens generally in the same circumstances.

2. The Contracting States shall use their best endeavours consistently with their laws and constitutions to secure the settlement of such refugees in the territories, other than the metropolitan territory, for whose international relations they are responsible.

Chapter IV: Welfare

Article 20. Rationing

Where a rationing system exists, which applies to the population at large and regulates the general distribution of products in short supply, refugees shall be accorded the same treatment as nationals.

Article 21. Housing

As regards housing, the Contracting States, in so far as the matter is regulated by laws or regulations or is subject to the control of public authorities, shall accord to refugees lawfully staying in their territory treatment as favourable as possible and, in any event, not less favourable than that accorded to aliens generally in the same circumstances.

Article 22. Public education

1. The Contracting States shall accord to refugees the same treatment as is accorded to nationals with respect to elementary education.

2. The Contracting States shall accord to refugees treatment as favourable as possible, and, in any event, not less favourable than that accorded to aliens generally in the same circumstances, with respect to education other than elementary education and, in particular, as regards access to studies, the recognition of foreign school certificates, diplomas and degrees, the remission of fees and charges and the award of scholarships.

Article 23. Public relief

The Contracting States shall accord to refugees lawfully staying in their territory the same treatment with respect to public relief and assistance as is accorded to their nationals.

Article 24. Labour legislation and social security

1. The Contracting States shall accord to refugees lawfully staying in their territory the same treatment as is accorded to nationals in respect of the following matters:

(a) In so far as such matters are governed by laws or regulations or are subject to the control of administrative authorities: remuneration, including family allowances where these form part of remuneration, hours of work, overtime arrangements, holidays with pay, restrictions on home work, minimum age of employment, apprenticeship and training, women's work and the work of young persons, and the enjoyment of the benefits of collective bargaining;

(b) Social security (legal provisions in respect of employment injury, occupational diseases, maternity, sickness, disability, old age, death, unemployment, family responsibilities and any other contingency which, according to national laws or regulations, is covered by a social security scheme), subject to the following limitations:

(i) There may be appropriate arrangements for the maintenance of acquired rights and rights in course of acquisition;

(ii) National laws or regulations of the country of residence may prescribe special arrangements concerning benefits or portions of benefits which are payable wholly out of public funds, and concerning allowances paid to persons who do not fulfill the contribution conditions prescribed for the award of a normal pension.

2. The right to compensation for the death of a refugee resulting from employment injury or from occupational disease shall not be affected by the fact that the residence of the beneficiary is outside the territory of the Contracting State.

3. The Contracting States shall extend to refugees the benefits of agreements concluded between them, or which may be concluded between them in the future, concerning the maintenance of acquired rights and rights in the process of acquisition in regard to social security, subject only to the conditions which apply to nationals of the States signatory to the agreements in question.

4. The Contracting States will give sympathetic consideration to extending to refugees

so far as possible the benefits of similar agreements which may at any time be in force between such Contracting States and non-contracting States.

Chapter V: Administrative Measures

Article 25. Administrative assistance

1. When the exercise of a right by a refugee would normally require the assistance of authorities of a foreign country to whom he cannot have recourse, the Contracting States in whose territory he is residing shall arrange that such assistance be afforded to him by their own authorities or by an international authority.

2. The authority or authorities mentioned in paragraph 1 shall deliver or cause to be delivered under their supervision to refugees such documents or certifications as would normally be delivered to aliens by or through their national authorities.

3. Documents or certifications so delivered shall stand in the stead of the official instruments delivered to aliens by or through their national authorities, and shall be given credence in the absence of proof to the contrary.

4. Subject to such exceptional treatment as may be granted to indigent persons, fees may be charged for the services mentioned herein, but such fees shall be moderate and commensurate with those charged to nationals for similar services.

5. The provisions of this article shall be without prejudice to Articles 27 and 28.

Article 26. Freedom of movement

Each Contracting State shall accord to refugees lawfully in its territory the right to choose their place of residence and to move freely within its territory subject to any regulations applicable to aliens generally in the same circumstances.

Article 27. Identity papers

The Contracting States shall issue identity papers to any refugee in their territory who does not possess a valid travel document.

Article 28. Travel documents

1 . The Contracting States shall issue to refugees lawfully staying in their territory travel documents for the purpose of travel outside their territory, unless compelling reasons of national security or public order otherwise require, and the provisions of the Schedule to this Convention shall apply with respect to such documents. The Contracting States may issue such a travel document to any other refugee in their territory; they shall in particular give sympathetic consideration to the issue of such a travel document to refugees in their territory who are unable to obtain a travel document from the country of their lawful residence.

2. Travel documents issued to refugees under previous international agreements by Parties thereto shall be recognized and treated by the Contracting States in the same way as if they had been issued pursuant to this article.

Article 29. Fiscal charges

1. The Contracting States shall not impose upon refugees duties, charges or taxes, of any description whatsoever, other or higher than those which are or may be levied on their nationals in similar situations.

2. Nothing in the above paragraph shall prevent the application to refugees of the laws and regulations concerning charges in respect of the issue to aliens of administrative documents including identity papers.

Article 30. Transfer of assets

1. A Contracting State shall, in conformity with its laws and regulations, permit refugees to transfer assets which they have brought into its territory, to another country where they have been admitted for the purposes of resettlement.

2. A Contracting State shall give sympathetic consideration to the application of refugees for permission to transfer assets wherever they may be and which are necessary for their resettlement in another country to which they have been admitted.

Article 31. Refugees unlawfully in the country of refuge

1. The Contracting States shall not impose penalties, on account of their illegal entry or presence, on refugees who, coming directly from a territory where their life or freedom was threatened in the sense of Article 1, enter or are present in their territory without authorization, provided they present themselves without delay to the authorities and show good cause for their illegal entry or presence.

2. The Contracting States shall not apply to the movements of such refugees restrictions other than those which are necessary and such restrictions shall only be applied until their status in the country is regularized or they obtain admission into another country. The Contracting States shall allow such refugees a reasonable period and all the necessary facilities to obtain admission into another country.

Article 32. Expulsion

1. The Contracting States shall not expel a refugee lawfully in their territory save on grounds of national security or public order.

2. The expulsion of such a refugee shall be only in pursuance of a decision reached in accordance with due process of law. Except where compelling reasons of national

security otherwise require, the refugee shall be allowed to submit evidence to clear himself, and to appeal to and be represented for the purpose before competent authority or a person or persons specially designated by the competent authority.

3. The Contracting States shall allow such a refugee a reasonable period within which to seek legal admission into another country. The Contracting States reserve the right to apply during that period such internal measures as they may deem necessary.

Article 33. Prohibition of expulsion or return ("refoulement")

1. No Contracting State shall expel or return ("refouler") a refugee in any manner whatsoever to the frontiers of territories where his life or freedom would be threatened on account of his race, religion, nationality, membership of a particular social group or political opinion.

2. The benefit of the present provision may not, however, be claimed by a refugee whom there are reasonable grounds for regarding as a danger to the security of the country in which he is, or who, having been convicted by a final judgement of a particularly serious crime, constitutes a danger to the community of that country.

Article 34. Naturalization

The Contracting States shall as far as possible facilitate the assimilation and naturalization of refugees. They shall in particular make every effort to expedite naturalization proceedings and to reduce as far as possible the charges and costs of such proceedings.

Chapter VI: Executory and Transitory Provisions

Article 35. Co-operation of the national authorities with the United Nations

1. The Contracting States undertake to co-operate with the Office of the United Nations High Commissioner for Refugees, or any other agency of the United Nations which may succeed it, in the exercise of its functions, and shall in particular facilitate its duty of supervising the application of the provisions of this Convention.

2. In order to enable the Office of the High Commissioner or any other agency of the United Nations which may succeed it, to make reports to the competent organs of the United Nations, the Contracting States undertake to provide them in the appropriate form with information and statistical data requested concerning:

(a) The condition of refugees,

(b) The implementation of this Convention, and

(c) Laws, regulations and decrees which are, or may hereafter be, in force relating to refugees.

Article 36. Information on national legislation

The Contracting States shall communicate to the Secretary-General of the United Nations the laws and regulations which they may adopt to ensure the application of this Convention.

Article 37. Relation to previous conventions

Without prejudice to Article 28, paragraph 2, of this Convention, this Convention replaces, as between Parties to it, the Arrangements of 5 July 1922, 31 May 1924, 12 May 1926, 30 June 1928 and 30 July 1935, the Conventions of 28 October 1933 and 10 February 1938, the Protocol of 14 September 1939 and the Agreement of 15 October 1946.

. . .

Chapter 7
International Convention on the Protection of the Rights of All Migrant Workers and Members of Their Families (excerpts)

Preamble

The States Parties to the present Convention,

Taking into account the principles embodied in the basic instruments of the United Nations concerning human rights, in particular the Universal Declaration of Human Rights, the International Covenant on Economic, Social and Cultural Rights, the International Covenant on Civil and Political Rights, the International Convention on the Elimination of All Forms of Racial Discrimination, the Convention on the Elimination of All Forms of Discrimination Against Women and the Convention on the Rights of the Child,

Taking into account also the principles and standards set forth in the relevant instruments elaborated within the framework of the International Labour Organisation, especially the Convention concerning Migration for Employment (No. 97), the Convention concerning Migrations in Abusive Conditions and the Promotion of Equality of Opportunity and Treatment of Migrant Workers (No.143), the Recommendation concerning Migration for Employment (No. 86), the Recommendation concerning Migrant Workers (No.151), the Convention concerning Forced or Compulsory Labour (No. 29) and the Convention concerning Abolition of Forced Labour (No. 105),

Reaffirming the importance of the principles contained in the Convention against Discrimination in Education of the United Nations Educational, Scientific and Cultural Organization,

Recalling the Convention against Torture and Other Cruel, Inhuman or Degrading Treatment or Punishment, the Declaration of the Fourth United Nations Congress on the Prevention of Crime and the Treatment of Offenders, the Code of Conduct for Law Enforcement Officials, and the Slavery Conventions,

Adopted by General Assembly resolution 45/158 of 18 December 1990, *entry into force* 1 January 2003.

Recalling that one of the objectives of the International Labour Organisation, as stated in its Constitution, is the protection of the interests of workers when employed in countries other than their own, and bearing in mind the expertise and experience of that organization in matters related to migrant workers and members of their families,

Recognizing the importance of the work done in connection with migrant workers and members of their families in various organs of the United Nations, in particular in the Commission on Human Rights and the Commission for Social Development, and in the Food and Agriculture Organization of the United Nations, the United Nations Educational, Scientific and Cultural Organization and the World Health Organization, as well as in other international organizations,

Recognizing also the progress made by certain States on a regional or bilateral basis towards the protection of the rights of migrant workers and members of their families, as well as the importance and usefulness of bilateral and multilateral agreements in this field,

Realizing the importance and extent of the migration phenomenon, which involves millions of people and affects a large number of States in the international community,

Aware of the impact of the flows of migrant workers on States and people concerned, and desiring to establish norms which may contribute to the harmonization of the attitudes of States through the acceptance of basic principles concerning the treatment of migrant workers and members of their families,

Considering the situation of vulnerability in which migrant workers and members of their families frequently-find themselves owing, among other things, to their absence from their State of origin and to the difficulties they may encounter arising from their presence in the State of employment,

Convinced that the rights of migrant workers and members of their families have not been sufficiently recognized everywhere and therefore require appropriate international protection,

Taking into account the fact that migration is often the cause of serious problems for the members of the families of migrant workers as well as for the workers themselves, in particular because of the scattering of the family,

Bearing in mind that the human problems involved in migration are even more serious in the case of irregular migration and convinced therefore that appropriate action should be encouraged in order to prevent and eliminate clandestine movements and trafficking in migrant workers, while at the same time assuring the protection of their fundamental human rights,

Considering that workers who are non-documented or in an irregular situation are frequently employed under less favourable conditions of work than other workers and that certain employers find this an inducement to seek such labour in order to reap the benefits of unfair competition,

Considering also that recourse to the employment of migrant workers who are in an irregular situation will be discouraged if the fundamental human rights of all migrant workers are more widely recognized and, moreover, that granting certain additional rights to migrant workers and members of their families in a regular situation will encourage all migrants and employers to respect and comply with the laws and procedures established by the States concerned,

Convinced, therefore, of the need to bring about the international protection of the rights of all migrant workers and members of their families, reaffirming and establishing basic norms in a comprehensive convention which could be applied universally,

Have agreed as follows:

Part I: Scope and Definitions

Article 1

1. The present Convention is applicable, except as otherwise provided hereafter, to all migrant workers and members of their families without distinction of any kind such as sex, race, colour, language, religion or conviction, political or other opinion, national, ethnic or social origin, nationality, age, economic position, property, marital status, birth or other status.

2. The present Convention shall apply during the entire migration process of migrant workers and members of their families, which comprises preparation for migration, departure, transit and the entire period of stay and remunerated activity in the State of employment as well as return to the State of origin or the State of habitual residence.

Article 2

For the purposes of the present Convention:

1. The term "migrant worker" refers to a person who is to be engaged, is engaged or has been engaged in a remunerated activity in a State of which he or she is not a national.

2. (a) The term "frontier worker" refers to a migrant worker who retains his or her habitual residence in a neighbouring State to which he or she normally returns every day or at least once a week;

(b) The term "seasonal worker" refers to a migrant worker whose work by its character is dependent on seasonal conditions and is performed only during part of the year;

(c) The term "seafarer," which includes a fisherman, refers to a migrant worker employed on board a vessel registered in a State of which he or she is not a national;

(d) The term "worker on an offshore installation" refers to a migrant worker employed on an offshore installation that is under the jurisdiction of a State of which he or she is not a national;

(e) The term "itinerant worker" refers to a migrant worker who, having his or her habitual residence in one State, has to travel to another State or States for short periods, owing to the nature of his or her occupation;

(f) The term "project-tied worker" refers to a migrant worker admitted to a State of employment for a defined period to work solely on a specific project being carried out in that State by his or her employer;

(g) The term "specified-employment worker" refers to a migrant worker:

(i) Who has been sent by his or her employer for a restricted and defined period of time to a State of employment to undertake a specific assignment or duty; or

(ii) Who engages for a restricted and defined period of time in work that requires professional, commercial, technical or other highly specialized skill; or

(iii) Who, upon the request of his or her employer in the State of employment, engages for a restricted and defined period of time in work whose nature is transitory or brief; and who is required to depart from the State of employment either at the expiration of his or her authorized period of stay, or earlier if he or she no longer undertakes that specific assignment or duty or engages in that work;

(h) The term "self-employed worker" refers to a migrant worker who is engaged in a remunerated activity otherwise than under a contract of employment and who earns his or her living through this activity normally working alone or together with members of his or her family, and to any other migrant worker recognized as self-employed by applicable legislation of the State of employment or bilateral or multilateral agreements.

Article 3

The present Convention shall not apply to:

(a) Persons sent or employed by international organizations and agencies or persons sent or employed by a State outside its territory to perform official functions, whose admission and status are regulated by general international law or by specific international agreements or conventions;

(b) Persons sent or employed by a State or on its behalf outside its territory who participate in development programmes and other co-operation programmes, whose admission and status are regulated by agreement with the State of employment and who, in accordance with that agreement, are not considered migrant workers;

(c) Persons taking up residence in a State different from their State of origin as investors;

(d) Refugees and stateless persons, unless such application is provided for in the relevant national legislation of, or international instruments in force for, the State Party concerned;

(e) Students and trainees;

(f) Seafarers and workers on an offshore installation who have not been admitted to take up residence and engage in a remunerated activity in the State of employment.

Article 4

For the purposes of the present Convention the term ''members of the family" refers to persons married to migrant workers or having with them a relationship that, according to applicable law, produces effects equivalent to marriage, as well as their dependent children and other dependent persons who are recognized as members of the family by applicable legislation or applicable bilateral or multilateral agreements between the States concerned.

Article 5

For the purposes of the present Convention, migrant workers and members of their families:

(a) Are considered as documented or in a regular situation if they are authorized to enter, to stay and to engage in a remunerated activity in the State of employment pursuant to the law of that State and to international agreements to which that State is a party;

(b) Are considered as non-documented or in an irregular situation if they do not comply with the conditions provided for in subparagraph (a) of the present article.

Article 6

For the purposes of the present Convention:

(a) The term "State of origin" means the State of which the person concerned is a national;

(b) The term "State of employment" means a State where the migrant worker is to be engaged, is engaged or has been engaged in a remunerated activity, as the case may be;

(c) The term "State of transit" means any State through which the person concerned passes on any journey to the State of employment or from the State of employment to the State of origin or the State of habitual residence.

Part II: Non-Discrimination with Respect to Rights

Article 7

States Parties undertake, in accordance with the international instruments concerning human rights, to respect and to ensure to all migrant workers and members of their families within their territory or subject to their jurisdiction the rights provided for in the present Convention without distinction of any kind such as to sex, race, colour, language, religion or conviction, political or other opinion, national, ethnic or social origin, nationality, age, economic position, property, marital status, birth or other status.

Part III: Human Rights of All Migrant Workers and Members of Their Families

Article 8

1. Migrant workers and members of their families shall be free to leave any State,

including their State of origin. This right shall not be subject to any restrictions except those that are provided by law, are necessary to protect national security, public order (ordre public), public health or morals or the rights and freedoms of others and are consistent with the other rights recognized in the present part of the Convention.

2. Migrant workers and members of their families shall have the right at any time to enter and remain in their State of origin.

Article 9

The right to life of migrant workers and members of their families shall be protected by law.

Article 10

No migrant worker or member of his or her family shall be subjected to torture or to cruel, inhuman or degrading treatment or punishment.

Article 11

1. No migrant worker or member of his or her family shall be held in slavery or servitude.

2. No migrant worker or member of his or her family shall be required to perform forced or compulsory labour.

3. Paragraph 2 of the present article shall not be held to preclude, in States where imprisonment with hard labour may be imposed as a punishment for a crime, the performance of hard labour in pursuance of a sentence to such punishment by a competent court.

4. For the purpose of the present article the term "forced or compulsory labour" shall not include:

(a) Any work or service not referred to in paragraph 3 of the present article normally required of a person who is under detention in consequence of a lawful order of a court or of a person during conditional release from such detention;

(b) Any service exacted in cases of emergency or calamity threatening the life or well-being of the community;

(c) Any work or service that forms part of normal civil obligations so far as it is imposed also on citizens of the State concerned.

Article 12

1. Migrant workers and members of their families shall have the right to freedom of thought, conscience and religion. This right shall include freedom to have or to adopt a religion or belief of their choice and freedom either individually or in community

with others and in public or private to manifest their religion or belief in worship, observance, practice and teaching.

2. Migrant workers and members of their families shall not be subject to coercion that would impair their freedom to have or to adopt a religion or belief of their choice.

3. Freedom to manifest one's religion or belief may be subject only to such limitations as are prescribed by law and are necessary to protect public safety, order, health or morals or the fundamental rights and freedoms of others.

4. States Parties to the present Convention undertake to have respect for the liberty of parents, at least one of whom is a migrant worker, and, when applicable, legal guardians to ensure the religious and moral education of their children in conformity with their own convictions.

Article 13

1. Migrant workers and members of their families shall have the right to hold opinions without interference.

2. Migrant workers and members of their families shall have the right to freedom of expression; this right shall include freedom to seek, receive and impart information and ideas of all kinds, regardless of frontiers, either orally, in writing or in print, in the form of art or through any other media of their choice.

3. The exercise of the right provided for in paragraph 2 of the present article carries with it special duties and responsibilities. It may therefore be subject to certain restrictions, but these shall only be such as are provided by law and are necessary:

(a) For respect of the rights or reputation of others;

(b) For the protection of the national security of the States concerned or of public order (ordre public) or of public health or morals;

(c) For the purpose of preventing any propaganda for war;

(d) For the purpose of preventing any advocacy of national, racial or religious hatred that constitutes incitement to discrimination, hostility or violence.

Article 14

No migrant worker or member of his or her family shall be subjected to arbitrary or unlawful interference with his or her privacy, family, home, correspondence or other communications, or to unlawful attacks on his or her honour and reputation. Each migrant worker and member of his or her family shall have the right to the protection of the law against such interference or attacks.

Article 15

No migrant worker or member of his or her family shall be arbitrarily deprived of property, whether owned individually or in association with others. Where, under the legislation in force in the State of employment, the assets of a migrant worker or a member of his or her family are expropriated in whole or in part, the person concerned shall have the right to fair and adequate compensation.

Article 16

1. Migrant workers and members of their families shall have the right to liberty and security of person.

2. Migrant workers and members of their families shall be entitled to effective protection by the State against violence, physical injury, threats and intimidation, whether by public officials or by private individuals, groups or institutions.

3. Any verification by law enforcement officials of the identity of migrant workers or members of their families shall be carried out in accordance with procedure established by law.

4. Migrant workers and members of their families shall not be subjected individually or collectively to arbitrary arrest or detention; they shall not be deprived of their liberty except on such grounds and in accordance with such procedures as are established by law.

5. Migrant workers and members of their families who are arrested shall be informed at the time of arrest as far as possible in a language they understand of the reasons for their arrest and they shall be promptly informed in a language they understand of any charges against them.

6. Migrant workers and members of their families who are arrested or detained on a criminal charge shall be brought promptly before a judge or other officer authorized by law to exercise judicial power and shall be entitled to trial within a reasonable time or to release. It shall not be the general rule that while awaiting trial they shall be detained in custody, but release may be subject to guarantees to appear for trial, at any other stage of the judicial proceedings and, should the occasion arise, for the execution of the judgement.

7. When a migrant worker or a member of his or her family is arrested or committed to prison or custody pending trial or is detained in any other manner:

(a) The consular or diplomatic authorities of his or her State of origin or of a State representing the interests of that State shall, if he or she so requests, be informed without delay of his or her arrest or detention and of the reasons therefor;

(b) The person concerned shall have the right to communicate with the said authorities. Any communication by the person concerned to the said authorities shall be forwarded without delay, and he or she shall also have the right to receive communications sent by the said authorities without delay;

(c) The person concerned shall be informed without delay of this right and of rights deriving from relevant treaties, if any, applicable between the States concerned, to correspond and to meet with representatives of the said authorities and to make arrangements with them for his or her legal representation.

8. Migrant workers and members of their families who are deprived of their liberty by arrest or detention shall be entitled to take proceedings before a court, in order that that court may decide without delay on the lawfulness of their detention and order their release if the detention is not lawful. When they attend such proceedings, they shall have the assistance, if necessary without cost to them, of an interpreter, if they cannot understand or speak the language used.

9. Migrant workers and members of their families who have been victims of unlawful arrest or detention shall have an enforceable right to compensation.

Article 17

1. Migrant workers and members of their families who are deprived of their liberty shall be treated with humanity and with respect for the inherent dignity of the human person and for their cultural identity.

2. Accused migrant workers and members of their families shall, save in exceptional circumstances, be separated from convicted persons and shall be subject to separate treatment appropriate to their status as unconvicted persons. Accused juvenile persons shall be separated from adults and brought as speedily as possible for adjudication.

3. Any migrant worker or member of his or her family who is detained in a State of transit or in a State of employment for violation of provisions relating to migration shall be held, in so far as practicable, separately from convicted persons or persons detained pending trial.

4. During any period of imprisonment in pursuance of a sentence imposed by a court of law, the essential aim of the treatment of a migrant worker or a member of his or her family shall be his or her reformation and social rehabilitation. Juvenile offenders shall be separated from adults and be accorded treatment appropriate to their age and legal status.

5. During detention or imprisonment, migrant workers and members of their families shall enjoy the same rights as nationals to visits by members of their families.

6. Whenever a migrant worker is deprived of his or her liberty, the competent authorities of the State concerned shall pay attention to the problems that may be posed for members of his or her family, in particular for spouses and minor children.

7. Migrant workers and members of their families who are subjected to any form of detention or imprisonment in accordance with the law in force in the State of employment or in the State of transit shall enjoy the same rights as nationals of those States who are in the same situation.

8. If a migrant worker or a member of his or her family is detained for the purpose of verifying any infraction of provisions related to migration, he or she shall not bear any costs arising therefrom.

Article 18

1. Migrant workers and members of their families shall have the right to equality with nationals of the State concerned before the courts and tribunals. In the determination of any criminal charge against them or of their rights and obligations in a suit of law, they shall be entitled to a fair and public hearing by a competent, independent and impartial tribunal established by law.

2. Migrant workers and members of their families who are charged with a criminal offence shall have the right to be presumed innocent until proven guilty according to law.

3. In the determination of any criminal charge against them, migrant workers and members of their families shall be entitled to the following minimum guarantees:

(a) To be informed promptly and in detail in a language they understand of the nature and cause of the charge against them;

(b) To have adequate time and facilities for the preparation of their defence and to communicate with counsel of their own choosing;

(c) To be tried without undue delay;

(d) To be tried in their presence and to defend themselves in person or through legal assistance of their own choosing; to be informed, if they do not have legal assistance, of this right; and to have legal assistance assigned to them, in any case where the interests of justice so require and without payment by them in any such case if they do not have sufficient means to pay;

(e) To examine or have examined the witnesses against them and to obtain the attendance and examination of witnesses on their behalf under the same conditions as witnesses against them;

(f) To have the free assistance of an interpreter if they cannot understand or speak the language used in court;

(g) Not to be compelled to testify against themselves or to confess guilt.

4. In the case of juvenile persons, the procedure shall be such as will take account of their age and the desirability of promoting their rehabilitation.

5. Migrant workers and members of their families convicted of a crime shall have the right to their conviction and sentence being reviewed by a higher tribunal according to law.

6. When a migrant worker or a member of his or her family has, by a final decision, been convicted of a criminal offence and when subsequently his or her conviction has been reversed or he or she has been pardoned on the ground that a new or newly discovered fact shows conclusively that there has been a miscarriage of justice, the person who has suffered punishment as a result of such conviction shall be compensated according to law, unless it is proved that the non-disclosure of the unknown fact in time is wholly or partly attributable to that person.

7. No migrant worker or member of his or her family shall be liable to be tried or punished again for an offence for which he or she has already been finally convicted or acquitted in accordance with the law and penal procedure of the State concerned.

Article 19

1. No migrant worker or member of his or her family shall be held guilty of any criminal offence on account of any act or omission that did not constitute a criminal offence under national or international law at the time when the criminal offence was committed, nor shall a heavier penalty be imposed than the one that was applicable at the time when it was committed. If, subsequent to the commission of the offence, provision is made by law for the imposition of a lighter penalty, he or she shall benefit thereby.

2. Humanitarian considerations related to the status of a migrant worker, in particular with respect to his or her right of residence or work, should be taken into account in imposing a sentence for a criminal offence committed by a migrant worker or a member of his or her family.

Article 20

1. No migrant worker or member of his or her family shall be imprisoned merely on the ground of failure to fulfill a contractual obligation.

2. No migrant worker or member of his or her family shall be deprived of his or her authorization of residence or work permit or expelled merely on the ground of failure to fulfill an obligation arising out of a work contract unless fulfillment of that obligation constitutes a condition for such authorization or permit.

Article 21

It shall be unlawful for anyone, other than a public official duly authorized by law, to confiscate, destroy or attempt to destroy identity documents, documents authorizing entry to or stay, residence or establishment in the national territory or work permits. No authorized confiscation of such documents shall take place without delivery of a detailed receipt. In no case shall it be permitted to destroy the passport or equivalent document of a migrant worker or a member of his or her family.

Article 22

1. Migrant workers and members of their families shall not be subject to measures of collective expulsion. Each case of expulsion shall be examined and decided individually.

2. Migrant workers and members of their families may be expelled from the territory of a State Party only in pursuance of a decision taken by the competent authority in accordance with law.

3. The decision shall be communicated to them in a language they understand. Upon their request where not otherwise mandatory, the decision shall be communicated to them in writing and, save in exceptional circumstances on account of national security, the reasons for the decision likewise stated. The persons concerned shall be informed of these rights before or at the latest at the time the decision is rendered.

4. Except where a final decision is pronounced by a judicial authority, the person concerned shall have the right to submit the reason he or she should not be expelled and to have his or her case reviewed by the competent authority, unless compelling reasons of national security require otherwise. Pending such review, the person concerned shall have the right to seek a stay of the decision of expulsion.

5. If a decision of expulsion that has already been executed is subsequently annulled, the person concerned shall have the right to seek compensation according to law and the earlier decision shall not be used to prevent him or her from re-entering the State concerned.

6. In case of expulsion, the person concerned shall have a reasonable opportunity before or after departure to settle any claims for wages and other entitlements due to him or her and any pending liabilities.

7. Without prejudice to the execution of a decision of expulsion, a migrant worker or a member of his or her family who is subject to such a decision may seek entry into a State other than his or her State of origin.

8. In case of expulsion of a migrant worker or a member of his or her family the costs of expulsion shall not be borne by him or her. The person concerned may be required to pay his or her own travel costs.

9. Expulsion from the State of employment shall not in itself prejudice any rights of a migrant worker or a member of his or her family acquired in accordance with the law of that State, including the right to receive wages and other entitlements due to him or her.

Article 23

Migrant workers and members of their families shall have the right to have recourse to the protection and assistance of the consular or diplomatic authorities of their State of origin or of a State representing the interests of that State whenever the rights recognized in the present Convention are impaired. In particular, in case of expulsion, the person concerned shall be informed of this right without delay and the authorities of the expelling State shall facilitate the exercise of such right.

Article 24

Every migrant worker and every member of his or her family shall have the right to recognition everywhere as a person before the law.

Article 25

1. Migrant workers shall enjoy treatment not less favourable than that which applies to nationals of the State of employment in respect of remuneration and:

(a) Other conditions of work, that is to say, overtime, hours of work, weekly rest, holidays with pay, safety, health, termination of the employment relationship and any other conditions of work which, according to national law and practice, are covered by these terms;

(b) Other terms of employment, that is to say, minimum age of employment, restriction on home work and any other matters which, according to national law and practice, are considered a term of employment.

2. It shall not be lawful to derogate in private contracts of employment from the principle of equality of treatment referred to in paragraph 1 of the present article.

3. States Parties shall take all appropriate measures to ensure that migrant workers are not deprived of any rights derived from this principle by reason of any irregularity in their stay or employment. In particular, employers shall not be relieved of any legal or contractual obligations, nor shall their obligations be limited in any manner by reason of such irregularity.

Article 26

1. States Parties recognize the right of migrant workers and members of their families:

To take part in meetings and activities of trade unions and of any other associations established in accordance with law, with a view to protecting their economic, social, cultural and other interests, subject only to the rules of the organization concerned;

(b) To join freely any trade union and any such association as aforesaid, subject only to the rules of the organization concerned;

(c) To seek the aid and assistance of any trade union and of any such association as aforesaid.

2. No restrictions may be placed on the exercise of these rights other than those that are prescribed by law and which are necessary in a democratic society in the interests of national security, public order (ordre public) or the protection of the rights and freedoms of others.

Article 27

1. With respect to social security, migrant workers and members of their families shall enjoy in the State of employment the same treatment granted to nationals in so far as they fulfill the requirements provided for by the applicable legislation of that State and the applicable bilateral and multilateral treaties. The competent authorities of the State of origin and the State of employment can at any time establish the necessary arrangements to determine the modalities of application of this norm.

2. Where the applicable legislation does not allow migrant workers and members of their families a benefit, the States concerned shall examine the possibility of reimbursing interested persons the amount of contributions made by them with respect to that benefit on the basis of the treatment granted to nationals who are in similar circumstances.

Article 28

Migrant workers and members of their families shall have the right to receive any medical care that is urgently required for the preservation of their life or the avoidance of irreparable harm to their health on the basis of equality of treatment with nationals of the State concerned. Such emergency medical care shall not be refused them by reason of any irregularity with regard to stay or employment.

Article 29

Each child of a migrant worker shall have the right to a name, to registration of birth and to a nationality.

Article 30

Each child of a migrant worker shall have the basic right of access to education on the basis of equality of treatment with nationals of the State concerned. Access to public pre-school educational institutions or schools shall not be refused or limited by reason of the irregular situation with respect to stay or employment of either parent or by reason of the irregularity of the child's stay in the State of employment.

Article 31

1. States Parties shall ensure respect for the cultural identity of migrant workers and members of their families and shall not prevent them from maintaining their cultural links with their State of origin.

2. States Parties may take appropriate measures to assist and encourage efforts in this respect.

Article 32

Upon the termination of their stay in the State of employment, migrant workers and members of their families shall have the right to transfer their earnings and savings and, in accordance with the applicable legislation of the States concerned, their personal effects and belongings.

Article 33

1. Migrant workers and members of their families shall have the right to be informed

by the State of origin, the State of employment or the State of transit as the case may be concerning:

(a) Their rights arising out of the present Convention;

(b) The conditions of their admission, their rights and obligations under the law and practice of the State concerned and such other matters as will enable them to comply with administrative or other formalities in that State.

2. States Parties shall take all measures they deem appropriate to disseminate the said information or to ensure that it is provided by employers, trade unions or other appropriate bodies or institutions. As appropriate, they shall co-operate with other States concerned.

3. Such adequate information shall be provided upon request to migrant workers and members of their families, free of charge, and, as far as possible, in a language they are able to understand.

Article 34

Nothing in the present part of the Convention shall have the effect of relieving migrant workers and the members of their families from either the obligation to comply with the laws and regulations of any State of transit and the State of employment or the obligation to respect the cultural identity of the inhabitants of such States.

Article 35

Nothing in the present part of the Convention shall be interpreted as implying the regularization of the situation of migrant workers or members of their families who are non-documented or in an irregular situation or any right to such regularization of their situation, nor shall it prejudice the measures intended to ensure sound and equitable- conditions for international migration as provided in part VI of the present Convention.

Part IV: Other Rights of Migrant Workers and Members of Their Families Who Are Documented or in a Regular Situation

Article 36

Migrant workers and members of their families who are documented or in a regular situation in the State of employment shall enjoy the rights set forth in the present part of the Convention in addition to those set forth in part III.

Article 37

Before their departure, or at the latest at the time of their admission to the State of employment, migrant workers and members of their families shall have the right to be fully informed by the State of origin or the State of employment, as appropriate, of all conditions applicable to their admission and particularly those concerning their stay and the remunerated activities in which they may engage as well as of the requirements they must satisfy in the State of employment and the authority to which they must address themselves for any modification of those conditions.

Article 38

1. States of employment shall make every effort to authorize migrant workers and members of the families to be temporarily absent without effect upon their authorization to stay or to work, as the case may be. In doing so, States of employment shall take into account the special needs and obligations of migrant workers and members of their families, in particular in their States of origin.

2. Migrant workers and members of their families shall have the right to be fully informed of the terms on which such temporary absences are authorized.

Article 39

1. Migrant workers and members of their families shall have the right to liberty of movement in the territory of the State of employment and freedom to choose their residence there.

2. The rights mentioned in paragraph 1 of the present article shall not be subject to any restrictions except those that are provided by law, are necessary to protect national security, public order (ordre public), public health or morals, or the rights and freedoms of others and are consistent with the other rights recognized in the present Convention.

Article 40

1. Migrant workers and members of their families shall have the right to form associations and trade unions in the State of employment for the promotion and protection of their economic, social, cultural and other interests.

2. No restrictions may be placed on the exercise of this right other than those that are prescribed by law and are necessary in a democratic society in the interests of national security, public order (ordre public) or the protection of the rights and freedoms of others.

Article 41

1. Migrant workers and members of their families shall have the right to participate in public affairs of their State of origin and to vote and to be elected at elections of that State, in accordance with its legislation.

2. The States concerned shall, as appropriate and in accordance with their legislation, facilitate the exercise of these rights.

Article 42

1. States Parties shall consider the establishment of procedures or institutions through which account may be taken, both in States of origin and in States of employment, of special needs, aspirations and obligations of migrant workers and members of their families and shall envisage, as appropriate, the possibility for migrant workers and members of their families to have their freely chosen representatives in those institutions.

2. States of employment shall facilitate, in accordance with their national legislation, the consultation or participation of migrant workers and members of their families in decisions concerning the life and administration of local communities.

3. Migrant workers may enjoy political rights in the State of employment if that State, in the exercise of its sovereignty, grants them such rights.

Article 43

1. Migrant workers shall enjoy equality of treatment with nationals of the State of employment in relation to:

(a) Access to educational institutions and services subject to the admission requirements and other regulations of the institutions and services concerned;

(b) Access to vocational guidance and placement services;

(c) Access to vocational training and retraining facilities and institutions;

(d) Access to housing, including social housing schemes, and protection against exploitation in respect of rents;

(e) Access to social and health services, provided that the requirements for participation in the respective schemes are met;

(f) Access to co-operatives and self-managed enterprises, which shall not imply a change of their migration status and shall be subject to the rules and regulations of the bodies concerned;

(g) Access to and participation in cultural life.

2. States Parties shall promote conditions to ensure effective equality of treatment to enable migrant workers to enjoy the rights mentioned in paragraph 1 of the present article whenever the terms of their stay, as authorized by the State of employment, meet the appropriate requirements.

3. States of employment shall not prevent an employer of migrant workers from establishing housing or social or cultural facilities for them. Subject to Article 70 of the present Convention, a State of employment may make the establishment of such facilities subject to the requirements generally applied in that State concerning their installation.

Article 44

1. States Parties, recognizing that the family is the natural and fundamental group unit

of society and is entitled to protection by society and the State, shall take appropriate measures to ensure the protection of the unity of the families of migrant workers.

2. States Parties shall take measures that they deem appropriate and that fall within their competence to facilitate the reunification of migrant workers with their spouses or persons who have with the migrant worker a relationship that, according to applicable law, produces effects equivalent to marriage, as well as with their minor dependent unmarried children.

3. States of employment, on humanitarian grounds, shall favourably consider granting equal treatment, as set forth in paragraph 2 of the present article, to other family members of migrant workers.

Article 45

1. Members of the families of migrant workers shall, in the State of employment, enjoy equality of treatment with nationals of that State in relation to:

(a) Access to educational institutions and services, subject to the admission requirements and other regulations of the institutions and services concerned;

(b) Access to vocational guidance and training institutions and services, provided that requirements for participation are met;

(c) Access to social and health services, provided that requirements for participation in the respective schemes are met;

(d) Access to and participation in cultural life.

2. States of employment shall pursue a policy, where appropriate in collaboration with the States of origin, aimed at facilitating the integration of children of migrant workers in the local school system, particularly in respect of teaching them the local language.

3. States of employment shall endeavour to facilitate for the children of migrant workers the teaching of their mother tongue and culture and, in this regard, States of origin shall collaborate whenever appropriate.

4. States of employment may provide special schemes of education in the mother tongue of children of migrant workers, if necessary in collaboration with the States of origin.

Article 46

Migrant workers and members of their families shall, subject to the applicable legislation of the States concerned, as well as relevant international agreements and the obligations of the States concerned arising out of their participation in customs unions, enjoy exemption from import and export duties and taxes in respect of their personal and household effects as well as the equipment necessary to engage in the remunerated activity for which they were admitted to the State of employment:

(a) Upon departure from the State of origin or State of habitual residence;

(b) Upon initial admission to the State of employment;

(c) Upon final departure from the State of employment;

(d) Upon final return to the State of origin or State of habitual residence.

Article 47

1. Migrant workers shall have the right to transfer their earnings and savings, in particular those funds necessary for the support of their families, from the State of employment to their State of origin or any other State. Such transfers shall be made in conformity with procedures established by applicable legislation of the State concerned and in conformity with applicable international agreements.

2. States concerned shall take appropriate measures to facilitate such transfers.

Article 48

1. Without prejudice to applicable double taxation agreements, migrant workers and members of their families shall, in the matter of earnings in the State of employment:

(a) Not be liable to taxes, duties or charges of any description higher or more onerous than those imposed on nationals in similar circumstances;

(b) Be entitled to deductions or exemptions from taxes of any description and to any tax allowances applicable to nationals in similar circumstances, including tax allowances for dependent members of their families.

2. States Parties shall endeavour to adopt appropriate measures to avoid double taxation of the earnings and savings of migrant workers and members of their families.

Article 49

1. Where separate authorizations to reside and to engage in employment are required by national legislation, the States of employment shall issue to migrant workers authorization of residence for at least the same period of time as their authorization to engage in remunerated activity.

2. Migrant workers who in the State of employment are allowed freely to choose their remunerated activity shall neither be regarded as in an irregular situation nor shall they lose their authorization of residence by the mere fact of the termination of their remunerated activity prior to the expiration of their work permits or similar authorizations.

3. In order to allow migrant workers referred to in paragraph 2 of the present article sufficient time to find alternative remunerated activities, the authorization of residence shall not be withdrawn at least for a period corresponding to that during which they may be entitled to unemployment benefits.

Article 50

1. In the case of death of a migrant worker or dissolution of marriage, the State of employment shall favourably consider granting family members of that migrant worker residing in that State on the basis of family reunion an authorization to stay; the State of employment shall take into account the length of time they have already resided in that State.

2. Members of the family to whom such authorization is not granted shall be allowed before departure a reasonable period of time in order to enable them to settle their affairs in the State of employment.

3. The provisions of paragraphs 1 and 2 of the present article may not be interpreted as adversely affecting any right to stay and work otherwise granted to such family members by the legislation of the State of employment or by bilateral and multilateral treaties applicable to that State.

Article 51

Migrant workers who in the State of employment are not permitted freely to choose their remunerated activity shall neither be regarded as in an irregular situation nor shall they lose their authorization of residence by the mere fact of the termination of their remunerated activity prior to the expiration of their work permit, except where the authorization of residence is expressly dependent upon the specific remunerated activity for which they were admitted. Such migrant workers shall have the right to seek alternative employment, participation in public work schemes and retraining during the remaining period of their authorization to work, subject to such conditions and limitations as are specified in the authorization to work.

Article 52

1. Migrant workers in the State of employment shall have the right freely to choose their remunerated activity, subject to the following restrictions or conditions.

2. For any migrant worker a State of employment may:

(a) Restrict access to limited categories of employment, functions, services or activities where this is necessary in the interests of this State and provided for by national legislation;

(b) Restrict free choice of remunerated activity in accordance with its legislation concerning recognition of occupational qualifications acquired outside its territory. However, States Parties concerned shall endeavour to provide for recognition of such qualifications.

3. For migrant workers whose permission to work is limited in time, a State of employment may also:

(a) Make the right freely to choose their remunerated activities subject to the condition that the migrant worker has resided lawfully in its territory for the purpose of remunerated activity for a period of time prescribed in its national legislation that should not exceed two years;

(b) Limit access by a migrant worker to remunerated activities in pursuance of a policy of granting priority to its nationals or to persons who are assimilated to them for these purposes by virtue of legislation or bilateral or multilateral agreements. Any such limitation shall cease to apply to a migrant worker who has resided lawfully in its territory for the purpose of remunerated activity for a period of time prescribed in its national legislation that should not exceed five years.

4. States of employment shall prescribe the conditions under which a migrant worker who has been admitted to take up employment may be authorized to engage in work on his or her own account. Account shall be taken of the period during which the worker has already been lawfully in the State of employment.

Article 53

1. Members of a migrant worker's family who have themselves an authorization of residence or admission that is without limit of time or is automatically renewable shall be permitted freely to choose their remunerated activity under the same conditions as are applicable to the said migrant worker in accordance with Article 52 of the present Convention.

2. With respect to members of a migrant worker's family who are not permitted freely to choose their remunerated activity, States Parties shall consider favourably granting them priority in obtaining permission to engage in a remunerated activity over other workers who seek admission to the State of employment, subject to applicable bilateral and multilateral agreements.

Article 54

1. Without prejudice to the terms of their authorization of residence or their permission to work and the rights provided for in Articles 25 and 27 of the present Convention, migrant workers shall enjoy equality of treatment with nationals of the State of employment in respect of:

(a) Protection against dismissal;

(b) Unemployment benefits;

(c) Access to public work schemes intended to combat unemployment;

(d) Access to alternative employment in the event of loss of work or termination of other remunerated activity, subject to Article 52 of the present Convention.

2. If a migrant worker claims that the terms of his or her work contract have been violated by his or her employer, he or she shall have the right to address his or her case to the competent authorities of the State of employment, on terms provided for in Article 18, paragraph 1, of the present Convention.

Article 55

Migrant workers who have been granted permission to engage in a remunerated activity, subject to the conditions attached to such permission, shall be entitled to equality of treatment with nationals of the State of employment in the exercise of that remunerated activity.

Article 56

1. Migrant workers and members of their families referred to in the present part of the Convention may not be expelled from a State of employment, except for reasons defined in the national legislation of that State, and subject to the safeguards established in part III.

2. Expulsion shall not be resorted to for the purpose of depriving a migrant worker or a member of his or her family of the rights arising out of the authorization of residence and the work permit.

3. In considering whether to expel a migrant worker or a member of his or her family, account should be taken of humanitarian considerations and of the length of time that the person concerned has already resided in the State of employment.

Part V: Provisions Applicable to Particular Categories of Migrant Workers and of Their Families

Article 57

The particular categories of migrant workers and members of their families specified in the present part of the Convention who are documented or in a regular situation shall enjoy the rights set forth in part III and, except as modified below, the rights set forth in part IV.

Article 58

1. Frontier workers, as defined in Article 2, paragraph 2 (a), of the present Convention, shall be entitled to the rights provided for in part IV that can be applied to them by reason of their presence and work in the territory of the State of employment, taking into account that they do not have their habitual residence in that State.

2. States of employment shall consider favourably granting frontier workers the right freely to choose their remunerated activity after a specified period of time. The granting of that right shall not affect their status as frontier workers.

Article 59

1. Seasonal workers, as defined in Article 2, paragraph 2 (b), of the present Convention, shall be entitled to the rights provided for in part IV that can be applied to them by reason of their presence and work in the territory of the State of employment and

that are compatible with their status in that State as seasonal workers, taking into account the fact that they are present in that State for only part of the year.

2. The State of employment shall, subject to paragraph 1 of the present article, consider granting seasonal workers who have been employed in its territory for a significant period of time the possibility of taking up other remunerated activities and giving them priority over other workers who seek admission to that State, subject to applicable bilateral and multilateral agreements.

Article 60

Itinerant workers, as defined in Article 2, paragraph 2 (a), of the present Convention, shall be entitled to the rights provided for in part IV that can be granted to them by reason of their presence and work in the territory of the State of employment and that are compatible with their status as itinerant workers in that State.

Article 61

1. Project-tied workers, as defined in Article 2, paragraph 2 (f) of the present Convention, and members of their families shall be entitled to the rights provided for in part IV except the provisions of Article 43, paragraphs 1 (b) and (c), Article 43, paragraph 1 (d), as it pertains to social housing schemes, Article 45, paragraph 1 (b), and Articles 52 to 55).

2. If a project-tied worker claims that the terms of his or her work contract have been violated by his or her employer, he or she shall have the right to address his or her case to the competent authorities of the State which has jurisdiction over that employer, on terms provided for in Article 18, paragraph 1, of the present Convention.

3. Subject to bilateral or multilateral agreements in force for them, the States Parties concerned shall endeavour to enable project-tied workers to remain adequately protected by the social security systems of their States of origin or habitual residence during their engagement in the project. States Parties concerned shall take appropriate measures with the aim of avoiding any denial of rights or duplication of payments in this respect.

4. Without prejudice to the provisions of Article 47 of the present Convention and to relevant bilateral or multilateral agreements, States Parties concerned shall permit payment of the earnings of project-tied workers in their State of origin or habitual residence.

Article 62

1. Specified-employment workers as defined in Article 2, paragraph 2 (g), of the present Convention, shall be entitled to the rights provided for in part IV, except the provisions of Article 43, paragraphs 1 (b) and (c), Article 43, paragraph 1 (d), as it pertains to social housing schemes, Article 52, and Article 54, paragraph 1 (d).

2. Members of the families of specified-employment workers shall be entitled to the rights relating to family members of migrant workers provided for in part IV of the present Convention, except the provisions of Article 53.

Article 63

1. Self-employed workers, as defined in Article 2, paragraph 2 (h), of the present Convention, shall be entitled to the rights provided for in part IV with the exception of those rights which are exclusively applicable to workers having a contract of employment.

2. Without prejudice to Articles 52 and 79 of the present Convention, the termination of the economic activity of the self-employed workers shall not in itself imply the withdrawal of the authorization for them or for the members of their families to stay or to engage in a remunerated activity in the State of employment except where the authorization of residence is expressly dependent upon the specific remunerated activity for which they were admitted.

Part VI: Promotion of Sound, Equitable, Humane and Lawful Conditions Connection with International Migration of Workers and Members of Their Families

Article 64

1. Without prejudice to Article 79 of the present Convention, the States Parties concerned shall as appropriate consult and co-operate with a view to promoting sound, equitable and humane conditions in connection with international migration of workers and members of their families.

2. In this respect, due regard shall be paid not only to labour needs and resources, but also to the social, economic, cultural and other needs of migrant workers and members of their families involved, as well as to the consequences of such migration for the communities concerned.

Article 65

1. States Parties shall maintain appropriate services to deal with questions concerning international migration of workers and members of their families. Their functions shall include, inter alia:

(a) The formulation and implementation of policies regarding such migration;

(b) An exchange of information, consultation and co-operation with the competent authorities of other States Parties involved in such migration;

(c) The provision of appropriate information, particularly to employers, workers and their organizations on policies, laws and regulations relating to migration and employment, on agreements concluded with other States concerning migration and on other relevant matters;

(d) The provision of information and appropriate assistance to migrant workers and members of their families regarding requisite authorizations and formalities and arrangements for departure, travel, arrival, stay, remunerated activities, exit and return, as well as on conditions of work and life in the State of employment and on customs, currency, tax and other relevant laws and regulations.

2. States Parties shall facilitate as appropriate the provision of adequate consular and other services that are necessary to meet the social, cultural and other needs of migrant workers and members of their families.

Article 66

1. Subject to paragraph 2 of the present article, the right to undertake operations with a view to the recruitment of workers for employment in another State shall be restricted to:

(a) Public Service or bodies of the state in which such operations take place;

(b) Public services or bodies of the State of employment on the basis of agreement between the States concerned;

(c) A body established by virtue of a bilateral or multilateral agreement.

2. Subject to any authorization, approval and supervision by the public authorities of the States Parties concerned as may be established pursuant to the legislation and practice of those States, agencies, prospective employers or persons acting on their behalf may also be permitted to undertake the said operations.

Article 67

1. States Parties concerned shall co-operate as appropriate in the adoption of measures regarding the orderly return of migrant workers and members of their families to the State of origin when they decide to return or their authorization of residence or employment expires or when they are in the State of employment in an irregular situation.

2. Concerning migrant workers and members of their families in a regular situation, States Parties concerned shall co-operate as appropriate, on terms agreed upon by those States, with a view to promoting adequate economic conditions for their resettlement and to facilitating their durable social and cultural reintegration in the State of origin.

Article 68

1. States Parties, including States of transit, shall collaborate with a view to preventing and eliminating illegal or clandestine movements and employment of migrant workers in an irregular situation. The measures to be taken to this end within the jurisdiction of each State concerned shall include:

(a) Appropriate measures against the dissemination of misleading information relating to emigration and immigration;

(b) Measures to detect and eradicate illegal or clandestine movements of migrant workers and members of their families and to impose effective sanctions on persons, groups or entities which organize, operate or assist in organizing or operating such movements;

(c) Measures to impose effective sanctions on persons, groups or entities which use violence, threats or intimidation against migrant workers or members of their families in an irregular situation.

2. States of employment shall take all adequate and effective measures to eliminate employment in their territory of migrant workers in an irregular situation, including, whenever appropriate, sanctions on employers of such workers. The rights of migrant workers vis-à-vis their employer arising from employment shall not be impaired by these measures.

Article 69

1. States Parties shall, when there are migrant workers and members of their families within their territory in an irregular situation, take appropriate measures to ensure that such a situation does not persist.

2. Whenever States Parties concerned consider the possibility of regularizing the situation of such persons in accordance with applicable national legislation and bilateral or multilateral agreements, appropriate account shall be taken of the circumstances of their entry, the duration of their stay in the States of employment and other relevant considerations, in particular those relating to their family situation.

Article 70

States Parties shall take measures not less favourable than those applied to nationals to ensure that working and living conditions of migrant workers and members of their families in a regular situation are in keeping with the standards of fitness, safety, health and principles of human dignity.

Article 71

1. States Parties shall facilitate, whenever necessary, the repatriation to the State of origin of the bodies of deceased migrant workers or members of their families.

2. As regards compensation matters relating to the death of a migrant worker or a member of his or her family, States Parties shall, as appropriate, provide assistance to the persons concerned with a view to the prompt settlement of such matters. Settlement of these matters shall be carried out on the basis of applicable national law in accordance with the provisions of the present Convention and any relevant bilateral or multilateral agreements.

Part VII: Application of the Convention

Article 72

1. (a) For the purpose of reviewing the application of the present Convention, there shall be established a Committee on the Protection of the Rights of All Migrant Workers and Members of Their Families (hereinafter referred to as "the Committee");

(b) The Committee shall consist, at the time of entry into force of the present Convention, of ten and, after the entry into force of the Convention for the forty-first State Party, of fourteen experts of high moral standing, impartiality and recognized competence in the field covered by the Convention.

2. (a) Members of the Committee shall be elected by secret ballot by the States Parties from a list of persons nominated by the States Parties, due consideration being given to equitable geographical distribution, including both States of origin and States of employment, and to the representation of the principal legal system. Each State Party may nominate one person from among its own nationals;

(b) Members shall be elected and shall serve in their personal capacity.

3. The initial election shall be held no later than six months after the date of the entry into force of the present Convention and subsequent elections every second year. At least four months before the date of each election, the Secretary-General of the United Nations shall address a letter to all States Parties inviting them to submit their nominations within two months. The Secretary-General shall prepare a list in alphabetical order of all persons thus nominated, indicating the States Parties that have nominated them, and shall submit it to the States Parties not later than one month before the date of the corresponding election, together with the curricula vitae of the persons thus nominated.

4. Elections of members of the Committee shall be held at a meeting of States Parties convened by the Secretary-General at United Nations Headquarters. At that meeting, for which two thirds of the States Parties shall constitute a quorum, the persons elected to the Committee shall be those nominees who obtain the largest number of votes and an absolute majority of the votes of the States Parties present and voting.

5. (a) The members of the Committee shall serve for a term of four years. However, the terms of five of the members elected in the first election shall expire at the end of two years; immediately after the first election, the names of these five members shall be chosen by lot by the Chairman of the meeting of States Parties;

(b) The election of the four additional members of the Committee shall be held in accordance with the provisions of paragraphs 2, 3 and 4 of the present article, following the entry into force of the Convention for the forty-first State Party. The term of two of the additional members elected on this occasion shall expire at the end of two years; the names of these members shall be chosen by lot by the Chairman of the meeting of States Parties;

(c) The members of the Committee shall be eligible for re-election if renominated.

6. If a member of the Committee dies or resigns or declares that for any other cause he or she can no longer perform the duties of the Committee, the State Party that nominated

the expert shall appoint another expert from among its own nationals for the remaining part of the term. The new appointment is subject to the approval of the Committee.

7. The Secretary-General of the United Nations shall provide the necessary staff and facilities for the effective performance of the functions of the Committee.

8. The members of the Committee shall receive emoluments from United Nations resources on such terms and conditions as the General Assembly may decide.

9. The members of the Committee shall be entitled to the facilities, privileges and immunities of experts on mission for the United Nations as laid down in the relevant sections of the Convention on the Privileges and Immunities of the United Nations.

Article 73

1. States Parties undertake to submit to the Secretary-General of the United Nations for consideration by the Committee a report on the legislative, judicial, administrative and other measures they have taken to give effect to the provisions of the present Convention:

(a) Within one year after the entry into force of the Convention for the State Party concerned;

(b) Thereafter every five years and whenever the Committee so requests.

2. Reports prepared under the present article shall also indicate factors and difficulties, if any, affecting the implementation of the Convention and shall include information on the characteristics of migration flows in which the State Party concerned is involved.

3. The Committee shall decide any further guidelines applicable to the content of the reports.

4. States Parties shall make their reports widely available to the public in their own countries.

Article 74

1. The Committee shall examine the reports submitted by each State Party and shall transmit such comments as it may consider appropriate to the State Party concerned. This State Party may submit to the Committee observations on any comment made by the Committee in accordance with the present article. The Committee may request supplementary information from States Parties when considering these reports.

2. The Secretary-General of the United Nations shall, in due time before the opening of each regular session of the Committee, transmit to the Director-General of the International Labour Office copies of the reports submitted by States Parties concerned and information relevant to the consideration of these reports, in order to enable the Office to assist the Committee with the expertise the Office may provide regarding those matters dealt with by the present Convention that fall within the sphere of competence of the International Labour Organisation. The Committee shall consider in its deliberations such comments and materials as the Office may provide.

3. The Secretary-General of the United Nations may also, after consultation with the Committee, transmit to other specialized agencies as well as to intergovernmental organizations, copies of such parts of these reports as may fall within their competence.

4. The Committee may invite the specialized agencies and organs of the United Nations, as well as intergovernmental organizations and other concerned bodies to submit, for consideration by the Committee, written information on such matters dealt with in the present Convention as fall within the scope of their activities.

5. The International Labour Office shall be invited by the Committee to appoint representatives to participate, in a consultative capacity, in the meetings of the Committee.

6. The Committee may invite representatives of other specialized agencies and organs of the United Nations, as well as of intergovernmental organizations, to be present and to be heard in its meetings whenever matters falling within their field of competence are considered.

7. The Committee shall present an annual report to the General Assembly of the United Nations on the implementation of the present Convention, containing its own considerations and recommendations, based, in particular, on the examination of the reports and any observations presented by States Parties.

8. The Secretary-General of the United Nations shall transmit the annual reports of the Committee to the States Parties to the present Convention, the Economic and Social Council, the Commission on Human Rights of the United Nations, the Director-General of the International Labour Office and other relevant organizations.

Article 75

1. The Committee shall adopt its own rules of procedure.

2. The Committee shall elect its officers for a term of two years.

3. The Committee shall normally meet annually.

4. The meetings of the Committee shall normally be held at United Nations Headquarters.

Article 76

1. A State Party to the present Convention may at any time declare under this article that it recognizes the competence of the Committee to receive and consider communications to the effect that a State Party claims that another State Party is not fulfilling its obligations under the present Convention. Communications under this article may be received and considered only if submitted by a State Party that has made a declaration recognizing in regard to itself the competence of the Committee. No communication shall be received by the Committee if it concerns a State Party which has not made such a declaration. Communications received under this article shall be dealt with in accordance with the following procedure:

(a) If a State Party to the present Convention considers that another State Party is not fulfilling its obligations under the present Convention, it may, by written communication, bring the matter to the attention of that State Party. The State Party may also inform the Committee of the matter. Within three months after the receipt of the communication the receiving State shall afford the State that sent the communication an explanation, or any other statement in writing clarifying the matter which should include, to the extent possible and pertinent, reference to domestic procedures and remedies taken, pending or available in the matter;

(b) If the matter is not adjusted to the satisfaction of both States Parties concerned within six months after the receipt by the receiving State of the initial communication, either State shall have the right to refer the matter to the Committee, by notice given to the Committee and to the other State;

(c) The Committee shall deal with a matter referred to it only after it has ascertained that all available domestic remedies have been invoked and exhausted in the matter, in conformity with the generally recognized principles of international law. This shall not be the rule where, in the view of the Committee, the application of the remedies is unreasonably prolonged;

(d) Subject to the provisions of subparagraph (c) of the present paragraph, the Committee shall make available its good offices to the States Parties concerned with a view to a friendly solution of the matter on the basis of the respect for the obligations set forth in the present Convention;

(e) The Committee shall hold closed meetings when examining communications under the present article;

(f) In any matter referred to it in accordance with subparagraph (b) of the present paragraph, the Committee may call upon the States Parties concerned, referred to in subparagraph (b), to supply any relevant information;

(g) The States Parties concerned, referred to in subparagraph (b) of the present paragraph, shall have the right to be represented when the matter is being considered by the Committee and to make submissions orally and/or in writing;

(h) The Committee shall, within twelve months after the date of receipt of notice under subparagraph (b) of the present paragraph, submit a report, as follows:

(i) If a solution within the terms of subparagraph (d) of the present paragraph is reached, the Committee shall confine its report to a brief statement of the facts and of the solution reached;

(ii) If a solution within the terms of subparagraph (d) is not reached, the Committee shall, in its report, set forth the relevant facts concerning the issue between the States Parties concerned. The written submissions and record of the oral submissions made by the States Parties concerned shall be attached to the report. The Committee may also communicate only to the States Parties concerned any views that it may consider relevant to the issue between them. In every matter, the report shall be communicated to the States Parties concerned.

2. The provisions of the present article shall come into force when ten States Parties to the present Convention have made a declaration under paragraph 1 of the present article. Such declarations shall be deposited by the States Parties with the Secretary-General of the United Nations, who shall transmit copies thereof to the other States Parties. A declaration may be withdrawn at any time by notification to the Secretary-General. Such a withdrawal shall not prejudice the consideration of any matter that is the subject of a communication already transmitted under the present article; no further communication by any State Party shall be received under the present article after the notification of withdrawal of the declaration has been received by the Secretary-General, unless the State Party concerned has made a new declaration.

Article 77

1. A State Party to the present Convention may at any time declare under the present article that it recognizes the competence of the Committee to receive and consider communications from or on behalf of individuals subject to its jurisdiction who claim that their individual rights as established by the present Convention have been violated by that State Party. No communication shall be received by the Committee if it concerns a State Party that has not made such a declaration.

2. The Committee shall consider inadmissible any communication under the present article which is anonymous or which it considers to be an abuse of the right of submission of such communications or to be incompatible with the provisions of the present Convention.

3. The Committee shall not consider any communication from an individual under the present article unless it has ascertained that:

(a) The same matter has not been, and is not being, examined under another procedure of international investigation or settlement;

(b) The individual has exhausted all available domestic remedies; this shall not be the rule where, in the view of the Committee, the application of the remedies is unreasonably prolonged or is unlikely to bring effective relief to that individual.

4. Subject to the provisions of paragraph 2 of the present article, the Committee shall bring any communications submitted to it under this article to the attention of the State Party to the present Convention that has made a declaration under paragraph 1 and is alleged to be violating any provisions of the Convention. Within six months, the receiving State shall submit to the Committee written explanations or statements clarifying the matter and the remedy, if any, that may have been taken by that State.

5. The Committee shall consider communications received under the present article in the light of all information made available to it by or on behalf of the individual and by the State Party concerned.

6. The Committee shall hold closed meetings when examining communications under the present article.

7. The Committee shall forward its views to the State Party concerned and to the individual.

8. The provisions of the present article shall come into force when ten States Parties to the present Convention have made declarations under paragraph 1 of the present article. Such declarations shall be deposited by the States Parties with the Secretary-General of the United Nations, who shall transmit copies thereof to the other States Parties. A declaration may be withdrawn at any time by notification to the Secretary-General. Such a withdrawal shall not prejudice the consideration of any matter that is the subject of a communication already transmitted under the present article; no further communication by or on behalf of an individual shall be received under the present article after the notification of withdrawal of the declaration has been received by the Secretary-General, unless the State Party has made a new declaration.

Article 78

The provisions of Article 76 of the present Convention shall be applied without prejudice to any procedures for settling disputes or complaints in the field covered by the present Convention laid down in the constituent instruments of, or in conventions adopted by, the United Nations and the specialized agencies and shall not prevent the States Parties from having recourse to any procedures for settling a dispute in accordance with international agreements in force between them.

Part VIII: General Provisions

Article 79

Nothing in the present Convention shall affect the right of each State Party to establish the criteria governing admission of migrant workers and members of their families. Concerning other matters related to their legal situation and treatment as migrant workers and members of their families, States Parties shall be subject to the limitations set forth in the present Convention.

Article 80

Nothing in the present Convention shall be interpreted as impairing the provisions of the Charter of the United Nations and of the constitutions of the specialized agencies which define the respective responsibilities of the various organs of the United Nations and of the specialized agencies in regard to the matters dealt with in the present Convention.

Article 81

1. Nothing in the present Convention shall affect more favourable rights or freedoms granted to migrant workers and members of their families by virtue of:

(a) The law or practice of a State Party; or

(b) Any bilateral or multilateral treaty in force for the State Party concerned.

2. Nothing in the present Convention may be interpreted as implying for any State, group or person any right to engage in any activity or perform any act that would impair any of the rights and freedoms as set forth in the present Convention.

Article 82

The rights of migrant workers and members of their families provided for in the present Convention may not be renounced. It shall not be permissible to exert any form of pressure upon migrant workers and members of their families with a view to their relinquishing or foregoing any of the said rights. It shall not be possible to derogate by contract from rights recognized in the present Convention. States Parties shall take appropriate measures to ensure that these principles are respected.

Article 83

Each State Party to the present Convention undertakes:

(a) To ensure that any person whose rights or freedoms as herein recognized are violated shall have an effective remedy, notwithstanding that the violation has been committed by persons acting in an official capacity;

(b) To ensure that any persons seeking such a remedy shall have his or her claim reviewed and decided by competent judicial, administrative or legislative authorities, or by any other competent authority provided for by the legal system of the State, and to develop the possibilities of judicial remedy;

(c) To ensure that the competent authorities shall enforce such remedies when granted.

Article 84

Each State Party undertakes to adopt the legislative and other measures that are necessary to implement the provisions of the present Convention.

. . .

Chapter 8
ILO Convention No. 29 Concerning Forced Labour (excerpts)

Article 1

1. Each Member of the International Labour Organisation which ratifies this Convention undertakes to suppress the use of forced or compulsory labour in all its forms within the shortest possible period.

2. With a view to this complete suppression, recourse to forced or compulsory labour may be had, during the transitional period, for public purposes only and as an exceptional measure, subject to the conditions and guarantees hereinafter provided.

3. At the expiration of a period of five years after the coming into force of this Convention, and when the Governing Body of the International Labour Office prepares the report provided for in Article 31 below, the said Governing Body shall consider the possibility of the suppression of forced or compulsory labour in all its forms without a further transitional period and the desirability of placing this question on the agenda of the Conference.

Article 2

1. For the purposes of this Convention the term "forced or compulsory labour" shall mean all work or service which is exacted from any person under the menace of any penalty and for which the said person has not offered himself voluntarily.

2. Nevertheless, for the purposes of this Convention the term "forced or compulsory labour" shall not include:

(a) Any work or service exacted in virtue of compulsory military service laws for work of a purely military character;

(b) Any work or service which forms part of the normal civic obligations of the citizens of a fully self-governing country;

Adopted 28 June 1930 by the General Conference of the International Labour Organisation, *entry into force* 1 May 1932, in accordance with Article 28.

(c) Any work or service exacted from any person as a consequence of a conviction in a court of law, provided that the said work or service is carried out under the supervision and control of a public authority and that the said person is not hired to or placed at the disposal of private individuals, companies or associations;

(d) Any work or service exacted in cases of emergency, that is to say, in the event of war or of a calamity or threatened calamity, such as fire, flood, famine, earthquake, violent epidemic or epizootic diseases, invasion by animal, insect or vegetable pests, and in general any circumstance that would endanger the existence or the well-being of the whole or part of the population;

(e) Minor communal services of a kind which, being performed by the members of the community in the direct interest of the said community, can therefore be considered as normal civic obligations incumbent upon the members of the community, provided that the members of the community or their direct representatives shall have the right to be consulted in regard to the need for such services.

Article 3

For the purposes of this Convention the term "competent authority" shall mean either an authority of the metropolitan country or the highest central authority in the territory concerned.

Article 4

1. The competent authority shall not impose or permit the imposition of forced or compulsory labour for the benefit of private individuals, companies or associations.

2. Where such forced or compulsory labour for the benefit of private individuals, companies or associations exists at the date on which a Member's ratification of this Convention is registered by the Director-General of the International Labour Office, the Member shall completely suppress such forced or compulsory labour from the date on which this Convention comes into force for that Member.

Article 5

1. No concession granted to private individuals, companies or associations shall involve any form of forced or compulsory labour for the production or the collection of products which such private individuals, companies or associations utilise or in which they trade.

2. Where concessions exist containing provisions involving such forced or compulsory labour, such provisions shall be rescinded as soon as possible, in order to comply with Article 1 of this Convention.

Article 6

Officials of the administration, even when they have the duty of encouraging the populations under their charge to engage in some form of labour, shall not put constraint upon the said populations or upon any individual members thereof to work for private individuals, companies or associations.

Article 7

1. Chiefs who do not exercise administrative functions shall not have recourse to forced or compulsory labour.

2. Chiefs who exercise administrative functions may, with the express permission of the competent authority, have recourse to forced or compulsory labour, subject to the provisions of Article 10 of this Convention.

3. Chiefs who are duly recognised and who do not receive adequate remuneration in other forms may have the enjoyment of personal services, subject to due regulation and provided that all necessary measures are taken to prevent abuses.

Article 8

1. The responsibility for every decision to have recourse to forced or compulsory labour shall rest with the highest civil authority in the territory concerned.

2. Nevertheless, that authority may delegate powers to the highest local authorities to exact forced or compulsory labour which does not involve the removal of the workers from their place of habitual residence. That authority may also delegate, for such periods and subject to such conditions as may be laid down in the regulations provided for in Article 23 of this Convention, powers to the highest local authorities to exact forced or compulsory labour which involves the removal of the workers from their place of habitual residence for the purpose of facilitating the movement of officials of the administration, when on duty, and for the transport of Government stores.

Article 9

Except as otherwise provided for in Article 10 of this Convention, any authority competent to exact forced or compulsory labour shall, before deciding to have recourse to such labour, satisfy itself:

(a) That the work to be done or the service to be rendered is of important direct interest for the community called upon to do the work or render the service;

(b) That the work or service is of present or imminent necessity;

(c) That it has been impossible to obtain voluntary labour for carrying out the work or rendering the service by the offer of rates of wages and conditions of labour not less favourable than those prevailing in the area concerned for similar work or service; and

(d) That the work or service will not lay too heavy a burden upon the present population, having regard to the labour available and its capacity to undertake the work.

Article 10

1. Forced or compulsory labour exacted as a tax and forced or compulsory labour to which recourse is had for the execution of public works by chiefs who exercise administrative functions shall be progressively abolished.

2. Meanwhile, where forced or compulsory labour is exacted as a tax, and where recourse is had to forced or compulsory labour for the execution of public works by chiefs who exercise administrative functions, the authority concerned shall first satisfy itself:

(a) That the work to be done or the service to be rendered is of important direct interest for the community called upon to do the work or render the service;

(b) That the work or the service is of present or imminent necessity;

(c) That the work or service will not lay too heavy a burden upon the present population, having regard to the labour available and its capacity to undertake the work;

(d) That the work or service will not entail the removal of the workers from their place of habitual residence;

(e) That the execution of the work or the rendering of the service will be directed in accordance with the exigencies of religion, social life and agriculture.

Article 11

1. Only adult able-bodied males who are of an apparent age of not less than 18 and not more than 45 years may be called upon for forced or compulsory labour. Except in respect of the kinds of labour provided for in Article 10 of this Convention, the following limitations and conditions shall apply:

(a) Whenever possible prior determination by a medical officer appointed by the administration that the persons concerned are not suffering from any infectious or contagious disease and that they are physically fit for the work required and for the conditions under which it is to be carried out;

(b) Exemption of school teachers and pupils and of officials of the administration in general;

(c) The maintenance in each community of the number of adult able-bodied men indispensable for family and social life;

(d) Respect for conjugal and family ties.

2. For the purposes of subparagraph (c) of the preceding paragraph, the regulations provided for in Article 23 of this Convention shall fix the proportion of the resident adult able-bodied males who may be taken at any one time for forced or compulsory labour, provided always that this proportion shall in no case exceed 25 percent. In fixing this proportion the competent authority shall take account of the density of the population, of its social and physical development, of the seasons, and of the work which must be done by the persons concerned on their own behalf in their locality, and, generally, shall have regard to the economic and social necessities of the normal life of the community concerned.

Article 12

1. The maximum period for which any person may be taken for forced or compulsory labour of all kinds in any one period of twelve months shall not exceed sixty days, including the time spent in going to and from the place of work.

2. Every person from whom forced or compulsory labour is exacted shall be furnished with a certificate indicating the periods of such labour which he has completed.

Article 13

1. The normal working hours of any person from whom forced or compulsory labour is exacted shall be the same as those prevailing in the case of voluntary labour, and the hours worked in excess of the normal working hours shall be remunerated at the rates prevailing in the case of overtime for voluntary labour.

2. A weekly day of rest shall be granted to all persons from whom forced or compulsory labour of any kind is exacted and this day shall coincide as far as possible with the day fixed by tradition or custom in the territories or regions concerned.

Article 14

1. With the exception of the forced or compulsory labour provided for in Article 10 of this Convention, forced or compulsory labour of all kinds shall be remunerated in cash at rates not less than those prevailing for similar kinds of work either in the district in which the labour is employed or in the district from which the labour is recruited, whichever may be the higher.

2. In the case of labour to which recourse is had by chiefs in the exercise of their administrative functions, payment of wages in accordance with the provisions of the preceding paragraph shall be introduced as soon as possible.

3. The wages shall be paid to each worker individually and not to his tribal chief or to any other authority.

4. For the purpose of payment of wages the days spent in travelling to and from the place of work shall be counted as working days.

5. Nothing in this article shall prevent ordinary rations being given as a part of wages, such rations to be at least equivalent in value to the money payment they are taken to represent, but deductions from wages shall not be made either for the payment of taxes or for special food, clothing or accommodation supplied to a worker for the purpose of maintaining him in a fit condition to carry on his work under the special conditions of any employment, or for the supply of tools.

Article 15

1. Any laws or regulations relating to workmen's compensation for accidents or sickness arising out of the employment of the worker and any laws or regulations providing compensation for the dependants of deceased or incapacitated workers which are or shall be in force in the territory concerned shall be equally applicable to persons from whom forced or compulsory labour is exacted and to voluntary workers.

2. In any case it shall be an obligation on any authority employing any worker on forced or compulsory labour to ensure the subsistence of any such worker who, by accident or sickness arising out of his employment, is rendered wholly or partially incapable of providing for himself, and to take measures to ensure the maintenance of any persons actually dependent upon such a worker in the event of his incapacity or decease arising out of his employment.

Article 16

1. Except in cases of special necessity, persons from whom forced or compulsory labour is exacted shall not be transferred to districts where the food and climate differ so considerably from those to which they have been accustomed as to endanger their health.

2. In no case shall the transfer of such workers be permitted unless all measures relating to hygiene and accommodation which are necessary to adapt such workers to the conditions and to safeguard their health can be strictly applied.

3. When such transfer cannot be avoided, measures of gradual habituation to the new conditions of diet and of climate shall be adopted on competent medical advice.

4. In cases where such workers are required to perform regular work to which they are not accustomed, measures shall be taken to ensure their habituation to it, especially as regards progressive training, the hours of work and the provision of rest intervals, and any increase or amelioration of diet which may be necessary.

Article 17

Before permitting recourse to forced or compulsory labour for works of construction or maintenance which entail the workers remaining at the workplaces for considerable periods, the competent authority shall satisfy itself:

(1) That all necessary measures are taken to safeguard the health of the workers and to guarantee the necessary medical care, and, in particular, (a) that the workers are medically examined before commencing the work and at fixed intervals during the period of service, (b) that there is an adequate medical staff, provided with the dispensaries, infirmaries, hospitals and equipment necessary to meet all requirements, and (c) that the sanitary conditions of the workplaces, the supply of drinking water, food, fuel, and cooking utensils, and, where necessary, of housing and clothing are satisfactory;

(2) That definite arrangements are made to ensure the subsistence of the families of the workers, in particular by facilitating the remittance, by a safe method, of part of the wages to the family, at the request or with the consent of the workers;

(3) That the journey of the workers to and from the workplaces are made at the expense and under the responsibility of the administration, which shall facilitate such journeys by making the fullest use of all available means of transport;

(4) That, in case of illness or accident causing incapacity to work of a certain duration, the worker is repatriated at the expense of the administration;

(5) That any worker who may wish to remain as a voluntary worker at the end of his period of forced or compulsory labour is permitted to do so without, for a period of two years, losing his right to repatriation free of expense to himself.

Article 18

1. Forced or compulsory labour for the transport of persons or goods, such as the labour of porters or boatmen, shall be abolished within the shortest possible period. Meanwhile the competent authority shall promulgate regulations determining, inter alia, (a) that such labour shall only be employed for the purpose of facilitating the movement of officials of the administration, when on duty, or for the transport of Government stores, or, in cases of very urgent necessity, the transport of persons other than officials, (b) that the workers so employed shall be medically certified to be physically fit, where medical examination is possible, and that where such medical examination is not practicable the person employing such workers shall be held responsible for ensuring that they are physically fit and not suffering from any infectious or contagious diseases, (c) the maximum load which these workers may carry, (d) the maximum distance from their homes to which they may be taken, (e) the maximum number of days per month or other period for which they may be taken, including the days spent in returning to their homes, and (f) the persons entitled to demand this form of forced or compulsory labour and the extent to which they are entitled to demand it.

2. In fixing the maxima referred to under (c), (d) and (e) in the foregoing paragraph, the competent authority shall have regard to all relevant factors, including the physical development of the population from which the workers are recruited, the nature of the country through which they must travel and the climatic conditions.

3. The competent authority shall further provide that the normal daily journey of such workers shall not exceed a distance corresponding to an average working day of eight hours, it being understood that account shall be taken not only of the weight to be carried and the distance to be covered, but also of the nature of the road, the season and all other relevant factors, and that, where hours of journey in excess of the normal daily journey are exacted, they shall be remunerated at rates higher than the normal rates.

Article 19

1. The competent authority shall only authorise recourse to compulsory cultivation as a method of precaution against famine or a deficiency of food supplies and always under the condition that the food or produce shall remain the property of the individuals or the community producing it.

2. Nothing in this article shall be construed as abrogating the obligation on members of a community, where production is organised on a communal basis by virtue of law or custom and where the procedure or any profit accruing from the sale thereof remain the property of the community, to perform the work demanded by the community by virtue of law or custom.

Article 20

Collective punishment laws under which a community may be punished for crimes committed by any of its members shall not contain provisions for forced or compulsory labour by the community as one of the methods of punishment.

Article 21

Forced or compulsory labour shall not be used for work underground in mines.

Article 22

The annual reports that Members which ratify this Convention agree to make to the International Labour Office, pursuant to the provisions of Article 22 of the Constitution of the International Labour Organisation, on the measures they have taken to give effect to the provisions of this Convention, shall contain as full information as possible, in respect of each territory concerned, regarding the extent to which recourse has been had to forced or compulsory labour in that territory, the purposes for which it has been employed, the sickness and death rates, hours of work, methods of payment of wages and rates of wages, and any other relevant information.

Article 23

1. To give effect to the provisions of this Convention the competent authority shall issue complete and precise regulations governing the use of forced or compulsory labour.

2. These regulations shall contain, inter alia, rules permitting any person from whom forced or compulsory labour is exacted to forward all complaints relative to the conditions of labour to the authorities and ensuring that such complaints will be examined and taken into consideration.

Article 24

Adequate measures shall in all cases be taken to ensure that the regulations governing the employment of forced or compulsory labour are strictly applied, either by extending the duties of any existing labour inspectorate which has been established for the inspection of voluntary labour to cover the inspection of forced or compulsory labour or in some other appropriate manner. Measures shall also be taken to ensure that the regulations are brought to the knowledge of persons from whom such labour is exacted.

Article 25

The illegal exaction of forced or compulsory labour shall be punishable as a penal offence, and it shall be an obligation on any Member ratifying this Convention to ensure that the penalties imposed by law are really adequate and are strictly enforced.

Article 26

1. Each Member of the International Labour Organization which ratifies this Convention undertakes to apply it to the territories placed under its sovereignty, jurisdiction, protection, suzerainty, tutelage or authority, so far as it has the right to accept obligations affecting matters of internal jurisdiction; provided that, if such Member may desire to take advantage of the provisions of Article 35 of the Constitution of the International Labour Organisation, it shall append to its ratification a declaration stating:

(1) The territories to which it intends to apply the provisions of this Convention without modification;

(2) The territories to which it intends to apply the provisions of this Convention with modifications, together with details of the said modifications;

(3) The territories in respect of which it reserves its decision.

2. The aforesaid declaration shall be deemed to be an integral part of the ratification and shall have the force of ratification. It shall be open to any Member, by a subsequent declaration, to cancel in whole or in part the reservations made, in pursuance of the provisions of subparagraphs (2) and (3) of this article, in the original declaration.

. . .

Chapter 9
ILO Convention No. 105 Concerning the Abolition of Forced Labour (excerpts)

Article 1

Each Member of the International Labour Organization which ratifies this Convention undertakes to suppress and not to make use of any form of forced or compulsory labour—

(a) as a means of political coercion or education or as a punishment for holding or expressing political views or views ideologically opposed to the established political, social or economic system;

(b) as a method of mobilizing and using labour for purposes of economic development;

(c) as a means of labour discipline;

(d) as a punishment for having participating in strikes;

(e) as a means of racial, social, national or religious discrimination.

Article 2

Each Member of the International Labour Organization which ratifies this Convention undertakes to take effective measures to secure the immediate and complete abolition of forced or compulsory labour as a specified in Article 1 of this Convention.

Article 3

The formal ratifications of this Convention shall be communicated to the Director-General of the International Labour Office for registration.

Adopted 25 June 1957 by the General Conference of the International Labour Organization, *entry into force* 17 January 1959, in accordance with Article 4.

Chapter 10
ILO Convention No. 111 Concerning Discrimination in Respect of Employment and Occupation (excerpts)

Article 1

1. For the purpose of this Convention the term "discrimination" includes —

(a) any distinction, exclusion or preference made on the basis or race, colour, sex, religion, political opinion, national extraction or social origin, which has the effect of nullifying or impairing equality of opportunity or treatment in employment or occupation;

(b) such other distinction, exclusion or preference which has the effect of nullifying or impairing equality of opportunity or treatment in employment or occupation as may be determined by the Member concerned after consultation with representative employers' and workers' organizations, where such exist, and with other appropriate bodies.

2. Any distinction, exclusion or preference in respect of a particular job based on the inherent requirements thereof shall not be deemed to be discrimination.

3. For the purpose of this Convention the terms "employment" and "occupation" include access to vocational training, access to employment and to particular occupations, and terms and condition if employment.

Article 2

Each Member for which this Convention is in force undertakes to declare and pursue a national policy designed to promote, by methods appropriate to national conditions and practice, equality of opportunity and treatment in respect of employment and occupation, with a view to eliminating any discrimination in respect thereof.

Article 3

Each Member for which this Convention is in force undertakes, by methods appropriate to national conditions and practice—

Adopted on 25 June 1958 by the General Conference of the International Labour Organization, *entry into force* 15 June 1960, in accordance with Article 8.

(a) to seek co-operation of employers' and workers' organizations and other appropriate bodies in promote the acceptance and observance of this policy;

(b) to enact such legislation and to promote such educational programmes as may be calculated to secure the acceptance and observance of this policy;

(c) to repeal any statutory provisions and modify any administrative instructions or practices which are inconsistent with the policy;

(d) to pursue the policy in respect of employment under the direct control of a national authority;

(e) to ensure observance of the policy in the activities of vocational guidance, vocational training and placement services under the direction of a national authority;

(f) to indicate in its annual report on the application of the Convention the action taken in pursuance of the policy and the results secured by such action.

Article 4

Any measures affecting an individual who is justifiably suspected of, or engaged in, activities prejudicial to the security of the State shall not be deemed to be discrimination, provided that the individual concerned shall have the right to appeal to a competent body established in accordance with national practice.

Article 5

1. Special measures of protection or assistance provided for in the other Conventions or Recommendations adopted by the International Labour Conference shall not be deemed to be discrimination.

2. Any Member may, after consultation with representative employers' and workers' organizations, where such exist, determine that other special measures designed to meet the particular requirements of persons who, for reasons such as sex, age, disablement, family responsibilities or social or cultural status, are generally recognized to require special protection or assistance, shall not be deemed to be discrimination.

. . .

Chapter 11

ILO Convention No. 117 Concerning Basic Aims and Standards of Social Policy (excerpts)

Part I: General Principles

Article 1

1. All policies shall be primarily directed to the well-being and development of the population and to the promotion of its desire for social progress.

2. All policies of more general application shall be formulated with due regard to their effect upon the well-being of the population.

Part II: Improvement of Standards of Living

Article 2

The improvement of standards of living shall be regarded as the principal objective in the planning of economic development.

Article 3

1. All practicable measures shall be taken in the planning of economic development to harmonise such development with the healthy evolution of the communities concerned.

2. In particular, efforts shall be made to avoid the disruption of family life and of traditional social units, especially by—

(a) close study of the causes and effect of migratory movements and appropriate action where necessary;

(b) the promotion of town and village planning in areas where economic needs result in the concentration of population;

Adopted 22 June 1962 by the General Conference of the International Labour Organisation, *entry into force* 23 April 1964, in accordance with Article 18.

(c) the prevention and elimination of congestion in urban areas;

(d) the improvement of living conditions in rural areas and the establishment of suitable industries in rural areas where adequate manpower is available.

Article 4

The measures to be considered by the competent authorities for the promotion of productive capacity and the improvement of standards of living of agricultural producers shall include—

(a) the elimination to the fullest practicable extent of the causes of chronic indebtedness;

(b) the control of the alienation of agricultural land to non-agriculturalists so as to ensure that such alienation takes place only when it is in the best interests of the country;

(c) the control, by the enforcement of adequate laws or regulations, of the ownership and use of land resources to ensure that they are used, with due regard to customary rights, in the best interests of the inhabitants of the country;

(d) the supervision of tenancy arrangements and of working conditions with a view to securing for tenants and labourers the highest practicable standards of living and an equitable share in any advantages which may result from improvements in productivity or in price levels;

(e) the reduction of production and distribution costs by all practicable means and in particular by forming, encouraging and assisting producers' and consumers' co-operatives.

Article 5

1. Measures shall be taken to secure for independent producers and wage earners conditions which will give them scope to improve living standards by their own efforts and will ensure the maintenance of minimum standards of living as ascertained by means of official inquiries into living conditions, conducted after consultation with the representative organisations of employers and workers.

2. In ascertaining the minimum standards of living, account shall be taken of such essential family needs of the workers as food and its nutritive value, housing, clothing, medical care and education.

Part III: Provisions Concerning Migrant Workers

Article 6

Where the circumstances under which workers are employed involve their living away from their homes, the terms and conditions of their employment shall take account of their normal family needs.

Article 7

Where the labour resources of one area are used on a temporary basis for the benefit of another area, measures shall be taken to encourage the transfer of part of the workers' wages and savings from the area of labour utilisation to the area of labour supply.

Article 8

1. Where the labour resources of a country are used in an area under a different administration, the competent authorities of the countries concerned shall, whenever necessary or desirable, enter into agreements for the purpose of regulating matters of common concern arising in connection with the application of the provisions of this Convention.

2. Such agreements shall provide that the worker shall enjoy protection and advantages not less than those enjoyed by workers resident in the area of labour utilisation.

3. Such agreements shall provide for facilities for enabling the worker to transfer part of his wages and savings to his home.

Article 9

Where workers and their families move from low-cost to higher-cost areas, account shall be taken of the increased cost of living resulting from the change.

Part IV: Remuneration of Workers and Related Questions

Article 10

1. The fixing of minimum wages by collective agreements freely negotiated between trade unions which are representative of the workers concerned and employers or employers' organisations shall be encouraged.

2. Where no adequate arrangements exist for the fixing of minimum wages by collective agreement, the necessary arrangements shall be made whereby minimum rates of wages can be fixed in consultation with representatives of the employers and workers, including representatives of their respective organisations, where such exist.

3. The necessary measures shall be taken to ensure that the employers and workers concerned are informed of the minimum wage rates in force and that wages are not paid at less than these rates in cases where they are applicable.

4. A worker to whom minimum rates are applicable and who, since they became applicable, has been paid wages at less than these rates shall be entitled to recover, by judicial or other means authorised by law, the amount by which he has been underpaid, subject to such limitation of time as may be determined by law or regulation.

Article 11

1. The necessary measures shall be taken to ensure the proper payment of all wages earned and employers shall be required to keep registers of wage payments, to issue to workers statements of wage payments and to take other appropriate steps to facilitate the necessary supervision.

2. Wages shall normally be paid in legal tender only.

3. Wages shall normally be paid direct to the individual worker.

4. The substitution of alcohol or other spirituous beverages for all or any part of wages for services performed by the worker shall be prohibited.

5. Payment of wages shall not be made in taverns or stores, except in the case of workers employed therein.

6. Unless there is an established local custom to the contrary, and the competent authority is satisfied that the continuance of this custom is desired by the workers, wages shall be paid regularly at such intervals as will lessen the likelihood of indebtedness among the wage earners.

7. Where food, housing, clothing and other essential supplies and services form part of remuneration, all practicable steps shall be taken by the competent authority to ensure that they are adequate and their cash value properly assessed.

8. All practicable measures shall be taken —

(a) to inform the workers of their wage rights;

(b) to prevent any unauthorised deductions from wages; and

(c) to restrict the amounts deductible from wages in respect of supplies and services forming part of remuneration to the proper cash value thereof.

Article 12

1. The maximum amounts and manner of repayment of advances on wages shall be regulated by the competent authority.

2. The competent authority shall limit the amount of advances which may be made to a worker in consideration of his taking up employment; the amount of advances permitted shall be clearly explained to the worker.

3. Any advance in excess of the amount laid down by the competent authority shall be legally irrecoverable and may not be recovered by the withholding of amounts of pay due to the worker at a later date.

Article 13

1. Voluntary forms of thrift shall be encouraged among wage earners and independent producers.

2. All practicable measures shall be taken for the protection of wage earners and independent producers against usury, in particular by action aiming at the reduction of rates of interest on loans, by the control of the operations of money lenders, and by the encouragement of facilities for borrowing money for appropriate purposes through co-operative credit organisations or through institutions which are under the control of the competent authority.

Part V: Non-Discrimination on Grounds of Race, Colour, Sex, Belief, Tribal Association, or Trade Union Affiliation

Article 14

1. It shall be an aim of policy to abolish all discrimination among workers on grounds of race, colour, sex, belief, tribal association or trade union affiliation in respect of—

(a) labour legislation and agreements which shall afford equitable economic treatment to all those lawfully resident or working in the country;

(b) admission to public or private employment;

(c) conditions of engagement and promotion;

(d) opportunities for vocational training;

(e) conditions of work;

(f) health, safety and welfare measures;

(g) discipline;

(h) participation in the negotiation of collective agreements;

(i) wage rates, which shall be fixed according to the principle of equal pay for work of equal value in the same operation and undertaking.

2. All practicable measures shall be taken to lessen, by raising the rates applicable to the lower-paid workers, any existing differences in wage rates due to discrimination by reason of race, colour, sex, belief, tribal association or trade union affiliation.

3. Workers from one country engaged for employment in another country may be granted in addition to their wages benefits in cash or in kind to meet any reasonable personal or family expenses resulting from employment away from their homes.

4. The foregoing provisions of this article shall be without prejudice to such measures as the competent authority may think it necessary or desirable to take for the safeguarding of motherhood and for ensuring the health, safety and welfare of women workers.

Part VI: Education and Training

Article 15

1. Adequate provision shall be made to the maximum extent possible under local

conditions, for the progressive development of broad systems of education, vocational training and apprenticeship, with a view to the effective preparation of children and young persons of both sexes for a useful occupation.

2. National laws or regulations shall prescribe the school-leaving age and the minimum age for and conditions of employment.

3. In order that the child population may be able to profit by existing facilities for education and in order that the extension of such facilities may not be hindered by a demand for child labour, the employment of persons below the school-leaving age during the hours when the schools are in session shall be prohibited in areas where educational facilities are provided on a scale adequate for the majority of the children of school age.

Article 16

1. In order to secure high productivity through the development of skilled labour, training in new techniques of production shall be provided in suitable cases.

2. Such training shall be organised by or under the supervision of the competent authorities, in consultation with the employers' and workers' organisations of the country from which the trainees come and of the country of training.

. . .

Chapter 12
ILO Convention No. 122 Concerning Employment Policy (excerpts)

Article 1

1. With a view to stimulating economic growth and development, raising levels of living, meeting manpower requirements and overcoming unemployment and underemployment, each Member shall declare and pursue, as a major goal, an active policy designed to promote full, productive and freely chosen employment.

2. The said policy shall aim at ensuring that:

(a) There is work for all who are available for and seeking work;

(b) Such work is as productive as possible;

(c) There is freedom of choice of employment and the fullest possible opportunity for each worker to qualify for, and to use his skills and endowments in, a job for which he is well suited, irrespective of race, colour, sex, religion, political opinion, national extraction or social origin.

3. The said policy shall take due account of the stage and level of economic development and the mutual relationships between employment objectives and other economic and social objectives, and shall be pursued by methods that are appropriate to national conditions and practices.

Article 2

Each Member shall, by such methods and to such extent as may be appropriate under national conditions:

(a) Decide on and keep under review, within the framework of a coordinated economic and social policy, the measures to be adopted for attaining the objectives specified in Article 1;

Adopted 9 July 1964 by the General Conference of the International Labour Organisation, *entry into force* 15 July 1966, in accordance with Article 5.

(b) Take such steps as may be needed, including when appropriate the establishment of programmes, for the application of these measures.

Article 3

In the application of this Convention, representatives of the persons affected by the measures to be taken, and in particular representatives of employers and workers, shall be consulted concerning employment policies, with a view to taking fully into account their experience and views and securing their full co-operation in formulating and enlisting support for such policies.

. . .

Chapter 13

ILO Convention No. 154 Concerning the Promotion of Collective Bargaining (excerpts)

Part I: Scope and Definitions

Article 1

1. This Convention applies to all branches of economic activity.

2. The extent to which the guarantees provided for in this Convention apply to the armed forces and the police may be determined by national laws or regulations or national practice.

3. As regards the public service, special modalities of application of this Convention may be fixed by national laws or regulations or national practice.

Article 2

For the purpose of this Convention the term "collective bargaining" extends to all negotiations which take place between an employer, a group of employers or one or more employers' organisations, on the one hand, and one or more workers' organisations, on the other, for:

(a) Determining working conditions and terms of employment; and/or

(b) Regulating relations between employers and workers; and/or

(c) Regulating relations between employers or their organisations and a workers' organisation or workers' organisations.

Article 3

1. Where national law or practice recognises the existence of workers' representatives as defined in Article 3, subparagraph (b), of the Workers' Representatives Convention,

Adopted 19 June 1981 by the General Conference of the International Labour Organisation, *entry into force* 11 August 1983, in accordance with Article 11.

1971, national law or practice may determine the extent to which the term "collective bargaining" shall also extend, for the purpose of this Convention, to negotiations with these representatives.

2. Where, in pursuance of paragraph I of this Article, the term "collective bargaining" also includes negotiations with the workers' representatives referred to in that paragraph, appropriate measures shall be taken, wherever necessary, to ensure that the existence of these representatives is not used to undermine the position of the workers' organisations concerned.

Part II: Methods of Application

Article 4

The provisions of this Convention shall, in so far as they are not otherwise made effective by means of collective agreements, arbitration awards or in such other manner as may be consistent with national practice, be given effect by national laws or regulations.

Part III: Promotion of Collective Bargaining

Article 5

1. Measures adapted to national conditions shall be taken to promote collective bargaining.

2. The aims of the measures referred to in paragraph 1 of this Article shall be the following:

(a) Collective bargaining should be made possible for all employers and all groups of workers in the branches of activity covered by this Convention;

(b) Collective bargaining should be progressively extended to all matters covered by subparagraphs (a), (b) and (c) of Article 2 of this Convention;

(c) The establishment of rules of procedure agreed between employers' and workers' organisations should be encouraged;

(d) Collective bargaining should not be hampered by the absence of rules governing the procedure to be used or by the inadequacy or inappropriateness of such rules;

(e) Bodies and procedures for the settlement of labour disputes should be so conceived as to contribute to the promotion of collective bargaining.

Article 6

The provisions of this Convention do not preclude the operation of industrial relations systems in which collective bargaining takes place within the framework of conciliation and/or arbitration machinery or institutions, in which machinery or institutions the parties to the collective bargaining process voluntarily participate.

Article 7

Measures taken by public authorities to encourage and promote the development of collective bargaining shall be the subject of prior consultation and, whenever possible, agreement between public authorities and employers' and workers' organisations.

Article 8

The measures taken with a view to promoting collective bargaining shall not be so conceived or applied as to hamper the freedom of collective bargaining.

. . .

Chapter 14
ILO Convention No. 168 Concerning Employment, Promotion, and Protection Against Unemployment (excerpts)

I: General Provisions

Article 1

In this Convention:

(a) The term "legislation" includes any social security rules as well as laws and regulations;

(b) The term "prescribed" means determined by or in virtue of national legislation.

Article 2

Each Member shall take appropriate steps to co-ordinate its system of protection against unemployment and its employment policy. To this end, it shall seek to ensure that its system of protection against unemployment, and in particular the methods of providing unemployment benefit, contribute to the promotion of full, productive and freely chosen employment, and are not such as to discourage employers from offering and workers from seeking productive employment.

Article 3

The provisions of this Convention shall be implemented in consultation and co-operation with the organisations of employers and workers, in accordance with national practice.

Article 4

1. Each Member which ratifies this Convention may, by a declaration accompanying

Adopted 21 June 1988 by the General Conference of the International Labour Organisation, *entry into force* 17 October 1991, in accordance with Article 33.

its ratification, exclude the provisions of Part VII from the obligations accepted by ratification.

2. Each Member which has made a declaration under paragraph 1 above may withdraw it at any time by a subsequent declaration.

Article 5

1. Each Member may avail itself, by a declaration accompanying its ratification, of at most two of the temporary exceptions provided for in Article 10, paragraph 4, Article 11, paragraph 3, Article 15, paragraph 2, Article 18, paragraph 2, Article 19, paragraph 4, Article 23, paragraph 2, Article 24, paragraph 2, and Article 25, paragraph 2. Such a declaration shall state the reasons which justify these exceptions.

2. Notwithstanding the provisions of paragraph 1 above, a Member, where it is justified by the extent of protection of its social security system, may avail itself, by a declaration accompanying its ratification, of the temporary exceptions provided for in Article 10, paragraph 4, Article 11, paragraph 3, Article 15, paragraph 2, Article 18, paragraph 2, Article 19, paragraph 4, Article 23, paragraph 2, Article 24, paragraph 2 and Article 25, paragraph 2.

2. Such a declaration shall state the reasons which justify these exceptions.

3. Each Member which has made a declaration under paragraph 1 or paragraph 2 shall include in its reports on the application of this Convention submitted under Article 22 of the Constitution of the International Labour Organisation a statement in respect of each exception of which it avails itself:

(a) That its reason for doing so subsists; or

(b) That it renounces its right to avail itself of the exception in question as from a stated date.

4. Each Member which has made a declaration under paragraph 1 or paragraph 2 shall, as appropriate to the terms of such declaration and as circumstances permit:

(a) Cover the contingency of partial unemployment;

(b) Increase the number of persons protected;

(c) Increase the amount of the benefits;

(d) Reduce the length of the waiting period;

(e) Extend the duration of payment of benefits;

(f) Adapt statutory social security schemes to the occupational circumstances of part-time workers;

(g) Endeavour to ensure the provision of medical care to persons in receipt of unemployment benefit and their dependants;

(h) Endeavour to guarantee that the periods during which such benefit is paid will be taken into account for the acquisition of the right to social security benefits and, where appropriate, the calculation of disability, old-age and survivors' benefit.

Article 6

1. Each Member shall ensure equality of treatment for all persons protected, without discrimination on the basis of race, colour, sex, religion, political opinion, national extraction, nationality, ethnic or social origin, disability or age.

2. The provisions of paragraph 1 shall not prevent the adoption of special measures which are justified by the circumstances of identified groups under the schemes referred to in Article 12, paragraph 2, or are designed to meet the specific needs of categories of persons who have particular problems in the labour market, in particular disadvantaged groups, or the conclusion between States of bilateral or multilateral agreements relating to unemployment benefits on the basis of reciprocity.

II: Promotion of Productive Employment

Article 7

Each Member shall declare as a priority objective a policy designed to promote full, productive and freely chosen employment by all appropriate means, including social security. Such means should include, inter alia, employment services, vocational training and vocational guidance.

Article 8

1. Each Member shall endeavour to establish, subject to national law and practice, special programmes to promote additional job opportunities and employment assistance and to encourage freely chosen and productive employment for identified categories of disadvantaged persons having or liable to have difficulties in finding lasting employment such as women, young workers, disabled persons, older workers, the long-term unemployed, migrant workers lawfully resident in the country and workers affected by structural change.

2. Each Member shall specify, in its reports under Article 22 of the Constitution of the International Labour Organisation, the categories of persons for whom it undertakes to promote employment programmes.

3. Each Member shall endeavour to extend the promotion of productive employment progressively to a greater number of categories than the number initially covered.

Article 9

The measures envisaged in this Part shall be taken in the light of the Human Resources

Development Convention and Recommendation, 1975, and the Employment Policy (Supplementary Provisions) Recommendation, 1984.

III: Contingencies Covered

Article 10

1. The contingencies covered shall include, under prescribed conditions, full unemployment defined as the loss of earnings due to inability to obtain suitable employment with due regard to the provisions of Article 21, paragraph 2, in the case of a person capable of working, available for work and actually seeking work.

2. Each Member shall endeavour to extend the protection of the Convention, under prescribed conditions, to the following contingencies:

(a) Loss of earnings due to partial unemployment, defined as a temporary reduction in the normal or statutory hours of work; and

(b) Suspension or reduction of earnings due to a temporary suspension of work, without any break in the employment relationship for reasons of, in particular, an economic, technological, structural or similar nature.

3. Each Member shall in addition endeavour to provide the payment of benefits to part-time workers who are actually seeking full-time work. The total of benefits and earnings from their part-time work may be such as to maintain incentives to take up full-time work.

4. Where a declaration made in virtue of Article 5 is in force, the implementation of paragraphs 2 and 3 above may be deferred.

IV: Persons Protected

Article 11

1. The persons protected shall comprise prescribed classes of employees, constituting not less than 85 percent of all employees, including public employees and apprentices.

2. Notwithstanding the provisions of paragraph 1 above, public employees whose employment up to normal retiring age is guaranteed by national laws or regulations may be excluded from protection.

3. Where a declaration made in virtue of Article 5 is in force, the persons protected shall comprise:

(a) Prescribed classes of employees constituting not less than 50 percent of all employees; or

(b) Where specifically justified by the level of development, prescribed classes of employees constituting not less than 50 percent of all employees in industrial workplaces employing 20 persons or more.

V: Methods of Protection

Article 12

1. Unless it is otherwise provided in this Convention, each Member may determine the method or methods of protection by which it chooses to put into effect the provisions of the Convention, whether by a contributory or non-contributory system, or by a combination of such systems.

2. Nevertheless, if the legislation of a Member protects all residents whose resources, during the contingency, do not exceed prescribed limits, the protection afforded may be limited, in the light of the resources of the beneficiary and his or her family, in accordance with the provisions of Article 16.

VI: Benefit to Be Provided

Article 13

Benefits provided in the form of periodical payments to the unemployed may be related to the methods of protection.

Article 14

In cases of full unemployment, benefits shall be provided in the form of periodical payments calculated in such a way as to provide the beneficiary with partial and transitional wage replacement and, at the same time, to avoid creating disincentives either to work or to employment creation.

Article 15

1. In cases of full unemployment and suspension of earnings due to a temporary suspension of work without any break in the employment relationship, when this contingency is covered, benefits shall be provided in the form of periodical payments, calculated as follows:

(a) Where these benefits are based on the contributions of or on behalf of the person protected or on previous earnings, they shall be fixed at not less than 50 percent of previous earnings, it being permitted to fix a maximum for the amount of the benefit or for the earnings to be taken into account, which may be related, for example, to the wage of a skilled manual employee or to the average wage of workers in the region concerned;

(b) Where such benefits are not based on contributions or previous earnings, they shall be fixed at not less than 50 percent of the statutory minimum wage or of the wage of an ordinary labourer, or at a level which provides the minimum essential for basic living expenses, whichever is the highest;

2. Where a declaration made in virtue of Article 5 is in force, the amount of the benefits shall be equal:

(a) To not less than 45 percent of the previous earnings; or

(b) To not less than 45 percent of the statutory minimum wage or of the wage of an ordinary labourer but no less than a level which provides the minimum essential for basic living expenses.

3. If appropriate, the percentages specified in paragraphs 1 and 2 may be reached by comparing net periodical payments after tax and contributions with net earnings after tax and contributions.

Article 16

Notwithstanding the provisions of Article 15, the benefit provided beyond the initial period specified in Article 19, paragraph 2 (a), as well as benefits paid by a Member in accordance with Article 12, paragraph 2, may be fixed after taking account of other resources, beyond a prescribed limit, available to the beneficiary and his or her family, in accordance with a prescribed scale. In any case, these benefits, in combination with any other benefits to which they may be entitled, shall guarantee them healthy and reasonable living conditions in accordance with national standards.

Article 17

1. Where the legislation of a Member makes the right to unemployment benefit conditional upon the completion of a qualifying period, this period shall not exceed the length deemed necessary to prevent abuse.

2. Each Member shall endeavour to adapt the qualifying period to the occupational circumstances of seasonal workers.

Article 18

1. If the legislation of a Member provides that the payment of benefit in cases of full employment should begin only after the expiry of a waiting period, such period shall not exceed seven days.

2. Where a declaration made in virtue of Article 5 is in force, the length of the waiting period shall not exceed ten days.

3. In the case of seasonal workers the waiting period specified in paragraph 1 above may be adapted to their occupational circumstances.

Article 19

1. The benefits provided in cases of full unemployment and suspension of earnings due

to a temporary suspension of work without any break in the employment relationship shall be paid throughout these contingencies.

2. Nevertheless, in the case of full unemployment:

(a) The initial duration of payment of the benefit provided for in Article 15 may be limited to 26 weeks in each spell of unemployment, or to 39 weeks over any period of 24 months;

(b) In the event of unemployment continuing beyond this initial period of benefit, the duration of payment of benefit, which may be calculated in the light of the resources of the beneficiary and his or her family in accordance with the provisions of Article 16, may be limited to a prescribed period.

3. If the legislation of a Member provides that the initial duration of payment of the benefit provided for in Article 15 shall vary with the length of the qualifying period, the average duration fixed for the payment of benefits shall be at least 26 weeks.

4. Where a declaration made in virtue of Article 5 is in force, the duration of payment of benefit may be limited to 13 weeks over any period of 12 months or to an average of 13 weeks if the legislation provides that the initial duration of payment shall vary with the length of the qualifying period.

5. In the cases envisaged in paragraph 2 (b) above, each Member shall endeavour to grant appropriate additional assistance to the persons concerned with a view to permitting them to find productive and freely chosen employment, having recourse in particular to the measures specified in Part II.

6. The duration of payment of benefit to seasonal workers may be adapted to their occupational circumstances, without prejudice to the provisions of paragraph 2 (b) above.

Article 20

The benefit to which a protected person would have been entitled in the cases of full or partial unemployment or suspension of earnings due to a temporary suspension of work without any break in the employment relationship may be refused, withdrawn, suspended or reduced to the extent prescribed:

(a) For as long as the person concerned is absent from the territory of the Member;

(b) When it has been determined by the competent authority that the person concerned had deliberately contributed to his or her own dismissal;

(c) When it has been determined by the competent authority that the person concerned has left employment voluntarily without just cause;

(d) During the period of a labour dispute, when the person concerned has stopped work to take part in a labour dispute or when he or she is prevented from working as a direct result of a stoppage of work due to this labour dispute;

(e) When the person concerned has attempted to obtain or has obtained benefits fraudulently;

(f) When the person concerned has failed without just cause to use the facilities available for placement, vocational guidance, training, retraining or redeployment in suitable work;

(g) As long as the person concerned is in receipt of another income maintenance benefit provided for in the legislation of the Member concerned, except a family benefit, provided that the part of the benefit which is suspended does not exceed that other benefit.

Article 21

1. The benefit to which a protected person would have been entitled in the case of full unemployment may be refused, withdrawn, suspended or reduced, to the extent prescribed, when the person concerned refuses to accept suitable employment.

2. In assessing the suitability of employment, account shall be taken, in particular, under prescribed conditions and to an appropriate extent, of the age of unemployed persons, their length of service in their former occupation, their acquired experience, the length of their period of unemployment, the labour market situation, the impact of the employment in question on their personal and family situation and whether the employment is vacant as a direct result of a stoppage of work due to an on-going labour dispute.

Article 22

When protected persons have received directly from their employer or from any other source under national laws or regulations or collective agreements, severance pay, the principal purpose of which is to contribute towards compensating them for the loss of earnings suffered in the event of full unemployment:

(a) The unemployment benefit to which the persons concerned would be entitled may be suspended for a period corresponding to that during which the severance pay compensates for the loss of earnings suffered; or

(b) The severance pay may be reduced by an amount corresponding to the value converted into a lump sum of the unemployment benefit to which the persons concerned are entitled for a period corresponding to that during which the severance pay compensates for the loss of earnings suffered, as each Member may decide.

Article 23

1. Each Member whose legislation provides for the right to medical care and makes it directly or indirectly conditional upon occupational activity shall endeavour to ensure,

under prescribed conditions, the provision of medical care to persons in receipt of unemployment benefit and to their dependants.

2. Where a declaration made in virtue of Article 5 is in force, the implementation of paragraph 1 above may be deferred.

Article 24

1. Each Member shall endeavour to guarantee to persons in receipt of unemployment benefit, under prescribed conditions, that the periods during which benefits are paid will be taken into consideration:

(a) For acquisition of the right to and, where appropriate, calculation of disability, old-age and survivors' benefit, and

(b) For acquisition of the right to medical care and sickness, maternity and family benefit after the end of unemployment, when the legislation of the Member concerned provides for such benefits and makes them directly or indirectly conditional upon occupational activity.

2. Where a declaration made in virtue of Article 5 is in force, the implementation of paragraph 1 above may be deferred.

Article 25

1. Each Member shall ensure that statutory social security schemes which are based on occupational activity are adjusted to the occupational circumstances of part-time workers, unless their hours of work or earnings can be considered, under prescribed conditions, as negligible.

2. Where a declaration made in virtue of Article 5 is in force, the implementation of paragraph 1 above may be deferred.

VII: Special Provisions for New Applicants for Employment

Article 26

1. Members shall take account of the fact that there are many categories of persons seeking work who have never been, or have ceased to be, recognised as unemployed or have never been, or have ceased to be, covered by schemes for the protection of the unemployed. Consequently, at least three of the following ten categories of persons seeking work shall receive social benefits, in accordance with prescribed terms and conditions:

(a) Young persons who have completed their vocational training;

(b) Young persons who have completed their studies;

(c) Young persons who have completed their compulsory military service;

(d) Persons after a period devoted to bringing up a child or caring for someone who is sick, disabled or elderly;

(e) Persons whose spouse had died, when they are not entitled to a survivor's benefit;

(f) Divorced or separated persons;

(g) Released prisoners;

(h) Adults, including disabled persons, who have completed a period of training;

(i) Migrant workers on return to their home country, except in so far as they have acquired rights under the legislation of the country where they last worked;

(j) Previously self-employed persons.

2. Each Member shall specify, in its reports under Article 22 of the Constitution of the International Labour Organisation, the categories of persons listed in paragraph 1 above which it undertakes to protect.

3. Each Member shall endeavour to extend protection progressively to a greater number of categories than the number initially protected.

VIII: Legal, Administrative and Financial Guarantees

Article 27

1. In the event of refusal, withdrawal, suspension or reduction of benefit or dispute as to its amount, claimants shall have the right to present a complaint to the body administering the benefit scheme and to appeal thereafter to an independent body. They shall be informed in writing of the procedures available, which shall be simple and rapid.

2. The appeal procedure shall enable the claimant, in accordance with national law and practice, to be represented or assisted by a qualified person of the claimant's choice or by a delegate of a representative workers' organisation or by a delegate of an organisation representative of protected persons.

Article 28

Each Member shall assume general responsibility for the sound administration of the institutions and services entrusted with the application of the Convention.

Article 29

1. When the administration is directly entrusted to a government department responsible to Parliament, representatives of the protected persons and of the employers

shall be associated in the administration in an advisory capacity, under prescribed conditions.

2. When the administration is not entrusted to a government department responsible to Parliament:

(a) Representatives of the protected persons shall participate in the administration or be associated therewith in an advisory capacity under prescribed conditions;

(b) National laws or regulations may also provide for the participation of employers' representatives;

(c) The laws or regulations may further provide for the participation of representatives of the public authorities.

Article 30

In cases where subsidies are granted by the State or the social security system in order to safeguard employment, Members shall take the necessary steps to ensure that the payments are expended only for the intended purpose and to prevent fraud or abuse by those who receive such payments.

Article 31

This Convention revises the Unemployment Provision Convention, 1934.

. . .

Chapter 15
ILO Convention No. 169 Concerning Indigenous and Tribal Peoples in Independent Countries (excerpts)

Part I: General Policy

Article 1

1. This Convention applies to:

(a) Tribal peoples in independent countries whose social, cultural and economic conditions distinguish them from other sections of the national community, and whose status is regulated wholly or partially by their own customs or traditions or by special laws or regulations;

(b) Peoples in independent countries who are regarded as indigenous on account of their descent from the populations which inhabited the country, or a geographical region to which the country belongs, at the time of conquest or colonisation or the establishment of present State boundaries and who, irrespective of their legal status, retain some or all of their own social, economic, cultural and political institutions.

2. Self-identification as indigenous or tribal shall be regarded as a fundamental criterion for determining the groups to which the provisions of this Convention apply.

3. The use of the term "peoples" in this Convention shall not be construed as having any implications as regards the rights which may attach to the term under international law.

Article 2

1. Governments shall have the responsibility for developing, with the participation of the peoples concerned, co-ordinated and systematic action to protect the rights of these peoples and to guarantee respect for their integrity.

Adopted 27 June 1989 by the General Conference of the International Labour Organisation, *entry into force* 5 September 1991.

2. Such action shall include measures for:

(a) Ensuring that members of these peoples benefit on an equal footing from the rights and opportunities which national laws and regulations grant to other members of the population;

(b) Promoting the full realisation of the social, economic and cultural rights of these peoples with respect for their social and cultural identity, their customs and traditions and their institutions;

(c) Assisting the members of the peoples concerned to eliminate socio-economic gaps that may exist between indigenous and other members of the national community, in a manner compatible with their aspirations and ways of life.

Article 3

1. Indigenous and tribal peoples shall enjoy the full measure of human rights and fundamental freedoms without hindrance or discrimination. The provisions of the Convention shall be applied without discrimination to male and female members of these peoples.

2. No form of force or coercion shall be used in violation of the human rights and fundamental freedoms of the peoples concerned, including the rights contained in this Convention.

Article 4

1. Special measures shall be adopted as appropriate for safeguarding the persons, institutions, property, labour, cultures and environment of the peoples concerned.

2. Such special measures shall not be contrary to the freely-expressed wishes of the peoples concerned.

3. Enjoyment of the general rights of citizenship, without discrimination, shall not be prejudiced in any way by such special measures.

Article 5

In applying the provisions of this Convention:

(a) The social, cultural, religious and spiritual values and practices of these peoples shall be recognised and protected, and due account shall be taken of the nature of the problems which face them both as groups and as individuals;

(b) The integrity of the values, practices and institutions of these peoples shall be respected;

(c) Policies aimed at mitigating the difficulties experienced by these peoples in facing new conditions of life and work shall be adopted, with the participation and co-operation of the peoples affected.

Article 6

1. In applying the provisions of this Convention, Governments shall:

(a) Consult the peoples concerned, through appropriate procedures and in particular through their representative institutions, whenever consideration is being given to legislative or administrative measures which may affect them directly;

(b) Establish means by which these peoples can freely participate, to at least the same extent as other sectors of the population, at all levels of decision-making in elective institutions and administrative and other bodies responsible for policies and programmes which concern them;

(c) Establish means for the full development of these peoples' own institutions and initiatives, and in appropriate cases provide the resources necessary for this purpose.

2. The consultations carried out in application of this Convention shall be undertaken, in good faith and in a form appropriate to the circumstances, with the objective of achieving agreement or consent to the proposed measures.

Article 7

1. The peoples concerned shall have the right to decide their own priorities for the process of development as it affects their lives, beliefs, institutions and spiritual well-being and the lands they occupy or otherwise use, and to exercise control, to the extent possible, over their own economic, social and cultural development. In addition, they shall participate in the formulation, implementation and evaluation of plans and programmes for national and regional development which may affect them directly.

2. The improvement of the conditions of life and work and levels of health and education of the peoples concerned, with their participation and co-operation, shall be a matter of priority in plans for the overall economic development of areas they inhabit. Special projects for development of the areas in question shall also be so designed as to promote such improvement.

3. Governments shall ensure that, whenever appropriate, studies are carried out, in co-operation with the peoples concerned, to assess the social, spiritual, cultural and environmental impact on them of planned development activities. The results of these studies shall be considered as fundamental criteria for the implementation of these activities.

4. Governments shall take measures, in co-operation with the peoples concerned, to protect and preserve the environment of the territories they inhabit.

Article 8

1. In applying national laws and regulations to the peoples concerned, due regard shall be had to their customs or customary laws.

2. These peoples shall have the right to retain their own customs and institutions, where these are not incompatible with fundamental rights defined by the national legal system and with internationally recognized human rights. Procedures shall be established, whenever necessary, to resolve conflicts which may arise in the application of this principle.

3. The application of paragraphs 1 and 2 of this Article shall not prevent members of these peoples from exercising the rights granted to all citizens and from assuming the corresponding duties.

Article 9

1. To the extent compatible with the national legal system and internationally recognised human rights, the methods customarily practised by the peoples concerned for dealing with offences committed by their members shall be respected.

2. The customs of these peoples in regard to penal matters shall be taken into consideration by the authorities and courts dealing with such cases.

Article 10

1. In imposing penalties laid down by general law on members of these peoples account shall be taken of their economic, social and cultural characteristics.

2. Preference shall be given to methods of punishment other than confinement in prison.

Article 11

The exaction from members of the peoples concerned of compulsory personal services in any form, whether paid or unpaid, shall be prohibited and punishable by law, except in cases prescribed by law for all citizens.

Article 12

The peoples concerned shall be safeguarded against the abuse of their rights and shall be able to take legal proceedings, either individually or through their representative bodies, for the effective protection of these rights. Measures shall be taken to ensure that members of these peoples can understand and be understood in legal proceedings where necessary through the provision of interpretation or by other effective means.

Part II: Land

Article 13

1. In applying the provisions of this Part of the Convention governments shall respect the special importance for the cultures and spiritual values of the peoples concerned of their relationship with the lands or territories, or both as applicable, which they occupy or otherwise use, and in particular the collective aspects of this relationship.

2. The use of the term "lands" in Articles 15 and 16 shall include the concept of territories, which covers the total environment of the areas which the peoples concerned occupy or otherwise use.

Article 14

1. The rights of ownership and possession of the peoples concerned over the lands which they traditionally occupy shall be recognised. In addition, measures shall be taken in appropriate cases to safeguard the right of the peoples concerned to use lands not exclusively occupied by them, but to which they have traditionally had access for their subsistence and traditional activities. Particular attention shall be paid to the situation of nomadic peoples and shifting cultivators in this respect.

2. Governments shall take steps as necessary to identify the lands which the peoples concerned traditionally occupy, and to guarantee effective protection of their rights of ownership and possession.

3. Adequate procedures shall be established within the national legal system to resolve land claims by the peoples concerned.

Article 15

1. The rights of the peoples concerned to the natural resources pertaining to their lands shall be specially safeguarded. These rights include the right of these peoples to participate in the use, management and conservation of these resources.

2. In cases in which the State retains the ownership of mineral or sub-surface resources or rights to other resources pertaining to lands, governments shall establish or maintain procedures through which they shall consult these peoples, with a view to ascertaining whether and to what degree their interests would be prejudiced, before undertaking or permitting any programmes for the exploration or exploitation of such resources pertaining to their lands. The peoples concerned shall wherever possible participate in the benefits of such activities, and shall receive fair compensation for any damages which they may sustain as a result of such activities.

Article 16

1. Subject to the following paragraphs of this Article, the peoples concerned shall not be removed from the lands which they occupy.

2. Where the relocation of these peoples is considered necessary as an exceptional measure, such relocation shall take place only with their free and informed consent. Where their consent cannot be obtained, such relocation shall take place only following appropriate procedures established by national laws and regulations, including public inquiries where appropriate, which provide the opportunity for effective representation of the peoples concerned.

3. Whenever possible, these peoples shall have the right to return to their traditional lands, as soon as the grounds for relocation cease to exist.

4. When such return is not possible, as determined by agreement or, in the absence of such agreement, through appropriate procedures, these peoples shall be provided in all possible cases with lands of quality and legal status at least equal to that of the lands previously occupied by them, suitable to provide for their present needs and future development. Where the peoples concerned express a preference for compensation in money or in kind, they shall be so compensated under appropriate guarantees.

5. Persons thus relocated shall be fully compensated for any resulting loss or injury.

Article 17

1. Procedures established by the peoples concerned for the transmission of land rights among members of these peoples shall be respected.

2. The peoples concerned shall be consulted whenever consideration is being given to their capacity to alienate their lands or otherwise transmit their rights outside their own community.

3. Persons not belonging to these peoples shall be prevented from taking advantage of their customs or of lack of understanding of the laws on the part of their members to secure the ownership, possession or use of land belonging to them.

Article 18

Adequate penalties shall be established by law for unauthorised intrusion upon, or use of, the lands of the peoples concerned, and governments shall take measures to prevent such offences.

Article 19

National agrarian programmes shall secure to the peoples concerned treatment equivalent to that accorded to other sectors of the population with regard to:

(a) The provision of more land for these peoples when they have not the area necessary for providing the essentials of a normal existence, or for any possible increase in their numbers;

(b) The provision of the means required to promote the development of the lands which these peoples already possess.

Part III: Recruitment and Conditions of Employment

Article 20

1. Governments shall, within the framework of national laws and regulations, and in co-operation with the peoples concerned, adopt special measures to ensure the effective protection with regard to recruitment and conditions of employment of workers belonging to these peoples, to the extent that they are not effectively protected by laws applicable to workers in general.

2. Governments shall do everything possible to prevent any discrimination between workers belonging to the peoples concerned and other workers, in particular as regards:

(a) Admission to employment, including skilled employment, as well as measures for promotion and advancement;

(b) Equal remuneration for work of equal value;

(c) Medical and social assistance, occupational safety and health, all social security benefits and any other occupationally related benefits, and housing;

(d) The right of association and freedom for all lawful trade union activities, and the right to conclude collective agreements with employers or employers' organisations.

3. The measures taken shall include measures to ensure:

(a) That workers belonging to the peoples concerned, including seasonal, casual and migrant workers in agricultural and other employment, as well as those employed by labour contractors, enjoy the protection afforded by national law and practice to other such workers in the same sectors, and that they are fully informed of their rights under labour legislation and of the means of redress available to them;

(b) That workers belonging to these peoples are not subjected to working conditions hazardous to their health, in particular through exposure to pesticides or other toxic substances;

(c) That workers belonging to these peoples are not subjected to coercive recruitment systems, including bonded labour and other forms of debt servitude;

(d) That workers belonging to these peoples enjoy equal opportunities and equal treatment in employment for men and women and protection from sexual harassment.

4. Particular attention shall be paid to the establishment of adequate labour inspection services in areas where workers belonging to the peoples concerned undertake wage employment, in order to ensure compliance with the provisions of this Part of this Convention.

Part IV: Vocational Training, Handicrafts and Rural Industries

Article 21

Members of the peoples concerned shall enjoy opportunities at least equal to those of other citizens in respect of vocational training measures.

Article 22

1. Measures shall be taken to promote the voluntary participation of members of the peoples concerned in vocational training programmes of general application.

2. Whenever existing programmes of vocational training of general application do not meet the special needs of the peoples concerned, governments shall, with the participation of these peoples, ensure the provision of special training programmes and facilities.

3. Any special training programmes shall be based on the economic environment, social and cultural conditions and practical needs of the peoples concerned. Any studies made in this connection shall be carried out in co-operation with these peoples, who shall be consulted on the organisation and operation of such programmes. Where feasible, these peoples shall progressively assume responsibility for the organisation and operation of such special training programmes, if they so decide.

Article 23

1. Handicrafts, rural and community-based industries, and subsistence economy and traditional activities of the peoples concerned, such as hunting, fishing, trapping and gathering, shall be recognised as important factors in the maintenance of their cultures and in their economic self-reliance and development. Governments shall, with the participation of these peoples and whenever appropriate, ensure that these activities are strengthened and promoted.

2. Upon the request of the peoples concerned, appropriate technical and financial assistance shall be provided wherever possible, taking into account the traditional technologies and cultural characteristics of these peoples, as well as the importance of sustainable and equitable development.

Part V: Social Security and Health

Article 24

Social security schemes shall be extended progressively to cover the peoples concerned, and applied without discrimination against them.

Article 25

1. Governments shall ensure that adequate health services are made available to the peoples concerned, or shall provide them with resources to allow them to design and deliver such services under their own responsibility and control, so that they may enjoy the highest attainable standard of physical and mental health.

2. Health services shall, to the extent possible, be community-based. These services shall be planned and administered in co-operation with the peoples concerned and

take into account their economic, geographic, social and cultural conditions as well as their traditional preventive care, healing practices and medicines.

3. The health care system shall give preference to the training and employment of local community health workers, and focus on primary health care while maintaining strong links with other levels of health care services.

4. The provision of such health services shall be co-ordinated with other social, economic and cultural measures in the country.

Part VI: Education and Means of Communication

Article 26

Measures shall be taken to ensure that members of the peoples concerned have the opportunity to acquire education at all levels on at least an equal footing with the rest of the national community.

Article 27

1. Education programmes and services for the peoples concerned shall be developed and implemented in co-operation with them to address their special needs, and shall incorporate their histories, their knowledge and technologies, their value systems and their further social, economic and cultural aspirations. They shall participate in the formulation, implementation and evaluation of plans and programmes for national and regional development which may affect them directly.

2. The competent authority shall ensure the training of members of these peoples and their involvement in the formulation and implementation of education programmes, with a view to the progressive transfer of responsibility for the conduct of these programmes to these peoples as appropriate.

3. In addition, governments shall recognise the right of these peoples to establish their own educational institutions and facilities, provided that such institutions meet minimum standards established by the competent authority in consultation with these peoples. Appropriate resources shall be provided for this purpose.

Article 28

1. Children belonging to the peoples concerned shall, wherever practicable, be taught to read and write in their own indigenous language or in the language most commonly used by the group to which they belong. When this is not practicable, the competent authorities shall undertake consultations with these peoples with a view to the adoption of measures to achieve this objective.

2. Adequate measures shall be taken to ensure that these peoples have the opportunity to attain fluency in the national language or in one of the official languages of the country.

3. Measures shall be taken to preserve and promote the development and practice of the indigenous languages of the peoples concerned.

Article 29

The imparting of general knowledge and skills that will help children belonging to the peoples concerned to participate fully and on an equal footing in their own community and in the national community shall be an aim of education for these peoples.

Article 30

1. Governments shall adopt measures appropriate to the traditions and cultures of the peoples concerned, to make known to them their rights and duties, especially in regard to labour, economic opportunities, education and health matters, social welfare and their rights deriving from this Convention.

2. If necessary, this shall be done by means of written translations and through the use of mass communications in the languages of these peoples.

Article 31

Educational measures shall be taken among all sections of the national community, and particularly among those that are in most direct contact with the peoples concerned, with the object of eliminating prejudices that they may harbour in respect of these peoples. To this end, efforts shall be made to ensure that history textbooks and other educational materials provide a fair, accurate and informative portrayal of the societies and cultures of these peoples.

Part VII: Contacts and Co-Operation Across Borders

Article 32

Governments shall take appropriate measures, including by means of international agreements, to facilitate contacts and co-operation between indigenous and tribal peoples across borders, including activities in the economic, social, cultural, spiritual and environmental fields.

Part VIII: Administration

Article 33

1. The governmental authority responsible for the matters covered in this Convention shall ensure that agencies or other appropriate mechanisms exist to administer the

programmes affecting the peoples concerned, and shall ensure that they have the means necessary for the proper fulfilment of the functions assigned to them.

2. These programmes shall include:

(a) The planning, co-ordination, execution and evaluation, in co- operation with the peoples concerned, of the measures provided for in this Convention;

(b) The proposing of legislative and other measures to the competent authorities and supervision of the application of the measures taken, in co-operation with the peoples concerned.

Part IX: General Provisions

Article 34

The nature and scope of the measures to be taken to give effect to this Convention shall be determined in a flexible manner, having regard to the conditions characteristic of each country.

Article 35

The application of the provisions of this Convention shall not adversely affect rights and benefits of the peoples concerned pursuant to other Conventions and Recommendations, international instruments, treaties, or national laws, awards, custom or agreements.

. . .

Chapter 16
Convention Against Discrimination in Education (excerpts)

The General Conference of the United Nations Educational, Scientific and Cultural Organization, meeting in Paris from 14 November to 15 December 1960, at its eleventh session,

Recalling that the Universal Declaration of Human Rights asserts the principle of non-discrimination and proclaims that every person has the right to education,

Considering that discrimination in education is a violation of rights enunciated in that Declaration,

Considering that, under the terms of its Constitution, the United Nations Educational, Scientific and Cultural Organization has the purpose of instituting collaboration among the nations with a view to furthering for all universal respect for human rights and equality of educational opportunity,

Recognizing that, consequently, the United Nations Educational, Scientific and Cultural Organization, while respecting the diversity of national educational systems, has the duty not only to proscribe any form of discrimination in education but also to promote equality of opportunity and treatment for all in education,

Having before it proposals concerning the different aspects of discrimination in education, constituting item 17.1.4 of the agenda of the session,

Having decided at its tenth session that this question should be made the subject of an international convention as well as of recommendations to Member States,

Adopts this Convention on the fourteenth day of December 1960.

Article 1

1. For the purpose of this Convention, the term "discrimination" includes any distinction, exclusion, limitation or preference which, being based on race, colour, sex, language,

Adopted by the General Conference of the United Nations Educational, Scientific and Cultural Organization 14 December 1960, *entry into force* 22 May 1962, in accordance with Article 14.

religion, political or other opinion, national or social origin, economic condition or birth, has the purpose or effect of nullifying or impairing equality of treatment in education and in particular:

(a) Of depriving any person or group of persons of access to education of any type or at any level;

(b) Of limiting any person or group of persons to education of an inferior standard;

(c) Subject to the provisions of Article 2 of this Convention, of establishing or maintaining separate educational systems or institutions for persons or groups of persons; or

(d) Of inflicting on any person or group of persons conditions which are incompatible with the dignity of man.

2. For the purposes of this Convention, the term "education" refers to all types and levels of education, and includes access to education, the standard and quality of education, and the conditions under which it is given.

Article 2

When permitted in a State, the following situations shall not be deemed to constitute discrimination, within the meaning of Article 1 of this Convention:

(a) The establishment or maintenance of separate educational systems or institutions for pupils of the two sexes, if these systems or institutions offer equivalent access to education, provide a teaching staff with qualifications of the same standard as well as school premises and equipment of the same quality, and afford the opportunity to take the same or equivalent courses of study;

(b) The establishment or maintenance, for religious or linguistic reasons, of separate educational systems or institutions offering an education which is in keeping with the wishes of the pupil's parents or legal guardians, if participation in such systems or attendance at such institutions is optional and if the education provided conforms to such standards as may be laid down or approved by the competent authorities, in particular for education of the same level;

(c) The establishment or maintenance of private educational institutions, if the object of the institutions is not to secure the exclusion of any group but to provide educational facilities in addition to those provided by the public authorities, if the institutions are conducted in accordance with that object, and if the education provided conforms with such standards as may be laid down or approved by the competent authorities, in particular for education of the same level.

Article 3

In order to eliminate and prevent discrimination within the meaning of this Convention, the States Parties thereto undertake:

(a) To abrogate any statutory provisions and any administrative instructions and to discontinue any administrative practices which involve discrimination in education;

(b) To ensure, by legislation where necessary, that there is no discrimination in the admission of pupils to educational institutions;

(c) Not to allow any differences of treatment by the public authorities between nationals, except on the basis of merit or need, in the matter of school fees and the grant of scholarships or other forms of assistance to pupils and necessary permits and facilities for the pursuit of studies in foreign countries;

(d) Not to allow, in any form of assistance granted by the public authorities to educational institutions, any restrictions or preference based solely on the ground that pupils belong to a particular group;

(e) To give foreign nationals resident within their territory the same access to education as that given to their own nationals.

Article 4

The States Parties to this Convention undertake furthermore to formulate, develop and apply a national policy which, by methods appropriate to the circumstances and to national usage, will tend to promote equality of opportunity and of treatment in the matter of education and in particular:

(a) To make primary education free and compulsory; make secondary education in its different forms generally available and accessible to all; make higher education equally accessible to all on the basis of individual capacity; assure compliance by all with the obligation to attend school prescribed by law;

(b) To ensure that the standards of education are equivalent in all public education institutions of the same level, and that the conditions relating to the quality of education provided are also equivalent;

(c) To encourage and intensify by appropriate methods the education of persons who have not received any primary education or who have not completed the entire primary education course and the continuation of their education on the basis of individual capacity;

(d) To provide training for the teaching profession without discrimination.

Article 5

1. The States Parties to this Convention agree that:

(a) Education shall be directed to the full development of the human personality and to the strengthening of respect for human rights and fundamental freedoms; it shall promote understanding, tolerance and friendship among all nations, racial or religious groups, and shall further the activities of the United Nations for the maintenance of peace;

(b) It is essential to respect the liberty of parents and, where applicable, of legal guardians, firstly to choose for their children institutions other than those maintained by the public authorities but conforming to such minimum educational standards as may be laid down or approved by the competent authorities and, secondly, to ensure in a manner consistent with the procedures followed in the State for the application of its legislation, the religious and moral education of the children in conformity with their own convictions; and no person or group of persons should be compelled to receive religious instruction inconsistent with his or their conviction;

(c) It is essential to recognize the right of members of national minorities to carry on their own educational activities, including the maintenance of schools and, depending on the educational policy of each State, the use or the teaching of their own language, provided, however:

(i) That this right is not exercised in a manner which prevents the members of these minorities from understanding the culture and language of the community as a whole and from participating in its activities, or which prejudices national sovereignty;

(ii) That the standard of education is not lower than the general standard laid down or approved by the competent authorities; and

(iii) That attendance at such schools is optional.

2. The States Parties to this Convention undertake to take all necessary measures to ensure the application of the principles enunciated in paragraph 1 of this article.

. . .

Chapter 17
Geneva Convention for the Amelioration of the Condition of the Wounded and Sick in Armed Forces in the Field (excerpts)

Chapter I: General Provisions

Article 1

The High Contracting Parties undertake to respect and to ensure respect for the present Convention in all circumstances.

Article 2

In addition to the provisions which shall be implemented in peacetime, the present Convention shall apply to all cases of declared war or of any other armed conflict which may arise between two or more of the High Contracting Parties, even if the state of war is not recognized by one of them.

The Convention shall also apply to all cases of partial or total occupation of the territory of a High Contracting Party, even if the said occupation meets with no armed resistance.

Although one of the Powers in conflict may not be a party to the present Convention, the Powers who are parties thereto shall remain bound by it in their mutual relations. They shall furthermore be bound by the Convention in relation to the said Power, if the latter accepts and applies the provisions thereof.

Article 3

In the case of armed conflict not of an international character occurring in the territory of one of the High Contracting Parties, each Party to the conflict shall be bound to apply, as a minimum, the following provisions:

Adopted 12 August 1949 by the Diplomatic Conference for the Establishment of International Conventions for the Protection of Victims of War, held in Geneva from 21 April to 12 August 1949, *entry into force* 21 October 1950.

1. Persons taking no active part in the hostilities, including members of armed forces who have laid down their arms and those placed hors de combat by sickness, wounds, detention, or any other cause, shall in all circumstances be treated humanely, without any adverse distinction founded on race, colour, religion or faith, sex, birth or wealth, or any other similar criteria.

To this end, the following acts are and shall remain prohibited at any time and in any place whatsoever with respect to the above-mentioned persons:

(a) Violence to life and person, in particular murder of all kinds, mutilation, cruel treatment and torture;

(b) Taking of hostages;

(c) Outrages upon personal dignity, in particular humiliating and degrading treatment;

(d) The passing of sentences and the carrying out of executions without previous judgment pronounced by a regularly constituted court, affording all the judicial guarantees which are recognized as indispensable by civilized peoples.

2. The wounded and sick shall be collected and cared for.

An impartial humanitarian body, such as the International Committee of the Red Cross, may offer its services to the Parties to the conflict.

The Parties to the conflict should further endeavour to bring into force, by means of special agreements, all or part of the other provisions of the present Convention.

The application of the preceding provisions shall not affect the legal status of the Parties to the conflict.

Article 4

Neutral Powers shall apply by analogy the provisions of the present Convention to the wounded and sick, and to members of the medical personnel and to chaplains of the armed forces of the Parties to the conflict, received or interned in their territory, as well as to dead persons found.

Article 5

For the protected persons who have fallen into the hands of the enemy, the present Convention shall apply until their final repatriation.

. . .

Chapter II: Wounded and Sick

Article 12

Members of the armed forces and other persons mentioned in the following Article, who are wounded or sick, shall be respected and protected in all circumstances.

They shall be treated humanely and cared for by the Party to the conflict in whose power they may be, without any adverse distinction founded on sex, race, nationality, religion, political opinions, or any other similar criteria. Any attempts upon their lives, or violence to their persons, shall be strictly prohibited; in particular, they shall not be murdered or exterminated, subjected to torture or to biological experiments; they shall not willfully be left without medical assistance and care, nor shall conditions exposing them to contagion or infection be created.

Only urgent medical reasons will authorize priority in the order of treatment to be administered.

Women shall be treated with all consideration due to their sex.

The Party to the conflict which is compelled to abandon wounded or sick to the enemy shall, as far as military considerations permit, leave with them a part of its medical personnel and material to assist in their care.

. . .

Chapter 18
Geneva Convention for the Amelioration of the Condition of Wounded, Sick and Shipwrecked Members of Armed Forces at Sea (excerpts)

Chapter I: General Provisions

Article 1

The High Contracting Parties undertake to respect and to ensure respect for the present Convention in all circumstances.

Article 2

In addition to the provisions which shall be implemented in peacetime, the present Convention shall apply to all cases of declared war or of any other armed conflict which may arise between two or more of the High Contracting Parties, even if the state of war is not recognized by one of them.

The Convention shall also apply to all cases of partial or total occupation of the territory of a High Contracting Party, even if the said occupation meets with no armed resistance.

Although one of the Powers in conflict may not be a party to the present Convention, the Powers who are parties thereto shall remain bound by it in their mutual relations. They shall furthermore be bound by the Convention in relation to the said Power, if the latter accepts and applies the provisions thereof.

Article 3

In the case of armed conflict not of an international character occurring in the territory of one of the High Contracting Parties, each Party to the conflict shall be bound to apply, as a minimum, the following provisions:

Adopted 12 August 1949 by the Diplomatic Conference for the Establishment of International Conventions for the Protection of Victims of War, held in Geneva from 21 April to 12 August 1949, *entry into force* 21 October 1950.

1. Persons taking no active part in the hostilities, including members of armed forces who have laid down their arms and those placed hors de combat by sickness, wounds, detention, or any other cause, shall in all circumstances be treated humanely, without any adverse distinction founded on race, colour, religion or faith, sex, birth or wealth, or any other similar criteria. To this end, the following acts are and shall remain prohibited at any time and in any place whatsoever with respect to the above-mentioned persons:

(a) Violence to life and person, in particular murder of all kinds, mutilation, cruel treatment and torture;

(b) Taking of hostages;

(c) Outrages upon personal dignity, in particular, humiliating and degrading treatment;

(d) The passing of sentences and the carrying out of executions without previous judgment pronounced by a regularly constituted court, affording all the judicial guarantees which are recognized as indispensable by civilized peoples.

2. The wounded, sick and shipwrecked shall be collected and cared for.

An impartial humanitarian body, such as the International Committee of the Red Cross, may offer its services to the Parties to the conflict.

The Parties to the conflict should further endeavour to bring into force, by means of special agreements, all or part of the other provisions of the present Convention.

The application of the preceding provisions shall not affect the legal status of the Parties to the conflict.

Article 4

In case of hostilities between land and naval forces of Parties to the conflict, the provisions of the present Convention shall apply only to forces on board ship.

Forces put ashore shall immediately become subject to the provisions of the Geneva Convention for the Amelioration of the Condition of the Wounded and Sick in Armed Forces in the Field of August 12, 1949.

. . .

Chapter II: Wounded, Sick and Shipwrecked

Article 12

Members of the armed forces and other persons mentioned in the following Article, who are at sea and who are wounded, sick or shipwrecked, shall be respected and protected in all circumstances, it being understood that the term "shipwreck" means shipwreck from any cause and includes forced landings at sea by or from aircraft.

Such persons shall be treated humanely and cared for by the Parties to the conflict in whose power they may be, without any adverse distinction founded on sex, race, nationality, religion, political opinions, or any other similar criteria. Any attempts upon their lives, or violence to their persons, shall be strictly prohibited; in particular, they shall not be murdered or exterminated, subjected to torture or to biological experiments; they shall not willfully be left without medical assistance and care, nor shall conditions exposing them to contagion or infection be created.

Only urgent medical reasons will authorize priority in the order of treatment to be administered. Women shall be treated with all consideration due to their sex.

. . .

Chapter 19
Geneva Convention Relative to the Treatment of Prisoners of War (excerpts)

Part I: General Provisions

Article 1

The High Contracting Parties undertake to respect and to ensure respect for the present Convention in all circumstances.

Article 2

In addition to the provisions which shall be implemented in peace time, the present Convention shall apply to all cases of declared war or of any other armed conflict which may arise between two or more of the High Contracting Parties, even if the state of war is not recognized by one of them.

The Convention shall also apply to all cases of partial or total occupation of the territory of a High Contracting Party, even if the said occupation meets with no armed resistance.

Although one of the Powers in conflict may not be a party to the present Convention, the Powers who are parties thereto shall remain bound by it in their mutual relations. They shall furthermore be bound by the Convention in relation to the said Power, if the latter accepts and applies the provisions thereof.

Article 3

In the case of armed conflict not of an international character occurring in the territory of one of the High Contracting Parties, each party to the conflict shall be bound to apply, as a minimum, the following provisions:

Adopted 12 August 1949 by the Diplomatic Conference for the Establishment of International Conventions for the Protection of Victims of War, held in Geneva from 21 April to 12 August 1949, *entry into force* 21 October 1950.

1. Persons taking no active part in the hostilities, including members of armed forces who have laid down their arms and those placed hors de combat by sickness, wounds, detention, or any other cause, shall in all circumstances be treated humanely, without any adverse distinction founded on race, colour, religion or faith, sex, birth or wealth, or any other similar criteria.

To this end the following acts are and shall remain prohibited at any time and in any place whatsoever with respect to the above-mentioned persons:

(a) Violence to life and person, in particular murder of all kinds, mutilation, cruel treatment and torture;

(b) Taking of hostages;

(c) Outrages upon personal dignity, in particular, humiliating and degrading treatment;

(d) The passing of sentences and the carrying out of executions without previous judgment pronounced by a regularly constituted court affording all the judicial guarantees which are recognized as indispensable by civilized peoples.

2. The wounded and sick shall be collected and cared for.

An impartial humanitarian body, such as the International Committee of the Red Cross, may offer its services to the Parties to the conflict.

The Parties to the conflict should further endeavour to bring into force, by means of special agreements, all or part of the other provisions of the present Convention.

The application of the preceding provisions shall not affect the legal status of the Parties to the conflict.

Article 4

A. Prisoners of war, in the sense of the present Convention, are persons belonging to one of the following categories, who have fallen into the power of the enemy:

1. Members of the armed forces of a Party to the conflict as well as members of militias or volunteer corps forming part of such armed forces.

2. Members of other militias and members of other volunteer corps, including those of organized resistance movements, belonging to a Party to the conflict and operating in or outside their own territory, even if this territory is occupied, provided that such militias or volunteer corps, including such organized resistance movements, fulfill the following conditions:

(a) That of being commanded by a person responsible for his subordinates;

(b) That of having a fixed distinctive sign recognizable at a distance;

(c) That of carrying arms openly;

(d) That of conducting their operations in accordance with the laws and customs of war.

3. Members of regular armed forces who profess allegiance to a government or an authority not recognized by the Detaining Power.

4. Persons who accompany the armed forces without actually being members thereof, such as civilian members of military aircraft crews, war correspondents, supply contractors, members of labour units or of services responsible for the welfare of the armed forces, provided that they have received authorization from the armed forces which they accompany, who shall provide them for that purpose with an identity card similar to the annexed model.

5. Members of crews, including masters, pilots and apprentices, of the merchant marine and the crews of civil aircraft of the Parties to the conflict, who do not benefit by more favourable treatment under any other provisions of international law.

6. Inhabitants of a non-occupied territory, who on the approach of the enemy spontaneously take up arms to resist the invading forces, without having had time to form themselves into regular armed units, provided they carry arms openly and respect the laws and customs of war.

B. The following shall likewise be treated as prisoners of war under the present Convention:

1. Persons belonging, or having belonged, to the armed forces of the occupied country, if the occupying Power considers it necessary by reason of such allegiance to intern them, even though it has originally liberated them while hostilities were going on outside the territory it occupies, in particular where such persons have made an unsuccessful attempt to rejoin the armed forces to which they belong and which are engaged in combat, or where they fail to comply with a summons made to them with a view to internment.

2. The persons belonging to one of the categories enumerated in the present Article, who have been received by neutral or non-belligerent Powers on their territory and whom these Powers are required to intern under international law, without prejudice to any more favourable treatment which these Powers may choose to give and with the exception of Articles 8, 10, 15, 30, fifth paragraph, 58–67, 92, 126 and, where diplomatic relations exist between the Parties to the conflict and the neutral or non-belligerent Power concerned, those Articles concerning the Protecting Power. Where such diplomatic relations exist, the Parties to a conflict on whom these persons depend shall be allowed to perform towards them the functions of a Protecting Power as provided in the present Convention, without prejudice to the functions which these Parties normally exercise in conformity with diplomatic and consular usage and treaties.

C. This Article shall in no way affect the status of medical personnel and chaplains as provided for in Article 33 of the present Convention.

. . .

Part II: General Protection of Prisoners of War

Article 12

Prisoners of war are in the hands of the enemy Power, but not of the individuals or military units who have captured them. Irrespective of the individual responsibilities that may exist, the Detaining Power is responsible for the treatment given them.

Prisoners of war may only be transferred by the Detaining Power to a Power which is a party to the Convention and after the Detaining Power has satisfied itself of the willingness and ability of such transferee Power to apply the Convention. When prisoners of war are transferred under such circumstances, responsibility for the application of the Convention rests on the Power accepting them while they are in its custody.

Nevertheless if that Power fails to carry out the provisions of the Convention in any important respect, the Power by whom the prisoners of war were transferred shall, upon being notified by the Protecting Power, take effective measures to correct the situation or shall request the return of the prisoners of war. Such requests must be complied with.

Article 13

Prisoners of war must at all times be humanely treated. Any unlawful act or omission by the Detaining Power causing death or seriously endangering the health of a prisoner of war in its custody is prohibited, and will be regarded as a serious breach of the present Convention. In particular, no prisoner of war may be subjected to physical mutilation or to medical or scientific experiments of any kind which are not justified by the medical, dental or hospital treatment of the prisoner concerned and carried out in his interest.

Likewise, prisoners of war must at all times be protected, particularly against acts of violence or intimidation and against insults and public curiosity.

Measures of reprisal against prisoners of war are prohibited.

Article 14

Prisoners of war are entitled in all circumstances to respect for their persons and their honour. Women shall be treated with all the regard due to their sex and shall in all cases benefit by treatment as favourable as that granted to men. Prisoners of war shall retain the full civil capacity which they enjoyed at the time of their capture. The Detaining Power may not restrict the exercise, either within or without its own territory, of the rights such capacity confers except in so far as the captivity requires.

Article 15

The Power detaining prisoners of war shall be bound to provide free of charge for their maintenance and for the medical attention required by their state of health.

Article 16

Taking into consideration the provisions of the present Convention relating to rank and sex, and subject to any privileged treatment which may be accorded to them by reason of their state of health, age or professional qualifications, all prisoners of war shall be treated alike by the Detaining Power, without any adverse distinction based on race, nationality, religious belief or political opinions, or any other distinction founded on similar criteria.

Part III: Captivity

Section I: Beginning of Captivity

. . .

Article 18

All effects and articles of personal use, except arms, horses, military equipment and military documents shall remain in the possession of prisoners of war, likewise their metal helmets and gas masks and like articles issued for personal protection. Effects and articles used for their clothing or feeding shall likewise remain in their possession, even if such effects and articles belong to their regulation military equipment.

At no time should prisoners of war be without identity documents. The Detaining Power shall supply such documents to prisoners of war who possess none.

Badges of rank and nationality, decorations and articles having above all a personal or sentimental value may not be taken from prisoners of war.

Sums of money carried by prisoners of war may not be taken away from them except by order of an officer, and after the amount and particulars of the owner have been recorded in a special register and an itemized receipt has been given, legibly inscribed with the name, rank and unit of the person issuing the said receipt. Sums in the currency of the Detaining Power, or which are changed into such currency at the prisoner's request, shall be placed to the credit of the prisoner's account as provided in Article 64.

The Detaining Power may withdraw articles of value from prisoners of war only for reasons of security; when such articles are withdrawn, the procedure laid down for sums of money impounded shall apply.

Such objects, likewise the sums taken away in any currency other than that of the Detaining Power and the conversion of which has not been asked for by the owners, shall be kept in the custody of the Detaining Power and shall be returned in their initial shape to prisoners of war at the end of their captivity.

. . .

Section II: Internment of Prisoners of War

Chapter I: General Observations

Article 21

The Detaining Power may subject prisoners of war to internment. It may impose on them the obligation of not leaving, beyond certain limits, the camp where they are interned, or if the said camp is fenced in, of not going outside its perimeter. Subject to the provisions of the present Convention relative to penal and disciplinary sanctions, prisoners of war may not be held in close confinement except where necessary to safeguard their health and then only during the continuation of the circumstances which make such confinement necessary.

Prisoners of war may be partially or wholly released on parole or promise, insofar as is allowed by the laws of the Power on which they depend. Such measures shall be taken particularly in cases where this may contribute to the improvement of their state of health. No prisoner of war shall be compelled to accept liberty on parole or promise.

Upon the outbreak of hostilities, each Party to the conflict shall notify the adverse Party of the laws and regulations allowing or forbidding its own nationals to accept liberty on parole or promise. Prisoners of war who are paroled or who have given their promise in conformity with the laws and regulations so notified, are bound on their personal honour scrupulously to fulfill, both towards the Power on which they depend and towards the Power which has captured them, the engagements of their paroles or promises. In such cases, the Power on which they depend is bound neither to require nor to accept from them any service incompatible with the parole or promise given.

Article 22

Prisoners of war may be interned only in premises located on land and affording every guarantee of hygiene and healthfulness. Except in particular cases which are justified by the interest of the prisoners themselves, they shall not be interned in penitentiaries.

Prisoners of war interned in unhealthy areas, or where the climate is injurious for them, shall be removed as soon as possible to a more favourable climate.

The Detaining Power shall assemble prisoners of war in camps or camp compounds according to their nationality, language and customs, provided that such prisoners shall not be separated from prisoners of war belonging to the armed forces with which they were serving at the time of their capture, except with their consent.

. . .

Chapter II: Quarters, Food and Clothing of Prisoners of War

Article 25

Prisoners of war shall be quartered under conditions as favourable as those for the forces of the Detaining Power who are billeted in the same area. The said conditions shall make allowance for the habits and customs of the prisoners and shall in no case be prejudicial to their health.

The foregoing provisions shall apply in particular to the dormitories of prisoners of war as regards both total surface and minimum cubic space, and the general installations, bedding and blankets.

The premises provided for the use of prisoners of war individually or collectively, shall be entirely protected from dampness and adequately heated and lighted, in particular between dusk and lights out. All precautions must be taken against the danger of fire.

In any camps in which women prisoners of war, as well as men, are accommodated, separate dormitories shall be provided for them.

Article 26

The basic daily food rations shall be sufficient in quantity, quality and variety to keep prisoners of war in good health and to prevent loss of weight or the development of nutritional deficiencies. Account shall also be taken of the habitual diet of the prisoners.

The Detaining Power shall supply prisoners of war who work with such additional rations as are necessary for the labour on which they are employed.

Sufficient drinking water shall be supplied to prisoners of war. The use of tobacco shall be permitted.

Prisoners of war shall, as far as possible, be associated with the preparation of their meals; they may be employed for that purpose in the kitchens. Furthermore, they shall be given the means of preparing, themselves, the additional food in their possession.

Adequate premises shall be provided for messing.

Collective disciplinary measures affecting food are prohibited.

Article 27

Clothing, underwear and footwear shall be supplied to prisoners of war in sufficient quantities by the Detaining Power, which shall make allowance for the climate of the region where the prisoners are detained. Uniforms of enemy armed forces captured by the Detaining Power should, if suitable for the climate, be made available to clothe prisoners of war.

The regular replacement and repair of the above articles shall be assured by the Detaining Power. In addition, prisoners of war who work shall receive appropriate clothing, wherever the nature of the work demands.

Article 28

Canteens shall be installed in all camps, where prisoners of war may procure foodstuffs, soap and tobacco and ordinary articles in daily use. The tariff shall never be in excess of local market prices. The profits made by camp canteens shall be used for the benefit of the prisoners; a special fund shall be created for this purpose. The prisoners' representative shall have the right to collaborate in the management of the canteen and of this fund.

When a camp is closed down, the credit balance of the special fund shall be handed to an international welfare organization, to be employed for the benefit of prisoners of war of the same nationality as those who have contributed to the fund. In case of a general repatriation, such profits shall be kept by the Detaining Power, subject to any agreement to the contrary between the Powers concerned.

Chapter III: Hygiene and Medical Attention

Article 29

The Detaining Power shall be bound to take all sanitary measures necessary to ensure the cleanliness and healthfulness of camps and to prevent epidemics.

Prisoners of war shall have for their use, day and night, conveniences which conform to the rules of hygiene and are maintained in a constant state of cleanliness. In any camps in which women prisoners of war are accommodated, separate conveniences shall be provided for them.

Also, apart from the baths and showers with which the camps shall be furnished, prisoners of war shall be provided with sufficient water and soap for their personal toilet and for washing their personal laundry; the necessary installations, facilities and time shall be granted them for that purpose.

Article 30

Every camp shall have an adequate infirmary where prisoners of war may have the attention they require, as well as appropriate diet. Isolation wards shall, if necessary, be set aside for cases of contagious or mental disease.

Prisoners of war suffering from serious disease, or whose condition necessitates special treatment, a surgical operation or hospital care, must be admitted to any military or civilian medical unit where such treatment can be given, even if their repatriation is contemplated in the near future. Special facilities shall be afforded for the care to be given to the disabled, in particular to the blind, and for their rehabilitation, pending repatriation.

Prisoners of war shall have the attention, preferably, of medical personnel of the Power on which they depend and, if possible, of their nationality.

Prisoners of war may not be prevented from presenting themselves to the medical authorities for examination. The detaining authorities shall, upon request, issue to every prisoner who has undergone treatment, an official certificate indicating the nature of his illness or injury, and the duration and kind of treatment received. A duplicate of this certificate shall be forwarded to the Central Prisoners of War Agency.

The costs of treatment, including those of any apparatus necessary for the maintenance of prisoners of war in good health, particularly dentures and other artificial appliances, and spectacles, shall be borne by the Detaining Power.

Article 31

Medical inspections of prisoners of war shall be held at least once a month. They shall include the checking and the recording of the weight of each prisoner of war. Their purpose shall be, in particular, to supervise the general state of health, nutrition and cleanliness of prisoners and to detect contagious diseases, especially tuberculosis, malaria and venereal disease. For this purpose the most efficient methods available shall be employed, e.g. periodic mass miniature radiography for the early detection of tuberculosis.

. . .

Chapter V: Religious, Intellectual and Physical Activities

Article 34

Prisoners of war shall enjoy complete latitude in the exercise of their religious duties, including attendance at the service of their faith, on condition that they comply with the disciplinary routine prescribed by the military authorities.

Adequate premises shall be provided where religious services may be held.

. . .

Article 41

In every camp the text of the present Convention and its Annexes and the contents of any special agreement provided for in Article 6, shall be posted, in the prisoners' own language, at places where all may read them. Copies shall be supplied, on request, to the prisoners who cannot have access to the copy which has been posted.

Regulations, orders, notices and publications of every kind relating to the conduct of prisoners of war shall be issued to them in a language which they understand. Such regulations, orders and publications shall be posted in the manner described above and copies shall be handed to the prisoners' representative. Every order and command addressed to prisoners of war individually must likewise be given in a language which they understand.

. . .

Section III: Labour of Prisoners of War

Article 49

The Detaining Power may utilize the labour of prisoners of war who are physically fit, taking into account their age, sex, rank and physical aptitude, and with a view particularly to maintaining them in a good state of physical and mental health.

Non-commissioned officers who are prisoners of war shall only be required to do supervisory work. Those not so required may ask for other suitable work which shall, so far as possible, be found for them.

If officers or persons of equivalent status ask for suitable work, it shall be found for them, so far as possible, but they may in no circumstances be compelled to work.

Article 50

Besides work connected with camp administration, installation or maintenance, prisoners of war may be compelled to do only such work as is included in the following classes:

(a) Agriculture;

(b) Industries connected with the production or the extraction of raw materials, and manufacturing industries, with the exception of metallurgical, machinery and chemical industries; public works and building operations which have no military character or purpose;

(c) Transport and handling of stores which are not military in character or purpose;

(d) Commercial business and arts and crafts;

(e) Domestic service;

(f) Public utility services having no military character or purpose.

Should the above provisions be infringed, prisoners of war shall be allowed to exercise their right of complaint, in conformity with Article 78.

Article 51

Prisoners of war must be granted suitable working conditions, especially as regards accommodation, food, clothing and equipment; such conditions shall not be inferior to those enjoyed by nationals of the Detaining Power employed in similar work; account shall also be taken of climatic conditions.

The Detaining Power, in utilizing the labour of prisoners of war, shall ensure that in areas in which prisoners are employed, the national legislation concerning the protection of labour, and, more particularly, the regulations for the safety of workers, are duly applied.

Prisoners of war shall receive training and be provided with the means of protection suitable to the work they will have to do and similar to those accorded to the nationals of the Detaining Power. Subject to the provisions of Article 52, prisoners may be submitted to the normal risks run by these civilian workers.

Conditions of labour shall in no case be rendered more arduous by disciplinary measures.

Article 52

Unless he be a volunteer, no prisoner of war may be employed on labour which is of an unhealthy or dangerous nature.

No prisoner of war shall be assigned to labour which would be looked upon as humiliating for a member of the Detaining Power's own forces.

The removal of mines or similar devices shall be considered dangerous labour.

Article 53

The duration of the daily labour of prisoners of war, including the time of the journey to and fro, shall not be excessive, and must in no case exceed that permitted for civilian workers in the district, who are nationals of the Detaining Power and employed on the same work.

Prisoners of war must be allowed, in the middle of the day's work, a rest of not less than one hour. This rest will be the same as that to which workers of the Detaining Power are entitled, if the latter is of longer duration. They shall be allowed in addition a rest of twenty-four consecutive hours every week, preferably on Sunday or the day of rest in their country of origin. Furthermore, every prisoner who has worked for one year shall be granted a rest of eight consecutive days, during which his working pay shall be paid him.

If methods of labour such as piece-work are employed, the length of the working period shall not be rendered excessive thereby.

Article 54

The working pay due to prisoners of war shall be fixed in accordance with the provisions of Article 62 of the present Convention.

Prisoners of war who sustain accidents in connection with work, or who contract a disease in the course, or in consequence of their work, shall receive all the care their condition may require. The Detaining Power shall furthermore deliver to such prisoners of war a medical certificate enabling them to submit their claims to the Power on which they depend, and shall send a duplicate to the Central Prisoners of War Agency provided for in Article 123.

. . .

Article 62

Prisoners of war shall be paid a fair working rate of pay by the detaining authorities direct. The rate shall be fixed by the said authorities, but shall at no time be less than one-fourth of one Swiss franc for a full working day. The Detaining Power shall inform prisoners of war, as well as the Power on which they depend, through the intermediary of the Protecting Power, of the rate of daily working pay that it has fixed.

Working pay shall likewise be paid by the detaining authorities to prisoners of war permanently detailed to duties or to a skilled or semi-skilled occupation in connection with the administration, installation or maintenance of camps, and to the prisoners who are required to carry out spiritual or medical duties on behalf of their comrades.

The working pay of the prisoners' representative, of his advisers, if any, and of his assistants, shall be paid out of the fund maintained by canteen profits. The scale of this working pay shall be fixed by the prisoners' representative and approved by the camp commander. If there is no such fund, the detaining authorities shall pay these prisoners a fair working rate of pay.

. . .

Article 71

Prisoners of war shall be allowed to send and receive letters and cards. If the Detaining Power deems it necessary to limit the number of letters and cards sent by each prisoner of war, the said number shall not be less than two letters and four cards monthly, exclusive of the capture cards provided for in Article 70, and conforming as closely as possible to the models annexed to the present Convention. Further limitations may be imposed only if the Protecting Power is satisfied that it would be in the interests of the prisoners of war concerned to do so owing to difficulties of translation caused by the Detaining Power's inability to find sufficient qualified linguists to carry out the necessary censorship. If limitations must be placed on the correspondence addressed to prisoners of war, they may be ordered only by the Power on which the prisoners depend, possibly at the request of the Detaining Power. Such letters and cards must be conveyed by the most rapid method at the disposal of the Detaining Power; they may not be delayed or retained for disciplinary reasons.

Prisoners of war who have been without news for a long period, or who are unable to receive news from their next of kin or to give them news by the ordinary postal route, as well as those who are at a great distance from their homes, shall be permitted to send telegrams, the fees being charged against the prisoners of war's accounts with the Detaining Power or paid in the currency at their disposal. They shall likewise benefit by this measure in cases of urgency.

As a general rule, the correspondence of prisoners of war shall be written in their native language. The Parties to the conflict may allow correspondence in other languages.

Sacks containing prisoner of war mail must be securely sealed and labelled so as clearly to indicate their contents, and must be addressed to offices of destination.

Article 72

Prisoners of war shall be allowed to receive by post or by any other means individual parcels or collective shipments containing, in particular, foodstuffs, clothing, medical supplies and articles of a religious, educational or recreational character which may meet their needs, including books, devotional articles, scientific equipment, examination papers, musical instruments, sports outfits and materials allowing prisoners of war to pursue their studies or their cultural activities.

Such shipments shall in no way free the Detaining Power from the obligations imposed upon it by virtue of the present Convention.

The only limits which may be placed on these shipments shall be those proposed by the Protecting Power in the interest of the prisoners themselves, or by the International Committee of the Red Cross or any other organization giving assistance to the prisoners, in respect of their own shipments only, on account of exceptional strain on transport or communications.

The conditions for the sending of individual parcels and collective relief shall, if necessary, be the subject of special agreements between the Powers concerned, which may in no case delay the receipt by the prisoners of relief supplies. Books may not be included in parcels of clothing and foodstuffs. Medical supplies shall, as a rule, be sent in collective parcels.

. . .

Section VI: Relations Between Prisoners of War and the Authorities

Chapter I: Complaints of Prisoners of War Respecting the Conditions of Captivity

Article 78

Prisoners of war shall have the right to make known to the military authorities in whose power they are, their requests regarding the conditions of captivity to which they are subjected.

They shall also have the unrestricted right to apply to the representatives of the Protecting Powers either through their prisoners' representative or, if they consider it necessary, directly, order to draw their attention to any points on which they may have complaints to make regarding their conditions of captivity.

These requests and complaints shall not be limited nor considered to be a part of the correspondence quota referred to in Article 71. They must be transmitted immediately. Even if they are recognized to be unfounded, they may not give rise to any punishment.

Prisoners' representatives may send periodic reports on the situation in the camps and the needs of the prisoners of war to the representatives of the Protecting Powers.

. . .

Article 129

The High Contracting Parties undertake to enact any legislation necessary to provide effective penal sanctions for persons committing, or ordering to be committed, any of the grave breaches of the present Convention defined in the following Article.

Each High Contracting Party shall be under the obligation to search for persons alleged to have committed, or to have ordered to be committed, such grave breaches, and shall bring such persons, regardless of their nationality, before its own courts. It may also, if it prefers, and in accordance with the provisions of its own legislation, hand such persons over for trial to another High Contracting Party concerned, provided such High Contracting Party has made out a prima facie case.

Each High Contracting Party shall take measures necessary for the suppression of all acts contrary to the provisions of the present Convention other than the grave breaches defined in the following Article.

In all circumstances, the accused persons shall benefit by safeguards of proper trial and defence, which shall not be less favourable than those provided by Article 105 and those following of the present Convention.

Article 130

Grave breaches to which the preceding Article relates shall be those involving any of the following acts, if committed against persons or property protected by the Convention: willful killing, torture or inhuman treatment, including biological experiments, willfully causing great suffering or serious injury to body or health, compelling a prisoner of war to serve in the forces of the hostile Power, or willfully depriving a prisoner of war of the rights of fair and regular trial prescribed in this Convention.

Article 131

No High Contracting Party shall be allowed to absolve itself or any other High Contracting Party of any liability incurred by itself or by another High Contracting Party in respect of breaches referred to in the preceding Article.

. . .

Chapter 20
Geneva Convention Relative to the Protection of Civilian Persons in Time of War (excerpts)

Part I: General Provisions

Article 1

The High Contracting Parties undertake to respect and to ensure respect for the present Convention in all circumstances.

Article 2

In addition to the provisions which shall be implemented in peacetime, the present Convention shall apply to all cases of declared war or of any other armed conflict which may arise between two or more of the High Contracting Parties, even if the state of war is not recognized by one of them.

The Convention shall also apply to all cases of partial or total occupation of the territory of a High Contracting Party, even if the said occupation meets with no armed resistance.

Although one of the Powers in conflict may not be a party to the present Convention, the Powers who are parties thereto shall remain bound by it in their mutual relations. They shall furthermore be bound by the Convention in relation to the said Power, if the latter accepts and applies the provisions thereof.

Article 3

In the case of armed conflict not of an international character occurring in the territory of one of the High Contracting Parties, each Party to the conflict shall be bound to apply, as a minimum, the following provisions:

Adopted 12 August 1949 by the Diplomatic Conference for the Establishment of International Conventions for the Protection of Victims of War, held in Geneva from 21 April to 12 August 1949, *entry into force* 21 October 1950.

1. Persons taking no active part in the hostilities, including members of armed forces who have laid down their arms and those placed hors de combat by sickness, wounds, detention, or any other cause, shall in all circumstances be treated humanely, without any adverse distinction founded on race, colour, religion or faith, sex, birth or wealth, or any other similar criteria.

To this end, the following acts are and shall remain prohibited at any time and in any place whatsoever with respect to the above-mentioned persons:

(a) Violence to life and person, in particular murder of all kinds, mutilation, cruel treatment and torture;

(b) Taking of hostages;

(c) Outrages upon personal dignity, in particular humiliating and degrading treatment;

(d) The passing of sentences and the carrying out of executions without previous judgment pronounced by a regularly constituted court, affording all the judicial guarantees which are recognized as indispensable by civilized peoples.

2. The wounded and sick shall be collected and cared for.

An impartial humanitarian body, such as the International Committee of the Red Cross, may offer its services to the Parties to the conflict.

The Parties to the conflict should further endeavour to bring into force, by means of special agreements, all or part of the other provisions of the present Convention.

The application of the preceding provisions shall not affect the legal status of the Parties to the conflict.

Article 4

Persons protected by the Convention are those who, at a given moment and in any manner whatsoever, find themselves, in case of a conflict or occupation, in the hands of a Party to the conflict or Occupying Power of which they are not nationals.

Nationals of a State which is not bound by the Convention are not protected by it. Nationals of a neutral State who find themselves in the territory of a belligerent State, and nationals of a co-belligerent State, shall not be regarded as protected persons while the State of which they are nationals has normal diplomatic representation in the State in whose hands they are.

The provisions of Part II are, however, wider in application, as defined in Article 13.

Persons protected by the Geneva Convention for the Amelioration of the Condition of the Wounded and Sick in Armed Forces in the Field of August 12, 1949, or by the Geneva Convention for the Amelioration of the Condition of Wounded, Sick and Shipwrecked Members of Armed Forces at Sea of August 12, 1949, or by the Geneva

Convention relative to the Treatment of Prisoners of War of August 12, 1949, shall not be considered as protected persons within the meaning of the present Convention.

Article 5

Where, in the territory of a Party to the conflict, the latter is satisfied that an individual protected person is definitely suspected of or engaged in activities hostile to the security of the State, such individual person shall not be entitled to claim such rights and privileges under the present Convention as would, if exercised in the favour of such individual person, be prejudicial to the security of such State.

Where in occupied territory an individual protected person is detained as a spy or saboteur, or as a person under definite suspicion of activity hostile to the security of the Occupying Power, such person shall, in those cases where absolute military security so requires, be regarded as having forfeited rights of communication under the present Convention.

In each case, such persons shall nevertheless be treated with humanity, and in case of trial, shall not be deprived of the rights of fair and regular trial prescribed by the present Convention. They shall also be granted the full rights and privileges of a protected person under the present Convention at the earliest date consistent with the security of the State or Occupying Power, as the case may be.

. . .

Article 8

Protected persons may in no circumstances renounce in part or in entirety the rights secured to them by the present Convention, and by the special agreements referred to in the foregoing Article, if such there be.

. . .

Part II: General Protection of Populations Against Certain Consequences of War

Article 13

The provisions of Part II cover the whole of the populations of the countries in conflict, without any adverse distinction based, in particular, on race, nationality, religion or political opinion, and are intended to alleviate the sufferings caused by war.

Article 14

In time of peace, the High Contracting Parties and, after the outbreak of hostilities, the Parties thereto, may establish in their own territory and, if the need arises, in occupied areas, hospital and safety zones and localities so organized as to protect from the effects of war, wounded, sick and aged persons, children under fifteen, expectant mothers and mothers of children under seven.

Upon the outbreak and during the course of hostilities, the Parties concerned may conclude agreements on mutual recognition of the zones and localities they have created. They may for this purpose implement the provisions of the Draft Agreement annexed to the present Convention, with such amendments as they may consider necessary.

The Protecting Powers and the International Committee of the Red Cross are invited to lend their good offices in order to facilitate the institution and recognition of these hospital and safety zones and localities.

Article 15

Any Party to the conflict may, either directly or through a neutral State or some humanitarian organization, propose to the adverse Party to establish, in the regions where fighting is taking place, neutralized zones intended to shelter from the effects of war the following persons, without distinction:

(a) Wounded and sick combatants or non-combatants;

(b) Civilian persons who take no part in hostilities, and who, while they reside in the zones, perform no work of a military character.

When the Parties concerned have agreed upon the geographical position, administration, food supply and supervision of the proposed neutralized zone, a written agreement shall be concluded and signed by the representatives of the Parties to the conflict. The agreement shall fix the beginning and the duration of the neutralization of the zone.

Article 16

The wounded and sick, as well as the infirm, and expectant mothers, shall be the object of particular protection and respect.

As far as military considerations allow, each Party to the conflict shall facilitate the steps taken to search for the killed and wounded, to assist the shipwrecked and other persons exposed to grave danger, and to protect them against pillage and ill-treatment.

Article 17

The Parties to the conflict shall endeavour to conclude local agreements for the removal from besieged or encircled areas, of wounded, sick, infirm, and aged persons, children and maternity cases, and for the passage of ministers of all religions, medical personnel and medical equipment on their way to such areas.

Article 18

Civilian hospitals organized to give care to the wounded and sick, the infirm and maternity cases, may in no circumstances be the object of attack, but shall at all times be respected and protected by the Parties to the conflict.

States which are Parties to a conflict shall provide all civilian hospitals with certificates showing that they are civilian hospitals and that the buildings which they occupy are not used for any purpose which would deprive these hospitals of protection in accordance with Article 19.

Civilian hospitals shall be marked by means of the emblem provided for in Article 38 of the Geneva Convention for the Amelioration of the Condition of the Wounded and Sick in Armed Forces in the Field of August 12, 1949, but only if so authorized by the State.

The Parties to the conflict shall, insofar as military considerations permit, take the necessary steps to make the distinctive emblems indicating civilian hospitals clearly visible to the enemy land, air and naval forces in order to obviate the possibility of any hostile action.

In view of the dangers to which hospitals may be exposed by being close to military objectives, it is recommended that such hospitals be situated as far as possible from such objectives.

Article 19

The protection to which civilian hospitals are entitled shall not cease unless they are used to commit, outside their humanitarian duties, acts harmful to the enemy. Protection may, however, cease only after due warning has been given, naming, in all appropriate cases, a reasonable time limit, and after such warning has remained unheeded.

The fact that sick or wounded members of the armed forces are nursed in these hospitals, or the presence of small arms and ammunition taken from such combatants which have not yet been handed to the proper service, shall not be considered to be acts harmful to the enemy.

Article 20

Persons regularly and solely engaged in the operation and administration of civilian hospitals, including the personnel engaged in the search for, removal and transporting of and caring for wounded and sick civilians, the infirm and maternity cases, shall be respected and protected.

In occupied territory and in zones of military operations, the above personnel shall be recognizable by means of an identity card certifying their status, bearing the photograph of the holder and embossed with the stamp of the responsible authority, and also by means of a stamped, water-resistant armlet which they shall wear on the left arm while carrying out their duties. This armlet shall be issued by the State and shall bear the emblem provided for in Article 38 of the Geneva Convention for the Amelioration of the Condition of the Wounded and Sick in Armed Forces in the Field of August 12, 1949.

Other personnel who are engaged in the operation and administration of civilian hospitals shall be entitled to respect and protection and to wear the armlet, as provided in and under the conditions prescribed in this Article, while they are employed on such duties. The identity card shall state the duties on which they are employed.

The management of each hospital shall at all times hold at the disposal of the competent national or occupying authorities an up-to-date list of such personnel.

Article 21

Convoys of vehicles or hospital trains on land or specially provided vessels on sea, conveying wounded and sick civilians, the infirm and maternity cases, shall be respected and protected in the same manner as the hospitals provided for in Article 18, and shall be marked, with the consent of the State, by the display of the distinctive emblem provided for in Article 38 of the Geneva Convention for the Amelioration of the Condition of the Wounded and Sick in Armed Forces in the Field of August 12, 1949.

Article 22

Aircraft exclusively employed for the removal of wounded and sick civilians, the infirm and maternity cases, or for the transport of medical personnel and equipment, shall not be attacked, but shall be respected while flying at heights, times and on routes specifically agreed upon between all the Parties to the conflict concerned.

They may be marked with the distinctive emblem provided for in Article 38 of the Geneva Convention for the Amelioration of the Condition of the Wounded and Sick in Armed Forces in the Field of August 12, 1949.

Unless agreed otherwise, flights over enemy or enemy-occupied territory are prohibited.

Such aircraft shall obey every summons to land. In the event of a landing thus imposed, the aircraft with its occupants may continue its flight after examination, if any.

Article 23

Each High Contracting Party shall allow the free passage of all consignments of medical and hospital stores and objects necessary for religious worship intended only for civilians of another High Contracting Party, even if the latter is its adversary. It shall likewise permit the free passage of all consignments of essential foodstuffs, clothing and tonics intended for children under fifteen, expectant mothers and maternity cases.

The obligation of a High Contracting Party to allow the free passage of the consignments indicated in the preceding paragraph is subject to the condition that this Party is satisfied that there are no serious reasons for fearing:

(a) That the consignments may be diverted from their destination;

(b) That the control may not be effective; or

(c) That a definite advantage may accrue to the military efforts or economy of the enemy through the substitution of the above-mentioned consignments for goods which would otherwise be provided or produced by the enemy or through the release of such material, services or facilities as would otherwise be required for the production of such goods.

The Power which allows the passage of the consignments indicated in the first paragraph of this Article may make such permission conditional on the distribution to the persons benefited there by being made under the local supervision of the Protecting Powers.

Such consignments shall be forwarded as rapidly as possible, and the Power which permits their free passage shall have the right to prescribe the technical arrangements under which such passage is allowed.

Article 24

The Parties to the conflict shall take the necessary measures to ensure that children under fifteen, who are orphaned or are separated from their families as a result of the war, are not left to their own resources, and that their maintenance, the exercise of their religion and their education are facilitated in all circumstances. Their education shall, as far as possible, be entrusted to persons of a similar cultural tradition.

The Parties to the conflict shall facilitate the reception of such children in a neutral country for the duration of the conflict with the consent of the Protecting Power, if any, and under due safeguards for the observance of the principles stated in the first paragraph.

They shall, furthermore, endeavour to arrange for all children under twelve to be identified by the wearing of identity discs, or by some other means.

. . .

Part III: Status and Treatment of Protected Persons

Section I: Provisions Common to the Territories of the Parties to the Conflict and to Occupied Territories

Article 27

Protected persons are entitled, in all circumstances, to respect for their persons, their honour, their family rights, their religious convictions and practices, and their manners and customs. They shall at all times be humanely treated, and shall be protected especially against all acts of violence or threats thereof and against insults and public curiosity.

Women shall be especially protected against any attack on their honour, in particular against rape, enforced prostitution, or any form of indecent assault.

Without prejudice to the provisions relating to their state of health, age and sex, all protected persons shall be treated with the same consideration by the Party to the conflict in whose power they are, without any adverse distinction based, in particular, on race, religion or political opinion.

However, the Parties to the conflict may take such measures of control and security in regard to protected persons as may be necessary as a result of the war.

. . .

Article 32

The High Contracting Parties specifically agree that each of them is prohibited from taking any measure of such a character as to cause the physical suffering or extermination of protected persons in their hands. This prohibition applies not only to murder, torture, corporal punishment, mutilation and medical or scientific experiments not necessitated by the medical treatment of a protected person but also to any other measures of brutality whether applied by civilian or military agents.

Article 33

No protected person may be punished for an offence he or she has not personally committed. Collective penalties and likewise all measures of intimidation or of terrorism are prohibited.

Pillage is prohibited.

Reprisals against protected persons and their property are prohibited.

Article 34

The taking of hostages is prohibited.

Section II: Aliens in the Territory of a Party to the Conflict

Article 35

All protected persons who may desire to leave the territory at the outset of, or during a conflict, shall be entitled to do so, unless their departure is contrary to the national interests of the State. The applications of such persons to leave shall be decided in accordance with regularly established procedures and the decision shall be taken as rapidly as possible. Those persons permitted to leave may provide themselves with the necessary funds for their journey and take with them a reasonable amount of their effects and articles of personal use.

If any such person is refused permission to leave the territory, he shall be entitled to have such refusal reconsidered as soon as possible by an appropriate court or administrative board designated by the Detaining Power for that purpose.

Upon request, representatives of the Protecting Power shall, unless reasons of security prevent it, or the persons concerned object, be furnished with the reasons for refusal of any request for permission to leave the territory and be given, as expeditiously as possible, the names of all persons who have been denied permission to leave.

Article 36

Departures permitted under the foregoing Article shall be carried out in satisfactory conditions as regards safety, hygiene, sanitation and food. All costs in connection therewith, from the point of exit in the territory of the Detaining Power, shall be borne by the country of destination, or, in the case of accommodation in a neutral country, by the Power whose nationals are benefited. The practical details of such movements may, if necessary, be settled by special agreements between the Powers concerned.

The foregoing shall not prejudice such special agreements as may be concluded between Parties to the conflict concerning the exchange and repatriation of their nationals in enemy hands.

Article 37

Protected persons who are confined pending proceedings or serving a sentence involving loss of liberty shall during their confinement be humanely treated.

As soon as they are released, they may ask to leave the territory in conformity with the foregoing Articles.

Article 38

With the exception of special measures authorized by the present Convention, in particular by Articles 27 and 41 thereof, the situation of protected persons shall continue to be regulated, in principle, by the provisions concerning aliens in time of peace. In any case, the following rights shall be granted to them:

1. They shall be enabled to receive the individual or collective relief that may be sent to them.

2. They shall, if their state of health so requires, receive medical attention and hospital treatment to the same extent as the nationals of the State concerned.

3. They shall be allowed to practise their religion and to receive spiritual assistance from ministers of their faith.

4. If they reside in an area particularly exposed to the dangers of war, they shall be authorized to move from that area to the same extent as the nationals of the State concerned.

5. Children under fifteen years, pregnant women and mothers of children under seven years shall benefit by any preferential treatment to the same extent as the nationals of the State concerned.

Article 39

Protected persons who, as a result of the war, have lost their gainful employment, shall be granted the opportunity to find paid employment. That opportunity shall, subject to security considerations and to the provisions of Article 40, be equal to that enjoyed by the nationals of the Power in whose territory they are.

Where a Party to the conflict applies to a protected person methods of control which result in his being unable to support himself, and especially if such a person is prevented for reasons of security from finding paid employment on reasonable conditions, the said Party shall ensure his support and that of his dependents.

Protected persons may in any case receive allowances from their home country, the Protecting Power, or the relief societies referred to in Article 30.

Article 40

Protected persons may be compelled to work only to the same extent as nationals of the Party to the conflict in whose territory they are.

If protected persons are of enemy nationality, they may only be compelled to do work which is normally necessary to ensure the feeding, sheltering, clothing, transport and health of human beings and which is not directly related to the conduct of military operations.

In the cases mentioned in the two preceding paragraphs, protected persons compelled to work shall have the benefit of the same working conditions and of the same safeguards as national workers, in particular as regards wages, hours of labour, clothing and equipment, previous training and compensation for occupational accidents and diseases.

If the above provisions are infringed, protected persons shall be allowed to exercise their right of complaint in accordance with Article 30.

. . .

Section III: Occupied Territories

Article 47

Protected persons who are in occupied territory shall not be deprived, in any case or in any manner whatsoever, of the benefits of the present Convention by any change introduced, as the result of the occupation of a territory, into the institutions or government of the said territory, nor by any agreement concluded between the authorities of the occupied territories and the Occupying Power, nor by any annexation by the latter of the whole or part of the occupied territory.

Article 48

Protected persons who are not nationals of the Power whose territory is occupied may avail themselves of the right to leave the territory subject to the provisions of Article 35, and decisions thereon shall be taken according to the procedure which the Occupying Power shall establish in accordance with the said Article.

Article 49

Individual or mass forcible transfers, as well as deportations of protected persons from occupied territory to the territory of the Occupying Power or to that of any other country, occupied or not, are prohibited, regardless of their motive.

Nevertheless, the Occupying Power may undertake total or partial evacuation of a given area if the security of the population or imperative military reasons do demand. Such evacuations may not involve the displacement of protected persons outside the bounds of the occupied territory except when for material reasons it is impossible to avoid such displacement. Persons thus evacuated shall be transferred back to their homes as soon as hostilities in the area in question have ceased.

The Occupying Power undertaking such transfers or evacuations shall ensure, to the greatest practicable extent, that proper accommodation is provided to receive the protected persons, that the removals are effected in satisfactory conditions of hygiene, health, safety and nutrition, and that members of the same family are not separated.

The Protecting Power shall be informed of any transfers and evacuations as soon as they have taken place.

The Occupying Power shall not detain protected persons in an area particularly exposed to the dangers of war unless the security of the population or imperative military reasons so demand.

The Occupying Power shall not deport or transfer parts of its own civilian population into the territory it occupies.

Article 50

The Occupying Power shall, with the cooperation of the national and local authorities, facilitate the proper working of all institutions devoted to the care and education of children.

The Occupying Power shall take all necessary steps to facilitate the identification of children and the registration of their parentage. It may not, in any case, change their personal status, nor enlist them in formations or organizations subordinate to it.

Should the local institutions be inadequate for the purpose, the Occupying Power shall make arrangements for the maintenance and education, if possible by persons of their own nationality, language and religion, of children who are orphaned or separated from their parents as a result of the war and who cannot be adequately cared for by a near relative or friend.

A special section of the Bureau set up in accordance with Article 136 shall be responsible for taking all necessary steps to identify children whose identity is in doubt. Particulars of their parents or other near relatives should always be recorded if available.

The Occupying Power shall not hinder the application of any preferential measures in regard to food, medical care and protection against the effects of war, which may have been adopted prior to the occupation in favour of children under fifteen years, expectant mothers, and mothers of children under seven years.

Article 51

The Occupying Power may not compel protected persons to serve in its armed or auxiliary forces. No pressure or propaganda which aims at securing voluntary enlistment is permitted.

The Occupying Power may not compel protected persons to work unless they are over eighteen years of age, and then only on work which is necessary either for the needs of the army of occupation, or for the public utility services, or for the feeding, sheltering, clothing, transportation or health of the population of the occupied country. Protected persons may not be compelled to undertake any work which would involve them in the obligation of taking part in military operations. The Occupying Power may not compel protected persons to employ forcible means to ensure the security of the installations where they are performing compulsory labour.

The work shall be carried out only in the occupied territory where the persons whose services have been requisitioned are. Every such person shall, so far as possible, be kept in his usual place of employment. Workers shall be paid a fair wage and the work shall be proportionate to their physical and intellectual capacities. The legislation in force in the occupied country concerning working conditions, and safeguards as regards, in particular, such matters as wages, hours of work, equipment, preliminary training and compensation for occupational accidents and diseases, shall be applicable to the protected persons assigned to the work referred to in this Article.

In no case shall requisition of labour lead to a mobilization of workers in an organization of a military or semi-military character.

Article 52

No contract, agreement or regulation shall impair the right of any worker, whether voluntary or not and wherever he may be, to apply to the representatives of the Protecting Power in order to request the said Power's intervention.

All measures aiming at creating unemployment or at restricting the opportunities offered to workers in an occupied territory, in order to induce them to work for the Occupying Power, are prohibited.

Article 53

Any destruction by the Occupying Power of real or personal property belonging individually or collectively to private persons, or to the State, or to other public authorities, or to social or cooperative organizations, is prohibited, except where such destruction is rendered absolutely necessary by military operations.

. . .

Article 55

To the fullest extent of the means available to it the Occupying Power has the duty of ensuring the food and medical supplies of the population; it should, in particular, bring in the necessary foodstuffs, medical stores and other articles if the resources of the occupied territory are inadequate.

The Occupying Power may not requisition foodstuffs, articles or medical supplies available in the occupied territory, except for use by the occupation forces and administration personnel, and then only if the requirements of the civilian population have been taken into account. Subject to the provisions of other international Conventions, the Occupying Power shall make arrangements to ensure that fair value is paid for any requisitioned goods.

The Protecting Power shall, at any time, be at liberty to verify the state of the food and medical supplies in occupied territories, except where temporary restrictions are made necessary by imperative military requirements.

Article 56

To the fullest extent of the means available to it, the Occupying Power has the duty of ensuring and maintaining, with the cooperation of national and local authorities, the medical and hospital establishments and services, public health and hygiene in the occupied territory, with particular reference to the adoption and application of the prophylactic and preventive measures necessary to combat the spread of contagious diseases and epidemics. Medical personnel of all categories shall be allowed to carry out their duties.

If new hospitals are set up in occupied territory and if the competent organs of the occupied State are not operating there, the occupying authorities shall, if necessary, grant them the recognition provided for in Article 18. In similar circumstances, the occupying authorities shall also grant recognition to hospital personnel and transport vehicles under the provisions of Articles 20 and 21.

In adopting measures of health and hygiene and in their implementation, the Occupying Power shall take into consideration the moral and ethical susceptibilities of the population of the occupied territory.

Article 57

The Occupying Power may requisition civilian hospitals only temporarily and only in cases of urgent necessity for the care of military wounded and sick, and then on condition that suitable arrangements are made in due time for the care and treatment of the patients and for the needs of the civilian population for hospital accommodation.

The material and stores of civilian hospitals cannot be requisitioned so long as they are necessary for the needs of the civilian population.

Article 58

The Occupying Power shall permit ministers of religion to give spiritual assistance to the members of their religious communities.

The Occupying Power shall also accept consignments of books and articles required for religious needs and shall facilitate their distribution in occupied territory.

Article 59

If the whole or part of the population of an occupied territory is inadequately supplied, the Occupying Power shall agree to relief schemes on behalf of the said population, and shall facilitate them by all the means at its disposal.

Such schemes, which may be undertaken either by States or by impartial humanitarian organizations such as the International Committee of the Red Cross, shall consist, in particular, of the provision of consignments of foodstuffs, medical supplies and clothing.

All Contracting Parties shall permit the free passage of these consignments and shall guarantee their protection.

A Power granting free passage to consignments on their way to territory occupied by an adverse Party to the conflict shall, however, have the right to search the consignments, to regulate their passage according to prescribed times and routes, and to be reasonably satisfied through the Protecting Power that these consignments are to be used for the relief of the needy population and are not to be used for the benefit of the Occupying Power.

. . .

Article 62

Subject to imperative reasons of security, protected persons in occupied territories shall be permitted to receive the individual relief consignments sent to them.

. . .

Article 76

Protected persons accused of offences shall be detained in the occupied country, and if convicted they shall serve their sentences therein. They shall, if possible, be separated from other detainees and shall enjoy conditions of food and hygiene which will be sufficient to keep them in good health, and which will be at least equal to those obtaining in prisons in the occupied country.

They shall receive the medical attention required by their state of health.

They shall also have the right to receive any spiritual assistance which they may require.

Women shall be confined in separate quarters and shall be under the direct supervision of women.

Proper regard shall be paid to the special treatment due to minors.

Protected persons who are detained shall have the right to be visited by delegates of the Protecting Power and of the International Committee of the Red Cross, in accordance with the provisions of Article 143.

Such persons shall have the right to receive at least one relief parcel monthly.

. . .

Section IV: Regulations for the Treatment of Internees

Chapter I: General Provisions

Article 79

The Parties to the conflict shall not intern protected persons, except in accordance with the provisions of Articles 41, 42, 43, 68 and 78.

Article 80

Internees shall retain their full civil capacity and shall exercise such attendant rights as may be compatible with their status.

Article 81

Parties to the conflict who intern protected persons shall be bound to provide free of charge for their maintenance, and to grant them also the medical attention required by their state of health.

No deduction from the allowances, salaries or credits due to the internees shall be made for the repayment of these costs.

The Detaining Power shall provide for the support of those dependent on the internees, if such dependants are without adequate means of support or are unable to earn a living.

Article 82

The Detaining Power shall, as far as possible, accommodate the internees according to their nationality, language and customs. Internees who are nationals of the same country shall not be separated merely because they have different languages.

Throughout the duration of their internment, members of the same family, and in particular parents and children, shall be lodged together in the same place of internment, except when separation of a temporary nature is necessitated for reasons of employment or health or for the purposes of enforcement of the provisions of Chapter IX of the present Section. Internees may request that their children who are left at liberty without parental care shall be interned with them.

Wherever possible, interned members of the same family shall be housed in the same premises and given separate accommodation from other internees, together with facilities for leading a proper family life.

Chapter II: Places of Internment

. . .

Article 85

The Detaining Power is bound to take all necessary and possible measures to ensure that protected persons shall, from the outset of their internment, be accommodated in buildings or quarters which afford every possible safeguard as regards hygiene and health, and provide efficient protection against the rigours of the climate and the effects of the war. In no case shall permanent places of internment be situated in unhealthy areas or in districts the climate of which is injurious to the internees. In all cases where the district in which a protected person is temporarily interned is in an unhealthy area or has a climate which is harmful to his health, he shall be removed to a more suitable place of internment as rapidly as circumstances permit.

The premises shall be fully protected from dampness, adequately heated and lighted, in particular between dusk and lights out. The sleeping quarters shall be sufficiently spacious and well ventilated, and the internees shall have suitable bedding and sufficient blankets, account being taken of the climate, and the age, sex, and state of health of the internees.

Internees shall have for their use, day and night, sanitary conveniences which conform to the rules of hygiene and are constantly maintained in a state of cleanliness. They shall be provided with sufficient water and soap for their daily personal toilet and for washing their personal laundry; installations and facilities necessary for this purpose shall be granted to them.

Showers or baths shall also be available. The necessary time shall be set aside for washing and for cleaning.

Whenever it is necessary, as an exceptional and temporary measure, to accommodate women internees who are not members of a family unit in the same place of internment as men, the provision of separate sleeping quarters and sanitary conveniences for the use of such women internees shall be obligatory.

Article 86

The Detaining Power shall place at the disposal of interned persons, of whatever denomination, premises suitable for the holding of their religious services.

Article 87

Canteens shall be installed in every place of internment, except where other suitable facilities are available. Their purpose shall be to enable internees to make purchases, at prices not higher than local market prices, of foodstuffs and articles of everyday use, including soap and tobacco, such as would increase their personal well-being and comfort.

Profits made by canteens shall be credited to a welfare fund to be set up for each place of internment, and administered for the benefit of the internees attached to such place of internment. The Internee Committee provided for in Article 102 shall have the right to check the management of the canteen and of the said fund.

When a place of internment is closed down, the balance of the welfare fund shall be transferred to the welfare fund of a place of internment for internees of the same nationality, or, if such a place does not exist, to a central welfare fund which shall be administered for the benefit of all internees remaining in the custody of the Detaining Power. In case of a general release, the said profits shall be kept by the Detaining Power, subject to any agreement to the contrary between the Powers concerned.

Article 88

In all places of internment exposed to air raids and other hazards of war, shelters adequate in number and structure to ensure the necessary protection shall be installed. In case of alarms, the internees shall be free to enter such shelters as quickly as possible, excepting those who remain for the protection of their quarters against the aforesaid hazards. Any protective measures taken in favour of the population shall also apply to them.

All due precautions must be taken in places of internment against the danger of fire.

Chapter III: Food and Clothing

Article 89

Daily food rations for internees shall be sufficient in quantity, quality and variety to keep internees in a good state of health and prevent the development of nutritional deficiencies. Account shall also be taken of the customary diet of the internees.

Internees shall also be given the means by which they can prepare for themselves any additional food in their possession.

Sufficient drinking water shall be supplied to internees. The use of tobacco shall be permitted.

Internees who work shall receive additional rations in proportion to the kind of labour which they perform.

Expectant and nursing mothers and children under fifteen years of age shall be given additional food, in proportion to their physiological needs.

Article 90

When taken into custody, internees shall be given all facilities to provide themselves with the necessary clothing, footwear and change of underwear, and later on, to procure further supplies if required. Should any internees not have sufficient clothing, account being taken of the climate, and be unable to procure any, it shall be provided free of charge to them by the Detaining Power.

The clothing supplied by the Detaining Power to internees and the outward markings placed on their own clothes shall not be ignominious nor expose them to ridicule.

Workers shall receive suitable working outfits, including protective clothing, whenever the nature of their work so requires.

Chapter IV: Hygiene and Medical Attention

Article 91

Every place of internment shall have an adequate infirmary, under the direction of a qualified doctor, where internees may have the attention they require, as well as an appropriate diet. Isolation wards shall be set aside for cases of contagious or mental diseases.

Maternity cases and internees suffering from serious diseases, or whose condition requires special treatment, a surgical operation or hospital care, must be admitted to any institution where adequate treatment can be given and shall receive care not inferior to that provided for the general population.

Internees shall, for preference, have the attention of medical personnel of their own nationality.

Internees may not be prevented from presenting themselves to the medical authorities for examination. The medical authorities of the Detaining Power shall, upon request, issue to every internee who has undergone treatment an official certificate showing the nature of his illness or injury, and the duration and nature of the treatment given. A duplicate of this certificate shall be forwarded to the Central Agency provided for in Article 140.

Treatment, including the provision of any apparatus necessary for the maintenance of internees in good health, particularly dentures and other artificial appliances and spectacles, shall be free of charge to the internee.

Article 92

Medical inspections of internees shall be made at least once a month. Their purpose shall be, in particular, to supervise the general state of health, nutrition and cleanliness of internees, and to detect contagious diseases, especially tuberculosis, malaria, and venereal diseases. Such inspections shall include, in particular, the checking of weight of each internee and, at least once a year, radioscopic examination.

Chapter V: Religious, Intellectual and Physical Activities

. . .

Article 95

The Detaining Power shall not employ internees as workers, unless they so desire. Employment which, if undertaken under compulsion by a protected person not in internment, would involve a breach of Articles 40 or 51 of the present Convention, and employment on work which is of a degrading or humiliating character are in any case prohibited. After a working period of six weeks, internees shall be free to give up work at any moment, subject to eight days' notice.

These provisions constitute no obstacle to the right of the Detaining Power to employ interned doctors, dentists and other medical personnel in their professional capacity on behalf of their fellow internees, or to employ internees for administrative and maintenance work in places of internment and to detail such persons for work in the kitchens or for other domestic tasks, or to require such persons to undertake duties connected with the protection of internees against aerial bombardment or other war risks. No internee may, however, be required to perform tasks for which he is, in the opinion of a medical officer, physically unsuited.

The Detaining Power shall take entire responsibility for all working conditions, for medical attention, for the payment of wages, and for ensuring that all employed internees receive compensation for occupational accidents and diseases. The standards prescribed for the said working conditions and for compensation shall be in accordance with the national laws and regulations, and with the existing practice; they shall in no case be inferior to those obtaining for work of the same nature in the same district. Wages for work done shall be determined on an equitable basis by special agreements between the internees, the Detaining Power, and, if the case arises, employers other than the Detaining Power, due regard being paid to the obligation of the Detaining Power to provide for free maintenance of internees and for the medical attention which their state of health may require. Internees permanently detailed for categories of work mentioned in the third paragraph of this Article shall be paid fair wages by the Detaining Power. The working conditions and the scale of compensation for occupational accidents and diseases to internees thus detailed shall not be inferior to those applicable to work of the same nature in the same district.

. . .

Chapter VI: Personal Proper and Financial Resources

Article 97

Internees shall be permitted to retain articles of personal use. Monies, cheques, bonds, etc., and valuables in their possession may not be taken from them except in accordance with established procedure. Detailed receipts shall be given therefor.

The amounts shall be paid into the account of every internee as provided for in Article 98. Such amounts may not be converted into any other currency unless legislation in force in the territory in which the owner is interned so requires or the internee gives his consent.

Articles which have above all a personal or sentimental value may not be taken away.

A woman internee shall not be searched except by a woman.

On release or repatriation, internees shall be given all articles, monies or other valuables taken from them during internment and shall receive in currency the balance of any credit to their accounts kept in accordance with Article 98, with the exception of any articles or amounts withheld by the Detaining Power by virtue of its legislation in force. If the property of an internee is so withheld, the owner shall receive a detailed receipt.

Family or identity documents in the possession of internees may not be taken away without a receipt being given. At no time shall internees be left without identity documents. If they have none, they shall be issued with special documents drawn up by the detaining authorities, which will serve as their identity papers until the end of their internment.

Internees may keep on their persons a certain amount of money, in cash or in the shape of purchase coupons, to enable them to make purchases.

Article 98

All internees shall receive regular allowances sufficient to enable them to purchase goods and articles, such as tobacco, toilet requisites, etc. Such allowances may take the form of credits or purchase coupons.

Furthermore, internees may receive allowances from the Power to which they owe allegiance, the Protecting Powers, the organizations which may assist them, or their families, as well as the income on their property in accordance with the law of the Detaining Power. The amount of allowances granted by the Power to which they owe allegiance shall be the same for each category of internees (infirm, sick, pregnant women, etc.), but may not be allocated by that Power or distributed by the Detaining Power on the basis of discrimination between internees which are prohibited by Article 27 of the present Convention.

The Detaining Power shall open a regular account for every internee, to which shall be credited the allowances named in the present Article, the wages earned and the remittances received, together with such sums taken from him as may be available under the legislation in force in the territory in which he is interned. Internees shall be granted all facilities consistent with the legislation in force in such territory to make remittances to their families and to other dependants. They may draw from their accounts the amounts necessary for their personal expenses, within the limits fixed by the Detaining Power. They shall at all times be afforded reasonable facilities for consulting and obtaining copies of their accounts. A statement of accounts shall be furnished to the Protecting Power on request, and shall accompany the internee in case of transfer.

. . .

Chapter X: Transfers of Internees

Article 127

The transfer of internees shall always be effected humanely. As a general rule, it shall be carried out by rail or other means of transport, and under conditions at least equal to those obtaining for the forces of the Detaining Power in their changes of station. If, as an exceptional measure, such removals have to be effected on foot, they may not take place unless the internees are in a fit state of health, and may not in any case expose them to excessive fatigue.

The Detaining Power shall supply internees during transfer with drinking water and food sufficient in quantity, quality and variety to maintain them in good health, and also with the necessary clothing, adequate shelter and the necessary medical attention. The Detaining Power shall take all suitable precautions to ensure their safety during transfer, and shall establish before their departure a complete list of all internees transferred.

Sick, wounded or infirm internees and maternity cases shall not be transferred if the journey would be seriously detrimental to them, unless their safety imperatively so demands.

If the combat zone draws close to a place of internment, the internees in the said place shall not be transferred unless their removal can be carried out in adequate conditions of safety, or unless they are exposed to greater risks by remaining on the spot than by being transferred.

When making decisions regarding the transfer of internees, the Detaining Power shall take their interests into account and, in particular, shall not do anything to increase the difficulties of repatriating them or returning them to their own homes.

Article 128

In the event of transfer, internees shall be officially advised of their departure and of their new postal address. Such notification shall be given in time for them to pack their luggage and inform their next of kin.

They shall be allowed to take with them their personal effects, and the correspondence and parcels which have arrived for them. The weight of such baggage may be limited if the conditions of transfer so require, but in no case to less than 25 kilograms per internee.

Mail and parcels addressed to their former place of internment shall be forwarded to them without delay.

The commandant of the place of internment shall take, in agreement with the Internee Committee, any measures needed to ensure the transport of the internees' community property and of the luggage the internees are unable to take with them in consequence of restrictions imposed by virtue of the second paragraph.

. . .

Article 146

The High Contracting Parties undertake to enact any legislation necessary to provide effective penal sanctions for persons committing, or ordering to be committed, any of the grave breaches of the present Convention defined in the following article.

Each High Contracting Party shall be under the obligation to search for persons alleged to have committed, or to have ordered to be committed, such grave breaches, and shall bring such persons, regardless of their nationality, before its own courts. It may also, if it prefers, and in accordance with the provisions of its own legislation, hand such persons over for trial to another High Contracting Party concerned, provided such High Contracting Party has made out a prima facie case.

Each High Contracting Party shall take measures necessary for the suppression of all acts contrary to the provisions of the present Convention other than the grave breaches defined in the following article.

In all circumstances, the accused persons shall benefit by safeguards of proper trial and defence, which shall not be less favourable than those provided by Article 105 and those following of the Geneva Convention relative to the Treatment of Prisoners of War of 12 August, 1949.

Article 147

Grave breaches to which the preceding Article relates shall be those involving any of the following acts, if committed against persons or property protected by the present Convention: willful killing, torture or inhuman treatment, including biological experiments, willfully causing great suffering or serious injury to body or health, unlawful deportation or transfer or unlawful confinement of a protected person, compelling a protected person to serve in the forces of a hostile Power, or willfully depriving a protected person of the rights of fair and regular trial prescribed in the present Convention, taking of hostages and extensive destruction and appropriation of property, not justified by military necessity and carried out unlawfully and wantonly.

Article 148

No High Contracting Party shall be allowed to absolve itself or any other High Contracting Party of any liability incurred by itself or by another High Contracting Party in respect of breaches referred to in the preceding article.

. . .

Chapter 21
Geneva Protocol 1 Relating to the Protection of Victims of International Armed Conflicts (excerpts)

Preamble

The High Contracting Parties,

Proclaiming their earnest wish to see peace prevail among peoples,

Recalling that every State has the duty, in conformity with the Charter of the United Nations, to refrain in its international relations from the threat or use of force against the sovereignty, territorial integrity or political independence of any State, or in any other manner inconsistent with the purposes of the United Nations.

Believing it necessary nevertheless to reaffirm and develop the provisions protecting the victims of armed conflicts and to supplement measures intended to reinforce their application,

Expressing their conviction that nothing in this Protocol or in the Geneva Conventions of 12 August 1949 can be construed as legitimizing or authorizing any act of aggression or any other use of force inconsistent with the Charter of the United Nations,

Reaffirming further that the provisions of the Geneva Conventions of 12 August 1949 and of this Protocol must be fully applied in all circumstances to all persons who are protected by those instruments, without any adverse distinction based on the nature or origin of the armed conflict or on the causes espoused by or attributed to the Parties to the conflicts,

Have agreed on the following:

Adopted 8 June 1977 by the Diplomatic Conference on the Reaffirmation and Development of International Humanitarian Law applicable in Armed Conflicts, *entry into force* 7 December 1979, in accordance with Article 95.

Part I: General Provisions

Article 1. General principles and scope of application

1. The High Contracting Parties undertake to respect and to ensure respect for this Protocol in all circumstances.

2. In cases not covered by this Protocol or by other international agreements, civilians and combatants remain under the protection and authority of the principles of international law derived from established custom, from the principles of humanity and from the dictates of public conscience.

3. This Protocol, which supplements the Geneva Conventions of 12 August 1949 for the protection of war victims, shall apply in the situations referred to in Article 2 common to those Conventions.

4. The situations referred to in the preceding paragraph include armed conflicts in which peoples are fighting against colonial domination and alien occupation and against racist regimes in the exercise of their right of self-determination, as enshrined in the Charter of the United Nations and the Declaration on Principles of International Law concerning Friendly Relations and Co-operation among States in accordance with the Charter of the United Nations.

. . .

Article 10. Protection and care

1. All the wounded, sick and shipwrecked, to whichever Party they belong, shall be respected and protected.

2. In all circumstances they shall be treated humanely and shall receive, to the fullest extent practicable and with the least possible delay, the medical care and attention required by their condition. There shall be no distinction among them founded on any grounds other than medical ones.

Article 11. Protection of persons

1. The physical or mental health and integrity of persons who are in the power of the adverse Party or who are interned, detained or otherwise deprived of liberty as a result of a situation referred to in Article 1 shall not be endangered by any unjustified act or omission. Accordingly, it is prohibited to subject the persons described in this Article to any medical procedure which is not indicated by the state of health of the person concerned and which is not consistent with generally accepted medical standards which would be applied under similar medical circumstances to persons who are nationals of the Party conducting the procedure and who are in no way deprived of liberty.

2. It is, in particular, prohibited to carry out on such persons, even with their consent:

(a) Physical mutilations;

(b) Medical or scientific experiments;

(c) Removal of tissue or organs for transplantation,

except where these acts are justified in conformity with the conditions provided for in paragraph 1.

3. Exceptions to the prohibition in paragraph 2 (c) may be made only in the case of donations of blood for transfusion or of skin for grafting, provided that they are given voluntarily and without any coercion or inducement, and then only for therapeutic purposes, under conditions consistent with generally accepted medical standards and controls designed for the benefit of both the donor and the recipient.

4. Any willful act or omission which seriously endangers the physical or mental health or integrity of any person who is in the power of a Party other than the one on which he depends and which either violates any of the prohibitions in paragraphs 1 and 2 or fails to comply with the requirements of paragraph 3 shall be a grave breach of this Protocol.

5. The persons described in paragraph 1 have the right to refuse any surgical operation. In case of refusal, medical personnel shall endeavour to obtain a written statement to that effect, signed or acknowledged by the patient.

6. Each Party to the conflict shall keep a medical record for every donation of blood for transfusion or skin for grafting by persons referred to in paragraph 1 if that donation is made under the responsibility of that Party. In addition, each Party to the conflict shall endeavour to keep a record of all medical procedures undertaken with respect to any person who is interned, detained or otherwise deprived of liberty as a result of a situation referred to in Article 1. These records shall be available at all times for inspection by the Protecting Power.

. . .

Article 15. Protection of civilian medical and religious personnel

1. Civilian medical personnel shall be respected and protected.

2. If needed, all available help shall be afforded to civilian medical personnel in an area where civilian medical services are disrupted by reason of combat activity.

3. The Occupying Power shall afford civilian medical personnel in occupied territories every assistance to enable them to perform, to the best of their ability, their humanitarian functions. The Occupying Power may not require that, in the performance of those functions, such personnel shall give priority to the treatment of any person except on medical grounds. They shall not be compelled to carry out tasks which are not compatible with their humanitarian mission.

4. Civilian medical personnel shall have access to any place where their services are essential, subject to such supervisory and safety measures as the relevant Party to the conflict may deem necessary.

5. Civilian religious personnel shall be respected and protected. The provisions of the Conventions and of this Protocol concerning the protection and identification of medical personnel shall apply equally to such persons.

Article 16. General protection of medical duties

1. Under no circumstances shall any person be punished for carrying out medical activities compatible with medical ethics, regardless of the person benefiting therefrom.

2. Persons engaged in medical activities shall not be compelled to perform acts or to carry out work contrary to the rules of medical ethics or to other medical rules designed for the benefit of the wounded and sick or to the provisions of the Conventions or of this Protocol, or to refrain from performing acts or from carrying out work required by those rules and provisions.

3. No person engaged in medical activities shall be compelled to give to anyone belonging either to an adverse Party, or to his own Party except as required by the law of the latter Party, any information concerning the wounded and sick who are, or who have been, under his care, if such information would, in his opinion, prove harmful to the patients concerned or to their families. Regulations for the compulsory notification of communicable diseases shall, however, be respected.

Article 17. Role of the civilian population and of aid societies

1. The civilian population shall respect the wounded, sick and shipwrecked, even if they belong to the adverse Party, and shall commit no act of violence against them. The civilian population and aid societies, such as national Red Cross (Red Crescent, Red Lion and Sun) Societies, shall be permitted, even on their own initiative, to collect and care for the wounded, sick and shipwrecked, even in invaded or occupied areas. No one shall be harmed, prosecuted, convicted or punished for such humanitarian acts.

2. The Parties to the conflict may appeal to the civilian population and the aid societies referred to in paragraph 1 to collect and care for the wounded, sick and shipwrecked, and to search for the dead and report their location; they shall grant both protection and the necessary facilities to those who respond to this appeal. If the adverse Party gains or regains control of the area, that Party also shall afford the same protection and facilities for so long as they are needed.

. . .

Article 53. Protection of cultural objects and of places of worship

Without prejudice to the provisions of the Hague Convention for the Protection of

Cultural Property in the Event of Armed Conflict of 14 May 1954, and of other relevant international instruments, it is prohibited:

(a) To commit any acts of hostility directed against the historic monuments, works of art or places of worship which constitute the cultural or spiritual heritage of peoples;

(b) To use such objects in support of the military effort;

(c) To make such objects the object of reprisals.

Article 54. Protection of objects indispensable to the survival of the civilian population

1. Starvation of civilians as a method of warfare is prohibited.

2. It is prohibited to attack, destroy, remove or render useless objects indispensable to the survival of the civilian population, such as foodstuffs, agricultural areas for the production of foodstuffs, crops, livestock, drinking water installations and supplies and irrigation works, for the specific purpose of denying them for their sustenance value to the civilian population or to the adverse Party, whatever the motive, whether in order to starve out civilians, to cause them to move away, or for any other motive.

3. The prohibitions in paragraph 2 shall not apply to such of the objects covered by it as are used by an adverse Party:

(a) As sustenance solely for the members of its armed forces; or

(b) If not as sustenance, then in direct support of military action, provided, however, that in no event shall actions against these objects be taken which may be expected to leave the civilian population with such inadequate food or water as to cause its starvation or force its movement.

4. These objects shall not be made the object of reprisals.

5. In recognition of the vital requirements of any Party to the conflict in the defence of its national territory against invasion, derogation from the prohibitions contained in paragraph 2 may be made by a Party to the conflict within such territory under its own control where required by imperative military necessity.

Article 55. Protection of the natural environment

1. Care shall be taken in warfare to protect the natural environment against widespread, long-term and severe damage. This protection includes a prohibition of the use of methods or means of warfare which are intended or may be expected to cause such damage to the natural environment and thereby to prejudice the health or survival of the population.

2. Attacks against the natural environment by way of reprisals are prohibited.

. . .

Chapter IV: Precautionary Measures

Article 57. Precautions in attack

1. In the conduct of military operations, constant care shall be taken to spare the civilian population, civilians and civilian objects.

2. With respect to attacks, the following precautions shall be taken:

(a) Those who plan or decide upon an attack shall:

(i) Do everything feasible to verify that the objectives to be attacked are neither civilians nor civilian objects and are not subject to special protection but are military objectives within the meaning of paragraph 2 of Article 52 and that it is not prohibited by the provisions of this Protocol to attack them;

(ii) Take all feasible precautions in the choice of means and methods of attack with a view to avoiding, and in any event to minimizing, incidental loss of civilian life, injury to civilians and damage to civilian objects;

(iii) Refrain from deciding to launch any attack which may be expected to cause incidental loss of civilian life, injury to civilians, damage to civilian objects, or a combination thereof, which would be excessive in relation to the concrete and direct military advantage anticipated;

(b) An attack shall be cancelled or suspended if it becomes apparent that the objective is not a military one or is subject to special protection or that the attack may be expected to cause incidental loss of civilian life, injury to civilians, damage to civilian objects, or a combination thereof, which would be excessive in relation to the concrete and direct military advantage anticipated;

(c) Effective advance warning shall be given of attacks which may affect the civilian population, unless circumstances do not permit.

3. When a choice is possible between several military objectives for obtaining a similar military advantage, the objective to be selected shall be that the attack on which may be expected to cause the least danger to civilian lives and to civilian objects.

4. In the conduct of military operations at sea or in the air, each Party to the conflict shall, in conformity with its rights and duties under the rules of international law applicable in armed conflict, take all reasonable precautions to avoid losses of civilian lives and damage to civilian objects.

5. No provision of this Article may be construed as authorizing any attacks against the civilian population, civilians or civilian objects.

Article 58. Precautions against the effects of attacks

The Parties to the conflict shall, to the maximum extent feasible:

(a) Without prejudice to Article 49 of the Fourth Convention, endeavour to remove the civilian population, individual civilians and civilian objects under their control from the vicinity of military objectives;

(b) Avoid locating military objectives within or near densely populated areas;

(c) Take the other necessary precautions to protect the civilian population, individual civilians and civilian objects under their control against the dangers resulting from military operations.

. . .

Section II: Relief in Favour of the Civilian Population

. . .

Article 69. Basic needs in occupied territories

1. In addition to the duties specified in Article 55 of the Fourth Convention concerning food and medical supplies, the Occupying Power shall, to the fullest extent of the means available to it and without any adverse distinction, also ensure the provision of clothing, bedding, means of shelter, other supplies essential to the survival of the civilian population of the occupied territory and objects necessary for religious worship.

2. Relief actions for the benefit of the civilian population of occupied territories are governed by Articles 59, 60, 61, 62, 108, 109, 110 and 111 of the Fourth Convention, and by Article 71 of this Protocol, and shall be implemented without delay.

Article 70. Relief actions

1. If the civilian population of any territory under the control of a Party to the conflict, other than occupied territory, is not adequately provided with the supplies mentioned in Article 69, relief actions which are humanitarian and impartial in character and conducted without any adverse distinction shall be undertaken, subject to the agreement of the Parties concerned in such relief actions. Offers of such relief shall not be regarded as interference in the armed conflict or as unfriendly acts. In the distribution of relief consignments, priority shall be given to those persons, such as children, expectant mothers, maternity cases and nursing mothers, who, under the Fourth Convention or under this Protocol, are to be accorded privileged treatment or special protection.

2. The Parties to the conflict and each High Contracting Party shall allow and facilitate rapid and unimpeded passage of all relief consignments, equipment and personnel provided in accordance with this Section, even if such assistance is destined for the civilian population of the adverse Party.

3. The Parties to the conflict and each High Contracting Party which allow the passage of relief consignments, equipment and personnel in accordance with paragraph 2:

(a) Shall have the right to prescribe the technical arrangements, including search, under which such passage is permitted;

(b) May make such permission conditional on the distribution of this assistance being made under the local supervision of a Protecting Power;

(c) Shall, in no way whatsoever, divert relief consignments from the purpose for which they are intended nor delay their forwarding, except in cases of urgent necessity in the interest of the civilian population concerned.

4. The Parties to the conflict shall protect relief consignments and facilitate their rapid distribution.

5. The Parties to the conflict and each High Contracting Party concerned shall encourage and facilitate effective international co-ordination of the relief actions referred to in paragraph 1.

. . .

Section III: Treatment of Persons in the Power of a Party to the Conflict

Chapter I: Field of Application and Protection of Persons and Objects

Article 72. Field of application

The provisions of this Section are additional to the rules concerning humanitarian protection of civilians and civilian objects in the power of a Party to the conflict contained in the Fourth Convention, particularly Parts I and m thereof, as well as to other applicable rules of international law relating to the protection of fundamental human rights during international armed conflict.

. . .

Article 75. Fundamental guarantees

1. In so far as they are affected by a situation referred to in Article 1 of this Protocol, persons who are in the power of a Party to the conflict and who do not benefit from more favourable treatment under the Conventions or under this Protocol shall be treated humanely in all circumstances and shall enjoy, as a minimum, the protection provided by this Article without any adverse distinction based upon race, colour, sex, language, religion or belief, political or other opinion, national or social origin, wealth, birth or other status, or on any other similar criteria. Each Party shall respect the person, honour, convictions and religious practices of all such persons.

2. The following acts are and shall remain prohibited at any time and in any place whatsoever, whether committed by civilian or by military agents:

(a) Violence to the life, health, or physical or mental well-being of persons, in particular:

(i) Murder;

(ii) Torture of all kinds, whether physical or mental;

(iii) Corporal punishment; and

(iv) Mutilation;

(b) Outrages upon personal dignity, in particular humiliating and degrading treatment, enforced prostitution and any form of indecent assault;

(c) The taking of hostages;

(d) Collective punishments; and

(e) Threats to commit any of the foregoing acts.

3. Any person arrested, detained or interned for actions related to the armed conflict shall be informed promptly, in a language he understands, of the reasons why these measures have been taken. Except in cases of arrest or detention for penal offences, such persons shall be released with the minimum delay possible and in any event as soon as the circumstances justifying the arrest, detention or internment have ceased to exist.

4. No sentence may be passed and no penalty may be executed on a person found guilty of a penal offence related to the armed conflict except pursuant to a conviction pronounced by an impartial and regularly constituted court respecting the generally recognized principles of regular judicial procedure, which include the following:

(a) The procedure shall provide for an accused to be informed without delay of the particulars of the offence alleged against him and shall afford the accused before and during his trial all necessary rights and means of defence;

(b) No one shall be convicted of an offence except on the basis of individual penal responsibility;

(c) No one shall be accused or convicted of a criminal offence on account of any act or omission which did not constitute a criminal offence under the national or international law to which he was subject at the time when it was committed; nor shall a heavier penalty be imposed than that which was applicable at the time when the criminal offence was committed; if, after the commission of the offence, provision is made by law for the imposition of a lighter penalty, the offender shall benefit thereby;

(d) Anyone charged with an offence is presumed innocent until proved guilty according to law;

(e) Anyone charged with an offence shall have the right to be tried in his presence;

(f) No one shall be compelled to testify against himself or to confess guilt;

(g) Anyone charged with an offence shall have the right to examine, or have examined, the witnesses against him and to obtain the attendance and examination of witnesses on his behalf under the same conditions as witnesses against him;

(h) No one shall be prosecuted or punished by the same Party for an offence in respect of which a final judgement acquitting or convicting that person has been previously pronounced under the same law and judicial procedure;

(i) Anyone prosecuted for an offence shall have the right to have the judgement pronounced publicly; and

(j) A convicted person shall be advised on conviction of his judicial and other remedies and of the time-limits within which they may be exercised.

5. Women whose liberty has been restricted for reasons related to the armed conflict shall be held in quarters separated from men's quarters. They shall be under the immediate supervision of women. Nevertheless, in cases where families are detained or interned, they shall, whenever possible, be held in the same place and accommodated as family units.

6. Persons who are arrested, detained or interned for reasons related to the armed conflict shall enjoy the protection provided by this Article until their final release, repatriation or re-establishment, even after the end of the armed conflict.

7. In order to avoid any doubt concerning the prosecution and trial of persons accused of war crimes or crimes against humanity, the following principles shall apply:

(a) Persons who are accused of such crimes should be submitted for the purpose of prosecution and trial in accordance with the applicable rules of international law; and

(b) Any such persons who do not benefit from more favourable treatment under the Conventions or this Protocol shall be accorded the treatment provided by this Article, whether or not the crimes of which they are accused constitute grave breaches of the Conventions or of this Protocol.

8. No provision of this Article may be construed as limiting or infringing any other more favourable provision granting greater protection, under any applicable rules of international law, to persons covered by paragraph 1.

Chapter II: Measures in Favour of Women and Children

Article 76. Protection of women

1. Women shall be the object of special respect and shall be protected in particular against rape, forced prostitution and any other form of indecent assault.

2. Pregnant women and mothers having dependent infants who are arrested, detained or interned for reasons related to the armed conflict, shall have their cases considered with the utmost priority.

3. To the maximum extent feasible, the Parties to the conflict shall endeavour to avoid the pronouncement of the death penalty on pregnant women or mothers having dependent infants, for an offense related to the armed conflict. The death penalty for such offences shall not be executed on such women.

Article 77. Protection of children

1. Children shall be the object of special respect and shall be protected against any form of indecent assault. The Parties to the conflict shall provide them with the care and aid they require, whether because of their age or for any other reason.

2. The Parties to the conflict shall take all feasible measures in order that children who have not attained the age of fifteen years do not take a direct part in hostilities and, in particular, they shall refrain from recruiting them into their armed forces. In recruiting among those persons who have attained the age of fifteen years but who have not attained the age of eighteen years, the Parties to the conflict shall endeavour to give priority to those who are oldest.

3. If, in exceptional cases, despite the provisions of paragraph 2, children who have not attained the age of fifteen years take a direct part in hostilities and fall into the power of an adverse Party, they shall continue to benefit from the special protection accorded by this Article, whether or not they are prisoners of war.

4. If arrested, detained or interned for reasons related to the armed conflict, children shall be held in quarters separate from the quarters of adults, except where families are accommodated as family units as provided in Article 75, paragraph 5.

5. The death penalty for an offence related to armed conflict shall not be executed on persons who had not attained the age of eighteen years at the time the offence was committed.

. . .

Section II: Repression of Breaches of the Conventions and of This Protocol

Article 85. Repression of breaches of this Protocol

1. The provisions of the Conventions relating to the repression of breaches and grave breaches, supplemented by this Section, shall apply to the repression of breaches and grave breaches of this Protocol.

2. Acts described as grave breaches in the Conventions are grave breaches of this Protocol if committed against persons in the power of an adverse Party protected by Articles 44, 45 and 73 of this Protocol, or against the wounded, sick and shipwrecked of the adverse Party who are protected by this Protocol, or against those medical or religious personnel, medical units or medical transports which are under the control of the adverse Party and are protected by this Protocol.

3. In addition to the grave breaches defined in Article 11, the following acts shall be regarded as grave breaches of this Protocol, when committed willfully, in violation of the relevant provisions of this Protocol, and causing death or serious injury to body or health:

(a) Making the civilian population or individual civilians the object of attack;

(b) Launching an indiscriminate attack affecting the civilian population or civilian objects in the knowledge that such attack will cause excessive loss of life, injury to civilians or damage to civilian objects, as defined in Article 57, paragraph 2 (a) (iii);

(c) Launching an attack against works or installations containing dangerous forces in the knowledge that such attack will cause excessive loss of life, injury to civilians or damage to civilian objects, as defined in Article 57, paragraph 2 (a) (iii);

(d) Making non-defended localities and demilitarized zones the object of attack;

(e) Making a person the object of attack in the knowledge that he is hors de combat;

(f) The perfidious use, in violation of Article 37, of the distinctive emblem of the red cross, red crescent or red lion and sun or of other protective signs recognized by the Conventions or this Protocol.

4. In addition to the grave breaches defined in the preceding paragraphs and in the Conventions, the following shall be regarded as grave breaches of this Protocol, when committed willfully and in violation of the Conventions of the Protocol;

(a) The transfer by the Occupying Power of parts of its own civilian population into the territory it occupies, or the deportation or transfer of all or parts of the population of the occupied territory within or outside this territory, in violation of Article 49 of the Fourth Convention;

(b) Unjustifiable delay in the repatriation of prisoners of war or civilians;

(c) Practices of apartheid and other inhuman and degrading practices involving outrages upon personal dignity, based on racial discrimination;

(d) Making the clearly-recognized historic monuments, works of art or places of worship which constitute the cultural or spiritual heritage of peoples and to which special protection has been given by special arrangement, for example, within the framework of a competent international organization, the object of attack, causing as a result extensive destruction thereof, where there is no evidence of the violation by the adverse Party of Article 53, sub-paragraph (b), and when such historic monuments, works of art and places of worship are not located in the immediate proximity of military objectives;

(e) Depriving a person protected by the Conventions or referred to in paragraph 2 of this Article of the rights of fair and regular trial.

5. Without prejudice to the application of the Conventions and of this Protocol, grave breaches of these instruments shall be regarded as war crimes.

Article 86. Failure to act

1. The High Contracting Parties and the Parties to the conflict shall repress grave breaches, and take measures necessary to suppress all other breaches, of the Conventions or of this Protocol which result from a failure to act when under a duty to do so.

2. The fact that a breach of the Conventions or of this Protocol was committed by a subordinate does not absolve his superiors from penal or disciplinary responsibility, as the case may be, if they knew, or had information which should have enabled them to conclude in the circumstances at the time, that he was committing or was going to commit such a breach and if they did not take all feasible measures within their power to prevent or repress the breach.

Article 87. Duty of commanders

1. The High Contracting Parties and the Parties to the conflict shall require military commanders, with respect to members of the armed forces under their command and other persons under their control, to prevent and, where necessary, to suppress and to report to competent authorities breaches of the Conventions and of this Protocol.

2. In order to prevent and suppress breaches, High Contracting Parties and Parties to the conflict shall require that, commensurate with their level of responsibility, commanders ensure that members of the armed forces under their command are aware of their obligations under the Conventions and this Protocol.

3. The High Contracting Parties and Parties to the conflict shall require any commander who is aware that subordinates or other persons under his control are going to commit or have committed a breach of the Conventions or of this Protocol, to initiate such steps as are necessary to prevent such violations of the Conventions or this Protocol, and, where appropriate, to initiate disciplinary or penal action against violators thereof.

. . .

Chapter 22
Geneva Protocol 2 Relating to the Protection of Victims of Non-International Armed Conflicts (excerpts)

Preamble

The High Contracting Parties,

Recalling that the humanitarian principles enshrined in Article 3 common to the Geneva Conventions of 12 August 1949 constitute the foundation of respect for the human person in cases of armed conflict not of an international character,

Recalling furthermore that international instruments relating to human rights offer a basic protection to the human person,

Emphasizing the need to ensure a better protection for the victims of those armed conflicts,

Recalling that, in cases not covered by the law in force, the human person remains under the protection of the principles of humanity and the dictates of the public conscience,

Have agreed on the following:

Part I: Scope of This Protocol

Article 1. Material field of application

1. This Protocol, which develops and supplements Article 3 common to the Geneva Conventions of 12 August 1949 without modifying its existing conditions of application, shall apply to all armed conflicts which are not covered by Article 1 of the Protocol Additional to the Geneva Conventions of 12 August 1949, and relating to the Protection

Adopted 8 June 1977 by the Diplomatic Conference on the Reaffirmation and Development of International Humanitarian Law applicable in Armed Conflicts, *entry into force* 7 December 1978, in accordance with Article 23.

of Victims of International Armed Conflicts (Protocol I) and which take place in the territory of a High Contracting Party between its armed forces and dissident armed forces or other organized armed groups which, under responsible command, exercise such control over a part of its territory as to enable them to carry out sustained and concerted military operations and to implement this Protocol.

2. This Protocol shall not apply to situations of internal disturbances and tensions, such as riots, isolated and sporadic acts of violence and other acts of a similar nature, as not being armed conflicts.

Article 2. Personal field of application

1. This Protocol shall be applied without any adverse distinction founded on race, colour, sex, language, religion or belief, political or other opinion, national or social origin, wealth, birth or other status, or on any other similar criteria (hereinafter referred to as "adverse distinction") to all persons affected by an armed conflict as defined in Article 1.

2. At the end of the armed conflict, all the persons who have been deprived of their liberty or whose liberty has been restricted for reasons related to such conflict, as well as those deprived of their liberty or whose liberty is restricted after the conflict for the same reasons, shall enjoy the protection of Articles 5 and 6 until the end of such deprivation or restriction of liberty.

Article 3. Non-intervention

1. Nothing in this Protocol shall be invoked for the purpose of affecting the sovereignty of a State or the responsibility of the government, by all legitimate means, to maintain or re-establish law and order in the State or to defend the national unity and territorial integrity of the State.

2. Nothing in this Protocol shall be invoked as a justification for intervening, directly or indirectly, for any reason whatever, in the armed conflict or in the internal or external affairs of the High Contracting Party in the territory of which that conflict occurs.

Part II: Humane Treatment

Article 4. Fundamental guarantees

1. All persons who do not take a direct part or who have ceased to take part in hostilities, whether or not their liberty has been restricted, are entitled to respect for their person, honour and convictions and religious practices. They shall in all circumstances be treated humanely, without any adverse distinction. It is prohibited to order that there shall be no survivors.

2. Without prejudice to the generality of the foregoing, the following acts against the

persons referred to in paragraph 1 are and shall remain prohibited at any time and in any place whatsoever:

(a) Violence to the life, health and physical or mental well-being of persons, in particular murder as well as cruel treatment such as torture, mutilation or any form of corporal punishment;

(b) Collective punishments;

(c) Taking of hostages;

(d) Acts of terrorism;

(e) Outrages upon personal dignity, in particular humiliating and degrading treatment, rape, enforced prostitution and any form of indecent assault;

(f) Slavery and the slave trade in all their forms;

(g) Pillage;

(h) Threats to commit any of the foregoing acts.

3. Children shall be provided with the care and aid they require, and in particular:

(a) They shall receive an education, including religious and moral education, in keeping with the wishes of their parents, or in the absence of parents, of those responsible for their care;

(b) All appropriate steps shall be taken to facilitate the reunion of families temporarily separated;

(c) Children who have not attained the age of fifteen years shall neither be recruited in the armed forces or groups nor allowed to take part in hostilities;

(d) The special protection provided by this Article to children who have not attained the age of fifteen years shall remain applicable to them if they take a direct part in hostilities despite the provisions of sub-paragraph (c) and are captured;

(e) Measures shall be taken, if necessary, and whenever possible with the consent of their parents or persons who by law or custom are primarily responsible for their care, to remove children temporarily from the area in which hostilities are taking place to a safer area within the country and ensure that they are accompanied by persons responsible for their safety and well-being.

Article 5. Persons whose liberty has been restricted

1. In addition to the provisions of Article 4, the following provisions shall be respected as a minimum with regard to persons deprived of their liberty for reasons related to the armed conflict, whether they are interned or detained:

(a) The wounded and the sick shall be treated in accordance with Article 7;

(b) The persons referred to in this paragraph shall, to the same extent as the local civilian population, be provided with food and drinking water and be afforded safeguards as regards health and hygiene and protection against the rigours of the climate and the dangers of the armed conflict;

(c) They shall be allowed to receive individual or collective relief;

(d) They shall be allowed to practise their religion and, if requested and appropriate, to receive spiritual assistance from persons, such as chaplains, performing religious functions;

(e) They shall, if made to work, have the benefit of working conditions and safeguards similar to those enjoyed by the local civilian population.

2. Those who are responsible for the internment or detention of the persons referred to in paragraph 1 shall also, within the limits of their capabilities, respect the following provisions relating to such persons:

(a) Except when men and women of a family are accommodated together, women shall be held in quarters separated from those of men and shall be under the immediate supervision of women;

(b) They shall be allowed to send and receive letters and cards, the number of which may be limited by the competent authority if it deems necessary;

(c) Places of internment and detention shall not be located close to the combat zone. The persons referred to in paragraph 1 shall be evacuated when the places where they are interned or detained become particularly exposed to danger arising out of the armed conflict, if their evacuation can be carried out under adequate conditions of safety;

(d) They shall have the benefit of medical examinations;

(e) Their physical or mental health and integrity shall not be endangered by an unjustified act or omission. Accordingly, it is prohibited to subject the persons described in this Article to any medical procedure which is not indicated by the state of health of the person concerned, and which is not consistent with the generally accepted medical standards applied to free persons under similar medical circumstances.

3. Persons who are not covered by paragraph 1 but whose liberty has been restricted in any way whatsoever for reasons related to the armed conflict shall be treated humanely in accordance with Article 4 and with paragraphs 1 (a), (c) and (d), and 2 (b) of this Article.

4. If it is decided to release persons deprived of their liberty, necessary measures to ensure their safety shall be taken by those so deciding.

. . .

Part III: Wounded, Sick and Shipwrecked

Article 7. Protection and care

1. All the wounded, sick and shipwrecked, whether or not they have taken part in the armed conflict, shall be respected and protected.

2. In all circumstances they shall be treated humanely and shall receive, to the fullest extent practicable and with the least possible delay, the medical care and attention required by their condition. There shall be no distinction among them founded on any grounds other than medical ones.

. . .

Article 9. Protection of medical and religious personnel

1. Medical and religious personnel shall be respected and protected and shall be granted all available help for the performance of their duties. They shall not be compelled to carry out tasks which are not compatible with their humanitarian mission.

2. In the performance of their duties medical personnel may not be required to give priority to any person except on medical grounds.

Article 10. General protection of medical duties

1. Under no circumstances shall any person be punished for having carried out medical activities compatible with medical ethics, regardless of the person benefiting therefrom.

2. Persons engaged in medical activities shall neither be compelled to perform acts or to carry out work contrary to, nor be compelled to refrain from acts required by, the rules of medical ethics or other rules designed for the benefit of the wounded and sick, or this Protocol.

3. The professional obligations of persons engaged in medical activities regarding information which they may acquire concerning the wounded and sick under their care shall, subject to national law, be respected.

4. Subject to national law, no person engaged in medical activities may be penalized in any way for refusing or failing to give information concerning the wounded and sick who are, or who have been, under his care.

Article 11. Protection of medical units and transports

1. Medical units and transports shall be respected and protected at all times and shall not be the object of attack.

2. The protection to which medical units and transports are entitled shall not cease unless they are used to commit hostile acts, outside their humanitarian function. Protection may, however, cease only after a warning has been given setting, whenever appropriate, a reasonable time-limit, and after such warning has remained unheeded.

. . .

Part IV: Civilian Population

Article 13. Protection of the civilian population

1. The civilian population and individual civilians shall enjoy general protection against the dangers arising from military operations. To give effect to this protection, the following rules shall be observed in all circumstances.

2. The civilian population as such, as well as individual civilians, shall not be the object of attack. Acts or threats of violence the primary purpose of which is to spread terror among the civilian population are prohibited.

3. Civilians shall enjoy the protection afforded by this Part, unless and for such time as they take a direct part in hostilities.

Article 14. Protection of objects indispensable to the survival of the civilian population

Starvation of civilians as a method of combat is prohibited. It is therefore prohibited to attack, destroy, remove or render useless, for that purpose, objects indispensable to the survival of the civilian population, such as foodstuffs, agricultural areas for the production of foodstuffs, crops, livestock, drinking water installations and supplies and irrigation works.

. . .

Article 16. Protection of cultural objects and of places of worship

Without prejudice to the provisions of The Hague Convention for the Protection of Cultural Property in the Event of Armed Conflict of 14 May 1954, it is prohibited to commit any acts of hostility directed against historic monuments, works of art or places of worship which constitute the cultural or spiritual heritage of peoples, and to use them in support of the military effort.

Article 17. Prohibition of forced movement of civilians

1. The displacement of the civilian population shall not be ordered for reasons related to the conflict unless the security of the civilians involved or imperative military reasons so demand. Should such displacements have to be carried out, all possible measures shall be taken in order that the civilian population may be received under satisfactory conditions of shelter, hygiene, health, safety and nutrition.

2. Civilians shall not be compelled to leave their own territory for reasons connected with the conflict.

. . .

B. DECLARATIONS

Chapter 1
Universal Declaration of Human Rights

Preamble

Whereas recognition of the inherent dignity and of the equal and inalienable rights of all members of the human family is the foundation of freedom, justice and peace in the world,

Whereas disregard and contempt for human rights have resulted in barbarous acts which have outraged the conscience of mankind, and the advent of a world in which human beings shall enjoy freedom of speech and belief and freedom from fear and want has been proclaimed as the highest aspiration of the common people,

Whereas it is essential, if man is not to be compelled to have recourse, as a last resort, to rebellion against tyranny and oppression, that human rights should be protected by the rule of law,

Whereas it is essential to promote the development of friendly relations between nations,

Whereas the peoples of the United Nations have in the Charter reaffirmed their faith in fundamental human rights, in the dignity and worth of the human person and in the equal rights of men and women and have determined to promote social progress and better standards of life in larger freedom,

Whereas Member States have pledged themselves to achieve, in co-operation with the United Nations, the promotion of universal respect for and observance of human rights and fundamental freedoms,

Whereas a common understanding of these rights and freedoms is of the greatest importance for the full realization of this pledge,

Now, therefore, the General Assembly,

Proclaims this Universal Declaration of Human Rights as a common standard of achievement for all peoples and all nations, to the end that every individual and every organ of society, keeping this Declaration constantly in mind, shall strive by teaching

Adopted and proclaimed by General Assembly resolution 217 A (III) of 10 December 1948.

and education to promote respect for these rights and freedoms and by progressive measures, national and international, to secure their universal and effective recognition and observance, both among the peoples of Member States themselves and among the peoples of territories under their jurisdiction.

Article 1

All human beings are born free and equal in dignity and rights. They are endowed with reason and conscience and should act towards one another in a spirit of brotherhood.

Article 2

Everyone is entitled to all the rights and freedoms set forth in this Declaration, without distinction of any kind, such as race, colour, sex, language, religion, political or other opinion, national or social origin, property, birth or other status. Furthermore, no distinction shall be made on the basis of the political, jurisdictional or international status of the country or territory to which a person belongs, whether it be independent, trust, non-self-governing or under any other limitation of sovereignty.

Article 3

Everyone has the right to life, liberty and security of person.

Article 4

No one shall be held in slavery or servitude; slavery and the slave trade shall be prohibited in all their forms.

Article 5

No one shall be subjected to torture or to cruel, inhuman or degrading treatment or punishment.

Article 6

Everyone has the right to recognition everywhere as a person before the law.

Article 7

All are equal before the law and are entitled without any discrimination to equal protection of the law. All are entitled to equal protection against any discrimination in violation of this Declaration and against any incitement to such discrimination.

Article 8

Everyone has the right to an effective remedy by the competent national tribunals for acts violating the fundamental rights granted him by the constitution or by law.

Article 9

No one shall be subjected to arbitrary arrest, detention or exile.

Article 10

Everyone is entitled in full equality to a fair and public hearing by an independent and impartial tribunal, in the determination of his rights and obligations and of any criminal charge against him.

Article 11

(1) Everyone charged with a penal offence has the right to be presumed innocent until proved guilty according to law in a public trial at which he has had all the guarantees necessary for his defence.

(2) No one shall be held guilty of any penal offence on account of any act or omission which did not constitute a penal offence, under national or international law, at the time when it was committed. Nor shall a heavier penalty be imposed than the one that was applicable at the time the penal offence was committed.

Article 12

No one shall be subjected to arbitrary interference with his privacy, family, home or correspondence, nor to attacks upon his honour and reputation. Everyone has the right to the protection of the law against such interference or attacks.

Article 13

(1) Everyone has the right to freedom of movement and residence within the borders of each state.

(2) Everyone has the right to leave any country, including his own, and to return to his country.

Article 14

(1) Everyone has the right to seek and to enjoy in other countries asylum from persecution.

(2) This right may not be invoked in the case of prosecutions genuinely arising from non-political crimes or from acts contrary to the purposes and principles of the United Nations.

Article 15

(1) Everyone has the right to a nationality.

(2) No one shall be arbitrarily deprived of his nationality nor denied the right to change his nationality.

Article 16

(1) Men and women of full age, without any limitation due to race, nationality or religion, have the right to marry and to found a family. They are entitled to equal rights as to marriage, during marriage and at its dissolution.

(2) Marriage shall be entered into only with the free and full consent of the intending spouses.

(3) The family is the natural and fundamental group unit of society and is entitled to protection by society and the State.

Article 17

(1) Everyone has the right to own property alone as well as in association with others.

(2) No one shall be arbitrarily deprived of his property.

Article 18

Everyone has the right to freedom of thought, conscience and religion; this right includes freedom to change his religion or belief, and freedom, either alone or in community with others and in public or private, to manifest his religion or belief in teaching, practice, worship and observance.

Article 19

Everyone has the right to freedom of opinion and expression; this right includes freedom to hold opinions without interference and to seek, receive and impart information and ideas through any media and regardless of frontiers.

Article 20

(1) Everyone has the right to freedom of peaceful assembly and association.

(2) No one may be compelled to belong to an association.

Article 21

(1) Everyone has the right to take part in the government of his country, directly or through freely chosen representatives.

(2) Everyone has the right of equal access to public service in his country.

(3) The will of the people shall be the basis of the authority of government; this will shall be expressed in periodic and genuine elections which shall be by universal and equal suffrage and shall be held by secret vote or by equivalent free voting procedures.

Article 22

Everyone, as a member of society, has the right to social security and is entitled to realization, through national effort and international co-operation and in accordance with the organization and resources of each State, of the economic, social and cultural rights indispensable for his dignity and the free development of his personality.

Article 23

(1) Everyone has the right to work, to free choice of employment, to just and favourable conditions of work and to protection against unemployment.

(2) Everyone, without any discrimination, has the right to equal pay for equal work.

(3) Everyone who works has the right to just and favourable remuneration ensuring for himself and his family an existence worthy of human dignity, and supplemented, if necessary, by other means of social protection.

(4) Everyone has the right to form and to join trade unions for the protection of his interests.

Article 24

Everyone has the right to rest and leisure, including reasonable limitation of working hours and periodic holidays with pay.

Article 25

(1) Everyone has the right to a standard of living adequate for the health and well-being of himself and of his family, including food, clothing, housing and medical care and necessary social services, and the right to security in the event of unemployment, sickness, disability, widowhood, old age or other lack of livelihood in circumstances beyond his control.

(2) Motherhood and childhood are entitled to special care and assistance. All children, whether born in or out of wedlock, shall enjoy the same social protection.

Article 26

(1) Everyone has the right to education. Education shall be free, at least in the elementary and fundamental stages. Elementary education shall be compulsory. Technical and professional education shall be made generally available and higher education shall be equally accessible to all on the basis of merit.

(2) Education shall be directed to the full development of the human personality and to the strengthening of respect for human rights and fundamental freedoms. It shall promote understanding, tolerance and friendship among all nations, racial or religious groups, and shall further the activities of the United Nations for the maintenance of peace.

(3) Parents have a prior right to choose the kind of education that shall be given to their children.

Article 27

(1) Everyone has the right freely to participate in the cultural life of the community, to enjoy the arts and to share in scientific advancement and its benefits.

(2) Everyone has the right to the protection of the moral and material interests resulting from any scientific, literary or artistic production of which he is the author.

Article 28

Everyone is entitled to a social and international order in which the rights and freedoms set forth in this Declaration can be fully realized.

Article 29

(1) Everyone has duties to the community in which alone the free and full development of his personality is possible.

(2) In the exercise of his rights and freedoms, everyone shall be subject only to such limitations as are determined by law solely for the purpose of securing due recognition and respect for the rights and freedoms of others and of meeting the just requirements of morality, public order and the general welfare in a democratic society.

(3) These rights and freedoms may in no case be exercised contrary to the purposes and principles of the United Nations.

Article 30

Nothing in this Declaration may be interpreted as implying for any State, group or person any right to engage in any activity or to perform any act aimed at the destruction of any of the rights and freedoms set forth herein.

Chapter 2
Declaration on Social Progress and Development

The General Assembly,

Mindful of the pledge of Members of the United Nations under the Charter to take joint and separate action in co-operation with the Organization to promote higher standards of living, full employment and conditions of economic and social progress and development,

Reaffirming faith in human rights and fundamental freedoms and in the principles of peace, of the dignity and worth of the human person, and of social justice proclaimed in the Charter,

Recalling the principles of the Universal Declaration of Human Rights, the International Covenants on Human Rights, the Declaration of the Rights of the Child, the Declaration on the Granting of Independence to Colonial Countries and Peoples, the International Convention on the Elimination of All Forms of Racial Discrimination, the United Nations Declaration on the Elimination of All Forms of Racial Discrimination, the Declaration on the Promotion among Youth of the Ideals of Peace, Mutual Respect and Understanding between Peoples, the Declaration on the Elimination of Discrimination against Women and of resolutions of the United Nations,

Bearing in mind the standards already set for social progress in the constitutions, conventions, recommendations and resolutions of the International Labour Organisation, the Food and Agriculture Organization of the United Nations, the United Nations Educational, Scientific and Cultural Organization, the World Health Organization, the United Nations Children's Fund and of other organizations concerned,

Convinced that man can achieve complete fulfilment of his aspirations only within a just social order and that it is consequently of cardinal importance to accelerate social and economic progress everywhere, thus contributing to international peace and solidarity,

Convinced that international peace and security on the one hand, and social progress

Proclaimed by General Assembly resolution 2542 (XXIV) of 11 December 1969.

and economic development on the other, are closely interdependent and influence each other,

Persuaded that social development can be promoted by peaceful coexistence, friendly relations and co-operation among States with different social, economic or political systems,

Emphasizing the interdependence of economic and social development in the wider process of growth and change, as well as the importance of a strategy of integrated development which takes full account at all stages of its social aspects,

Regretting the inadequate progress achieved in the world social situation despite the efforts of States and the international community,

Recognizing that the primary responsibility for the development of the developing countries rests on those countries themselves and acknowledging the pressing need to narrow and eventually close the gap in the standards of living between economically more advanced and developing countries and, to that end, that Member States shall have the responsibility to pursue internal and external policies designed to promote social development throughout the world, and in particular to assist developing countries to accelerate their economic growth,

Recognizing the urgency of devoting to works of peace and social progress resources being expended on armaments and wasted on conflict and destruction,

Conscious of the contribution that science and technology can render towards meeting the needs common to all humanity,

Believing that the primary task of all States and international organizations is to eliminate from the life of society all evils and obstacles to social progress, particularly such evils as inequality, exploitation, war, colonialism and racism,

Desirous of promoting the progress of all mankind towards these goals and of overcoming all obstacles to their realization,

Solemnly proclaims this Declaration on Social Progress and Development and calls for national and international action for its use as a common basis for social development policies:

Part I: Principles

Article 1

All peoples and all human beings, without distinction as to race, colour, sex, language, religion, nationality, ethnic origin, family or social status, or political or other conviction, shall have the right to live in dignity and freedom and to enjoy the fruits of social progress and should, on their part, contribute to it.

Article 2

Social progress and development shall be founded on respect for the dignity and value of the human person and shall ensure the promotion of human rights and social justice, which requires:

(a) The immediate and final elimination of all forms of inequality, exploitation of peoples and individuals, colonialism and racism, including nazism and apartheid, and all other policies and ideologies opposed to the purposes and principles of the United Nations;

(b) The recognition and effective implementation of civil and political rights as well as of economic, social and cultural rights without any discrimination.

Article 3

The following are considered primary conditions of social progress and development:

(a) National independence based on the right of peoples to self- determination;

(b) The principle of non-interference in the internal affairs of States;

(c) Respect for the sovereignty and territorial integrity of States;

(d) Permanent sovereignty of each nation over its natural wealth and resources;

(e) The right and responsibility of each State and, as far as they are concerned, each nation and people to determine freely its own objectives of social development, to set its own priorities and to decide in conformity with the principles of the Charter of the United Nations the means and methods of their achievement without any external interference;

(f) Peaceful coexistence, peace, friendly relations and co-operation among States irrespective of differences in their social, economic or political systems.

Article 4

The family as a basic unit of society and the natural environment for the growth and well-being of all its members, particularly children and youth, should be assisted and protected so that it may fully assume its responsibilities within the community. Parents have the exclusive right to determine freely and responsibly the number and spacing of their children.

Article 5

Social progress and development require the full utilization of human resources, including, in particular:

(a) The encouragement of creative initiative under conditions of enlightened public opinion;

(b) The dissemination of national and international information for the purpose of making individuals aware of changes occurring in society as a whole;

(c) The active participation of all elements of society, individually or through associations, in defining and in achieving the common goals of development with full respect for the fundamental freedoms embodied in the Universal Declaration of Human Rights;

(d) The assurance to disadvantaged or marginal sectors of the population of equal opportunities for social and economic advancement in order to achieve an effectively integrated society.

Article 6

Social development requires the assurance to everyone of the right to work and the free choice of employment.

Social progress and development require the participation of all members of society in productive and socially useful labour and the establishment, in conformity with human rights and fundamental freedoms and with the principles of justice and the social function of property, of forms of ownership of land and of the means of production which preclude any kind of exploitation of man, ensure equal rights to property for all and create conditions leading to genuine equality among people.

Article 7

The rapid expansion of national income and wealth and their equitable distribution among all members of society are fundamental to all social progress, and they should therefore be in the forefront of the preoccupations of every State and Government.

The improvement in the position of the developing countries in international trade resulting among other things from the achievement of favourable terms of trade and of equitable and remunerative prices at which developing countries market their products is necessary in order to make it possible to increase national income and in order to advance social development.

Article 8

Each Government has the primary role and ultimate responsibility of ensuring the social progress and well-being of its people, of planning social development measures as part of comprehensive development plans, of encouraging and co-ordinating or integrating all national efforts towards this end and of introducing necessary changes in the social structure. In planning social development measures, the diversity of the needs of developing and developed areas, and of urban and rural areas, within each country, shall be taken into due account.

Article 9

Social progress and development are the common concerns of the international community, which shall supplement, by concerted international action, national efforts to raise the living standards of peoples.

Social progress and economic growth require recognition of the common interest of all nations in the exploration, conservation, use and exploitation, exclusively for peaceful purposes and in the interests of all mankind, of those areas of the environment such as outer space and the sea-bed and ocean floor and the subsoil thereof, beyond the limits of national jurisdiction, in accordance with the purposes and principles of the Charter of the United Nations.

Part II: Objectives

Social progress and development shall aim at the continuous raising of the material and spiritual standards of living of all members of society, with respect for and in compliance with human rights and fundamental freedoms, through the attainment of the following main goals:

Article 10

(a) The assurance at all levels of the right to work and the right of everyone to form trade unions and workers' associations and to bargain collectively; promotion of full productive employment and elimination of unemployment and under-employment; establishment of equitable and favourable conditions of work for all, including the improvement of health and safety conditions; assurance of just remuneration for labour without any discrimination as well as a sufficiently high minimum wage to ensure a decent standard of living; the protection of the consumer;

(b) The elimination of hunger and malnutrition and the guarantee of the right to proper nutrition;

(c) The elimination of poverty; the assurance of a steady improvement in levels of living and of a just and equitable distribution of income;

(d) The achievement of the highest standards of health and the provision of health protection for the entire population, if possible free of charge;

(e) The eradication of illiteracy and the assurance of the right to universal access to culture, to free compulsory education at the elementary level and to free education at all levels; the raising of the general level of life-long education;

(f) The provision for all, particularly persons in low income groups and large families, of adequate housing and community services.

Social progress and development shall aim equally at the progressive attainment of the following main goals:

Article 11

(a) The provision of comprehensive social security schemes and social welfare services; the establishment and improvement of social security and insurance schemes for all persons who, because of illness, disability or old age, are temporarily or permanently unable to earn a living, with a view to ensuring a proper standard of living for such persons and for their families and dependants;

(b) The protection of the rights of the mother and child; concern for the upbringing and health of children; the provision of measures to safeguard the health and welfare of women and particularly of working mothers during pregnancy and the infancy of their children, as well as of mothers whose earnings are the sole source of livelihood for the family; the granting to women of pregnancy and maternity leave and allowances without loss of employment or wages;

(c) The protection of the rights and the assuring of the welfare of children, the aged and the disabled; the provision of protection for the physically or mentally disadvantaged;

(d) The education of youth in, and promotion among them of, the ideals of justice and peace, mutual respect and understanding among peoples; the promotion of full participation of youth in the process of national development;

(e) The provision of social defence measures and the elimination of conditions leading to crime and delinquency especially juvenile delinquency;

(f) The guarantee that all individuals, without discrimination of any kind, are made aware of their rights and obligations and receive the necessary aid in the exercise and safeguarding of their rights.

Social progress and development shall further aim at achieving the following main objectives:

Article 12

(a) The creation of conditions for rapid and sustained social and economic development, particularly in the developing countries; change in international economic relations; new and effective methods of international co-operation in which equality of opportunity should be as much a prerogative of nations as of individuals within a nation;

(b) The elimination of all forms of discrimination and exploitation and all other practices and ideologies contrary to the purposes and principles of the Charter of the United Nations;

(c) The elimination of all forms of foreign economic exploitation, particularly that practised by international monopolies, in order to enable the people of every country to enjoy in full the benefits of their national resources.

Social progress and development shall finally aim at the attainment of the following main goals:

Article 13

(a) Equitable sharing of scientific and technological advances by developed and developing countries, and a steady increase in the use of science and technology for the benefit of the social development of society;

(b) The establishment of a harmonious balance between scientific, technological and material progress and the intellectual, spiritual, cultural and moral advancement of humanity;

(c) The protection and improvement of the human environment.

Part III: Means and Methods

On the basis of the principles set forth in this Declaration, the achievement of the objectives of social progress and development requires the mobilization of the necessary resources by national and international action, with particular attention to such means and methods as:

Article 14

(a) Planning for social progress and development as an integrated part of balanced overall development planning;

(b) The establishment, where necessary, of national systems for framing and carrying out social policies and programmes, and the promotion by the countries concerned of planned regional development, taking into account differing regional conditions and needs, particularly the development of regions which are less favoured or under-developed by comparison with the rest of the country;

(c) The promotion of basic and applied social research, particularly comparative international research applied to the planning and execution of social development programmes.

Article 15

(a) The adoption of measures, to ensure the effective participation, as appropriate, of all the elements of society in the preparation and execution of national plans and programmes of economic and social development;

(b) The adoption of measures for an increasing rate of popular participation in the economic, social, cultural and political life of countries through national governmental bodies, non-governmental organizations, co-operatives, rural associations, workers' and employers' organizations and women's and youth organizations, by such methods as national and regional plans for social and economic progress and community development, with a view to achieving a fully integrated national society, accelerating the process of social mobility and consolidating the democratic system;

(c) Mobilization of public opinion, at both national and international levels, in support of the principles and objectives of social progress and development;

(d) The dissemination of social information, at the national and the international level, to make people aware of changing circumstances in society as a whole, and to educate the consumer.

Article 16

(a) Maximum mobilization of all national resources and their rational and efficient utilization; promotion of increased and accelerated productive investment in social and economic fields and of employment; orientation of society towards the development process;

(b) Progressively increasing provision of the necessary budgetary and other resources required for financing the social aspects of development;

(c) Achievement of equitable distribution of national income, utilizing, inter alia, the fiscal system and government spending as an instrument for the equitable distribution and redistribution of income in order to promote social progress;

(d) The adoption of measures aimed at prevention of such an outflow of capital from developing countries as would be detrimental to their economic and social development.

Article 17

(a) The adoption of measures to accelerate the process of industrialization, especially in developing countries, with due regard for its social aspects, in the interests of the entire population; development of an adequate organization and legal framework conducive to an uninterrupted and diversified growth of the industrial sector; measures to overcome the adverse social effects which may result from urban development and industrialization, including automation; maintenance of a proper balance between rural and urban development, and in particular, measures designed to ensure healthier living conditions, especially in large industrial centres;

(b) Integrated planning to meet the problems of urbanization and urban development;

(c) Comprehensive rural development schemes to raise the level s of living of the rural populations and to facilitate such urban-rural relationships and population distribution as will promote balanced national development and social progress;

(d) Measures for appropriate supervision of the utilization of land in the interests of society.

The achievement of the objectives of social progress and development equally requires the implementation of the following means and methods:

Article 18

(a) The adoption of appropriate legislative, administrative and other measures ensuring to everyone not only political and civil rights, but also the full realization of economic, social and cultural rights without any discrimination;

(b) The promotion of democratically based social and institutional reforms and motivation for change basic to the elimination of all forms of discrimination and exploitation and conducive to high rates of economic and social progress, to include land reform, in which the ownership and use of land will be made to serve best the objectives of social justice and economic development;

(c) The adoption of measures to boost and diversify agricultural production through, inter alia, the implementation of democratic agrarian reforms, to ensure an adequate and well-balanced supply of food, its equitable distribution among the whole population and the improvement of nutritional standards;

(d) The adoption of measures to introduce, with the participation of the Government, low-cost housing programmes in both rural and urban areas;

(e) Development and expansion of the system of transportation and communications, particularly in developing countries.

Article 19

(a) The provision of free health services to the whole population and of adequate preventive and curative facilities and welfare medical services accessible to all;

(b) The enactment and establishment of legislative measures and administrative regulations with a view to the implementation of comprehensive programmes of social security schemes and social welfare services and to the improvement and co-ordination of existing services;

(c) The adoption of measures and the provision of social welfare services to migrant workers and their families, in conformity with the provisions of Convention No. 97 of the International Labour Organisation and other international instruments relating to migrant workers;

(d) The institution of appropriate measures for the rehabilitation of mentally or physically disabled persons, especially children and youth, so as to enable them to the fullest possible extent to be useful members of society- these measures shall include the provision of treatment and technical appliances, education, vocational and social guidance, training and selective placement, and other assistance required-and the creation of social conditions in which the handicapped are not discriminated against because of their disabilities.

Article 20

(a) The provision of full democratic freedoms to trade unions; freedom of association for all workers, including the right to bargain collectively and to strike; recognition of the right to form other organizations of working people; the provision for the growing participation of trade unions in economic and social development; effective participation of all members in trade unions in the deciding of economic and social issues which affect their interests;

(b) The improvement of health and safety conditions for workers, by means of appropriate technological and legislative measures and the provision of the material prerequisites for the implementation of those measures, including the limitation of working hours;

(c) The adoption of appropriate measures for the development of harmonious industrial relations.

Article 21

(a) The training of national personnel and cadres, including administrative, executive, professional and technical personnel needed for social development and for overall development plans and policies;

(b) The adoption of measures to accelerate the extension and improvement of general, vocational and technical education and of training and retraining, which should be provided free at all levels;

(c) Raising the general level of education; development and expansion of national information media, and their rational and full use towards continuing education of the whole population and towards encouraging its participation in social development activities; the constructive use of leisure, particularly that of children and adolescents;

(d) The formulation of national and international policies and measures to avoid the "brain drain" and obviate its adverse effects.

Article 22

(a) The development and co-ordination of policies and measures designed to strengthen the essential functions of the family as a basic unit of society;

(b) The formulation and establishment, as needed, of programmes in the field of population, within the framework of national demographic policies and as part of the welfare medical services, including education, training of personnel and the provision to families of the knowledge and means necessary to enable them to exercise their right to determine freely and responsibly the number and spacing of their children;

(c) The establishment of appropriate child-care facilities in the interest of children and working parents. The achievement of the objectives of social progress and development finally requires the implementation of the following means and methods:

Article 23

(a) The laying down of economic growth rate targets for the developing countries within the United Nations policy for development, high enough to lead to a substantial acceleration of their rates of growth;

(b) The provision of greater assistance on better terms; the implementation of the aid volume target of a minimum of 1 per cent of the gross national product at market prices of economically advanced countries; the general easing of the terms of lending to the developing countries through low interest rates on loans and long grace periods for the repayment of loans, and the assurance that the allocation of such loans will be based strictly on socioeconomic criteria free of any political considerations;

(c) The provision of technical, financial and material assistance, both bilateral and multilateral, to the fullest possible extent and on favourable terms, and improved co-ordination of international assistance for the achievement of the social objectives of national development plans;

(d) The provision to the developing countries of technical, financial and material assistance and of favourable conditions to facilitate the direct exploitation of their national resources and natural wealth by those countries with a view to enabling the peoples of those countries to benefit fully from their national resources;

(e) The expansion of international trade based on principles of equality and non-discrimination, the rectification of the position of developing countries in international trade by equitable terms of trade, a general nonreciprocal and non-discriminatory system of preferences for the exports of developing countries to the developed countries, the establishment and implementation of general and comprehensive commodity agreements, and the financing of reasonable buffer stocks by international institutions.

Article 24

(a) Intensification of international co-operation with a view to ensuring the international exchange of information, knowledge and experience concerning social progress and development;

(b) The broadest possible international technical, scientific and cultural co-operation and reciprocal utilization of the experience of countries with different economic and social systems and different levels of development, on the basis of mutual advantage and strict observance of and respect for national sovereignty;

(c) Increased utilization of science and technology for social and economic development; arrangements for the transfer and exchange of technology, including know-how and patents, to the developing countries.

Article 25

(a) The establishment of legal and administrative measures for the protection and improvement of the human environment, at both national and international level;

(b) The use and exploitation, in accordance with the appropriate international regimes, of the resources of areas of the environment such as outer space and the sea-bed and ocean floor and the subsoil thereof, beyond the limits of national jurisdiction, in order to supplement national resources available for the achievement of economic and social progress and development in every country, irrespective of its geographical location, special consideration being given to the interests and needs of the developing countries.

Article 26

Compensation for damages, be they social or economic in nature- including restitution and reparations-caused as a result of aggression and of illegal occupation of territory by the aggressor.

Article 27

(a) The achievement of general and complete disarmament and the channelling of the progressively released resources to be used for economic and social progress for the welfare of people everywhere and, in particular, for the benefit of developing countries;

(b) The adoption of measures contributing to disarmament, including, inter alia, the complete prohibition of tests of nuclear weapons, the prohibition of the development, production and stockpiling of chemical and bacteriological (biological) weapons and the prevention of the pollution of oceans and inland waters by nuclear wastes.

Chapter 3
Declaration on Race and Racial Prejudice

Preamble

The General Conference of the United Nations Educational, Scientific and Cultural Organization, meeting at Paris at its twentieth session, from 24 October to 28 November 1978,

Whereas it is stated in the Preamble to the Constitution of UNESCO, adopted on 16 November 1945, that "the great and terrible war which has now ended was a war made possible by the denial of the democratic principles of the dignity, equality and mutual respect of men, and by the propagation, in their place, through ignorance and prejudice, of the doctrine of the inequality of men and races," and whereas, according to Article I of the said Constitution, the purpose of UNESCO "is to contribute to peace and security by promoting collaboration among the nations through education, science and culture in order to further universal respect for justice, for the rule of law and for the human rights and fundamental freedoms which are affirmed for the peoples of the world, without distinction of race, sex, language or religion, by the Charter of the United Nations,"

Recognizing that, more than three decades after the founding of UNESCO, these principles are just as significant as they were when they were embodied in its Constitution,

Mindful of the process of decolonization and other historical changes which have led most of the peoples formerly under foreign rule to recover their sovereignty, making the international community a universal and diversified whole and creating new opportunities of eradicating the scourge of racism and of putting an end to its odious manifestations in all aspects of social and political life, both nationally and internationally,

Convinced that the essential unity of the human race and consequently the fundamental equality of all human beings and all peoples, recognized in the loftiest expressions of philosophy, morality and religion, reflect an ideal towards which ethics and science are converging today,

Adopted and proclaimed by the General Conference of the United Nations Educational, Scientific and Cultural Organization on 27 November 1978.

Convinced that all peoples and all human groups, whatever their composition or ethnic origin, contribute according to their own genius to the progress of the civilizations and cultures which, in their plurality and as a result of their interpenetration, constitute the common heritage of mankind,

Confirming its attachment to the principles proclaimed in the United Nations Charter and the Universal Declaration of Human Rights and its determination to promote the implementation of the International Covenants on Human Rights as well as the Declaration on the Establishment of a New International Economic Order,

Determined also to promote the implementation of the United Nations Declaration and the International Convention on the Elimination of All Forms of Racial Discrimination,

Noting the Convention on the Prevention and Punishment of the Crime of Genocide, the International Convention on the Suppression and Punishment of the Crime of Apartheid and the Convention on the Non-Applicability of Statutory Limitations to War Crimes and Crimes against Humanity,

Recalling also the international instruments already adopted by UNESCO, including in particular the Convention and Recommendation against Discrimination in Education, the Recommendation concerning the Status of Teachers, the Declaration of the Principles of International Cultural Co-operation, the Recommendation concerning Education for International Understanding, Co-operation and Peace and Education relating to Human Rights and Fundamental Freedoms, the Recommendations on the Status of Scientific Researchers, and the Recommendation on participation by the people at large in cultural life and their contribution to it,

Bearing in mind the four statements on the race question adopted by experts convened by UNESCO,

Reaffirming its desire to play a vigorous and constructive part in the implementation of the programme of the Decade for Action to Combat Racism and Racial Discrimination, as defined by the General Assembly of the United Nations at its twenty-eighth session,

Noting with the gravest concern that racism, racial discrimination, colonialism and apartheid continue to afflict the world in ever-changing forms, as a result both of the continuation of legislative provisions and government and administrative practices contrary to the principles of human rights and also of the continued existence of political and social structures, and of relationships and attitudes, characterized by injustice and contempt for human beings and leading to the exclusion, humiliation and exploitation, or to the forced assimilation, of the members of disadvantaged groups,

Expressing its indignation at these offences against human dignity, deploring the obstacles they place in the way of mutual understanding between peoples and alarmed at the danger of their seriously disturbing international peace and security,

Adopts and solemnly proclaims this Declaration on Race and Racial Prejudice:

Article 1

1. All human beings belong to a single species and are descended from a common stock. They are born equal in dignity and rights and all form an integral part of humanity.

2. All individuals and groups have the right to be different, to consider themselves as different and to be regarded as such. However, the diversity of life styles and the right to be different may not, in any circumstances, serve as a pretext for racial prejudice; they may not justify either in law or in fact any discriminatory practice whatsoever, nor provide a ground for the policy of apartheid, which is the extreme form of racism.

3. Identity of origin in no way affects the fact that human beings can and may live differently, nor does it preclude the existence of differences based on cultural, environmental and historical diversity nor the right to maintain cultural identity.

4. All peoples of the world possess equal faculties for attaining the highest level in intellectual, technical, social, economic, cultural and political development.

5. The differences between the achievements of the different peoples are entirely attributable to geographical, historical, political, economic, social and cultural factors. Such differences can in no case serve as a pretext for any rank-ordered classification of nations or peoples.

Article 2

1. Any theory which involves the claim that racial or ethnic groups are inherently superior or inferior, thus implying that some would be entitled to dominate or eliminate others, presumed to be inferior, or which bases value judgements on racial differentiation, has no scientific foundation and is contrary to the moral and ethical principles of humanity.

2. Racism includes racist ideologies, prejudiced attitudes, discriminatory behaviour, structural arrangements and institutionalized practices resulting in racial inequality as well as the fallacious notion that discriminatory relations between groups are morally and scientifically justifiable; it is reflected in discriminatory provisions in legislation or regulations and discriminatory practices as well as in anti-social beliefs and acts; it hinders the development of its victims, perverts those who practise it, divides nations internally, impedes international co-operation and gives rise to political tensions between peoples; it is contrary to the fundamental principles of international law and, consequently, seriously disturbs international peace and security.

3. Racial prejudice, historically linked with inequalities in power, reinforced by economic and social differences between individuals and groups, and still seeking today to justify such inequalities, is totally without justification.

Article 3

Any distinction, exclusion, restriction or preference based on race, colour, ethnic or national origin or religious intolerance motivated by racist considerations, which destroys or compromises the sovereign equality of States and the right of peoples to self-determination, or which limits in an arbitrary or discriminatory manner the right of every human being and group to full development is incompatible with the requirements of an international order which is just and guarantees respect for human rights; the right to full development implies equal access to the means of personal and collective advancement and fulfilment in a climate of respect for the values of civilizations and cultures, both national and world-wide.

Article 4

1. Any restriction on the complete self-fulfilment of human beings and free communication between them which is based on racial or ethnic considerations is contrary to the principle of equality in dignity and rights; it cannot be admitted.

2. One of the most serious violations of this principle is represented by apartheid, which, like genocide, is a crime against humanity, and gravely disturbs international peace and security.

3. Other policies and practices of racial segregation and discrimination constitute crimes against the conscience and dignity of mankind and may lead to political tensions and gravely endanger international peace and security.

Article 5

1. Culture, as a product of all human beings and a common heritage of mankind, and education in its broadest sense, offer men and women increasingly effective means of adaptation, enabling them not only to affirm that they are born equal in dignity and rights, but also to recognize that they should respect the right of all groups to their own cultural identity and the development of their distinctive cultural life within the national and international contexts, it being understood that it rests with each group to decide in complete freedom on the maintenance, and, if appropriate, the adaptation or enrichment of the values which it regards as essential to its identity.

2. States, in accordance with their constitutional principles and procedures, as well as all other competent authorities and the entire teaching profession, have a responsibility to see that the educational resources of all countries are used to combat racism, more especially by ensuring that curricula and textbooks include scientific and ethical considerations concerning human unity and diversity and that no invidious distinctions are made with regard to any people; by training teachers to achieve these ends; by making the resources of the educational system available to all groups of the population without racial restriction or discrimination; and by taking appropriate steps to remedy the handicaps from which certain racial or ethnic groups suffer with regard to their level of education and standard of living and in particular to prevent such handicaps from being passed on to children.

3. The mass media and those who control or serve them, as well as all organized groups within national communities, are urged-with due regard to the principles embodied in the Universal Declaration of Human Rights, particulary the principle of freedom of expression—to promote understanding, tolerance and friendship among individuals and groups and to contribute to the eradication of racism, racial discrimination and racial prejudice, in particular by refraining from presenting a stereotyped, partial, unilateral or tendentious picture of individuals and of various human groups. Communication between racial and ethnic groups must be a reciprocal process, enabling them to express themselves and to be fully heard without let or hindrance. The mass media should therefore be freely receptive to ideas of individuals and groups which facilitate such communication.

Article 6

1. The State has prime responsibility for ensuring human rights and fundamental freedoms on an entirely equal footing in dignity and rights for all individuals and all groups.

2. So far as its competence extends and in accordance with its constitutional principles and procedures, the State should take all appropriate steps, inter alia by legislation, particularly in the spheres of education, culture and communication, to prevent, prohibit and eradicate racism~ racist propaganda, racial segregation and apartheid and to encourage the dissemination of knowledge and the findings of appropriate research in natural and social sciences on the causes and prevention of racial prejudice and racist attitudes with due regard to the principles embodied in the Universal Declaration of Human Rights and in the International Covenant on Civil and Political Rights.

3. Since laws proscribing racial discrimination are not in themselves sufficient, it is also incumbent on States to supplement them by administrative machinery for the systematic investigation of instances of racial discrimination, by a comprehensive framework of legal remedies against acts of racial discrimination, by broadly based education and research programmes designed to combat racial prejudice and racial discrimination and by programmes of positive political, social, educational and cultural measures calculated to promote genuine mutual respect among groups. Where circumstances warrant, special programmes should be undertaken to promote the advancement of disadvantaged groups and, in the case of nationals, to ensure their effective participation in the decision-making processes of the community.

Article 7

In addition to political, economic and social measures, law is one of the principal means of ensuring equality in dignity and rights among individuals, and of curbing any propaganda, any form of organization or any practice which is based on ideas or theories referring to the alleged superiority of racial or ethnic groups or which seeks to justify or encourage racial hatred and discrimination in any form. States should adopt such legislation as is appropriate to this end and see that it is given effect and applied by all their services, with due regard to the principles embodied in the Universal Declaration of Human Rights. Such legislation should form part of a political, economic and social framework conducive to its implementation. Individuals and other legal entities, both public and private, must conform with such legislation and use all appropriate means to help the population as a whole to understand and apply it.

Article 8

1. Individuals, being entitled to an economic, social, cultural and legal order, on the national and international planes, such as to allow them to exercise all their capabilities on a basis of entire equality of rights and opportunities, have corresponding duties towards their fellows, towards the society in which they live and towards the international community. They are accordingly under an obligation to promote harmony among the peoples, to combat racism and racial prejudice and to assist by every means available to them in eradicating racial discrimination in all its forms.

2. In the field of racial prejudice and racist attitudes and practices, specialists in natural and social sciences and cultural studies, as well as scientific organizations and associations, are called upon to undertake objective research on a wide interdisciplinary basis; all States should encourage them to this end.

3. It is, in particular, incumbent upon such specialists to ensure, by all means available to them, that their research findings are not misinterpreted, and also that they assist the public in understanding such findings.

Article 9

1. The principle of the equality in dignity and rights of all human beings and all peoples, irrespective of race, colour and origin, is a generally accepted and recognized principle of international law. Consequently any form of racial discrimination practised by a State constitutes a violation of international law giving rise to its international responsibility.

2. Special measures must be taken to ensure equality in dignity and rights for individuals and groups wherever necessary, while ensuring that they are not such as to appear racially discriminatory. In this respect, particular attention should be paid to racial or ethnic groups which are socially or economically disadvantaged, so as to afford them, on a completely equal footing and without discrimination or restriction, the protection of the laws and regulations and the advantages of the social measures in force, in particular in regard to housing, employment and health; to respect the authenticity of their culture and values; and to facilitate their social and occupational advancement, especially through education.

3. Population groups of foreign origin, particularly migrant workers and their families

who contribute to the development of the host country, should benefit from appropriate measures designed to afford them security and respect for their dignity and cultural values and to facilitate their adaptation to the host environment and their professional advancement with a view to their subsequent reintegration in their country of origin and their contribution to its development; steps should be taken to make it possible for their children to be taught their mother tongue.

4. Existing disequilibria in international economic relations contribute to the exacerbation of racism and racial prejudice; all States should consequently endeavour to contribute to the restructuring of the international economy on a more equitable basis.

Article 10

International organizations, whether universal or regional, governmental or non-governmental, are called upon to co-operate and assist, so far as their respective fields of competence and means allow, in the full and complete implementation of the principles set out in this Declaration, thus contributing to the legitimate struggle of all men, born equal in dignity and rights, against the tyranny and oppression of racism, racial segregation, apartheid and genocide, so that all the peoples of the world may be forever delivered from these scourges.

Chapter 4
Declaration on the Rights of Persons Belonging to National or Ethnic, Religious and Linguistic Minorities

The General Assembly,

Reaffirming that one of the basic aims of the United Nations, as proclaimed in the Charter, is to promote and encourage respect for human rights and for fundamental freedoms for all, without distinction as to race, sex, language or religion,

Reaffirming faith in fundamental human rights, in the dignity and worth of the human person, in the equal rights of men and women and of nations large and small,

Desiring to promote the realization of the principles contained in the Charter, the Universal Declaration of Human Rights, the Convention on the Prevention and Punishment of the Crime of Genocide, the International Convention on the Elimination of All Forms of Racial Discrimination, the International Covenant on Civil and Political Rights, the International Covenant on Economic, Social and Cultural Rights, the Declaration on the Elimination of All Forms of Intolerance and of Discrimination Based on Religion or Belief, and the Convention on the Rights of the Child, as well as other relevant international instruments that have been adopted at the universal or regional level and those concluded between individual States Members of the United Nations,

Inspired by the provisions of article 27 of the International Covenant on Civil and Political Rights concerning the rights of persons belonging to ethnic, religious or linguistic minorities,

Considering that the promotion and protection of the rights of persons belonging to national or ethnic, religious and linguistic minorities contribute to the political and social stability of States in which they live,

Emphasizing that the constant promotion and realization of the rights of persons belonging to national or ethnic, religious and linguistic minorities, as an integral part of the development of society as a whole and within a democratic framework based on

Adopted by General Assembly resolution 47/135 of 18 December 1992.

the rule of law, would contribute to the strengthening of friendship and cooperation among peoples and States,

Considering that the United Nations has an important role to play regarding the protection of minorities,

Bearing in mind the work done so far within the United Nations system, in particular by the Commission on Human Rights, the Subcommission on Prevention of Discrimination and Protection of Minorities and the bodies established pursuant to the International Covenants on Human Rights and other relevant international human rights instruments in promoting and protecting the rights of persons belonging to national or ethnic, religious and linguistic minorities,

Taking into account the important work which is done by intergovernmental and non-governmental organizations in protecting minorities and in promoting and protecting the rights of persons belonging to national or ethnic, religious and linguistic minorities,

Recognizing the need to ensure even more effective implementation of international human rights instruments with regard to the rights of persons belonging to national or ethnic, religious and linguistic minorities,

Proclaims this Declaration on the Rights of Persons Belonging to National or Ethnic, Religious and Linguistic Minorities:

Article 1

1. States shall protect the existence and the national or ethnic, cultural, religious and linguistic identity of minorities within their respective territories and shall encourage conditions for the promotion of that identity.

2. States shall adopt appropriate legislative and other measures to achieve those ends.

Article 2

1. Persons belonging to national or ethnic, religious and linguistic minorities (hereinafter referred to as persons belonging to minorities) have the right to enjoy their own culture, to profess and practise their own religion, and to use their own language, in private and in public, freely and without interference or any form of discrimination.

2. Persons belonging to minorities have the right to participate effectively in cultural, religious, social, economic and public life.

3. Persons belonging to minorities have the right to participate effectively in decisions on the national and, where appropriate, regional level concerning the minority to which they belong or the regions in which they live, in a manner not incompatible with national legislation.

4. Persons belonging to minorities have the right to establish and maintain their own associations.

5. Persons belonging to minorities have the right to establish and maintain, without any discrimination, free and peaceful contacts with other members of their group and with persons belonging to other minorities, as well as contacts across frontiers with citizens of other States to whom they are related by national or ethnic, religious or linguistic ties.

Article 3

1. Persons belonging to minorities may exercise their rights, including those set forth in the present Declaration, individually as well as in community with other members of their group, without any discrimination.

2. No disadvantage shall result for any person belonging to a minority as the consequence of the exercise or non-exercise of the rights set forth in the present Declaration.

Article 4

1. States shall take measures where required to ensure that persons belonging to minorities may exercise fully and effectively all their human rights and fundamental freedoms without any discrimination and in full equality before the law.

2. States shall take measures to create favourable conditions to enable persons belonging to minorities to express their characteristics and to develop their culture, language, religion, traditions and customs, except where specific practices are in violation of national law and contrary to international standards.

3. States should take appropriate measures so that, wherever possible, persons belonging to minorities may have adequate opportunities to learn their mother tongue or to have instruction in their mother tongue.

4. States should, where appropriate, take measures in the field of education, in order to encourage knowledge of the history, traditions, language and culture of the minorities existing within their territory. Persons belonging to minorities should have adequate opportunities to gain knowledge of the society as a whole.

5. States should consider appropriate measures so that persons belonging to minorities may participate fully in the economic progress and development in their country.

Article 5

1. National policies and programmes shall be planned and implemented with due regard for the legitimate interests of persons belonging to minorities.

2. Programmes of cooperation and assistance among States should be planned and implemented with due regard for the legitimate interests of persons belonging to minorities.

Article 6

States should cooperate on questions relating to persons belonging to minorities, inter alia, exchanging information and experiences, in order to promote mutual understanding and confidence.

Article 7

States should cooperate in order to promote respect for the rights set forth in the present Declaration.

Article 8

1. Nothing in the present Declaration shall prevent the fulfillment of international obligations of States in relation to persons belonging to minorities. In particular, States shall fulfill in good faith the obligations and commitments they have assumed under international treaties and agreements to which they are parties.

2. The exercise of the rights set forth in the present Declaration shall not prejudice the enjoyment by all persons of universally recognized human rights and fundamental freedoms.

3. Measures taken by States to ensure the effective enjoyment of the rights set forth in the present Declaration shall not prima facie be considered contrary to the principle of equality contained in the Universal Declaration of Human Rights.

4. Nothing in the present Declaration may be construed as permitting any activity contrary to the purposes and principles of the United Nations, including sovereign equality, territorial integrity and political independence of States.

Article 9

The specialized agencies and other organizations of the United Nations system shall contribute to the full realization of the rights and principles set forth in the present Declaration, within their respective fields of competence.

Chapter 5
Universal Declaration on the Eradication of Hunger and Malnutrition

The World Food Conference,

Convened by the General Assembly of the United Nations and entrusted with developing ways and means whereby the international community, as a whole, could take specific action to resolve the world food problem within the broader context of development and international economic co-operation,

Adopts the following Declaration:

Universal Declaration on the Eradication of Hunger and Malnutrition

Recognizing that:

(a) The grave food crisis that is afflicting the peoples of the developing countries where most of the world's hungry and ill-nourished live and where more than two thirds of the world's population produce about one third of the world's food—an imbalance which threatens to increase in the next 10 years—is not only fraught with grave economic and social implications, but also acutely jeopardizes the most fundamental principles and values associated with the right to life and human dignity as enshrined in the Universal Declaration of Human Rights;

(b) The elimination of hunger and malnutrition, included as one of the objectives in the United Nations Declaration on Social Progress and Development, and the elimination of the causes that determine this situation are the common objectives of all nations;

(c) The situation of the peoples afflicted by hunger and malnutrition arises from their historical circumstances, especially social inequalities, including in many cases alien and colonial domination, foreign occupation, racial discrimination, apartheid and neo-colonialism in all its forms, which continue to be among the greatest obstacles to the full emancipation and progress of the developing countries and all the peoples involved;

Adopted on 16 November 1974 by the World Food Conference and endorsed by General Assembly resolution 3348 (XXIX) of 17 December 1974.

(d) This situation has been aggravated in recent years by a series of crises to which the world economy has been subjected, such as the deterioration in the international monetary system, the inflationary increase in import costs, the heavy burdens imposed by external debt on the balance of payments of many developing countries, a rising food demand partly due to demographic pressure, speculation, and a shortage of, and increased costs for, essential agricultural inputs;

(e) These phenomena should be considered within the framework of the on-going negotiations on the Charter of Economic Rights and Duties of States, and the General Assembly of the United Nations should be urged unanimously to agree upon, and to adopt, a Charter that will be an effective instrument for the establishment of new international economic relations based on principles of equity and justice;

(f) All countries, big or small, rich or poor, are equal. All countries have the full right to participate in the decisions on the food problem;

(g) The well-being of the peoples of the world largely depends on the adequate production and distribution of food as well as the establishment of a world food security system which would ensure adequate availability of, and reasonable prices for, food at all times, irrespective of periodic fluctuations and vagaries of weather and free of political and economic pressures, and should thus facilitate, amongst other things, the development process of developing countries;

(h) Peace and justice encompass an economic dimension helping the solution of the world economic problems, the liquidation of under-development, offering a lasting and definitive solution of the food problem for all peoples and guaranteeing to all countries the right to implement freely and effectively their development programmes. To this effect, it is necessary to eliminate threats and resort to force and to promote peaceful co-operation between States to the fullest extent possible, to apply the principles of non-interference in the internal affairs of other States, full equality of rights and respect of national independence and sovereignty, as well as to encourage the peaceful co-operation between all States, irrespective of their political, social and economic systems. The further improvement of international relations will create better conditions for international co-operation in all fields which should make possible large financial and material resources to be used, inter alia, for developing agricultural production and substantially improving world food security;

(i) For a lasting solution of the food problem all efforts should be made to eliminate the widening gaps which today separate developed and developing countries and to bring about a new international economic order. It should be possible for all countries to participate actively and effectively in the new international economic relations by the establishment of suitable international systems, where appropriate, capable of producing adequate action in order to establish just and equitable relations in international economic co-operation;

(j) Developing countries reaffirm their belief that the primary responsibility for ensuring their own rapid development rests with themselves. They declare, therefore, their readiness to continue to intensify their individual and collective efforts with a view to expanding their mutual co-operation in the field of agricultural development and food production, including the eradication of hunger and malnutrition;

(k) Since, for various reasons, many developing countries are not yet always able to meet their own food needs, urgent and effective international action should be taken to assist them, free of political pressures,

Consistent with the aims and objectives of the Declaration on the Establishment of a New International Economic Order and the Programme of Action adopted by the General Assembly at its sixth special session,

The Conference consequently solemnly proclaims:

1. Every man, woman and child has the inalienable right to be free from hunger and malnutrition in order to develop fully and maintain their physical and mental faculties. Society today already possesses sufficient resources, organizational ability and technology and hence the competence to achieve this objective. Accordingly, the eradication of hunger is a common objective of all the countries of the international community, especially of the developed countries and others in a position to help.

2. It is a fundamental responsibility of Governments to work together for higher food production and a more equitable and efficient distribution of food between countries and within countries. Governments should initiate immediately a greater concerted attack on chronic malnutrition and deficiency diseases among the vulnerable and lower income groups. In order to ensure adequate nutrition for all, Governments should formulate appropriate food and nutrition policies integrated in overall socio-economic and agricultural development plans based on adequate knowledge of available as well as potential food resources. The importance of human milk in this connection should be stressed on nutritional grounds.

3. Food problems must be tackled during the preparation and implementation of national plans and programmes for economic and social development, with emphasis on their humanitarian aspects.

4. It is a responsibility of each State concerned, in accordance with its sovereign judgement and internal legislation, to remove the obstacles to food production and to provide proper incentives to agricultural producers. Of prime importance for the attainment of these objectives are effective measures of socio-economic transformation by agrarian, tax, credit and investment policy reform and the reorganization of rural structures, such as the reform of the conditions of ownership, the encouragement of producer and consumer co-operatives, the mobilization of the full potential of human resources, both male and female, in the developing countries for an integrated rural development and the involvement of small farmers, fishermen and landless workers in attaining the required food production and employment targets. Moreover, it is necessary to recognize the key role of women in agricultural production and rural economy in many countries, and to ensure that appropriate education, extension programmes and financial facilities are made available to women on equal terms with men.

5. Marine and inland water resources are today becoming more important than ever as a source of food and economic prosperity. Accordingly, action should be taken to promote a rational exploitation of these resources, preferably for direct consumption, in order to contribute to meeting the food requirements of all peoples.

6. The efforts to increase food production should be complemented by every endeavour to prevent wastage of food in all its forms.

7. To give impetus to food production in developing countries and in particular in the least developed and most seriously affected among them, urgent and effective international action should be taken, by the developed countries and other countries in a position to do so, to provide them with sustained additional technical and financial assistance on favourable terms and in a volume sufficient to their needs on the basis of bilateral and multilateral arrangements. This assistance must be free of conditions inconsistent with the sovereignty of the receiving States.

8. All countries, and primarily the highly industrialized countries, should promote the advancement of food production technology and should make all efforts to promote the transfer, adaptation and dissemination of appropriate food production technology for the benefit of the developing countries and, to that end, they should inter alia make all efforts to disseminate the results of their research work to Governments and scientific institutions of developing countries in order to enable them to promote a sustained agricultural development.

9. To assure the proper conservation of natural resources being utilized, or which might be utilized, for food production, all countries must collaborate in order to facilitate the preservation of the environment, including the marine environment.

10. All developed countries and others able to do so should collaborate technically and financially with the developing countries in their efforts to expand land and water resources for agricultural production and to assure a rapid increase in the availability, at fair costs, of agricultural inputs such as fertilizers and other chemicals, high-quality seeds, credit and technology. Co-operation among developing countries, in this connection, is also important.

11. All States should strive to the utmost to readjust, where appropriate, their agricultural policies to give priority to food production, recognizing, in this connection the interrelationship between the world food problem and international trade. In the determination of attitudes towards farm support programmes for domestic food production, developed countries should take into account, as far as possible, the interest of the food-exporting developing countries, in order to avoid detrimental effect on their exports. Moreover, all countries should co-operate to devise effective steps to deal with the problem of stabilizing world markets and promoting equitable and remunerative prices, where appropriate through international arrangements, to improve access to markets through reduction or elimination of tariff and non-tariff barriers on the products of interest to the developing countries, to substantially increase the export earnings of these countries, to contribute to the diversification of their exports, and

apply to them, in the multilateral trade negotiations, the principles as agreed upon in the Tokyo Declaration, including the concept of non-reciprocity and more favourable treatment.

12. As it is the common responsibility of the entire international community to ensure the availability at all times of adequate world supplies of basic food-stuffs by way of appropriate reserves, including emergency reserves, all countries should co-operate in the establishment of an effective system of world food security by:

Participating in and supporting the operation of the Global Information and Early Warning System on Food and Agriculture;

Adhering to the objectives, policies and guidelines of the proposed International Undertaking on World Food Security as endorsed by the World Food Conference;

Earmarking, where possible, stocks or funds for meeting international emergency food requirements as envisaged in the proposed International Undertaking on World Food Security and developing international guidelines to provide for the co-ordination and the utilization of such stocks;

Co-operating in the provision of food aid for meeting emergency and nutritional needs as well as for stimulating rural employment through development projects.

All donor countries should accept and implement the concept of forward planning of food aid and make all efforts to provide commodities and/or financial assistance that will ensure adequate quantities of grains and other food commodities.

Time is short. Urgent and sustained action is vital. The Conference, therefore, calls upon all peoples expressing their will as individuals, and through their Governments, and non-governmental organizations, to work together to bring about the end of the age-old scourge of hunger.

The Conference affirms:

The determination of the participating States to make full use of the United Nations system in the implementation of this Declaration and the other decisions adopted by the Conference.

Chapter 6

Declaration on the Rights of Disabled Persons

The General Assembly,

Mindful of the pledge made by Member States, under the Charter of the United Nations to take joint and separate action in co-operation with the Organization to promote higher standards of living, full employment and conditions of economic and social progress and development,

Reaffirming its faith in human rights and fundamental freedoms and in the principles of peace, of the dignity and worth of the human person and of social justice proclaimed in the Charter,

Recalling the principles of the Universal Declaration of Human Rights, the International Covenants on Human Rights, the Declaration of the Rights of the Child and the Declaration on the Rights of Mentally Retarded Persons, as well as the standards already set for social progress in the constitutions, conventions, recommendations and resolutions of the International Labour Organisation, the United Nations Educational, Scientific and Cultural Organization, the World Health Organization, the United Nations Children's Fund and other organizations concerned,

Recalling also Economic and Social Council resolution 1921 (LVIII) of 6 May 1975 on the prevention of disability and the rehabilitation of disabled persons,

Emphasizing that the Declaration on Social Progress and Development has proclaimed the necessity of protecting the rights and assuring the welfare and rehabilitation of the physically and mentally disadvantaged,

Bearing in mind the necessity of preventing physical and mental disabilities and of assisting disabled persons to develop their abilities in the most varied fields of activities and of promoting their integration as far as possible in normal life,

Aware that certain countries, at their present stage of development, can devote only limited efforts to this end,

Proclaimed by General Assembly resolution 3447 (XXX) of 9 December 1975.

Proclaims this Declaration on the Rights of Disabled Persons and calls for national and international action to ensure that it will be used as a common basis and frame of reference for the protection of these rights:

1. The term "disabled person" means any person unable to ensure by himself or herself, wholly or partly, the necessities of a normal individual and/or social life, as a result of deficiency, either congenital or not, in his or her physical or mental capabilities.

2. Disabled persons shall enjoy all the rights set forth in this Declaration. These rights shall be granted to all disabled persons without any exception whatsoever and without distinction or discrimination on the basis of race, colour, sex, language, religion, political or other opinions, national or social origin, state of wealth, birth or any other situation applying either to the disabled person himself or herself or to his or her family.

3. Disabled persons have the inherent right to respect for their human dignity. Disabled persons, whatever the origin, nature and seriousness of their handicaps and disabilities, have the same fundamental rights as their fellow-citizens of the same age, which implies first and foremost the right to enjoy a decent life, as normal and full as possible.

4. Disabled persons have the same civil and political rights as other human beings; paragraph 7 of the Declaration on the Rights of Mentally Retarded Persons applies to any possible limitation or suppression of those rights for mentally disabled persons.

5. Disabled persons are entitled to the measures designed to enable them to become as self-reliant as possible.

6. Disabled persons have the right to medical, psychological and functional treatment, including prosthetic and orthetic appliances, to medical and social rehabilitation, education, vocational training and rehabilitation, aid, counselling, placement services and other services which will enable them to develop their capabilities and skills to the maximum and will hasten the processes of their social integration or reintegration.

7. Disabled persons have the right to economic and social security and to a decent level of living. They have the right, according to their capabilities, to secure and retain employment or to engage in a useful, productive and remunerative occupation and to join trade unions.

8. Disabled persons are entitled to have their special needs taken into consideration at all stages of economic and social planning.

9. Disabled persons have the right to live with their families or with foster parents and to participate in all social, creative or recreational activities. No disabled person shall be subjected, as far as his or her residence is concerned, to differential treatment other than that required by his or her condition or by the improvement which he or she may derive therefrom. If the stay of a disabled person in a specialized establishment is indispensable, the environment and living conditions therein shall be as close as possible to those of the normal life of a person of his or her age.

10. Disabled persons shall be protected against all exploitation, all regulations and all treatment of a discriminatory, abusive or degrading nature.

11. Disabled persons shall be able to avail themselves of qualified legal aid when such aid proves indispensable for the protection of their persons and property. If judicial proceedings are instituted against them, the legal procedure applied shall take their physical and mental condition fully into account.

12. Organizations of disabled persons may be usefully consulted in all matters regarding the rights of disabled persons.

13. Disabled persons, their families and communities shall be fully informed, by all appropriate means, of the rights contained in this Declaration.

Chapter 7
Declaration on the Right to Development

The General Assembly,

Bearing in mind the purposes and principles of the Charter of the United Nations relating to the achievement of international co-operation in solving international problems of an economic, social, cultural or humanitarian nature, and in promoting and encouraging respect for human rights and fundamental freedoms for all without distinction as to race, sex, language or religion,

Recognizing that development is a comprehensive economic, social, cultural and political process, which aims at the constant improvement of the well-being of the entire population and of all individuals on the basis of their active, free and meaningful participation in development and in the fair distribution of benefits resulting therefrom,

Considering that under the provisions of the Universal Declaration of Human Rights everyone is entitled to a social and international order in which the rights and freedoms set forth in that Declaration can be fully realized,

Recalling the provisions of the International Covenant on Economic, Social and Cultural Rights and of the International Covenant on Civil and Political Rights,

Recalling further the relevant agreements, conventions, resolutions, recommendations and other instruments of the United Nations and its specialized agencies concerning the integral development of the human being, economic and social progress and development of all peoples, including those instruments concerning decolonization, the prevention of discrimination, respect for and observance of, human rights and fundamental freedoms, the maintenance of international peace and security and the further promotion of friendly relations and co-operation among States in accordance with the Charter,

Recalling the right of peoples to self-determination, by virtue of which they have the right freely to determine their political status and to pursue their economic, social and cultural development,

Recalling also the right of peoples to exercise, subject to the relevant provisions of both

Adopted by General Assembly resolution 41/128 of 4 December 1986.

International Covenants on Human Rights, full and complete sovereignty over all their natural wealth and resources,

Mindful of the obligation of States under the Charter to promote universal respect for and observance of human rights and fundamental freedoms for all without distinction of any kind such as race, colour, sex, language, religion, political or other opinion, national or social origin, property, birth or other status,

Considering that the elimination of the massive and flagrant violations of the human rights of the peoples and individuals affected by situations such as those resulting from colonialism, neo-colonialism, apartheid, all forms of racism and racial discrimination, foreign domination and occupation, aggression and threats against national sovereignty, national unity and territorial integrity and threats of war would contribute to the establishment of circumstances propitious to the development of a great part of mankind,

Concerned at the existence of serious obstacles to development, as well as to the complete fulfilment of human beings and of peoples, constituted, inter alia, by the denial of civil, political, economic, social and cultural rights, and considering that all human rights and fundamental freedoms are indivisible and interdependent and that, in order to promote development, equal attention and urgent consideration should be given to the implementation, promotion and protection of civil, political, economic, social and cultural rights and that, accordingly, the promotion of, respect for and enjoyment of certain human rights and fundamental freedoms cannot justify the denial of other human rights and fundamental freedoms,

Considering that international peace and security are essential elements for the realization of the right to development,

Reaffirming that there is a close relationship between disarmament and development and that progress in the field of disarmament would considerably promote progress in the field of development and that resources released through disarmament measures should be devoted to the economic and social development and well-being of all peoples and, in particular, those of the developing countries,

Recognizing that the human person is the central subject of the development process and that development policy should therefore make the human being the main participant and beneficiary of development,

Recognizing that the creation of conditions favourable to the development of peoples and individuals is the primary responsibility of their States,

Aware that efforts at the international level to promote and protect human rights should be accompanied by efforts to establish a new international economic order,

Confirming that the right to development is an inalienable human right and that equality of opportunity for development is a prerogative both of nations and of individuals who make up nations,

Proclaims the following Declaration on the Right to Development:

Article 1

1. The right to development is an inalienable human right by virtue of which every human person and all peoples are entitled to participate in, contribute to, and enjoy economic, social, cultural and political development, in which all human rights and fundamental freedoms can be fully realized.

2. The human right to development also implies the full realization of the right of peoples to self-determination, which includes, subject to the relevant provisions of both International Covenants on Human Rights, the exercise of their inalienable right to full sovereignty over all their natural wealth and resources.

Article 2

1. The human person is the central subject of development and should be the active participant and beneficiary of the right to development.

2. All human beings have a responsibility for development, individually and collectively, taking into account the need for full respect for their human rights and fundamental freedoms as well as their duties to the community, which alone can ensure the free and complete fulfilment of the human being, and they should therefore promote and protect an appropriate political, social and economic order for development.

3. States have the right and the duty to formulate appropriate national development policies that aim at the constant improvement of the well-being of the entire population and of all individuals, on the basis of their active, free and meaningful participation in development and in the fair distribution of the benefits resulting therefrom.

Article 3

1. States have the primary responsibility for the creation of national and international conditions favourable to the realization of the right to development.

2. The realization of the right to development requires full respect for the principles of international law concerning friendly relations and co-operation among States in accordance with the Charter of the United Nations.

3. States have the duty to co-operate with each other in ensuring development and eliminating obstacles to development. States should realize their rights and fulfil their duties in such a manner as to promote a new international economic order based on sovereign equality, interdependence, mutual interest and co-operation among all States, as well as to encourage the observance and realization of human rights.

Article 4

1. States have the duty to take steps, individually and collectively, to formulate international development policies with a view to facilitating the full realization of the right to development.

2. Sustained action is required to promote more rapid development of developing countries. As a complement to the efforts of developing countries, effective international co-operation is essential in providing these countries with appropriate means and facilities to foster their comprehensive development.

Article 5

States shall take resolute steps to eliminate the massive and flagrant violations of the human rights of peoples and human beings affected by situations such as those resulting from apartheid, all forms of racism and racial discrimination, colonialism, foreign domination and occupation, aggression, foreign interference and threats against national sovereignty, national unity and territorial integrity, threats of war and refusal to recognize the fundamental right of peoples to self-determination.

Article 6

1. All States should co-operate with a view to promoting, encouraging and strengthening universal respect for and observance of all human rights and fundamental freedoms for all without any distinction as to race, sex, language or religion.

2. All human rights and fundamental freedoms are indivisible and interdependent; equal attention and urgent consideration should be given to the implementation, promotion and protection of civil, political, economic, social and cultural rights.

3. States should take steps to eliminate obstacles to development resulting from failure to observe civil and political rights, as well as economic social and cultural rights.

Article 7

All States should promote the establishment, maintenance and strengthening of international peace and security and, to that end, should do their utmost to achieve general and complete disarmament under effective international control, as well as to ensure that the resources released by effective disarmament measures are used for comprehensive development, in particular that of the developing countries.

Article 8

1. States should undertake, at the national level, all necessary measures for the realization of the right to development and shall ensure, inter alia, equality of opportunity for all in their access to basic resources, education, health services, food, housing, employment and the fair distribution of income. Effective measures should be undertaken to ensure that women have an active role in the development process. Appropriate economic and social reforms should be carried out with a view to eradicating all social injustices.

2. States should encourage popular participation in all spheres as an important factor in development and in the full realization of all human rights.

Article 9

1. All the aspects of the right to development set forth in the present Declaration are indivisible and interdependent and each of them should be considered in the context of the whole.

2. Nothing in the present Declaration shall be construed as being contrary to the purposes and principles of the United Nations, or as implying that any State, group or person has a right to engage in any activity or to perform any act aimed at the violation of the rights set forth in the Universal Declaration of Human Rights and in the International Covenants on Human Rights.

Article 10

Steps should be taken to ensure the full exercise and progressive enhancement of the right to development, including the formulation, adoption and implementation of policy, legislative and other measures at the national and international levels.

C. SUPPLEMENTARY UN STANDARDS AND RESOURCES

Chapter 1
CESCR General Comment No. 1 (1989) on Reporting by States Parties

1. The reporting obligations which are contained in part IV of the Covenant are designed principally to assist each State party in fulfilling its obligations under the Covenant and, in addition, to provide a basis on which the Council, assisted by the Committee, can discharge its responsibilities for monitoring States parties' compliance with their obligations and for facilitating the realization of economic, social and cultural rights in accordance with the provisions of the Covenant. The Committee considers that it would be incorrect to assume that reporting is essentially only a procedural matter designed solely to satisfy each State party's formal obligation to report to the appropriate international monitoring body. On the contrary, in accordance with the letter and spirit of the Covenant, the processes of preparation and submission of reports by States can, and indeed should, serve to achieve a variety of objectives.

2. A first objective, which is of particular relevance to the initial report required to be submitted within two years of the Covenant's entry into force for the State party concerned, is to ensure that a comprehensive review is undertaken with respect to national legislation, administrative rules and procedures, and practices in an effort to ensure the fullest possible conformity with the Covenant. Such a review might, for example, be undertaken in conjunction with each of the relevant national ministries or other authorities responsible for policy-making and implementation in the different fields covered by the Covenant.

3. A second objective is to ensure that the State party monitors the actual situation with respect to each of the rights on a regular basis and is thus aware of the extent to which the various rights are, or are not, being enjoyed by all individuals within its territory or under its jurisdiction. From the Committee's experience to date, it is clear that the fulfillment of this objective cannot be achieved only by the preparation of aggregate national statistics or estimates, but also requires that special attention be given to any worse-off regions or areas and to any specific groups or subgroups which appear to be particularly vulnerable or disadvantaged. Thus, the essential first step towards promoting the realization of economic, social and cultural rights is diagnosis and knowledge

UN Committee on Economic, Social and Cultural Rights. Original notes omitted.

of the existing situation. The Committee is aware that this process of monitoring and gathering information is a potentially time-consuming and costly one and that international assistance and cooperation, as provided for in Article 2, paragraph 1 and Articles 22 and 23 of the Covenant, may well be required in order to enable some States parties to fulfill the relevant obligations. If that is the case, and the State party concludes that it does not have the capacity to undertake the monitoring process which is an integral part of any process designed to promote accepted goals of public policy and is indispensable to the effective implementation of the Covenant, it may note this fact in its report to the Committee and indicate the nature and extent of any international assistance that it may need.

4. While monitoring is designed to give a detailed overview of the existing situation, the principal value of such an overview is to provide the basis for the elaboration of clearly stated and carefully targeted policies, including the establishment of priorities which reflect the provisions of the Covenant. Therefore, a third objective of the reporting process is to enable the Government to demonstrate that such principled policy-making has in fact been undertaken. While the Covenant makes this obligation explicit only in Article 14 in cases where "compulsory primary education, free of charge" has not yet been secured for all, a comparable obligation "to work out and adopt a detailed plan of action for the progressive implementation" of each of the rights contained in the Covenant is clearly implied by the obligation in Article 2, paragraph 1 "to take steps . . . by all appropriate means . . ."

5. A fourth objective of the reporting process it to facilitate public scrutiny of government policies with respect to economic, social and cultural rights and to encourage the involvement of the various economic, social and cultural sectors of society in the formulation, implementation and review of the relevant policies. In examining reports submitted to it to date, the Committee has welcomed the fact that a number of States parties, reflecting different political and economic systems, have encouraged inputs by such non-governmental groups into the preparation of their reports under the Covenant. Other States have ensured the widespread dissemination of their reports with a view to enabling comments to be made by the public at large. In these ways, the preparation of the report, and its consideration at the national level can come to be of at least as much value as the constructive dialogue conducted at the international level between the Committee and representatives of the reporting State.

6. A fifth objective is to provide a basis on which the State party itself, as well as the Committee, can effectively evaluate the extent to which progress has been made towards the realization of the obligations contained in the Covenant. For this purpose, it may be useful for States to identify specific benchmarks or goals against which their performance in a given area can be assessed. Thus, for example, it is generally agreed that it is important to set specific goals with respect to the reduction of infant mortality, the extent of vaccination of children, the intake of calories per person, the number of persons per health-care provider, etc. In many of these areas, global benchmarks are of limited use, whereas national or other more specific benchmarks can provide an extremely valuable indication of progress.

7. In this regard, the Committee wishes to note that the Covenant attaches particular importance to the concept of "progressive realization" of the relevant rights and, for that reason, the Committee urges States parties to include in their periodic reports information which shows the progress over time, with respect to the effective realization of the relevant rights. By the same token, it is clear that qualitative, as well as quantitative, data are required in order for an adequate assessment of the situation to be made.

8. A sixth objective is to enable the State party itself to develop a better understanding of the problems and shortcomings encountered in efforts to realize progressively the full range of economic, social and cultural rights. For this reason, it is essential that States parties report in detail on the "factors and difficulties" inhibiting such realization. This process of identification and recognition of the relevant difficulties then provides the framework within which more appropriate policies can be devised.

9. A seventh objective is to enable the Committee, and the States parties as a whole, to facilitate the exchange of information among States and to develop a better understanding of the common problems faced by States and a fuller appreciation of the type of measures which might be taken to promote effective realization of each of the rights contained in the Covenant. This part of the process also enables the Committee to identify the most appropriate means by which the international community might assist States, in accordance with Articles 22 and 23 of the Covenant. In order to underline the importance which the Committee attaches to this objective, a separate general comment on those articles will be discussed by the Committee at its fourth session.

Chapter 2
CESCR General Comment No. 2 (1990) on International Technical Assistance Measures (Article 22 of the Covenant)

1. Article 22 of the Covenant establishes a mechanism by which the Economic and Social Council may bring to the attention of relevant United Nations bodies any matters arising out of reports submitted under the Covenant "which may assist such bodies in deciding, each within its field of competence, on the advisability of international measures likely to contribute to the effective progressive implementation of the . . . Covenant." While the primary responsibility under Article 22 is vested in the Council, it is clearly appropriate for the Committee on Economic, Social and Cultural Rights to play an active role in advising and assisting the Council in this regard.

2. Recommendations in accordance with Article 22 may be made to any "organs of the United Nations, their subsidiary organs and specialized agencies concerned with furnishing technical assistance." The Committee considers that this provision should be interpreted so as to include virtually all United Nations organs and agencies involved in any aspect of international development cooperation. It would therefore be appropriate for recommendations in accordance with Article 22 to be addressed, *inter alia*, to the Secretary-General, subsidiary organs of the Council such as the Commission on Human Rights, the Commission on Social Development and the Commission on the Status of Women, other bodies such as UNDP, UNICEF and CDP, agencies such as the World Bank and IMF, and any of the other specialized agencies such as ILO, FAO, UNESCO and WHO.

3. Article 22 could lead either to recommendations of a general policy nature or to more narrowly focused recommendations relating to a specific situation. In the former context, the principal role of the Committee would seem to be to encourage greater attention to efforts to promote economic, social and cultural rights within the framework of international development cooperation activities undertaken by, or with the assistance of, the United Nations and its agencies. In this regard the Committee notes that the Commission on Human Rights, in its resolution 1989/13 of 2 March 1989,

Original notes omitted.

invited it "to give consideration to means by which the various United Nations agencies working in the field of development could best integrate measures designed to promote full respect for economic, social and cultural rights in their activities."

4. As a preliminary practical matter, the Committee notes that its own endeavours would be assisted, and the relevant agencies would also be better informed, if they were to take a greater interest in the work of the Committee. While recognizing that such an interest can be demonstrated in a variety of ways, the Committee observes that attendance by representatives of the appropriate United Nations bodies at its first four sessions has, with the notable exceptions of ILO, UNESCO and WHO, been very low. Similarly, pertinent materials and written information had been received from only a very limited number of agencies. The Committee considers that a deeper understanding of the relevance of economic, social and cultural rights in the context of international development cooperation activities would be considerably facilitated through greater interaction between the Committee and the appropriate agencies. At the very least, the day of general discussion on a specific issue, which the Committee undertakes at each of its sessions, provides an ideal context in which a potentially productive exchange of views can be undertaken.

5. On the broader issues of the promotion of respect for human rights in the context of development activities, the Committee has so far seen only rather limited evidence of specific efforts by United Nations bodies. It notes with satisfaction in this regard the initiative taken jointly by the Centre for Human Rights and UNDP in writing to United Nations Resident Representatives and other field-based officials, inviting their "suggestions and advice, in particular with respect to possible forms of cooperation in ongoing projects [identified] as having a human rights dimension or in new ones in response to a specific Government's request." The Committee has also been informed of long-standing efforts undertaken by ILO to link its own human rights and other international labour standards to its technical cooperation activities.

6. With respect to such activities, two general principles are important. The first is that the two sets of human rights are indivisible and interdependent. This means that efforts to promote one set of rights should also take full account of the other. United Nations agencies involved in the promotion of economic, social and cultural rights should do their utmost to ensure that their activities are fully consistent with the enjoyment of civil and political rights. In negative terms this means that the international agencies should scrupulously avoid involvement in projects which, for example, involve the use of forced labour in contravention of international standards, or promote or reinforce discrimination against individuals or groups contrary to the provisions of the Covenant, or involve large-scale evictions or displacement of persons without the provision of all appropriate protection and compensation. In positive terms, it means that, wherever possible, the agencies should act as advocates of projects and approaches which contribute not only to economic growth or other broadly defined objectives, but also to enhanced enjoyment of the full range of human rights.

7. The second principle of general relevance is that development cooperation activities

do not automatically contribute to the promotion of respect for economic, social and cultural rights. Many activities undertaken in the name of "development" have subsequently been recognized as ill-conceived and even counter-productive in human rights terms. In order to reduce the incidence of such problems, the whole range of issues dealt with in the Covenant should, wherever possible and appropriate, be given specific and careful consideration.

8. Despite the importance of seeking to integrate human rights concerns into development activities, it is true that proposals for such integration can too easily remain at a level of generality. Thus, in an effort to encourage the operationalization of the principle contained in Article 22 of the Covenant, the Committee wishes to draw attention to the following specific measures which merit consideration by the relevant bodies:

(a) As a matter of principle, the appropriate United Nations organs and agencies should specifically recognize the intimate relationship which should be established between development activities and efforts to promote respect for human rights in general, and economic, social and cultural rights in particular. The Committee notes in this regard the failure of each of the first three United Nations Development Decade Strategies to recognize that relationship and urges that the fourth such strategy, to be adopted in 1990, should rectify that omission;

(b) Consideration should be given by United Nations agencies to the proposal, made by the Secretary-General in a report of 1979 that a "human rights impact statement" be required to be prepared in connection with all major development cooperation activities;

(c) The training or briefing given to project and other personnel employed by United Nations agencies should include a component dealing with human rights standards and principles;

(d) Every effort should be made, at each phase of a development project, to ensure that the rights contained in the Covenants are duly taken into account. This would apply, for example, in the initial assessment of the priority needs of a particular country, in the identification of particular projects, in project design, in the implementation of the project, and in its final evaluation.

9. A matter which has been of particular concern to the Committee in the examination of the reports of States parties is the adverse impact of the debt burden and of the relevant adjustment measures on the enjoyment of economic, social and cultural rights in many countries. The Committee recognizes that adjustment programmes will often be unavoidable and that these will frequently involve a major element of austerity. Under such circumstances, however, endeavours to protect the most basic economic, social and cultural rights become more, rather than less, urgent. States parties to the Covenant, as well as the relevant United Nations agencies, should thus make a particular effort to ensure that such protection is, to the maximum extent possible, built-in to programmes and policies designed to promote adjustment. Such an approach, which is sometimes referred to as "adjustment with a human face" or as promoting "the human dimension of development" requires that the goal of protecting the rights of

the poor and vulnerable should become a basic objective of economic adjustment. Similarly, international measures to deal with the debt crisis should take full account of the need to protect economic, social and cultural rights through, inter alia, international cooperation. In many situations, this might point to the need for major debt relief initiatives.

10. Finally, the Committee wishes to draw attention to the important opportunity provided to States parties, in accordance with Article 22 of the Covenant, to identify in their reports any particular needs they might have for technical assistance or development cooperation.

Chapter 3
CESCR General Comment No. 3 (1990) on the Nature of States Parties Obligations (Article 2(1) of the Covenant)

1. Article 2 is of particular importance to a full understanding of the Covenant and must be seen as having a dynamic relationship with all of the other provisions of the Covenant. It describes the nature of the general legal obligations undertaken by States parties to the Covenant. Those obligations include both what may be termed (following the work of the International Law Commission) obligations of conduct and obligations of result. While great emphasis has sometimes been placed on the difference between the formulations used in this provision and that contained in the equivalent Article 2 of the International Covenant on Civil and Political Rights, it is not always recognized that there are also significant similarities. In particular, while the Covenant provides for progressive realization and acknowledges the constraints due to the limits of available resources, it also imposes various obligations which are of immediate effect. Of these, two are of particular importance in understanding the precise nature of States parties obligations. One of these, which is dealt with in a separate general comment, and which is to be considered by the Committee at its sixth session, is the "undertaking to guarantee" that relevant rights "will be exercised without discrimination. . . ."

2. The other is the undertaking in Article 2 (1) "to take steps," which in itself is not qualified or limited by other considerations. The full meaning of the phrase can also be gauged by noting some of the different language versions. In English the undertaking is "to take steps," in French it is "to act" ("s'engage à agir") and in Spanish it is "to adopt measures" ("a adoptar medidas"). Thus while the full realization of the relevant rights may be achieved progressively, steps towards that goal must be taken within a reasonably short time after the Covenant's entry into force for the States concerned. Such steps should be deliberate, concrete and targeted as clearly as possible towards meeting the obligations recognized in the Covenant.

3. The means which should be used in order to satisfy the obligation to take steps are stated in Article 2 (1) to be "all appropriate means, including particularly the adoption

Original notes omitted.

of legislative measures." The Committee recognizes that in many instances legislation is highly desirable and in some cases may even be indispensable. For example, it may be difficult to combat discrimination effectively in the absence of a sound legislative foundation for the necessary measures. In fields such as health, the protection of children and mothers, and education, as well as in respect of the matters dealt with in Articles 6 to 9, legislation may also be an indispensable element for many purposes.

4. The Committee notes that States parties have generally been conscientious in detailing at least some of the legislative measures that they have taken in this regard. It wishes to emphasize, however, that the adoption of legislative measures, as specifically foreseen by the Covenant, is by no means exhaustive of the obligations of States parties. Rather, the phrase "by all appropriate means" must be given its full and natural meaning. While each State party must decide for itself which means are the most appropriate under the circumstances with respect to each of the rights, the "appropriateness" of the means chosen will not always be self-evident. It is therefore desirable that States parties' reports should indicate not only the measures that have been taken but also the basis on which they are considered to be the most "appropriate" under the circumstances. However, the ultimate determination as to whether all appropriate measures have been taken remains one for the Committee to make.

5. Among the measures which might be considered appropriate, in addition to legislation, is the provision of judicial remedies with respect to rights which may, in accordance with the national legal system, be considered justiciable. The Committee notes, for example, that the enjoyment of the rights recognized, without discrimination, will often be appropriately promoted, in part, through the provision of judicial or other effective remedies. Indeed, those States parties which are also parties to the International Covenant on Civil and Political Rights are already obligated (by virtue of arts. 2 (paras. 1 and 3), 3 and 26) of that Covenant to ensure that any person whose rights or freedoms (including the right to equality and non-discrimination) recognized in that Covenant are violated, "shall have an effective remedy" (art. 2 (3) (a)). In addition, there are a number of other provisions in the International Covenant on Economic, Social and Cultural Rights, including Articles 3, 7 (a) (i), 8, 10 (3), 13 (2) (a), (3) and (4) and 15 (3), which would seem to be capable of immediate application by judicial and other organs in many national legal systems. Any suggestion that the provisions indicated are inherently non-self-executing would seem to be difficult to sustain.

6. Where specific policies aimed directly at the realization of the rights recognized in the Covenant have been adopted in legislative form, the Committee would wish to be informed, inter alia, as to whether such laws create any right of action on behalf of individuals or groups who feel that their rights are not being fully realized. In cases where constitutional recognition has been accorded to specific economic, social and cultural rights, or where the provisions of the Covenant have been incorporated directly into national law, the Committee would wish to receive information as to the extent to which these rights are considered to be justiciable (i.e. able to be invoked before the courts). The Committee would also wish to receive specific information as to any instances in which existing constitutional provisions relating to economic, social and cultural rights have been weakened or significantly changed.

7. Other measures which may also be considered "appropriate" for the purposes of Article 2 (1) include, but are not limited to, administrative, financial, educational and social measures.

8. The Committee notes that the undertaking "to take steps . . . by all appropriate means including particularly the adoption of legislative measures" neither requires nor precludes any particular form of government or economic system being used as the vehicle for the steps in question, provided only that it is democratic and that all human rights are thereby respected. Thus, in terms of political and economic systems the Covenant is neutral and its principles cannot accurately be described as being predicated exclusively upon the need for, or the desirability of a socialist or a capitalist system, or a mixed, centrally planned, or *laisser-faire* economy, or upon any other particular approach. In this regard, the Committee reaffirms that the rights recognized in the Covenant are susceptible of realization within the context of a wide variety of economic and political systems, provided only that the interdependence and indivisibility of the two sets of human rights, as affirmed inter alia in the preamble to the Covenant, is recognized and reflected in the system in question. The Committee also notes the relevance in this regard of other human rights and in particular the right to development.

9. The principal obligation of result reflected in Article 2 (1) is to take steps "with a view to achieving progressively the full realization of the rights recognized" in the Covenant. The term "progressive realization" is often used to describe the intent of this phrase. The concept of progressive realization constitutes a recognition of the fact that full realization of all economic, social and cultural rights will generally not be able to be achieved in a short period of time. In this sense the obligation differs significantly from that contained in Article 2 of the International Covenant on Civil and Political Rights which embodies an immediate obligation to respect and ensure all of the relevant rights. Nevertheless, the fact that realization over time, or in other words progressively, is foreseen under the Covenant should not be misinterpreted as depriving the obligation of all meaningful content. It is on the one hand a necessary flexibility device, reflecting the realities of the real world and the difficulties involved for any country in ensuring full realization of economic, social and cultural rights. On the other hand, the phrase must be read in the light of the overall objective, indeed the raison d'être, of the Covenant which is to establish clear obligations for States parties in respect of the full realization of the rights in question. It thus imposes an obligation to move as expeditiously and effectively as possible towards that goal. Moreover, any deliberately retrogressive measures in that regard would require the most careful consideration and would need to be fully justified by reference to the totality of the rights provided for in the Covenant and in the context of the full use of the maximum available resources.

10. On the basis of the extensive experience gained by the Committee, as well as by the body that preceded it, over a period of more than a decade of examining States parties' reports the Committee is of the view that a minimum core obligation to ensure the satisfaction of, at the very least, minimum essential levels of each of the rights is

incumbent upon every State party. Thus, for example, a State party in which any significant number of individuals is deprived of essential foodstuffs, of essential primary health care, of basic shelter and housing, or of the most basic forms of education is, prima facie, failing to discharge its obligations under the Covenant. If the Covenant were to be read in such a way as not to establish such a minimum core obligation, it would be largely deprived of its raison d'être. By the same token, it must be noted that any assessment as to whether a State has discharged its minimum core obligation must also take account of resource constraints applying within the country concerned. Article 2 (1) obligates each State party to take the necessary steps "to the maximum of its available resources." In order for a State party to be able to attribute its failure to meet at least its minimum core obligations to a lack of available resources it must demonstrate that every effort has been made to use all resources that are at its disposition in an effort to satisfy, as a matter of priority, those minimum obligations.

11. The Committee wishes to emphasize, however, that even where the available resources are demonstrably inadequate, the obligation remains for a State party to strive to ensure the widest possible enjoyment of the relevant rights under the prevailing circumstances. Moreover, the obligations to monitor the extent of the realization, or more especially of the non-realization, of economic, social and cultural rights, and to devise strategies and programmes for their promotion, are not in any way eliminated as a result of resource constraints. The Committee has already dealt with these issues in its General Comment 1 (1989).

12. Similarly, the Committee underlines the fact that even in times of severe resources constraints whether caused by a process of adjustment, of economic recession, or by other factors the vulnerable members of society can and indeed must be protected by the adoption of relatively low-cost targeted programmes. In support of this approach the Committee takes note of the analysis prepared by UNICEF entitled "Adjustment with a human face: protecting the vulnerable and promoting growth," the analysis by UNDP in its *Human Development Report 1990*, and the analysis by the World Bank in *World Development Report 1990*.

13. A final element of Article 2 (1), to which attention must be drawn, is that the undertaking given by all States parties is "to take steps, individually and through international assistance and cooperation, especially economic and technical. . . ." The Committee notes that the phrase "to the maximum of its available resources" was intended by the drafters of the Covenant to refer to both the resources existing within a State and those available from the international community through international cooperation and assistance. Moreover, the essential role of such cooperation in facilitating the full realization of the relevant rights is further underlined by the specific provisions contained in Articles 11, 15, 22 and 23. With respect to Article 22 the Committee has already drawn attention, in General Comment 2 (1990), to some of the opportunities and responsibilities that exist in relation to international cooperation. Article 23 also specifically identifies "the furnishing of technical assistance" as well as other activities, as being among the means of "international action for the achievement of the rights recognized. . ."

14. The Committee wishes to emphasize that in accordance with Articles 55 and 56 of the Charter of the United Nations, with well-established principles of international law, and with the provisions of the Covenant itself, international cooperation for development and thus for the realization of economic, social and cultural rights is an obligation of all States. It is particularly incumbent upon those States which are in a position to assist others in this regard. The Committee notes in particular the importance of the Declaration on the Right to Development adopted by the General Assembly in its resolution 41/128 of 4 December 1986 and the need for States parties to take full account of all of the principles recognized therein. It emphasizes that, in the absence of an active programme of international assistance and cooperation on the part of all those States that are in a position to undertake one, the full realization of economic, social and cultural rights will remain an unfulfilled aspiration in many countries. In this respect, the Committee also recalls the terms of its General Comment 2 (1990).

Chapter 4

CESCR General Comment No. 4 (1991) on the Right to Adequate Housing (Article 11(1) of the Covenant)

1. Pursuant to Article 11 (1) of the Covenant, States parties "recognize the right of everyone to an adequate standard of living for himself and his family, including adequate food, clothing and housing, and to the continuous improvement of living conditions." The human right to adequate housing, which is thus derived from the right to an adequate standard of living, is of central importance for the enjoyment of all economic, social and cultural rights.

2. The Committee has been able to accumulate a large amount of information pertaining to this right. Since 1979, the Committee and its predecessors have examined 75 reports dealing with the right to adequate housing. The Committee has also devoted a day of general discussion to the issue at each of its third (see E/1989/22, para. 312) and fourth sessions (E/1990/23, paras. 281–285). In addition, the Committee has taken careful note of information generated by the International Year of Shelter for the Homeless (1987) including the Global Strategy for Shelter to the Year 2000 adopted by the General Assembly in its resolution 42/191 of 11 December 1987. The Committee has also reviewed relevant reports and other documentation of the Commission on Human Rights and the Sub-Commission on Prevention of Discrimination and Protection of Minorities.

3. Although a wide variety of international instruments address the different dimensions of the right to adequate housing, Article 11 (1) of the Covenant is the most comprehensive and perhaps the most important of the relevant provisions.

4. Despite the fact that the international community has frequently reaffirmed the importance of full respect for the right to adequate housing, there remains a disturbingly large gap between the standards set in Article 11 (1) of the Covenant and the situation prevailing in many parts of the world. While the problems are often particularly acute in some developing countries which confront major resource and other constraints, the Committee observes that significant problems of homelessness and inadequate

Original notes omitted.

housing also exist in some of the most economically developed societies. The United Nations estimates that there are over 100 million persons homeless worldwide and over 1 billion inadequately housed. There is no indication that this number is decreasing. It seems clear that no State party is free of significant problems of one kind or another in relation to the right to housing.

5. In some instances, the reports of States parties examined by the Committee have acknowledged and described difficulties in ensuring the right to adequate housing. For the most part, however, the information provided has been insufficient to enable the Committee to obtain an adequate picture of the situation prevailing in the State concerned. This General Comment thus aims to identify some of the principal issues which the Committee considers to be important in relation to this right.

6. The right to adequate housing applies to everyone. While the reference to "himself and his family" reflects assumptions as to gender roles and economic activity patterns commonly accepted in 1966 when the Covenant was adopted, the phrase cannot be read today as implying any limitations upon the applicability of the right to individuals or to female-headed households or other such groups. Thus, the concept of "family" must be understood in a wide sense. Further, individuals, as well as families, are entitled to adequate housing regardless of age, economic status, group or other affiliation or status and other such factors. In particular, enjoyment of this right must, in accordance with Article 2 (2) of the Covenant, not be subject to any form of discrimination.

7. In the Committee's view, the right to housing should not be interpreted in a narrow or restrictive sense which equates it with, for example, the shelter provided by merely having a roof over one's head or views shelter exclusively as a commodity. Rather it should be seen as the right to live somewhere in security, peace and dignity. This is appropriate for at least two reasons. In the first place, the right to housing is integrally linked to other human rights and to the fundamental principles upon which the Covenant is premised. This "inherent dignity of the human person" from which the rights in the Covenant are said to derive requires that the term "housing" be interpreted so as to take account of a variety of other considerations, most importantly that the right to housing should be ensured to all persons irrespective of income or access to economic resources. Secondly, the reference in Article 11 (1) must be read as referring not just to housing but to adequate housing. As both the Commission on Human Settlements and the Global Strategy for Shelter to the Year 2000 have stated: "Adequate shelter means . . . adequate privacy, adequate space, adequate security, adequate lighting and ventilation, adequate basic infrastructure and adequate location with regard to work and basic facilities—all at a reasonable cost."

8. Thus the concept of adequacy is particularly significant in relation to the right to housing since it serves to underline a number of factors which must be taken into account in determining whether particular forms of shelter can be considered to constitute "adequate housing" for the purposes of the Covenant. While adequacy is determined in part by social, economic, cultural, climatic, ecological and other factors, the Committee believes that it is nevertheless possible to identify certain aspects of the

right that must be taken into account for this purpose in any particular context. They include the following:

(a) Legal security of tenure. Tenure takes a variety of forms, including rental (public and private) accommodation, cooperative housing, lease, owner-occupation, emergency housing and informal settlements, including occupation of land or property. Notwithstanding the type of tenure, all persons should possess a degree of security of tenure which guarantees legal protection against forced eviction, harassment and other threats. States parties should consequently take immediate measures aimed at conferring legal security of tenure upon those persons and households currently lacking such protection, in genuine consultation with affected persons and groups;

(b) Availability of services, materials, facilities and infrastructure. An adequate house must contain certain facilities essential for health, security, comfort and nutrition. All beneficiaries of the right to adequate housing should have sustainable access to natural and common resources, safe drinking water, energy for cooking, heating and lighting, sanitation and washing facilities, means of food storage, refuse disposal, site drainage and emergency services;

(c) Affordability. Personal or household financial costs associated with housing should be at such a level that the attainment and satisfaction of other basic needs are not threatened or compromised. Steps should be taken by States parties to ensure that the percentage of housing-related costs is, in general, commensurate with income levels. States parties should establish housing subsidies for those unable to obtain affordable housing, as well as forms and levels of housing finance which adequately reflect housing needs. In accordance with the principle of affordability, tenants should be protected by appropriate means against unreasonable rent levels or rent increases. In societies where natural materials constitute the chief sources of building materials for housing, steps should be taken by States parties to ensure the availability of such materials;

(d) Habitability. Adequate housing must be habitable, in terms of providing the inhabitants with adequate space and protecting them from cold, damp, heat, rain, wind or other threats to health, structural hazards, and disease vectors. The physical safety of occupants must be guaranteed as well. The Committee encourages States parties to comprehensively apply the Health Principles of Housing prepared by WHO which view housing as the environmental factor most frequently associated with conditions for disease in epidemiological analyses; i.e. inadequate and deficient housing and living conditions are invariably associated with higher mortality and morbidity rates;

(e) Accessibility. Adequate housing must be accessible to those entitled to it. Disadvantaged groups must be accorded full and sustainable access to adequate housing resources. Thus, such disadvantaged groups as the elderly, children, the physically disabled, the terminally ill, HIV-positive individuals, persons with persistent medical problems, the mentally ill, victims of natural disasters, people living in disaster-prone areas and other groups should be ensured some degree of priority consideration in the housing sphere. Both housing law and policy should take fully into account the special housing needs of these groups. Within many States parties increasing access to land by landless or impoverished segments of the society should constitute a central policy goal. Discernible governmental obligations need to be developed aiming to substantiate the right of all to a secure place to live in peace and dignity, including access to land as an entitlement;

(f) Location. Adequate housing must be in a location which allows access to employment options, health-care services, schools, child-care centres and other social facilities. This is true both in large cities and in rural areas where the temporal and financial costs of getting to and from the place of work can place excessive demands upon the budgets of poor households. Similarly, housing should not be built on polluted sites nor in immediate proximity to pollution sources that threaten the right to health of the inhabitants;

(g) Cultural adequacy. The way housing is constructed, the building materials used and the policies supporting these must appropriately enable the expression of cultural identity and diversity of housing. Activities geared towards development or modernization in the housing sphere should ensure that the cultural dimensions of housing are not sacrificed, and that, inter alia, modern technological facilities, as appropriate, are also ensured.

9. As noted above, the right to adequate housing cannot be viewed in isolation from other human rights contained in the two International Covenants and other applicable international instruments. Reference has already been made in this regard to the concept of human dignity and the principle of non-discrimination. In addition, the full enjoyment of other rights—such as the right to freedom of expression, the right to freedom of association (such as for tenants and other community-based groups), the right to freedom of residence and the right to participate in public decision-making—is indispensable if the right to adequate housing is to be realized and maintained by all groups in society. Similarly, the right not to be subjected to arbitrary or unlawful interference with one's privacy, family, home or correspondence constitutes a very important dimension in defining the right to adequate housing.

10. Regardless of the state of development of any country, there are certain steps which must be taken immediately. As recognized in the Global Strategy for Shelter and in other international analyses, many of the measures required to promote the right to housing would only require the abstention by the Government from certain practices and a commitment to facilitating "self-help" by affected groups. To the extent that any such steps are considered to be beyond the maximum resources available to a State party, it is appropriate that a request be made as soon as possible for international cooperation in accordance with Articles 11 (1), 22 and 23 of the Covenant, and that the Committee be informed thereof.

11. States parties must give due priority to those social groups living in unfavourable conditions by giving them particular consideration. Policies and legislation should correspondingly not be designed to benefit already advantaged social groups at the expense of others. The Committee is aware that external factors can affect the right to a continuous improvement of living conditions, and that in many States parties overall

living conditions declined during the 1980s. However, as noted by the Committee in its General Comment 2 (1990) (E/1990/23, annex III), despite externally caused problems, the obligations under the Covenant continue to apply and are perhaps even more pertinent during times of economic contraction. It would thus appear to the Committee that a general decline in living and housing conditions, directly attributable to policy and legislative decisions by States parties, and in the absence of accompanying compensatory measures, would be inconsistent with the obligations under the Covenant.

12. While the most appropriate means of achieving the full realization of the right to adequate housing will inevitably vary significantly from one State party to another, the Covenant clearly requires that each State party take whatever steps are necessary for that purpose. This will almost invariably require the adoption of a national housing strategy which, as stated in paragraph 32 of the Global Strategy for Shelter, "defines the objectives for the development of shelter conditions, identifies the resources available to meet these goals and the most cost-effective way of using them and sets out the responsibilities and time-frame for the implementation of the necessary measures." Both for reasons of relevance and effectiveness, as well as in order to ensure respect for other human rights, such a strategy should reflect extensive genuine consultation with, and participation by, all of those affected, including the homeless, the inadequately housed and their representatives. Furthermore, steps should be taken to ensure coordination between ministries and regional and local authorities in order to reconcile related policies (economics, agriculture, environment, energy, etc.) with the obligations under Article 11 of the Covenant.

13. Effective monitoring of the situation with respect to housing is another obligation of immediate effect. For a State party to satisfy its obligations under Article 11 (1) it must demonstrate, inter alia, that it has taken whatever steps are necessary, either alone or on the basis of international cooperation, to ascertain the full extent of homelessness and inadequate housing within its jurisdiction. In this regard, the revised general guidelines regarding the form and contents of reports adopted by the Committee (E/C.12/1991/1) emphasize the need to "provide detailed information about those groups within . . . society that are vulnerable and disadvantaged with regard to housing." They include, in particular, homeless persons and families, those inadequately housed and without ready access to basic amenities, those living in "illegal" settlements, those subject to forced evictions and low-income groups.

14. Measures designed to satisfy a State party's obligations in respect of the right to adequate housing may reflect whatever mix of public and private sector measures considered appropriate. While in some States public financing of housing might most usefully be spent on direct construction of new housing, in most cases, experience has shown the inability of Governments to fully satisfy housing deficits with publicly built housing. The promotion by States parties of "enabling strategies," combined with a full commitment to obligations under the right to adequate housing, should thus be encouraged. In essence, the obligation is to demonstrate that, in aggregate, the measures being taken are sufficient to realize the right for every individual in the shortest possible time in accordance with the maximum of available resources.

15. Many of the measures that will be required will involve resource allocations and policy initiatives of a general kind. Nevertheless, the role of formal legislative and administrative measures should not be underestimated in this context. The Global Strategy for Shelter (paras. 66–67) has drawn attention to the types of measures that might be taken in this regard and to their importance.

16. In some States, the right to adequate housing is constitutionally entrenched. In such cases the Committee is particularly interested in learning of the legal and practical significance of such an approach. Details of specific cases and of other ways in which entrenchment has proved helpful should thus be provided.

17. The Committee views many component elements of the right to adequate housing as being at least consistent with the provision of domestic legal remedies. Depending on the legal system, such areas might include, but are not limited to: (a) legal appeals aimed at preventing planned evictions or demolitions through the issuance of court-ordered injunctions; (b) legal procedures seeking compensation following an illegal eviction; (c) complaints against illegal actions carried out or supported by landlords (whether public or private) in relation to rent levels, dwelling maintenance, and racial or other forms of discrimination; (d) allegations of any form of discrimination in the allocation and availability of access to housing; and (e) complaints against landlords concerning unhealthy or inadequate housing conditions. In some legal systems it would also be appropriate to explore the possibility of facilitating class action suits in situations involving significantly increased levels of homelessness.

18. In this regard, the Committee considers that instances of forced eviction are prima facie incompatible with the requirements of the Covenant and can only be justified in the most exceptional circumstances, and in accordance with the relevant principles of international law.

19. Finally, Article 11 (1) concludes with the obligation of States parties to recognize "the essential importance of international cooperation based on free consent." Traditionally, less than 5 per cent of all international assistance has been directed towards housing or human settlements, and often the manner by which such funding is provided does little to address the housing needs of disadvantaged groups. States parties, both recipients and providers, should ensure that a substantial proportion of financing is devoted to creating conditions leading to a higher number of persons being adequately housed. International financial institutions promoting measures of structural adjustment should ensure that such measures do not compromise the enjoyment of the right to adequate housing. States parties should, when contemplating international financial cooperation, seek to indicate areas relevant to the right to adequate housing where external financing would have the most effect. Such requests should take full account of the needs and views of the affected groups.

Chapter 5
CESCR General Comment No. 5 (1994) on Persons with Disabilities

1. The central importance of the International Covenant on Economic, Social and Cultural Rights in relation to the human rights of persons with disabilities has frequently been underlined by the international community. Thus a 1992 review by the Secretary-General of the implementation of the World Programme of Action concerning Disabled Persons and the United Nations Decade of Disabled Persons concluded that "disability is closely linked to economic and social factors" and that "conditions of living in large parts of the world are so desperate that the provision of basic needs for all—food, water, shelter, health protection and education—must form the cornerstone of national programmes." Even in countries which have a relatively high standard of living, persons with disabilities are very often denied the opportunity to enjoy the full range of economic, social and cultural rights recognized in the Covenant.

2. The Committee on Economic, Social and Cultural Rights, and the working group which preceded it, have been explicitly called upon by both the General Assembly and the Commission on Human Rights to monitor the compliance of States parties to the Covenant with their obligation to ensure the full enjoyment of the relevant rights by persons with disabilities. The Committee's experience to date, however, indicates that States parties have devoted very little attention to this issue in their reports. This appears to be consistent with the Secretary-General's conclusion that "most Governments still lack decisive concerted measures that would effectively improve the situation" of persons with disabilities. It is therefore appropriate to review, and emphasize, some of the ways in which issues concerning persons with disabilities arise in connection with the obligations contained in the Covenant.

3. There is still no internationally accepted definition of the term "disability." For present purposes, however, it is sufficient to rely on the approach adopted in the Standard Rules of 1993, which state: "The term 'disability' summarizes a great number of different functional limitations occurring in any population . . . People may be disabled by physical, intellectual or sensory impairment, medical conditions or mental illness. Such impairments, conditions or illnesses may be permanent or transitory in nature."

Original notes omitted.

4. In accordance with the approach adopted in the Standard Rules, this General Comment uses the term "persons with disabilities" rather than the older term "disabled persons." It has been suggested that the latter term might be misinterpreted to imply that the ability of the individual to function as a person has been disabled.

5. The Covenant does not refer explicitly to persons with disabilities. Nevertheless, the Universal Declaration of Human Rights recognizes that all human beings are born free and equal in dignity and rights and, since the Covenant's provisions apply fully to all members of society, persons with disabilities are clearly entitled to the full range of rights recognized in the Covenant. In addition, insofar as special treatment is necessary, States parties are required to take appropriate measures, to the maximum extent of their available resources, to enable such persons to seek to overcome any disadvantages, in terms of the enjoyment of the rights specified in the Covenant, flowing from their disability. Moreover, the requirement contained in Article 2 (2) of the Covenant that the rights "enunciated . . . will be exercised without discrimination of any kind" based on certain specified grounds "or other status" clearly applies to discrimination on the grounds of disability.

6. The absence of an explicit, disability-related provision in the Covenant can be attributed to the lack of awareness of the importance of addressing this issue explicitly, rather than only by implication, at the time of the drafting of the Covenant over a quarter of a century ago. More recent international human rights instruments have, however, addressed the issue specifically. They include the Convention on the Rights of the Child (art. 23); the African Charter on Human and Peoples' Rights (art. 18 (4)); and the Additional Protocol to the American Convention on Human Rights in the Area of Economic, Social and Cultural Rights (art. 18). Thus it is now very widely accepted that the human rights of persons with disabilities must be protected and promoted through general, as well as specially designed, laws, policies and programmes.

7. In accordance with this approach, the international community has affirmed its commitment to ensuring the full range of human rights for persons with disabilities in the following instruments:

(a) the World Programme of Action concerning Disabled Persons, which provides a policy framework aimed at promoting "effective measures for prevention of disability, rehabilitation and the realization of the goals of 'full participation' of [persons with disabilities] in social life and development, and of 'equality'";

(b) the Guidelines for the Establishment and Development of National Coordinating Committees on Disability or Similar Bodies, adopted in 1990;

(c) the Principles for the Protection of Persons with Mental Illness and for the Improvement of Mental Health Care, adopted in 1991;

(d) the Standard Rules on the Equalization of Opportunities for Persons with Disabilities (hereinafter referred to as the "Standard Rules"), adopted in 1993, the purpose of which is to ensure that all persons with disabilities "may exercise the same rights and obligations as others." The Standard Rules are of major importance and constitute a particularly valuable reference guide in identifying more precisely the relevant obligations of States parties under the Covenant.

I. General Obligations of States Parties

8. The United Nations has estimated that there are more than 500 million persons with disabilities in the world today. Of that number, 80 percent live in rural areas in developing countries. Seventy percent of the total are estimated to have either limited or no access to the services they need. The challenge of improving the situation of persons with disabilities is thus of direct relevance to every State party to the Covenant. While the means chosen to promote the full realization of the economic, social and cultural rights of this group will inevitably differ significantly from one country to another, there is no country in which a major policy and programme effort is not required.

9. The obligation of States parties to the Covenant to promote progressive realization of the relevant rights to the maximum of their available resources clearly requires Governments to do much more than merely abstain from taking measures which might have a negative impact on persons with disabilities. The obligation in the case of such a vulnerable and disadvantaged group is to take positive action to reduce structural disadvantages and to give appropriate preferential treatment to people with disabilities in order to achieve the objectives of full participation and equality within society for all persons with disabilities. This almost invariably means that additional resources will need to be made available for this purpose and that a wide range of specially tailored measures will be required.

10. According to a report by the Secretary-General, developments over the past decade in both developed and developing countries have been especially unfavourable from the perspective of persons with disabilities: ". . . current economic and social deterioration, marked by low-growth rates, high unemployment, reduced public expenditure, current structural adjustment programmes and privatization, have negatively affected programmes and services . . . If the present negative trends continue, there is the risk that [persons with disabilities] may increasingly be relegated to the margins of society, dependent on ad hoc support." As the Committee has previously observed (General Comment No. 3 (Fifth session, 1990), para. 12), the duty of States parties to protect the vulnerable members of their societies assumes greater rather than less importance in times of severe resource constraints.

11. Given the increasing commitment of Governments around the world to market-based policies, it is appropriate in that context to emphasize certain aspects of States parties' obligations. One is the need to ensure that not only the public sphere, but also the private sphere, are, within appropriate limits, subject to regulation to ensure the equitable treatment of persons with disabilities. In a context in which arrangements for the provision of public services are increasingly being privatized and in which the free market is being relied on to an ever greater extent, it is essential that private employers, private suppliers of goods and services, and other non-public entities be subject to

both non-discrimination and equality norms in relation to persons with disabilities. In circumstances where such protection does not extend beyond the public domain, the ability of persons with disabilities to participate in the mainstream of community activities and to realize their full potential as active members of society will be severely and often arbitrarily constrained. This is not to imply that legislative measures will always be the most effective means of seeking to eliminate discrimination within the private sphere. Thus, for example, the Standard Rules place particular emphasis on the need for States to "take action to raise awareness in society about persons with disabilities, their rights, their needs, their potential and their contribution."

12. In the absence of government intervention there will always be instances in which the operation of the free market will produce unsatisfactory results for persons with disabilities, either individually or as a group, and in such circumstances it is incumbent on Governments to step in and take appropriate measures to temper, complement, compensate for, or override the results produced by market forces. Similarly, while it is appropriate for Governments to rely on private, voluntary groups to assist persons with disabilities in various ways, such arrangements can never absolve Governments from their duty to ensure full compliance with their obligations under the Covenant. As the World Programme of Action concerning Disabled Persons states, "the ultimate responsibility for remedying the conditions that lead to impairment and for dealing with the consequences of disability rests with Governments."

II. Means of Implementation

13. The methods to be used by States parties in seeking to implement their obligations under the Covenant towards persons with disabilities are essentially the same as those available in relation to other obligations (see General Comment No. 1 (Third session, 1989)). They include the need to ascertain, through regular monitoring, the nature and scope of the problems existing within the State; the need to adopt appropriately tailored policies and programmes to respond to the requirements thus identified; the need to legislate where necessary and to eliminate any existing discriminatory legislation; and the need to make appropriate budgetary provisions or, where necessary, seek international cooperation and assistance. In the latter respect, international cooperation in accordance with Articles 22 and 23 of the Covenant is likely to be a particularly important element in enabling some developing countries to fulfill their obligations under the Covenant.

14. In addition, it has been consistently acknowledged by the international community that policy-making and programme implementation in this area should be undertaken on the basis of close consultation with, and involvement of, representative groups of the persons concerned. For this reason, the Standard Rules recommend that everything possible be done to facilitate the establishment of national coordinating committees, or similar bodies, to serve as a national focal point on disability matters. In doing so, Governments should take account of the 1990 Guidelines for the

Establishment and Development of National Coordinating Committees on Disability or Similar Bodies.

III. The Obligation to Eliminate Discrimination on the Grounds of Disability

15. Both de jure and de facto discrimination against persons with disabilities have a long history and take various forms. They range from invidious discrimination, such as the denial of educational opportunities, to more "subtle" forms of discrimination such as segregation and isolation achieved through the imposition of physical and social barriers. For the purposes of the Covenant, "disability-based discrimination" may be defined as including any distinction, exclusion, restriction or preference, or denial of reasonable accommodation based on disability which has the effect of nullifying or impairing the recognition, enjoyment or exercise of economic, social or cultural rights. Through neglect, ignorance, prejudice and false assumptions, as well as through exclusion, distinction or separation, persons with disabilities have very often been prevented from exercising their economic, social or cultural rights on an equal basis with persons without disabilities. The effects of disability-based discrimination have been particularly severe in the fields of education, employment, housing, transport, cultural life, and access to public places and services.

16. Despite some progress in terms of legislation over the past decade, the legal situation of persons with disabilities remains precarious. In order to remedy past and present discrimination, and to deter future discrimination, comprehensive anti-discrimination legislation in relation to disability would seem to be indispensable in virtually all States parties. Such legislation should not only provide persons with disabilities with judicial remedies as far as possible and appropriate, but also provide for social-policy programmes which enable persons with disabilities to live an integrated, self-determined and independent life.

17. Anti-discrimination measures should be based on the principle of equal rights for persons with disabilities and the non-disabled, which, in the words of the World Programme of Action concerning Disabled Persons, "implies that the needs of each and every individual are of equal importance, that these needs must be made the basis for the planning of societies, and that all resources must be employed in such a way as to ensure, for every individual, equal opportunity for participation. Disability policies should ensure the access of [persons with disabilities] to all community services."

18. Because appropriate measures need to be taken to undo existing discrimination and to establish equitable opportunities for persons with disabilities, such actions should not be considered discriminatory in the sense of Article 2 (2) of the International Covenant on Economic, Social and Cultural Rights as long as they are based on the principle of equality and are employed only to the extent necessary to achieve that objective.

IV. Specific Provisions of the Covenant

A. Article 3. Equal rights for men and women

19. Persons with disabilities are sometimes treated as genderless human beings. As a result, the double discrimination suffered by women with disabilities is often neglected. Despite frequent calls by the international community for particular emphasis to be placed upon their situation, very few efforts have been undertaken during the decade. The neglect of women with disabilities is mentioned several times in the report of the Secretary-General on the implementation of the World Programme of Action. The Committee therefore urges States parties to address the situation of women with disabilities, with high priority being given in future to the implementation of economic, social and cultural rights-related programmes.

B. Articles 6–8. Rights relating to work

20. The field of employment is one in which disability-based discrimination has been prominent and persistent. In most countries the unemployment rate among persons with disabilities is two to three times higher than the unemployment rate for persons without disabilities. Where persons with disabilities are employed, they are mostly engaged in low-paid jobs with little social and legal security and are often segregated from the mainstream of the labour market. The integration of persons with disabilities into the regular labour market should be actively supported by States.

21. The "right of everyone to the opportunity to gain his living by work which he freely chooses or accepts" (art. 6 (1)) is not realized where the only real opportunity open to disabled workers is to work in so-called "sheltered" facilities under substandard conditions. Arrangements whereby persons with a certain category of disability are effectively confined to certain occupations or to the production of certain goods may violate this right. Similarly, in the light of Principle 13 (3) of the Principles for the Protection of Persons with Mental Illness and for the Improvement of Mental Health Care, "therapeutical treatment" in institutions which amounts to forced labour is also incompatible with the Covenant. In this regard, the prohibition on forced labour contained in the International Covenant on Civil and Political Rights is also of potential relevance.

22. According to the Standard Rules, persons with disabilities, whether in rural or urban areas, must have equal opportunities for productive and gainful employment in the labour market. For this to happen it is particularly important that artificial barriers to integration in general, and to employment in particular, be removed. As the International Labour Organisation has noted, it is very often the physical barriers that society has erected in areas such as transport, housing and the workplace which are then cited as the reason why persons with disabilities cannot be employed. For example, as long as workplaces are designed and built in ways that make them inaccessible to wheelchairs, employers will be able to "justify" their failure to employ wheelchair

users. Governments should also develop policies which promote and regulate flexible and alternative work arrangements that reasonably accommodate the needs of disabled workers.

23. Similarly, the failure of Governments to ensure that modes of transportation are accessible to persons with disabilities greatly reduces the chances of such persons finding suitable, integrated jobs, taking advantage of educational and vocational training, or commuting to facilities of all types. Indeed, the provision of access to appropriate and, where necessary, specially tailored forms of transportation is crucial to the realization by persons with disabilities of virtually all the rights recognized in the Covenant.

24. The "technical and vocational guidance and training programmes" required under Article 6 (2) of the Covenant should reflect the needs of all persons with disabilities, take place in integrated settings, and be planned and implemented with the full involvement of representatives of persons with disabilities.

25. The right to "the enjoyment of just and favourable conditions of work" (art. 7) applies to all disabled workers, whether they work in sheltered facilities or in the open labour market. Disabled workers may not be discriminated against with respect to wages or other conditions if their work is equal to that of non-disabled workers. States parties have a responsibility to ensure that disability is not used as an excuse for creating low standards of labour protection or for paying below minimum wages.

26. Trade union-related rights (art. 8) apply equally to workers with disabilities and regardless of whether they work in special work facilities or in the open labour market. In addition, Article 8, read in conjunction with other rights such as the right to freedom of association, serves to emphasize the importance of the right of persons with disabilities to form their own organizations. If these organizations are to be effective in "the promotion and protection of [the] economic and social interests" (art. 8 (1) (a)) of such persons, they should be consulted regularly by government bodies and others in relation to all matters affecting them; it may also be necessary that they be supported financially and otherwise so as to ensure their viability.

27. The International Labour Organization has developed valuable and comprehensive instruments with respect to the work-related rights of persons with disabilities, including in particular Convention No. 159 (1983) concerning vocational rehabilitation and employment of persons with disabilities. The Committee encourages States parties to the Covenant to consider ratifying that Convention.

C. Article 9. Social security

28. Social security and income-maintenance schemes are of particular importance for persons with disabilities. As stated in the Standard Rules, "States should ensure the provision of adequate income support to persons with disabilities who, owing to disability or disability-related factors, have temporarily lost or received a reduction in their income or have been denied employment opportunities." Such support should reflect

the special needs for assistance and other expenses often associated with disability. In addition, as far as possible, the support provided should also cover individuals (who are overwhelmingly female) who undertake the care of a person with disabilities. Such persons, including members of the families of persons with disabilities, are often in urgent need of financial support because of their assistance role.

29. Institutionalization of persons with disabilities, unless rendered necessary for other reasons, cannot be regarded as an adequate substitute for the social security and income-support rights of such persons.

D. Article 10. Protection of the family and of mothers and children

30. In the case of persons with disabilities, the Covenant's requirement that "protection and assistance" be rendered to the family means that everything possible should be done to enable such persons, when they so wish, to live with their families. Article 10 also implies, subject to the general principles of international human rights law, the right of persons with disabilities to marry and have their own family. These rights are frequently ignored or denied, especially in the case of persons with mental disabilities. In this and other contexts, the term "family" should be interpreted broadly and in accordance with appropriate local usage. States parties should ensure that laws and social policies and practices do not impede the realization of these rights. Persons with disabilities should have access to necessary counselling services in order to fulfill their rights and duties within the family.

31. Women with disabilities also have the right to protection and support in relation to motherhood and pregnancy. As the Standard Rules state, "persons with disabilities must not be denied the opportunity to experience their sexuality, have sexual relationships and experience parenthood." The needs and desires in question should be recognized and addressed in both the recreational and the procreational contexts. These rights are commonly denied to both men and women with disabilities worldwide. Both the sterilization of, and the performance of an abortion on, a woman with disabilities without her prior informed consent are serious violations of Article 10 (2).

32. Children with disabilities are especially vulnerable to exploitation, abuse and neglect and are, in accordance with Article 10 (3) of the Covenant (reinforced by the corresponding provisions of the Convention on the Rights of the Child), entitled to special protection.

E. Article 11. The right to an adequate standard of living

33. In addition to the need to ensure that persons with disabilities have access to adequate food, accessible housing and other basic material needs, it is also necessary to ensure that "support services, including assistive devices" are available "for persons with disabilities, to assist them to increase their level of independence in their daily living and to exercise their rights." The right to adequate clothing also assumes a special

significance in the context of persons with disabilities who have particular clothing needs, so as to enable them to function fully and effectively in society. Wherever possible, appropriate personal assistance should also be provided in this connection. Such assistance should be undertaken in a manner and spirit which fully respect the human rights of the person(s) concerned. Similarly, as already noted by the Committee in paragraph 8 of General Comment No. 4 (Sixth session, 1991), the right to adequate housing includes the right to accessible housing for persons with disabilities.

F. Article 12. The right to physical and mental health

34. According to the Standard Rules, "States should ensure that persons with disabilities, particularly infants and children, are provided with the same level of medical care within the same system as other members of society." The right to physical and mental health also implies the right to have access to, and to benefit from, those medical and social services—including orthopaedic devices—which enable persons with disabilities to become independent, prevent further disabilities and support their social integration. Similarly, such persons should be provided with rehabilitation services which would enable them "to reach and sustain their optimum level of independence and functioning." All such services should be provided in such a way that the persons concerned are able to maintain full respect for their rights and dignity.

G. Articles 13 and 14. The right to education

35. School programmes in many countries today recognize that persons with disabilities can best be educated within the general education system. Thus the Standard Rules provide that "States should recognize the principle of equal primary, secondary and tertiary educational opportunities for children, youth and adults with disabilities, in integrated settings." In order to implement such an approach, States should ensure that teachers are trained to educate children with disabilities within regular schools and that the necessary equipment and support are available to bring persons with disabilities up to the same level of education as their non-disabled peers. In the case of deaf children, for example, sign language should be recognized as a separate language to which the children should have access and whose importance should be acknowledged in their overall social environment.

H. Article 15. The right to take part in cultural life and enjoy the benefits of scientific progress

36. The Standard Rules provide that "States should ensure that persons with disabilities have the opportunity to utilize their creative, artistic and intellectual potential, not only for their own benefit, but also for the enrichment of their community, be they in urban or rural areas. . . . States should promote the accessibility to and availability of places for cultural performances and services. . . ." The same applies to places for recreation, sports and tourism.

37. The right to full participation in cultural and recreational life for persons with disabilities further requires that communication barriers be eliminated to the greatest extent possible. Useful measures in this regard might include "the use of talking books, papers written in simple language and with clear format and colours for persons with mental disability, [and] adapted television and theatre for deaf persons."

38. In order to facilitate the equal participation in cultural life of persons with disabilities, Governments should inform and educate the general public about disability. In particular, measures must be taken to dispel prejudices or superstitious beliefs against persons with disabilities, for example those that view epilepsy as a form of spirit possession or a child with disabilities as a form of punishment visited upon the family. Similarly, the general public should be educated to accept that persons with disabilities have as much right as any other person to make use of restaurants, hotels, recreation centres and cultural venues.

Chapter 6
CESCR General Comment No. 6 (1995) on the Economic, Social and Cultural Rights of Older Persons

1. Introduction

The world population is aging at a steady, quite spectacular rate. The total number of persons aged 60 and above rose from 200 million in 1950 to 400 million in 1982 and is projected to reach 600 million in the year 2001 and 1.2 billion by the year 2025, at which time over 70 percent of them will be living in what are today's developing countries. The number of people aged 80 and above has grown and continues to grow even more dramatically, going from 13 million in 1950 to over 50 million today and projected to increase to 137 million in 2025. This is the fastest growing population group in the world, projected to increase by a factor of ten between 1950 and 2025, compared with a factor of six for the group aged 60 and above and a factor of little more than three for the total population.

2. These figures are illustrations of a quiet revolution, but one which has far-reaching and unpredictable consequences and which is now affecting the social and economic structures of societies both at the world level and at the country level, and will affect them even more in future.

3. Most of the States parties to the Covenant, and the industrialized countries in particular, are faced with the task of adapting their social and economic policies to the aging of their populations, especially as regards social security. In the developing countries, the absence or deficiencies of social security coverage are being aggravated by the emigration of the younger members of the population and the consequent weakening of the traditional role of the family, the main support of older people.

2. Internationally Endorsed Policies in Relation to Older Persons

4. In 1982 the World Assembly on Aging adopted the Vienna International Plan of Action on Aging. This important document was endorsed by the General Assembly and is a very useful guide, for it details the measures that should be taken by Member States to safeguard the rights of older persons within the context of the rights proclaimed by

Original notes omitted.

the International Covenants on Human Rights. It contains 62 recommendations, many of which are of direct relevance to the Covenant.

5. In 1991 the General Assembly adopted the United Nations Principles for Older Persons which, because of their programmatic nature, is also an important document in the present context. It is divided into five sections which correlate closely to the rights recognized in the Covenant. "Independence" includes access to adequate food, water, shelter, clothing and health care. To these basic rights are added the opportunity to remunerated work and access to education and training. By "participation" is meant that older persons should participate actively in the formulation and implementation of policies that affect their well-being and share their knowledge and skills with younger generations, and should be able to form movements and associations. The section headed "care" proclaims that older persons should benefit from family care, health care and be able to enjoy human rights and fundamental freedoms when residing in a shelter, care or treatment facility. With regard to "self-fulfillment," the Principles that older persons should pursue opportunities for the full development of their potential through access to the educational, cultural, spiritual and recreational resources of their societies. Lastly, the section entitled "dignity" states that older persons should be able to live in dignity and security and be free of exploitation and physical or mental abuse, should be treated fairly, regardless of age, gender, racial or ethnic background, disability, financial situation or any other status, and be valued independently of their economic contribution.

6. In 1992, the General Assembly adopted eight global targets on aging for the year 2001 and a brief guide for setting national targets. In a number of important respects, these global targets serve to reinforce the obligations of States parties to the Covenant.

7. Also in 1992, and in commemoration of the tenth anniversary of the adoption of the Vienna International Plan of Action by the Conference on Aging, the General Assembly adopted the Proclamation on Aging in which it urged support of national initiatives on aging so that older women are given adequate support for their largely unrecognized contributions to society and older men are encouraged to develop social, cultural and emotional capacities which they may have been prevented from developing during breadwinning years; families are supported in providing care and all family members encouraged to cooperate in caregiving; and that international cooperation is expanded in the context of the strategies for reaching the global targets on aging for the year 2001. It also proclaimed the year 1999 as the International Year of Older Persons in recognition of humanity's demographic "coming of age."

8. The United Nations specialized agencies, especially the International Labour Organization, have also given attention to the problem of aging in their respective fields of competence.

3. The Rights of Older Persons in Relation to the International Covenant on Economic, Social and Cultural Rights

9. The terminology used to describe older persons varies considerably, even in international documents. It includes: "older persons," "the aged," "the elderly," "the third

age," "the aging," and, to denote persons more than 80 years of age, "the fourth age." The Committee opted for "older persons" (in French, *personnes âgées*; in Spanish, *personas mayores*), the term employed in General Assembly resolutions 47/5 and 48/98. According to the practice in the United Nations statistical services, these terms cover persons aged 60 and above (Eurostat, the statistical service of the European Union, considers "older persons" to mean persons aged 65 or above, since 65 is the most common age of retirement and the trend is towards later retirement still).

10. The International Covenant on Economic, Social and Cultural Rights does not contain any explicit reference to the rights of older persons, although Article 9 dealing with "the right of everyone to social security, including social insurance," implicitly recognizes the right to old-age benefits. Nevertheless, in view of the fact that the Covenant's provisions apply fully to all members of society, it is clear that older persons are entitled to enjoy the full range of rights recognized in the Covenant. This approach is also fully reflected in the Vienna International Plan of Action on Aging. Moreover, insofar as respect for the rights of older persons requires special measures to be taken, States parties are required by the Covenant to do so to the maximum of their available resources.

11. Another important issue is whether discrimination on the basis of age is prohibited by the Covenant. Neither the Covenant nor the Universal Declaration of Human Rights refers explicitly to age as one of the prohibited grounds. Rather than being seen as an intentional exclusion, this omission is probably best explained by the fact that, when these instruments were adopted, the problem of demographic aging was not as evident or as pressing as it is now.

12. This is not determinative of the matter, however, since the prohibition of discrimination on the grounds of "other status" could be interpreted as applying to age. The Committee notes that while it may not yet be possible to conclude that discrimination on the grounds of age is comprehensively prohibited by the Covenant, the range of matters in relation to which such discrimination can be accepted is very limited. Moreover, it must be emphasized that the unacceptableness of discrimination against older persons is underlined in many international policy documents and is confirmed in the legislation of the vast majority of States. In the few areas in which discrimination continues to be tolerated, such as in relation to mandatory retirement ages or access to tertiary education, there is a clear trend towards the elimination of such barriers. The Committee is of the view that States parties should seek to expedite this trend to the greatest extent possible.

13. Accordingly, the Committee on Economic, Social and Cultural Rights is of the view that States parties to the Covenant are obligated to pay particular attention to promoting and protecting the economic, social and cultural rights of older persons. The Committee's own role in this regard is rendered all the more important by the fact that, unlike the case of other population groups such as women and children, no comprehensive international convention yet exists in relation to the rights of older persons and no binding supervisory arrangements attach to the various sets of United Nations principles in this area.

14. By the end of its thirteenth session, the Committee and, before that, its predecessor, the Sessional Working Group of Governmental Experts, had examined 144 initial reports, 70 second periodic reports and 20 initial and periodic global reports on Articles 1 to 15. This examination made it possible to identify many of the problems that may be encountered in implementing the Covenant in a considerable number of States parties that represent all the regions of the world and have different political, socio-economic and cultural systems. The reports examined to date have not provided any information in a systematic way on the situation of older persons with regard to compliance with the Covenant, apart from information, of varying completeness, on the implementation of Article 9 relating to the right to social security.

15. In 1993, the Committee devoted a day of general discussion to this issue in order to plan its future activity in this area. Moreover, it has, at recent sessions, begun to attach substantially more importance to information on the rights of older persons and its questioning has elicited some very valuable information in some instances. Nevertheless, the Committee notes that the great majority of States parties reports continue to make little reference to this important issue. It therefore wishes to indicate that, in future, it will insist that the situation of older persons in relation to each of the rights recognized in the Covenant should be adequately addressed in all reports. The remainder of this General Comment identifies the specific issues which are relevant in this regard.

4. General Obligations of States Parties

16. Older persons as a group are as heterogeneous and varied as the rest of the population and their situation depends on a country's economic and social situation, on demographic, environmental cultural and employment factors and, at the individual level, on the family situation, the level of education, the urban or rural environment and the occupation of workers and retirees.

17. Side by side with older persons who are in good health and whose financial situation is acceptable, there are many who do not have adequate means of support, even in developed countries, and who feature prominently among the most vulnerable, marginal and unprotected groups. In times of recession and of restructuring of the economy, older persons are particularly at risk. As the Committee has previously stressed (General Comment No. 3 (1990), para. 12), even in times of severe resource constraints, States parties have the duty to protect the vulnerable members of society.

18. The methods that States parties use to fulfill the obligations they have assumed under the Covenant in respect of older persons will be basically the same as those for the fulfillment of other obligations (see General Comment No. 1 (1989)). They include the need to determine the nature and scope of problems within a State through regular monitoring, the need to adopt properly designed policies and programmes to meet requirements, the need to enact legislation when necessary and to eliminate any discriminatory legislation and the need to ensure the relevant budget support or, as appropriate, to request international cooperation. In the latter connection, international

cooperation in accordance with Articles 22 and 23 of the Covenant may be a particularly important way of enabling some developing countries to fulfill their obligations under the Covenant.

19. In this context, attention may be drawn to Global Target No. 1, adopted by the General Assembly in 1992, which calls for the establishment of national support infrastructures to promote policies and programmes on aging in national and international development plans and programmes. In this regard, the Committee notes that one of the United Nations Principles for Older Persons which Governments were encouraged to incorporate into their national programmes is that older persons should be able to form movements or associations of older persons.

5. Specific Provisions of the Covenant

Article 3. Equal rights of men and women

20. In accordance with Article 3 of the Covenant, by which States parties undertake "to ensure the equal right of men and women to the enjoyment of all economic, social and cultural rights," the Committee considers that States parties should pay particular attention to older women who, because they have spent all or part of their lives caring for their families without engaging in a remunerated activity entitling them to an old-age pension, and who are also not entitled to a widow's pension, are often in critical situations.

21. To deal with such situations and comply fully with Article 9 of the Covenant and paragraph 2 (h) of the Proclamation on Aging, States parties should institute non-contributory old-age benefits or other assistance for all persons, regardless of their sex, who find themselves without resources on attaining an age specified in national legislation. Given their greater life expectancy and the fact that it is more often they who have no contributory pensions, women would be the principal beneficiaries.

Articles 6 to 8. Rights relating to work

22. Article 6 of the Covenant requires States parties to take appropriate steps to safeguard the right of everyone to the opportunity to gain a living by work which is freely chosen or accepted. In this regard, the Committee, bearing in mind that older workers who have not reached retirement age often encounter problems in finding and keeping jobs, stresses the need for measures to prevent discrimination on grounds of age in employment and occupation.

23. The right "to the enjoyment of just and favourable conditions of work" (Covenant, art. 7) is of special importance for ensuring that older workers enjoy safe working conditions until their retirement. In particular, it is desirable, to employ older workers in circumstances in which the best use can be made of their experience and know-how.

24. In the years preceding retirement, retirement preparation programmes should be

implemented, with the participation of representative organizations of employers and workers and other bodies concerned, to prepare older workers to cope with their new situation. Such programmes should, in particular, provide older workers with information about: their rights and obligations as pensioners; the opportunities and conditions for continuing an occupational activity or undertaking voluntary work; means of combating detrimental effects of aging; facilities for adult education and cultural activities, and the use of leisure time.

25. The rights protected by Article 8 of the Covenant, namely, trade union rights, including after retirement age, must be applied to older workers.

Article 9. Right to social security

26. Article 9 of the Covenant provides generally that States parties "recognize the right of everyone to social security," without specifying the type or level of protection to be guaranteed. However, the term "social security" implicitly covers all the risks involved in the loss of means of subsistence for reasons beyond a person's control.

27. In accordance with Article 9 of the Covenant and the provisions concerning implementation of the ILO social security conventions—Convention No. 102 concerning Social Security (Minimum Standards) (1952) and Convention No. 128 concerning Invalidity, Old-Age and Survivors' Benefits (1967)—States parties must take appropriate measures to establish general regimes of compulsory old-age insurance, starting at a particular age, to be prescribed by national law.

28. In keeping with the recommendations contained in the two ILO Conventions mentioned above and Recommendation No. 162, the Committee invites States parties to establish retirement age so that it is flexible, depending on the occupations performed and the working ability of elderly persons, with due regard to demographic, economic and social factors.

29. In order to give effect to the provisions of Article 9 of the Covenant, States parties must guarantee the provision of survivors' and orphans' benefits on the death of the breadwinner who was covered by social security or receiving a pension.

30. Furthermore, as already observed in paragraphs 20 and 21, in order fully to implement the provisions of Article 9 of the Covenant, States parties should, within the limits of available resources, provide non-contributory old-age benefits and other assistance for all older persons, who, when reaching the age prescribed in national legislation, have not completed a qualifying period of contribution and are not entitled to an old-age pension or other social security benefit or assistance and have no other source of income.

Article 10. Protection of the family

31. On the basis of Article 10, paragraph 1, of the Covenant and Recommendations 25 and 29 of the Vienna International Plan of Action on Aging, States parties should

make all the necessary efforts to support, protect and strengthen the family and help it, in accordance with each society's system of cultural values, to respond to the needs of its dependent aging members. Recommendation 29 encourages Governments and non-governmental organizations to establish social services to support the whole family when there are elderly people at home and to implement measures especially for low-income families who wish to keep elderly people at home. This assistance should also be provided for persons living alone or elderly couples wishing to remain at home.

Article 11. Right to an adequate standard of living

32. Of the United Nations Principles for Older Persons, Principle 1, which stands at the beginning of the section relating to the independence of older persons, provides that: "Older persons should have access to adequate food, water, shelter, clothing and health care through the provision of income, family and community support and self-help." The Committee attaches great importance to this principle, which demands for older persons the rights contained in Article 11 of the Covenant.

33. Recommendations 19 to 24 of the Vienna International Plan of Action on Aging emphasize that housing for the elderly must be viewed as more than mere shelter and that, in addition to the physical, it has psychological and social significance which should be taken into account. Accordingly, national policies should help elderly persons to continue to live in their own homes as long as possible, through the restoration, development and improvement of homes and their adaptation to the ability of those persons to gain access to and use them (recommendation 19). Recommendation 20 stresses the need for urban rebuilding and development planning and law to pay special attention to the problems of the aging, assisting in securing their social integration, while Recommendation 22 draws attention to the need to take account of the functional capacity of the elderly in order to provide them with a better living environment and facilitate mobility and communication through the provision of adequate means of transport.

Article 12. Right to physical and mental health

34. With a view to the realization of the right of elderly persons to the enjoyment of a satisfactory standard of physical and mental health, in accordance with Article 12, paragraph 1, of the Covenant, States parties should take account of the content of Recommendations 1 to 17 of the Vienna International Plan of Action on Aging, which focus entirely on providing guidelines on health policy to preserve the health of the elderly and take a comprehensive view, ranging from prevention and rehabilitation to the care of the terminally ill.

35. Clearly, the growing number of chronic, degenerative diseases and the high hospitalization costs they involve cannot be dealt with only by curative treatment. In this regard, States parties should bear in mind that maintaining health into old age requires

investments during the entire life span, basically through the adoption of healthy lifestyles (food, exercise, elimination of tobacco and alcohol, etc.). Prevention, through regular checks suited to the needs of the elderly, plays a decisive role, as does rehabilitation, by maintaining the functional capacities of elderly persons, with a resulting decrease in the cost of investments in health care and social services.

Articles 13 to 15. Right to education and culture

36. Article 13, Paragraph 1, of the Covenant recognizes the right of everyone to education. In the case of the elderly, this right must be approached from two different and complementary points of view: (a) the right of elderly persons to benefit from educational programmes; and (b) making the know-how and experience of elderly persons available to younger generations.

37. With regard to the former, States parties should take account of: (a) the recommendations in Principle 16 of the United Nations Principles for Older Persons to the effect that older persons should have access to suitable education programmes and training and should, therefore, on the basis of their preparation, abilities and motivation, be given access to the various levels of education through the adoption of appropriate measures regarding literacy training, life-long education, access to university, etc.; and (b) Recommendation 47 of the Vienna International Plan of Action on Aging, which, in accordance with the concept of life-long education promulgated by the United Nations Educational, Scientific and Cultural Organization (UNESCO), recommends informal, community-based and recreation-oriented programmes for the elderly in order to develop their sense of self-reliance and the community's sense of responsibility. Such programmes should enjoy the support of national Governments and international organizations.

38. With regard to the use of the know-how and experience of older persons, as referred to in the part of the recommendations of the Vienna International Plan of Action on Aging dealing with education (paras. 74–76), attention is drawn to the important role that elderly and old persons still play in most societies as the transmitters of information, knowledge, traditions and spiritual values and to the fact that this important tradition should not be lost. Consequently, the Committee attaches particular importance to the message contained in Recommendation 44 of the Plan: "Educational programmes featuring the elderly as the teachers and transmitters of knowledge, culture and spiritual values should be developed."

39. In Article 15, paragraphs 1 (a) and (b), of the Covenant, States parties recognize the right of everyone to take part in cultural life and to enjoy the benefits of scientific progress and its applications. In this respect, the Committee urges States parties to take account of the recommendations contained in the United Nations Principles for Older Persons, and in particular of Principle 7: "Older persons should remain integrated in society, participate actively in the formulation and implementation of policies that directly affect their well-being and share their knowledge and skills with

younger generations"; and Principle 16: "Older persons should have access to the educational, cultural, spiritual and recreational resources of society."

40. Similarly, Recommendation 48 of the Vienna International Plan of Action on Aging encourages Governments and international organizations to support programmes aimed at providing the elderly with easier physical access to cultural institutions (museums, theatres, concert halls, cinemas, etc.).

41. Recommendation 50 stresses the need for Governments, non-governmental organizations and the aging themselves to make efforts to overcome negative stereotyped images of older persons as suffering from physical and psychological disabilities, incapable of functioning independently and having neither role nor status in society. These efforts, in which the media and educational institutions should also take part, are essential for achieving a society that champions the full integration of the elderly.

42. With regard to the right to enjoy the benefits of scientific progress and its applications, States parties should take account of Recommendations 60, 61 and 62 of the Vienna International Plan of Action and make efforts to promote research on the biological, mental and social aspects of aging and ways of maintaining functional capacities and preventing and delaying the start of chronic illnesses and disabilities. In this connection, it is recommended that States, intergovernmental organizations and non-governmental organizations should establish institutions specializing in the teaching of gerontology, geriatrics and geriatric psychology in countries where such institutions do not exist.

Chapter 7

CESCR General Comment No. 7 (1997) on Forced Evictions (Article 11(1), The Right to Adequate Housing)

1. In its General Comment No. 4 (1991), the Committee observed that all persons should possess a degree of security of tenure which guarantees legal protection against forced eviction, harassment and other threats. It concluded that forced evictions are prima facie incompatible with the requirements of the Covenant. Having considered a significant number of reports of forced evictions in recent years, including instances in which it has determined that the obligations of States parties were being violated, the Committee is now in a position to seek to provide further clarification as to the implications of such practices in terms of the obligations contained in the Covenant.

2. The international community has long recognized that the issue of forced evictions is a serious one. In 1976, the United Nations Conference on Human Settlements noted that special attention should be paid to "undertaking major clearance operations should take place only when conservation and rehabilitation are not feasible and relocation measures are made." In 1988, in the Global Strategy for Shelter to the Year 2000, adopted by the General Assembly in its resolution 43/181, the "fundamental obligation [of Governments] to protect and improve houses and neighbourhoods, rather than damage or destroy them" was recognized. Agenda 21 stated that "people should be protected by law against unfair eviction from their homes or land." In the Habitat Agenda Governments committed themselves to "protecting all people from, and providing legal protection and redress for, forced evictions that are contrary to the law, taking human rights into consideration; [and] when evictions are unavoidable, ensuring, as appropriate, that alternative suitable solutions are provided." The Commission on Human Rights has also indicated that "forced evictions are a gross violation of human rights." However, although these statements are important, they leave open one of the most critical issues, namely that of determining the circumstances under which forced evictions are permissible and of spelling out the types of protection required to ensure respect for the relevant provisions of the Covenant.

Original notes omitted.

3. The use of the term "forced evictions" is, in some respects, problematic. This expression seeks to convey a sense of arbitrariness and of illegality. To many observers, however, the reference to "forced evictions" is a tautology, while others have criticized the expression "illegal evictions" on the ground that it assumes that the relevant law provides adequate protection of the right to housing and conforms with the Covenant, which is by no means always the case. Similarly, it has been suggested that the term "unfair evictions" is even more subjective by virtue of its failure to refer to any legal framework at all. The international community, especially in the context of the Commission on Human Rights, has opted to refer to "forced evictions," primarily since all suggested alternatives also suffer from many such defects. The term "forced evictions" as used throughout this general comment is defined as the permanent or temporary removal against their will of individuals, families and/or communities from the homes and/or land which they occupy, without the provision of, and access to, appropriate forms of legal or other protection. The prohibition on forced evictions does not, however, apply to evictions carried out by force in accordance with the law and in conformity with the provisions of the International Covenants on Human Rights.

4. The practice of forced evictions is widespread and affects persons in both developed and developing countries. Owing to the interrelationship and interdependency which exist among all human rights, forced evictions frequently violate other human rights. Thus, while manifestly breaching the rights enshrined in the Covenant, the practice of forced evictions may also result in violations of civil and political rights, such as the right to life, the right to security of the person, the right to non-interference with privacy, family and home and the right to the peaceful enjoyment of possessions.

5. Although the practice of forced evictions might appear to occur primarily in heavily populated urban areas, it also takes place in connection with forced population transfers, internal displacement, forced relocations in the context of armed conflict, mass exoduses and refugee movements. In all of these contexts, the right to adequate housing and not to be subjected to forced eviction may be violated through a wide range of acts or omissions attributable to States parties. Even in situations where it may be necessary to impose limitations on such a right, full compliance with Article 4 of the Covenant is required so that any limitations imposed must be "determined by law only insofar as this may be compatible with the nature of these [i.e., economic, social and cultural] rights and solely for the purpose of promoting the general welfare in a democratic society."

6. Many instances of forced eviction are associated with violence, such as evictions resulting from international armed conflicts, internal strife and communal or ethnic violence.

7. Other instances of forced eviction occur in the name of development. Evictions may be carried out in connection with conflict over land rights, development and infrastructure projects, such as the construction of dams or other large-scale energy projects, with land acquisition measures associated with urban renewal, housing renovation, city beautification programmes, the clearing of land for agricultural purposes, unbridled speculation in land, or the holding of major sporting events like the Olympic Games.

8. In essence, the obligations of States parties to the Covenant in relation to forced evictions are based on Article 11.1, read in conjunction with other relevant provisions. In particular, Article 2.1 obliges States to use "all appropriate means" to promote the right to adequate housing. However, in view of the nature of the practice of forced evictions, the reference in Article 2.1 to progressive achievement based on the availability of resources will rarely be relevant. The State itself must refrain from forced evictions and ensure that the law is enforced against its agents or third parties who carry out forced evictions (as defined in paragraph 3 above). Moreover, this approach is reinforced by Article 17.1 of the International Covenant on Civil and Political Rights which complements the right not to be forcefully evicted without adequate protection. That provision recognizes, inter alia, the right to be protected against "arbitrary or unlawful interference" with one's home. It is to be noted that the State's obligation to ensure respect for that right is not qualified by considerations relating to its available resources.

9. Article 2.1 of the Covenant requires States parties to use "all appropriate means," including the adoption of legislative measures, to promote all the rights protected under the Covenant. Although the Committee has indicated in its General Comment No. 3 (1990) that such measures may not be indispensable in relation to all rights, it is clear that legislation against forced evictions is an essential basis upon which to build a system of effective protection. Such legislation should include measures which (a) provide the greatest possible security of tenure to occupiers of houses and land, (b) conform to the Covenant and (c) are designed to control strictly the circumstances under which evictions may be carried out. The legislation must also apply to all agents acting under the authority of the State or who are accountable to it. Moreover, in view of the increasing trend in some States towards the Government greatly reducing its responsibilities in the housing sector, States parties must ensure that legislative and other measures are adequate to prevent and, if appropriate, punish forced evictions carried out, without appropriate safeguards, by private persons or bodies. States parties should therefore review relevant legislation and policies to ensure that they are compatible with the obligations arising from the right to adequate housing and repeal or amend any legislation or policies that are inconsistent with the requirements of the Covenant.

10. Women, children, youth, older persons, indigenous people, ethnic and other minorities, and other vulnerable individuals and groups all suffer disproportionately from the practice of forced eviction. Women in all groups are especially vulnerable given the extent of statutory and other forms of discrimination which often apply in relation to property rights (including home ownership) or rights of access to property or accommodation, and their particular vulnerability to acts of violence and sexual abuse when they are rendered homeless. The non-discrimination provisions of Articles 2.2 and 3 of the Covenant impose an additional obligation upon Governments to ensure that, where evictions do occur, appropriate measures are taken to ensure that no form of discrimination is involved.

11. Whereas some evictions may be justifiable, such as in the case of persistent non-payment of rent or of damage to rented property without any reasonable cause, it is

incumbent upon the relevant authorities to ensure that they are carried out in a manner warranted by a law which is compatible with the Covenant and that all the legal recourses and remedies are available to those affected.

12. Forced eviction and house demolition as a punitive measure are also inconsistent with the norms of the Covenant. Likewise, the Committee takes note of the obligations enshrined in the Geneva Conventions of 1949 and Protocols thereto of 1977 concerning prohibitions on the displacement of the civilian population and the destruction of private property as these relate to the practice of forced eviction.

13. States parties shall ensure, prior to carrying out any evictions, and particularly those involving large groups, that all feasible alternatives are explored in consultation with the affected persons, with a view to avoiding, or at least minimizing, the need to use force. Legal remedies or procedures should be provided to those who are affected by eviction orders. States parties shall also see to it that all the individuals concerned have a right to adequate compensation for any property, both personal and real, which is affected. In this respect, it is pertinent to recall Article 2.3 of the International Covenant on Civil and Political Rights, which requires States parties to ensure "an effective remedy" for persons whose rights have been violated and the obligation upon the "competent authorities (to) enforce such remedies when granted."

14. In cases where eviction is considered to be justified, it should be carried out in strict compliance with the relevant provisions of international human rights law and in accordance with general principles of reasonableness and proportionality. In this regard it is especially pertinent to recall General Comment 16 of the Human Rights Committee, relating to Article 17 of the International Covenant on Civil and Political Rights, which states that interference with a person's home can only take place "in cases envisaged by the law." The Committee observed that the law "should be in accordance with the provisions, aims and objectives of the Covenant and should be, in any event, reasonable in the particular circumstances." The Committee also indicated that "relevant legislation must specify in detail the precise circumstances in which such interferences may be permitted."

15. Appropriate procedural protection and due process are essential aspects of all human rights but are especially pertinent in relation to a matter such as forced evictions which directly invokes a large number of the rights recognized in both the International Covenants on Human Rights. The Committee considers that the procedural protections which should be applied in relation to forced evictions include: (a) an opportunity for genuine consultation with those affected; (b) adequate and reasonable notice for all affected persons prior to the scheduled date of eviction; (c) information on the proposed evictions, and, where applicable, on the alternative purpose for which the land or housing is to be used, to be made available in reasonable time to all those affected; (d) especially where groups of people are involved, government officials or their representatives to be present during an eviction; (e) all persons carrying out the eviction to be properly identified; (f) evictions not to take place in particularly bad weather or at night unless the affected persons consent otherwise; (g) provision of

legal remedies; and (h) provision, where possible, of legal aid to persons who are in need of it to seek redress from the courts.

16. Evictions should not result in individuals being rendered homeless or vulnerable to the violation of other human rights. Where those affected are unable to provide for themselves, the State party must take all appropriate measures, to the maximum of its available resources, to ensure that adequate alternative housing, resettlement or access to productive land, as the case may be, is available.

17. The Committee is aware that various development projects financed by international agencies within the territories of State parties have resulted in forced evictions. In this regard, the Committee recalls its General Comment No. 2 (1990) which states, inter alia, that "international agencies should scrupulously avoid involvement in projects which, for example . . . promote or reinforce discrimination against individuals or groups contrary to the provisions of the Covenant, or involve large-scale evictions or displacement of persons without the provision of all appropriate protection and compensation. Every effort should be made, at each phase of a development project, to ensure that the rights contained in the Covenant are duly taken into account."

18. Some institutions, such as the World Bank and the Organisation for Economic Cooperation and Development (OECD) have adopted guidelines on relocation and/or resettlement with a view to limiting the scale of and human suffering associated with forced evictions. Such practices often accompany large-scale development projects, such as dam-building and other major energy projects. Full respect for such guidelines, insofar as they reflect the obligations contained in the Covenant, is essential on the part of both the agencies themselves and States parties to the Covenant. The Committee recalls in this respect the statement in the Vienna Declaration and Programme of Action to the effect that "while development facilitates the enjoyment of all human rights, the lack of development may not be invoked to justify the abridgement of internationally recognized human rights" (Part I, para. 10).

19. In accordance with the guidelines for reporting adopted by the Committee, State parties are requested to provide various types of information pertaining directly to the practice of forced evictions. This includes information relating to (a) the "number of persons evicted within the last five years and the number of persons currently lacking legal protection against arbitrary eviction or any other kind of eviction," (b) "legislation concerning the rights of tenants to security of tenure, to protection from eviction" and (c) "legislation prohibiting any form of eviction."

20. Information is also sought as to "measures taken during, inter alia, urban renewal programmes, redevelopment projects, site upgrading, preparation for international events (Olympics and other sporting competitions, exhibitions, conferences, etc.) 'beautiful city' campaigns, etc. which guarantee protection from eviction or guarantee rehousing based on mutual consent, by any persons living on or near to affected sites." However, few States parties have included the requisite information in their reports to the Committee. The Committee therefore wishes to emphasize the importance it attaches to the receipt of such information.

21. Some States parties have indicated that information of this nature is not available. The Committee recalls that effective monitoring of the right to adequate housing, either by the Government concerned or by the Committee, is not possible in the absence of the collection of appropriate data and would request all States parties to ensure that the necessary data is collected and is reflected in the reports submitted by them under the Covenant.

Chapter 8
CESCR General Comment No. 8 (1997) on the Relationship Between Economic Sanctions and Respect for Economic, Social and Cultural Rights

1. Economic sanctions are being imposed with increasing frequency, both internationally, regionally and unilaterally. The purpose of this general comment is to emphasize that, whatever the circumstances, such sanctions should always take full account of the provisions of the International Covenant on Economic, Social and Cultural Rights. The Committee does not in any way call into question the necessity for the imposition of sanctions in appropriate cases in accordance with Chapter VII of the Charter of the United Nations or other applicable international law. But those provisions of the Charter that relate to human rights (Articles 1, 55 and 56) must still be considered to be fully applicable in such cases.

2. During the 1990s the Security Council has imposed sanctions of varying kind and duration in relation to South Africa, Iraq/Kuwait, parts of the former Yugoslavia, Somalia, the Libyan Arab Jamahiriya, Liberia, Haiti, Angola, Rwanda and the Sudan. The impact of sanctions upon the enjoyment of economic, social and cultural rights has been brought to the Committee's attention in a number of cases involving States parties to the Covenant, some of which have reported regularly, thereby giving the Committee the opportunity to examine the situation carefully.

3. While the impact of sanctions varies from one case to another, the Committee is aware that they almost always have a dramatic impact on the rights recognized in the Covenant. Thus, for example, they often cause significant disruption in the distribution of food, pharmaceuticals and sanitation supplies, jeopardize the quality of food and the availability of clean drinking water, severely interfere with the functioning of basic health and education systems, and undermine the right to work. In addition, their unintended consequences can include reinforcement of the power of oppressive élites, the emergence, almost invariably, of a black market and the generation of huge windfall profits for the privileged élites which manage it, enhancement of the control

Original notes omitted.

of the governing élites over the population at large, and restriction of opportunities to seek asylum or to manifest political opposition. While the phenomena mentioned in the preceding sentence are essentially political in nature, they also have a major additional impact on the enjoyment of economic, social and cultural rights.

4. In considering sanctions, it is essential to distinguish between the basic objective of applying political and economic pressure upon the governing élite of the country to persuade them to conform to international law, and the collateral infliction of suffering upon the most vulnerable groups within the targeted country. For that reason, the sanctions regimes established by the Security Council now include humanitarian exemptions designed to permit the flow of essential goods and services destined for humanitarian purposes. It is commonly assumed that these exemptions ensure basic respect for economic, social and cultural rights within the targeted country.

5. However, a number of recent United Nations and other studies which have analysed the impact of sanctions have concluded that these exemptions do not have this effect. Moreover, the exemptions are very limited in scope. They do not address, for example, the question of access to primary education, nor do they provide for repairs to infrastructures which are essential to provide clean water, adequate health care, etc. The Secretary-General suggested in 1995 that there is a need to assess the potential impact of sanctions before they are imposed and to enhance arrangements for the provision of humanitarian assistance to vulnerable groups. In the following year, a major study prepared for the General Assembly by Ms Graça Machel, on the impact of armed conflict on children, stated that "humanitarian exemptions tend to be ambiguous and are interpreted arbitrarily and inconsistently. . . . Delays, confusion and the denial of requests to import essential humanitarian goods cause resource shortages. . . . [Their effects] inevitably fall most heavily on the poor." Most recently, an October 1997 United Nations report concluded that the review procedures established under the various sanctions committees established by the Security Council "remain cumbersome and aid agencies still encounter difficulties in obtaining approval for exempted supplies. . . . [The] committees neglect larger problems of commercial and governmental violations in the form of black-marketing, illicit trade, and corruption."

6. It is thus clear, on the basis of an impressive array of both country-specific and general studies, that insufficient attention is being paid to the impact of sanctions on vulnerable groups. Nevertheless, for various reasons, these studies have not examined specifically the nefarious consequences that ensue for the enjoyment of economic, social and cultural rights, per se. It is in fact apparent that in most, if not all, cases, those consequences have either not been taken into account at all or not given the serious consideration they deserve. There is thus a need to inject a human rights dimension into deliberations on this issue.

7. The Committee considers that the provisions of the Covenant, virtually all of which are also reflected in a range of other human rights treaties as well as the Universal Declaration of Human Rights, cannot be considered to be inoperative, or in any way inapplicable, solely because a decision has been taken that considerations of international

peace and security warrant the imposition of sanctions. Just as the international community insists that any targeted State must respect the civil and political rights of its citizens, so too must that State and the international community itself do everything possible to protect at least the core content of the economic, social and cultural rights of the affected peoples of that State.

8. While this obligation of every State is derived from the commitment in the Charter of the United Nations to promote respect for all human rights, it should also be recalled that every permanent member of the Security Council has signed the Covenant, although two (China and the United States) have yet to ratify it. Most of the non-permanent members at any given time are parties. Each of these States has undertaken, in conformity with Article 2, paragraph 1, of the Covenant to "take steps, individually and through international assistance and cooperation, especially economic and technical, to the maximum of its available resources, with a view to achieving progressively the full realization of the rights recognized in the present Covenant by all appropriate means. . . ." When the affected State is also a State party, it is doubly incumbent upon other States to respect and take account of the relevant obligations. To the extent that sanctions are imposed on States which are not parties to the Covenant, the same principles would in any event apply given the status of the economic, social and cultural rights of vulnerable groups as part of general international law, as evidenced, for example, by the near-universal ratification of the Convention on the Rights of the Child and the status of the Universal Declaration of Human Rights.

9. Although the Committee has no role to play in relation to decisions to impose or not to impose sanctions, it does, however, have a responsibility to monitor compliance by all States parties with the Covenant. When measures are taken which inhibit the ability of a State party to meet its obligations under the Covenant, the terms of sanctions and the manner in which they are implemented become appropriate matters for concern for the Committee.

10. The Committee believes that two sets of obligations flow from these considerations. The first set relates to the affected State. The imposition of sanctions does not in any way nullify or diminish the relevant obligations of that State party. As in other comparable situations, those obligations assume greater practical importance in times of particular hardship. The Committee is thus called upon to scrutinize very carefully the extent to which the State concerned has taken steps "to the maximum of its available resources" to provide the greatest possible protection for the economic, social and cultural rights of each individual living within its jurisdiction. While sanctions will inevitably diminish the capacity of the affected State to fund or support some of the necessary measures, the State remains under an obligation to ensure the absence of discrimination in relation to the enjoyment of these rights, and to take all possible measures, including negotiations with other States and the international community, to reduce to a minimum the negative impact upon the rights of vulnerable groups within the society.

11. The second set of obligations relates to the party or parties responsible for the imposition, maintenance or implementation of the sanctions, whether it be the international

community, an international or regional organization, or a State or group of States. In this respect, the Committee considers that there are three conclusions which follow logically from the recognition of economic, social and cultural human rights.

12. First, these rights must be taken fully into account when designing an appropriate sanctions regime. Without endorsing any particular measures in this regard, the Committee notes proposals such as those calling for the creation of a United Nations mechanism for anticipating and tracking sanctions impacts, the elaboration of a more transparent set of agreed principles and procedures based on respect for human rights, the identification of a wider range of exempt goods and services, the authorization of agreed technical agencies to determine necessary exemptions, the creation of a better resourced set of sanctions committees, more precise targeting of the vulnerabilities of those whose behaviour the international community wishes to change, and the introduction of greater overall flexibility.

13. Second, effective monitoring, which is always required under the terms of the Covenant, should be undertaken throughout the period that sanctions are in force. When an external party takes upon itself even partial responsibility for the situation within a country (whether under Chapter VII of the Charter or otherwise), it also unavoidably assumes a responsibility to do all within its power to protect the economic, social and cultural rights of the affected population.

14. Third, the external entity has an obligation "to take steps, individually and through international assistance and cooperation, especially economic and technical" in order to respond to any disproportionate suffering experienced by vulnerable groups within the targeted country.

15. In anticipating the objection that sanctions must, almost by definition, result in the grave violations of economic, social and cultural rights if they are to achieve their objectives, the Committee notes the conclusion of a major United Nations study to the effect that "decisions to reduce the suffering of children or minimize other adverse consequences can be taken without jeopardizing the policy aim of sanctions." This applies equally to the situation of all vulnerable groups.

16. In adopting this general comment the sole aim of the Committee is to draw attention to the fact that the inhabitants of a given country do not forfeit their basic economic, social and cultural rights by virtue of any determination that their leaders have violated norms relating to international peace and security. The aim is not to give support or encouragement to such leaders, nor is it to undermine the legitimate interests of the international community in enforcing respect for the provisions of the Charter of the United Nations and the general principles of international law. Rather, it is to insist that lawlessness of one kind should not be met by lawlessness of another kind which pays no heed to the fundamental rights that underlie and give legitimacy to any such collective action.

Chapter 9
CESCR General Comment No. 9 (1998) on the Domestic Application of the Covenant

A. The Duty to Give Effect to the Covenant in the Domestic Legal Order

1. In its General Comment No. 3 (1990) on the nature of States parties' obligations (art. 2, para. 1, of the Covenant) the Committee addressed issues relating to the nature and scope of States parties' obligations. The present general comment seeks to elaborate further certain elements of the earlier statement. The central obligation in relation to the Covenant is for States parties to give effect to the rights recognized therein. By requiring Governments to do so "by all appropriate means," the Covenant adopts a broad and flexible approach which enables the particularities of the legal and administrative systems of each State, as well as other relevant considerations, to be taken into account.

2. But this flexibility coexists with the obligation upon each State party to use all the means at its disposal to give effect to the rights recognized in the Covenant. In this respect, the fundamental requirements of international human rights law must be borne in mind. Thus the Covenant norms must be recognized in appropriate ways within the domestic legal order, appropriate means of redress, or remedies, must be available to any aggrieved individual or group, and appropriate means of ensuring governmental accountability must be put in place.

3. Questions relating to the domestic application of the Covenant must be considered in the light of two principles of international law. The first, as reflected in Article 27 of the Vienna Convention on the Law of Treaties, is that "[A] party may not invoke the provisions of its internal law as justification for its failure to perform a treaty." In other words, States should modify the domestic legal order as necessary in order to give effect to their treaty obligations. The second principle is reflected in Article 8 of the Universal Declaration of Human Rights, according to which "Everyone has the right to an effective remedy by the competent national tribunals for acts violating the fundamental rights granted him by the constitution or by law." The International Covenant

Original notes omitted.

on Economic, Social and Cultural Rights contains no direct counterpart to Article 2, paragraph 3 (b), of the International Covenant on Civil and Political Rights, which obligates States parties to, *inter alia*, "develop the possibilities of judicial remedy." Nevertheless, a State party seeking to justify its failure to provide any domestic legal remedies for violations of economic, social and cultural rights would need to show either that such remedies are not "appropriate means" within the terms of Article 2, paragraph 1, of the International Covenant on Economic, Social and Cultural Rights or that, in view of the other means used, they are unnecessary. It will be difficult to show this and the Committee considers that, in many cases, the other means used could be rendered ineffective if they are not reinforced or complemented by judicial remedies.

B. The Status of the Covenant in the Domestic Legal Order

4. In general, legally binding international human rights standards should operate directly and immediately within the domestic legal system of each State party, thereby enabling individuals to seek enforcement of their rights before national courts and tribunals. The rule requiring the exhaustion of domestic remedies reinforces the primacy of national remedies in this respect. The existence and further development of international procedures for the pursuit of individual claims is important, but such procedures are ultimately only supplementary to effective national remedies.

5. The Covenant does not stipulate the specific means by which it is to be implemented in the national legal order. And there is no provision obligating its comprehensive incorporation or requiring it to be accorded any specific type of status in national law. Although the precise method by which Covenant rights are given effect in national law is a matter for each State party to decide, the means used should be appropriate in the sense of producing results which are consistent with the full discharge of its obligations by the State party. The means chosen are also subject to review as part of the Committee's examination of the State party's compliance with its obligations under the Covenant.

6. An analysis of State practice with respect to the Covenant shows that States have used a variety of approaches. Some States have failed to do anything specific at all. Of those that have taken measures, some States have transformed the Covenant into domestic law by supplementing or amending existing legislation, without invoking the specific terms of the Covenant. Others have adopted or incorporated it into domestic law, so that its terms are retained intact and given formal validity in the national legal order. This has often been done by means of constitutional provisions according priority to the provisions of international human rights treaties over any inconsistent domestic laws. The approach of States to the Covenant depends significantly upon the approach adopted to treaties in general in the domestic legal order.

7. But whatever the preferred methodology, several principles follow from the duty to give effect to the Covenant and must therefore be respected. First, the means of implementation chosen must be adequate to ensure fulfilment of the obligations under the

Covenant. The need to ensure justiciability (see para. 10 below) is relevant when determining the best way to give domestic legal effect to the Covenant rights. Second, account should be taken of the means which have proved to be most effective in the country concerned in ensuring the protection of other human rights. Where the means used to give effect to the Covenant on Economic, Social and Cultural Rights differ significantly from those used in relation to other human rights treaties, there should be a compelling justification for this, taking account of the fact that the formulations used in the Covenant are, to a considerable extent, comparable to those used in treaties dealing with civil and political rights.

8. Third, while the Covenant does not formally oblige States to incorporate its provisions in domestic law, such an approach is desirable. Direct incorporation avoids problems that might arise in the translation of treaty obligations into national law, and provides a basis for the direct invocation of the Covenant rights by individuals in national courts. For these reasons, the Committee strongly encourages formal adoption or incorporation of the Covenant in national law.

C. The Role of Legal Remedies: Legal or Judicial Remedies?

9. The right to an effective remedy need not be interpreted as always requiring a judicial remedy. Administrative remedies will, in many cases, be adequate and those living within the jurisdiction of a State party have a legitimate expectation, based on the principle of good faith, that all administrative authorities will take account of the requirements of the Covenant in their decision-making. Any such administrative remedies should be accessible, affordable, timely and effective. An ultimate right of judicial appeal from administrative procedures of this type would also often be appropriate. By the same token, there are some obligations, such as (but by no means limited to) those concerning non-discrimination, in relation to which the provision of some form of judicial remedy would seem indispensable in order to satisfy the requirements of the Covenant. In other words, whenever a Covenant right cannot be made fully effective without some role for the judiciary, judicial remedies are necessary.

Justiciability

10. In relation to civil and political rights, it is generally taken for granted that judicial remedies for violations are essential. Regrettably, the contrary assumption is too often made in relation to economic, social and cultural rights. This discrepancy is not warranted either by the nature of the rights or by the relevant Covenant provisions. The Committee has already made clear that it considers many of the provisions in the Covenant to be capable of immediate implementation. Thus, in General Comment No. 3 (1990) it cited, by way of example, Articles 3; 7, paragraph (a) (i); 8; 10, paragraph 3; 13, paragraph 2 (a); 13, paragraph 3; 13, paragraph 4; and 15, paragraph 3. It is important in this regard to distinguish between justiciability (which refers to those matters which are appropriately resolved by the courts) and norms which are self-executing (capable

of being applied by courts without further elaboration). While the general approach of each legal system needs to be taken into account, there is no Covenant right which could not, in the great majority of systems, be considered to possess at least some significant justiciable dimensions. It is sometimes suggested that matters involving the allocation of resources should be left to the political authorities rather than the courts. While the respective competences of the various branches of government must be respected, it is appropriate to acknowledge that courts are generally already involved in a considerable range of matters which have important resource implications. The adoption of a rigid classification of economic, social and cultural rights which puts them, by definition, beyond the reach of the courts would thus be arbitrary and incompatible with the principle that the two sets of human rights are indivisible and interdependent. It would also drastically curtail the capacity of the courts to protect the rights of the most vulnerable and disadvantaged groups in society.

Self-executing

11. The Covenant does not negate the possibility that the rights it contains may be considered self-executing in systems where that option is provided for. Indeed, when it was being drafted, attempts to include a specific provision in the Covenant to the effect that it be considered "non-self-executing" were strongly rejected. In most States, the determination of whether or not a treaty provision is self-executing will be a matter for the courts, not the executive or the legislature. In order to perform that function effectively, the relevant courts and tribunals must be made aware of the nature and implications of the Covenant and of the important role of judicial remedies in its implementation. Thus, for example, when Governments are involved in court proceedings, they should promote interpretations of domestic laws which give effect to their Covenant obligations. Similarly, judicial training should take full account of the justiciability of the Covenant. It is especially important to avoid any a priori assumption that the norms should be considered to be non-self-executing. In fact, many of them are stated in terms which are at least as clear and specific as those in other human rights treaties, the provisions of which are regularly deemed by courts to be self-executing.

D. The Treatment of the Covenant in Domestic Courts

12. In the Committee's guidelines for States' reports, States are requested to provide information as to whether the provisions of the Covenant "can be invoked before, and directly enforced by, the Courts, other tribunals or administrative authorities." Some States have provided such information, but greater importance should be attached to this element in future reports. In particular, the Committee requests that States parties provide details of any significant jurisprudence from their domestic courts that makes use of the provisions of the Covenant.

13. On the basis of available information, it is clear that State practice is mixed. The Committee notes that some courts have applied the provisions of the Covenant either

directly or as interpretive standards. Other courts are willing to acknowledge, in principle, the relevance of the Covenant for interpreting domestic law, but in practice, the impact of the Covenant on the reasoning or outcome of cases is very limited. Still other courts have refused to give any degree of legal effect to the Covenant in cases in which individuals have sought to rely on it. There remains extensive scope for the courts in most countries to place greater reliance upon the Covenant.

14. Within the limits of the appropriate exercise of their functions of judicial review, courts should take account of Covenant rights where this is necessary to ensure that the State's conduct is consistent with its obligations under the Covenant. Neglect by the courts of this responsibility is incompatible with the principle of the rule of law, which must always be taken to include respect for international human rights obligations.

15. It is generally accepted that domestic law should be interpreted as far as possible in a way which conforms to a State's international legal obligations. Thus, when a domestic decision maker is faced with a choice between an interpretation of domestic law that would place the State in breach of the Covenant and one that would enable the State to comply with the Covenant, international law requires the choice of the latter. Guarantees of equality and non-discrimination should be interpreted, to the greatest extent possible, in ways which facilitate the full protection of economic, social and cultural rights.

Chapter 10

CESCR General Comment No. 10 (1998) on the Role of National Human Rights Institutions in the Protection of Economic, Social and Cultural Rights

1. Article 2, paragraph 1, of the Covenant obligates each State party "to take steps . . . with a view to achieving progressively the full realization of the [Covenant] rights . . . by all appropriate means." The Committee notes that one such means, through which important steps can be taken, is the work of national institutions for the promotion and protection of human rights. In recent years there has been a proliferation of these institutions and the trend has been strongly encouraged by the General Assembly and the Commission on Human Rights. The Office of the United Nations High Commissioner for Human Rights has established a major programme to assist and encourage States in relation to national institutions.

2. These institutions range from national human rights commissions through Ombudsman offices, public interest or other human rights "advocates," to "defensores del pueblo." In many cases, the institution has been established by the Government, enjoys an important degree of autonomy from the executive and the legislature, takes full account of international human rights standards which are applicable to the country concerned, and is mandated to perform various activities designed to promote and protect human rights. Such institutions have been established in States with widely differing legal cultures and regardless of their economic situation.

3. The Committee notes that national institutions have a potentially crucial role to play in promoting and ensuring the indivisibility and interdependence of all human rights. Unfortunately, this role has too often either not been accorded to the institution or has been neglected or given a low priority by it. It is therefore essential that full attention be given to economic, social and cultural rights in all of the relevant activities of these institutions. The following list is indicative of the types of activities that can be, and in some instances already have been, undertaken by national institutions in relation to these rights:

Original notes omittted.

(a) The promotion of educational and information programmes designed to enhance awareness and understanding of economic, social and cultural rights, both within the population at large and among particular groups such as the public service, the judiciary, the private sector and the labour movement;

(b) The scrutinizing of existing laws and administrative acts, as well as draft bills and other proposals, to ensure that they are consistent with the requirements of the International Covenant on Economic, Social and Cultural Rights;

(c) Providing technical advice, or undertaking surveys in relation to economic, social and cultural rights, including at the request of the public authorities or other appropriate agencies;

(d) The identification of national-level benchmarks against which the realization of Covenant obligations can be measured;

(e) Conducting research and inquiries designed to ascertain the extent to which particular economic, social and cultural rights are being realized, either within the State as a whole or in areas or in relation to communities of particular vulnerability;

(f) Monitoring compliance with specific rights recognized under the Covenant and providing reports thereon to the public authorities and civil society; and

(g) Examining complaints alleging infringements of applicable economic, social and cultural rights standards within the State.

4. The Committee calls upon States parties to ensure that the mandates accorded to all national human rights institutions include appropriate attention to economic, social and cultural rights and requests States parties to include details of both the mandates and the principal relevant activities of such institutions in their reports submitted to the Committee.

Chapter 11

CESCR General Comment No. 11 (1999) on Plans of Action for Primary Education (Article 14 of the Covenant)

1. Article 14 of the International Covenant on Economic, Social and Cultural Rights requires each State party which has not been able to secure compulsory primary education, free of charge, to undertake, within two years, to work out and adopt a detailed plan of action for the progressive implementation, within a reasonable number of years, to be fixed in the plan, of the principle of compulsory primary education free of charge for all. In spite of the obligations undertaken in accordance with Article 14, a number of States parties have neither drafted nor implemented a plan of action for free and compulsory primary education.

2. The right to education, recognized in Articles 13 and 14 of the Covenant, as well as in a variety of other international treaties, such as the Convention on the Rights of the Child and the Convention on the Elimination of All Forms of Discrimination against Women, is of vital importance. It has been variously classified as an economic right, a social right and a cultural right. It is all of these. It is also, in many ways, a civil right and a political right, since it is central to the full and effective realization of those rights as well. In this respect, the right to education epitomizes the indivisibility and interdependence of all human rights.

3. In line with its clear and unequivocal obligation under Article 14, every State party is under a duty to present to the Committee a plan of action drawn up along the lines specified in paragraph 8 below. This obligation needs to be scrupulously observed in view of the fact that in developing countries, 130 million children of school age are currently estimated to be without access to primary education, of whom about two thirds are girls. The Committee is fully aware that many diverse factors have made it difficult for States parties to fulfill their obligation to provide a plan of action. For example, the structural adjustment programmes that began in the 1970s, the debt crises that followed in the 1980s and the financial crises of the late 1990s, as well as other factors, have greatly exacerbated the extent to which the right to primary education is being

Original notes omitted.

denied. These difficulties, however, cannot relieve States parties of their obligation to adopt and submit a plan of action to the Committee, as provided for in Article 14 of the Covenant.

4. Plans of action prepared by States parties to the Covenant in accordance with Article 14 are especially important as the work of the Committee has shown that the lack of educational opportunities for children often reinforces their subjection to various other human rights violations. For instance, these children, who may live in abject poverty and not lead healthy lives, are particularly vulnerable to forced labour and other forms of exploitation. Moreover, there is a direct correlation between, for example, primary school enrollment levels for girls and major reductions in child marriages.

5. Article 14 contains a number of elements which warrant some elaboration in the light of the Committee's extensive experience in examining State party reports.

6. Compulsory. The element of compulsion serves to highlight the fact that neither parents, nor guardians, nor the State are entitled to treat as optional the decision as to whether the child should have access to primary education. Similarly, the prohibition of gender discrimination in access to education, required also by Articles 2 and 3 of the Covenant, is further underlined by this requirement. It should be emphasized, however, that the education offered must be adequate in quality, relevant to the child and must promote the realization of the child's other rights.

7. Free of charge. The nature of this requirement is unequivocal. The right is expressly formulated so as to ensure the availability of primary education without charge to the child, parents or guardians. Fees imposed by the Government, the local authorities or the school, and other direct costs, constitute disincentives to the enjoyment of the right and may jeopardize its realization. They are also often highly regressive in effect. Their elimination is a matter which must be addressed by the required plan of action. Indirect costs, such as compulsory levies on parents (sometimes portrayed as being voluntary, when in fact they are not), or the obligation to wear a relatively expensive school uniform, can also fall into the same category. Other indirect costs may be permissible, subject to the Committee's examination on a case-by-case basis. This provision of compulsory primary education in no way conflicts with the right recognized in Article 13.3 of the Covenant for parents and guardians "to choose for their children schools other than those established by the public authorities."

8. Adoption of a detailed plan. The State party is required to adopt a plan of action within two years. This must be interpreted as meaning within two years of the Covenant's entry into force of the State concerned, or within two years of a subsequent change in circumstances which has led to the non-observance of the relevant obligation. This obligation is a continuing one and States parties to which the provision is relevant by virtue of the prevailing situation are not absolved from the obligation as a result of their past failure to act within the two-year limit. The plan must cover all of the actions which are necessary in order to secure each of the requisite component parts of the right and must be sufficiently detailed so as to ensure the comprehensive

realization of the right. Participation of all sections of civil society in the drawing up of the plan is vital and some means of periodically reviewing progress and ensuring accountability are essential. Without those elements, the significance of the article would be undermined.

9. Obligations. A State party cannot escape the unequivocal obligation to adopt a plan of action on the grounds that the necessary resources are not available. If the obligation could be avoided in this way, there would be no justification for the unique requirement contained in Article 14 which applies, almost by definition, to situations characterized by inadequate financial resources. By the same token, and for the same reason, the reference to "international assistance and cooperation" in Article 2.1 and to "international action" in Article 23 of the Covenant are of particular relevance in this situation. Where a State party is clearly lacking in the financial resources and/or expertise required to "work out and adopt" a detailed plan, the international community has a clear obligation to assist.

10. Progressive implementation. The plan of action must be aimed at securing the progressive implementation of the right to compulsory primary education, free of charge, under Article 14. Unlike the provision in Article 2.1, however, Article 14 specifies that the target date must be "within a reasonable number of years" and moreover, that the time-frame must "be fixed in the plan." In other words, the plan must specifically set out a series of targeted implementation dates for each stage of the progressive implementation of the plan. This underscores both the importance and the relative inflexibility of the obligation in question. Moreover, it needs to be stressed in this regard that the State party's other obligations, such as non-discrimination, are required to be implemented fully and immediately.

11. The Committee calls upon every State party to which Article 14 is relevant to ensure that its terms are fully complied with and that the resulting plan of action is submitted to the Committee as an integral part of the reports required under the Covenant. Further, in appropriate cases, the Committee encourages States parties to seek the assistance of relevant international agencies, including the International Labour Organization (ILO), the United Nations Development Programme (UNDP), the United Nations Educational, Scientific and Cultural Organization (UNESCO), the United Nations Children's Fund (UNICEF), the International Monetary Fund (IMF) and the World Bank, in relation both to the preparation of plans of action under Article 14 and their subsequent implementation. The Committee also calls upon the relevant international agencies to assist States parties to the greatest extent possible to meet their obligations on an urgent basis.

Chapter 12
CESCR General Comment No. 12 (1999) on the Right to Adequate Food (Article 11 of the Covenant)

Introduction and basic premises

1. The human right to adequate food is recognized in several instruments under international law. The International Covenant on Economic, Social and Cultural Rights deals more comprehensively than any other instrument with this right. Pursuant to Article 11.1 of the Covenant, States parties recognize "the right of everyone to an adequate standard of living for himself and his family, including adequate food, clothing and housing, and to the continuous improvement of living conditions," while pursuant to Article 11.2 they recognize that more immediate and urgent steps may be needed to ensure "the fundamental right to freedom from hunger and malnutrition." The human right to adequate food is of crucial importance for the enjoyment of all rights. It applies to everyone; thus the reference in Article 11.1 to "himself and his family" does not imply any limitation upon the applicability of this right to individuals or to female-headed households.

2. The Committee has accumulated significant information pertaining to the right to adequate food through examination of States parties' reports over the years since 1979. The Committee has noted that while reporting guidelines are available relating to the right to adequate food, only few States parties have provided information sufficient and precise enough to enable the Committee to determine the prevailing situation in the countries concerned with respect to this right and to identify the obstacles to its realization. This General Comment aims to identify some of the principal issues which the Committee considers to be important in relation to the right to adequate food. Its preparation was triggered by the request of Member States during the 1996 World Food Summit, for a better definition of the rights relating to food in Article 11 of the Covenant, and by a special request to the Committee to give particular attention to the Summit Plan of Action in monitoring the implementation of the specific measures provided for in Article 11 of the Covenant.

Original notes omitted.

3. In response to these requests, the Committee reviewed the relevant reports and documentation of the Commission on Human Rights and of the Sub-Commission on Prevention of Discrimination and Protection of Minorities on the right to adequate food as a human right; devoted a day of general discussion to this issue at its seventeenth session in 1997, taking into consideration the draft international code of conduct on the human right to adequate food prepared by international non-governmental organizations; participated in two expert consultations on the right to adequate food as a human right organized by the Office of the United Nations High Commissioner for Human Rights (OHCHR), in Geneva in December 1997, and in Rome in November 1998 co-hosted by the Food and Agriculture Organization of the United Nations (FAO), and noted their final reports. In April 1999 the Committee participated in a symposium on "The substance and politics of a human rights approach to food and nutrition policies and programmes," organized by the Administrative Committee on Co-ordination/ Sub-Committee on Nutrition of the United Nations at its twenty-sixth session in Geneva and hosted by OHCHR.

4. The Committee affirms that the right to adequate food is indivisibly linked to the inherent dignity of the human person and is indispensable for the fulfillment of other human rights enshrined in the International Bill of Human Rights. It is also inseparable from social justice, requiring the adoption of appropriate economic, environmental and social policies, at both the national and international levels, oriented to the eradication of poverty and the fulfillment of all human rights for all.

5. Despite the fact that the international community has frequently reaffirmed the importance of full respect for the right to adequate food, a disturbing gap still exists between the standards set in Article 11 of the Covenant and the situation prevailing in many parts of the world. More than 840 million people throughout the world, most of them in developing countries, are chronically hungry; millions of people are suffering from famine as the result of natural disasters, the increasing incidence of civil strife and wars in some regions and the use of food as a political weapon. The Committee observes that while the problems of hunger and malnutrition are often particularly acute in developing countries, malnutrition, under-nutrition and other problems which relate to the right to adequate food and the right to freedom from hunger, also exist in some of the most economically developed countries. Fundamentally, the roots of the problem of hunger and malnutrition are not lack of food but lack of *access to* available food, inter alia because of poverty, by large segments of the world's population

Normative content of Article 11, paragraphs 1 and 2

6. The right to adequate food is realized when every man, woman and child, alone or in community with others, has physical and economic access at all times to adequate food or means for its procurement. The right to adequate food shall therefore not be interpreted in a narrow or restrictive sense which equates it with a minimum package of calories, proteins and other specific nutrients. The right to adequate food will have to be realized progressively. However, States have a core obligation to take the necessary

action to mitigate and alleviate hunger as provided for in paragraph 2 of Article 11, even in times of natural or other disasters.

Adequacy and sustainability of food availability and access

7. The concept of adequacy is particularly significant in relation to the right to food since it serves to underline a number of factors which must be taken into account in determining whether particular foods or diets that are accessible can be considered the most appropriate under given circumstances for the purposes of Article 11 of the Covenant. The notion of sustainability is intrinsically linked to the notion of adequate food or food security, implying food being accessible for both present and future generations. The precise meaning of "adequacy" is to a large extent determined by prevailing social, economic, cultural, climatic, ecological and other conditions, while "sustainability" incorporates the notion of long-term availability and accessibility.

8. The Committee considers that the core content of the right to adequate food implies:

The availability of food in a quantity and quality sufficient to satisfy the dietary needs of individuals, free from adverse substances, and acceptable within a given culture;

The accessibility of such food in ways that are sustainable and that do not interfere with the enjoyment of other human rights.

9. Dietary needs implies that the diet as a whole contains a mix of nutrients for physical and mental growth, development and maintenance, and physical activity that are in compliance with human physiological needs at all stages throughout the life cycle and according to gender and occupation. Measures may therefore need to be taken to maintain, adapt or strengthen dietary diversity and appropriate consumption and feeding patterns, including breast-feeding, while ensuring that changes in availability and access to food supply as a minimum do not negatively affect dietary composition and intake.

10. Free from adverse substances sets requirements for food safety and for a range of protective measures by both public and private means to prevent contamination of foodstuffs through adulteration and/or through bad environmental hygiene or inappropriate handling at different stages throughout the food chain; care must also be taken to identify and avoid or destroy naturally occurring toxins.

11. Cultural or consumer acceptability implies the need also to take into account, as far as possible, perceived non nutrient-based values attached to food and food consumption and informed consumer concerns regarding the nature of accessible food supplies.

12. Availability refers to the possibilities either for feeding oneself directly from productive land or other natural resources, or for well-functioning distribution, processing and market systems that can move food from the site of production to where it is needed in accordance with demand.

13. Accessibility encompasses both economic and physical accessibility:

Economic accessibility implies that personal or household financial costs associated with the acquisition of food for an adequate diet should be at a level such that the attainment and satisfaction of other basic needs are not threatened or compromised. Economic accessibility applies to any acquisition pattern or entitlement through which people procure their food and is a measure of the extent to which it is satisfactory for the enjoyment of the right to adequate food. Socially vulnerable groups such as landless persons and other particularly impoverished segments of the population may need attention through special programmes. Physical accessibility implies that adequate food must be accessible to everyone, including physically vulnerable individuals, such as infants and young children, elderly people, the physically disabled, the terminally ill and persons with persistent medical problems, including the mentally ill. Victims of natural disasters, people living in disaster-prone areas and other specially disadvantaged groups may need special attention and sometimes priority consideration with respect to accessibility of food. A particular vulnerability is that of many indigenous population groups whose access to their ancestral lands may be threatened.

Obligations and violations

14. The nature of the legal obligations of States parties are set out in Article 2 of the Covenant and has been dealt with in the Committee's General Comment No. 3 (1990). The principal obligation is to take steps to achieve progressively the full realization of the right to adequate food. This imposes an obligation to move as expeditiously as possible towards that goal. Every State is obliged to ensure for everyone under its jurisdiction access to the minimum essential food which is sufficient, nutritionally adequate and safe, to ensure their freedom from hunger.

15. The right to adequate food, like any other human right, imposes three types or levels of obligations on States parties: the obligations to respect, to protect and to fulfill. In turn, the obligation to fulfill incorporates both an obligation to facilitate and an obligation to provide. The obligation to respect existing access to adequate food requires States parties not to take any measures that result in preventing such access. The obligation to protect requires measures by the State to ensure that enterprises or individuals do not deprive individuals of their access to adequate food. The obligation to fulfill (facilitate) means the State must pro-actively engage in activities intended to strengthen people's access to and utilization of resources and means to ensure their livelihood, including food security. Finally, whenever an individual or group is unable, for reasons beyond their control, to enjoy the right to adequate food by the means at their disposal, States have the obligation to fulfill (provide) that right directly. This obligation also applies for persons who are victims of natural or other disasters.

16. Some measures at these different levels of obligations of States parties are of a more immediate nature, while other measures are more of a long-term character, to achieve progressively the full realization of the right to food.

17. Violations of the Covenant occur when a State fails to ensure the satisfaction of, at the very least, the minimum essential level required to be free from hunger. In determining which actions or omissions amount to a violation of the right to food, it is important to distinguish the inability from the unwillingness of a State party to comply. Should a State party argue that resource constraints make it impossible to provide access to food for those who are unable by themselves to secure such access, the State has to demonstrate that every effort has been made to use all the resources at its disposal in an effort to satisfy, as a matter of priority, those minimum obligations. This follows from Article 2.1 of the Covenant, which obliges a State party to take the necessary steps to the maximum of its available resources, as previously pointed out by the Committee in its General Comment No. 3, paragraph 10. A State claiming that it is unable to carry out its obligation for reasons beyond its control therefore has the burden of proving that this is the case and that it has unsuccessfully sought to obtain international support to ensure the availability and accessibility of the necessary food.

18. Furthermore, any discrimination in access to food, as well as to means and entitlements for its procurement, on the grounds of race, colour, sex, language, age, religion, political or other opinion, national or social origin, property, birth or other status with the purpose or effect of nullifying or impairing the equal enjoyment or exercise of economic, social and cultural rights constitutes a violation of the Covenant.

19. Violations of the right to food can occur through the direct action of States or other entities insufficiently regulated by States. These include: the formal repeal or suspension of legislation necessary for the continued enjoyment of the right to food; denial of access to food to particular individuals or groups, whether the discrimination is based on legislation or is pro-active; the prevention of access to humanitarian food aid in internal conflicts or other emergency situations; adoption of legislation or policies which are manifestly incompatible with pre-existing legal obligations relating to the right to food; and failure to regulate activities of individuals or groups so as to prevent them from violating the right to food of others, or the failure of a State to take into account its international legal obligations regarding the right to food when entering into agreements with other States or with international organizations.

20. While only States are parties to the Covenant and are thus ultimately accountable for compliance with it, all members of society—individuals, families, local communities, non-governmental organizations, civil society organizations, as well as the private business sector—have responsibilities in the realization of the right to adequate food. The State should provide an environment that facilitates implementation of these responsibilities. The private business sector—national and transnational—should pursue its activities within the framework of a code of conduct conducive to respect of the right to adequate food, agreed upon jointly with the Government and civil society.

Implementation at the national level

21. The most appropriate ways and means of implementing the right to adequate food will inevitably vary significantly from one State party to another. Every State will have

a margin of discretion in choosing its own approaches, but the Covenant clearly requires that each State party take whatever steps are necessary to ensure that everyone is free from hunger and as soon as possible can enjoy the right to adequate food. This will require the adoption of a national strategy to ensure food and nutrition security for all, based on human rights principles that define the objectives, and the formulation of policies and corresponding benchmarks. It should also identify the resources available to meet the objectives and the most cost-effective way of using them.

22. The strategy should be based on a systematic identification of policy measures and activities relevant to the situation and context, as derived from the normative content of the right to adequate food and spelled out in relation to the levels and nature of State parties' obligations referred to in paragraph 15 of the present general comment. This will facilitate coordination between ministries and regional and local authorities and ensure that related policies and administrative decisions are in compliance with the obligations under Article 11 of the Covenant.

23. The formulation and implementation of national strategies for the right to food requires full compliance with the principles of accountability, transparency, people's participation, decentralization, legislative capacity and the independence of the judiciary. Good governance is essential to the realization of all human rights, including the elimination of poverty and ensuring a satisfactory livelihood for all.

24. Appropriate institutional mechanisms should be devised to secure a representative process towards the formulation of a strategy, drawing on all available domestic expertise relevant to food and nutrition. The strategy should set out the responsibilities and time-frame for the implementation of the necessary measures.

25. The strategy should address critical issues and measures in regard to *all* aspects of the food system, including the production, processing, distribution, marketing and consumption of safe food, as well as parallel measures in the fields of health, education, employment and social security. Care should be taken to ensure the most sustainable management and use of natural and other resources for food at the national, regional, local and household levels.

26. The strategy should give particular attention to the need to prevent discrimination in access to food or resources for food. This should include: guarantees of full and equal access to economic resources, particularly for women, including the right to inheritance and the ownership of land and other property, credit, natural resources and appropriate technology; measures to respect and protect self-employment and work which provides a remuneration ensuring a decent living for wage earners and their families (as stipulated in Article 7 (a) (ii) of the Covenant); maintaining registries on rights in land (including forests).

27. As part of their obligations to protect people's resource base for food, States parties should take appropriate steps to ensure that activities of the private business sector and civil society are in conformity with the right to food.

28. Even where a State faces severe resource constraints, whether caused by a process of economic adjustment, economic recession, climatic conditions or other factors,

measures should be undertaken to ensure that the right to adequate food is especially fulfilled for vulnerable population groups and individuals.

Benchmarks and framework legislation

29. In implementing the country-specific strategies referred to above, States should set verifiable benchmarks for subsequent national and international monitoring. In this connection, States should consider the adoption of a framework law as a major instrument in the implementation of the national strategy concerning the right to food. The framework law should include provisions on its purpose; the targets or goals to be achieved and the time-frame to be set for the achievement of those targets; the means by which the purpose could be achieved described in broad terms, in particular the intended collaboration with civil society and the private sector and with international organizations; institutional responsibility for the process; and the national mechanisms for its monitoring, as well as possible recourse procedures. In developing the benchmarks and framework legislation, States parties should actively involve civil society organizations.

30. Appropriate United Nations programmes and agencies should assist, upon request, in drafting the framework legislation and in reviewing the sectoral legislation. FAO, for example, has considerable expertise and accumulated knowledge concerning legislation in the field of food and agriculture. The United Nations Children's Fund (UNICEF) has equivalent expertise concerning legislation with regard to the right to adequate food for infants and young children through maternal and child protection including legislation to enable breast-feeding, and with regard to the regulation of marketing of breast milk substitutes.

Monitoring

31. States parties shall develop and maintain mechanisms to monitor progress towards the realization of the right to adequate food for all, to identify the factors and difficulties affecting the degree of implementation of their obligations, and to facilitate the adoption of corrective legislation and administrative measures, including measures to implement their obligations under Articles 2.1 and 23 of the Covenant.

Remedies and accountability

32. Any person or group who is a victim of a violation of the right to adequate food should have access to effective judicial or other appropriate remedies at both national and international levels. All victims of such violations are entitled to adequate reparation, which may take the form of restitution, compensation, satisfaction or guarantees of non-repetition. National Ombudsmen and human rights commissions should address violations of the right to food.

33. The incorporation in the domestic legal order of international instruments recognizing the right to food, or recognition of their applicability, can significantly enhance the scope and effectiveness of remedial measures and should be encouraged in all cases. Courts would then be empowered to adjudicate violations of the core content of the right to food by direct reference to obligations under the Covenant.

34. Judges and other members of the legal profession are invited to pay greater attention to violations of the right to food in the exercise of their functions.

35. States parties should respect and protect the work of human rights advocates and other members of civil society who assist vulnerable groups in the realization of their right to adequate food.

International obligations

States parties

36. In the spirit of Article 56 of the Charter of the United Nations, the specific provisions contained in Articles 11, 2.1, and 23 of the Covenant and the Rome Declaration of the World Food Summit, States parties should recognize the essential role of international cooperation and comply with their commitment to take joint and separate action to achieve the full realization of the right to adequate food. In implementing this commitment, States parties should take steps to respect the enjoyment of the right to food in other countries, to protect that right, to facilitate access to food and to provide the necessary aid when required. States parties should, in international agreements whenever relevant, ensure that the right to adequate food is given due attention and consider the development of further international legal instruments to that end.

37. States parties should refrain at all times from food embargoes or similar measures which endanger conditions for food production and access to food in other countries. Food should never be used as an instrument of political and economic pressure. In this regard, the Committee recalls its position, stated in its General Comment No. 8, on the relationship between economic sanctions and respect for economic, social and cultural rights.

States and international organizations

38. States have a joint and individual responsibility, in accordance with the Charter of the United Nations, to cooperate in providing disaster relief and humanitarian assistance in times of emergency, including assistance to refugees and internally displaced persons. Each State should contribute to this task in accordance with its ability. The role of the World Food Programme (WFP) and the Office of the United Nations High Commissioner for Refugees (UNHCR), and increasingly that of UNICEF and FAO is of particular importance in this respect and should be strengthened. Priority in food aid should be given to the most vulnerable populations.

39. Food aid should, as far as possible, be provided in ways which do not adversely affect local producers and local markets, and should be organized in ways that facilitate the return to food self-reliance of the beneficiaries. Such aid should be based on the needs of the intended beneficiaries. Products included in international food trade or aid programmes must be safe and culturally acceptable to the recipient population.

The United Nations and other international organizations

40. The role of the United Nations agencies, including through the United Nations Development Assistance Framework (UNDAF) at the country level, in promoting the realization of the right to food is of special importance. Coordinated efforts for the realization of the right to food should be maintained to enhance coherence and interaction among all the actors concerned, including the various components of civil society. The food organizations, FAO, WFP and the International Fund for Agricultural Development (IFAD) in conjunction with the United Nations Development Programme (UNDP), UNICEF, the World Bank and the regional development banks, should cooperate more effectively, building on their respective expertise, on the implementation of the right to food at the national level, with due respect to their individual mandates.

Chapter 13

CESCR General Comment No. 13 (1999) on the Right to Education (Article 13 of the Covenant)

The right to education

1. Education is both a human right in itself and an indispensable means of realizing other human rights. As an empowerment right, education is the primary vehicle by which economically and socially marginalized adults and children can lift themselves out of poverty and obtain the means to participate fully in their communities. Education has a vital role in empowering women, safeguarding children from exploitative and hazardous labour and sexual exploitation, promoting human rights and democracy, protecting the environment, and controlling population growth. Increasingly, education is recognized as one of the best financial investments States can make. But the importance of education is not just practical: a well-educated, enlightened and active mind, able to wander freely and widely, is one of the joys and rewards of human existence.

2. The International Covenant on Economic, Social and Cultural Rights (ICESCR) devotes two Articles to the right to education, Articles 13 and 14. Article 13, the longest provision in the Covenant, is the most wide-ranging and comprehensive Article on the right to education in international human rights law. The Committee has already adopted General Comment 11 on Article 14 (plans of action for primary education); General Comment 11 and the present general comment are complementary and should be considered together. The Committee is aware that for millions of people throughout the world, the enjoyment of the right to education remains a distant goal. Moreover, in many cases, this goal is becoming increasingly remote. The Committee is also conscious of the formidable structural and other obstacles impeding the full implementation of Article 13 in many States parties.

3. With a view to assisting States parties' implementation of the Covenant and the fulfillment of their reporting obligations, this general comment focuses on the normative content of Article 13 (Part I, paras. 4–42), some of the obligations arising from it (Part II, paras. 43–57), and some illustrative violations (Part II, paras. 58–59). Part III briefly

Original notes omitted.

remarks upon the obligations of actors other than States parties. The general comment is based upon the Committee's experience in examining States parties, reports over many years.

I. Normative Content of Article 13

Article 13 (1). Aims and objectives of education

4. States parties agree that all education, whether public or private, formal or non-formal, shall be directed towards the aims and objectives identified in Article 13 (1). The Committee notes that these educational objectives reflect the fundamental purposes and principles of the United Nations as enshrined in Articles 1 and 2 of the Charter. For the most part, they are also found in Article 26 (2) of the Universal Declaration of Human Rights, although Article 13 (1) adds to the Declaration in three respects: education shall be directed to the human personality's "sense of dignity," it shall "enable all persons to participate effectively in a free society," and it shall promote understanding among all "ethnic" groups, as well as nations and racial and religious groups. Of those educational objectives which are common to Article 26 (2) of the Universal Declaration of Human Rights and Article 13 (1) of the Covenant, perhaps the most fundamental is that "education shall be directed to the full development of the human personality."

5. The Committee notes that since the General Assembly adopted the Covenant in 1966, other international instruments have further elaborated the objectives to which education should be directed. Accordingly, the Committee takes the view that States parties are required to ensure that education conforms to the aims and objectives identified in Article 13 (1), as interpreted in the light of the World Declaration on Education for All (Jomtien, Thailand, 1990) (art. 1), the Convention on the Rights of the Child (art. 29 (1)), the Vienna Declaration and Programme of Action (Part I, para. 33 and Part II, para. 80), and the Plan of Action for the United Nations Decade for Human Rights Education (para. 2). While all these texts closely correspond to Article 13 (1) of the Covenant, they also include elements which are not expressly provided for in Article 13 (1), such as specific references to gender equality and respect for the environment. These new elements are implicit in, and reflect a contemporary interpretation of Article 13 (1). The Committee obtains support for this point of view from the widespread endorsement that the previously mentioned texts have received from all regions of the world.

Article 13 (2). The right to receive an education—some general remarks

6. While the precise and appropriate application of the terms will depend upon the conditions prevailing in a particular State party, education in all its forms and at all levels shall exhibit the following interrelated and essential features:

(a) Availability—functioning educational institutions and programmes have to be available in sufficient quantity within the jurisdiction of the State party. What they require to function depends upon numerous factors, including the developmental context within which they operate; for example, all institutions and programmes are likely to require buildings or other protection from the elements, sanitation facilities for both sexes, safe drinking water, trained teachers receiving domestically competitive salaries, teaching materials, and so on; while some will also require facilities such as a library, computer facilities and information technology;

(b) Accessibility—educational institutions and programmes have to be accessible to everyone, without discrimination, within the jurisdiction of the State party. Accessibility has three overlapping dimensions:

Non-discrimination—education must be accessible to all, especially the most vulnerable groups, in law and fact, without discrimination on any of the prohibited grounds (see paras. 31–37 on non-discrimination);

Physical accessibility—education has to be within safe physical reach, either by attendance at some reasonably convenient geographic location (e.g. a neighbourhood school) or via modern technology (e.g. access to a "distance learning" programme);

Economic accessibility—education has to be affordable to all. This dimension of accessibility is subject to the differential wording of Article 13 (2) in relation to primary, secondary and higher education: whereas primary education shall be available "free to all," States parties are required to progressively introduce free secondary and higher education;

(c) Acceptability—the form and substance of education, including curricula and teaching methods, have to be acceptable (e.g., relevant, culturally appropriate and of good quality) to students and, in appropriate cases, parents; this is subject to the educational objectives required by Article 13 (1) and such minimum educational standards as may be approved by the State (see art. 13 (3) and (4));

(d) Adaptability—education has to be flexible so it can adapt to the needs of changing societies and communities and respond to the needs of students within their diverse social and cultural settings.

7. When considering the appropriate application of these "interrelated and essential features" the best interests of the student shall be a primary consideration.

Article 13 (2) (a). The right to primary education

8. Primary education includes the elements of availability, accessibility, acceptability and adaptability which are common to education in all its forms and at all levels.

9. The Committee obtains guidance on the proper interpretation of the term "primary education" from the World Declaration on Education for All which states: "The main delivery system for the basic education of children outside the family is primary schooling. Primary education must be universal, ensure that the basic learning needs of all children are satisfied, and take into account the culture, needs and opportunities of

the community" (art. 5). "[B]asic learning needs" are defined in Article 1 of the World Declaration. While primary education is not synonymous with basic education, there is a close correspondence between the two. In this regard, the Committee endorses the position taken by UNICEF: "Primary education is the most important component of basic education."

10. As formulated in Article 13 (2) (a), primary education has two distinctive features: it is "compulsory" and "available free to all." For the Committee's observations on both terms, see paragraphs 6 and 7 of General Comment 11 on Article 14 of the Covenant.

Article 13 (2) (b). The right to secondary education

11. Secondary education includes the elements of availability, accessibility, acceptability and adaptability which are common to education in all its forms and at all levels.

12. While the content of secondary education will vary among States parties and over time, it includes completion of basic education and consolidation of the foundations for life-long learning and human development. It prepares students for vocational and higher educational opportunities. Article 13 (2) (b) applies to secondary education "in its different forms," thereby recognizing that secondary education demands flexible curricula and varied delivery systems to respond to the needs of students in different social and cultural settings. The Committee encourages "alternative" educational programmes which parallel regular secondary school systems.

13. According to Article 13 (2) (b), secondary education "shall be made generally available and accessible to all by every appropriate means, and in particular by the progressive introduction of free education." The phrase "generally available" signifies, firstly, that secondary education is not dependent on a student's apparent capacity or ability and, secondly, that secondary education will be distributed throughout the State in such a way that it is available on the same basis to all. For the Committee's interpretation of "accessible," see paragraph 6 above. The phrase "every appropriate means" reinforces the point that States parties should adopt varied and innovative approaches to the delivery of secondary education in different social and cultural contexts.

14. "[P]rogressive introduction of free education" means that while States must prioritize the provision of free primary education, they also have an obligation to take concrete steps towards achieving free secondary and higher education. For the Committee's general observations on the meaning of the word "free," see paragraph 7 of General Comment 11 on Article 14.

Technical and vocational education

15. Technical and vocational education (TVE) forms part of both the right to education and the right to work (art. 6 (2)). Article 13 (2) (b) presents TVE as part of secondary education, reflecting the particular importance of TVE at this level of education.

Article 6 (2), however, does not refer to TVE in relation to a specific level of education; it comprehends that TVE has a wider role, helping "to achieve steady economic, social and cultural development and full and productive employment." Also, the Universal Declaration of Human Rights states that "Technical and professional education shall be made generally available" (art. 26 (1)). Accordingly, the Committee takes the view that TVE forms an integral element of all levels of education.

16. An introduction to technology and to the world of work should not be confined to specific TVE programmes but should be understood as a component of general education. According to the UNESCO Convention on Technical and Vocational Education (1989), TVE consists of "all forms and levels of the educational process involving, in addition to general knowledge, the study of technologies and related sciences and the acquisition of practical skills, know-how, attitudes and understanding relating to occupations in the various sectors of economic and social life" (art. 1 (a)). This view is also reflected in certain ILO Conventions. Understood in this way, the right to TVE includes the following aspects:

(a) It enables students to acquire knowledge and skills which contribute to their personal development, self-reliance and employability and enhances the productivity of their families and communities, including the State party's economic and social development;

(b) It takes account of the educational, cultural and social background of the population concerned; the skills, knowledge and levels of qualification needed in the various sectors of the economy; and occupational health, safety and welfare;

(c) Provides retraining for adults whose current knowledge and skills have become obsolete owing to technological, economic, employment, social or other changes;

(d) It consists of programmes which give students, especially those from developing countries, the opportunity to receive TVE in other States, with a view to the appropriate transfer and adaptation of technology;

(e) It consists, in the context of the Covenant's non-discrimination and equality provisions, of programmes which promote the TVE of women, girls, out-of-school youth, unemployed youth, the children of migrant workers, refugees, persons with disabilities and other disadvantaged groups.

Article 13 (2) (c). The right to higher education

17. Higher education includes the elements of availability, accessibility, acceptability and adaptability which are common to education in all its forms at all levels.

18. While Article 13 (2) (c) is formulated on the same lines as Article 13 (2) (b), there are three differences between the two provisions. Article 13 (2) (c) does not include a reference to either education "in its different forms" or specifically to TVE. In the Committee's opinion, these two omissions reflect only a difference of emphasis between Article 13 (2) (b) and (c). If higher education is to respond to the needs of students in

different social and cultural settings, it must have flexible curricula and varied delivery systems, such as distance learning; in practice, therefore, both secondary and higher education have to be available "in different forms." As for the lack of reference in Article 13 (2) (c) to technical and vocational education, given Article 6 (2) of the Covenant and Article 26 (1) of the Universal Declaration, TVE forms an integral component of all levels of education, including higher education.

19. The third and most significant difference between Article 13 (2) (b) and (c) is that while secondary education "shall be made generally available and accessible to all," higher education "shall be made equally accessible to all, on the basis of capacity." According to Article 13 (2) (c), higher education is not to be "generally available," but only available "on the basis of capacity." The "capacity" of individuals should be assessed by reference to all their relevant expertise and experience.

20. So far as the wording of Article 13 (2) (b) and (c) is the same (e.g., "the progressive introduction of free education"), see the previous comments on Article 13 (2) (b).

Article 13 (2) (d). The right to fundamental education

21. Fundamental education includes the elements of availability, accessibility, acceptability and adaptability which are common to education in all its forms and at all levels.

22. In general terms, fundamental education corresponds to basic education as set out in the World Declaration on Education for All. By virtue of Article 13 (2) (d), individuals "who have not received or completed the whole period of their primary education" have a right to fundamental education, or basic education as defined in the World Declaration on Education for All.

23. Since everyone has the right to the satisfaction of their "basic learning needs" as understood by the World Declaration, the right to fundamental education is not confined to those "who have not received or completed the whole period of their primary education." The right to fundamental education extends to all those who have not yet satisfied their "basic learning needs."

24. It should be emphasized that enjoyment of the right to fundamental education is not limited by age or gender; it extends to children, youth and adults, including older persons. Fundamental education, therefore, is an integral component of adult education and life-long learning. Because fundamental education is a right of all age groups, curricula and delivery systems must be devised which are suitable for students of all ages.

Article 13 (2) (e). A school system; adequate fellowship system; material conditions of teaching staff

25. The requirement that the "development of a system of schools at all levels shall be actively pursued" means that a State party is obliged to have an overall developmental strategy for its school system. The strategy must encompass schooling at all levels, but

the Covenant requires States parties to prioritize primary education (see para. 51). "[A]ctively pursued" suggests that the overall strategy should attract a degree of governmental priority and, in any event, must be implemented with vigour.

26. The requirement that "an adequate fellowship system shall be established" should be read with the Covenant's non-discrimination and equality provisions; the fellowship system should enhance equality of educational access for individuals from disadvantaged groups.

27. While the Covenant requires that "the material conditions of teaching staff shall be continuously improved," in practice the general working conditions of teachers have deteriorated, and reached unacceptably low levels, in many States parties in recent years. Not only is this inconsistent with Article 13 (2) (e), but it is also a major obstacle to the full realization of students' right to education. The Committee also notes the relationship between Articles 13 (2) (e), 2 (2), 3 and 6–8 of the Covenant, including the right of teachers to organize and bargain collectively; draws the attention of States parties to the joint UNESCO-ILO Recommendation Concerning the Status of Teachers (1966) and the UNESCO Recommendation Concerning the Status of Higher-Education Teaching Personnel (1997); and urges States parties to report on measures they are taking to ensure that all teaching staff enjoy the conditions and status commensurate with their role.

Article 13 (3) and (4). The right to educational freedom

28. Article 13 (3) has two elements, one of which is that States parties undertake to respect the liberty of parents and guardians to ensure the religious and moral education of their children in conformity with their own convictions. The Committee is of the view that this element of Article 13 (3) permits public school instruction in subjects such as the general history of religions and ethics if it is given in an unbiased and objective way, respectful of the freedoms of opinion, conscience and expression. It notes that public education that includes instruction in a particular religion or belief is inconsistent with Article 13 (3) unless provision is made for non-discriminatory exemptions or alternatives that would accommodate the wishes of parents and guardians.

29. The second element of Article 13 (3) is the liberty of parents and guardians to choose other than public schools for their children, provided the schools conform to "such minimum educational standards as may be laid down or approved by the State." This has to be read with the complementary provision, Article 13 (4), which affirms "the liberty of individuals and bodies to establish and direct educational institutions," provided the institutions conform to the educational objectives set out in Article 13 (1) and certain minimum standards. These minimum standards may relate to issues such as admission, curricula and the recognition of certificates. In their turn, these standards must be consistent with the educational objectives set out in Article 13 (1).

30. Under Article 13 (4), everyone, including non-nationals, has the liberty to establish and direct educational institutions. The liberty also extends to "bodies," i.e., legal persons

or entities. It includes the right to establish and direct all types of educational institutions, including nurseries, universities and institutions for adult education. Given the principles of non-discrimination, equal opportunity and effective participation in society for all, the State has an obligation to ensure that the liberty set out in Article 13 (4) does not lead to extreme disparities of educational opportunity for some groups in society.

Article 13. Special topics of broad application

Non-discrimination and equal treatment

31. The prohibition against discrimination enshrined in Article 2 (2) of the Covenant is subject to neither progressive realization nor the availability of resources; it applies fully and immediately to all aspects of education and encompasses all internationally prohibited grounds of discrimination. The Committee interprets Articles 2 (2) and 3 in the light of the UNESCO Convention against Discrimination in Education, the relevant provisions of the Convention on the Elimination of All Forms of Discrimination against Women, the International Convention on the Elimination of All Forms of Racial Discrimination, the Convention on the Rights of the Child and the ILO Indigenous and Tribal Peoples Convention, 1989 (Convention No. 169), and wishes to draw particular attention to the following issues.

32. The adoption of temporary special measures intended to bring about de facto equality for men and women and for disadvantaged groups is not a violation of the right to non-discrimination with regard to education, so long as such measures do not lead to the maintenance of unequal or separate standards for different groups, and provided they are not continued after the objectives for which they were taken have been achieved.

33. In some circumstances, separate educational systems or institutions for groups defined by the categories in Article 2 (2) shall be deemed not to constitute a breach of the Covenant. In this regard, the Committee affirms Article 2 of the UNESCO Convention against Discrimination in Education (1960).

34. The Committee takes note of Article 2 of the Convention on the Rights of the Child and Article 3 (e) of the UNESCO Convention against Discrimination in Education and confirms that the principle of non-discrimination extends to all persons of school age residing in the territory of a State party, including non-nationals, and irrespective of their legal status.

35. Sharp disparities in spending policies that result in differing qualities of education for persons residing in different geographic locations may constitute discrimination under the Covenant.

36. The Committee affirms paragraph 35 of its General Comment 5, which addresses the issue of persons with disabilities in the context of the right to education,

and paragraphs 36–42 of its General Comment 6, which address the issue of older persons in relation to Articles 13–15 of the Covenant.

37. States parties must closely monitor education—including all relevant policies, institutions, programmes, spending patterns and other practices—so as to identify and take measures to redress any de facto discrimination. Educational data should be disaggregated by the prohibited grounds of discrimination.

Academic freedom and institutional autonomy

38. In the light of its examination of numerous States parties' reports, the Committee has formed the view that the right to education can only be enjoyed if accompanied by the academic freedom of staff and students. Accordingly, even though the issue is not explicitly mentioned in Article 13, it is appropriate and necessary for the Committee to make some observations about academic freedom. The following remarks give particular attention to institutions of higher education because, in the Committee's experience, staff and students in higher education are especially vulnerable to political and other pressures which undermine academic freedom. The Committee wishes to emphasize, however, that staff and students throughout the education sector are entitled to academic freedom and many of the following observations have general application.

39. Members of the academic community, individually or collectively, are free to pursue, develop and transmit knowledge and ideas, through research, teaching, study, discussion, documentation, production, creation or writing. Academic freedom includes the liberty of individuals to express freely opinions about the institution or system in which they work, to fulfill their functions without discrimination or fear of repression by the State or any other actor, to participate in professional or representative academic bodies, and to enjoy all the internationally recognized human rights applicable to other individuals in the same jurisdiction. The enjoyment of academic freedom carries with it obligations, such as the duty to respect the academic freedom of others, to ensure the fair discussion of contrary views, and to treat all without discrimination on any of the prohibited grounds.

40. The enjoyment of academic freedom requires the autonomy of institutions of higher education. Autonomy is that degree of self-governance necessary for effective decision-making by institutions of higher education in relation to their academic work, standards, management and related activities. Self-governance, however, must be consistent with systems of public accountability, especially in respect of funding provided by the State. Given the substantial public investments made in higher education, an appropriate balance has to be struck between institutional autonomy and accountability. While there is no single model, institutional arrangements should be fair, just and equitable, and as transparent and participatory as possible.

Discipline in schools

41. In the Committee's view, corporal punishment is inconsistent with the fundamental guiding principle of international human rights law enshrined in the Preambles to

the Universal Declaration of Human Rights and both Covenants: the dignity of the individual. Other aspects of school discipline may also be inconsistent with human dignity, such as public humiliation. Nor should any form of discipline breach other rights under the Covenant, such as the right to food. A State party is required to take measures to ensure that discipline which is inconsistent with the Covenant does not occur in any public or private educational institution within its jurisdiction. The Committee welcomes initiatives taken by some States parties which actively encourage schools to introduce "positive," non-violent approaches to school discipline.

Limitations on Article 13

42. The Committee wishes to emphasize that the Covenant's limitations clause, Article 4, is primarily intended to be protective of the rights of individuals rather than permissive of the imposition of limitations by the State. Consequently, a State party which closes a university or other educational institution on grounds such as national security or the preservation of public order has the burden of justifying such a serious measure in relation to each of the elements identified in Article 4.

II. States Parties' Obligations and Violations

General legal obligations

43. While the Covenant provides for progressive realization and acknowledges the constraints due to the limits of available resources, it also imposes on States parties various obligations which are of immediate effect. States parties have immediate obligations in relation to the right to education, such as the "guarantee" that the right "will be exercised without discrimination of any kind" (art. 2 (2)) and the obligation "to take steps" (art. 2 (1)) towards the full realization of Article 13. Such steps must be "deliberate, concrete and targeted" towards the full realization of the right to education.

44. The realization of the right to education over time, that is "progressively," should not be interpreted as depriving States parties' obligations of all meaningful content. Progressive realization means that States parties have a specific and continuing obligation "to move as expeditiously and effectively as possible" towards the full realization of Article 13.

45. There is a strong presumption of impermissibility of any retrogressive measures taken in relation to the right to education, as well as other rights enunciated in the Covenant. If any deliberately retrogressive measures are taken, the State party has the burden of proving that they have been introduced after the most careful consideration of all alternatives and that they are fully justified by reference to the totality of the rights provided for in the Covenant and in the context of the full use of the State party's maximum available resources.

46. The right to education, like all human rights, imposes three types or levels of obligations on States parties: the obligations to respect, protect and fulfill. In turn, the

obligation to fulfill incorporates both an obligation to facilitate and an obligation to provide.

47. The obligation to respect requires States parties to avoid measures that hinder or prevent the enjoyment of the right to education. The obligation to protect requires States parties to take measures that prevent third parties from interfering with the enjoyment of the right to education. The obligation to fulfill (facilitate) requires States to take positive measures that enable and assist individuals and communities to enjoy the right to education. Finally, States parties have an obligation to fulfill (provide) the right to education. As a general rule, States parties are obliged to fulfill (provide) a specific right in the Covenant when an individual or group is unable, for reasons beyond their control, to realize the right themselves by the means at their disposal. However, the extent of this obligation is always subject to the text of the Covenant.

48. In this respect, two features of Article 13 require emphasis. First, it is clear that Article 13 regards States as having principal responsibility for the direct provision of education in most circumstances; States parties recognize, for example, that the "development of a system of schools at all levels shall be actively pursued" (art. 13 (2) (e)). Secondly, given the differential wording of Article 13 (2) in relation to primary, secondary, higher and fundamental education, the parameters of a State party's obligation to fulfill (provide) are not the same for all levels of education. Accordingly, in light of the text of the Covenant, States parties have an enhanced obligation to fulfill (provide) regarding the right to education, but the extent of this obligation is not uniform for all levels of education. The Committee observes that this interpretation of the obligation to fulfill (provide) in relation to Article 13 coincides with the law and practice of numerous States parties.

Specific legal obligations

49. States parties are required to ensure that curricula, for all levels of the educational system, are directed to the objectives identified in Article 13 (1). They are also obliged to establish and maintain a transparent and effective system which monitors whether or not education is, in fact, directed to the educational objectives set out in Article 13 (1).

50. In relation to Article 13 (2), States have obligations to respect, protect and fulfill each of the "essential features" (availability, accessibility, acceptability, adaptability) of the right to education. By way of illustration, a State must respect the availability of education by not closing private schools; protect the accessibility of education by ensuring that third parties, including parents and employers, do not stop girls from going to school; fulfill (facilitate) the acceptability of education by taking positive measures to ensure that education is culturally appropriate for minorities and indigenous peoples, and of good quality for all; fulfill (provide) the adaptability of education by designing and providing resources for curricula which reflect the contemporary needs of students in a changing world; and fulfill (provide) the availability of education by actively developing a system of schools, including building classrooms, delivering programmes, providing teaching materials, training teachers and paying them domestically competitive salaries.

51. As already observed, the obligations of States parties in relation to primary, secondary, higher and fundamental education are not identical. Given the wording of Article 13 (2), States parties are obliged to prioritize the introduction of compulsory, free primary education. This interpretation of Article 13 (2) is reinforced by the priority accorded to primary education in Article 14. The obligation to provide primary education for all is an immediate duty of all States parties.

52. In relation to Article 13 (2) (b)–(d), a State party has an immediate obligation "to take steps" (art. 2 (1)) towards the realization of secondary, higher and fundamental education for all those within its jurisdiction. At a minimum, the State party is required to adopt and implement a national educational strategy which includes the provision of secondary, higher and fundamental education in accordance with the Covenant. This strategy should include mechanisms, such as indicators and benchmarks on the right to education, by which progress can be closely monitored.

53. Under Article 13 (2) (e), States parties are obliged to ensure that an educational fellowship system is in place to assist disadvantaged groups. The obligation to pursue actively the "development of a system of schools at all levels" reinforces the principal responsibility of States parties to ensure the direct provision of the right to education in most circumstances.

54. States parties are obliged to establish "minimum educational standards" to which all educational institutions established in accordance with Article 13 (3) and (4) are required to conform. They must also maintain a transparent and effective system to monitor such standards. A State party has no obligation to fund institutions established in accordance with Article 13 (3) and (4); however, if a State elects to make a financial contribution to private educational institutions, it must do so without discrimination on any of the prohibited grounds.

55. States parties have an obligation to ensure that communities and families are not dependent on child labour. The Committee especially affirms the importance of education in eliminating child labour and the obligations set out in Article 7 (2) of the Worst Forms of Child Labour Convention, 1999 (Convention No. 182). Additionally, given Article 2 (2), States parties are obliged to remove gender and other stereotyping which impedes the educational access of girls, women and other disadvantaged groups.

56. In its General Comment 3, the Committee drew attention to the obligation of all States parties to take steps, "individually and through international assistance and cooperation, especially economic and technical," towards the full realization of the rights recognized in the Covenant, such as the right to education. See the Committee's General Comment 3, paras. 13–14. Articles 2 (1) and 23 of the Covenant, Article 56 of the Charter of the United Nations, Article 10 of the World Declaration on Education for All, and Part I, paragraph 34 of the Vienna Declaration and Programme of Action all reinforce the obligation of States parties in relation to the provision of international assistance and cooperation for the full realization of the right to education. In relation to the negotiation and ratification of international agreements, States parties

should take steps to ensure that these instruments do not adversely impact upon the right to education. Similarly, States parties have an obligation to ensure that their actions as members of international organizations, including international financial institutions, take due account of the right to education.

57. In its General Comment 3, the Committee confirmed that States parties have "a minimum core obligation to ensure the satisfaction of, at the very least, minimum essential levels" of each of the rights enunciated in the Covenant, including "the most basic forms of education." In the context of Article 13, this core includes an obligation: to ensure the right of access to public educational institutions and programmes on a non-discriminatory basis; to ensure that education conforms to the objectives set out in Article 13 (1); to provide primary education for all in accordance with Article 13 (2) (a); to adopt and implement a national educational strategy which includes provision for secondary, higher and fundamental education; and to ensure free choice of education without interference from the State or third parties, subject to conformity with "minimum educational standards" (art. 13 (3) and (4)).

Violations

58. When the normative content of Article 13 (Part I) is applied to the general and specific obligations of States parties (Part II), a dynamic process is set in motion which facilitates identification of violations of the right to education. Violations of Article 13 may occur through the direct action of States parties (acts of commission) or through their failure to take steps required by the Covenant (acts of omission).

59. By way of illustration, violations of Article 13 include: the introduction or failure to repeal legislation which discriminates against individuals or groups, on any of the prohibited grounds, in the field of education; the failure to take measures which address de facto educational discrimination; the use of curricula inconsistent with the educational objectives set out in Article 13 (1); the failure to maintain a transparent and effective system to monitor conformity with Article 13 (1); the failure to introduce, as a matter of priority, primary education which is compulsory and available free to all; the failure to take "deliberate, concrete and targeted" measures towards the progressive realization of secondary, higher and fundamental education in accordance with Article 13 (2) (b)-(d); the prohibition of private educational institutions; the failure to ensure private educational institutions conform to the "minimum educational standards" required by Article 13 (3) and (4); the denial of academic freedom of staff and students; the closure of educational institutions in times of political tension in nonconformity with Article 4.

III. Obligations of Actors Other Than States Parties

60. Given Article 22 of the Covenant, the role of the United Nations agencies, including at the country level through the United Nations Development Assistance Framework

(UNDAF), is of special importance in relation to the realization of Article 13. Coordinated efforts for the realization of the right to education should be maintained to improve coherence and interaction among all the actors concerned, including the various components of civil society. UNESCO, the United Nations Development Programme, UNICEF, ILO, the World Bank, the regional development banks, the International Monetary Fund and other relevant bodies within the United Nations system should enhance their cooperation for the implementation of the right to education at the national level, with due respect to their specific mandates, and building on their respective expertise. In particular, the international financial institutions, notably the World Bank and IMF, should pay greater attention to the protection of the right to education in their lending policies, credit agreements, structural adjustment programmes and measures taken in response to the debt crisis. When examining the reports of States parties, the Committee will consider the effects of the assistance provided by all actors other than States parties on the ability of States to meet their obligations under Article 13. The adoption of a human rights-based approach by United Nations specialized agencies, programmes and bodies will greatly facilitate implementation of the right to education.

Chapter 14
CESCR General Comment No. 14 (2000) on the Right to the Highest Attainable Standard of Health (Article 12)

1. Health is a fundamental human right indispensable for the exercise of other human rights. Every human being is entitled to the enjoyment of the highest attainable standard of health conducive to living a life in dignity. The realization of the right to health may be pursued by numerous, complementary approaches, such as the formulation of health policies, or the implementation of health programmes developed by the World Health Organization (WHO), or the adoption of specific legal instruments. Moreover, the right to health includes certain components which are legally enforceable.

2. The human right to health is recognized in numerous international instruments. Article 25(1) of the Universal Declaration of Human Rights affirms: "Everyone has a right to a standard of living adequate for the health of himself and his family, including food, clothing, housing, and medical care and necessary social services." The International Covenant on Economic, Social and Cultural Rights provides the most comprehensive article on the right to health in international human rights law. According to Article 12 (1) of the Covenant, States Parties recognize "the right of everyone to the enjoyment of the highest attainable standard of physical and mental health, while Article 12 (2) enumerates, by way of illustration, a number of "steps to be taken by the States parties [. . .] to achieve the full realization of this right." Additionally, the right to health is recognized, inter alia, in Article 5 (e) (iv) of the International Convention on the Elimination of All Forms of Racial Discrimination of 1965, in Articles 11 (1) (f) and 12 of the Convention on the Elimination of All Forms of Discrimination Against Women of 1979 and in Article 24 of the Convention on the Rights of the Child of 1989. Several regional human rights instruments also recognize the right to health, such as the European Social Charter of 1961 as revised (Article 11), the African Charter on Human and Peoples' Rights of 1981 (Article 16) and the Additional Protocol to the American Convention on Human Rights in the Area of Economic, Social and Cultural Rights of 1988 (Article 10). Similarly, the right to health has been proclaimed by the Commission on Human Rights, as well as in the Vienna Declaration and Programme of Action of 1993 and other international instruments.

Original notes omitted.

3. The right to health is closely related to and dependent upon the realization of other human rights, as contained in the International Bill of Rights, including the rights to food, housing, work, education, human dignity, life, non-discrimination, equality, the prohibition against torture, privacy, access to information, and the freedoms of association, assembly and movement. These and other rights and freedoms address integral components of the right to health.

4. In drafting Article 12 of the Covenant, the General Assembly's Third Committee did not adopt the definition of health contained in the preamble to the Constitution of WHO which conceptualizes health as "a state of complete physical, mental and social well-being and not merely the absence of disease or infirmity." However, the reference in Article 12 (1) of the Covenant to "the highest attainable standard of physical and mental health" is not confined to the right to health care. On the contrary, the drafting history and the express wording of Article 12 (2) acknowledge that the right to health embraces a wide range of socio-economic factors that promote conditions whereby people can lead a healthy life, and extends to the underlying determinants of health, such as food and nutrition, housing, access to safe and potable water and sanitation, safe and healthy working conditions, and a healthy environment.

5. The Committee is aware that, for millions of people throughout the world, the full enjoyment of the right to health still remains a distant goal. Moreover, in many cases, especially for those living in poverty, this goal is becoming increasingly remote. The Committee recognizes the formidable structural and other obstacles that result from international and other factors beyond the control of States, and impeding the full realization of Article 12 in many States parties.

6. With a view to assisting States parties' implementation of the Covenant and the fulfillment of their reporting obligations, this General Comment focuses on the normative content of Article 12 (Part I), States parties' obligations (Part II), violations (Part III), and implementation at the national level (Part IV), while Part V deals with the obligations of actors other than States parties. The General Comment is based on the Committee's experience in examining States parties' reports over many years.

I. Normative Content of Article 12

7. Article 12 (1) provides a definition of the right to health, while Article 12 (2) enumerates illustrative, non-exhaustive examples of States parties' obligations.

8. The right to health is not to be understood as a right to be healthy. The right to health contains both freedoms and entitlements. Freedoms include the right to control one's health and body, including sexual and reproductive freedom, and the right to be free from interference, such as the right to be free from torture, non-consensual medical treatment and experimentation. By contrast, the entitlements include the right to a system of health protection, which provides equality of opportunity for people to enjoy the highest attainable level of health.

9. The notion of "the highest attainable standard of health" in Article 12 (1) takes into account both the individual's biological and socio-economic preconditions and a State's available resources. There are a number of aspects which cannot be addressed solely within the relationship between States and individuals, in particular, good health cannot be ensured by a State, nor can States provide protection against every possible cause of human ill health. Thus, genetic factors, individual susceptibility to ill health and the adoption of unhealthy or risky lifestyles may play an important role with respect to an individual's health. Consequently, the right to health must be understood as a right to the enjoyment of a variety of facilities, goods, services and conditions necessary for the realization of the highest attainable standard of health.

10. Since the adoption of the two UN Covenants in 1966 the world health situation has changed dramatically and the notion of health has undergone substantial changes and has also widened in scope. More determinants of health are being taken into consideration, such as resource distribution and gender differences. A wider definition of health also takes into account such socially-related concerns as violence and armed conflict. Moreover, formerly unknown diseases, such as Human Immunodeficiency Virus and Acquired Immunodeficiency Syndrome (HIV/AIDS), and others that have become more widespread, such as cancer, as well as the rapid growth of the world population, have created new obstacles for the realization of the right to health which need to be taken into account when interpreting Article 12.

11. The Committee interprets the right to health, as defined in Article 12 (1), as an inclusive right extending not only to timely and appropriate health care but also to the underlying determinants of health, such as access to safe and potable water and adequate sanitation, an adequate supply of safe food, nutrition and housing, healthy occupational and environmental conditions and access to health-related education and information, including on sexual and reproductive health. A further important aspect is the participation of the population in all health-related decision-making at the community, national and international levels.

12. The right to health in all its forms and at all levels contains the following interrelated and essential terms, the precise application of which will depend on the conditions prevailing in a particular State party:

(1) Availability—functioning public health and health care facilities, goods and services, as well as programmes, have to be available in sufficient quantity within the State party. The precise nature of the facilities, goods and services will vary according to numerous factors, including the State party's developmental level. They will include, however, the underlying determinants of health, such as safe and potable drinking water and sanitation facilities, hospitals, clinics and other health-related buildings, trained medical and professional personnel receiving domestically competitive salaries and essential drugs, as defined by WHO's Action Programme on Essential Drugs.

(2) Accessibility—health facilities, goods and services have to be accessible to everyone without discrimination, within the jurisdiction of the State party. Accessibility has four overlapping dimensions:

(i) Non-discrimination—health facilities, goods and services must be accessible to all, especially the most vulnerable or marginalized sections of the population, in law and fact, without discrimination on any of the prohibited grounds.

(ii) Physical accessibility—health facilities, goods and services must be within safe physical reach for all parts of the population, especially for vulnerable or marginalized groups, such as ethnic minorities and indigenous populations, women, children, adolescents, older persons, persons with disabilities, and persons with HIV/AIDS. Accessibility also implies that medical services and underlying determinants of health, such as safe and potable water and adequate sanitary facilities, are within safe physical reach, including in rural areas. Accessibility further includes adequate access to buildings for persons with disabilities.

(iii) Economic accessibility (affordability)—health facilities, goods and services must be affordable for all. Payment for health care services, as well as services related to the underlying determinants of health, have to be based on the principle of equity ensuring that these services, whether privately or publicly provided, are affordable for all, including socially disadvantaged groups. Equity demands that poorer households should not be disproportionately burdened with health expenses as compared to richer households.

(iv) Information accessibility—Accessibility includes the right to seek, receive and impart information and ideas concerning health issues. However, accessibility of information should not impair the right to have personal health data treated with confidentiality.

(3) Acceptability—all health facilities, goods and services must be respectful of medical ethics and culturally appropriate, i.e. respectful of the culture of individuals, minorities, peoples and communities, sensitive to gender and life-cycle requirements, as well as being designed to respect confidentiality and improve the health status of those concerned.

(4) Quality—as well as being culturally acceptable, health facilities, goods and services must also be scientifically and medically appropriate and of good quality. This requires, inter alia, skilled medical personnel, scientifically approved and unexpired drugs and hospital equipment, safe and potable water, and adequate sanitation.

13. The non-exhaustive catalogue of examples in Article 12 (2) provides guidance in defining the action to be taken by States. It gives specific generic examples of measures arising from the broad definition of the right to health contained in paragraph 1, thereby illustrating the content of that right, as exemplified in the following paragraphs.

Article 12 (2) a. The right to maternal, child and reproductive health

14. "The provision for the reduction of the stillbirth-rate and of infant mortality and for the healthy development of the child" (art. 12 (2) a) may be understood as requiring measures to improve child and maternal health, sexual and reproductive health services, including access to family planning, pre- and post-natal care, emergency obstetric services and access to information, as well as to resources necessary to act on that information.

Article 12 (2) b. The right to healthy natural and workplace environments

15. "The improvement of all aspects of environmental and industrial hygiene" (art. 12 (2) b) includes, inter alia, preventive measures in respect of occupational accidents and diseases; the requirement to ensure an adequate supply of safe and potable water and basic sanitation; the prevention and reduction of the population's exposure to harmful substances such as radiation and harmful chemicals or other detrimental environmental conditions that directly or indirectly impact upon human health. Furthermore, industrial hygiene refers to the minimization of, so far as is reasonably practicable, the causes of health hazards inherent in the working environment. Article 12 (2) (b) also embraces adequate housing and safe and hygienic working conditions, an adequate supply of food and proper nutrition, and discourages the abuse of alcohol, and the use of tobacco, drugs and other harmful substances.

Article 12 (2) (c). The right to prevention, treatment and control of diseases

16. "The prevention, treatment and control of epidemic, endemic, occupational and other diseases" (art. 12 (2) c) requires the establishment of prevention and education programmes for behaviour-related health concerns such as sexually transmitted diseases, in particular HIV/AIDS, and those adversely affecting sexual and reproductive health, and the promotion of social determinants of good health, such as environmental safety, education, economic development and gender equity. The right to treatment includes the creation of a system of urgent medical care in cases of accidents, epidemics, and similar health hazards, and the provision of disaster relief and humanitarian assistance in emergency situations. The control of diseases refers to States' individual and joint efforts to, inter alia, make available relevant technologies, using and improving epidemiological surveillance and data collection on a disaggregated basis, the implementation or enhancement of immunization programmes and other strategies of infectious disease control.

Article 12 (2) (d). The right to health facilities, goods and services

17. "The creation of conditions which would assure to all medical service and medical attention in the event of sickness" (art. 12 (2) d), both physical and mental, includes the provision of equal and timely access to basic preventive, curative, rehabilitative health services, and health education; regular screening programmes; appropriate treatment of prevalent diseases, illnesses, injuries and disabilities, preferably at community level; the provision of essential drugs; and appropriate mental health treatment and care. A further important aspect is the improvement and furtherance of participation of the population in the provision of preventive and curative health services, such as the organization of the health sector, the insurance system and, in particular participation in political decisions relating to the right to health taken at both the community and national levels.

Article 12. Special topics of broad application

Non-discrimination and equal treatment

18. By virtue of Articles 2 (2) and 3, the Covenant proscribes any discrimination in access to health care and underlying determinants of health, as well as to means and entitlements for their procurement, on the grounds of race, colour, sex, language, religion, political or other opinion, national or social origin, property, birth, physical or mental disability, health status (including HIV/AIDS), sexual orientation and civil, political, social or other status, which has the intention or effect of nullifying or impairing the equal enjoyment or exercise of the right to health. The Committee stresses that many measures, such as most strategies and programmes designed to eliminate health-related discrimination, can be pursued with minimum resource implications through the adoption, modification or abrogation of legislation or the dissemination of information. The Committee recalls General Comment No. 3, paragraph 12, which states that even in times of severe resource limitations, the vulnerable or marginalized members of society must be protected by the adoption of relatively low-cost targeted programmes.

19. With respect to the right to health, equality of access to health care and health services has to be emphasized. States have a special obligation to provide those who do not have sufficient means with the necessary health insurance and health care facilities, and to prevent any discrimination on internationally prohibited grounds in the provision of health care and health services, especially with respect to the core obligations of the right to health. Inappropriate health resource allocation can lead to discrimination that may not be overt. For example, investments should not disproportionately favour expensive curative health services which are often accessible only to a small, privileged fraction of the population, rather than primary and preventive health care benefiting a far larger part of the population.

Gender perspective

20. The Committee recommends that States integrate a gender perspective in their health-related policies, planning, programmes and research in order to promote better health for both women and men. A gender-based approach recognizes that biological and socio-cultural factors play a significant role in influencing the health of men and women. The disaggregation of health and socio-economic data according to sex is essential for identifying and remedying inequalities in health.

Women and the right to health

21. To eliminate discrimination against women, there is a need to develop and implement a comprehensive national strategy for promoting women's right to health throughout their life span. Such a strategy should include interventions aimed at the prevention and treatment of diseases affecting women, as well as policies to provide access to a full range of high quality and affordable health care, including sexual and

reproductive services. A major goal should be reducing women's health risks, particularly lowering rates of maternal mortality and protecting women from domestic violence. The realisation of women's right to health requires the removal of all barriers interfering with access to health services, education and information, including in the area of sexual and reproductive health. It is also important to undertake preventive, promotive, and remedial action to shield women from the impact of harmful traditional cultural practices and norms that deny full reproductive rights to women.

Children and adolescents

22. Article 12 (2) (a) outlines the need to take measures to reduce infant mortality and promote the healthy development of infants and children. Subsequent international human rights instruments recognize that children and adolescents have the right to the enjoyment of the highest standard of health and access to facilities for the treatment of illness. The Convention on the Rights of the Child directs States to ensure access to essential health services for the child and his or her family, including pre- and post-natal care for mothers. The Convention links these goals with ensuring access to child-friendly information about preventive and health-promoting behaviour and support to families and communities in implementing these practices. Implementation of the principle of non-discrimination requires that girls, as well as boys, have equal access to adequate nutrition, safe environments, and physical as well as mental health services. There is a need to adopt effective and appropriate measures to abolish harmful traditional practices affecting the health of children, particularly girls, including early marriage, female genital mutilation, preferential feeding and care of male children. Children with disabilities should be given the opportunity to enjoy a fulfilling and decent life and to participate within their community.

23. States parties should provide a safe and supportive environment for adolescents, that ensures the opportunity to participate in decisions affecting their health, to build life-skills, to acquire appropriate information, to receive counselling and to negotiate the health-behaviour choices they make. The realization of the right to health of adolescents is dependent on the development of youth-friendly health care, which respects confidentiality and privacy, and includes appropriate sexual and reproductive health services.

24. In all policies and programmes aimed at guaranteeing the right to health of children and adolescents their best interests shall be a primary consideration.

Older persons

25. With regard to the realization of the right to health of older persons, the Committee, in accordance with paragraphs 34 and 35 of General Comment No. 6 (1995), reaffirms the importance of an integrated approach, combining elements of preventive, curative and rehabilitative health treatment. Such measures should be based on periodical check-ups for both sexes; physical as well as psychological rehabilitative measures

aimed at maintaining the functionality and autonomy of older persons; and attention and care for chronically and terminally ill persons, sparing them avoidable pain and enabling them to die with dignity.

Persons with disabilities

26. The Committee reaffirms paragraph 34 of its General Comment No. 5, which addresses the issue of persons with disabilities in the context of the right to physical and mental health. Moreover, the Committee stresses the need to ensure that not only the public health sector but also private providers of health services and facilities comply with the principle of non-discrimination in relation to persons with disabilities.

Indigenous peoples

27. In the light of emerging international law and practice and the recent measures taken by States in relation to indigenous peoples, the Committee deems it useful to identify elements that would help to define indigenous peoples' right to health in order to better enable States with indigenous peoples to implement the provisions contained in Article 12 of the Covenant. The Committee considers that indigenous peoples have the right to specific measures to improve their access to health services and care. These health services should be culturally appropriate, taking into account traditional preventive care, healing practices and medicines. States should provide resources for indigenous peoples to design, deliver and control such services so that they may enjoy the highest attainable standard of physical and mental health. The vital medicinal plants, animals and minerals necessary to the full enjoyment of health of indigenous peoples should also be protected. The Committee notes that, in indigenous communities, the health of the individual is often linked to the health of the society as a whole and has a collective dimension. In this respect, the Committee considers that development-related activities that lead to the displacement of indigenous peoples against their will from their traditional territories and environment, denying them their sources of nutrition and breaking their symbiotic relationship with their lands, has a deleterious effect on their health.

Limitations

28. Issues of public health are sometimes used by States as grounds for limiting the exercise of other fundamental rights. The Committee wishes to emphasize that the Covenant's limitation clause, Article 4, is primarily intended to protect the rights of individuals rather than to permit the imposition of limitations by States. Consequently a State party which, for example, restricts the movement of, or incarcerates, persons with transmissible diseases such as HIV/AIDS, refuses to allow doctors to treat persons believed to be opposed to a government, or fails to provide immunization against the community's major infectious diseases, on grounds such as national security or the

preservation of public order, has the burden of justifying such serious measures in relation to each of the elements identified in Article 4. Such restrictions must be in accordance with the law, including international human rights standards, compatible with the nature of the rights protected by the Covenant, in the interest of legitimate aims pursued, and strictly necessary for the promotion of the general welfare in a democratic society.

29. In line with Article 5 (1), such limitations must be proportional, i.e. the least restrictive alternative must be adopted where several types of limitations are available. Even where such limitations on grounds of protecting public health are basically permitted, they should be of limited duration and subject to review.

II. States Parties' Obligations

General legal obligations

30. While the Covenant provides for progressive realization and acknowledges the constraints due to the limits of available resources, it also imposes on States parties various obligations which are of immediate effect. States parties have immediate obligations in relation to the right to health, such as the guarantee that the right will be exercised without discrimination of any kind (Article 2(2)) and the obligation to take steps (Article 2(1)) towards the full realization of Article 12. Such steps must be deliberate, concrete and targeted towards the full realization of the right to health.

31. The progressive realization of the right to health over a period of time should not be interpreted as depriving States parties' obligations of all meaningful content. Rather, progressive realization means that States parties have a specific and continuing obligation to move as expeditiously and effectively as possible towards the full realization of Article 12.

32. As with all other rights in the Covenant, there is a strong presumption that retrogressive measures taken in relation to the right to health are impermissible. If any deliberately retrogressive measures are taken, the State party has the burden of proving that they have been introduced after the most careful consideration of all alternatives and that they are duly justified by reference to the totality of the rights provided for in the Covenant in the context of the full use of the State party's maximum available resources.

33. The right to health, like all human rights, imposes three types or levels of obligations on States parties: the obligations to respect, protect and fulfill. In turn, the obligation to fulfill contains obligations to facilitate, provide and promote. The obligation to respect requires States to refrain from interfering directly or indirectly with the enjoyment of the right to health. The obligation to protect requires States to take measures that prevent third parties from interfering with Article 12 guarantees. Finally, the obligation to fulfill requires States to adopt appropriate legislative, administrative, budgetary, judicial, promotional and other measures towards the full realization of the right to health.

Specific legal obligations

34. In particular, States are under the obligation to respect the right to health by, inter alia, refraining from denying or limiting equal access for all persons, including prisoners or detainees, minorities, asylum seekers and illegal immigrants, to preventive, curative and palliative health services; abstaining from enforcing discriminatory practices as a state policy; and abstaining from imposing discriminatory practices related to women's health status and needs. Furthermore, obligations to respect include a State's obligation to refrain from prohibiting or impeding traditional preventive care, healing practices and medicines, from marketing unsafe drugs and from applying coercive medical treatments, unless on an exceptional basis for the treatment of mental illness or the prevention and control of communicable diseases. Such exceptional cases should be subject to specific and restrictive conditions, respecting best practices and applicable international standards, including the UN Principles for the Protection of Persons with Mental Illness and the Improvement of Mental Health Care. In addition, States should refrain from limiting access to contraceptives and other means of maintaining sexual and reproductive health, from censoring, withholding or intentionally misrepresenting health-related information, including sexual education and information, as well as from preventing people's participation in health-related matters. States should also refrain from unlawfully polluting air, water, and soil, e.g., through industrial waste from State-owned facilities, from using or testing nuclear, biological or chemical weapons if such testing results in the release of substances harmful to human health, and from limiting access to health services as a punitive measure, e.g., during armed conflicts in violation of international humanitarian law.

35. Obligations to protect include, inter alia, the duties of States to adopt legislation or to take other measures ensuring equal access to health care and health-related services provided by third parties; to ensure that privatization of the health sector does not constitute a threat to the availability, accessibility, acceptability and quality of health facilities, goods and services; to control the marketing of medical equipment and medicines by third parties; and to ensure that medical practitioners and other health professionals meet appropriate standards of education, skill, and ethical codes of conduct. States are also obliged to ensure that harmful social or traditional practices do not interfere with access to pre- and post-natal care and family-planning; to prevent third parties from coercing women to undergo traditional practices, e.g. female genital mutilation; and to take measures to protect all vulnerable or marginalized groups of society, in particular women, children, adolescents and older persons, in the light of gender-based expressions of violence. States should also ensure that third parties do not limit people's access to health-related information and services.

36. The obligation to fulfill requires States parties, inter alia, to give sufficient recognition to the right to health in the national political and legal systems, preferably by way of legislative implementation, and to adopt a national health policy with a detailed plan for realizing the right to health. States must ensure provision of health care, including immunization programmes against the major infectious diseases, and ensure equal access for all to the underlying determinants of health, such as nutritiously safe

food and potable drinking water, basic sanitation, and adequate housing and living conditions. Public health infrastructures should provide for sexual and reproductive health services, including safe motherhood, particularly in rural areas. States have to ensure the appropriate training of doctors and other medical personnel, the provision of a sufficient number of hospitals, clinics and other health-related facilities, and the promotion and support of the establishment of institutions providing counseling and mental health services, with due regard to equitable distribution throughout the country. Further obligations include the provision of a public, private or mixed health insurance system which is affordable for all, the promotion of medical research and health education, as well as information campaigns, in particular with respect to HIV/AIDS, sexual and reproductive health, traditional practices, domestic violence, the abuse of alcohol and the use of cigarettes, drugs and other harmful substances. States are also required to adopt measures against environmental and occupational health hazards and against any other threat as demonstrated by epidemiological data. For this purpose they should formulate and implement national policies aimed at reducing and eliminating pollution of air, water and soil, including pollution by heavy metals such as lead from gasoline. Furthermore, States parties are required to formulate, implement and periodically review a coherent national policy on occupational accidents and diseases by minimizing risks, as well as to provide a coherent national policy on occupational safety and health services.

37. The obligation to fulfill (facilitate) requires States, inter alia, to take positive measures that enable and assist individuals and communities to enjoy the right to health. States parties are also obliged to fulfill (provide) a specific right contained in the Covenant when an individual or group is unable, for reasons beyond their control, to realize that right themselves by the means at their disposal. The obligation to fulfill (promote) the right to health requires States to undertake actions that create, maintain and restore the health of the population. Such obligations include:

(1) fostering recognition of factors favouring positive health results, e.g. research and provision of information;

(2) ensuring that health services are culturally appropriate and that health care staff are trained to recognize and respond to the specific needs of vulnerable or marginalized groups;

(3) ensuring that the State meets its obligations in the dissemination of appropriate information relating to healthy lifestyles and nutrition, harmful traditional practices and the availability of services;

(4) supporting people in making informed choices about their health.

International obligations

38. In its General Comment No. 3, the Committee drew attention to the obligation of all States parties to take steps, individually and through international assistance and cooperation, especially economic and technical towards the full realization of the

rights recognized in the Covenant, such as the right to health. In the spirit of Article 56 of the Charter of the United Nations, the specific provisions of the Covenant (Articles 12, 2 (1), 22 and 23) and the Alma-Ata Declaration on Primary Health Care, States parties should recognize the essential role of international co-operation and comply with their commitment to take joint and separate action to achieve the full realisation of the right to health. In this regard, States parties are referred to the Declaration of Alma-Ata which proclaims that the existing gross inequality in the health status of the people particularly between developed and developing countries as well as within countries is politically, socially and economically unacceptable and is, therefore, of common concern to all countries."

39. To comply with their international obligations in relation to Article 12, States parties have to respect the enjoyment of the right to health in other countries, and to prevent third parties from violating the right in other countries, if they are able to influence these third parties by way of legal or political means, in accordance with the Charter of the United Nations and applicable international law. Depending on the availability of resources, States should facilitate access to essential health facilities, goods and services in other countries, wherever possible and provide the necessary aid when required. States parties should ensure that the right to health is given due attention in international agreements and, to that end, should consider the development of further legal instruments. In relation to the conclusion of other international agreements, States parties should take steps to ensure that these instruments do not adversely impact upon the right to health. Similarly, States parties have an obligation to ensure that their actions as members of international organizations take due account of the right to health. Accordingly, States parties which are members of international financial institutions, notably the International Monetary Fund, the World Bank and regional development banks, should pay greater attention to the protection of the right to health in influencing the lending policies, credit agreements and international measures of these institutions.

40. States parties have a joint and individual responsibility, in accordance with the Charter of the United Nations and relevant resolutions of the UN General Assembly and of the World Health Assembly, to co-operate in providing disaster relief and humanitarian assistance in times of emergency, including assistance to refugees and internally displaced persons. Each State should contribute to this task to the maximum of its capacities. Priority in the provision of international medical aid, distribution and management of resources, such as safe and potable water, food and medical supplies and financial aid should be given to the most vulnerable or marginalized groups of the population. Moreover, given that some diseases are easily transmissible beyond the frontiers of a State, there is a collective responsibility on the international community to address this problem. The economically developed States parties have a special responsibility and interest to assist the poorer developing States in this regard.

41. States parties should refrain at all times from imposing embargoes or similar measures restricting the supply of another State with adequate medicines and medical equipment. Restrictions on such goods should never be used as an instrument of political

and economic pressure. In this regard, the Committee recalls its position, stated in General Comment No. 8, on the relationship between economic sanctions and respect for economic, social and cultural rights.

42. While only States are parties to the Covenant and thus ultimately accountable for compliance with it, all members of society—individuals, including health professionals, families, local communities, inter-governmental and non-governmental organisations, civil society organisations, as well as the private business sector—have responsibilities regarding the realization of the right to health. State parties should therefore provide for an environment which facilitates the discharge of these responsibilities.

Core obligations

43. In General Comment No. 3, the Committee confirms that States parties have a core obligation to ensure the satisfaction of, at the very least, minimum essential levels of each of the rights enunciated in the Covenant, including essential primary health care. Read in conjunction with more contemporary instruments, such as the Programme of Action of the International Conference on Population and Development, the Declaration of Alma-Ata provides compelling guidance on the core obligations arising from Article 12. Accordingly, in the Committee's view, this core includes at least the following obligations:

(1) to ensure the right of access to health facilities, goods and services on a nondiscriminatory basis, especially for vulnerable or marginalized groups;

(2) to ensure access to the minimum essential food which is sufficient, nutritionally adequate and safe, to ensure freedom from hunger to everyone;

(3) to ensure access to basic shelter, housing and sanitation and an adequate supply of safe and potable water;

(4) to provide essential drugs, as from time to time defined by WHO's Action Programme on Essential Drugs;

(5) to ensure equitable distribution of all health facilities, goods and services;

(6) to adopt and implement a national public health strategy and plan of action, on the basis of epidemiological evidence, addressing the health concerns of the whole population; the strategy and plan of action shall be devised, and periodically reviewed, on the basis of a participatory and transparent process; they shall include methods, such as right to health indicators and benchmarks, by which progress can be closely monitored; the process by which the strategy and plan of action is devised, as well as their content, shall give particular attention to all vulnerable or marginalized groups.

44. The Committee also confirms that obligations of comparable priority include the following:

(1) to ensure reproductive, maternal (pre-natal as well as post-natal) and child health care;

(2) to provide immunization against the community's major infectious diseases;

(3) to take measures to prevent, treat and control epidemic and endemic diseases;

(4) to provide education and access to information concerning the main health problems in the community, including methods of preventing and controlling them;

(5) to provide appropriate training for health personnel, including education on health and human rights.

45. For the avoidance of any doubt, the Committee wishes to emphasise that it is particularly incumbent on States parties and other actors are in a position to assist others, to provide "international assistance and cooperation, especially economic and technical" which enable developing countries to fulfil their core and other obligations indicated in Paragraphs 43 and 44 above.

III. Violations

46. When the normative content of Article 12 (Part I) is applied to the obligations of States parties (Part II), a dynamic process is set in motion which facilitates identification of violations of the right to health. The following paragraphs provide illustrations of violations of Article 12.

47. In determining which actions or omissions amount to a violation of the right to health, it is important to distinguish the inability from the unwillingness of a State party to comply with its obligations under Article 12. This follows from Article 12 (1) which speaks of the highest attainable standard of health, as well as from Article 2 (1) of the Covenant, which obliges each State party to take the necessary steps to the maximum of its available resources. A State which is unwilling to use the maximum of its available resources for the realization of the right to health is in violation of its obligations under Article 12. If resource constraints render it impossible for a State to comply fully with its Covenant obligations, it has the burden of justifying that every effort has nevertheless been made to use all available resources at its disposal in order to satisfy, as a matter of priority, the obligations as outlined above. It should be stressed, however, that a State party cannot, under any circumstances whatsoever, justify its non-compliance with the core obligations set out in paragraph 43 above which are non-derogable.

48. Violations of the right to health can occur through the direct action of States or other entities insufficiently regulated by States. The adoption of any retrogressive measures incompatible with the core obligations under the right to health, as outlined in paragraph 43 above, constitutes a violation of the right to health. Violations through acts of commission include the formal repeal or suspension of legislation necessary for the continued enjoyment of the right to health or the adoption of legislation or policies which are manifestly incompatible with pre-existing domestic or international legal obligations in relation to the right to health.

49. Violations of the right to health can also occur through the omission or failure of States to take necessary measures arising from legal obligations. Violations through acts of omission include the failure to take appropriate steps towards the full realization of

everyone's right to the enjoyment of the highest attainable standard of physical and mental health, the failure to have a national policy on occupational safety and health as well as occupational health services and the failure to enforce relevant laws.

Violations of the obligation to respect

50. Violations of the obligation to respect are those state actions, policies or laws that contravene the standards set out in Article 12 of the Covenant and are likely to result in bodily harm, unnecessary morbidity and preventable mortality. Examples include the denial of access to health facilities, goods and services to particular individuals or groups as a result of de iure or de facto discrimination; the deliberate withholding or misrepresentation of information vital to health protection or treatment; the suspension of legislation or the adoption of laws or policies that interfere with the enjoyment of any of the components of the right to health; and the failure of the State to take into account its legal obligations regarding the right to health when entering into bilateral or multilateral agreements with other States, international organizations and other entities, such as multinational corporations.

Violations of the obligation to protect

51. Violations of the obligation to protect follow from the failure of a State to take all necessary measures to safeguard persons within their jurisdiction from infringements of the right to health by third parties. This category includes such omissions as the failure to regulate the activities of individuals, groups, or corporations so as to prevent them from violating the right to health of others; the failure to protect consumers and workers from practices detrimental to health, e.g., by employers and manufacturers of medicines or food; the failure to discourage production, marketing, and consumption of tobacco, narcotics, and other harmful substances; the failure to protect women against violence or to prosecute perpetrators; the failure to discourage the continued observance of harmful traditional medical or cultural practices; and the failure to enact or enforce laws to prevent the pollution of water, air and soil by extractive and manufacturing industries.

Violations of the obligation to fulfill

52. Violations of the obligation to fulfill occur through the failure of States parties to take all necessary steps to ensure the realization of the right to health. Examples include the failure to adopt or implement a national health policy designed to ensure the right to health for everyone; insufficient expenditure or misallocation of public resources which results in the non-enjoyment of the right to health by individuals or groups, particularly the vulnerable or marginalized; the failure to monitor the realization of the right to health at the national level, for example, by identifying right to health indicators and benchmarks; the failure to take measures to reduce the inequitable distribution

of health facilities, goods and services; the failure to adopt a gender-sensitive approach to health; and the failure to reduce infant and maternal mortality rates.

IV. Implementation at the National Level

Framework legislation

53. The most appropriate feasible measures to implement the right to health will vary significantly from one State to another. Every State has a margin of discretion in assessing which measures are most suitable to meet its specific circumstances. The Covenant, however, clearly imposes a duty on each State to take whatever steps are necessary to ensure that everyone has access to health facilities, goods and services so that they can enjoy, as soon as possible, the highest attainable standard of physical and mental health. This requires the adoption of a national strategy to ensure the enjoyment of the right to health to all, based on human rights principles which define the objectives of that strategy, and the formulation of policies and corresponding right to health indicators and benchmarks. The national health strategy should also identify the resources available to attain defined objectives, as well as the most cost-effective way of using those resources.

54. The formulation and implementation of national health strategies and plans of action should respect, inter alia, the principles of non-discrimination and people's participation. In particular, the right of individuals and groups to participate in decision-making processes, which may affect their development, must be an integral component of any policy, programme or strategy developed to discharge governmental obligations under Article 12. Promoting health must involve effective community action in setting priorities, making decisions, planning, implementing and evaluating strategies to achieve better health. Effective provision of health services can only be assured if people's participation is secured by States.

55. The national health strategy and plan of action should also be based on the principles of accountability, transparency and independence of the judiciary since good governance is essential to the effective implementation of all human rights, including the realization of the right to health. In order to create a favourable climate for the realization of the right, States parties should take appropriate steps to ensure that the private business sector and civil society are aware of, and consider the importance of, the right to health in pursuing their activities.

56. States should consider the adoption of a framework law to operationalize their right to health national strategy. The framework law should establish national mechanisms for monitoring the implementation of national health strategies and plans of action. It should include provisions on the targets to be achieved and the time-frame for their achievement; the means by which right to health benchmarks could be achieved; the intended collaboration with civil society, including health experts, the private sector and international organizations; institutional responsibility for the

implementation of the right to health national strategy and plan of action; and possible recourse procedures. In monitoring progress towards the realization of the right to health, States parties should identify the factors and difficulties affecting implementation of their obligations.

Right to health indicators and benchmarks

57. National health strategies should identify appropriate right to health indicators and benchmarks. The indicators should be designed to monitor, at the national and international levels, the state party's obligations under Article 12. States may obtain guidance on appropriate right to health indicators, which should address different aspects of the right to health, from the on-going work of WHO and UNICEF in this field. Right to health indicators require disaggregation on the prohibited grounds of discrimination.

58. Having identified appropriate right to health indicators, States parties are invited to set appropriate national benchmarks in relation to each indicator. During the periodic reporting procedure the Committee will engage in a process of scoping with the State party. Scoping involves the joint consideration by the State party and the Committee of the indicators and national benchmarks which will then provide the targets to be achieved during the next reporting period. In the following five years, the State party will use these national benchmarks to help monitor its implementation of Article 12. Thereafter, in the subsequent reporting process, the State party and the Committee will consider whether or not the benchmarks have been achieved, and the reasons for any difficulties that may have been encountered.

Remedies and accountability

59. Any person or group who is a victim of a violation of the right to health should have access to effective judicial or other appropriate remedies at both national and international levels. All victims of such violations should be entitled to adequate reparation, which may take the form of restitution, compensation, satisfaction or guarantees of non-repetition. National ombudsmen, human rights commissions, consumer forums, patients' rights associations or similar institutions should address violations of the right to health.

60. The incorporation in the domestic legal order of international instruments recognizing the right to health can significantly enhance the scope and effectiveness of remedial measures and should be encouraged in all cases. Incorporation enables courts to adjudicate violations of the right to health, or at least its core obligations, by direct reference to the Covenant.

61. Judges and members of the legal profession should be encouraged by States parties to pay greater attention to violations of the right to health in the exercise of their functions.

62. States parties should respect, protect, facilitate and promote the work of human

rights advocates and other members of civil society with a view to assisting vulnerable or marginalised groups in the realization of their right to health.

V. Obligations of Actors Other Than States Parties

63. The role of the United Nations agencies and programmes, and in particular the key function assigned to WHO in realizing the right to health at the international, regional and country levels, is of particular importance, as is the function of UNICEF in relation to the right to health of children. When formulating and implementing their right to health national strategies, States parties should avail themselves of WHO's technical assistance and cooperation. Further, when preparing their reports, States parties should utilise the extensive information and advisory services of WHO as regards data collection, disaggregation, and the development of right to health indicators and benchmarks.

64. Moreover, co-ordinated efforts for the realization of the right to health should be maintained to enhance the interaction among all the actors concerned, including the various components of civil society. In conformity with Articles 22 and 23 of the Covenant, WHO, ILO, UNDP, UNICEF, UNFPA, the World Bank, regional development banks, the International Monetary Fund, WTO and other relevant bodies within the UN system, should co-operate effectively with States parties, building on their respective expertise, in relation to the implementation of the right to health at national levels, with due respect to their individual mandates. In particular, the international financial institutions, notably the World Bank and IMF, should pay greater attention to the protection of the right to health in their lending policies, credit agreements and structural adjustment programmes. When examining the reports of States parties, and their ability to meet the obligations under Article 12, the Committee will consider the effects of the assistance provided by all other actors. The adoption of a human rights-based approach by United Nations specialized agencies, programmes and bodies will greatly facilitate implementation of the right to health. In the course of its examination of States parties' reports, the Committee will also consider the role of health professional associations and other NGOs in relation to the States' obligations under Article 12.

65. The role of WHO, the Office of the United Nations High Commissioner for Refugees (UNHCR), the International Committee of the Red Cross/Red Crescent and UNICEF, as well as non-governmental organizations and national medical associations, is of particular importance in relation to disaster relief and humanitarian assistance in times of emergencies, including assistance to refugees and internally displaced persons. Priority in the provision of international medical aid, distribution and management of resources, such as safe and potable water, food and medical supplies and financial aid should be given to the most vulnerable or marginalized groups of the population.

Chapter 15
Revised General Guidelines Regarding the Form and Contents of Reports to be Submitted by States Parties Under Articles 16 and 17 of the ICESCR (1991)

A. Part of the Report Relating to General Provisions of the Covenant

Article 1 of the Covenant

In what manner has the right to self-determination been implemented?

Article 2 of the Covenant

1. To what extent and in what manner are non-nationals not guaranteed the rights recognized in the Covenant? What justification is there for any difference?

2. Which of the rights are specifically subject to non-discrimination provisions in national law? Attach the text of such provisions.

3. If your State participates in development cooperation, is any effort made to ensure that it is used, on a priority basis, to promote the realization of economic, social and cultural rights?

B. Part of the Report Relating to Specific Rights

Article 6 of the Covenant

1. If your State is a party to any of the following Conventions:

International Labour Organisation (ILO) Employment Policy Convention, 1964 (No. 122)

ILO Discrimination (Employment and Occupation) Convention, 1958 (No. 111)

International Convention on the Elimination of all Forms of Racial Discrimination

Convention on the Elimination of all Forms of Discrimination Against Women and has already submitted reports to the supervisory committee(s) concerned which are relevant to the provisions of Article 6, you may wish to refer to the respective parts of those reports rather than repeat the information here. However, all matters which arise under the present Covenant and are not covered fully in those reports should be dealt with in the present report.

2. (a) Please supply information on the situation, level and trends of employment, unemployment and underemployment in your country, in respect of both the aggregate and particular categories of workers such as women, young persons, older workers and disabled workers. Please compare the respective situation 10 years ago and 5 years ago. Which persons, groups, regions or areas do you consider particularly vulnerable or disadvantaged with regard to employment?

(b) Please describe the principal policies pursued and measures taken with a view to ensuring that there is work for all who are available for and seeking work.

(c) Please indicate what measures have been adopted to ensure that work is as productive as possible.

(d) Please indicate what provisions ensure that there is freedom of choice of employment and that conditions of employment do not infringe upon fundamental political and economic freedoms of the individual.

(e) Please describe the technical and vocational training programmes that exist in your country, their effective mode of operation and their practical availability.

(f) Please state whether particular difficulties have been encountered in attaining the objectives of full, productive and freely chosen employment, and indicate how far these difficulties have been overcome.

3. (a) Please indicate whether there exist in your country any distinctions, exclusions, restrictions or preferences, be it in law or in administrative practices or in practical relationships, between persons or groups of persons, made on the basis of race, colour, sex, religion, political opinion, nationality or social origin, which have the effect of nullifying or impairing the recognition, enjoyment or exercise of equality of opportunity or treatment in employment or occupation. What steps are taken to eliminate such discrimination?

(b) Please supply information on the actual situation in your country regarding vocational guidance and training, employment and occupation of persons according to their race, colour, sex, religion, and national origin.

(c) Please indicate the main cases in which a distinction, exclusion or preference based on any of the above-named conditions is not considered in your country as discrimination, owing to the inherent requirements of a particular job. Please indicate any difficulties in application, disputes or controversies which have arisen in relation to such conditions.

4. Please indicate what proportion of the working population of your country holds

more than one full-time job in order to secure an adequate standard of living for themselves and their families. Describe this development over time.

5. In case of subsequent reports, give a short review of changes, if any, in national legislation, court decisions, as well as administrative rules, procedures and practices during the reporting period affecting the right to work.

6. Please indicate the role of international assistance in the full realization of the right enshrined in Article 6.

Article 7 of the Covenant

1. If your State is a party to any of the following ILO Conventions:

Minimum Wage-Fixing Convention, 1970 (No. 131)

Equal Remuneration Convention, 1951 (No. 100)

Weekly Rest (Industry) Convention, 1921 (No. 14)

Weekly Rest (Commerce and Offices) Convention, 1957 (No. 106)

Holidays with Pay Convention (Revised), 1970 (No. 132)

Labour Inspection Convention, 1947 (No. 81)

Labour Inspection (Agriculture) Convention, 1969 (No. 129)

Occupational Safety and Health Convention, 1981 (No. 155)

and has already submitted reports to the ILO Committee of Experts on the Application of Conventions and Recommendations which are relevant to the provisions of Article 7 you may wish to refer to the respective parts of those reports rather than repeat the information here. However, all matters which arise under the present Covenant and are not covered fully in those reports should be dealt within the present report.

2. (a) Please supply information on the principal methods used for fixing wages.

(b) Please indicate whether a system of minimum wages has been established, and specify the groups of wage earners to which it applies, the number of persons covered by each group as well as the competent authority for determining these groups. Are there any wage earners remaining outside the protection of the system of minimum wages in law or in fact?

(i) Do these minimum wages have the force of law and in which ways are they secured against erosion?

(ii) To what extent and by which methods are the needs of workers and their families as well as economic factors taken into consideration and reconciled with each other in determining the level of minimum wages? What standards, goals and bench-marks are relevant in this respect?

(iii) Please describe briefly the machinery set up for fixing, monitoring and adjusting minimum wages;

(iv) Please supply information on the development of average and minimum wages 10 years ago, 5 years ago and at present, set against the respective development of the cost of living;

(v) Please indicate whether, in practice, the system of minimum wages is supervised effectively.

(c) Please indicate whether there exists in your country any inequality in remuneration for work of equal value, infringements of the principle of equal pay for equal work, or conditions of work for women which are inferior to those enjoyed by men.

(i) What steps are taken to eliminate such discrimination? Please describe the successes and failures of these steps with regard to the various groups that are discriminated against;

(ii) Please indicate what methods, if any, have been adopted to promote an objective appraisal of jobs on the basis of the work to be performed.

(d) Please indicate the income distribution of employees, both in the public and private sector taking into account both remuneration and non-monetary benefits. If available, give data on the remuneration of comparable jobs in the public and private sector.

3. What legal, administrative or other provisions exist that prescribe minimum conditions of occupational health and safety. How are these provisions enforced in practice and in which areas do they not apply?

(a) Please indicate which categories of workers, if any, are excluded from existing schemes by law and what other categories benefit from such schemes only insufficiently or not at all.

(b) Please provide statistical or other information on how the number, nature and frequency of occupational accidents (particularly with fatal results) and diseases have developed over time (10 years ago, 5 years as compared with the present).

4. Please supply information on the actual realization in your country of the principle of equal opportunity for promotion.

(a) Which groups of workers are currently deprived of such equal opportunity? In particular, what is the situation of women in this respect?

(b) What steps are taken to eliminate such inequality? Please describe the successes and failures of these steps with regard to the various disadvantaged groups.

5. Please describe the laws and practices in your country regarding rest, leisure, reasonable limitations of working hours, periodic holidays with pay and remuneration for public holidays.

(a) Indicate the factors and difficulties affecting the degree of realization of these rights.

(b) Indicate which categories of workers are excluded by law or in practice, or both, from the enjoyment of which of these rights. What measures are contemplated or currently taken to remedy this situation?

6. In case of subsequent reports, give a short review of changes, if any, in national legislation, court decisions, or administrative rules, procedures and practices during the reporting period affecting the right to just and favourable conditions of work.

7. Please indicate the role of international assistance in the full realization of the right enshrined in article.

Article 8 of the Covenant

1. If your State is a party to any of the following Conventions:

International Covenant on Civil and Political Rights

ILO Freedom of Association and Protection of the Right to Organise Convention, 1948 (No. 87)

ILO Right to Organise and Collective Bargaining Convention, 1949 (No. 98)

ILO Labour Relations (Public Service) Convention, 1978 (No. 151)

and has already submitted reports to the supervisory committee(s) concerned which are relevant to the provisions of Article 8, you may wish to refer to the respective parts of those reports rather than repeat the information here. However, all matters which arise under the present Covenant and are not covered fully in those reports should be dealt with in the present report.

2. Please indicate what substantive or formal conditions, if any, must be fulfilled in order to join and form the trade union of one's choice.

(a) Please specify whether there exist any special legal provisions regarding the establishment of trade unions by certain categories of workers and, eventually, what these special provisions are, how they have been applied in practice, as well as the number of persons subjected to them.

(b) Are there any restrictions placed upon the exercise of the right to join and form trade unions by workers? Please provide a detailed account of the legal provisions prescribing such restrictions and their application in practice over time.

(c) Please supply information on how your Government secures the right of trade unions to federate and join international trade union organizations. What legal and practical restrictions are placed upon the exercise of this right?

(d) Please indicate in detail what conditions or limitations are placed upon the right of trade unions to function freely. Which trade unions have been adversely affected in practice by these conditions or limitations? What measures are being taken to promote free collective bargaining?

(e) Please supply data on the number and structure of trade unions established in your country, and on their respective membership.

3. Please indicate whether in your country workers are granted the possibility to strike as a matter of constitutional or legal right. If your answer is in the negative, what other legal or factual approach is used to guarantee the exercise of this right?

(a) What restrictions are placed upon the exercise of the right to strike? Please provide a detailed account of the legal provisions governing such restrictions and their application in practice over time.

(b) Please indicate whether there exist any special legal provisions regarding the exercise of the right to strike by certain categories of workers and what these special provisions are, how they have been applied in practice, as well as the number of workers subjected to them.

4. Please indicate whether any restrictions are placed upon the exercise of the rights mentioned in paragraphs 2 and 3 above by members of the armed forces, the police or the administration of the State. How have such restrictions been applied in actual practice?

5. In case of subsequent reports, give a short review of changes, if any, in national legislation, court decisions, as well as administrative rules, procedures and practices during the reporting period affecting the rights enshrined in Article 8.

Article 9 of the Covenant

1. If your State is a party to the ILO Social Security (Minimum Standards) Convention, 1952 (No. 102) or to other relevant subsequent ILO Conventions (Nos. 121, 128, 130 and 168) and has already submitted reports to the supervisory committee(s) concerned which are relevant to the provisions of Article 9, you may wish to refer to the respective parts of those reports rather than repeat the information here. However, all matters which arise under the present Covenant and are not covered fully in those reports should be dealt with in the present report.

2. Please indicate which of the following branches of social security exist in your country:

Medical care

Cash sickness benefits

Maternity benefits

Old-age benefits

Invalidity benefits

Survivors' benefits

Employment injury benefits

Unemployment benefits

Family benefits.

3. Please describe for each branch existing in your country the main features of the schemes in force, indicating the comprehensiveness of the coverage provided, both in the aggregate and with respect to different groups within the society, the nature and level of benefits, and the method of financing the schemes.

4. Please indicate what percentage of your GNP as well as of your national and/or regional budget(s) is spent on social security. How does this compare with the situation 10 years ago? What reasons are there for any changes?

5. Please indicate whether in your country the formal (public) social security schemes described are supplemented by any informal (private) arrangements. If such is the case, please describe these arrangements and the inter-relationships between them and the formal (public) schemes.

6. Please indicate whether in your country there are any groups which do not enjoy the right to social security at all or which do so to a significantly lesser degree than the majority of the population. In particular, what is the situation of women in that respect? Please give particulars of such non-enjoyment of social security.

(a) Please indicate what measures are regarded as necessary by your Government in order to realize the right to social security for the groups mentioned above.

(b) Please explain the policy measures your Government has taken, to the maximum of its available resources, to implement the right to social security for these groups. Give a calendar and time-related bench-marks for measuring your achievements in this regard.

(c) Please describe the effect of these measures on the situation of the vulnerable and disadvantaged groups in point, and report the successes, problems and shortcomings of such measures.

7. In case of subsequent reports, give a short review of changes, if any, in national legislation, court decisions, as well as administrative rules, procedures and practices during the reporting period affecting the right to social security.

8. Please indicate the role of international assistance in the full realization of the right enshrined in Article 9.

Article 10 of the Covenant

1. If your State is a party to any of the following Conventions:

International Covenant on Civil and Political Rights

Convention on the Rights of the Child

Convention on the Elimination of all Forms of Discrimination Against Women

ILO Maternity Protection Convention (Revised) 1952 (No. 103)

ILO Minimum Age Convention, 1973 (No. 138)

or to any other ILO convention on the protection of children and young persons in relation to employment and work, and if your Government has already submitted reports to the supervisory committee(s) concerned which are relevant to the provisions of Article 10, you may wish to refer to the respective parts of those reports rather than repeat the information here. However, all matters which arise under the present Covenant and are not covered fully in these reports should be dealt with in the present report.

2. Please indicate what meaning is given in your society to the term "family."

3. Please indicate the age at which in your country children are deemed to attain their majority for different purposes.

4. Please supply information on the ways and means, both formal and informal, employed in your country to grant assistance and protection to the family. In particular:

(a) How does your country guarantee the right of men and, particularly, women to enter into marriage with their full and free consent and to establish a family? Please indicate and eventually give particulars about cases where the measures taken were not successful in abolishing practices adversely affecting the enjoyment of this right.

(b) By what measures does your country facilitate the establishment of a family as well as maintain, strengthen and protect it, particularly while it is responsible for the care and education of dependent children? Despite these measures, are there families which do not enjoy the benefit of such protection and assistance at all or which do so to a significantly lesser degree than the majority of the population? Please give details of these situations. Are extended families or other forms of familial organization recognized in determining the availability or applicability of these measures, particularly with respect to government benefits?

(c) With regard to shortcomings visible under subparagraphs (a) or (b), what measures are contemplated to remedy the situation?

5. Please provide information on your system of maternity protection.

(a) In particular:

(i) Describe the scope of the scheme of protection;

(ii) Indicate the total length of the maternity leave and of the period of compulsory leave after confinement;

(iii) Describe the cash, medical and other social security benefits granted during these periods;

(iv) Indicate how these benefits have been developed over time.

(b) Please indicate whether there are in your society groups of women who do not enjoy any maternity protection at all or which do so to a significantly lesser degree than the majority. Please give details of these situations. What measures are being taken or contemplated to remedy this situation? Please describe the effect of these measures on the situation of the vulnerable and disadvantaged groups in point and report on successes, problems and shortcomings of such measures.

6. Please describe the special measures of protection and assistance on behalf of children and young persons, especially measures to protect them from economic and social exploitation or to prevent their employment in work harmful to their morals or health or dangerous to life or likely to hamper their normal development.

(a) What are the age limits in your country below which the paid employment of child labour in different occupations is prohibited?

(b) Please specify how many children, and of which age groups, engage in paid employment, and to what extent.

(c) Please specify to what extent children are being employed in their families' households, farms or businesses.

(d) Please indicate whether there are in your country any groups of children and young persons which do not enjoy the measures of protection and assistance at all or which do so to a significantly lesser degree than the majority. In particular, what is the respective situation of orphans, children without living biological parents, young girls, children who are abandoned or deprived of their family environment, as well as physically or mentally handicapped children?

(e) How are the persons mentioned in the preceding paragraph informed of their respective rights?

(f) Please give details of any difficulties and shortcomings. How have such adverse situations developed over time? What measures are being taken to remedy these situations? Please describe the effect of these measures over time and report on successes, problems and shortcomings.

7. In case of subsequent reports, give a short review of changes, if any, in national legislation, court decisions as well as administrative rules, procedures and practices during the reporting period affecting the right enshrined in Article 10.

8. Please describe the role of international assistance in the full realization of the right enshrined in Article 10.

Article 11 of the Covenant

1. (a) Please supply information on the current standard of living of your population, in respect of both the aggregate and different socio-economic, cultural, and other groups within the society. How has the standard of living changed over time (e.g., compared with 10 years ago and 5 years ago) with regard to these different groups? Has there been a continuous improvement of living conditions for the entire population or for what groups?

(b) In case your Government has recently submitted reports relevant to the situation with respect to all or some of the rights contained in Article 11 to the United Nations or a specialized agency, you may wish to refer to the relevant parts of those reports rather than repeat the information here.

(c) Please indicate the per capita GNP for the poorest 40 per cent of your population. Is there a "poverty line" in existence in your country and, if so, what is the basis for this line?

(d) Please indicate your country's Physical Quality of Life Index.

2. The right to adequate food

(a) Please provide a general overview of the extent to which the right to adequate food has been realized in your country. Describe the sources of information that exist in this regard, including nutritional surveys and other monitoring arrangements.

(b) Please provide detailed information (including statistical data broken down in terms of different geographical areas) on the extent to which hunger and/or malnutrition exists in your country. This information should deal in particular with the following issues:

(i) The situation of especially vulnerable or disadvantaged groups, including:

Landless peasants
Marginalized peasants
Rural workers
Rural unemployed
Urban unemployed
Urban poor
Migrant workers
Indigenous peoples
Children
Elderly people
Other especially affected groups;

(ii) Any significant differences in the situation of men and women within each of the above groups;

(iii) The changes that have taken place over the past five years with respect to the situation of each of the above groups.

(c) During the reporting period, have there been any changes in national policies, laws and practices negatively affecting the access to adequate food by these groups or sectors or within the worse-off regions? If so, please describe these changes and evaluate their impact.

(d) Please indicate what measures are considered necessary by your Government to guarantee access to adequate food for each of the vulnerable or disadvantaged groups mentioned above and for the worse-off areas, and for the full implementation of the right to food for both men and women. Indicate the measures taken and specify time-related goals and nutritional bench-marks for measuring achievements in this regard.

(e) Please indicate in what ways measures taken to improve methods of production, conservation and distribution of food by making full use of technical and scientific knowledge have contributed towards, or have impeded the realization of the right to adequate food. Please describe the impact of these measures in terms of ecological sustainability and the protection and conservation of food producing resources.

(f) Please indicate what measures are taken to disseminate knowledge of the principles of nutrition and specify whether any significant groups or sectors within society seem to lack such knowledge.

(g) Please describe any measures of agrarian reform taken by your Government to ensure that the agrarian system is efficiently utilized in order to promote food security at household level without negatively affecting human dignity both in the rural and urban settings taking into account Articles 6 to 8 of the Covenant. Describe the measures taken:

(i) To legislate to this effect;

(ii) To enforce existing law to this effect;

(iii) To facilitate monitoring through governmental and non-governmental organizations.

(h) Please describe and evaluate the measures taken by your Government in order to ensure an equitable distribution, in terms of both production and trade, of world food supplies in relation to need, taking into account the problems of both food-importing and food-exporting countries.

3. The right to adequate housing

(a) Please furnish detailed statistical information about the housing situation in your country.

(b) Please provide detailed information about those groups within your society that are vulnerable and disadvantaged with regard to housing. Indicate, in particular:

(i) The number of homeless individuals and families;

(ii) The number of individuals and families currently inadequately housed and without ready access to basic amenities such as water, heating (if necessary), waste disposal, sanitation facilities, electricity, postal services, etc. (insofar as you consider these amenities relevant in your country). Include the number of people living in over-crowded, damp, structurally unsafe housing or other conditions which affect health;

(iii) The number of persons currently classified as living in "illegal" settlements or housing;

(iv) The number of persons evicted within the last five years and the number of persons currently lacking legal protection against arbitrary eviction or any other kind of eviction;

(v) The number of persons whose housing expenses are above any government-set limit of affordability, based upon ability to pay or as a ratio of income;

(vi) The number of persons on waiting lists for obtaining accommodation, the average length of waiting time and measures taken to decrease such lists as well as to assist those on such lists in finding temporary housing;

(vii) The number of persons in different types of housing tenure by: social or public housing; private rental sector; owner-occupiers; "illegal" sector; and other.

(c) Please provide information on the existence of any laws affecting the realization of the right to housing, including:

(i) Legislation which gives substance to the right to housing in terms of defining the content of this right;

(ii) Legislation such as housing acts, homeless person acts, municipal corporation acts, etc;

(iii) Legislation relevant to land use, land distribution; land allocation, land zoning, land ceilings, expropriations including provisions for compensation; land planning, including procedures for community participation;

(iv) Legislation concerning the rights of tenants to security of tenure, to protection from eviction; to housing finance and rental control (or subsidy), housing affordability, etc;

(v) Legislation concerning building codes, building regulations and standards and the provision of infrastructure;

(vi) Legislation prohibiting any and all forms of discrimination in the housing sector, including groups not traditionally protected;

(vii) Legislation prohibiting any form of eviction;

(viii) Any legislative repeal or reform of existing laws which detracts from the fulfillment of the right to housing;

(ix) Legislation restricting speculation on housing or property, particularly when such peculation has a negative impact on the fulfillment of housing rights for all sectors of society;

(x) Legislative measures conferring legal title to those living in the "illegal" sector;

(xi) Legislation concerning environmental planning and health in housing and human settlements.

(d) Please provide information on all other measures taken to fulfill the right to housing, including:

(i) Measures taken to encourage "enabling strategies" whereby local community-based organizations and the "informal sector" can build housing and related services. Are such organizations free to operate? Do they receive Government funding?

(ii) Measures taken by the State to build housing units and to increase other construction of affordable, rental housing;

(iii) Measures taken to release unutilized, under-utilized or mis-utilized land;

(iv) Financial measures taken by the State including details of the budget of the Ministry of Housing or other relevant Ministry as a percentage of the national budget;

(v) Measures taken to ensure that international assistance for housing and human settlements is used to fulfill the needs of the most disadvantaged groups;

(vi) Measures taken to encourage the development of small and intermediate urban centres, especially at the rural level;

(vii) Measures taken during, inter alia, urban renewal programmes, redevelopment projects, site upgrading, preparation for international events (Olympics, expositions, conferences, etc.), "beautiful city campaigns," etc., which guarantee protection from eviction or guaranteed rehousing based on mutual agreement, by any persons living on or near to affected sites;

(e) During the reporting period, have there been any changes in national policies, laws and practices negatively affecting the right to adequate housing? If so, please describe the changes and evaluate their impact.

4. Please give details on any difficulties or shortcomings encountered in the fulfillment of the rights enshrined in Article 11 and on the measures taken to remedy these situations (if not already described in the present report).

5. Please indicate the role of international assistance in the full realization of the rights enshrined in Article 11.

Article 12 of the Covenant

1. Please supply information on the physical and mental health of your population, in respect of both the aggregate and the different groups within your society. How has the health situation changed over time with regard to these groups? In case your Government has recently submitted reports on the health situation in your country to the World Health Organization (WHO) you may wish to refer to the relevant parts of these reports rather than repeat the information here.

2. Please indicate whether your country has a national health policy. Please indicate whether a commitment to the WHO primary health care approach has been adopted as part of the health policy of your country. If so, what measures have been taken to implement primary health care?

3. Please indicate what percentage of your GNP as well as of your national and/or regional budget(s) is spent on health. What percentage of those resources is allocated to primary health care? How does this compare with 5 years ago and 10 years ago?

4. Please provide, where available, indicators as defined by the WHO, relating to the following issues:

(a) Infant mortality rate (in addition to the national value, please provide the rate by sex, urban/rural division, and also, if possible, by socio-economic or ethnic group and geographical area. Please include national definitions of urban/rural and other subdivisions);

(b) Population access to safe water (please disaggregate urban/rural);

(c) Population access to adequate excreta disposal facilities (please disaggregate urban/rural);

(d) Infants immunized against diphtheria, pertussis, tetanus, measles, poliomyelitis and tuberculosis (please disaggregate urban/rural and by sex);

(e) Life expectancy (please disaggregate urban/rural, by socio-economic group and by sex);

(f) Proportion of the population having access to trained personnel for the treatment of common diseases and injuries, with regular supply of 20 essential drugs, within one hour's walk or travel;

(g) Proportion of pregnant women having access to trained personnel during pregnancy and proportion attended by such personnel for delivery. Please provide figures on the maternity mortality rate, both before and after childbirth;

(h) Proportion of infants having access to trained personnel for care.

(Please provide breakdowns by urban/rural and socio-economic groups for indicators (f) to (h).)

5. Can it be discerned from the breakdowns of the indicators employed in paragraph 4, or by other means, that there are any groups in your country whose health situation is significantly worse than that of the majority of the population? Please define these groups as precisely as possible and give details. Which geographical areas in your country, if any, are worse off with regard to the health of their population?

(a) During the reporting period, have there been any changes in national policies, laws and practices negatively affecting the health situation of these groups or areas? If so, please describe these changes and their impact.

(b) Please indicate what measures are considered necessary by your Government to improve the physical and mental health situation of such vulnerable and disadvantaged groups or in such worse-off areas.

(c) Please explain the policy measures your Government has taken, to the maximum of available resources, to realize such improvement. Indicate time-related goals and bench-marks for measuring your achievements in this regard.

(d) Please describe the effect of these measures on the health situation of the vulnerable and disadvantaged groups or worse-off areas under consideration, and report on the successes, problems and shortcomings of these measures.

(e) Please describe the measures taken by your Government in order to reduce the stillbirth-rate and infant mortality and to provide for the healthy development of the child.

(f) Please list the measures taken by your Government to improve all aspects of environmental and industrial hygiene.

(g) Please describe the measures taken by your Government to prevent, treat and control epidemic, endemic, occupational and other diseases.

(h) Please describe the measures taken by your Government to assure to all medical service and medical attention in the event of sickness.

(i) Please describe the effect of the measures listed in subparagraphs (e) to (h) on the situation of the vulnerable and disadvantaged groups in your society and in any worse-off areas. Report on difficulties and failures as well as on positive results.

6. Please indicate the measures taken by your Government to ensure that the rising costs of health care for the elderly do not lead to infringements of these persons right to health.

7. Please indicate what measures have been taken in your country to maximize community participation in the planning, organization, operation and control of primary health care.

8. Please indicate what measures have been taken in your country to provide education concerning prevailing health problems and the measures of preventing and controlling them.

9. Please indicate the role of international assistance in the full realization of the right enshrined in Article 12.

Article 13 of the Covenant

1. With a view to achieving in your country the full realization of the right of everyone to education:

(a) How does your Government discharge its obligation to provide for primary education that is compulsory and available free to all? (If primary education is not compulsory and/or free of charge, see especially Article 14.)

(b) Is secondary education, including technical and vocational secondary education, generally available and accessible to all? To what extent is such secondary education free of charge?

(c) To what extent is general access to higher education realized in your country? What are the costs of such higher education? Is free education established or being introduced progressively?

(d) What efforts have you made to establish a system of fundamental education for those persons who have not received or completed the whole period of their primary education?

In case your Government has recently submitted reports relevant to the situation with respect to the right contained in Article 13 to the United Nations or a specialized agency, you may wish to refer to the relevant parts of those reports rather than repeat the information here.

2. What difficulties have you encountered in the realization of the right to education, as spelt out in paragraph 1? What time-related goals and bench-marks has your Government set in this respect?

3. Please provide statistics on literacy, enrollment in fundamental education with information on rural areas, adult and continuing education, drop-out rates at all levels of education as well as graduating rates at all levels (please disaggregate, if possible, according to sex, religion, etc.). Also provide information on measures taken to promote literacy, with data on the scope of the programmes, target population, financing and enrollment, as well as graduation statistics by age group, sex, etc. Please report on the positive results of these measures as well as on difficulties and failures.

4. Please provide information on the percentage of your budget (or, if necessary, regional budgets) spent on education. Describe your system of schools, your activity in building new schools, the vicinity of schools, particularly in rural areas, as well as the schooling schedules.

5. To what extent is equal access to the different levels of education and measures to promote literacy enjoyed in practice? For instance:

(a) What is the ratio of men and women making use of the different levels of education and taking part in these measures?

(b) With regard to practical enjoyment of the right to these levels of education and measures to promote literacy, are there any particularly vulnerable and disadvantaged groups? Indicate, for instance, to what extent young girls, children of low-income groups, children in rural areas, children who are physically or mentally disabled, children of immigrants and of migrant workers, children belonging to linguistic, racial, religious or other minorities, and children of indigenous people, enjoy the right to literacy and education spelt out in Article 12.

(c) What actions is your Government taking or contemplating in order to introduce or guarantee equal access to all levels of education within your country, for instance in the form of anti-discriminatory measures, financial incentives, fellowships, positive or affirmative action? Please describe the effect of such measures.

(d) Please describe the language facilities provided to this effect, such as the availability of teaching in the mother tongue of the students.

6. Please describe the conditions of teaching staff at all levels in your country, having

regard to the Recommendation concerning the Status of Teachers, adopted on 5 October 1966 by the Special Intergovernmental Conference on the Status of Teachers, convened by UNESCO. How do teachers' salaries compare to salaries of (other) civil servants? How has this ratio developed over time? What measures does your country take or contemplate to improve the living conditions of teaching staff?

7. What proportion of schools at all levels in your country is not established and administered by the Government? Have any difficulties been encountered by those wishing to establish or to gain access to those schools?

8. During the reporting period, have there been any changes in national policies, laws and practices negatively affecting the right enshrined in Article 13? If so, please describe these changes and evaluate their impact.

9. Please indicate the role of international assistance in the full realization of the right enshrined in Article 13.

Article 14 of the Covenant

If compulsory and free primary education in your country is not currently enjoyed, please provide details on the required plan of action for the progressive implementation, within a reasonable number of years fixed in this plan, of this principle. What particular difficulties have you encountered in the realization of this plan of action? Please indicate the role of international assistance in this respect.

Article 15 of the Covenant

1. Please describe the legislative and other measures adopted by or in your State to realize the right of everyone to take part in the cultural life which he or she considers pertinent, and to manifest his or her own culture. In particular, provide information on the following:

(a) Availability of funds for the promotion of cultural development and popular participation in cultural life, including public support for private initiative.

(b) The institutional infrastructure established for the implementation of policies to promote popular participation in culture, such as cultural centres, museums, libraries, theatres, cinemas, and in traditional arts and crafts.

(c) Promotion of cultural identity as a factor of mutual appreciation among individuals, groups, nations and regions.

(d) Promotion of awareness and enjoyment of the cultural heritage of national ethnic groups and minorities and of indigenous peoples.

(e) Role of mass media and communications media in promoting participation in cultural life.

(f) Preservation and presentation of mankind's cultural heritage.

(g) Legislation protecting the freedom of artistic creation and performance, including the freedom to disseminate the results of such activities, as well as an indication of any restrictions or limits imposed on the freedom.

(h) Professional education in the field of culture and art.

(i) Any other measures taken for the conservation, development and diffusion of culture.

Please report on positive effects as well as on difficulties and failures, particularly concerning indigenous and other disadvantaged and particularly vulnerable groups.

2. Please describe the legislative and other measures taken to realize the right of everyone to enjoy the benefits of scientific progress and its applications, including those aimed at the conservation, development and diffusion of science. In particular, provide information on the following:

(a) Measures taken to ensure the application of scientific progress for the benefit of everyone, including measures aimed at the preservation of mankind's natural heritage and at promoting a healthy and pure environment and information on the institutional infrastructures established for that purpose.

(b) Measures taken to promote the diffusion of information on scientific progress.

(c) Measures taken to prevent the use of scientific and technical progress for purposes which are contrary to the enjoyment of all human rights, including the rights to life, health, personal freedom, privacy and the like.

(d) Any restrictions which are placed upon the exercise of this right, with details of the legal provisions prescribing such restrictions.

3. Please describe the legislative and other measures taken to realize the right of everyone to benefit from the protection of the moral and material interests resulting from any scientific, literary or artistic work of which he or she is the author. In particular, supply information on the practical measures aimed at the full implementation of this right, including provision of the necessary conditions for scientific, literary and artistic activities, and the protection of intellectual property rights resulting from such activities. What difficulties have affected the degree of realization of this right?

4. What steps has your Government taken for the conservation, development and diffusion of science and culture? Please describe in particular:

(a) Measures at the constitutional level, within the national educational system and by means of the communications media.

(b) All other practical steps taken to promote such conservation, development and diffusion.

5. Please describe the legal, administrative and judicial system designed to respect and protect the freedom indispensable for scientific research and creative activity, in particular:

(a) Measures designed to promote enjoyment of this freedom including the creation of all necessary conditions and facilities for scientific research and creative activity.

(b) Measures taken to guarantee the freedom of exchange of scientific, technical and cultural information, views and experience between scientists, writers, creative workers, artists and other creative individuals and their respective institutions.

(c) Measures taken to support learned societies, academies of science, professional associations, unions of workers and other organizations and institutions engaged in scientific research and creative activities.

What difficulties have affected the degree of realization of this freedom?

6. Please describe the legislative and other measures by which your Government encourages and develops international contacts and co-operation in the scientific and cultural fields, including measures taken for:

(a) The fullest utilization, by all the States concerned, of the facilities afforded by their adherence to regional and international conventions, agreements and other instruments in the scientific and cultural fields.

(b) Participation by scientists, writers, artists and others involved in scientific research or creative activity, in international scientific and cultural conferences, seminars, symposiums, etc.

What factors and difficulties have affected the development of international co-operation in these fields?

7. During the reporting period, have there been any changes in national policies, laws and practices negatively affecting the rights enshrined in Article 15? If so, please describe these changes and evaluate their impact.

8. In case your Government has recently submitted reports relevant to the situation with respect to the rights contained in Article 15 to the United Nations or a specialized agency, you may wish to refer to the relevant parts of those reports rather than repeat the information here.

9. Please indicate the role of international assistance in the full realization of the rights enshrined in Article 15.

Chapter 16
CEDAW General Recommendation No. 13 (1989) on Equal Remuneration for Work of Equal Value

The Committee on the Elimination of Discrimination Against Women,

Recalling International Labour Organisation Convention No. 100 concerning Equal Remuneration for Men and Women Workers for Work of Equal Value, which has been ratified by a large majority of States parties to the Convention on the Elimination of All Forms of Discrimination against Women,

Recalling also that it has considered 51 initial and 5 second periodic reports of States parties since 1983,

Considering that although reports of States parties indicate that, even though the principle of equal remuneration for work of equal value has been accepted in the legislation of many countries, more remains to be done to ensure the application of that principle in practice, in order to overcome the gender-segregation in the labour market,

Recommends to the States parties to the Convention on the Elimination of All Forms of Discrimination against Women that:

1. In order to implement fully the Convention on the Elimination of All Forms of Discrimination against Women, those States parties that have not yet ratified ILO Convention No. 100 should be encouraged to do so;

2. They should consider the study, development and adoption of job evaluation systems based on gender-neutral criteria that would facilitate the comparison of the value of those jobs of a different nature, in which women presently predominate, with those jobs in which men presently predominate, and they should include the results achieved in their reports to the Committee on the Elimination of Discrimination against Women;

3. They should support, as far as practicable, the creation of implementation machinery and encourage the efforts of the parties to collective agreements, where they apply, to ensure the application of the principle of equal remuneration for work of equal value.

Convention on the Elimination of All Forms of Discrimination Against Women. Original notes omitted.

Chapter 17
CEDAW General Recommendation No. 16 (1991) on Unpaid Women Workers in Rural and Urban Family Enterprises

The Committee on the Elimination of Discrimination Against Women,

Bearing in mind Articles 2 (c) and 11 (c), (d) and (e) of the Convention on the Elimination of All Forms of Discrimination against Women and general recommendation No. 9 (eighth session, 1989) on statistical data concerning the situation of women,

Taking into consideration that a high percentage of women in the States parties work without payment, social security and social benefits in enterprises owned usually by a male member of the family,

Noting that the reports presented to the Committee on the Elimination of Discrimination against Women generally do not refer to the problem of unpaid women workers of family enterprises,

Affirming that unpaid work constitutes a form of women's exploitation that is contrary to the Convention,

Recommends that States parties:

(1) Include in their reports to the Committee information on the legal and social situation of unpaid women working in family enterprises;

(2) Collect statistical data on women who work without payment, social security and social benefits in enterprises owned by a family member, and include these data in their report to the Committee;

(3) Take the necessary steps to guarantee payment, social security and social benefits for women who work without such benefits in enterprises owned by a family member.

Chapter 18

CEDAW General Recommendation No. 18 (1991) on Disabled Women

The Committee on the Elimination of Discrimination against Women,

Taking into consideration particularly Article 3 of the Convention on the Elimination of All Forms of Discrimination against Women,

Having considered more than 60 periodic reports of States parties, and having recognized that they provide scarce information on disabled women,

Concerned about the situation of disabled women, who suffer from a double discrimination linked to their special living conditions,

Recalling paragraph 296 of the Nairobi Forward-looking Strategies for the Advancement of Women, in which disabled women are considered as a vulnerable group under the heading "areas of special concern,"

Affirming its support for the World Programme of Action concerning Disabled Persons (1982),

Recommends that States parties provide information on disabled women in their periodic reports, and on measures taken to deal with their particular situation, including special measures to ensure that they have equal access to education and employment, health services and social security, and to ensure that they can participate in all areas of social and cultural life.

Chapter 19
CEDAW General Recommendation No. 24 (1999) on Women and Health

1. The Committee on the Elimination of Discrimination against Women, affirming that access to health care, including reproductive health, is a basic right under the Convention on the Elimination of All Forms of Discrimination against Women, decided at its twentieth session, pursuant to Article 21, to elaborate a general recommendation on Article 12 of the Convention.

Background

2. States parties' compliance with Article 12 of the Convention is central to the health and well-being of women. It requires States to eliminate discrimination against women in their access to health-care services throughout the life cycle, particularly in the areas of family planning, pregnancy and confinement and during the post-natal period. The examination of reports submitted by States parties pursuant to Article 18 of the Convention demonstrates that women's health is an issue that is recognized as a central concern in promoting the health and well-being of women. For the benefit of States parties and those who have a particular interest in and concern with the issues surrounding women's health, the present general recommendation seeks to elaborate the Committee's understanding of Article 12 and to address measures to eliminate discrimination in order to realize the right of women to the highest attainable standard of health.

3. Recent United Nations world conferences have also considered these objectives. In preparing this general recommendation, the Committee has taken into account relevant programmes of action adopted at United Nations world conferences and, in particular, those of the 1993 World Conference on Human Rights, the 1994 International Conference on Population and Development and the 1995 Fourth World Conference on Women. The Committee has also noted the work of the World Health Organization (WHO), the United Nations Population Fund (UNFPA) and other United Nations bodies. It has collaborated with a large number of non-governmental organizations with a special expertise in women's health in preparing this general recommendation.

Original notes omitted.

4. The Committee notes the emphasis that other United Nations instruments place on the right to health and to the conditions that enable good health to be achieved. Among such instruments are the Universal Declaration of Human Rights, the International Covenant on Economic, Social and Cultural Rights, the International Covenant on Civil and Political Rights, the Convention on the Rights of the Child and the Convention on the Elimination of All Forms of Racial Discrimination.

5. The Committee refers also to its earlier general recommendations on female circumcision, human immunodeficiency virus/acquired immunodeficiency syndrome (HIV/AIDS), disabled women, violence against women and equality in family relations, all of which refer to issues that are integral to full compliance with Article 12 of the Convention.

6. While biological differences between women and men may lead to differences in health status, there are societal factors that are determinative of the health status of women and men and can vary among women themselves. For that reason, special attention should be given to the health needs and rights of women belonging to vulnerable and disadvantaged groups, such as migrant women, refugee and internally displaced women, the girl child and older women, women in prostitution, indigenous women and women with physical or mental disabilities.

7. The Committee notes that the full realization of women's right to health can be achieved only when States parties fulfill their obligation to respect, protect and promote women's fundamental human right to nutritional well-being throughout their lifespan by means of a food supply that is safe, nutritious and adapted to local conditions. To this end, States parties should take steps to facilitate physical and economic access to productive resources, especially for rural women, and to otherwise ensure that the special nutritional needs of all women within their jurisdiction are met.

Article 12

8. Article 12 reads as follows:

"1. States parties shall take all appropriate measures to eliminate discrimination against women in the field of health care in order to ensure, on a basis of equality of men and women, access to health-care services, including those related to family planning.

2. Notwithstanding the provisions of paragraph 1 of this article, States parties shall ensure to women appropriate services in connection with pregnancy, confinement and the post-natal period, granting free services where necessary, as well as adequate nutrition during pregnancy and lactation."

States parties are encouraged to address the issue of women's health throughout the woman's lifespan. For the purposes of the present general recommendation, therefore, "women" includes girls and adolescents. The general recommendation will set out the Committee's analysis of the key elements of Article 12.

Key elements

Article 12 (1)

9. States parties are in the best position to report on the most critical health issues affecting women in that country. Therefore, in order to enable the Committee to evaluate whether measures to eliminate discrimination against women in the field of health care are appropriate, States parties must report on their health legislation, plans and policies for women with reliable data disaggregated by sex on the incidence and severity of diseases and conditions hazardous to women's health and nutrition and on the availability and cost-effectiveness of preventive and curative measures. Reports to the Committee must demonstrate that health legislation, plans and policies are based on scientific and ethical research and assessment of the health status and needs of women in that country and take into account any ethnic, regional or community variations or practices based on religion, tradition or culture.

10. States parties are encouraged to include in their reports information on diseases, health conditions and conditions hazardous to health that affect women or certain groups of women differently from men, as well as information on possible intervention in this regard.

11. Measures to eliminate discrimination against women are considered to be inappropriate if a health-care system lacks services to prevent, detect and treat illnesses specific to women. It is discriminatory for a State party to refuse to provide legally for the performance of certain reproductive health services for women. For instance, if health service providers refuse to perform such services based on conscientious objection, measures should be introduced to ensure that women are referred to alternative health providers.

12. States parties should report on their understanding of how policies and measures on health care address the health rights of women from the perspective of women's needs and interests and how it addresses distinctive features and factors that differ for women in comparison to men, such as:

(a) Biological factors that differ for women in comparison with men, such as their menstrual cycle, their reproductive function and menopause. Another example is the higher risk of exposure to sexually transmitted diseases that women face;

(b) Socio-economic factors that vary for women in general and some groups of women in particular. For example, unequal power relationships between women and men in the home and workplace may negatively affect women's nutrition and health. They may also be exposed to different forms of violence which can affect their health. Girl children and adolescent girls are often vulnerable to sexual abuse by older men and family members, placing them at risk of physical and psychological harm and unwanted and early pregnancy. Some cultural or traditional practices such as female genital mutilation also carry a high risk of death and disability;

(c) Psychosocial factors that vary between women and men include depression in general and post-partum depression in particular as well as other psychological conditions, such as those that lead to eating disorders such as anorexia and bulimia;

(d) While lack of respect for the confidentiality of patients will affect both men and women, it may deter women from seeking advice and treatment and thereby adversely affect their health and well-being. Women will be less willing, for that reason, to seek medical care for diseases of the genital tract, for contraception or for incomplete abortion and in cases where they have suffered sexual or physical violence.

13. The duty of States parties to ensure, on a basis of equality of men and women, access to health-care services, information and education implies an obligation to respect, protect and fulfill women's rights to health care. States parties have the responsibility to ensure that legislation and executive action and policy comply with these three obligations. They must also put in place a system that ensures effective judicial action. Failure to do so will constitute a violation of Article 12.

14. The obligation to respect rights requires States parties to refrain from obstructing action taken by women in pursuit of their health goals. States parties should report on how public and private health-care providers meet their duties to respect women's rights to have access to health care. For example, States parties should not restrict women's access to health services or to the clinics that provide those services on the ground that women do not have the authorization of husbands, partners, parents or health authorities, because they are unmarried or because they are women. Other barriers to women's access to appropriate health care include laws that criminalize medical procedures only needed by women punish women who undergo those procedures.

15. The obligation to protect rights relating to women's health requires States parties, their agents and officials to take action to prevent and impose sanctions for violations of rights by private persons and organizations. Since gender-based violence is a critical health issue for women, States parties should ensure:

(a) The enactment and effective enforcement of laws and the formulation of policies, including health-care protocols and hospital procedures to address violence against women and sexual abuse of girl children and the provision of appropriate health services;

(b) Gender-sensitive training to enable health-care workers to detect and manage the health consequences of gender-based violence;

(c) Fair and protective procedures for hearing complaints and imposing appropriate sanctions on health-care professionals guilty of sexual abuse of women patients;

(d) The enactment and effective enforcement of laws that prohibit female genital mutilation and marriage of girl children.

16. States parties should ensure that adequate protection and health services, including trauma treatment and counselling, are provided for women in especially difficult circumstances, such as those trapped in situations of armed conflict and women refugees.

17. The duty to fulfill rights places an obligation on States parties to take appropriate legislative, judicial, administrative, budgetary, economic and other measures to the maximum extent of their available resources to ensure that women realize their rights to health care. Studies such as those that emphasize the high maternal mortality and morbidity rates worldwide and the large numbers of couples who would like to limit their family size but lack access to or do not use any form of contraception provide an important indication for States parties of possible breaches of their duties to ensure women's access to health care. The Committee asks States parties to report on what they have done to address the magnitude of women's ill-health, in particular when it arises from preventable conditions, such as tuberculosis and HIV/AIDS. The Committee is concerned about the evidence that States are relinquishing these obligations as they transfer State health functions to private agencies. States and parties cannot absolve themselves of responsibility in these areas by delegating or transferring these powers to private sector agencies. States parties should therefore report on what they have done to organize governmental processes and all structures through which public power is exercised to promote and protect women's health. They should include information on positive measures taken to curb violations of women's rights by third parties and to protect their health and the measures they have taken to ensure the provision of such services.

18. The issues of HIV/AIDS and other sexually transmitted diseases are central to the rights of women and adolescent girls to sexual health. Adolescent girls and women in many countries lack adequate access to information and services necessary to ensure sexual health. As a consequence of unequal power relations based on gender, women and adolescent girls are often unable to refuse sex or insist on safe and responsible sex practices. Harmful traditional practices, such as female genital mutilation, polygamy, as well as marital rape, may also expose girls and women to the risk of contracting HIV/AIDS and other sexually transmitted diseases. Women in prostitution are also particularly vulnerable to these diseases. States parties should ensure, without prejudice or discrimination, the right to sexual health information, education and services for all women and girls, including those who have been trafficked, even if they are not legally resident in the country. In particular, States parties should ensure the rights of female and male adolescents to sexual and reproductive health education by properly trained personnel in specially designed programmes that respect their right to privacy and confidentiality.

19. In their reports, States parties should identify the test by which they assess whether women have access to health care on a basis of equality of men and women in order to demonstrate compliance with Article 12. In applying these tests, States parties should bear in mind the provisions of Article 1 of the Convention. Reports should therefore include comments on the impact that health policies, procedures, laws and protocols have on women when compared with men.

20. Women have the right to be fully informed, by properly trained personnel, of their options in agreeing to treatment or research, including likely benefits and potential adverse effects of proposed procedures and available alternatives.

21. States parties should report on measures taken to eliminate barriers that women face in access to health-care services and what measures they have taken to ensure women timely and affordable access to such services. Barriers include requirements or conditions that prejudice women's access, such as high fees for health-care services, the requirement for preliminary authorization by spouse, parent or hospital authorities, distance from health facilities and the absence of convenient and affordable public transport.

22. States parties should also report on measures taken to ensure access to quality health-care services, for example, by making them acceptable to women. Acceptable services are those that are delivered in a way that ensures that a woman gives her fully informed consent, respects her dignity, guarantees her confidentiality and is sensitive to her needs and perspectives. States parties should not permit forms of coercion, such as non-consensual sterilization, mandatory testing for sexually transmitted diseases or mandatory pregnancy testing as a condition of employment that violate women's rights to informed consent and dignity.

23. In their reports, States parties should state what measures they have taken to ensure timely access to the range of services that are related to family planning, in particular, and to sexual and reproductive health in general. Particular attention should be paid to the health education of adolescents, including information and counselling on all methods of family planning.

24. The Committee is concerned about the conditions of health-care services for older women, not only because women often live longer than men and are more likely than men to suffer from disabling and degenerative chronic diseases, such as osteoporosis and dementia, but because they often have the responsibility for their ageing spouses. Therefore, States parties should take appropriate measures to ensure the access of older women to health services that address the handicaps and disabilities associated with ageing.

25. Women with disabilities, of all ages, often have difficulty with physical access to health services. Women with mental disabilities are particularly vulnerable, while there is limited understanding, in general, of the broad range of risks to mental health to which women are disproportionately susceptible as a result of gender discrimination, violence, poverty, armed conflict, dislocation and other forms of social deprivation. States parties should take appropriate measures to ensure that health services are sensitive to the needs of women with disabilities and are respectful of their human rights and dignity.

Article 12 (2)

26. Reports should also include what measures States parties have taken to ensure women appropriate services in connection with pregnancy, confinement and the post-natal period. Information on the rates at which these measures have reduced maternal mortality and morbidity in their countries, in general, and in vulnerable groups, regions and communities, in particular, should also be included.

27. States parties should include in their reports how they supply free services where necessary to ensure safe pregnancies, childbirth and post-partum periods for women. Many women are at risk of death or disability from pregnancy-related causes because they lack the funds to obtain or access the necessary services, which include antenatal, maternity and post-natal services. The Committee notes that it is the duty of States parties to ensure women's right to safe motherhood and emergency obstetric services and they should allocate to these services the maximum extent of available resources.

Other relevant articles in the Convention

28. When reporting on measures taken to comply with Article 12, States parties are urged to recognize its interconnection with other articles in the Convention that have a bearing on women's health. Those articles include Article 5 (b), which requires States parties to ensure that family education includes a proper understanding of maternity as a social function; Article 10, which requires States parties to ensure equal access to education, thus enabling women to access health care more readily and reducing female student drop-out rates, which are often a result of premature pregnancy; Article 10 (h), which requires that States parties provide to women and girls access to specific educational information to help ensure the health and well-being of families, including information and advice on family planning; Article 11, which is concerned, in part, with the protection of women's health and safety in working conditions, including the safeguarding of the reproductive function, special protection from harmful types of work during pregnancy and with the provision of paid maternity leave; Article 14, paragraph 2 (b), which requires States parties to ensure access for rural women to adequate health-care facilities, including information, counselling and services in family planning, and (h), which obliges States parties to take all appropriate measures to ensure adequate living conditions, particularly housing, sanitation, electricity and water supply, transport and communications, all of which are critical for the prevention of disease and the promotion of good health care; and Article 16, paragraph 1 (e), which requires States parties to ensure that women have the same rights as men to decide freely and responsibly on the number and spacing of their children and to have access to the information, education and means to enable them to exercise those rights. Article 16, paragraph 2 proscribes the betrothal and marriage of children, an important factor in preventing the physical and emotional harm which arise from early childbirth.

Recommendations for government action

29. States parties should implement a comprehensive national strategy to promote women's health throughout their lifespan. This will include interventions aimed at both the prevention and treatment of diseases and conditions affecting women, as well as responding to violence against women, and will ensure universal access for all women to a full range of high-quality and affordable health care, including sexual and reproductive health services.

30. States parties should allocate adequate budgetary, human and administrative resources to ensure that women's health receives a share of the overall health budget comparable with that for men's health, taking into account their different health needs.

31. States parties should also, in particular:

(a) Place a gender perspective at the centre of all policies and programmes affecting women's health and should involve women in the planning, implementation and monitoring of such policies and programmes and in the provision of health services to women;

(b) Ensure the removal of all barriers to women's access to health services, education and information, including in the area of sexual and reproductive health, and, in particular, allocate resources for programmes directed at adolescents for the prevention and treatment of sexually transmitted diseases, including HIV/AIDS;

(c) Prioritize the prevention of unwanted pregnancy through family planning and sex education and reduce maternal mortality rates through safe motherhood services and prenatal assistance. When possible, legislation criminalizing abortion should be amended, in order to withdraw punitive measures imposed on women who undergo abortion;

(d) Monitor the provision of health services to women by public, non-governmental and private organizations, to ensure equal access and quality of care;

(e) Require all health services to be consistent with the human rights of women, including the rights to autonomy, privacy, confidentiality, informed consent and choice;

(f) Ensure that the training curricula of health workers include comprehensive, mandatory, gender-sensitive courses on women's health and human rights, in particular gender-based violence.

D. WORLD CONFERENCES

Chapter 1
Vienna Declaration and Plan of Action (excerpts)

The World Conference on Human Rights,

Considering that the promotion and protection of human rights is a matter of priority for the international community, and that the Conference affords a unique opportunity to carry out a comprehensive analysis of the international human rights system and of the machinery for the protection of human rights, in order to enhance and thus promote a fuller observance of those rights, in a just and balanced manner,

Recognizing and affirming that all human rights derive from the dignity and worth inherent in the human person, and that the human person is the central subject of human rights and fundamental freedoms, and consequently should be the principal beneficiary and should participate actively in the realization of these rights and freedoms,

Reaffirming their commitment to the purposes and principles contained in the Charter of the United Nations and the Universal Declaration of Human Rights,

Reaffirming the commitment contained in Article 56 of the Charter of the United Nations to take joint and separate action, placing proper emphasis on developing effective international cooperation for the realization of the purposes set out in Article 55, including universal respect for, and observance of, human rights and fundamental freedoms for all,

Emphasizing the responsibilities of all States, in conformity with the Charter of the United Nations, to develop and encourage respect for human rights and fundamental freedoms for all, without distinction as to race, sex, language or religion,

Recalling the Preamble to the Charter of the United Nations, in particular the determination to reaffirm faith in fundamental human rights, in the dignity and worth of the human person, and in the equal rights of men and women and of nations large and small,

Recalling also the determination expressed in the Preamble of the Charter of the United Nations to save succeeding generations from the scourge of war, to establish

Adopted by the World Conference on Human Rights on 25 June 1993.

conditions under which justice and respect for obligations arising from treaties and other sources of international law can be maintained, to promote social progress and better standards of life in larger freedom, to practice tolerance and good neighbourliness, and to employ international machinery for the promotion of the economic and social advancement of all peoples,

Emphasizing that the Universal Declaration of Human Rights, which constitutes a common standard of achievement for all peoples and all nations, is the source of inspiration and has been the basis for the United Nations in making advances in standard setting as contained in the existing international human rights instruments, in particular the International Covenant on Civil and Political Rights and the International Covenant on Economic, Social and Cultural Rights.

Considering the major changes taking place on the international scene and the aspirations of all the peoples for an international order based on the principles enshrined in the Charter of the United Nations, including promoting and encouraging respect for human rights and fundamental freedoms for all and respect for the principle of equal rights and self-determination of peoples, peace, democracy, justice, equality, rule of law, pluralism, development, better standards of living and solidarity,

Deeply concerned by various forms of discrimination and violence, to which women continue to be exposed all over the world,

Recognizing that the activities of the United Nations in the field of human rights should be rationalized and enhanced in order to strengthen the United Nations machinery in this field and to further the objectives of universal respect for observance of international human rights standards,

Having taken into account the Declarations adopted by the three regional meetings at Tunis, San José and Bangkok and the contributions made by Governments, and bearing in mind the suggestions made by intergovernmental and non-governmental organizations, as well as the studies prepared by independent experts during the preparatory process leading to the World Conference on Human Rights,

Welcoming the International Year of the World's Indigenous People 1993 as a reaffirmation of the commitment of the international community to ensure their enjoyment of all human rights and fundamental freedoms and to respect the value and diversity of their cultures and identities,

Recognizing also that the international community should devise ways and means to remove the current obstacles and meet challenges to the full realization of all human rights and to prevent the continuation of human rights violations resulting thereof throughout the world,

Invoking the spirit of our age and the realities of our time which call upon the peoples of the world and all States Members of the United Nations to rededicate themselves to the global task of promoting and protecting all human rights and fundamental freedoms so as to secure full and universal enjoyment of these rights,

Determined to take new steps forward in the commitment of the international community with a view to achieving substantial progress in human rights endeavours by an increased and sustained effort of international cooperation and solidarity,

Solemnly adopts the Vienna Declaration and Programme of Action.

1. The World Conference on Human Rights reaffirms the solemn commitment of all States to fulfill their obligations to promote universal respect for, and observance and protection of, all human rights and fundamental freedoms for all in accordance with the Charter of the United Nations, other instruments relating to human rights, and international law. The universal nature of these rights and freedoms is beyond question.

2. In this framework, enhancement of international cooperation in the field of human rights is essential for the full achievement of the purposes of the United Nations.

3. Human rights and fundamental freedoms are the birthright of all human beings; their protection and promotion is the first responsibility of Governments.

4. The promotion and protection of all human rights and fundamental freedoms must be considered as a priority objective of the United Nations in accordance with its purposes and principles, in particular the purpose of international cooperation. In the framework of these purposes and principles, the promotion and protection of all human rights is a legitimate concern of the international community. The organs and specialized agencies related to human rights should therefore further enhance the coordination of their activities based on the consistent and objective application of international human rights instruments.

5. All human rights are universal, indivisible and interdependent and interrelated. The international community must treat human rights globally in a fair and equal manner, on the same footing, and with the same emphasis. While the significance of national and regional particularities and various historical, cultural and religious backgrounds must be borne in mind, it is the duty of States, regardless of their political, economic and cultural systems, to promote and protect all human rights and fundamental freedoms.

6. The efforts of the United Nations system towards the universal respect for, and observance of, human rights and fundamental freedoms for all, contribute to the stability and well-being necessary for peaceful and friendly relations among nations, and to improved conditions for peace and security as well as social and economic development, in conformity with the Charter of the United Nations.

7. The processes of promoting and protecting human rights should be conducted in conformity with the purposes and principles of the Charter of the United Nations, and international law.

8. Democracy, development and respect for human rights and fundamental freedoms are interdependent and mutually reinforcing. Democracy is based on the freely expressed will of the people to determine their own political, economic, social and cultural systems and their full participation in all aspects of their lives. In the context of the above, the promotion and protection of human rights and fundamental freedoms

at the national and international levels should be universal and conducted without conditions attached. The international community should support the strengthening and promoting of democracy, development and respect for human rights and fundamental freedoms in the entire world.

9. The World Conference on Human Rights reaffirms that least developed countries committed to the process of democratization and economic reforms, many of which are in Africa, should be supported by the international community in order to succeed in their transition to democracy and economic development.

10. The World Conference on Human Rights reaffirms the right to development, as established in the Declaration on the Right to Development, as a universal and inalienable right and an integral part of fundamental human rights.

As stated in the Declaration on the Right to Development, the human person is the central subject of development.

While development facilitates the enjoyment of all human rights, the lack of development may not be invoked to justify the abridgement of internationally recognized human rights.

States should cooperate with each other in ensuring development and eliminating obstacles to development. The international community should promote effective international cooperation for the realization of the right to development and the elimination of obstacles to development.

Lasting progress towards the implementation of the right to development requires effective development policies at the national level, as well as equitable economic relations and a favourable economic environment at the international level.

11. The right to development should be fulfilled so as to meet equitably the developmental and environmental needs of present and future generations. The World Conference on Human Rights recognizes that illicit dumping of toxic and dangerous substances and waste potentially constitutes a serious threat to the human rights to life and health of everyone.

Consequently, the World Conference on Human Rights calls on all States to adopt and vigorously implement existing conventions relating to the dumping of toxic and dangerous products and waste and to cooperate in the prevention of illicit dumping.

Everyone has the right to enjoy the benefits of scientific progress and its applications. The World Conference on Human Rights notes that certain advances, notably in the biomedical and life sciences as well as in information technology, may have potentially adverse consequences for the integrity, dignity and human rights of the individual, and calls for international cooperation to ensure that human rights and dignity are fully respected in this area of universal concern.

12. The World Conference on Human Rights calls upon the international community to make all efforts to help alleviate the external debt burden of developing countries,

in order to supplement the efforts of the Governments of such countries to attain the full realization of the economic, social and cultural rights of their people.

13. There is a need for States and international organizations, in cooperation with non-governmental organizations, to create favourable conditions at the national, regional and international levels to ensure the full and effective enjoyment of human rights. States should eliminate all violations of human rights and their causes, as well as obstacles to the enjoyment of these rights.

14. The existence of widespread extreme poverty inhibits the full and effective enjoyment of human rights; its immediate alleviation and eventual elimination must remain a high priority for the international community.

15. Respect for human rights and for fundamental freedoms without distinction of any kind is a fundamental rule of international human rights law. The speedy and comprehensive elimination of all forms of racism and racial discrimination, xenophobia and related intolerance is a priority task for the international community. Governments should take effective measures to prevent and combat them. Groups, institutions, intergovernmental and non-governmental organizations and individuals are urged to intensify their efforts in cooperating and coordinating their activities against these evils.

. . .

18. The human rights of women and of the girl-child are an inalienable, integral and indivisible part of universal human rights. The full and equal participation of women in political, civil, economic, social and cultural life, at the national, regional and international levels, and the eradication of all forms of discrimination on grounds of sex are priority objectives of the international community.

Gender-based violence and all forms of sexual harassment and exploitation, including those resulting from cultural prejudice and international trafficking, are incompatible with the dignity and worth of the human person, and must be eliminated. This can be achieved by legal measures and through national action and international cooperation in such fields as economic and social development, education, safe maternity and health care, and social support.

The human rights of women should form an integral part of the United Nations human rights activities, including the promotion of all human rights instruments relating to women.

The World Conference on Human Rights urges Governments, institutions, intergovernmental and non-governmental organizations to intensify their efforts for the protection and promotion of human rights of women and the girl child.

19. Considering the importance of the promotion and protection of the rights of persons belonging to minorities and the contribution of such promotion and protection to the political and social stability of the States in which such persons live, The World Conference on Human Rights reaffirms the obligation of States to ensure that persons

belonging to minorities may exercise fully and effectively all human rights and fundamental freedoms without any discrimination and in full equality before the law in accordance with the Declaration on the Rights of Persons Belonging to National or Ethnic, Religious and Linguistic Minorities.

The persons belonging to minorities have the right to enjoy their own culture, to profess and practise their own religion and to use their own language in private and in public, freely and without interference or any form of discrimination.

20. The World Conference on Human Rights recognizes the inherent dignity and the unique contribution of indigenous people to the development and plurality of society and strongly reaffirms the commitment of the international community to their economic, social and cultural well-being and their enjoyment of the fruits of sustainable development. States should ensure the full and free participation of indigenous people in all aspects of society, in particular in matters of concern to them. Considering the importance of the promotion and protection of the rights of indigenous people, and the contribution of such promotion and protection to the political and social stability of the States in which such people live, States should, in accordance with international law, take concerted positive steps to ensure respect for all human rights and fundamental freedoms of indigenous people, on the basis of equality and non-discrimination, and recognize the value and diversity of their distinct identities, cultures and social organization.

21. The World Conference on Human Rights, welcoming the early ratification of the Convention on the Rights of the Child by a large number of States and noting the recognition of the human rights of children in the World Declaration on the Survival, Protection and Development of Children and Plan of Action adopted by the World Summit for Children, urges universal ratification of the Convention by 1995 and its effective implementation by States parties through the adoption of all the necessary legislative, administrative and other measures and the allocation to the maximum extent of the available resources. In all actions concerning children, non-discrimination and the best interest of the child should be primary considerations and the views of the child given due weight. National and international mechanisms and programmes should be strengthened for the defence and protection of children, in particular, the girl-child, abandoned children, street children, economically and sexually exploited children, including through child pornography, child prostitution or sale of organs, children victims of diseases including acquired immunodeficiency syndrome, refugee and displaced children, children in detention, children in armed conflict, as well as children victims of famine and drought and other emergencies. International cooperation and solidarity should be promoted to support the implementation of the Convention on the Rights of the Child should be a priority in the United Nations system-wide action on human rights.

The World Conference on Human Rights also stresses that the child for the full and harmonious development of his or her personality should grow up in a family environment which accordingly merits broader protection.

22. Special attention needs to be paid to ensuring non-discrimination, and the equal enjoyment of all human rights and fundamental freedoms by disabled persons, including their active participation in all aspects of society.

. . .

24. Great importance must be given to the promotion and protection of the human rights of persons belonging to groups which have been rendered vulnerable, including migrant workers, the elimination of all forms of discrimination against them, and the strengthening and more effective implementation of existing human rights instruments. States have an obligation to create and maintain adequate measures at the national level, in particular in the fields of education, health and social support, for the promotion and protection of the rights of persons in vulnerable sectors of their populations and to ensure the participation of those among them who are interested in finding a solution to their own problems.

25. The World Conference on Human Rights affirms that extreme poverty and social exclusion constitute a violation of human dignity and that urgent steps are necessary to achieve better knowledge of extreme poverty and its causes, including those related to the problem of development, in order to promote the human rights of the poorest, and to put an end to extreme poverty and social exclusion and to promote the enjoyment of the fruits of social progress. It is essential for States to foster participation by the poorest people in the decision-making process by the community in which they live, the promotion of human rights and efforts to combat extreme poverty.

. . .

30. The World Conference on Human Rights also expresses its dismay and condemnation that gross and systematic violations and situations that constitute serious obstacles to the full enjoyment of all human rights continue to occur in different parts of the world. Such violations and obstacles include, as well as torture and cruel, inhuman and degrading treatment or punishment, summary and arbitrary executions, disappearances, arbitrary detentions, all forms of racism, racial discrimination and apartheid, foreign occupation and alien domination, xenophobia, poverty, hunger and other denials of economic, social and cultural rights, religious intolerance, terrorism, discrimination against women and lack of the rule of law.

. . .

33. The World Conference on Human Rights reaffirms that States are duty-bound, as stipulated in the Universal Declaration of Human Rights and the International Covenant on Economic, Social and Cultural Rights and in other international human rights instruments, to ensure that education is aimed at strengthening the respect of human rights and fundamental freedoms. The World Conference on Human Rights emphasizes the importance of incorporating the subject of human rights education programmes and calls upon States to do so. Education should promote understanding, tolerance, peace and friendly relations between the nations and all racial or religious

groups and encourage the development of United Nations activities in pursuance of these objectives. Therefore, education on human rights and the dissemination of proper information, both theoretical and practical, play an important role in the promotion and respect of human rights with regard to all individuals without distinction of any kind such as race, sex, language or religion, and this should be integrated in the education policies at the national as well as international levels. The World Conference on Human Rights notes that resource constraints and institutional inadequacies may impede the immediate realization of these objectives.

Chapter 2
Beijing Declaration: Fourth World Conference on Women

1. We, the Governments participating in the Fourth World Conference on Women,

2. Gathered here in Beijing in September 1995, the year of the fiftieth anniversary of the founding of the United Nations,

3. Determined to advance the goals of equality, development and peace for all women everywhere in the interest of all humanity,

4. Acknowledging the voices of all women everywhere and taking note of the diversity of women and their roles and circumstances, honouring the women who paved the way and inspired by the hope present in the world's youth,

5. Recognize that the status of women has advanced in some important respects in the past decade but that progress has been uneven, inequalities between women and men have persisted and major obstacles remain, with serious consequences for the well-being of all people,

6. Also recognize that this situation is exacerbated by the increasing poverty that is affecting the lives of the majority of the world's people, in particular women and children, with origins in both the national and international domains,

7. Dedicate ourselves unreservedly to addressing these constraints and obstacles and thus enhancing further the advancement and empowerment of women all over the world, and agree that this requires urgent action in the spirit of determination, hope, co-operation and solidarity, now and to carry us forward into the next century.

We reaffirm our commitment to:

8. The equal rights and inherent human dignity of women and men and other purposes and principles enshrined in the Charter of the United Nations, to the Universal Declaration of Human Rights and other international human rights instruments, in particular the Convention on the Elimination of All Forms of Discrimination against Women and the Convention on the Rights of the Child, as well as the Declaration on the Elimination of Violence against Women and the Declaration on the Right to Development;

Adopted by the Fourth World Conference on Women, held in Beijing, 4–15 September 1995. Programme of Action available from www.un.org/womenwatch.

9. Ensure the full implementation of the human rights of women and of the girl child as an inalienable, integral and indivisible part of all human rights and fundamental freedoms;

10. Build on consensus and progress made at previous United Nations conferences and summits - on women in Nairobi in 1985, on children in New York in 1990, on environment and development in Rio de Janeiro in1992, on human rights in Vienna in 1993, on population and development in Cairo in 1994 and on social development in Copenhagen in 1995 with the objective of achieving equality, development and peace;

11. Achieve the full and effective implementation of the Nairobi Forward-looking Strategies for the Advancement of Women;

12. The empowerment and advancement of women, including the right to freedom of thought, conscience, religion and belief, thus contributing to the moral, ethical, spiritual and intellectual needs of women and men individually or in community with others and thereby guaranteeing them the possibility of realizing their full potential in society and shaping their lives in accordance with their own aspirations.

We are convinced that:

13. Women's empowerment and their full participation on the basis of equality in all spheres of society, including participation in the decision-making process and access to power, are fundamental for the achievement of equality, development and peace;

14. Women's rights are human rights;

15. Equal rights, opportunities and access to resources, equal sharing of responsibilities for the family by men and women, and a harmonious partnership between them are critical to their well-being and that of their families as well as to the consolidation of democracy;

16. Eradication of poverty based on sustained economic growth, social development, environmental protection and social justice requires the involvement of women in economic and social development, equal opportunities and the full and equal participation of women and men as agents and beneficiaries of people-centred sustainable development;

17. The explicit recognition and reaffirmation of the right of all women to control all aspects of their health, in particular their own fertility, is basic to their empowerment;

18. Local, national, regional and global peace is attainable and is inextricably linked with the advancement of women, who are a fundamental force for leadership, conflict resolution and the promotion of lasting peace at all levels;

19. It is essential to design, implement and monitor, with the full participation of women, effective, efficient and mutually reinforcing gender-sensitive policies and programmes, including development policies and programmes, at all levels that will foster the empowerment and advancement of women;

20. The participation and contribution of all actors of civil society, particularly women's groups and networks and other non-governmental organizations and community-based organizations, with full respect for their autonomy, in cooperation with Governments, are important to the effective implementation and follow-up of the Platform for Action;

21. The implementation of the Platform for Action requires commitment from Governments and the international community. By making national and international commitments for action, including those made at the Conference, Governments and the international community recognize the need to take priority action for the empowerment and advancement of women.

We are determined to:

22. Intensify efforts and actions to achieve the goals of the Nairobi Forward-looking Strategies for the Advancement of Women by the end of this century;

23. Ensure the full enjoyment by women and the girl child of all human rights and fundamental freedoms and take effective action against violations of these rights and freedoms;

24. Take all necessary measures to eliminate all forms of discrimination against women and the girl child and remove all obstacles to gender equality and the advancement and empowerment of women;

25. Encourage men to participate fully in all actions towards equality;

26. Promote women's economic independence, including employment, and eradicate the persistent and increasing burden of poverty on women by addressing the structural causes of poverty through changes in economic structures, ensuring equal access for all women, including those in rural areas, as vital development agents, to productive resources, opportunities and public services;

27. Promote people-centred sustainable development, including sustained economic growth, through the provision of basic education, life-long education, literacy and training, and primary health care for girls and women;

28. Take positive steps to ensure peace for the advancement of women and, recognizing the leading role that women have played in the peace movement, work actively towards general and complete disarmament under strict and effective international control, and support negotiations on the conclusion, without delay, of a universal and multilaterally and effectively verifiable comprehensive nuclear-test-ban treaty which contributes to nuclear disarmament and the prevention of the proliferation of nuclear weapons in all its aspects;

29. Prevent and eliminate all forms of violence against women and girls;

30. Ensure equal access to and equal treatment of women and men in education and health care and enhance women's sexual and reproductive health as well as education;

31. Promote and protect all human rights of women and girls;

32. Intensify efforts to ensure equal enjoyment of all human rights and fundamental freedoms for all women and girls who face multiple barriers to their empowerment and advancement because of such factors as their race, age, language, ethnicity, culture, religion, or disability, or because they are indigenous people;

33. Ensure respect for international law, including humanitarian law, in order to protect women and girls in particular;

34. Develop the fullest potential of girls and women of all ages, ensure their full and equal participation in building a better world for all and enhance their role in the development process.

We are determined to:

35. Ensure women's equal access to economic resources, including land, credit, science and technology, vocational training, information, communication and markets, as a means to further the advancement and empowerment of women and girls, including through the enhancement of their capacities to enjoy the benefits of equal access to these resources, *inter alia,* by means of international cooperation;

36. Ensure the success of the Platform for Action, which will require a strong commitment on the part of Governments, international organizations and institutions at all levels. We are deeply convinced that economic development, social development and environmental protection are interdependent and mutually reinforcing components of sustainable development, which is the framework for our efforts to achieve a higher quality of life for all people. Equitable social development that recognizes empowering the poor, particularly women living in poverty, to utilize environmental resources sustainably is a necessary foundation for sustainable development. We also recognize that broad-based and sustained economic growth in the context of sustainable development is necessary to sustain social development and social justice. The success of the Platform for Action will also require adequate mobilization of resources at the national and international levels as well as new and additional resources to the developing countries from all available funding mechanisms, including multilateral, bilateral and private sources for the advancement of women; financial resources to strengthen the capacity of national, subregional, regional and international institutions; a commitment to equal rights, equal responsibilities and equal opportunities and to the equal participation of women and men in all national, regional and international bodies and policy-making processes; and the establishment or strengthening of mechanisms at all levels for accountability to the world's women;

37. Ensure also the success of the Platform for Action in countries with economies in transition, which will require continued international co-operation and assistance;

38. We hereby adopt and commit ourselves as Governments to implement the following Platform for Action, ensuring that a gender perspective is reflected in all our policies and programmes. We urge the United Nations system, regional and international financial institutions, other relevant regional and international institutions and all women and men, as well as non-governmental organizations, with full respect for their autonomy, and all sectors of civil society, in co-operation with Governments, to fully commit themselves and contribute to the implementation of this Platform for Action.

Chapter 3
Copenhagen Declaration on Social Development

1. For the first time in history, at the invitation of the United Nations, we gather as heads of State and Government to recognize the significance of social development and human well-being for all and to give to these goals the highest priority both now and into the twenty-first century.

2. We acknowledge that the people of the world have shown in different ways an urgent need to address profound social problems, especially poverty, unemployment and social exclusion, that affect every country. It is our task to address both their underlying and structural causes and their distressing consequences in order to reduce uncertainty and insecurity in the life of people.

3. We acknowledge that our societies must respond more effectively to the material and spiritual needs of individuals, their families and the communities in which they live throughout our diverse countries and regions. We must do so not only as a matter of urgency but also as a matter of sustained and unshakeable commitment through the years ahead.

4. We are convinced that democracy and transparent and accountable governance and administration in all sectors of society are indispensable foundations for the realization of social and people-centred sustainable development.

5. We share the conviction that social development and social justice are indispensable for the achievement and maintenance of peace and security within and among our nations. In turn, social development and social justice cannot be attained in the absence of peace and security or in the absence of respect for all human rights and fundamental freedoms. This essential interdependence was recognized 50 years ago in the Charter of the United Nations and has since grown ever stronger.

6. We are deeply convinced that economic development, social development and

Adopted by the World Summit for Social Development, held in Copenhagen 6–12 March 1995. Original notes omitted.

environmental protection are interdependent and mutually reinforcing components of sustainable development, which is the framework for our efforts to achieve a higher quality of life for all people. Equitable social development that recognizes empowering the poor to utilize environmental resources sustainably is a necessary foundation for sustainable development. We also recognize that broad-based and sustained economic growth in the context of sustainable development is necessary to sustain social development and social justice.

7. We recognize, therefore, that social development is central to the needs and aspirations of people throughout the world and to the responsibilities of Governments and all sectors of civil society. We affirm that, in both economic and social terms, the most productive policies and investments are those that empower people to maximize their capacities, resources and opportunities. We acknowledge that social and economic development cannot be secured in a sustainable way without the full participation of women and that equality and equity between women and men is a priority for the international community and as such must be at the centre of economic and social development.

8. We acknowledge that people are at the centre of our concerns for sustainable development and that they are entitled to a healthy and productive life in harmony with the environment.

9. We gather here to commit ourselves, our Governments and our nations to enhancing social development throughout the world so that all men and women, especially those living in poverty, may exercise the rights, utilize the resources and share the responsibilities that enable them to lead satisfying lives and to contribute to the well-being of their families, their communities and humankind. To support and promote these efforts must be the overriding goals of the international community, especially with respect to people suffering from poverty, unemployment and social exclusion.

10. We make this solemn commitment on the eve of the fiftieth anniversary of the United Nations, with a determination to capture the unique possibilities offered by the end of the cold war to promote social development and social justice. We reaffirm and are guided by the principles of the Charter of the United Nations and by agreements reached at relevant international conferences, including the World Summit for Children, held at New York in 1990;

11. We gather here in Copenhagen in a Summit of hope, commitment and action. We gather with full awareness of the difficulty of the tasks that lie ahead but with a conviction that major progress can be achieved, must be achieved and will be achieved.

12. We commit ourselves to this Declaration and Programme of Action for enhancing social development and ensuring human well-being for all throughout the world now and into the twenty-first century. We invite all people in all countries and in all walks of life, as well as the international community, to join us in our common cause.

A. Current Social Situation and Reasons for Convening the Summit

13. We are witnessing in countries throughout the world the expansion of prosperity for some, unfortunately accompanied by an expansion of unspeakable poverty for others. This glaring contradiction is unacceptable and needs to be corrected through urgent actions.

14. Globalization, which is a consequence of increased human mobility, enhanced communications, greatly increased trade and capital flows, and technological developments, opens new opportunities for sustained economic growth and development of the world economy, particularly in developing countries. Globalization also permits countries to share experiences and to learn from one another's achievements and difficulties, and promotes a cross-fertilization of ideals, cultural values and aspirations. At the same time, the rapid processes of change and adjustment have been accompanied by intensified poverty, unemployment and social disintegration. Threats to human well-being, such as environmental risks, have also been globalized. Furthermore, the global transformations of the world economy are profoundly changing the parameters of social development in all countries. The challenge is how to manage these processes and threats so as to enhance their benefits and mitigate their negative effects upon people.

15. There has been progress in some areas of social and economic development:

(a) The global wealth of nations has multiplied sevenfold in the past 50 years and international trade has grown even more dramatically;

(b) Life expectancy, literacy and primary education, and access to basic health care, including family planning, have increased in the majority of countries and average infant mortality has been reduced, including in developing countries;

(c) Democratic pluralism, democratic institutions and fundamental civil liberties have expanded. Decolonization efforts have achieved much progress, while the elimination of apartheid is a historic achievement.

16. Yet we recognize that far too many people, particularly women and children, are vulnerable to stress and deprivation. Poverty, unemployment and social disintegration too often result in isolation, marginalization and violence. The insecurity that many people, in particular vulnerable people, face about the future—their own and their children's—is intensifying:

(a) Within many societies, in both developed and developing countries, the gap between rich and poor has increased. Furthermore, despite the fact that some developing countries are growing rapidly the gap between developed and many developing countries, particularly the least developed countries, has widened;

(b) More than one billion people in the world live in abject poverty, most of whom go hungry every day. A large proportion, the majority of whom are women, have very limited access to income, resources, education, health care or nutrition, particularly in Africa and the least developed countries;

(c) There are also serious social problems of a different nature and magnitude in countries with economies in transition and countries experiencing fundamental political, economic and social transformations;

(d) The major cause of the continued deterioration of the global environment is the unsustainable pattern of consumption and production, particularly in industrialized countries, which is a matter of grave concern, aggravating poverty and imbalances;

(e) Continued growth in the world's population, its structure and distribution, and its relationship with poverty and social and gender inequality challenge the adaptive capacities of Governments, individuals, social institutions and the natural environment;

(f) Over 120 million people world wide are officially unemployed and many more are underemployed. Too many young people, including those with formal education, have little hope of finding productive work;

(g) More women than men live in absolute poverty and the imbalance continues to grow, with serious consequences for women and their children. Women carry a disproportionate share of the problems of coping with poverty, social disintegration, unemployment, environmental degradation and the effects of war;

(h) One of the world's largest minorities, more than 1 in 10, are people with disabilities, who are too often forced into poverty, unemployment and social isolation. In addition, in all countries older persons may be particularly vulnerable to social exclusion, poverty and marginalization;

(i) Millions of people world wide are refugees or internally displaced persons. The tragic social consequences have a critical effect on the social stability and development of their home countries, their host countries and their respective regions.

17. While these problems are global in character and affect all countries, we clearly acknowledge that the situation of most developing countries, and particularly of Africa and the least developed countries, is critical and requires special attention and action. We also acknowledge that these countries, which are undergoing fundamental political, economic and social transformation, including countries in the process of consolidating peace and democracy, require the support of the international community.

18. Countries with economies in transition, which are also undergoing fundamental political, economic and social transformation, require the support of the international community as well.

19. Other countries that are undergoing fundamental political, economic and social transformation require the support of the international community as well.

20. The goals and objectives of social development require continuous efforts to reduce and eliminate major sources of social distress and instability for the family and for society.

We pledge to place particular focus on and give priority attention to the fight against the world-wide conditions that pose severe threats to the health, safety, peace, security and well-being of our people. Among these conditions are chronic hunger; malnutrition; illicit drug problems; organized crime; corruption; foreign occupation; armed conflicts; illicit arms trafficking, terrorism, intolerance and incitement to racial, ethnic, religious and other hatreds; xenophobia; and endemic, communicable and chronic diseases. To this end, coordination and cooperation at the national level and especially at the regional and international levels should be further strengthened.

21. In this context, the negative impact on development of excessive military expenditures, the arms trade, and investment for arms production and acquisition must be addressed.

22. Communicable diseases constitute a serious health problem in all countries and are a major cause of death globally; in many cases, their incidence is increasing. These diseases are a hindrance to social development and are often the cause of poverty and social exclusion. The prevention, treatment and control of these diseases, covering a spectrum from tuberculosis and malaria to the human immunodeficiency virus/ acquired immunodeficiency syndrome (HIV/AIDS), must be given the highest priority.

23. We can continue to hold the trust of the people of the world only if we make their needs our priority. We know that poverty, lack of productive employment and social disintegration are an offence to human dignity. We also know that they are negatively reinforcing and represent a waste of human resources and a manifestation of ineffectiveness in the functioning of markets and economic and social institutions and processes.

24. Our challenge is to establish a people-centred framework for social development to guide us now and in the future, to build a culture of cooperation and partnership, and to respond to the immediate needs of those who are most affected by human distress. We are determined to meet this challenge and promote social development throughout the world.

B. Principles and Goals

25. We heads of State and Government are committed to a political, economic, ethical and spiritual vision for social development that is based on human dignity, human rights, equality, respect, peace, democracy, mutual responsibility and cooperation, and full respect for the various religious and ethical values and cultural backgrounds of people. Accordingly, we will give the highest priority in national, regional and international policies and actions to the promotion of social progress, justice and the betterment of the human condition, based on full participation by all.

26. To this end, we will create a framework for action to:

(a) Place people at the centre of development and direct our economies to meet human needs more effectively;

(b) Fulfill our responsibility for present and future generations by ensuring equity among generations and protecting the integrity and sustainable use of our environment;

(c) Recognize that, while social development is a national responsibility, it cannot be successfully achieved without the collective commitment and efforts of the international community;

(d) Integrate economic, cultural and social policies so that they become mutually supportive, and acknowledge the interdependence of public and private spheres of activity;

(e) Recognize that the achievement of sustained social development requires sound, broadly based economic policies;

(f) Promote democracy, human dignity, social justice and solidarity at the national, regional and international levels; ensure tolerance, non-violence, pluralism and non-discrimination, with full respect for diversity within and among societies;

(g) Promote the equitable distribution of income and greater access to resources through equity and equality of opportunity for all;

(h) Recognize the family as the basic unit of society, and acknowledge that it plays a key role in social development and as such should be strengthened, with attention to the rights, capabilities and responsibilities of its members. In different cultural, political and social systems various forms of family exist. It is entitled to receive comprehensive protection and support;

(i) Ensure that disadvantaged and vulnerable persons and groups are included in social development, and that society acknowledges and responds to the consequences of disability by securing the legal rights of the individual and by making the physical and social environment accessible;

(j) Promote universal respect for, and observance and protection of, all human rights and fundamental freedoms for all, including the right to development; promote the effective exercise of rights and the discharge of responsibilities at all levels of society; promote equality and equity between women and men; protect the rights of children and youth; and promote the strengthening of social integration and civil society;

(k) Reaffirm the right of self-determination of all peoples, in particular of peoples under colonial or other forms of alien domination or foreign occupation, and the importance of the effective realization of this right, as enunciated, inter alia, in the Vienna Declaration and Programme of Action adopted at the World Conference on Human Rights;

(l) Support progress and security for people and communities whereby every member of society is enabled to satisfy his or her basic human needs and to realize his or her personal dignity, safety and creativity;

(m) Recognize and support indigenous people in their pursuit of economic and social development, with full respect for their identity, traditions, forms of social organization and cultural values;

(n) Underline the importance of transparent and accountable governance and administration in all public and private national and international institutions;

(o) Recognize that empowering people, particularly women, to strengthen their own capacities is a main objective of development and its principal resource. Empowerment requires the full participation of people in the formulation, implementation and evaluation of decisions determining the functioning and well-being of our societies;

(p) Assert the universality of social development and outline a new and strengthened approach to social development, with a renewed impetus for international cooperation and partnership;

(q) Improve the possibility of older persons achieving a better life;

(r) Recognize that the new information technologies and new approaches to access to and use of technologies by people living in poverty can help in fulfilling social development goals; and therefore recognize the need to facilitate access to such technologies;

(s) Strengthen policies and programmes that improve, ensure and broaden the participation of women in all spheres of political, economic, social and cultural life, as equal partners, and improve their access to all resources needed for the full exercise of their fundamental rights;

(t) Create the political, legal, material and social conditions that allow for the voluntary repatriation of refugees in safety and dignity to their countries of origin, and the voluntary and safe return of internally displaced persons to their places of origin and their smooth reintegration into their societies;

(u) Emphasize the importance of the return of all prisoners of war, persons missing in action and hostages to their families, in accordance with international conventions, in order to reach full social development.

27. We acknowledge that it is the primary responsibility of States to attain these goals. We also acknowledge that these goals cannot be achieved by States alone. The international community, the United Nations, the multilateral financial institutions, all regional organizations and local authorities, and all actors of civil society need to positively contribute their own share of efforts and resources in order to reduce inequalities among people and narrow the gap between developed and developing countries in a global effort to reduce social tensions, and to create greater social and economic stability and security. Radical political, social and economic changes in the countries with economies in transition have been accompanied by a deterioration in their economic and social situation. We invite all people to express their personal commitment to enhancing the human condition through concrete actions in their own fields of activities and through assuming specific civic responsibilities.

C. Commitments

28. Our global drive for social development and the recommendations for action contained in the Programme of Action are made in a spirit of consensus and international

cooperation, in full conformity with the purposes and principles of the Charter of the United Nations, recognizing that the formulation and implementation of strategies, policies, programmes and actions for social development are the responsibility of each country and should take into account the economic, social and environmental diversity of conditions in each country, with full respect for the various religious and ethical values, cultural backgrounds and philosophical convictions of its people, and in conformity with all human rights and fundamental freedoms. In this context, international cooperation is essential for the full implementation of social development programmes and actions.

29. On the basis of our common pursuit of social development, which aims at social justice, solidarity, harmony and equality within and among countries, with full respect for national sovereignty and territorial integrity, as well as policy objectives, development priorities and religious and cultural diversity, and full respect for all human rights and fundamental freedoms, we launch a global drive for social progress and development embodied in the following commitments.

Commitment 1

We commit ourselves to creating an economic, political, social, cultural and legal environment that will enable people to achieve social development.

To this end, at the national level, we will:

(a) Provide a stable legal framework, in accordance with our constitutions, laws and procedures, and consistent with international law and obligations, which includes and promotes equality and equity between women and men, full respect for all human rights and fundamental freedoms and the rule of law, access to justice, the elimination of all forms of discrimination, transparent and accountable governance and administration and the encouragement of partnership with free and representative organizations of civil society;

(b) Create an enabling economic environment aimed at promoting more equitable access for all to income, resources and social services;

(c) Reinforce, as appropriate, the means and capacities for people to participate in the formulation and implementation of social and economic policies and programmes through decentralization, open management of public institutions and strengthening the abilities and opportunities of civil society and local communities to develop their own organizations, resources and activities;

(d) Reinforce peace by promoting tolerance, non-violence and respect for diversity, and by settling disputes by peaceful means;

(e) Promote dynamic, open, free markets, while recognizing the need to intervene in markets, to the extent necessary, to prevent or counteract market failure, promote stability and long-term investment, ensure fair competition and ethical conduct, and harmonize economic and social development, including the development and implementation of appropriate programmes that would entitle and enable people living in poverty and the disadvantaged, especially women, to participate fully and productively in the economy and society;

(f) Reaffirm, promote and strive to ensure the realization of the rights set out in relevant international instruments and declarations, such as the Universal Declaration of Human Rights, the Covenant on Economic, Social and Cultural Rights and the Declaration on the Right to Development, including those relating to education, food, shelter, employment, health and information, particularly in order to assist people living in poverty;

(g) Create the comprehensive conditions to allow for the voluntary repatriation of refugees in safety and dignity to their countries of origin, and the voluntary and safe return of internally displaced persons to their places of origin and their smooth reintegration into their societies.

At the international level, we will:

(h) Promote international peace and security and make and support all efforts to settle international disputes by peaceful means in accordance with the Charter of the United Nations;

(i) Strengthen international cooperation for achieving social development;

(j) Promote and implement policies to create a supportive external economic environment, through, inter alia, cooperation in the formulation and implementation of macroeconomic policies, trade liberalization, mobilization and/or provision of new and additional financial resources that are both adequate and predictable and mobilized in a way that maximizes the availability of such resources for sustainable development, using all available funding sources and mechanisms, enhanced financial stability, and more equitable access of developing countries to global markets, productive investments and technologies and appropriate knowledge, with due consideration to the needs of countries with economies in transition;

(k) Strive to ensure that international agreements relating to trade, investment, technology, debt and official development assistance are implemented in a manner that promotes social development;

(l) Support, particularly through technical and financial cooperation, the efforts of developing countries to achieve rapid, broadly based sustainable development. Particular consideration should be given to the special needs of small island and land-locked developing countries and the least developed countries;

(m) Support, through appropriate international cooperation, the efforts of countries with economies in transition to achieve rapid broadly based sustainable development;

(n) Reaffirm and promote all human rights, which are universal, indivisible, interdependent and interrelated, including the right to development as a universal and inalienable right and an integral part of fundamental human rights, and strive to ensure that they are respected, protected and observed.

Commitment 2

We commit ourselves to the goal of eradicating poverty in the world, through decisive national actions and international cooperation, as an ethical, social, political and economic imperative of humankind.

To this end, at the national level, in partnership with all actors of civil society and in the context of a multidimensional and integrated approach, we will:

(a) Formulate or strengthen, as a matter of urgency, and preferably by the year 1996, the International Year for the Eradication of Poverty, national policies and strategies geared to substantially reducing overall poverty in the shortest possible time, reducing inequalities and eradicating absolute poverty by a target date to be specified by each country in its national context;

(b) Focus our efforts and policies to address the root causes of poverty and to provide for the basic needs of all. These efforts should include the elimination of hunger and malnutrition; the provision of food security, education, employment and livelihood, primary health-care services including reproductive health care, safe drinking water and sanitation, and adequate shelter; and participation in social and cultural life. Special priority will be given to the needs and rights of women and children, who often bear the greatest burden of poverty, and to the needs of vulnerable and disadvantaged groups and persons;

(c) Ensure that people living in poverty have access to productive resources, including credit, land, education and training, technology, knowledge and information, as well as to public services, and participate in decision-making on a policy and regulatory environment that would enable them to benefit from expanding employment and economic opportunities;

(d) Develop and implement policies to ensure that all people have adequate economic and social protection during unemployment, ill health, maternity, child-rearing, widowhood, disability and old age;

(e) Ensure that national budgets and policies are oriented, as necessary, to meeting basic needs, reducing inequalities and targeting poverty, as a strategic objective;

(f) Seek to reduce inequalities, increase opportunities and access to resources and income, and remove any political, legal, economic and social factors and constraints that foster and sustain inequality.

At the international level, we will:

(g) Strive to ensure that the international community and international organizations, particularly the multilateral financial institutions, assist developing countries and all countries in need in their efforts to achieve our overall goal of eradicating poverty and ensuring basic social protection;

(h) Encourage all international donors and multilateral development banks to support policies and programmes for the attainment, in a sustained manner, of the specific efforts of the developing countries and all countries in need relating to people-centred sustainable development and to meeting basic needs for all; to assess their existing programmes in consultation with the concerned developing countries to ensure the achievement of the agreed programme objectives; and to seek to ensure that their own policies and programmes will advance the attainment of agreed development goals that focus on meeting basic needs for all and eradicating absolute poverty. Efforts should be made to ensure that participation by the people concerned is an integral part of such programmes;

(i) Focus attention on and support the special needs of countries and regions in which there are substantial concentrations of people living in poverty, in particular in South Asia, and which therefore face serious difficulties in achieving social and economic development.

Commitment 3

We commit ourselves to promoting the goal of full employment as a basic priority of our economic and social policies, and to enabling all men and women to attain secure and sustainable livelihoods through freely chosen productive employment and work.

To this end, at the national level, we will:

(a) Put the creation of employment, the reduction of unemployment and the promotion of appropriately and adequately remunerated employment at the centre of strategies and policies of Governments, with full respect for workers' rights and with the participation of employers, workers and their respective organizations, giving special attention to the problems of structural, long-term unemployment and underemployment of youth, women, people with disabilities, and all other disadvantaged groups and individuals;

(b) Develop policies to expand work opportunities and productivity in both rural and urban sectors by achieving economic growth, investing in human resource development, promoting technologies that generate productive employment, and encouraging self-employment, entrepreneurship, and small and medium-sized enterprises;

(c) Improve access to land, credit, information, infrastructure and other productive resources for small and micro-enterprises, including those in the informal sector, with particular emphasis on the disadvantaged sectors of society;

(d) Develop policies to ensure that workers and employers have the education, information and training needed to adapt to changing economic conditions, technologies and labour markets;

(e) Explore innovative options for employment creation and seek new approaches to generating income and purchasing power;

(f) Foster policies that enable people to combine their paid work with their family responsibilities;

(g) Pay particular attention to women's access to employment, the protection of their position in the labour market and the promotion of equal treatment of women and men, in particular with respect to pay;

(h) Take due account of the importance of the informal sector in our employment development strategies with a view to increasing its contribution to the eradication of poverty and to social integration in developing countries, and to strengthening its linkages with the formal economy;

(i) Pursue the goal of ensuring quality jobs, and safeguard the basic rights and interests of workers and to this end, freely promote respect for relevant International Labour Organization conventions, including those on the prohibition of forced and child labour, the freedom of association, the right to organize and bargain collectively, and the principle of non-discrimination.

At the international level, we will:

(j) Ensure that migrant workers benefit from the protections provided by relevant national and international instruments, take concrete and effective measures against the exploitation of migrant workers, and encourage all countries to consider the ratification and full implementation of the relevant international instruments on migrant workers;

(k) Foster international cooperation in macroeconomic policies, liberalization of trade and investment so as to promote sustained economic growth and the creation of employment, and exchange experiences on successful policies and programmes aimed at increasing employment and reducing unemployment.

Commitment 4

We commit ourselves to promoting social integration by fostering societies that are stable, safe and just and that are based on the promotion and protection of all human rights, as well as on non-discrimination, tolerance, respect for diversity, equality of opportunity, solidarity, security, and participation of all people, including disadvantaged and vulnerable groups and persons.

To this end, at the national level, we will:

(a) Promote respect for democracy, the rule of law, pluralism and diversity, tolerance and responsibility, non-violence and solidarity by encouraging educational systems, communication media and local communities and organizations to raise people's understanding and awareness of all aspects of social integration;

(b) Formulate or strengthen policies and strategies geared to the elimination of discrimination in all its forms and the achievement of social integration based on equality and respect for human dignity;

(c) Promote access for all to education, information, technology and know-how as essential means for enhancing communication and participation in civil, political, economic, social and cultural life, and ensure respect for civil, political, economic, social and cultural rights;

(d) Ensure the protection and full integration into the economy and society of disadvantaged and vulnerable groups and persons;

(e) Formulate or strengthen measures to ensure respect for and protection of the human rights of migrants, migrant workers and their families, to eliminate the increasing acts of racism and xenophobia in sectors of many societies, and to promote greater harmony and tolerance in all societies;

(f) Recognize and respect the right of indigenous people to maintain and develop their identity, culture and interests, support their aspirations for social justice and provide an environment that enables them to participate in the social, economic and political life of their country;

(g) Foster the social protection and full integration into the economy and society of veterans, including veterans and victims of the Second World War and other wars;

(h) Acknowledge and encourage the contribution of people of all age groups as equally and vitally important for the building of a harmonious society, and foster dialogue between generations in all parts of society;

(i) Recognize and respect cultural, ethnic and religious diversity, promote and protect the rights of persons belonging to national, ethnic, religious or linguistic minorities, and take measures to facilitate their full participation in all aspects of the political, economic, social, religious and cultural life of their societies and in the economic progress and social development of their countries;

(j) Strengthen the ability of local communities and groups with common concerns to develop their own organizations and resources and to propose policies relating to social development, including through the activities of non-governmental organizations;

(k) Strengthen institutions that enhance social integration, recognizing the central role of the family and providing it with an environment that assures its protection and support. In different cultural, political and social systems, various forms of the family exist;

(l) Address the problems of crime, violence and illicit drugs as factors of social disintegration.

At the international level, we will:

(m) Encourage the ratification of, the avoidance as far as possible of the resort to reservations to, and the implementation of international instruments and adherence to internationally recognized declarations relevant to the elimination of discrimination and the promotion and protection of all human rights;

(n) Further enhance international mechanisms for the provision of humanitarian and financial assistance to refugees and host countries and promote appropriate shared responsibility;

(o) Promote international cooperation and partnership on the basis of equality, mutual respect and mutual benefit.

Commitment 5

We commit ourselves to promoting full respect for human dignity and to achieving equality and equity between women and men, and to recognizing and enhancing the participation and leadership roles of women in political, civil, economic, social and cultural life and in development.

To this end, at the national level, we will:

(a) Promote changes in attitudes, structures, policies, laws and practices in order to eliminate all obstacles to human dignity, equality and equity in the family and in society, and promote full and equal participation of urban and rural women and women with disabilities in social, economic and political life, including in the formulation, implementation and follow-up of public policies and programmes;

(b) Establish structures, policies, objectives and measurable goals to ensure gender balance and equity in decision-making processes at all levels, broaden women's political, economic, social and cultural opportunities and independence, and support the empowerment of women, including through their various organizations, especially those of indigenous women, those at the grass-roots level, and those of poverty-stricken communities, including through affirmative action, where necessary, and also through measures to integrate a gender perspective in the design and implementation of economic and social policies;

(c) Promote full and equal access of women to literacy, education and training, and remove all obstacles to their access to credit and other productive resources and to their ability to buy, hold and sell property and land equally with men;

(d) Take appropriate measures to ensure, on the basis of equality of men and women, universal access to the widest range of health-care services, including those relating to reproductive health care, consistent with the Programme of Action of the International Conference on Population and Development;

(e) Remove the remaining restrictions on women's rights to own land, inherit property or borrow money, and ensure women's equal right to work;

(f) Establish policies, objectives and goals that enhance the equality of status, welfare and opportunity of the girl child, especially in regard to health, nutrition, literacy and education, recognizing that gender discrimination starts at the earliest stages of life;

(g) Promote equal partnership between women and men in family and community life and society, emphasize the shared responsibility of men and women in the care of children and support for older family members, and emphasize men's shared responsibility and promote their active involvement in responsible parenthood and responsible sexual and reproductive behaviour;

(h) Take effective measures, including through the enactment and enforcement of laws, and implement policies to combat and eliminate all forms of discrimination, exploitation, abuse and violence against women and girl children, in accordance with relevant international instruments and declarations;

(i) Promote and protect the full and equal enjoyment by women of all human rights and fundamental freedoms;

(j) Formulate or strengthen policies and practices to ensure that women are enabled to participate fully in paid work and in employment through such measures as positive action, education, training, appropriate protection under labour legislation, and facilitating the provision of quality child care and other support services.

At the international level, we will:

(k) Promote and protect women's human rights and encourage the ratification of, if possible by the year 2000, the avoidance, as far as possible, of the resort to reservations to, and the implementation of the provisions of the Convention on the Elimination of All Forms of Discrimination against Women and other relevant instruments, as well as the implementation of the Nairobi Forward-looking Strategies for the Advancement of Women, the Geneva Declaration for Rural Women, and the Programme of Action of the International Conference on Population and Development;

(l) Give specific attention to the preparations for the Fourth World Conference on Women, to be held at Beijing in September 1995, and to the implementation and follow-up of the conclusions of that Conference;

(m) Promote international cooperation to assist developing countries, at their request, in their efforts to achieve equality and equity and the empowerment of women;

(n) Devise suitable means to recognize and make visible the full extent of the work of women and all their contributions to the national economy, including contributions in the unremunerated and domestic sectors.

Commitment 6

We commit ourselves to promoting and attaining the goals of universal and equitable access to quality education, the highest attainable standard of physical and mental health, and the access of all to primary health care, making particular efforts to rectify inequalities relating to social conditions and without distinction as to race, national origin, gender, age or disability; respecting and promoting our common and particular cultures; striving to strengthen the role of culture in development; preserving the essential bases of people-centred sustainable development; and contributing to the full development of human resources and to social development. The purpose of these activities is to eradicate poverty, promote full and productive employment and foster social integration.

To this end, at the national level, we will:

(a) Formulate and strengthen time-bound national strategies for the eradication of illiteracy and universalization of basic education, which includes early childhood education, primary education and education for the illiterate, in all communities, in particular for the introduction, if possible, of national languages in the educational system and by support of the various means of non-formal education, striving to attain the highest possible standard of learning;

(b) Emphasize lifelong learning by seeking to improve the quality of education to ensure that people of all ages are provided with useful knowledge, reasoning ability, skills, and the ethical and social values required to develop their full capacities in health and dignity and to participate fully in the social, economic and political process of development. In this regard, women and girls should be considered a priority group;

(c) Ensure that children, particularly girls, enjoy their rights and promote the exercise of those rights by making education, adequate nutrition and health care accessible to them, consistent with the Convention on the Rights of the Child, and recognizing the rights, duties and responsibilities of parents and other persons legally responsible for children;

(d) Take appropriate and affirmative steps to enable all children and adolescents to attend and complete school and to close the gender gap in primary, secondary, vocational and higher education;

(e) Ensure full and equal access to education for girls and women, recognizing that investing in women's education is the key element in achieving social equality, higher productivity and social returns in terms of health, lower infant mortality and the reduced need for high fertility;

(f) Ensure equal educational opportunities at all levels for children, youth and adults with disabilities, in integrated settings, taking full account of individual differences and situations;

(g) Recognize and support the right of indigenous people to education in a manner that is responsive to their specific needs, aspirations and cultures, and ensure their full access to health care;

(h) Develop specific educational policies, with gender perspective, and design appropriate mechanisms at all levels of society in order to accelerate the conversion of general and specific information available world wide into knowledge, and the conversion of that knowledge into creativity, increased productive capacity and active participation in society;

(i) Strengthen the links between labour market and education policies, realizing that education and vocational training are vital elements in job creation and in combating unemployment and social exclusion in our societies, and emphasize the role of higher education and scientific research in all plans of social development;

(j) Develop broad-based education programmes that promote and strengthen respect for all human rights and fundamental freedoms, including the right to development, promote the values of tolerance, responsibility and respect for the diversity and rights of others, and provide training in peaceful conflict resolution, in recognition of the United Nations Decade for Human Rights Education (1995–2005);

(k) Focus on learning acquisition and outcome, broaden the means and scope of basic education, enhance the environment for learning and strengthen partnerships among Governments, non-governmental organizations, the private sector, local communities, religious groups and families to achieve the goal of education for all;

(l) Establish or strengthen both school-based and community-based health education programmes for children, adolescents and adults, with special attention to girls and women, on a whole range of health issues, as one of the prerequisites for social development, recognizing the rights, duties and responsibilities of parents and other persons legally responsible for children consistent with the Convention on the Rights of the Child;

(m) Expedite efforts to achieve the goals of national Health-for-All strategies, based on equality and social justice in line with the Alma-Ata Declaration on Primary Health Care, by developing or updating country action plans or programmes to ensure universal, non-discriminatory access to basic health services, including sanitation and drinking water, to protect health, and to promote nutrition education and preventive health programmes;

(n) Strive to ensure that persons with disabilities have access to rehabilitation and other independent living services and assistive technology to enable them to maximize their well-being, independence and full participation in society;

(o) Ensure an integrated and intersectoral approach so as to provide for the protection and promotion of health for all in economic and social development, taking cognizance of the health dimensions of policies in all sectors;

(p) Seek to attain the maternal and child health objectives, especially the objectives of reducing child and maternal mortality, of the World Summit for Children, the United Nations Conference on Environment and Development and the International Conference on Population and Development;

(q) Strengthen national efforts to address more effectively the growing HIV/AIDS pandemic by providing necessary education and prevention services, working to ensure that appropriate care and support services are available and accessible to those affected by HIV/AIDS, and taking all necessary steps to eliminate every form of discrimination against and isolation of those living with HIV/AIDS;

(r) Promote, in all educational and health policies and programmes, environmental awareness, including awareness of unsustainable patterns of consumption and production.

At the international level, we will:

(s) Strive to ensure that international organizations, in particular the international financial institutions, support these objectives, integrating them into their policy programmes and operations as appropriate. This should be complemented by renewed bilateral and regional cooperation;

(t) Recognize the importance of the cultural dimension of development to ensure respect for cultural diversity and that of our common human cultural heritage. Creativity should be recognized and promoted;

(u) Request the specialized agencies, notably the United Nations Educational, Scientific and Cultural Organization and the World Health Organization, as well as other international organizations dedicated to the promotion of education, culture and health, to give greater emphasis to the overriding goals of eradicating poverty, promoting full and productive employment and fostering social integration;

(v) Strengthen intergovernmental organizations that utilize various forms of education to promote culture; disseminate information through education and communication media; help spread the use of technologies; and promote technical and professional training and scientific research;

(w) Provide support for stronger, better coordinated global actions against major diseases that take a heavy toll of human lives, such as malaria, tuberculosis, cholera, typhoid fever and HIV/AIDS; in this context, continue to support the joint and co-sponsored United Nations programme on HIV/AIDS;

(x) Share knowledge, experience and expertise and enhance creativity, for example by promoting the transfer of technology, in the design and delivery of effective education, training and health programmes and policies, including substance-abuse awareness, prevention and rehabilitation programmes, which will result, inter alia, in endogenous capacity-building;

(y) Intensify and coordinate international support for education and health programmes based on respect for human dignity and focused on the protection of all women and children, especially against exploitation, trafficking and harmful practices, such as child prostitution, female genital mutilation and child marriages.

Commitment 7

We commit ourselves to accelerating the economic, social and human resource development of Africa and the least developed countries.

To this end, we will:

(a) Implement, at the national level, structural adjustment policies, which should include social development goals, as well as effective development strategies that establish a more favourable climate for trade and investment, give priority to human resource development and further promote the development of democratic institutions;

(b) Support the domestic efforts of Africa and the least developed countries to implement economic reforms, programmes to increase food security, and commodity diversification efforts through international cooperation, including South-South cooperation and technical and financial assistance, as well as trade and partnership;

(c) Find effective, development-oriented and durable solutions to external debt problems, through the immediate implementation of the terms of debt forgiveness agreed upon in the Paris Club in December 1994, which encompass debt reduction, including cancellation or other debt-relief measures; invite the international financial institutions to examine innovative approaches to assist low-income countries with a high proportion of multilateral debt, with a view to alleviating their debt burdens; and develop techniques of debt conversion applied to social development programmes and projects in conformity with Summit priorities. These actions should take into account the mid-term review of the United Nations New Agenda for the Development of Africa in the 1990s and the Programme of Action for the Least Developed Countries for the 1990s, and should be implemented as soon as possible;

(d) Ensure the implementation of the strategies and measures for the development of Africa decided by the international community, and support the reform efforts, development strategies and programmes decided by the African countries and the least developed countries;

(e) Increase official development assistance, both overall and for social programmes, and improve its impact, consistent with countries' economic circumstances and capacities to assist, and consistent with commitments in international agreements;

(f) Consider ratifying the United Nations Convention to Combat Desertification in Those Countries Experiencing Serious Drought and/or Desertification, Particularly in Africa, and support African countries in the implementation of urgent action to combat desertification and mitigate the effects of drought;

(g) Take all necessary measures to ensure that communicable diseases, particularly HIV/AIDS, malaria and tuberculosis, do not restrict or reverse the progress made in economic and social development.

Commitment 8

We commit ourselves to ensuring that when structural adjustment programmes are agreed to they include social development goals, in particular eradicating poverty, promoting full and productive employment, and enhancing social integration.

To this end, at the national level, we will:

(a) Promote basic social programmes and expenditures, in particular those affecting the poor and the vulnerable segments of society, and protect them from budget reductions, while increasing the quality and effectiveness of social expenditures;

(b) Review the impact of structural adjustment programmes on social development, including, where appropriate, by means of gender-sensitive social impact assessments and other relevant methods, in order to develop policies to reduce their negative effects and improve their positive impact; the cooperation of international financial institutions in the review could be requested by interested countries;

(c) Promote, in the countries with economies in transition, an integrated approach to the transformation process, addressing the social consequences of reforms and human resource development needs;

(d) Reinforce the social development components of all adjustment policies and programmes, including those resulting from the globalization of markets and rapid technological change, by designing policies to promote more equitable and enhanced access to income and resources;

(e) Ensure that women do not bear a disproportionate burden of the transitional costs of such processes.

At the international level, we will:

(f) Work to ensure that multilateral development banks and other donors complement adjustment lending with enhanced targeted social development investment lending;

(g) Strive to ensure that structural adjustment programmes respond to the economic and social conditions, concerns and needs of each country;

(h) Enlist the support and cooperation of regional and international organizations and the United Nations system, in particular the Bretton Woods institutions, in the design, social management and assessment of structural adjustment policies, and in implementing social development goals and integrating them into their policies, programmes and operations.

Commitment 9

We commit ourselves to increasing significantly and/or utilizing more efficiently the resources allocated to social development in order to achieve the goals of the Summit through national action and regional and international cooperation.

To this end, at the national level, we will:

(a) Develop economic policies to promote and mobilize domestic savings and attract external resources for productive investment, and seek innovative sources of funding, both public and private, for social programmes, while ensuring their effective utilization;

(b) Implement macroeconomic and micro-economic policies to ensure sustained economic growth and sustainable development to support social development;

(c) Promote increased access to credit for small and micro-enterprises, including those in the informal sector, with particular emphasis on the disadvantaged sectors of society;

(d) Ensure that reliable statistics and statistical indicators are used to develop and assess social policies and programmes so that economic and social resources are used efficiently and effectively;

(e) Ensure that, in accordance with national priorities and policies, taxation systems are fair, progressive and economically efficient, cognizant of sustainable development concerns, and ensure effective collection of tax liabilities;

(f) In the budgetary process, ensure transparency and accountability in the use of public resources, and give priority to providing and improving basic social services;

(g) Undertake to explore new ways of generating new public and private financial resources, inter alia, through the appropriate reduction of excessive military expenditures, including global military expenditures and the arms trade, and investments for arms production and acquisition, taking into consideration national security requirements, so as to allow possible allocation of additional funds for social and economic development;

(h) Utilize and develop fully the potential and contribution of cooperatives for the attainment of social development goals, in particular the eradication of poverty, the generation of full and productive employment, and the enhancement of social integration.

At the international level, we will:

(i) Seek to mobilize new and additional financial resources that are both adequate and predictable and are mobilized in a way that maximizes the availability of such resources and uses all available funding sources and mechanisms, inter alia, multilateral, bilateral and private sources, including on concessional and grant terms;

(j) Facilitate the flow to developing countries of international finance, technology and human skill in order to realize the objective of providing new and additional resources that are both adequate and predictable;

(k) Facilitate the flow of international finance, technology and human skill towards the countries with economies in transition;

(l) Strive for the fulfilment of the agreed target of 0.7 per cent of gross national product for overall official development assistance as soon as possible, and increase the share of funding for social development programmes, commensurate with the scope and scale of activities required to achieve the objectives and goals of the present Declaration and the Programme of Action of the Summit;

(m) Increase the flow of international resources to meet the needs of countries facing problems relating to refugees and displaced persons;

(n) Support South-South cooperation, which can take advantage of the experience of developing countries that have overcome similar difficulties;

(o) Ensure the urgent implementation of existing debt-relief agreements and negotiate further initiatives, in addition to existing ones, to alleviate the debts of the poorest and heavily indebted low-income countries at an early date, especially through more favourable terms of debt forgiveness, including application of the terms of debt forgiveness agreed upon in the Paris Club in December 1994, which encompass debt reduction, including cancellation or other debt-relief measures; where appropriate, these countries should be given a reduction of their bilateral official debt sufficient to enable them to exit from the rescheduling process and resume growth and development; invite the international financial institutions to examine innovative approaches to assist low-income countries with a high proportion of multilateral debt, with a view to alleviating their debt burdens; develop techniques of debt conversion applied to social development programmes and projects in conformity with Summit priorities;

(p) Fully implement the Final Act of the Uruguay Round of multilateral trade negotiations as scheduled, including the complementary provisions specified in the Marrakesh Agreement establishing the World Trade Organization, in recognition of the fact that broadly based growth in incomes, employment and trade are mutually reinforcing, taking into account the need to assist African countries and the least developed countries in evaluating the impact of the implementation of the Final Act so that they can benefit fully;

(q) Monitor the impact of trade liberalization on the progress made in developing countries to meet basic human needs, giving particular attention to new initiatives to expand their access to international markets;

(r) Give attention to the needs of countries with economies in transition with respect to international cooperation and financial and technical assistance, stressing the need for the full integration of economies in transition into the world economy, in particular to improve market access for exports in accordance with multilateral trade rules, taking into account the needs of developing countries;

(s) Support United Nations development efforts by a substantial increase in resources for operational activities on a predictable, continuous and assured basis, commensurate with the increasing needs of developing countries, as stated in General Assembly resolution 47/199, and strengthen the capacity of the United Nations and the specialized agencies to fulfil their responsibilities in the implementation of the outcome of the World Summit for Social Development.

Commitment 10

We commit ourselves to an improved and strengthened framework for international, regional and subregional cooperation for social development, in a spirit of partnership, through the United Nations and other multilateral institutions.

To this end, at the national level, we will:

(a) Adopt the appropriate measures and mechanisms for implementing and monitoring the outcome of the World Summit for Social Development, with the assistance, upon request, of the specialized agencies, programmes and regional commissions of the United Nations system, with broad participation of all sectors of civil society.

At the regional level, we will:

(b) Pursue such mechanisms and measures as are necessary and appropriate in particular regions or subregions. The regional commissions, in cooperation with regional intergovernmental organizations and banks, could convene, on a biennial basis, a meeting at a high political level to evaluate progress made towards fulfilling the outcome of the Summit, exchange views on their respective experiences and adopt appropriate measures. The regional commissions should report, through the appropriate mechanisms, to the Economic and Social Council on the outcome of such meetings.

At the international level, we will:

(c) Instruct our representatives to the organizations and bodies of the United Nations system, international development agencies and multilateral development banks to enlist the support and cooperation of these organizations and bodies to take appropriate and coordinated measures for continuous and sustained progress in attaining the goals and commitments agreed to by the Summit. The United Nations and the Bretton Woods institutions should establish regular and substantive dialogue, including at the field level, for more effective and efficient coordination of assistance for social development;

(d) Refrain from any unilateral measure not in accordance with international law and the Charter of the United Nations that creates obstacles to trade relations among States;

(e) Strengthen the structure, resources and processes of the Economic and Social Council and its subsidiary bodies, and other organizations within the United Nations system that are concerned with economic and social development;

(f) Request the Economic and Social Council to review and assess, on the basis of reports of national Governments, the regional commissions, relevant functional commissions and specialized agencies, progress made by the international community towards implementing the outcome of the World Summit for Social Development, and to report to the General Assembly, accordingly, for its appropriate consideration and action;

(g) Request the General Assembly to hold a special session in the year 2000 for an overall review and appraisal of the implementation of the outcome of the Summit and to consider further actions and initiatives.

Chapter 4
Istanbul Declaration on Human Settlements

1. We, the Heads of State or Government and the official delegations of countries assembled at the United Nations Conference on Human Settlements (Habitat II) in Istanbul, Turkey from 3 to 14 June 1996, take this opportunity to endorse the universal goals of ensuring adequate shelter for all and making human settlements safer, healthier and more liveable, equitable, sustainable and productive. Our deliberations on the two major themes of the Conference—adequate shelter for all and sustainable human settlements development in an urbanizing world—have been inspired by the Charter of the United Nations and are aimed at reaffirming existing and forging new partnerships for action at the international, national and local levels to improve our living environment. We commit ourselves to the objectives, principles and recommendations contained in the Habitat Agenda and pledge our mutual support for its implementation.

2. We have considered, with a sense of urgency, the continuing deterioration of conditions of shelter and human settlements. At the same time, we recognize cities and towns as centres of civilization, generating economic development and social, cultural, spiritual and scientific advancement. We must take advantage of the opportunities presented by our settlements and preserve their diversity to promote solidarity among all our peoples.

3. We reaffirm our commitment to better standards of living in larger freedom for all humankind. We recall the first United Nations Conference on Human Settlements, held at Vancouver, Canada, the celebration of the International Year of Shelter for the Homeless and the Global Strategy for Shelter to the Year 2000, all of which have contributed to increased global awareness of the problems of human settlements and called for action to achieve adequate shelter for all. Recent United Nations world conferences, including, in particular, the United Nations Conference on Environment and Development, have given us a comprehensive agenda for the equitable attainment of peace, justice and democracy built on economic development, social development and environmental protection as interdependent and mutually reinforcing components of sustainable development. We have sought to integrate the outcomes of these conferences into the Habitat Agenda.

Adopted by the UN Conference on Human Settlements (Habitat II), held in Istanbul, 3–14 June 1996.

4. To improve the quality of life within human settlements, we must combat the deterioration of conditions that in most cases, particularly in developing countries, have reached crisis proportions. To this end, we must address comprehensively, inter alia, unsustainable consumption and production patterns, particularly in industrialized countries; unsustainable population changes, including changes in structure and distribution, giving priority consideration to the tendency towards excessive population concentration; homelessness; increasing poverty; unemployment; social exclusion; family instability; inadequate resources; lack of basic infrastructure and services; lack of adequate planning; growing insecurity and violence; environmental degradation; and increased vulnerability to disasters.

5. The challenges of human settlements are global, but countries and regions also face specific problems which need specific solutions. We recognize the need to intensify our efforts and cooperation to improve living conditions in the cities, towns and villages throughout the world, particularly in developing countries, where the situation is especially grave, and in countries with economies in transition. In this connection, we acknowledge that globalization of the world economy presents opportunities and challenges for the development process, as well as risks and uncertainties, and that achievement of the goals of the Habitat Agenda would be facilitated by, inter alia, positive actions on the issues of financing of development, external debt, international trade and transfer of technology. Our cities must be places where human beings lead fulfilling lives in dignity, good health, safety, happiness and hope.

6. Rural and urban development are interdependent. In addition to improving the urban habitat, we must also work to extend adequate infrastructure, public services and employment opportunities to rural areas in order to enhance their attractiveness, develop an integrated network of settlements and minimize rural-to-urban migration. Small- and medium-sized towns need special focus.

7. As human beings are at the centre of our concern for sustainable development, they are the basis for our actions as in implementing the Habitat Agenda. We recognize the particular needs of women, children and youth for safe, healthy and secure living conditions. We shall intensify our efforts to eradicate poverty and discrimination, to promote and protect all human rights and fundamental freedoms for all, and to provide for basic needs, such as education, nutrition and life-span health care services, and, especially, adequate shelter for all. To this end, we commit ourselves to improving the living conditions in human settlements in ways that are consonant with local needs and realities, and we acknowledge the need to address the global, economic, social and environmental trends to ensure the creation of better living environments for all people. We shall also ensure the full and equal participation of all women and men, and the effective participation of youth, in political, economic and social life. We shall promote full accessibility for people with disabilities, as well as gender equality in policies, programmes and projects for shelter and sustainable human settlements development. We make these commitments with particular reference to the more than one billion people living in absolute poverty and to the members of vulnerable and disadvantaged groups identified in the Habitat Agenda.

8. We reaffirm our commitment to the full and progressive realization of the right to adequate housing as provided for in international instruments. To that end, we shall seek the active participation of our public, private and non-governmental partners at all levels to ensure legal security of tenure, protection from discrimination and equal access to affordable, adequate housing for all persons and their families.

9. We shall work to expand the supply of affordable housing by enabling markets to perform efficiently and in a socially and environmentally responsible manner, enhancing access to land and credit and assisting those who are unable to participate in housing markets.

10. In order to sustain our global environment and improve the quality of living in our human settlements, we commit ourselves to sustainable patterns of production, consumption, transportation and settlements development; pollution prevention; respect for the carrying capacity of ecosystems; and the preservation of opportunities for future generations. In this connection, we shall cooperate in a spirit of global partnership to conserve, protect and restore the health and integrity of the Earth's ecosystem. In view of different contributions to global environmental degradation, we reaffirm the principle that countries have common but differentiated responsibilities. We also recognize that we must take these actions in a manner consistent with the precautionary principle approach, which shall be widely applied according to the capabilities of countries. We shall also promote healthy living environments, especially through the provision of adequate quantities of safe water and effective management of waste.

11. We shall promote the conservation, rehabilitation and maintenance of buildings, monuments, open spaces, landscapes and settlement patterns of historical, cultural, architectural, natural, religious and spiritual value.

12. We adopt the enabling strategy and the principles of partnership and participation as the most democratic and effective approach for the realization of our commitments. Recognizing local authorities as our closest partners, and as essential, in the implementation of the Habitat Agenda, we must, within the legal framework of each country, promote decentralization through democratic local authorities and work to strengthen their financial and institutional capacities in accordance with the conditions of countries, while ensuring their transparency, accountability and responsiveness to the needs of people, which are key requirements for Governments at all levels. We shall also increase our cooperation with parliamentarians, the private sector, labour unions and non-governmental and other civil society organizations with due respect for their autonomy. We shall also enhance the role of women and encourage socially and environmentally responsible corporate investment by the private sector. Local action should be guided and stimulated through local programmes based on Agenda 21, the Habitat Agenda, or any other equivalent programme, as well as drawing upon the experience of worldwide cooperation initiated in Istanbul by the World Assembly of Cities and Local Authorities, without prejudice to national policies, objectives, priorities and programmes. The enabling strategy includes a responsibility for Governments to

implement special measures for members of disadvantaged and vulnerable groups when appropriate.

13. As the implementation of the Habitat Agenda will require adequate funding, we must mobilize financial resources at the national and international levels, including new and additional resources from all sources—multilateral and bilateral, public and private. In this connection, we must facilitate capacity-building and promote the transfer of appropriate technology and know-how. Furthermore, we reiterate the commitments set out in recent United Nations conferences, especially those in Agenda 21 on funding and technology transfer.

14. We believe that the full and effective implementation of the Habitat Agenda will require the strengthening of the role and functions of the United Nations Centre for Human Settlements (Habitat), taking into account the need for the Centre to focus on well-defined and thoroughly developed objectives and strategic issues. To this end, we pledge our support for the successful implementation of the Habitat Agenda and its global plan of action. Regarding the implementation of the Habitat Agenda, we fully recognize the contribution of the regional and national action plans prepared for this Conference.

15. This Conference in Istanbul marks a new era of cooperation, an era of a culture of solidarity. As we move into the twenty-first century, we offer a positive vision of sustainable human settlements, a sense of hope for our common future and an exhortation to join a truly worthwhile and engaging challenge, that of building together a world where everyone can live in a safe home with the promise of a decent life of dignity, good health, safety, happiness and hope.

E. INTERPRETIVE TEXTS

Chapter 1

Limburg Principles on the Implementation of the International Covenant on Economic, Social and Cultural Rights

Introduction

(i) A group of distinguished experts in international law, convened by the International Commission of Jurists, the Faculty of Law of the University of Limburg (Maastricht, the Netherlands) and the Urban Morgan Institute for Human Rights, University of Cincinnati (Ohio, United States of America), met in Maastricht on 2–6 June 1986 to consider the nature and scope of the obligations of States Parties to the International Covenant on Economic, Social and Cultural Rights, the consideration of States Parties Reports by the newly constituted ECOSOC Committee on Economic, Social and Cultural Rights, and international co-operation under Part IV of the Covenant.

(ii) The 29 participants came from Australia, the Federal Republic of Germany, Hungary, Ireland, Mexico, Netherlands, Norway, Senegal, Spain, United Kingdom, United States of America, Yugoslavia, the United Nations Centre for Human Rights, the International Labour Organisation (ILO), the United Nations Educational, Scientific and Cultural Organization (UNESCO), the World Health Organization (WHO), the Commonwealth Secretariat, and the sponsoring organizations. Four of the participants were members of the ECOSOC Committee on Economic, Social and Cultural Rights.

(iii) The participants agreed unanimously upon the following principles which they believe reflect the present state of international law, with the exception of certain recommendations indicated by the use of the verb "should" instead of "shall."

Part I: The Nature and Scope of States Parties' Obligations

A. General Observations

1. Economic, social and cultural rights are an integral part of international human rights law. They are the subject of specific treaty obligations in various international

Original notes omitted.

instruments, notably the International Covenant on Economic, Social and Cultural Rights.

2. The International Covenant on Economic, Social and Cultural Rights, together with the International Covenant on Civil and Political Rights and the Optional Protocol, entered into force in 1976. The Covenants serve to elaborate the Universal Declaration of Human Rights: these instruments constitute the International Bill of Human Rights.

3. As human rights and fundamental freedoms are indivisible and interdependent, equal attention and urgent consideration should be given to the implementation, promotion and protection of both civil and political, and economic, social and cultural rights.

4. The International Covenant on Economic, Social and Cultural Rights (hereafter the Covenant) should, in accordance with the Vienna Convention on the Law of Treaties (Vienna, 1969), be interpreted in good faith, taking into account the object and purpose, the ordinary meaning, the preparatory work and the relevant practice.

5. The experience of the relevant specialized agencies as well as of United Nations bodies and intergovernmental organizations, including the United Nations working groups and special rapporteurs in the field of human rights, should be taken into account in the implementation of the Covenant and in monitoring States Parties' achievements.

6. The achievement of economic, social and cultural rights may be realized in a variety of political settings. There is no single road to their full realization. Successes and failures have been registered in both market and non-market economies, in both centralized and decentralized political structures.

7. States Parties must at all times act in good faith to fulfill the obligations they have accepted under the Covenant.

8. Although the full realization of the rights recognized in the Covenant is to be attained progressively, the application of some rights can be made justiciable immediately while other rights can become justiciable over time.

9. Non-governmental organizations can play an important role in promoting the implementation of the Covenant. This role should accordingly be facilitated at the national as well as the international level.

10. States Parties are accountable both to the international community and to their own people for their compliance with the obligations under the Covenant.

11. A concerted national effort to invoke the full participation of all sectors of society is, therefore, indispensable to achieving progress in realizing economic, social and cultural rights. Popular participation is required at all stages, including the formulation, application and review of national policies.

12. The supervision of compliance with the Covenant should be approached in a spirit of co-operation and dialogue. To this end, in considering the reports of States Parties, the Committee on Economic, Social and Cultural Rights, hereinafter called "the

Committee," should analyse the causes and factors impeding the realization of the rights covered under the Covenant and, where possible, indicate solutions. This approach should not preclude a finding, where the information available warrants such a conclusion, that a State Party has failed to comply with its obligations under the Covenant.

13. All organs monitoring the Covenant should pay special attention to the principles of non-discrimination and equality before the law when assessing States Parties' compliance with the Covenant.

14. Given the significance for development of the progressive realization of the rights set forth in the Covenant, particular attention should be given to measures to improve the standard of living of the poor and other disadvantaged groups, taking into account that special measures may be required to protect cultural rights of indigenous peoples and minorities.

15. Trends in international economic relations should be taken into account in assessing the efforts of the international community to achieve the Covenant's objectives.

B. Interpretative Principles Specifically Relating to Part II of the Covenant

Article 2 (1). "to take steps . . . by all appropriate means, including particularly the adoption of legislation"

16. All States Parties have an obligation to begin immediately to take steps towards full realization of the rights contained in the Covenant.

17. At the national level States Parties shall use all appropriate means, including legislative, administrative, judicial, economic, social and educational measures, consistent with the nature of the rights in order to fulfill their obligations under the Covenant.

18. Legislative measures alone are not sufficient to fulfill the obligations of the Covenant. It should be noted, however, that Article 2 (1) would often require legislative action to be taken in cases where existing legislation is in violation of the obligations assumed under the Covenant.

19. States Parties shall provide for effective remedies including, where appropriate, judicial remedies.

20. The appropriateness of the means to be applied in a particular State shall be determined by that State Party, and shall be subject to review by the United Nations Economic and Social Council, with the assistance of the Committee. Such review shall be without prejudice to the competence of the other organs established pursuant to the Charter of the United Nations.

"to achieve progressively the full realization of the rights"

21. The obligation "to achieve progressively the full realization of the rights" requires

States Parties to move as expeditiously as possible towards the realization of the rights. Under no circumstances shall this be interpreted as implying for States the right to defer indefinitely efforts to ensure full realization. On the contrary all States Parties have the obligation to begin immediately to take steps to fulfill their obligations under the Covenant.

22. Some obligations under the Covenant require immediate implementation in full by all States Parties, such as the prohibition of discrimination in Article 2 (2) of the Covenant.

23. The obligation of progressive achievement exists independently of the increase in resources; it requires effective use of resources available.

24. Progressive implementation can be effected not only by increasing resources, but also by the development of societal resources necessary for the realization by everyone of the rights recognized in the Covenant.

"to the maximum of its available resources"

25. States Parties are obligated regardless of the level of economic development, to ensure respect for minimum subsistence rights for all.

26. "Its available resources" refers to both the resources within a State and those available from the international community through international co-operation and assistance.

27. In determining whether adequate measures have been taken for the realization of the rights recognized in the Covenant attention shall be paid to equitable and effective use of and access to the available resources.

28. In the use of the available resources due priority shall be given to the realization of rights recognized in the Covenant, mindful of the need to assure to everyone the satisfaction of subsistence requirements as well as the provision of essential services.

"individually and through international assistance and co-operation, especially economic and technical"

29. International co-operation and assistance pursuant to the Charter of the United Nations (arts. 55 and 56) and the Covenant shall have in view as a matter of priority the realization of all human rights and fundamental freedoms, economic social and cultural as well as civil and political.

30. International co-operation and assistance must be directed towards the establishment of a social and international order in which the rights and freedoms set forth in the Covenant can be fully realized (cf. art. 28 Universal Declaration of Human Rights).

31. Irrespective of differences in their political, economic and social systems, States shall co-operate with one another to promote international social, economic and cultural progress, in particular the economic growth of developing countries, free from discrimination based on such differences.

32. States Parties shall take steps by international means to assist and co-operate in the realization of the rights recognized by the Covenant.

33. International co-operation and assistance shall be based on the sovereign equality of States and be aimed at the realization of the rights contained in the Covenant.

34. In undertaking international co-operation and assistance pursuant to Article 2 (1) the role of international organizations and the contribution of non-governmental organizations shall be kept in mind.

Article 2 (2). Non-discrimination

35. Article 2 (2) calls for immediate application and involves and explicit guarantee on behalf of the States Parties. It should, therefore, be made subject to judicial review and other recourse procedures.

36. The grounds of discrimination mentioned in Article 2 (2) are not exhaustive.

37. Upon becoming a party to the Covenant States shall eliminate de jure discrimination by abolishing without delay any discriminatory laws, regulations and practices (including acts of omission as well as commission) affecting the enjoyment of economic, social and cultural rights.

38. De facto discrimination occurring as a result of the unequal enjoyment of economic, social and cultural rights, on account of a lack of resources or otherwise, should be brought to an end as speedily as possible.

39. Special measures taken for the sole purpose of securing adequate advancement of certain groups or individuals requiring such protection as may be necessary in order to ensure to such groups or individuals equal enjoyment of economic, social and cultural rights shall not be deemed discrimination, provided, however, that such measures do not, as a consequence, lead to the maintenance of separate rights for different groups and that such measures shall not be continued after their intended objectives have been achieved.

40. Article 2 (2) demands from States Parties that they prohibit private persons and bodies from practising discrimination in any field of public life.

41. In the application of Article 2 (2) due regard should be paid to all relevant international instruments including the Declaration and Convention on the Elimination of all Forms of Racial Discrimination as well as to the activities of the supervisory committee (CERD) under the said Convention.

Article 2 (3). Non-nationals in developing countries

42. As a general rule the Covenant applies equally to nationals and non-nationals.

43. The purpose of Article 2 (3) was to end the domination of certain economic groups

of non-nationals during colonial times. In the light of this the exception in Article 2 (3) should be interpreted narrowly.

44. This narrow interpretation of Article 2 (3) refers in particular to the notion of economic rights and to the notion of developing countries. The latter notion refers to those countries which have gained independence and which fall within the appropriate United Nations classifications of developing countries.

Article 3. Equal rights for men and women

45. In the application of Article 3 due regard should be paid to the Declaration and Convention on the Elimination of All Forms of Discrimination against Women and other relevant instruments and the activities of the supervisory committee (CEDAW) under the said Convention.

Article 4. Limitations

46. Article 4 was primarily intended to be protective of the rights of individuals rather than permissive of the imposition of limitations by the State.

47. The article was not meant to introduce limitations on rights affecting the subsistence or survival of the individual or integrity of the person.

"determined by law"

48. No limitation on the exercise of economic, social and cultural rights shall be made unless provided for by national law of general application which is consistent with the Covenant and is in force at the time the limitation is applied.

49. Laws imposing limitations on the exercise of economic, social and cultural rights shall not be arbitrary or unreasonable or discriminatory.

50. Legal rules limiting the exercise of economic, social and cultural rights shall be clear and accessible to everyone.

51. Adequate safeguards and effective remedies shall be provided by law against illegal or abusive imposition on application of limitations on economic, social and cultural rights.

"promoting the general welfare"

52. This term shall be construed to mean furthering the well-being of the people as a whole.

"in a democratic society"

53. The expression "in a democratic society" shall be interpreted as imposing a further restriction on the application of limitations.

54. The burden is upon a State imposing limitations to demonstrate that the limitations do not impair the democratic functioning of the society.

55. While there is no single model of a democratic society, a society which recognizes and respects the human rights set forth in the United Nations Charter and the Universal Declaration of Human Rights may be viewed as meeting this definition.

"compatible with the nature of these rights"

56. The restriction "compatible with the nature of these rights" requires that a limitation shall not be interpreted or applied so as to jeopardize the essence of the right concerned.

Article 5

57. Article 5 (1) underlines the fact that there is no general, implied or residual right for a State to impose limitations beyond those which are specifically provided for in the law. None of the provisions in the law may be interpreted in such a way as to destroy "any of the rights or freedoms recognized." In addition Article 5 is intended to ensure that nothing in the Covenant shall be interpreted as impairing the inherent right of all peoples to enjoy and utilize fully and freely their natural wealth and resources.

58. The purpose of Article 5 (2) is to ensure that no provision in the Covenant shall be interpreted to prejudice the provisions of domestic law or any bilateral or multilateral treaties, conventions or agreements which are already in force, or may come into force, under which more favourable treatment would be accorded to the persons protected. Neither shall Article 5 (2) be interpreted to restrict the exercise of any human right protected to a greater extent by national or international obligations accepted by the State Party.

C. Interpretative Principles Specifically Relating to Part III of the Covenant

Article 8. "prescribed by law"

59. See the interpretative principles under the synonymous term "determined by law" in Article 4.

"necessary in a democratic society"

60. In addition to the interpretative principles listed under Article 4 concerning the phrase "in a democratic society," Article 8 imposes a greater restraint upon a State Party which is exercising limitations on trade union rights. It requires that such a limitation is indeed necessary. The term "necessary" implies that the limitation:

(a) responds to a pressing public or social need;

(b) pursues a legitimate aim; and

(c) is proportional to that aim.

61. Any assessment as to the necessity of a limitation shall be based upon objective considerations.

"national security"

62. National security may be invoked to justify measures limiting certain rights only when they are taken to protect the existence of the nation or its territorial integrity or political independence against force or threat of force.

63. National security cannot be invoked as a reason for imposing limitations to prevent merely local or relatively isolated threats to law and order.

64. National security cannot be used as a pretext for imposing vague or arbitrary limitations and may be invoked only when there exist adequate safeguards and effective remedies against abuse.

65. The systematic violation of economic, social and cultural rights undermines true national security and may jeopardize international peace and security. A State responsible for such violation shall not invoke national security as a justification for measures aimed at suppressing opposition to such violation or at perpetrating repressive practices against its population.

"public order (ordre public)"

66. The expression "public order (ordre public)" as used in the Covenant may be defined as the sum of rules which ensures the functioning of society or the set of fundamental principles on which a society is founded. Respect for economic, social and cultural rights is part of public order (ordre public).

67. Public order (ordre public) shall be interpreted in the context of the purpose of the particular economic, social and cultural rights which are limited on this ground.

68. State organs or agents responsible for the maintenance of public order (ordre public) shall be subject to controls in the exercise of their power through the parliament, courts, or other competent independent bodies.

"rights and freedoms of others"

69. The scope of the rights and freedoms of others that may act as a limitation upon rights in the Covenant extends beyond the rights and freedoms recognized in the Covenant.

D. Violations of Economic, Social and Cultural Rights

70. A failure by a State Party to comply with an obligation contained in the Covenant is, under international law, a violation of the Covenant.

71. In determining what amounts to a failure to comply, it must be borne in mind that the Covenant affords to a State Party a margin of discretion in selecting the means for carrying out its objects, and that factors beyond its reasonable control may adversely affect its capacity to implement particular rights.

72. A State Party will be in violation of the Covenant, inter alia, if:

• it fails to take a step which it is required to take by the Covenant;

• it fails to remove promptly obstacles which it is under a duty to remove to permit the immediate fulfillment of a right;

• it fails to implement without delay a right which it is required by the Covenant to provide immediately;

• it willfully fails to meet a generally accepted international minimum standard of achievement, which is within its powers to meet;

• it applies a limitation to a right recognized in the Covenant other than in accordance with the Covenant;

• it deliberately retards or halts the progressive realization of a right, unless it is acting within a limitation permitted by the Covenant or it does so due to a lack of available resources or force majeure;

• it fails to submit reports as required under the Covenant.

73. In accordance with international law each State Party to the Covenant has the right to express the view that another State Party is not complying with its obligations under the Covenant and to bring this to the attention of that State Party. Any dispute that may thus arise shall be settled in accordance with the relevant rules of international law relating to the peaceful settlement of disputes.

Part II: Consideration of States Parties' Reports and International Co-Operation Under Part IV of the Covenant

A. Preparation and Submission of Reports by States Parties

74. The effectiveness of the supervisory machinery provided in Part IV of the Covenant depends largely upon the duality and timeliness of reports by States Parties. Governments are therefore urged to make their reports as meaningful as possible. For this purpose they should develop adequate internal procedures for consultations with the competent government departments and agencies, compilation of relevant data, training of staff, acquisition of background documentation, and consultation with relevant non-governmental and international institutions.

75. The preparation of reports under Article 16 of the Covenant could be facilitated by the implementation of elements of the programme of advisory services and technical assistance as proposed by the chairmen of the main human rights supervisory organs in their 1984 report to the General Assembly (United Nations Doc. A39/484).

76. States Parties should view their reporting obligations as an opportunity for broad public discussion on goals and policies designed to realize economic, social and cultural rights. For this purpose wide publicity should be given to the reports, if possible

in draft. The preparation of reports should also be an occasion to review the extent to which relevant national policies adequately reflect the scope and content of each right, and to specify the means by which it is to be realized.

77. States Parties are encouraged to examine the possibility of involving non-governmental organizations in the preparation of their reports.

78. In reporting on legal steps taken to give effect to the Covenant, States Parties should not merely describe any relevant legislative provisions. They should specify, as appropriate, the judicial remedies, administrative procedures and other measures they have adopted for enforcing those rights and the practice under those remedies and procedures.

79. Quantitative information should be included in the reports of States Parties in order to indicate the extent to which the rights are protected in fact. Statistical information and information on budgetary allocations and expenditures should be presented in such a way as to facilitate the assessment of the compliance with Covenant obligations. States Parties should, where possible, adopt clearly defined targets and indicators in implementing the Covenant. Such targets and indicators should, as appropriate, be based on criteria established through international co-operation in order to increase the relevance and comparability of data submitted by States Parties in their reports.

80. Where necessary, governments should conduct or commission studies to enable them to fill gaps in information regarding progress made and difficulties encountered in achieving the observance of the Covenant rights.

81. Reports by States Parties should indicate the areas where more progress could be achieved through international co-operation and suggest economic and technical co-operation programmes that might be helpful toward that end.

82. In order to ensure a meaningful dialogue between the States Parties and the organs assessing their compliance with the provisions of the Covenant, States Parties should designate representatives who are fully familiar with the issues raised in the report.

B. Role of the Committee on Economic, Social and Cultural Rights

83. The Committee has been entrusted with assisting the Economic and Social Council in the substantive tasks assigned to it by the Covenant. In particular, its role is to consider States Parties reports and to make suggestions and recommendations of a general nature, including suggestions and recommendations as to fuller compliance with the Covenant by States Parties. The decision of the Economic and Social Council to replace its sessional Working Group by a Committee of independent experts should lead to a more effective supervision of the implementation by States Parties.

84. In order to enable it to discharge fully its responsibilities the Economic and Social Council should ensure that sufficient sessions are provided to the Committee. It is imperative that the necessary staff and facilities for the effective performance of the Committee's functions be provided, in accordance with ECOSOC resolution 1985/17.

85. In order to address the complexity of the substantive issues covered by the Covenant, the Committee might consider delegating certain tasks to its members. For example, drafting grounds could be established to prepare preliminary formulations or recommendations of a general nature or summaries of the information received. Rapporteurs could be appointed to assist the work of the Committee in particular to prepare reports on specific topics and for that purpose consult States Parties, specialized agencies and relevant experts and to draw up proposals regarding economic and technical assistance projects that could help overcome difficulties States Parties have encountered in fulfillling their Covenant obligations.

86. The Committee should, pursuant to Articles 22 and 23 of the Covenant, explore with other organs of the United Nations, specialized agencies and other concerned organizations, the possibilities of taking additional international measures likely to contribute to the progressive implementation of the Covenant.

87. The Committee should reconsider the current six-year cycle of reporting in view of the delays which have led to simultaneous consideration of reports submitted under different phases of the cycle. The Committee should also review the guidelines for States Parties to assist them in preparing reports and propose any necessary modifications.

88. The Committee should consider inviting States Parties to comment on selected topics leading to a direct and sustained dialogue with the Committee.

89. The Committee should devote adequate attention to the methodological issues involved in assessing compliance with the obligations contained in the Covenant. Reference to indicators, in so far as they may help measure progress made in the achievement of certain rights, may be useful in evaluating reports submitted under the Covenant. The Committee should take due account of the indicators selected by or in the framework of the specialized agencies and draw upon or promote additional research, in consultation with the specialized agencies concerned, where gaps have been identified.

90. Whenever the Committee is not satisfied that the information provided by a State Party is adequate for a meaningful assessment of progress achieved and difficulties encountered it should request supplementary information, specifying as necessary the precise issues or questions it would like the State Party to address.

91. In preparing its reports under ECOSOC resolution 1985/17, the Committee should consider, in addition to the "summary of its consideration of the reports," highlighting thematic issues raised during its deliberations.

C. Relations Between the Committee and Specialized Agencies, and Other International Organs

92. The establishment of the Committee should be seen as an opportunity to develop a positive and mutually beneficial relationship between the Committee and the specialized agencies and other international organs.

93. New arrangements under Article 18 of the Covenant should be considered where they could enhance the contribution of the specialized agencies to the work of the Committee. Given that the working methods with regard to the implementation of economic, social and cultural rights vary from one specialized agency to another, flexibility is appropriate in making such arrangements under Article 18.

94. It is essential for the proper supervision of the implementation of the Covenant under Part IV that a dialogue be developed between the specialized agencies and the Committee with respect to matters of common interest. In particular consultations should address the need for developing indicators for assessing compliance with the Covenant; drafting guidelines for the submission of reports by States Parties; making arrangements for submission of reports by the specialized agencies under Article 18. Consideration should also be given to any relevant procedures adopted in the agencies. Participation of their representatives in meetings of the Committee would be very valuable.

95. It would be useful if Committee members could visit specialized agencies concerned, learn through personal contact about programmes of the agencies relevant to the realization of the rights contained in the Covenant and discuss the possible areas of collaboration with those agencies.

96. Consultations should be initiated between the Committee and international financial institutions and development agencies to exchange information and share ideas on the distribution of available resources in relation to the realization of the rights recognized in the Covenant. These exchanges should consider the impact of international economic assistance on efforts by States Parties to implement the Covenant and possibilities of technical and economic co-operation under Article 22 of the Covenant.

97. The Commission on Human Rights, in addition to its responsibilities under Article 19 of the Covenant, should take into account the work of the Committee in its consideration of items on its agenda relating to economic, social and cultural rights.

98. The Covenant on Economic, Social and Cultural Rights is related to the Covenant on Civil and Political Rights. Although most rights can clearly be delineated as falling within the framework of one or other Covenant, there are several rights and provisions referred to in both instruments which are not susceptible to clear differentiation. Both Covenants moreover share common provisions and articles. It is important that consultative arrangements be established between the Economic, Social and Cultural Rights Committee and the Human Rights Committee.

99. Given the relevance of other international legal instruments to the Covenant, early consideration should be given by the Economic and Social Council to the need for developing effective consultative arrangements between the various supervisory bodies.

100. International and regional intergovernmental organizations concerned with the realization of economic, social and cultural rights are urged to develop measures, as appropriate, to promote the implementation of the Covenant.

101. As the Committee is a subsidiary organ of the Economic and Social Council, non-governmental organizations enjoying consultative status with the Economic and Social Council are urged to attend and follow the meetings of the Committee and, when appropriate, to submit information in accordance with ECOSOC resolution 1296 (XLIV).

102. The Committee should develop, in co-operation with intergovernmental organizations and non-governmental organizations as well as research institutes an agreed system for recording, storing and making accessible case law and other interpretative material relating to international instruments on economic, social and cultural rights.

103. As one of the measures recommended in Article 23 it is recommended that seminars be held periodically to review the work of the Committee and the progress made in the realization of economic, social and cultural rights by States Parties.

Chapter 2
Maastricht Guidelines on Violations of Economic, Social and Cultural Rights

Introduction

On the occasion of the 10th anniversary of the Limburg Principles on the Implementation of the International Covenant on Economic, Social and Cultural Rights (hereinafter "the Limburg Principles"), a group of more than thirty experts met in Maastricht from 22 to 26 January 1997 at the invitation of the International Commission of Jurists (Geneva, Switzerland), the Urban Morgan Institute on Human Rights (Cincinnati, Ohio, USA) and the Centre for Human Rights of the Faculty of Law of Maastricht University (the Netherlands). The objective of this meeting was to elaborate on the Limburg Principles as regards the nature and scope of violations of economic, social and cultural rights and appropriate responses and remedies.

The participants unanimously agreed on the following guidelines which they understand to reflect the evolution of international law since 1986. These guidelines are designed to be of use to all who are concerned with understanding and determining violations of economic, social and cultural rights and in providing remedies thereto, in particular monitoring and adjudicating bodies at the national, regional and international levels.

I: The Significance of Economic, Social and Cultural Rights

1. Since the Limburg Principles were adopted in 1986, economic and social conditions have declined at alarming rates for over 1.6 billion people, while they have advanced also at a dramatic pace for more than a quarter of the world's population. The gap between rich and poor has doubled in the last three decades, with the poorest fifth of the world's population receiving 1.4% of the global income and the richest fifth 85%. The impact of these disparities on the lives of people—especially the poor—is dramatic and renders the enjoyment of economic, social and cultural rights illusory for a significant portion of humanity.

2. Since the end of the Cold War, there has been a trend in all regions of the world to reduce the role of the state and to rely on the market to resolve problems of human welfare, often in response to conditions generated by international and national financial

markets and institutions and in an effort to attract investments from the multinational enterprises whose wealth and power exceed that of many states. It is no longer taken for granted that the realization of economic, social and cultural rights depends significantly on action by the state, although, as a matter of international law, the state remains ultimately responsible for guaranteeing the realization of these rights. While the challenge of addressing violations of economic, social and cultural rights is rendered more complicated by these trends, it is more urgent than ever to take these rights seriously and, therefore, to deal with the accountability of governments for failure to meet their obligations in this area.

3. There have also been significant legal developments enhancing economic, social and cultural rights since 1986, including the emerging jurisprudence of the Committee on Economic, Social and Cultural Rights and the adoption of instruments, such as the revised European Social Charter of 1996 and the Additional Protocol to the European Charter Providing for a System of Collective Complaints, and the San Salvador Protocol to the American Convention on Human Rights in the Area of Economic, Social and Cultural Rights of 1988. Governments have made firm commitments to address more effectively economic, social and cultural rights within the framework of seven UN World Summits conferences (1992–1996). Moreover, the potential exists for improved accountability for violations of economic, social and cultural rights through the proposed Optional Protocols to the International Covenant on Economic, Social and Cultural Rights and the Convention on the Elimination of All Forms of Discrimination Against Women. Significant developments within national civil society movements and regional and international NGOs in the field of economic, social and cultural rights have taken place.

4. It is now undisputed that all human rights are indivisible, interdependent, interrelated and of equal importance for human dignity. Therefore, states are as responsible for violations of economic, social and cultural rights as they are for violations of civil and political rights.

5. As in the case of civil and political rights, the failure by a State party to comply with a treaty obligation concerning economic, social and cultural rights is, under international law, a violation of that treaty. Building upon the Limburg Principles , the considerations below relate primarily to the International Covenant on Economic, Social and Cultural Rights (hereinafter "the Covenant"). They are equally relevant, however, to the interpretation and application of other norms of international and domestic law in the field of economic, social and cultural rights.

II: The Meaning of Violations of Economic, Social and Cultural Rights

Obligations to respect, protect and fulfill

6. Like civil and political rights, economic, social and cultural rights impose three different types of obligations on States: the obligations to respect, protect and fulfill. Failure

to perform any one of these three obligations constitutes a violation of such rights. The obligation to respect requires States to refrain from interfering with the enjoyment of economic, social and cultural rights. Thus, the right to housing is violated if the State engages in arbitrary forced evictions. The obligation to protect requires States to prevent violations of such rights by third parties. Thus, the failure to ensure that private employers comply with basic labour standards may amount to a violation of the right to work or the right to just and favourable conditions of work. The obligation to fulfil requires States to take appropriate legislative, administrative, budgetary, judicial and other measures towards the full realization of such rights. Thus, the failure of States to provide essential primary health care to those in need may amount to a violation.

Obligations of conduct and of result

7. The obligations to respect, protect and fulfill each contain elements of obligation of conduct and obligation of result. The obligation of conduct requires action reasonably calculated to realize the enjoyment of a particular right. In the case of the right to health, for example, the obligation of conduct could involve the adoption and implementation of a plan of action to reduce maternal mortality. The obligation of result requires States to achieve specific targets to satisfy a detailed substantive standard. With respect to the right to health, for example, the obligation of result requires the reduction of maternal mortality to levels agreed at the 1994 Cairo International Conference on Population and Development and the 1995 Beijing Fourth World Conference on Women.

Margin of discretion

8. As in the case of civil and political rights, States enjoy a margin of discretion in selecting the means for implementing their respective obligations. State practice and the application of legal norms to concrete cases and situations by international treaty monitoring bodies as well as by domestic courts have contributed to the development of universal minimum standards and the common understanding of the scope, nature and limitation of economic, social and cultural rights. The fact that the full realization of most economic, social and cultural rights can only be achieved progressively, which in fact also applies to most civil and political rights, does not alter the nature of the legal obligation of States which requires that certain steps be taken immediately and others as soon as possible. Therefore, the burden is on the State to demonstrate that it is making measurable progress toward the full realization of the rights in question. The State cannot use the "progressive realization" provisions in article 2 of the Covenant as a pretext for non-compliance. Nor can the State justify derogations or limitations of rights recognized in the Covenant because of different social, religious and cultural backgrounds.

Minimum core obligations

9. Violations of the Covenant occur when a State fails to satisfy what the Committee on

Economic, Social and Cultural Rights has referred to as "a minimum core obligation to ensure the satisfaction of, at the very least, minimum essential levels of each of the rights [. . .]. Thus, for example, a State party in which any significant number of individuals is deprived of essential foodstuffs, of essential primary health care, of basic shelter and housing, or of the most basic forms of education is, *prima facie*, violating the Covenant." Such minimum core obligations apply irrespective of the availability of resources of the country concerned or any other factors and difficulties.

Availability of resources

10. In many cases, compliance with such obligations may be undertaken by most States with relative ease, and without significant resource implications. In other cases, however, full realization of the rights may depend upon the availability of adequate financial and material resources. Nonetheless, as established by Limburg Principles 25–28, and confirmed by the developing jurisprudence of the Committee on Economic, Social and Cultural Rights, resource scarcity does not relieve States of certain minimum obligations in respect of the implementation of economic, social and cultural rights.

State policies

11. A violation of economic, social and cultural rights occurs when a State pursues, by action or omission, a policy or practice which deliberately contravenes or ignores obligations of the Covenant, or fails to achieve the required standard of conduct or result. Furthermore, any discrimination on grounds of race, colour, sex, language, religion, political or other opinion, national or social origin, property, birth or other status with the purpose or effect of nullifying or impairing the equal enjoyment or exercise of economic, social and cultural rights constitutes a violation of the Covenant.

Gender discrimination

12. Discrimination against women in relation to the rights recognized in the Covenant, is understood in light of the standard of equality for women under the Convention on the Elimination of All Forms of Discrimination Against Women. That standard requires the elimination of all forms of discrimination against women including gender discrimination arising out of social, cultural and other structural disadvantages.

Inability to comply

13. In determining which actions or omissions amount to a violation of an economic, social or cultural right, it is important to distinguish the inability from the unwillingness of a State to comply with its treaty obligations. A State claiming that it is unable to carry out its obligation for reasons beyond its control has the burden of proving that this is the case. A temporary closure of an educational institution due to an earthquake, for

instance, would be a circumstance beyond the control of the State, while the elimination of a social security scheme without an adequate replacement programme could be an example of unwillingness by the State to fulfill its obligations.

Violations through acts of commission

14. Violations of economic, social and cultural rights can occur through the direct action of States or other entities insufficiently regulated by States. Examples of such violations include:

(a) The formal removal or suspension of legislation necessary for the continued enjoyment of an economic, social and cultural right that is currently enjoyed;

(b) The active denial of such rights to particular individuals or groups, whether through legislated or enforced discrimination;

(c) The active support for measures adopted by third parties which are inconsistent with economic, social and cultural rights;

(d) The adoption of legislation or policies which are manifestly incompatible with pre-existing legal obligations relating to these rights, unless it is done with the purpose and effect of increasing equality and improving the realization of economic, social and cultural rights for the most vulnerable groups;

(e) The adoption of any deliberately retrogressive measure that reduces the extent to which any such right is guaranteed;

(f) The calculated obstruction of, or halt to, the progressive realization of a right protected by the Covenant, unless the State is acting within a limitation permitted by the Covenant or it does so due to a lack of available resources or force majeure;

(g) The reduction or diversion of specific public expenditure, when such reduction or diversion results in the non-enjoyment of such rights and is not accompanied by adequate measures to ensure minimum subsistence rights for everyone.

Violations through acts of omission

15. Violations of economic, social, cultural rights can also occur through the omission or failure of States to take necessary measures stemming from legal obligations. Examples of such violations include:

(a) The failure to take appropriate steps as required under the Covenant;

(b) The failure to reform or repeal legislation which is manifestly inconsistent with an obligation of the Covenant;

(c) The failure to enforce legislation or put into effect policies designed to implement provisions of the Covenant;

(d) The failure to regulate activities of individuals or groups so as to prevent them from violating economic, social and cultural rights;

(e) The failure to utilize the maximum of available resources towards the full realization of the Covenant;

(f) The failure to monitor the realization of economic, social and cultural rights, including the development and application of criteria and indicators for assessing compliance;

(g) The failure to remove promptly obstacles which it is under a duty to remove to permit the immediate fulfillment of a right guaranteed by the Covenant;

(h) The failure to implement without delay a right which it is required by the Covenant to provide immediately;

(i) The failure to meet a generally accepted international minimum standard of achievement, which is within its powers to meet;

(j) The failure of a State to take into account its international legal obligations in the field of economic, social and cultural rights when entering into bilateral or multilateral agreements with other States, international organizations or multinational corporations.

III: Responsibility for Violations

State responsibility

16. The violations referred to in section II are in principle imputable to the State within whose jurisdiction they occur. As a consequence, the State responsible must establish mechanisms to correct such violations, including monitoring investigation, prosecution, and remedies for victims.

Alien domination or occupation

17. Under circumstances of alien domination, deprivations of economic, social and cultural rights may be imputable to the conduct of the State exercising effective control over the territory in question. This is true under conditions of colonialism, other forms of alien domination and military occupation. The dominating or occupying power bears responsibility for violations of economic, social and cultural rights. There are also circumstances in which States acting in concert violate economic, social and cultural rights.

Acts by non-state entities

18. The obligation to protect includes the State's responsibility to ensure that private entities or individuals, including transnational corporations over which they exercise

jurisdiction, do not deprive individuals of their economic, social and cultural rights. States are responsible for violations of economic, social and cultural rights that result from their failure to exercise due diligence in controlling the behaviour of such non-state actors.

Acts by international organizations

19. The obligations of States to protect economic, social and cultural rights extend also to their participation in international organizations, where they act collectively. It is particularly important for States to use their influence to ensure that violations do not result from the programmes and policies of the organizations of which they are members. It is crucial for the elimination of violations of economic, social and cultural rights for international organizations, including international financial institutions, to correct their policies and practices so that they do not result in deprivation of economic, social and cultural rights. Member States of such organizations, individually or through the governing bodies, as well as the secretariat and nongovernmental organizations should encourage and generalize the trend of several such organizations to revise their policies and programmes to take into account issues of economic, social and cultural rights, especially when these policies and programmes are implemented in countries that lack the resources to resist the pressure brought by international institutions on their decision-making affecting economic, social and cultural rights.

IV: Victims of Violations

Individuals and groups

20. As is the case with civil and political rights, both individuals and groups can be victims of violations of economic, social and cultural rights. Certain groups suffer disproportionate harm in this respect such as lower-income groups, women, indigenous and tribal peoples, occupied populations, asylum seekers, refugees and internally displaced persons, minorities, the elderly, children, landless peasants, persons with disabilities and the homeless.

Criminal sanctions

21. Victims of violations of economic, social and cultural rights should not face criminal sanctions purely because of their status as victims, for example, through laws criminalizing persons for being homeless. Nor should anyone be penalized for claiming their economic, social and cultural rights.

V: Remedies and Other Responses to Violations

Access to remedies

22. Any person or group who is a victim of a violation of an economic, social or

cultural right should have access to effective judicial or other appropriate remedies at both national and international levels.

Adequate reparation

23. All victims of violations of economic, social and cultural rights are entitled to adequate reparation, which may take the form of restitution, compensation, rehabilitation and satisfaction or guarantees of non-repetition.

No official sanctioning of violations

24. National judicial and other organs must ensure that any pronouncements they may make do not result in the official sanctioning of a violation of an international obligation of the State concerned. At a minimum, national judiciaries should consider the relevant provisions of international and regional human rights law as an interpretive aide in formulating any decisions relating to violations of economic, social and cultural rights.

National institutions

25. Promotional and monitoring bodies such as national ombudsman institutions and human rights commissions, should address violations of economic, social and cultural rights as vigorously as they address violations of civil and political rights.

Domestic application of international instruments

26. The direct incorporation or application of international instruments recognizing economic, social and cultural rights within the domestic legal order can significantly enhance the scope and effectiveness of remedial measures and should be encouraged in all cases.

Impunity

27. States should develop effective measures to preclude the possibility of impunity of any violation of economic, social and cultural rights and to ensure that no person who may be responsible for violations of such rights has immunity from liability for their actions.

Role of the legal professions

28. In order to achieve effective judicial and other remedies for victims of violations of economic, social and cultural rights, lawyers, judges, adjudicators, bar associations and the legal community generally should pay far greater attention to these violations in

the exercise of their professions, as recommended by the International Commission of Jurists in the Bangalore Declaration and Plan of Action of 1995.

Special rapporteurs

29. In order to further strengthen international mechanisms with respect to preventing, early warning, monitoring and redressing violations of economic, social and cultural rights, the UN Commission on Human Rights should appoint thematic Special Rapporteurs in this field.

New standards

30. In order to further clarify the contents of States obligations to respect, protect and fulfill economic, social and cultural rights, States and appropriate international bodies should actively pursue the adoption of new standards on specific economic, social and cultural rights, in particular the right to work, to food, to housing and to health.

Optional protocols

31. The optional protocol providing for individual and group complaints in relation to the rights recognized in the Covenant should be adopted and ratified without delay. The proposed optional protocol to the Convention on the Elimination of All Forms of Discrimination Against Women should ensure that equal attention is paid to violations of economic, social and cultural rights. In addition, consideration should be given to the drafting of an optional complaints procedure under the Convention on the Rights of the Child.

Documenting and monitoring

32. Documenting and monitoring violations of economic, social and cultural rights should be carried out by all relevant actors, including NGOs, national governments and international organizations. It is indispensable that the relevant international organizations provide the support necessary for the implementation of international instruments in this field. The mandate of the United Nations High Commissioner for Human Rights includes the promotion of economic, social and cultural rights and it is essential that effective steps be taken urgently and that adequate staff and financial resources be devoted to this objective. Specialized agencies and other international organizations working in the economic and social spheres should also place appropriate emphasis upon economic, social and cultural rights as rights and, where they do not already do so, should contribute to efforts to respond to violations of these rights.

Chapter 3
Bangalore Declaration and Plan of Action Regarding Economic, Cultural and Social Rights and the Role of Lawyers

1. Between 23–25 October 1995 the International Commission of Jurists (ICJ), in conjunction with the Commission's Triennial Meeting, convened in Bangalore, India, a Conference on Economic, Social and Cultural Rights and the Role of Lawyers.

2. The Conference was inaugurated by the Hon Chief Justice of India (The Hon A. M. Ahmadi) and the Minister of State for External Affairs (the Hon S. Kurshid, M.P.) in the presence of distinguished jurists from every Continent.

3. The Conference recalled the long standing commitment of the ICJ to the indivisibility of human rights—economic, social, cultural, Civil and political. That commitment has been evidenced over the years by the Declaration of Delhi 1959, the Law of Lagos, 1961, the Limburg Principles on the. implementation of the International Covenant on Economic, Social and Cultural Rights, 1986 and the draft paper for the World Summit on Social Development, 1995, among many other ICJ activities concerned with the vital importance of economic, social and cultural rights for the attainment of the Rule of Law.

Reaffirming the Limburg Principles

4. The Conference re-affirmed the Limburg Principles. It considered regional perspectives on the realisation of economic, social and cultural rights. It examined the means of monitoring the attainment of such rights, including in respect of the compliance by States with their obligations under the International Covenant on Economic, Social and Cultural Rights (ICESCR). It considered the issues of the implementation of those rights and the justiciability of many of them for legal enforcement. It reviewed the steps which might be taken to achieve global endorsement of ICESCR in a way which promoted at once the universal application of the Covenant and its genuine application as an influence upon the conduct of states and others. It reflected upon the need for an Optional Protocol to the ICESCR akin to the First Optional Protocol to the International Covenant on Civil and Political Rights (ICCPR) allowing individual and

group communication to the United Nations Committee by individuals who had exhausted domestic remedies and who complained about the failure of Governments to conform to the ICESCR "by all appropriate means" and "to the maximum (of their) available resources," "progressively" and without discrimination, as the Covenant requires.

5. The participants reminded themselves that, in the words of the Limburg Principles:

Economic, Social and Cultural Rights are an integral part of international human rights law;

The ICESCR is part of the International Bill of Rights; as human rights and fundamental freedoms are indivisible and interdependent, equal attention and urgent consideration should be given to the implementation, promotion and protection of economic, social and cultural rights as well as civil and political rights; The achievement of economic, social and cultural rights may be realised in a variety of political settings. There is no single road to their full attainment;

Non-governmental Organisations, all sectors of society, Specialised Agencies and Officers of the United Nations and individuals have important functions to play in addition to the role of governments in attaining economic, social and cultural rights to their full measure; and trends in international and economic relations should be taken into account in assessing the efforts of the international covenant, to achieve the objectives of the ICESCR.

6. The participants noted that since the Limburg Principles were adopted, the collapse of the command economies in a number of countries of Central and Eastern Europe of Asia and to rapid alteration of the economic arrangements of many countries had altered, in ways which were then unpredictable, the context in which economic, social and cultural rights are to be attained.

7. The participants recalled that the 1993 World Conference on Human Rights in Vienna had reaffirmed the universality, interdependence and indivisibility of Economic, Social, Cultural, Civil and Political Rights and stressed the need for elaborating an Optional Protocol to the ICESCR aimed at establishing an international complaints system to monitor States compliance with their obligations in this field. By stressing both the human right to development and the importance of all human rights in achieving the goal of sustainable development, the Vienna Declaration and Programme of Action made an important contribution to linking the Human Rights discourse with development.

8. The Conference recalled the reaffirmation by the UN World Summit on Social Development, Copenhagen, 1995, of the universality, indivisibility, interdependence, and inter-relation of all human rights, including the right to development of people that human rights, whether economic, social and cultural or civil and political, are a legitimate concern of the international community. The Conference also recalled that the Summit's Final Declaration encourages the ratification and implementation by States of the ICESCR.

9. The Conference called attention to the acute disadvantages of women in the area of economic, social and cultural rights and to the need for taking steps to overcome obstacles facing women's full realisation of those rights. Jurists should co-operate with women and grass-roots organisations 'to formulate concrete measures to protect and promote economic, social and cultural rights of women, bearing in mind the "Platform for Action" formulated by the 1995 UN World Conference on Women in Beijing.

10. Consideration was given to the extent, variety, with and sometimes apparent incompatibility of reservations entered with ratifications of the ICESCR and other relevant treaties. The need for the development of the procedure for reviewing reservations or limiting their duration was supported. The participants were reminded of the general principles of the law of treaties limiting the operation of the incompatible reservations and of a recent ruling of the Committee on civil and political rights that such reservations would be disregarded as inconsistent with the act of ratification.

Jurists' doubts and neglect

11. Much time was devoted, as befitted a Conference of jurists, to examining the extent to which and means by which in domestic jurisdiction the human rights recognised in ICESCR and other relevant international instruments are, or may become, justiciable. The participants sought to analyse with complete candour the reasons, often myths, why jurists had been less involved in the pursuit of the attainment of economic, social and cultural rights. Amongst other reasons, they identified and considered, the beliefs of some jurists that economic, social and cultural rights are not really rights of a legally enforceable kind; such rights are variable in content, altering over time and resistant to precise legal enforcement; such rights, however important, are not really the specific domain of lawyers; such rights, for their attainment, involve typically, large expenditure of money which should better be left to government which is, or should be accountable to the people rather than to the courts whose members may have neither expertise nor the information with which to make decisions having a large economic or social significance. Whilst realisation of civil and political rights have clear economic costs, inherent in many if not most court decisions, the attainment of the "right to work", "right to housing" and other economic, social and cultural rights is much more likely to involve large issues of social and political policy in which lawyers have a role to play as politicians and citizens but a much lesser role to play as legal professionals. Several participants warned against the tendency for the law, its institutions and professionals to overreach their proper function and expertise and to illegalise issues which are more properly to be decided in a context and according to considerations larger than typically found in courts of law.

12. The participants acknowledged the foregoing concerns and opinions which, amongst others, help to explain the reluctance of jurists sometimes to become directly concerned with the realisation of economic, social and cultural rights by means of the techniques of the law and using the courts and other instruments of legal practice. The widespread ignorance of the ICESCR, not only amongst judges and lawyers but also

amongst governments and in the community was a matter of concern. But the participants reaffirmed the fact that economic, social and cultural rights are an essential part of the global mosaic of human rights. The participants recognised the important role of lawyers and judges in countries such as India to apply and judicially enforce economic, social and cultural rights in the context of the right to life, fair trial, equality before the law, equal protection of the law and other civil and political rights. They resolved that jurists in the future should play a greater part in the realisation of such rights, than they have in the past. Without in any way diminishing the vital work of lawyers in the attainment of civil and political rights, they affirmed that the realisation of economic, social and cultural rights is often of widen application and pressing urgency affecting every day, as such rights, do, all members of society. For lawyers to exclude themselves from a proper and constructive role in the realisation of such rights would be to deny them a function in a vital area of human rights. The task of the conference was, therefore, one of defining these activities in which lawyers *qua* lawyers might have a legitimate and constructive function and to promote within the judiciary and the legal profession in every land a realisation of the opportunities and obligations which fall to lawyers in this regard.

13. Impunity of perpetrators of grave and systematic violations of economic, social and cultural rights, including corruption of State officials is an obstacle to the enjoyment of economic, social and cultural rights which must be combated.

Follow-up to the Conference

14. The participants resolved to request the ICJ to publish and disseminate the proceedings of the Conference and to ensure that the papers and the record of the reflections of the participants be widely distributed and publicised with a view to enlarging the awareness amongst lawyers throughout the world of their proper and legitime functions in promoting and securing the attainment of the economic, social and cultural rights which belong to humanity. The record of the Conference will reflect the sense of urgency and sometimes of professional failure and indifference which has often marked, in the past, the response of lawyers to this area of human rights.

15. The participants also recommended that the IW publish and disseminate for widespread discussion and possible action, some of the suggestions which were made during the Conference. Other such suggestions appear in the papers and record of the Conference. Together such proposals constitute the Bangalore Action Plan for the better attainment of economic, social and cultural rights in every land. The Conference agreed that there is a need to raise awareness amongst judges and lawyers every where concerning their role in the realisation of economic, social and cultural rights. To that end, all agreed that the Action Plan which follows should be placed before jurists everywhere as a contribution to further reflection upon the role which they can play in the attainment of such rights. Lawyers have a vital role in such attainment as stated in the United Nations Basic Principles on the Role of Lawyers. Lack of involvement of lawyers in the realisation of more than half of the field of human rights, vital to humanity, is no longer acceptable.

Action Plan

Action—International

16. Among suggestions for action at an international level were:

16.1. Fresh action in the international community and specifically by the ICJ and other international and national human rights NGOs to attain universal ratification of ICESCR. While ratifications lacking integrity or accompanied by large reservations, are deplorable, the experience of recent years has been that it is ratification which renders a State susceptible to influence and pressure upon the subject matter of the treaty.

16.2. Specific pressure should be applied to obtain more ratification by countries in the Asian/Pacific region. Particularly in Asia and despite the rapid advances in many economies in the region, ratifications are few. New pressure should be added to correct this position. It should be supplemented by renewed consideration of the establishment of an effective regional or sub-regional mechanisms for dealing with complaints about derogations from fundamental human rights (including economic, social and cultural rights);

16.3. Renewed efforts should be directed towards the adoption of an Optional Protocol to the ICESCR. This would provide a complaints mechanism to permit international monitoring of complaints of departures from the rights expressed in the ICESCR. The conference considered the several drafts for such a protocol including the 1994 draft prepared by the Chairperson of the Committee on Economic, Social and Cultural Rights, the 1994 draft for CEDAW prepared in Maastricht and the 1995 draft prepared by a group of experts in Utrecht. The advantage of the several drafts were studied and a system which paid regard to the special needs of the international scrutiny of economic, social and cultural rights should be called for. The conference urged the ICJ to take a leading role and ensure that such a protocol should be adopted immediately.

16.4. The ICJ and other international human rights organisations should redouble their efforts to monitor and report upon departures in compliance with economic, social and cultural rights. Where necessary such NGOs should consider issuing 'alternative reports', to supplement the reports of member States under the ICESCR. They should also report to the communities affected upon the Governments' reports to the Committee so as to stimulate the political, legal and other action necessary to redress wrongs;

16.5. The treaty bodies of the United Nations having relevance in the fields of economic, social and cultural rights where they have not already done so should improve their facilities for cooperation and assistance by NGOs. Facilities should be provided to such NGOs to provide in a formal way assistance to the relevant bodies concerned. Pending such institutional reforms, the NGOs, should be imaginative and innovative in the provision of their assistance -even were not granted consultative status.

16.6. The role and responsibility of international financial institutions, inter-governmental, governmental and private, were recognised. The recently expressed concern about issues of economic, social and cultural human rights on the part of the World

Bank was welcomed. It is desirable that an ombudsman for the World Bank, be appointed to receive complaints and suggestions for the better attainment of the principles of ICESCR.

16.7. The need to ensure prompt, substantial and candid reports under the relevant treaties was emphasised. So was the need for NGOs to draw attention to default including by use of the national and international media;

16.8. The probability of seeking an advisory opinion of the International Court of Justice and the legality and equity of interest on debtor countries was raised.

16.9. Many participants emphasised the importance of viewing the attainment of economic, social and cultural rights in the international context in relation to other international moves including:

(i) monitoring progressive compliance of State obligations under the ICESCR, available resources including those resources devoted to arms purchases and debt repayment should be taken into account;

(ii) control of international trade in arms and the huge burden of military expenditure;

(iii) control and redress of corruption and offshore placement of corruptly obtained funds;

(iv) increase in the empowerment of women, including by general eduction and in particular by promoting the reproductive rights of women.

(v) reform of agricultural policies of certain developed countries arising from the uneconomic subsidisation of local agricultural production to the exclusion of markets for agricultural producers in developing countries.

(vi) improvement of the functioning of the regional systems and bodies with respect to the attainment of economic, social and cultural rights.

Action—national

17. Participants also suggested the following action, amongst others, at a national level:

17.1. An increase in the sensitisation of judges, lawyers, government officials and all those concerned with legal institutions about the terms and objectives of the ICESCR, its mechanism, other treaties of relevance and the vital importance for individuals of these aspects of human rights and the legitimate role of Jurists in attaining them. The role of universities, law colleges, judicial training courses and general media to promote greater awareness was emphasized;

17.2. The task of specifying those aspects of economic, social and cultural rights which were more readily susceptible to legal enforcement requires legal skills and imagination. It would be necessary to define legal obligations with precision, define what constitutes a violation; specify conditions to be taken as complaints; develop strategies for dealing with abuses or failures and provide legal vehicles in appropriate cases to secure the attainment of the objectives deemed desirable.

17.3. Among specific actions which could be taken, the following were endorsed:

17.3.1. Reform of Constitutional provisions, where necessary, to incorporate references to economic, social and cultural rights.

17.3.2. Revision of municipal law to state in precise and justiciable terms, the economic, social and cultural rights in a way susceptible to legal enforcement;

17.3.3. Reform of the Law of Standing and encouragement of public interest litigation such as has occurred in India, by test cases, to further and stimulate the political process into attention to economic, social and cultural rights;

17.3.4. Establishment and enhancement of the functions and powers of the ombudsman or of specialised ombudsmen, to provide an accessible and independent for receiving complaints against the Government and departure from the obligation to ensure the attainment of economic, social and cultural rights.

17.4. The conference endorsed the indispensability of an independent judiciary to the effective implementation of economic, social and cultural rights. Whilst the Judiciary is not the only means of securing the realisation of such rights, the existence of an independent judiciary is an essential requirement for the effective involvement of jurists in the enforcement by law of such rights, given that they are often sensitive, controversial and such as to require the balancing of competing and conflicting interests and values.

17.5. Among suggestions for attention to steps necessary to ensure real progress in the attainment of these ends, the following were endorsed:

17.5.1. The need for effective means of independent public legal aid and like assistance in appropriate cases;

17.5.2. The need for Bar Associations and Law Societies to provide pro bono services and to enlarge their agendas in the field of human rights and involve the service of their members in this regard.

17.5.3. The need to empower disadvantaged groups, including women, minorities, indigenous peoples and others lacking legal experience and confidence in the legal system, to come forward to claim and secure their rights and the need for court procedure, to adapt to their end.

17.5.4. The need for judges to domestically apply international human rights norms in the field of economic, social, and cultural rights. Where there is ambiguity in a local constitution or statutes, an apparent gap in the law, or inconsistency with the international standards, judges, should resolve the ambiguity, inconsistency or fill the gap by reference to the jurisprudence of international human rights bodies. Renewed efforts should be made, including by the IW, to promote existing principles such as the Bangalore Principles, on the Universal level with particular emphasis on economic, social and cultural rights.

Action—individual

18. Among actions that should be taken by jurists as individuals, the following are endorsed:

18.1. Action within Bar Associations and Law Societies to add a focus upon economic, social and cultural rights to the agenda of jurists for the attainment of human rights in full measure;

18.2. Action by jurists as legislators, community leaders and as citizens to enlarge governmental and community knowledge about and understanding of social, economic and cultural rights, so that the obligations of ICESCR and other relevant treaties will become better known;

18.3. Use by jurists, in addition to the courts and tribunals, of other independent organs such as the ombudsman, independent Human Rights Commissions, as well as national, regional and international bodies to promote the attainment of the standards of relevant treaties. In such States in which such institutions have not been established, jurists should promote their establishment. Jurists should work closely with the institutions of civil society to help promote and attain the objectives of the ICESCR and other relevant treaties.

Chapter 4
Guiding Principles on Internal Displacement

Introduction: scope and purpose

1. These Guiding Principles address the specific needs of internally displaced persons world wide. They identify rights and guarantees relevant to the protection of persons from forced displacement and to their protection and assistance during displacement as well as during return or resettlement and reintegration.

2. For the purposes of these Principles, internally displaced persons are persons or groups of persons who have been forced or obliged to flee or to leave their homes or places of habitual residence, in particular as a result of or in order to avoid the effects of armed conflict, situations of generalized violence, violations of human rights or natural or human-made disasters, and who have not crossed an internationally recognized State border.

3. These Principles reflect and are consistent with international human rights law and international humanitarian law. They provide guidance to:

(a) The Representative of the Secretary-General on internally displaced persons in carrying out his mandate;

(b) States when faced with the phenomenon of internal displacement;

(c) All other authorities, groups and persons in their relations with internally displaced persons; and

(d) Intergovernmental and non-governmental organizations when addressing internal displacement.

4. These Guiding Principles should be disseminated and applied as widely as possible.

Contained within the report of the Representative of the UN Secretary General on Internally Displaced Persons (E/CN.4/1998/53/Add. 2, dated 11 February 1998).

Section I—General Principles

Principle 1

1. Internally displaced persons shall enjoy, in full equality, the same rights and freedoms under international and domestic law as do other persons in their country. They shall not be discriminated against in the enjoyment of any rights and freedoms on the ground that they are internally displaced.

2. These Principles are without prejudice to individual criminal responsibility under international law, in particular relating to genocide, crimes against humanity and war crimes.

Principle 2

1. These Principles shall be observed by all authorities, groups and persons irrespective of their legal status and applied without any adverse distinction. The observance of these Principles shall not affect the legal status of any authorities, groups or persons involved.

2. These Principles shall not be interpreted as restricting, modifying or impairing the provisions of any international human rights or international humanitarian law instrument or rights granted to persons under domestic law. In particular, these Principles are without prejudice to the right to seek and enjoy asylum in other countries.

Principle 3

1. National authorities have the primary duty and responsibility to provide protection and humanitarian assistance to internally displaced persons within their jurisdiction.

2. Internally displaced persons have the right to request and to receive protection and humanitarian assistance from these authorities. They shall not be persecuted or punished for making such a request.

Principle 4

1. These Principles shall be applied without discrimination of any kind, such as race, colour, sex, language, religion or belief, political or other opinion, national, ethnic or social origin, legal or social status, age, disability, property, birth, or on any other similar criteria.

2. Certain internally displaced persons, such as children, especially unaccompanied minors, expectant mothers, mothers with young children, female heads of household, persons with disabilities and elderly persons, shall be entitled to protection and assistance required by their condition and to treatment which takes into account their special needs.

Section II—Principles Relating to Protection from Displacement

Principle 5

All authorities and international actors shall respect and ensure respect for their obligations under international law, including human rights and humanitarian law, in all circumstances, so as to prevent and avoid conditions that might lead to displacement of persons.

Principle 6

1. Every human being shall have the right to be protected against being arbitrarily displaced from his or her home or place of habitual residence.

2. The prohibition of arbitrary displacement includes displacement:

(a) When it is based on policies of apartheid, "ethnic cleansing" or similar practices aimed at/or resulting in altering the ethnic, religious or racial composition of the affected population;

(b) In situations of armed conflict, unless the security of the civilians involved or imperative military reasons so demand;

(c) In cases of large-scale development projects, which are not justified by compelling and overriding public interests;

(d) In cases of disasters, unless the safety and health of those affected requires their evacuation; and

(e) When it is used as a collective punishment.

3. Displacement shall last no longer than required by the circumstances.

Principle 7

1. Prior to any decision requiring the displacement of persons, the authorities concerned shall ensure that all feasible alternatives are explored in order to avoid displacement altogether. Where no alternatives exist, all measures shall be taken to minimize displacement and its adverse effects.

2. The authorities undertaking such displacement shall ensure, to the greatest practicable extent, that proper accommodation is provided to the displaced persons, that such displacements are effected in satisfactory conditions of safety, nutrition, health and hygiene, and that members of the same family are not separated.

3. If displacement occurs in situations other than during the emergency stages of armed conflicts and disasters, the following guarantees shall be complied with:

(a) A specific decision shall be taken by a State authority empowered by law to order such measures;

(b) Adequate measures shall be taken to guarantee to those to be displaced full information on the reasons and procedures for their displacement and, where applicable, on compensation and relocation;

(c) The free and informed consent of those to be displaced shall be sought;

(d) The authorities concerned shall endeavour to involve those affected, particularly women, in the planning and management of their relocation;

(e) Law enforcement measures, where required, shall be carried out by competent legal authorities; and

(f) The right to an effective remedy, including the review of such decisions by appropriate judicial authorities, shall be respected.

Principle 8

Displacement shall not be carried out in a manner that violates the rights to life, dignity, liberty and security of those affected.

Principle 9

States are under a particular obligation to protect against the displacement of indigenous peoples, minorities, peasants, pastoralists and other groups with a special dependency on and attachment to their lands.

Section III—Principles Relating to Protection During Displacement

Principle 10

1. Every human being has the inherent right to life which shall be protected by law. No one shall be arbitrarily deprived of his or her life. Internally displaced persons shall be protected in particular against:

(a) Genocide;

(b) Murder;

(c) Summary or arbitrary executions; and

(d) Enforced disappearances, including abduction or unacknowledged detention, threatening or resulting in death.

Threats and incitement to commit any of the foregoing acts shall be prohibited.

2. Attacks or other acts of violence against internally displaced persons who do not or no longer participate in hostilities are prohibited in all circumstances. Internally displaced persons shall be protected, in particular, against:

(a) Direct or indiscriminate attacks or other acts of violence, including the creation of areas wherein attacks on civilians are permitted;

(b) Starvation as a method of combat;

(c) Their use to shield military objectives from attack or to shield, favour or impede military operations;

(d) Attacks against their camps or settlements; and

(e) The use of anti-personnel landmines.

Principle 11

1. Every human being has the right to dignity and physical, mental and moral integrity.

2. Internally displaced persons, whether or not their liberty has been restricted, shall be protected in particular against:

(a) Rape, mutilation, torture, cruel, inhuman or degrading treatment or punishment, and other outrages upon personal dignity, such as acts of gender-specific violence, forced prostitution and any form of indecent assault;

(b) Slavery or any contemporary form of slavery, such as sale into marriage, sexual exploitation, or forced labour of children; and

(c) Acts of violence intended to spread terror among internally displaced persons.

Threats and incitement to commit any of the foregoing acts shall be prohibited.

Principle 12

1. Every human being has the right to liberty and security of person. No one shall be subjected to arbitrary arrest or detention.

2. To give effect to this right for internally displaced persons, they shall not be interned in or confined to a camp. If in exceptional circumstances such internment or confinement is absolutely necessary, it shall not last longer than required by the circumstances.

3. Internally displaced persons shall be protected from discriminatory arrest and detention as a result of their displacement.

4. In no case shall internally displaced persons be taken hostage.

Principle 13

1. In no circumstances shall displaced children be recruited nor be required or permitted to take part in hostilities.

2. Internally displaced persons shall be protected against discriminatory practices of

recruitment into any armed forces or groups as a result of their displacement. In particular any cruel, inhuman or degrading practices that compel compliance or punish non-compliance with recruitment are prohibited in all circumstances.

Principle 14

1. Every internally displaced person has the right to liberty of movement and freedom to choose his or her residence.

2. In particular, internally displaced persons have the right to move freely in and out of camps or other settlements.

Principle 15

Internally displaced persons have:

(a) The right to seek safety in another part of the country;

(b) The right to leave their country;

(c) The right to seek asylum in another country; and

(d) The right to be protected against forcible return to or resettlement in any place where their life, safety, liberty and/or health would be at risk.

Principle 16

1. All internally displaced persons have the right to know the fate and whereabouts of missing relatives.

2. The authorities concerned shall endeavour to establish the fate and whereabouts of internally displaced persons reported missing, and co-operate with relevant international organizations engaged in this task. They shall inform the next of kin on the progress of the investigation and notify them of any result.

3. The authorities concerned shall endeavour to collect and identify the mortal remains of those deceased, prevent their despoliation or mutilation, and facilitate the return of those remains to the next of kin or dispose of them respectfully.

4. Grave sites of internally displaced persons should be protected and respected in all circumstances. Internally displaced persons should have the right of access to the grave sites of their deceased relatives.

Principle 17

1. Every human being has the right to respect of his or her family life.

2. To give effect to this right for internally displaced persons, family members who wish to remain together shall be allowed to do so.

3. Families which are separated by displacement should be reunited as quickly as possible. All appropriate steps shall be taken to expedite the reunion of such families, particularly when children are involved. The responsible authorities shall facilitate inquiries made by family members and encourage and cooperate with the work of humanitarian organizations engaged in the task of family reunification.

4. Members of internally displaced families whose personal liberty has been restricted by internment or confinement in camps shall have the right to remain together.

Principle 18

1. All internally displaced persons have the right to an adequate standard of living.

2. At the minimum, regardless of the circumstances, and without discrimination, competent authorities shall provide internally displaced persons with and ensure safe access to:

(a) Essential food and potable water;

(b) Basic shelter and housing;

(c) Appropriate clothing; and

(d) Essential medical services and sanitation.

3. Special efforts should be made to ensure the full participation of women in the planning and distribution of these basic supplies.

Principle 19

1. All wounded and sick internally displaced persons as well as those with disabilities shall receive to the fullest extent practicable and with the least possible delay, the medical care and attention they require, without distinction on any grounds other than medical ones. When necessary, internally displaced persons shall have access to psychological and social services.

2. Special attention should be paid to the health needs of women, including access to female health care providers and services, such as reproductive health care, as well as appropriate counselling for victims of sexual and other abuses.

3. Special attention should also be given to the prevention of contagious and infectious diseases, including AIDS, among internally displaced persons.

Principle 20

1. Every human being has the right to recognition everywhere as a person before the law.

2. To give effect to this right for internally displaced persons, the authorities concerned shall issue to them all documents necessary for the enjoyment and exercise of their legal rights, such as passports, personal identification documents, birth certificates and marriage certificates. In particular, the authorities shall facilitate the issuance of new documents or the replacement of documents lost in the course of displacement, without imposing unreasonable conditions, such as requiring the return to one's area of habitual residence in order to obtain these or other required documents.

3. Women and men shall have equal rights to obtain such necessary documents and shall have the right to have such documentation issued in their own names.

Principle 21

1. No one shall be arbitrarily deprived of property and possessions.

2. The property and possessions of internally displaced persons shall in all circumstances be protected, in particular, against the following acts:

(a) Pillage;

(b) Direct or indiscriminate attacks or other acts of violence;

(c) Being used to shield military operations or objectives;

(d) Being made the object of reprisal; and

(e) Being destroyed or appropriated as a form of collective punishment.

3. Property and possessions left behind by internally displaced persons should be protected against destruction and arbitrary and illegal appropriation, occupation or use.

Principle 22

1. Internally displaced persons, whether or not they are living in camps, shall not be discriminated against as a result of their displacement in the enjoyment of the following rights:

(a) The rights to freedom of thought, conscience, religion or belief, opinion and expression;

(b) The right to seek freely opportunities for employment and to participate in economic activities;

(c) The right to associate freely and participate equally in community affairs;

(d) The right to vote and to participate in governmental and public affairs, including the right to have access to the means necessary to exercise this right; and

(e) The right to communicate in a language they understand.

Principle 23

1. Every human being has the right to education.

2. To give effect to this right for internally displaced persons, the authorities concerned shall ensure that such persons, in particular displaced children, receive education which shall be free and compulsory at the primary level. Education should respect their cultural identity, language and religion.

3. Special efforts should be made to ensure the full and equal participation of women and girls in educational programmes.

4. Education and training facilities shall be made available to internally displaced persons, in particular adolescents and women, whether or not living in camps, as soon as conditions permit.

Section IV—Principles Relating To Humanitarian Assistance

Principle 24

1. All humanitarian assistance shall be carried out in accordance with the principles of humanity and impartiality and without discrimination.

2. Humanitarian assistance to internally displaced persons shall not be diverted, in particular for political or military reasons.

Principle 25

1. The primary duty and responsibility for providing humanitarian assistance to internally displaced persons lies with national authorities.

2. International humanitarian organizations and other appropriate actors have the right to offer their services in support of the internally displaced. Such an offer shall not be regarded as an unfriendly act or an interference in a State's internal affairs and shall be considered in good faith. Consent thereto shall not be arbitrarily withheld, particularly when authorities concerned are unable or unwilling to provide the required humanitarian assistance.

3. All authorities concerned shall grant and facilitate the free passage of humanitarian assistance and grant persons engaged in the provision of such assistance rapid and unimpeded access to the internally displaced.

Principle 26

Persons engaged in humanitarian assistance, their transport and supplies shall be respected and protected. They shall not be the object of attack or other acts of violence.

Principle 27

1. International humanitarian organizations and other appropriate actors when providing assistance should give due regard to the protection needs and human rights of

internally displaced persons and take appropriate measures in this regard. In so doing, these organizations and actors should respect relevant international standards and codes of conduct.

2. The preceding paragraph is without prejudice to the protection responsibilities of international organizations mandated for this purpose, whose services may be offered or requested by States.

Section V—Principles Relating To Return, Resettlement And Reintegration

Principle 28

1. Competent authorities have the primary duty and responsibility to establish conditions, as well as provide the means, which allow internally displaced persons to return voluntarily, in safety and with dignity, to their homes or places of habitual residence, or to resettle voluntarily in another part of the country. Such authorities shall endeavour to facilitate the reintegration of returned or resettled internally displaced persons.

2. Special efforts should be made to ensure the full participation of internally displaced persons in the planning and management of their return or resettlement and reintegration.

Principle 29

1. Internally displaced persons who have returned to their homes or places of habitual residence or who have resettled in another part of the country shall not be discriminated against as a result of their having been displaced. They shall have the right to participate fully and equally in public affairs at all levels and have equal access to public services.

2. Competent authorities have the duty and responsibility to assist returned and/or resettled internally displaced persons to recover, to the extent possible, their property and possessions which they left behind or were dispossessed of upon their displacement. When recovery of such property and possessions is not possible, competent authorities shall provide or assist these persons in obtaining appropriate compensation or another form of just reparation.

Principle 30

All authorities concerned shall grant and facilitate for international humanitarian organizations and other appropriate actors, in the exercise of their respective mandates, rapid and unimpeded access to internally displaced persons to assist in their return or resettlement and reintegration.

Chapter 5

Comprehensive Human Rights Guidelines on Development-Based Displacement

Preamble

Recalling the human rights standards established pursuant to the International Bill of Human Rights,

Whereas many international treaties, resolutions, decisions, general comments, judgments and other texts have recognized and reaffirmed that forced evictions constitute violations of a wide range of internationally recognized human rights,

Recalling Economic and Social Council decision 1996/290, Commission on Human Rights Resolution 1993/77, and Sub-Commission on Prevention of Discrimination and Protection of Minorities resolution 1996/27,

Reaffirming that under international law every State has the obligation to respect and ensure respect for human rights and humanitarian law, including obligations to prevent violations, to investigate violations, to take appropriate action against violators, and to afford remedies and reparation to victims,

Reaffirming that development is a comprehensive economic, social, cultural and political process, which aims at the constant improvement of the well-being of the entire population and of all individuals on the basis of their active, free and meaningful participation in development and in the fair distribution of benefits resulting therefrom,

Whereas the Vienna Declaration and Plan of Action stipulated that while development facilitates the enjoyment of all human rights, the lack of development may not be invoked to justify the abridgment of internationally recognized human rights,

Recognizing the widespread nature of the practice of forced evictions and that when forced evictions are carried out this can occur in a variety of contexts including but not limited to conflicts over land rights, development and infrastructure projects, such as the construction of dams or other large-scale energy projects, land acquisition measures associated with urban renewal, housing renovation, city beautification programmes,

Adopted by the Expert Seminar on the Practice of Forced Evictions, Geneva, 11–13 June 1997.

the clearing of land for agricultural purposes or macro-urban projects, unbridled speculation in land, and the holding of major international events such as the Olympic Games,

Conscious that forced evictions intensify social conflict and inequality and invariably affect the poorest, most socially, economically, and vulnerable sectors of society, specifically women, children, and indigenous peoples,

Conscious also of guidelines developed by international financial and other institutions on involuntary displacement and resettlement,

Resolved to protect human rights and prevent violations due to the practice of forced evictions.

Section One: Background Issues

Scope and nature of the guidelines

1. The present Guidelines address the human rights implications of the practice of forced evictions associated with development-based displacement in urban and rural areas. The Guidelines reflect and are consistent with international human rights law and international humanitarian law and should be subject to the widest possible application.

2. Having due regard to all relevant definitions of the practice of forced evictions under international human rights provisions and instruments, the present Guidelines apply to instances of forced evictions in which there are acts and/or omissions involving the coerced and involuntary removal of individuals, groups and communities from their homes and/or lands and common property resources they occupy or are dependent upon, thus eliminating or limiting the possibility of an individual, group or community residing or working in a particular dwelling, residence or place.

3. While there are many similarities between the practice of forced evictions and internal displacement, population transfer, mass expulsions, mass exodus, ethnic cleansing and other practices involving the coerced and involuntary movement of people from their homes, lands and communities, forced evictions constitute a distinct practice under international law. Persons, groups and communities subjected to or threatened with forced evictions form, therefore, a distinct group under international human rights law.

4. Forced evictions constitute prima facie violations of a wide range of internationally recognized human rights and can only be carried out under exceptional circumstances and in full accordance with the present Guidelines and relevant provisions of international human rights law.

Section Two: General Obligations

5. While forced evictions can be carried out, sanctioned, demanded, proposed, initiated or tolerated by a variety of distinct actors, responsibility for forced evictions under

international law, ultimately, is held by States. This does not, however, relieve other entities from obligations in this regard, in particular occupying powers, international financial and other institutions or organizations, transnational corporations and individual third parties, including public and private landlords or land owners.

6. States should apply appropriate civil or criminal penalties against any person or entity, within its jurisdiction, whether public or private, who carries out any forced evictions, not in full conformity with applicable law and the present Guidelines.

7. States should object, through the appropriate international legal mechanisms, to the carrying out of forced evictions in other States when such forced evictions are not in full conformity with the present Guidelines and relevant provisions of international human rights law.

8. States should ensure that international organizations in which they are represented refrain from sponsoring or implementing any project, programme or policy which may involve the carrying out of forced evictions not in full conformity with international law and the present Guidelines.

Section Three: Preventative Obligations

The obligation of maximum effective protection

9. States should secure by all appropriate means, including the provision of security of tenure, the maximum degree of effective protection against the practice of forced evictions for all persons under their jurisdiction. In this regard, special consideration should be given to the rights of indigenous peoples, children and women, particularly female-headed households and other vulnerable groups. These obligations are of an immediate nature and are not qualified by resource-related considerations.

10. States should refrain from introducing any deliberately retrogressive measures with respect to de jure or de facto protection against forced evictions.

11. States should ensure that adequate and effective legal or other appropriate remedies are available to any persons claiming that his/her right of protection against forced evictions has been violated or is under threat of violation.

12. States should ensure that eviction impact assessments are carried out prior to the initiation of any project which could result in development-based displacement, with a view to fully securing the human rights of all potentially affected persons, groups and communities.

The obligation to prevent homelessness

13. States should ensure that no persons, groups or communities are rendered homeless or are exposed to the violation of any other human rights as a consequence of a forced eviction.

The obligation to adopt appropriate measures of law and policy

14. States should carry out comprehensive reviews of relevant national legislation with a view to ensuring the compatibility of such legislation with the norms contained in the present Guidelines and other relevant international human rights provisions. In this regard, special measures shall be taken to ensure that no forms of discrimination, statutory or otherwise, are applied in relation to property rights, housing rights and access to resources.

15. States should adopt appropriate legislation and policies to ensure the protection of individuals, groups and communities from forced eviction, having due regard to their best interests. States are encouraged to adopt constitutional provisions in this regard.

The obligation to explore all possible alternatives

16. States should fully explore all possible alternatives to any act involving forced eviction. In this regard, all affected persons, including women, children and indigenous peoples shall have the right to all relevant information and the right to full participation and consultation throughout the entire process and to propose any alternatives. In the event that agreement cannot be reached on the proposed alternative by the affected persons, groups and communities and the entity proposing the forced eviction in question, an independent body, such as a court of law, tribunal, or ombudsman may be called upon.

The obligation to expropriate only as a last resort

17. States should refrain, to the maximum possible extent, from compulsorily acquiring housing or land, unless such acts are legitimate and necessary and designed to facilitate the enjoyment of human rights through, for instance, measures of land reform or redistribution. If, as a last resort, States consider themselves compelled to undertake proceedings of expropriation or compulsory acquisition, such action shall be:

(a) determined and envisaged by law and norms regarding forced eviction, in so far as these are consistent internationally recognized human rights;

(b) solely for the purpose of protecting the general welfare in a democratic society;

(c) reasonable and proportional and

(d) in accordance with the present Guidelines.

Section Four: The Rights of All Persons

Integrity of the home

18. All persons have the right to adequate housing which includes, inter alia, the integrity

of the home and access to and protection of common property resources. The home and its occupants shall be protected against any acts of violence, threats of violence or other forms of harassment, in particular as they relate to women and children. The home and its occupants shall further be protected against any arbitrary or unlawful interference with privacy or respect of the home.

Assurances of security of tenure

19. All persons have a right to security of tenure which provides sufficient legal protection from forced eviction from one's home or land.

20. The present Guidelines shall apply to all persons, groups and communities irrespective of their tenure status.

Section Five: Legal Remedies

21. All persons threatened with forced eviction, notwithstanding the rationale or legal basis thereof, have the right to:

(a) a fair hearing before a competent, impartial and independent court or tribunal;

(b) legal counsel, and where necessary, sufficient legal aid;

(c) effective remedies.

22. States should adopt legislative measures prohibiting any forced evictions without a court order. The court shall consider all relevant circumstances of affected persons, groups and communities and any decision be in full accordance with principles of equality and justice and internationally recognized human rights.

23. All persons have a right to appeal any judicial or other decisions affecting their rights as established pursuant to the present Guidelines, to the highest national judicial authority.

Compensation

24. All persons subjected to any forced eviction not in full accordance with the present Guidelines, should have a right to compensation for any losses of land, personal, real or other property or goods, including rights or interests in property not recognized in national legislation, incurred in connection with a forced eviction. Compensation should include land and access to common property resources and should not be restricted to cash payments.

Restitution and return

25. All persons, groups and communities subjected to forced evictions have the right to, but shall not be forced to return to their homes, lands or places of origin.

Resettlements

26. In full cognizance of the contents of the present Guidelines there may be instances in which, in the public interest, or where the safety, health or enjoyment of human rights so demands, particular persons, groups and communities may be subject to resettlement. Such resettlement must occur in a just and equitable manner and in full accordance with law of general application.

27. All persons, groups and communities have the right to suitable resettlement which includes the right to alternative land or housing, which is safe, secure, accessible, affordable and habitable.

28. In determining the compatibility of resettlement with the present Guidelines, States should ensure that in the context of any case of resettlement the following criteria are adhered to:

(a) No resettlement shall take place until such a time that a full resettlement policy consistent with the present Guidelines and internationally recognized human rights is in place.

(b) Resettlement must ensure equal rights to women, children and indigenous populations and other vulnerable groups including the right to property ownership and access to resources. Resettlement policies should include programmes designed for women with respect to education, health, family welfare and employment opportunities.

(c) The actor proposing and/or carrying out the resettlement shall be required by law to pay for any costs associated therewith, including all resettlement costs.

(d) No affected persons, groups or communities, shall suffer detriment as far as their human rights are concerned nor shall their right to the continuous improvement of living conditions be subject to infringement. This applies equally to host communities at resettlement sites, and affected persons, groups and communities subjected to forced eviction.

(e) That affected persons, groups and communities provide their full and informed consent as regards the relocation site. The State shall provide all necessary amenities and services and economic opportunities.

(f) Sufficient information shall be provided to affected persons, groups and communities concerning all State projects as well as to the planning and implementation processes relating to the resettlement concerned, including information concerning the purpose to which the eviction dwelling or site is to be put and the persons, groups or communities who will benefit from the evicted site. Particular attention must be given to ensure that indigenous peoples, ethnic minorities, the landless, women and children are represented and included in this process.

(g) The entire resettlement process should be carried out in full consultation and participation with the affected persons, groups and communities. States should take into account in particular all alternate plans proposed by the affected persons, groups and communities.

(h) If after a full and fair public hearing, it is found that thee is a need to proceed with the resettlement, then the affected persons, groups and communities shall be given at least ninety (90) days notice prior to the date of the resettlement; and

(i) Local government officials and neutral observers, properly identified, shall be present during the resettlement so as to ensure that no force, violence, or intimidation is involved.

Section Six: Monitoring

29. The United Nations High Commissioner for Human Rights and other United Nations human rights institutions should seek by all possible means to secure full compliance with the present Guidelines.

Section Seven: Savings

Savings clause

30. The provisions contained within the present Guidelines are without prejudice to the provisions of any other international instrument or national law which ensures the enjoyment of all human rights as they relate to the practice of forced evictions.

F. UN HUMAN RIGHTS SPECIAL RAPPORTEURS

Chapter 1
The Realization of Economic, Social and Cultural Rights (excerpts)

. . .

IV. Conclusions: The Need for New Approaches

170. It does not seem far-fetched to accentuate that the failure of Governments, and indeed virtually all models of development pursued thus far, in creating conditions whereby the society-wide enjoyment of economic, social and cultural rights has occurred, indicates the pressing necessity of new approaches towards this category of rights. While legal approaches can obviously achieve a good deal, these must be coupled with an examination of broader social trends and political realities.

171. The multi-faceted achievements of the Committee on Economic, Social and Cultural Rights represent active advancements in this area of international law. The inclusion of an additional protocol on these rights to the American Convention on Human Rights of the Organization of American States (OAS), as well as recent changes to the enforcement mechanisms of the European Social Charter are also indicative of recent steps forward. Yet as important as these legally oriented steps are, it seems crucial (particularly for lawyers) to look beyond these issues at some of the underlying issues which require greater focus for the goal of achieving economic, social and cultural rights for everyone, everywhere. With a mandate as broad as that entrusted to the Special Rapporteur, only several of a broad range of approaches can be considered, prior to examining a lengthy list of what are intended to be concrete recommendations designed to promote the realization of economic, social and cultural rights as a whole.

A. Rediscovering the role of local government

172. The macro-dimensions of the legal issues dealt with most frequently at the international level have led many to ignore or at best under-emphasize the role played by

Final report submitted by Mr. Danilo Türk, Special Rapporteur to the Sub-Commission on Prevention of Distrimination and Protection of Minorities, E/CN.4/Sub.2/1992/16. Original footnotes omitted.

local government in areas affecting the realization of economic, social and cultural rights. As the decision-making structures of the United Nations are exclusively comprised of national Governments this situation is perhaps unsurprising. Nevertheless, a re-discovery of the capacity of local government in satisfying States' legal obligations needs to occur. At the very least, such an emphasis provides a crucial mechanism in promoting popular participation in the development process, as well as providing a means of representing local needs at the national level.

173. How then, could re-emphasizing local government potentially lead to an improvement in the status of economic, social and cultural rights. Re-orienting considering of city and municipal government implies expanding measures towards decentralization. As the United Nations Development Programme (UNDP) has pointed out:

"Decentralizing social services reduces costs, because it encourages the use of local resources and often holds down administrative costs . . . Decentralization usually creates an atmosphere that encourages initiative at all levels, from bottom to top. It thus promotes development that is more people-oriented, more sustainable and more relevant to people's needs and interests."

174. Throughout most of the developing world, however, local governments remain excessively weak, inefficient and very often unrepresentative. And often in conjunction with the adjustment process and the overall economic crisis, local government has weakened yet further, resulting in, *inter alia,* declining promotion of means for encouraging participation of people in the development process. Local governments in third world cities often have 1 percent of the revenue per capita available to most city or municipal governments in Europe and yet they have comparable levels of responsibility.

175. While the variation in the tasks apportioned to local government varies widely, as does the degree of political and economic capacities possessed by these decision-makers, a majority of the tasks for which city or municipal governments are responsible relate directly to areas of competence linked to economic, social and cultural rights. The regulation of land, housing, pollution control, health care, schools, emergency services, trade and production, the provision of water, sanitation and garbage collection and disposal are each predominantly the tasks of local government. UNDP has found, for instance, that decentralizing control over these areas can lead to substantial cost reductions, greater efficiency and wider positive impact in areas of education, health care, water and sanitation and food subsidies.

176. Caution should be exercised in this area, for there can be major drawbacks in decentralizing responsibility in this manner, such as making it more difficult to maintain and control desired quality standards for the services delivered, taking pressure off national government and re-apportioning blame to the local level, the prospect of reinforcing disparities between social groups, regions or local communities, and the risk that devolving power to the local level may provide greater powers to the local elite, who may be less responsive to those in need than central government. Nevertheless, an appraisal by the human rights community of the role of local government appears imperative.

B. Making popular participation real

177. Decades of pleas for increasing levels of participation in the development process, principles about which are included, for instance, in the 1986 Declaration on the Right to Development, have clearly yet to bear fruit.

178. According to one commentator:

"Though the World Bank claims that 'it seeks to meet the needs of the poorest people,' at no stage in what it refers to as 'the project cycle,' however, does it actually take time to ask the poor themselves how they perceive their needs; neither does it canvass their views on how they feel these needs might best be met. Indeed, from the identification of a possible Bank project right through to its *ex post* evaluation, the poor are entirely left out of the decision-making process—almost as if they did not exist."

179. Even the Bank itself has recognized this inadequacy, admitting in 1988 that:

"the principles guiding beneficiary participation in Bank-financed projects have been quite abstract and of limited operational impact. Beneficiaries were not assigned a role in the decision-making process, nor was their technological knowledge sought prior to designing project components."

Though non-governmental organization participation in World Bank projects has increased in the past three years, by far the greatest share of this "participation" was in project implementation, with substantially smaller emphasis being placed on design, advice, monitoring and evaluation.

180. The declining capacities of the State and the resolute inability of the market or private sector, coupled with measures of adjustment, and an overall global economic decline have led to the evolution of new citizen movements, new coalitions and new political processes, all but ignored in the literature of the international financial agencies and by much of the United Nations system. Within these new movements is where real participation occurs, where much of real development takes place and where the legitimate needs of people are increasingly being demanded.

181. Much debate has taken place recently about the obvious relationship between development, democracy and human rights, implying, of course, the issue of citizen participation in all political processes associated with development. One United Nations agency has provided support in the following terms:

"An essential part of any political process to benefit the poor is a high degree of participation. Encouraging the autonomy of citizens is, indeed, an end in itself. And participation is a means to ensure the efficient provision and more equitable distribution of goods and services. If people are involved in decision-making, policies and projects tend to be more realistic, more pragmatic and more sustainable."

C. Using indicators to monitor realization of economic, social and cultural rights

182. The previous three reports of the Special Rapporteur have addressed the potential

role of social and economic indicators as a tool in assessing State compliance with economic, social and cultural rights. The process of incorporating indicator usage into the human rights machinery will be addressed further in the upcoming Expert Seminar on Economic and Social Indicators and Their Use in Monitoring the Realization of Economic, Social and Cultural Rights. A working paper prepared by the Special Rapporteur and considered during the forty-third session of the Sub-Commission outlined some general principles on the use of indicators, tentative themes for the agenda of the seminar and the eventual goals of this meeting. While the inherent limitations of this approach have been recognized, this method of measuring the realization of economic, social and cultural rights has received general support.

183. The degree of seriousness which the human rights bodies have accorded indicator usage was reflected in the general discussion on indicators held at the sixth session of the Committee on Economic, Social and Cultural Rights. One issue raised on several occasions was that of the use of indicators in determining violations of the Covenant. This seems an interesting and constructive use of statistical measurements, and one which could be further incorporated into the work of all human rights bodies. Though one could envision many possible means of addressing violations in this manner, any rise in deprivation accountable to government policy and derived from indicators could be a first step towards employing this strategy. Clearly, the issue of violations of economic, social and cultural rights requires further development.

184. Towards this end, the appointment by the Commission of Human Rights of thematic special rapporteurs mandated to address specific economic, social and cultural rights could provide a useful basis for enhancing the effectiveness of existing mechanisms capable of monitoring violations of these standards. In the view of the Special Rapporteur, the issue of whether or not economic, social and cultural rights can be violated in a legal sense has been answered convincingly in the affirmative. The recent pronouncements of the Committee on Economic, Social and Cultural Rights, for instance, declaring the Dominican Republic to be in violation of the covenant represent critical and path-breaking steps in the monitoring of economic, social and cultural rights. Additionally, the Limburg Principles outline a wide range of State "failures" constituting violations of the Covenant, many of which are unquestionably infringed by a majority of the 106 States parties to the Covenant.

185. Both the upcoming Expert Seminar on Indicators and the 1993 World Conference on Human Rights could provide a venue for exploring in programmatic terms how most effectively to pursue the issue of violations of economic, social and cultural rights. It must be emphasized that approaching this issue from the angle of discrimination may serve as a useful starting point in attaining at least some degree of conceptual clarity concerning this type of violation. To apply discrimination-oriented criteria, however, it will be necessary to devote increased attention to areas of discriminatory behaviour generally ignored at the international level, in particular the grounds of social status, income level, medical status, age, property and sexual orientation.

186. Moreover, accent must be placed by the United Nations on developing means to

monitor consistently and reliably violations of economic, social and cultural rights, accompanied by renewed State party commitments and strengthened interpretation of the legal obligations found in Article 2.1 of the Covenant on Economic, Social and Cultural Rights. Obviously, the eventual adoption and entering into force of an Optional Protocol to the Covenant, enabling individuals and groups to submit formal communications to the Committee alleging violations of any of the rights found in that text, would substantially assist in furthering the debate and generating helpful jurisprudence on the issue. Work on the Optional Protocol should be continued as a matter of priority, with a view to giving the rights in the Covenant practical meaning for the hundreds of millions of citizens who have yet to benefit from the norms of the Covenant.

D. Creating standards or creating space?

187. There exists a strong tendency for lawyers and others involved with the law to advocate the creation of new standards when existing standards appear to be failing in achieving a certain goal. The first progress report addressed two specific issues which the Special Rapporteur viewed as areas where new standard-setting might be beneficial, namely, land rights and the right to adequate housing. Support by members of the Sub-Commission was clearly stronger for the latter than the former area. Standards, of course, need not always imply the creation of new instruments; judicial interpretation of existing norms can also in effect refine and provide conceptual clarity to rights which are currently in place, without recourse to new texts. This raises the question of whether the United Nations human rights bodies should perhaps focus more on the creation of space, broadly defined, than on creating standards.

188. Creating political, legal, social and economic space, implying the expansion of access to space, to decision-making, to individual, family and community choices and to de facto opportunity to assert, demand and claim economic, social and cultural rights are processes at least as critical to the attainment of these rights as is the creation of new legal or quasi-legal standards. The creation of these forms of "space," however, is much less concrete, more difficult to monitor with precision and less "legal" in nature than explicit standards.

189. A number of non-governmental organizations working in the field of economic, social and cultural rights and consulted by the Special Rapporteur put forth the interesting question: Is the goal of human rights to set limits and tell the State what to do, or to free space for people to find solutions to their problems by themselves?

190. New standards, the vast majority of which are totally unknown by the people they are allegedly designed to protect, even when ratified by States, are often ignored and also provide a useful "smokescreen," effectively providing a sense of legitimization in a certain area of the law, when the State in question has no intention of complying with it. The setting of new standards without accompanying measures of monitoring and enforcement is no guarantee that the issues addressed will be adhered to and fulfilled.

191. The creation of standards almost invariably assumes the pre-eminence of the State,

the market or a mixture of the two, in effect ignoring the resources, energies, wisdom and creativity of what is often called the "third sector," civil society or the people. To illustrate the importance of the third sector, we need only note that in the cities of the developing world, housing needs are met neither by the State nor by the market. In most urban areas between 60 and 90 percent of all housing built is constructed by the people themselves, without assistance from either the State or the market.

192. Creating space implies a solid recognition of the true, but often ignored fact that a large proportion of the obligations associated with economic, social and cultural rights are negative in nature, implying the duty of the State not to intervene in certain social processes. Moreover, this point relates to the reality that many aspects of these rights do not require substantial financial expenditure by the State, but rather, a concerted attempt on the part of the State to create the conditions necessary for the eventual fulfillment of these rights. Creating space means that the issue of official "legality" should not be employed by the State to deny citizens the ability to fulfilling there own needs when the State is unwilling or incapable of doing so. This would, for instance, apply to the right to work in the context of the "informal sector" or to the right to housing in the context of the "illegal" occupation of land. The creation of space by Governments can, in fact, lead to improvements in the livelihood of citizens by simply allowing people to create their own solutions to their own problems.

193. Allowing space for personal and community initiatives related to areas comprising economic, social and cultural rights should not be taken as a subjugation of State responsibility to respect, protect and fulfill these rights. People's movements, campaigns and initiatives aimed at satisfying citizens' needs should not be discouraged by States or viewed as a threat to social stability, but as perhaps one of the few means by which people who are organized can express themselves and create solutions for their many predicaments. What this approach recognizes, however, is the frequent inability of the State to intervene sufficiently or provide the necessary resources for these rights to be widely enjoyed. The State should allow these processes to flourish, while simultaneously acting in full accordance with any international obligations concerning these rights. It is in these areas that the relevance of "freedom" enters the domain of economic, social and cultural rights.

E. Humanizing adjustment

194. The debt and overall economic crisis of the 1980s, accompanied by the adjustment process carried out with such controversy during the past decade, has created both winners and losers. The fact that one social group in particular has benefited from this process while many other sectors have seen living standards decline raises a number of serious issues.

195. Recent figures concerning adjustment in Latin America and the Caribbean indicate that consumption per capita of the business sector increased by 16 percent

whereas consumption by labour declined by 25 percent. Many sources show that the social factions which have gained most from adjustment are top executives in private business linked with foreign capital, local agents of foreign concerns, and those importers and exporters able to obtain special access to foreign exchange in a situation of scarcity.

196. The European Network on Debt and Development has promoted a view, with which the Special Rapporteur agrees, that in order to make it consistent with the existing obligations of States concerning economic, social and cultural rights the policy package constituting adjustment should at a minimum address:

(a) The need substantially to increase the level and quality of popular participation, particularly by social sectors negatively affected by adjustment;

(b) The need for greater institutional transparency within the international financial institutions and levels of national government negotiating adjustment measures;

(c) The pressing need for economic adjustment in the industrialized world, which fully takes into account the international ramifications of domestic economic decision-making;

(d) The provision of the necessary level of financial and other resources, sufficient to attain the goals set by appropriately designed adjustment packages;

(e) The need to implement a truly case-by-case approach to adjustment programme design; and

(f) The defence and extension of investment in human resource development, particularly crucial in periods of adjustment.

F. Remembering cultural rights

197. Of the five major groupings of internationally recognized human rights (civil, political, economic, social and cultural), that of cultural rights receives by far the least amount of serious attention. It is thus interesting to note in this regard that the Committee on Economic, Social and Cultural Rights will consider a draft general comment on cultural rights at its seventh session later this year, which may provide clarity and substance to these often ignored, yet central, human rights.

198. In terms of overall respect for human rights, cultural rights, in particular the increasingly discussed right to cultural identity, clearly require further incorporation into the global human rights paradigm. The rights of indigenous peoples, peoples under foreign occupation, migrant workers, ethnic minorities' or foreign residents in countries other than their own, have significant (and often controversial) cultural dimensions. The centrality of the right to culture is obvious, for instance, with regard to the rights of indigenous peoples. Without affording full guarantees for their cultural rights, including the right not to assimilate and the right to cultural autonomy, the

protection offered to indigenous peoples by other rights can become practically meaningless. As Rodolfo Stavenhagen states:

"Only if collective ethnic minority rights are recognized as such, and specifically as human rights, can such communities survive in environments that are often hostile to their very existence and survival . . . If minority cultures have any role to play in the contemporary world, then their rights must be actively fostered and not only passively and reluctantly protected. Insofar as this is a question of human rights, only the minority ethnics themselves should be empowered to decide if or to what extent they want their cultures, societies, values and identities to survive in a rapidly changing world."

199. Devoting more attention to cultural rights may lay the foundation for dealing more constructively with issues such as: the system of cultural integration contrasted to policies of multiculturalism; the relationship between the rapidly advancing internationalization of culture and the right to maintain cultural autonomy; how foreign forces often quash cultural rights in territories they occupy, seeking to substantiate control, including cultural domination; the impact of population transfer upon the enjoyment of cultural rights; and the negative effects of disavowing cultural attributes in the development process. Preventing the expression of cultural rights, through limitations on religious practices, language, wearing traditional clothing, housing and in the education sphere, not only denies the exercise of a core human right, but also tends to create social tension and disarray.

200. The relationship between the expression of culture and the full realization of additional, economic and social, rights has been recognized both in the context of the right to food and the right to adequate housing as constituting a key component in the definition and eventual fulfillment of these rights. The study on the right to adequate food as a human right explicitly stated that "food must be . . . culturally adequate in the context of prevailing food patterns." Whereas General Comment No. 4 on the Right to Adequate Housing, adopted in 1991 by the Committee on Economic, Social and Cultural Rights, expressed the principle in the context of defining housing adequacy:

The way housing is constructed, the building materials used and the policies supporting these must appropriately enable the expression of cultural identity and diversity of housing. Activities geared towards development or modernization in the housing sphere should ensure that the cultural dimensions of housing are not sacrificed and that they should ensure, inter alia, modern technological facilities, as appropriate.

201. Though political, economic and development processes often ride roughshod over cultural heritage, cultural practices and the like, the time for the human rights community to take a stand supporting the right to culture is surely upon us. The relationship of culture to people being able to live a life of dignity and self-respect is beyond any dispute. Likewise, the cultural manifestations of many additional human rights, including food and housing, are clear. Rights associated with culture require inclusion into the human rights programme of the United Nations, international development policies and global economic processes.

V. RECOMMENDATIONS

. . .

C. Recommendations concerning States

218. The Special Rapporteur believes that, in accordance with the resolutions of the General Assembly and the Commission on Human Rights, States which have not yet done so should be encouraged to ratify the International Covenant on Economic, Social and Cultural Rights and other relevant international instruments. Corresponding legislation, policies and programmes should be adopted accordingly and the process of implementation strengthened. In this connection, special attention should be given to the Limburg Principles on the Implementation of the International Covenant on Economic, Social and Cultural Rights.

219. States parties to the International Covenant on Economic, Social and Cultural Rights should attach particular importance to the preparation of their reports in accordance with Articles 16 and 17 of the Covenant and taking into account the revised general guidelines on reporting and the general comments prepared by the Committee on Economic, Social and Cultural Rights.

220. The reporting obligation should be utilized as a process through which the realization of economic, social and cultural rights can be assisted. The various functions and phases of the reporting process, such as initial review, monitoring, policy formulation, public scrutiny, evaluation, identification of problems and exchange of information, should be pursued in a systematic and coherent manner. Preparation of reports should be timely and used as a means for streamlining policies related to the realization of economic, social and cultural rights.

221. The widest possible participation by citizens, community-based organizations and non-governmental organziations should be encouraged by States in the process of preparing and discussing the reports. These reports should be widely publicized within the States parties to the Covenant, with a view to promoting national dialogue as well as allowing citizens to examine the reports. Excerpts from States' reports should be disseminated through the mass media as a means of facilitating greater public involvement in the reporting process.

222. The reports should provide a coherent picture of the status of the realization of economic, social and cultural rights in each reporting State. In this context, particular attention should be paid to the development and analysis of coherent sets of economic and social indicators, the establishment of "benchmarks" of progress and of appropriate methods of legislative and policy review.

223. The emerging principle that minimum core obligations concerning economic, social and cultural rights exist and should be identified has to be promoted in the reporting process with the view to ensuring the satisfaction of basic levels of achievement of each of the rights enshrined in the International Covenant on Economic,

Social and Cultural Rights. In this connection, particular attention should be paid to General Comment No. 3 (1990) on the nature of States parties' obligations (art. 2, para. 1 of the Covenant) of the Committee on Economic, Social and Cultural Rights.

224. States should establish, whenever possible, appropriate judicial or administrative review mechanisms concerning economic, social and cultural rights. The identification of core obligations of States regarding these rights should facilitate justiciability of those economic, social and cultural rights which cannot, as yet, be considered justiciable in all States.

225. All relevant policies, legislation and programmes should be adapted, as appropriate, by States parties to reflect each State's international obligations concerning economic, social and cultural rights. Within pertinent ministries, specific programmes should be developed placing explicit emphasis upon strategies, methods and means for the realization of economic, social and cultural rights.

226. In accordance with the obligations arising from the Covenant and from other instruments in the field of economic, social and cultural rights, patterns of public spending should be analysed by States parties. This should include an in-depth consideration of the four relevant ratios suggested in the *Human Development Report* (1991), namely the public expenditure ratio, the social allocation ratio, the social priority ratio and the human expenditure ratio. Efforts should be made by States to achieve a rate of 5 percent within the human expenditure ratio, that is to say 5 percent of national income should be diverted to human priority concerns. Public spending must be consistent with the degree to which economic, social and cultural rights remain unrealized in a given country.

227. Practical measures aimed at reducing income disparity should be taken by States as a fundamental means for ensuring society-wide enjoyment of economic, social and cultural rights. Sustained and dedicated efforts are necessary to distribute more fairly both land and wealth within a designated society, in particular to benefit disadvantaged groups. It is important to note, in this connection, that there is a clear correlation between the enjoyment of economic, social and cultural rights and systems which seek to ensure an equitable distribution of income. Convincing efforts should also be made by States to increase the percentage of public revenues derived from measures of taxation (currently, some 10 percent in developing countries and over 30 percent in industrialized countries) and to promote the realization of economic, social and cultural rights.

228. In pursuit of the policy objectives mentioned in the preceding paragraphs, States should pay particular attention to the most disadvantaged groups and the extremely poor. In this connection, it is necessary to bear in mind that extreme poverty leads to the exclusion of the affected persons and to their consequent inability fully to realize their human rights. States should develop appropriate strategies aimed at reducing and ultimately eradicating extreme poverty. Such strategies should be the subject of wide public debate and be implemented at all levels including, in particular, the local level.

229. In the context of economic adjustment or stabilization measures, whether carried out alone or in cooperation with the international financial institutions, States should ensure that socially disadvantaged groups do not suffer disproportionately from the measures employed. The human impact of adjustment, particularly measures affecting the enjoyment of economic, social and cultural rights, should be subject to systematic review. Targeted subsidies, social safety nets and other compensatory measures, consistent with "adjustment with a human face" and measures for poverty alleviation and eradication, should be applied.

230. International cooperation and assistance represent an important potential for strengthening the policies and programmes of the developing countries aiming at a higher level of realization of economic, social and cultural rights. It is necessary to examine continuously existing policies of development assistance with a view to expanding the proportion of development assistance committed to human priority areas and social sectors. The *Human Development Report* (1990) offers particularly useful guidance in that regard. In the context of further evaluation of development assistance policies consideration should be given to the need for debt relief, where necessary, and for debt reductions for developing countries based, inter alia, on the global commitment to the realization of economic, social and cultural rights.

. . .

Chapter 2

The Right to Adequate Housing (excerpts)

. . .

8. The Special Rapporteur's working paper (1992) focused primarily on what he recognized as the primary causes of the global housing crisis and various legal issues relating to the human right to adequate housing. The principal reasons for the still widespread denial of housing rights throughout the world, according to the Special Rapporteur, were (i) the failures of government and development policies; (ii) housing discrimination; (iii) environmental health, disasters and housing; (iv) the withholding of information crucial to housing; (v) exploitation in the housing sphere; (vi) speculation and the commoditization of housing; (vii) forced evictions; (viii) armed conflict; (ix) the criminalization of housing; (x) structural adjustment programmes and debt; (xi) poverty and the deprivation of means; and (xii) the perpetuation of homelessness (E/CN.4/Sub.2/1992/15, paras. 22–57).

9. The Special Rapporteur's first progress report (E/CN.4/Sub.2/1993/15) provided a detailed legal analysis of the legal obligations of States to respect, protect and fulfill housing rights, resulting in the development of a synthesis of governmental obligations based on international legal standards. The first progress report also touched on the question of justiciability of housing rights and gave an overview of housing right jurisprudence.

10. One of the main misperceptions that the work on housing rights is subject to, and which is readily cited by those that do not accept the right to adequate housing as a human right, is that such acceptance would mean that every individual would start demanding a house, and that the resources at the disposal of States would be totally insufficient to meet such a demand. The Special Rapporteur has refuted such a narrow interpretation of the human rights approach in the following manner.

11. The Special Rapporteur submits that the legal recognition and obligations inherent in housing rights, at the most basic level, do not imply the following:

(a) That the State is required to build housing for the entire population;

Final report submitted by Mr. Rajindar Sachar, Special Rapporteur to the Sub-Commission on Prevention of Discrimination Against Minorities, E/CN.4/Sub.2/1995/12. Original footnotes omitted.

(b) That housing is to be provided free of charge by the State to all who request it;

(c) That the State must necessarily fulfill all aspects of this right immediately upon assuming duties to do so;

(d) That the State should exclusively entrust either itself or the unregulated market to ensuring this right to all; or

(e) That this right will manifest itself in precisely the same manner in all circumstances or locations.

Of course, qualifications must be made to some of these perspectives so that States do not misinterpret and abrogate State responsibility, particularly for highly disadvantaged groups such as the homeless, the disabled, victims of riots or ethnic strife, man-made and natural disasters and other groups unable to fulfill their housing rights on their own.

12. Conversely, the fundamental necessity of an adequate place to live in peace, dignity and security is such that a recognition of housing rights must be seen and interpreted, in the most general sense, to imply the following:

(a) That once such obligations have been formally accepted, the State will endeavour by all appropriate means possible to ensure everyone has access to housing resources adequate for health, well-being and security, consistent with other human rights;

(b) That a claim or demand can be made upon society for the provision of or access to housing resources should a person be homeless, inadequately housed or generally incapable of acquiring the bundle of entitlements implicitly linked with housing rights; and

(c) That the State, directly upon assuming legal obligations, will undertake a series of measures which indicate policy and legislative recognition of each of the constituent aspects of the right in question.

13. In his second progress report (1994), with a view to clarifying the nature of the right to adequate housing and the still common neglect of this norm, the Special Rapporteur outlined several misconceptions and misinterpretations of the right to adequate housing which continue to hinder efforts to fulfill this right in a universal sense. These are: (1) social housing is invariably suspect; (2) national wealth increases home ownership; (3) housing rights are less fundamental than property rights; (4) the private sector or the market will guarantee housing for all; (5) legislative recognition of housing rights is sufficient to ensure the realization of these rights; (6) housing rights are non-justiciable; (7) most housing is built by the public and private commercial sector; (8) measuring homelessness is impossible; (9) squatters are criminals; (10) housing is a problem only in the developing countries; (11) public expenditure on housing is sufficient; and (12) the right to adequate housing is unrelated to other social concerns (E/CN.4/Sub.2/1994/20, paras. 17–45).

14. The report also sought to remove the misconception of the lack of resources as an impediment to achieving housing rights. It is important to bear in mind that according

to UNCHS, about US$ 75 billion are required to meet the needs in housing. In that context reference may be made to the *1993 Report on the World Social Situation* which analyses government expenditure on, inter alia, housing in both developing and developed countries. While government expenditure on housing in developing countries rose slightly in 1990 compared to 1980, the proportion devoted to this sector remained on the whole low, increasing from 2.94 percent in 1980 to only 3.32 percent of the overall government outlays in 1990. Comparatively, government expenditure in 1990 for health amounted to 6.42 percent, nearly double that allocated to housing, while education received nearly 15 percent of public funds.

15. The plea of lack of resources sounds hollow in view of the finding of the United Nations Development Programme in 1992 that only a 3 percent reduction in arms expenditure per year during the 1990s would make available by the year 2000 an amount of US$ 1.2 trillion for the industrialized countries and an amount of $279 billion for the developing countries.

16. The Special Rapporteur began his mandate three years ago with the hope that the debate in the Subcommission might persuade Governments to show an enriched understanding of the human right to adequate housing, and, much more importantly, might lead to the taking of steps by all relevant actors towards eradicating the inestimable human suffering which so often goes hand in hand with the deprivation of housing rights. Unfortunately, the Special Rapporteur has all too little good news to report to the Subcommission, and is alarmed as ever at the ongoing, and in many cases systematic, violation of the housing rights of the growing underclass of humanity who are now so routinely ignored. We hear reports daily of growing economies, liberalization of trade regimes, globalization of the world market and other such fancy phrases, as if such things were all that mattered in our world and these issues were inherently good for humanity. Sadly, the Special Rapporteur can only express dismay at the enduring and rapidly growing despair of the world's least advantaged citizens as the rights which were meant to be bestowed upon them are increasingly denied or ignored. Such a state of affairs is evident in the next section in which the Special Rapporteur reviews his activities over the past year and takes stock of the developments within the United Nations system regarding housing rights.

Recent developments on housing rights

. . .

36. With specific reference to South Africa, the Special Rapporteur has received information on the results of a workshop on economic and social rights held in Johannesburg in April 1995 devoted to developing means of including—in a fully justiciable way—economic and social rights in the new South African Constitution. Special attention was given to formulating the right to adequate housing within the new constitution in a manner reflecting popular aspirations for a dignified life and which would be subject to judicial enforcement. The workshop framed a draft article on housing rights

for the consideration of the legislators, illustrating the fundamental proposition that economic and social rights can be included in the new Constitution in a manner such that they become rights of substance rather than unenforceable promises. The draft article reads as follows:

"Every person shall have the right to adequate housing, which shall include but is not limited to:

(a) Security of tenure and protection against arbitrary, unreasonable, punitive or unlawful eviction;

(b) Equitable access to appropriate land, services, building materials and amenities;

(c) Equitable access to credit, subsidies and financing on reasonable terms for disadvantaged households;

(d) Special measures to ensure adequate housing for households with special needs or lacking necessary resources;

(e) Provision of appropriate emergency housing where necessary."

. . .

A. The right to housing and women's rights

45. The Special Rapporteur has in an earlier report briefly mentioned the importance, in all areas of housing rights, of recognizing and promoting the critical role of women. From all information available to the Special Rapporteur it is abundantly clear that women across the world continue to suffer from discrimination in the attainment of all aspects of the right to housing: land security and inheritance of rights to land and property; access to credit facilities; access to information essential for participation in housing activities and in contributing to the improvement of the living environment; availability of essential housing services and resources including potable water, sanitation, fuel and fodder and access to appropriate housing projects, upgrading schemes and resettlement areas.

46. The issue of land security is of primary importance. It is clear that in most countries of the world women have neither a right to the home in which they were born nor to the home they live in after marriage. This essential homelessness of women is a major factor in limiting the valuable contribution women can make in gaining and retaining a home and, in turn, in building society. Even in countries where inheritance laws and laws governing rights to home ownership and security of tenure have changed, women are seldom able to exercise these rights. This has a debilitating affect, even leading to the conclusion that the most critical factor in the perpetuation of gender inequality and poverty is the continued discrimination faced by women in all matters of land and property.

47. In addition to the inequities of land ownership, women also continue to be the hardest hit by evictions and inadequate resettlement. As has been pointed out in a report of the Secretary-General to the Commission on the Status of Women, "Resettlement

and evictions should be avoided, since they particularly increase the vulnerability of women and children and because women bear the brunt of traumatized and dislocated communities."

48. In many parts of the world the growing energy crisis has also created unsustainable hardships for women who have to spend more and more of what could be productive time collecting water, fuel and fodder. During the past two decades the energy crisis has deepened and the availability of essential natural resources has declined owing to the adoption of models of economic growth that discriminate against women. This situation calls for a concerted effort by all concerned authorities.

49. The Special Rapporteur has stressed in his reports that gaining and securing the right to housing can lead to the attainment of other rights and create possibilities for the improvement of the living environment. As the Commission on the Status of Women has stated "Security of tenure promotes greater participation of women in community management. The feeling of belonging encourages investment in the improvement not only of the dwelling units but also the neighbourhood as a whole . . . This in turn, helps households escape the poverty trap and has a positive effect on the upbringing of children."

B. Children and housing rights

50. The physical and social development of children is closely linked to the environment in which they grow up and the living conditions they have to confront. The child's self-confidence and identity depends significantly on having access to a place to live in security and dignity. The absence of these conditions leads to the child being deprived of many basic rights such as the right to health, education, protection from economic exploitation and abuse and the right to a legal identity and citizenship. In a world where poverty and marginalization of vulnerable groups are on the rise the Special Rapporteur would like to stress the particular importance of the right to adequate housing for children. Particularly important is the need to focus on the structural causes in societies that are leading to the disintegration of family structures and the growing phenomenon of street children.

51. Recent developments in the United Nations system demonstrate the utility of the housing rights approach in addressing the basic survival and livelihood questions confronting different sectors of society. The Special Rapporteur is particularly encouraged by the adoption by the Subcommission at its forty-sixth session of resolution 1994/8, entitled "Children and the right to adequate housing." The Special Rapporteur welcomes, in particular, the linkage made in the resolution between housing rights, the prevalence of inadequate living conditions and the continued existence of widespread poverty. The resolution also makes the valuable point that "one of the areas where the indivisibility and interdependence of human rights and of the rights of children becomes most apparent is with respect to the existence of widespread poverty leading to inadequate housing and living conditions."

52. The Special Rapporteur is also encouraged by the clear recommendations set forth in the resolution to various entities concerned with the rights of children such as Governments, UNICEF and the Committee on the Rights of the Child. Given the importance that the Special Rapporteur has all along attached to the primacy of action by affected groups themselves, the resolution makes a welcome departure in insisting on the full participation of children themselves in the development of effective strategies for improving the housing and living conditions of children.

C. Land rights and the right to food

53. The Special Rapporteur has attempted in his reports to project the right to housing as a central aspect of the bundle of rights that protect the survival and livelihood of people and communities. For millions of people all over the world especially in rural areas, land is the principal resource for survival. This dependency on land is not limited to tribal or indigenous populations but encompasses small and marginal farmers and the rural agricultural labour that depends on land for livelihood. The failure by Governments to either adopt land reforms or implement the existing statutes, and the failure to arrest speculation and the commercialization of land, has resulted in a situation today where evictions, landlessness and homelessness are on the increase. Extensive studies demonstrate that particular groups are severely affected by the lack of access to land rights and the life-giving value of the attainment of these rights.

54. The Special Rapporteur sees land as being a basic housing resource and views land and housing rights as congruent entitlements. When housing is viewed as the right to a place to live in security and dignity (as international legal developments in recent years have done) it necessarily encompasses security of tenure and equitable access to land resources. The violations that affect access and entitlement to land also have an impact upon housing security and are among some of the most important causes of homelessness. The Special Rapporteur would like to argue that the two rights need to be viewed holistically and that a deeper understanding of their inherent linkages is necessary to strengthen the policy and legal interventions necessary to promote these essential survival and livelihood rights.

55. The denial of housing and land rights through the destruction of the natural resource base, the prevalence of forced evictions and the existence of inadequate resettlement and compensation policies reduces people and communities to a state of landlessness and homelessness that leads to hunger and malnutrition. The right to food or, as has been better expressed, the right to feed oneself, is therefore critically linked to the right to housing.

D. The right to health and the right to housing

56. The Special Rapporteur, indicated in his working paper that one of the causes of the global housing crisis was the continued existence of inadequate housing and living

conditions that lead to serious ill-health and daily problems of survival. In 1995, at the time of writing, the situation has, according to all available sources, not changed and if anything worsened. The *1995 World Health Report* of the World Health Organization is a telling testimony to the continued threat facing millions of the world's dwellers faced with the ravages of increasing poverty, lack of access to essential civic services (particularly potable water and sanitation) and the concomitant increase in disease and epidemics resulting from unhygienic and life-threatening disease conditions.

57. The need for interventions at all levels to remove the obstacles that prevent the existence of adequate housing and living conditions is an imperative facing all levels of society. In an attempt to identify the principles on which such action could be based the Special Rapporteur has found the work of WHO helpful. The principles put forward, for example, in the 1989 WHO publication entitled *Health Principles of Housing*, are useful starting points for devising policy measures to counter inadequate living conditions. In the section on "Principles related to health needs," the relationship between housing conditions and human health are set forth in six major principles: (i) protection against communicable diseases; (ii) protection against injuries, poisonings and chronic diseases; (iii) reducing psychological and social stresses to a minimum; (iv) improving the housing environment; (v) making informed use of housing and (vi) protecting populations at risk.

58. Under the first principle, the following conditions are stressed as being necessary to ensure adequate housing: safe water supply; sanitary excreta disposal; disposal of solid wastes; drainage of surface water; personal and domestic hygiene; safe food protection and structural safeguards against disease transmission. The same report states that "At its best, appropriate housing promotes physical and mental health. It provides people with psychological security, physical ties with their community and culture, and a means of expressing their individuality." The Special Rapporteur affirms these views that are in full conformity to the human rights approach and define the indivisible relationship between the right to health and the right to housing.

E. The human right to adequate housing and the indivisibility of all human rights

59. Throughout his mandate, the Special Rapporteur has stressed the indivisibility and interdependence of all human rights, while placing emphasis upon discussing the inherent, indispensable and permeable relationship between the full enjoyment of the right to adequate housing and certain civil and political rights. The Special Rapporteur is convinced that a wide range of civil and political rights will be compromised in the absence of measures geared towards respecting, protecting and ensuring the right to adequate housing. Conversely, violations of many civil and political rights have a direct bearing upon the enjoyment of housing rights. The examples of regional and international housing rights case-law contained in earlier reports of the Special Rapporteur exemplify the congruous nature of housing rights and civil and political rights. The indicators presented in this report also demonstrate the clear linkage between the two sets of rights.

60. It is now indisputable that rights including the right to privacy, the right to family life, the right to equal protection and benefit of the law, the right to gender equality, the right to be free from discrimination, the right to due process of law, the right to security of the person, the right to freedom of movement and the freedom to choose one's residence, the right to free association, the right to freedom of expression, the right to property, the right to remain in place, the right to seek, receive and impart information and other rights are intrinsically linked to the full realization of the right to adequate housing. To separate these rights from housing rights, as some conservative commentators have sought to do, undermines the principles of indivisibility and interdependence and disregards the fact that there are as many "negative" obligations incumbent upon States vis-à-vis housing rights as there are "positive" State duties.

61. While much can be said on this issue, the Special Rapporteur would like to simply reiterate the necessity of all human rights institutions, adjudicating bodies, Governments, non-governmental organizations and other relevant actors to consider fully and internalize the inherent linkage between the many human rights that have a direct impact upon housing rights.

III. Clarifying and Detailing the Justiciability of the Human Right to Adequate Housing

. . .

95. Based on the detailed analysis of the human right to adequate housing carried out by the Special Rapporteur since 1992, coupled with recent developments in this area, the following elements of this right must be viewed as inherently justiciable, whether in national, regional or international settings:

(a) Protection against arbitrary, unreasonable, punitive or unlawful forced evictions and/or demolitions;

(b) Security of tenure;

(c) Non-discrimination and equality of access in housing;

(d) Housing affordability and accessibility;

(e) Tenants' rights;

(f) The right to equality and equal protection and benefit of the law;

(g) Equality of access to land, basic civic services, building materials and amenities;

(h) Equitable access to credit, subsidies and financing on reasonable terms for disadvantaged groups;

(i) The right to special measures to ensure adequate housing for households with special needs or lacking necessary resources;

(j) The right to the provision of appropriate emergency housing to the poorest section of society;

(k) The right to participation in all aspects of the housing sphere;

(l) The right to a clean environment and safe and secure habitable housing.

96. The Special Rapporteur is therefore more than convinced that the right to adequate housing can be legally enforced against the States which are not fulfilling their obligations as mentioned above. The Special Rapporteur also believes that States must ensure the provision of domestic remedies for each of these fundamental aspects and core contents of the human right to adequate housing.

. . .

VII. Conclusions

144. Throughout his mandate, the Special Rapporteur has sought to identify, clarify and elaborate the legal sources of the human right to adequate housing under international law with a view to promoting the full realization of this right for all. The reports submitted to the Subcommission have shown beyond any doubt that this right exists widely throughout the body of international human rights law, as well as within a large number of national constitutions and domestic legislation. While specifics may differ among States, there can be no doubting that every nation has one or another degree of obligation to respect, protect and fulfill this right under law.

145. In many respects, this is perhaps the most important conclusion to be drawn from this study for it profoundly indicates that far too few Governments and other influential actors have acted upon the fundamental human right to adequate housing in a manner sufficiently reflecting the obligations associated with that right. While we must recognize both the inherent equality of all nations, peoples and citizens under international law in conjunction with our bountiful differences, which should only enrich a tolerant humanity, housing rights must be seen to transcend political distinctions of left and right, North and South, urban and rural areas, women and men, young and old and any other categorization. Housing rights belong to every child, every woman and every man and must be understood and acted upon with the same conviction, the same fortitude and the same determination everywhere.

146. An understanding of the clearly universal relevance and applicability of the human right to adequate housing should move all of us to do more to ensure that all people, everywhere, are guaranteed their legitimate right to housing as defined under international human rights law. Governments must do more, the United Nations must do more, the financially well-endowed must do more and civil society must do more; do more to halt housing rights violations, do more to protect the weakest and most vulnerable among us, do more to ensure the basic necessities of life and livelihood to all and do more to find and grasp the most effective means of guaranteeing an adequate place in which to live in peace, security and dignity.

147. Achieving this right for all within the foreseeable future is by no means beyond our common reach. If the world as a whole remains inadequately housed this will not

be due simply to a lack of resources, deficient finances or insufficient land or materials, as is so often argued today. Rather, it will be a continuation of the misguided status quo, a tragically inequitable distribution of income and resources within and between nations, an attachment to the fiction of the all-providing market, the treatment of housing as a dispensable commodity and the ongoing marginalization of economic, social and cultural rights that will be responsible for creating conditions such that more than 1 billion persons continue to languish without an adequate home, and live their lives with increasingly less likelihood of ever attaining their housing rights.

148. In his four reports the Special Rapporteur attempted to identify some of the conceptual, political and legal hurdles which have obstructed and continue to obstruct the enjoyment of this right by some one fifth of humanity. Some of the key causes of the global housing crisis were distinguished, as were a series of common misperceptions of housing and housing rights. The identification of these contributing factors to the denial of the human right to adequate housing were outlined in order to discern constructive ways and means of ending housing rights violations and of promoting the realization of this right. Indeed, viable solutions are both realistic and attainable.

149. The past several years have witnessed some important advances in the global struggle for housing rights: new housing rights legislation has appeared in several countries; some new or revised national Constitutions have enshrined the right to adequate housing; resolutions reaffirming this right have been adopted by several United Nations bodies; popular campaigns, often eloquently demanding housing rights, have emerged in nearly all of the world's regions; significant court rulings have protected housing rights, in the process creating important jurisprudence from a diverse range of adjudicating bodies, both internationally and nationally; some planned or pending housing rights violations were prevented before they occurred; an enriched housing rights literature has been produced; and, to a degree, we can note a nascent housing rights culture within the human rights community. These small yet meaningful strides are welcomed by the Special Rapporteur and it is sincerely hoped that future years will see the emergence of much expanded attention to this long under-emphasized human right by all relevant actors.

150. Despite these steps forward, how much has really improved during the past few years as far as housing rights are concerned? Has the world progressed or regressed? Are more people in full possession of their housing rights than ever before or have these rights been too often neglected or forgotten?

151. The Special Rapporteur deeply regrets that housing rights have unjustifiably remained a sadly empty promise for far too many people. In a growing number of countries more homes are actually destroyed each year than are built. The numbers of homeless persons continues to grow, whether in the streets of Brussels, Bombay, Budapest, Buenos Aires or Bangkok. Forced evictions continue to displace brutally many millions of persons from their homes year after year. So-called development projects are all too often praised and prioritized without critique, even when human rights violations take place in the process. National budgets devoted to housing those most

in need continue to decline and public expenditure on housing for the upper or middle classes all too often take precedence over homes for the poor. Unmerciful armed conflicts in dozens and dozens of nations have led to the massive destruction of homes and properties, and to millions of blameless residents being made homeless and forced to flee their dwellings and lands either as internally displaced persons or refugees. Blatant discrimination continues to be directed at certain ethnic, racial, indigenous, national and other groups and peoples, in the process actively denying them their lawful rights to dwell in peace and security. The slums of the world continue to grow, seemingly without end, and preventable deaths due entirely to man-made deprivation, destitution and abysmal housing and living conditions unnecessarily take away the lives of tens of millions of persons every year. More and more, women, children, minorities, the poor and the marginalized are effectively (and literally) left by the wayside of what is cleverly but callously passed off as "progress" and "development."

152. Virtually everyone reading this document will have no visible housing rights difficulties or housing discomforts to report. Indeed, those who are well housed—those of us who enjoy our housing rights—all too often fail to acknowledge our fortunate circumstances. We know where we will sleep tonight. We know where we will live tomorrow. We know where we will enjoy our rest and spend time with our friends and families. We know we will be protected from the oncoming storm and that our homes most likely protect, rather than harm, our health. We know we have somewhere to call home. We have somewhere to dwell. If we choose, we can simply take solace in our good fortune, enjoy it, improve it and leave it at that. However, to relax in our safe and comfortable dwellings—with our housing rights met—while a growing portion of humanity lives in perpetual insecurity and desperation might neither be the most ethical nor the wisest of paths to pursue.

153. The terrain is immense, the problems extraordinary and the millions affected are desperately yearning for interventions that will give them the chance to empower themselves. The housing rights approach is perfectly suited to tackling the gross violations that people facing inadequate housing and living conditions are at present confronted with. The Special Rapporteur's reports have attempted to show amply that the right to adequate housing is a basic human right, constituting a cornerstone right in the struggle being waged for survival and livelihood by people and communities across the world. Much more remains to be done and ways and means must be found by the United Nations to continue and expand the focus on this critical human right. The United Nations human rights programme must play a leadership role in such endeavours. In one sense the debate has really only just begun. It is the sincere hope of the Special Rapporteur that his contribution has highlighted both the substantial loss of dignity, skills and identity resulting from continued violations of the right to adequate housing and the promise inherent in this right as an empowering process for people and communities everywhere.

154. The conception of housing rights permeating the reports of the Special Rapporteur offers an alternative pedagogy, at once indigenous and modern, existential and liberating. The housing rights process provides a continuum between community,

nature and culture, embodying the assertion of a space and place rooted in the common human urge to be able to dwell somewhere in security and dignity. In the currently turbulent flux threatening to overtake issue-based struggles, any community empowered to assert its right to livelihood, housing and a secure existence is that much better off. The human right to adequate housing offers one such path, taking on a powerfully unifying meaning if it is recognized as a catalyst for social transformation—one that cuts across class, racial and ideological barriers.

VIII. Recommendations

155. The Special Rapporteur would like to conclude with a series of recommendations directed to a wide range of actors, each of whom can take meaningful steps to promote and ensure the full enjoyment of housing rights for everyone. The Special Rapporteur is convinced that the issues elaborated in this section are attainable and, indeed, crucial, if the right to adequate housing is to provide the necessary protection to the large part of humanity that is denied that right.

156. The following recommendations are directed to: States; States parties to the Covenant on Economic, Social and Cultural Rights; the United Nations human rights programme; the human rights treaty bodies; regional human rights organs; United Nations specialized agencies; other United Nations bodies; regional organizations; world conferences; and non-governmental and community-based organizations.

1. States

157. In accordance with resolutions adopted by the General Assembly and a wide range of relevant United Nations bodies, and as reaffirmed by the World Conference on Human Rights in the Vienna Declaration and Programme of Action, States which have not done so should ratify all international human rights treaties enshrining the right to adequate housing.

158. States should seek to reaffirm consistently the fundamental nature of the basic human right to adequate housing as recognized throughout international human rights law. Simultaneously, States should refrain from drawing up and adopting policies that arise from viewing housing as exclusively a "need" or "aspiration" or in any way detracting from the human rights dimensions of the right to adequate housing.

159. When addressing housing rights issues within any international forum, States should ensure that approaches are taken which are fully consistent with the international legal status of this right. In this regard, States should ensure that any statements made at international gatherings by delegations on behalf of their respective national Governments do not conflict with the fundamental nature of the human right to adequate housing. Specifically, States should ensure that positive action is taken regarding housing rights within the context of the Habitat II World Conference on Human Settlements, scheduled for June 1996, and that no retrograde steps are taken regarding these rights.

160. States parties should consider undertaking nationwide education campaigns promoting greater public awareness (both within the Government and throughout civil society) of the provisions of all international instruments that contain the right to housing and related rights.

161. States should seek to fully integrate the contents of General Comment No. 4 on the right to adequate housing (art. 11.1 of the Covenant on Economic, Social and Cultural Rights) into the relevant national legislative and policy domains.

162. With a view to clarifying, refining and strengthening the human right to adequate housing, all States proceeding with the elaboration of new, revised or amended national Constitutions, should give due attention to including housing rights provisions in these texts. The same principle should apply during the legislative process regarding any new or revised laws with a bearing in any way on the full realization of this right. In this regard, the adoption of comprehensive national housing rights acts should be positively contemplated by States.

163. Relevant national ministries, including housing, planning, environment, social welfare, industry, finance and others, in carrying out policy and implementing statutory duties should ensure that the housing rights obligations of the Government are fully complied with.

164. With a view to strengthening international legal standards relevant to the human right to adequate housing, States should give serious consideration to the possible adoption of an international convention on housing rights under the auspices of the United Nations, as addressed in the second progress report of the Special Rapporteur (E/CN.4/Sub.2/1994/20, chap. IX).

165. As far as national legislation, policies, programmes and practices are concerned, States should, at a minimum, ensure that no violations of the right to adequate housing such as those elaborated in the Special Rapporteur's first progress report (E/CN.4/Sub.2/1993/15, para. 144), are allowed to take place. In the event of any housing rights violations, States should undertake all necessary measures to halt any further violations and bring to justice any person(s) responsible for such infringements.

166. In accordance with the undisputed acceptance under international human rights law that forced evictions constitute "gross violations of human rights, in particular the right to adequate housing," States should scrupulously avoid sponsoring, tolerating or actively carrying out forced evictions of any type not in conformity with international human rights law.

167. Local and municipal governments, as public bodies, should pursue policies which are in full conformity with the international legal obligations of the national Government. In particular, local and municipal governments should refrain from sponsoring, tolerating or carrying out forced evictions not in conformity with international human rights law.

168. Development projects that lead to evictions should not be initiated until a full

resettlement policy is in place. Complete rehabilitation, in accordance with international law, must be ensured, taking into account the needs of special groups—women, children and the aged. Rehabilitation policies must ensure, in keeping with the provisions of the right to housing, basic amenities, services and livelihood opportunities.

169. States should ensure that women are guaranteed full equality of treatment regarding any and all aspects of the human right to adequate housing, with particular attention being paid to rights to land and/or property ownership and inheritance that influence decision-making processes.

170. The Special Rapporteur has repeatedly stressed that security of tenure is a cornerstone element of housing rights. States should, therefore, within the shortest possible time-frame, confer legal security of tenure to all persons and communities currently lacking such legal protection. In this regard, due attention should be given to regularizing human settlements where rights to security of tenure are not in place.

171. States that have not done so should prepare detailed and public assessments of the material reality of housing conditions and trends in their countries such that accurate housing policies and programmes can evolve. One manner of achieving this goal is through the periodic preparation of status reports on the state of housing and living conditions throughout the country. In the preparation of all reports and studies reflecting the state of housing and living conditions, the Special Rapporteur urges States to utilize indicators based on the human right to adequate housing.

172. In view of the continuing and massive denial of the right to adequate housing, all States should undertake clearly targeted and concerted action towards eradicating homelessness and inadequate housing conditions in a manner fully consistent with the right to adequate housing as recognized under international human rights law. In this respect, serious consideration should be given by States to the development of national housing rights strategies designed to ensure the enjoyment of housing rights by everyone within the shortest possible time-frame.

173. When developing national housing rights strategies, States should include reference within the strategies to:

(a) How most effectively to limit land and housing speculation in the interests of society-wide enjoyment of housing rights;

(b) The necessity of regulating the market in the manner which most appropriately ensures the full realization of housing rights;

(c) The need for extensive public debate on the strategy prior to adoption which includes the full participation of civil society;

(d) The imperative of the strategy being based on an accurate assessment of the scale of the housing problem in the country, including a clear prioritization to the housing rights of the poorest sectors of society; and

(e) Including within the strategy issues relating to accessible housing finance consistent with the proportion of the population that is yet to realize its housing rights.

174. In terms of implementing national housing rights strategies, which need to be linked to national housing rights acts, States should pursue the creation of statutory authorities on housing for the poor. These authorities should include the representation of NGOs and community-based organizations. All parties, public and private, should be made accountable to this authority. In addition, States should seek to incorporate in the mandate of existing human rights commissions mechanisms designed to prevent, halt or rectify violations of housing rights.

175. All relevant national judiciaries, tribunals, administrative organs and other adjudicating bodies should consider the International Covenant on Economic, Social and Cultural Rights and all other related international obligations generally, as interpretive aides in clarifying and enforcing domestic laws and they should ensure that domestic law is interpreted and applied in a manner that is consistent with that International Covenant and any other relevant ratified treaty.

176. States should give due regard to the provisions contained in article 27 of the Vienna Convention on the Law of Treaties, which provides that States parties may not invoke domestic law as an excuse for avoiding international obligations.

177. States should fully recognize the indispensable role played by civil society, including non-governmental and community-based organizations, throughout the housing process. Consequently, their contributions to the realization of housing rights should be recognized, promoted and ensured by States.

178. To facilitate the implementation of the recommendations that have been outlined above States may consider adopting the right to housing as an organizing principle of State policy and developing a hierarchy of policies that give due prominence to all economic, social and cultural rights.

2. States parties to the International Covenant on Economic, Social and Cultural Rights

179. States parties should undertake to carry out systematic legislative and policy reviews with a view to harmonizing laws and policy with the obligations arising from the provisions in the Covenant. States parties should duly alter any domestic laws clearly incompatible with the housing rights provisions of the Covenant, and should take it fully into account in adopting any new legislation.

180. In this respect, States parties should take into account the fact that many areas of legislation and policy, above and beyond those relating exclusively to housing, have a major bearing upon the degree to which the right of everyone to adequate housing is actually realized.

181. States parties should arrange for training programmes for the judiciary relating to the obligations arising under the Covenant with a view to ensuring the full applicability of the Covenant within domestic legal and judicial systems. Moreover, States parties should ensure that legal remedies relating to complaints based on the rights guaranteed in article 11.1 of the Covenant are available to everyone.

182. When the Committee on Economic, Social and Cultural Rights issues concluding observations to States parties that relate in any manner to the right to adequate housing established in article 11.1, States parties should duly implement any recommendations made to them by the Committee and take fully into account any other views concerning article 11.1 made by the Committee, in accordance with the basic principles of international law.

183. States parties should, in accordance with articles 16 and 17 of the Covenant, submit their reports to the Committee on time. Similarly, States parties should utilize the guidelines prepared by the Committee as a means of organizing their reports. All States reports should be widely publicized within the country prior to their consideration by the Committee. For this purpose the reports should be made directly available to NGOs and the civic society as a whole.

184. Governmental employees from any relevant ministry should be required to receive training and education relating to the housing rights provisions of the Covenant and the State obligations arising from the recognition of these rights.

185. States parties should support the adoption of an optional protocol to the Covenant providing individuals with the right to submit complaints alleging non-compliance with the Covenant to the Committee on Economic, Social and Cultural Rights for its consideration. Once adopted, States parties should ratify the protocol without reservation.

3. The United Nations human rights programme

186. The Subcommission on Prevention of Discrimination and Protection of Minorities should: (a) recommend that the Commission on Human Rights appoint a special rapporteur on housing rights; and (b) request the Secretary-General to compile all comments received from States, United Nations agencies, non-governmental organizations and others concerning the draft convention on housing rights contained in the second progress report and the indicators contained in the final report of the present Special Rapporteur.

187. The Working Group on Indigenous Populations of the Subcommission should be requested to devote sufficient attention to the housing and land rights of indigenous peoples, taking into account the special nature of these rights as far as indigenous peoples are concerned.

188. The Working Group on Communications of the Subcommission should be requested to look into complaints alleging gross and systematic violations of housing rights provisions under international law. Particular attention should be paid in this regard to instances of mass forced evictions, mass deportations, land confiscation, racial discrimination in the housing sphere, significant increases in homelessness or inadequate housing conditions, and so forth.

189. The Commission on Human Rights should, considering the current absence of an explicit Commission mechanism designed to monitor, promote and protect the human right to adequate housing, appoint a special rapporteur on housing rights. All country

rapporteurs of the Commission on Human Rights are encouraged to examine housing rights violations within the framework of their particular mandates.

190. The Special Representative of the Secretary-General on internally displaced persons should examine the fundamental relationship between the right to adequate housing and the rights of internally displaced persons, both as this right relates to the right not to be displaced as a consequence of projects and other alleged developmental programmes without provision having been made for adequate relocation and rehabilitation, and as it pertains to persons already internally displaced.

191. The High Commissioner for Human Rights should, in view of the indivisibility and interdependence of all human rights, more intensively promote economic, social and cultural rights, and should undertake concrete measures towards preventing violations of the human right to adequate housing as well as redressing past violations. In addition, the Special Rapporteur urges the High Commissioner to give specific attention to forced evictions, development-based displacement, indigenous peoples and forced evictions, and to following up any relevant concluding observations of the Committee on Economic, Social and Cultural Rights concerning these matters, where applicable.

192. The Centre for Human Rights should, in the context of its advisory services programme, include in needs assessment reports explicit references to matters and issues relating to the human right to adequate housing. In this respect, expertise should be developed within the advisory services programme on practical measures which could be promoted towards the full realization of the human right to adequate housing in States receiving advisory services. Additionally, the Centre should consider publishing the four reports of the Special Rapporteur in a single document in the relevant publication series.

4. *The human rights treaty bodies*

193. The Committee on Economic, Social and Cultural Rights should consider the development of housing rights indicators revealing and clarifying the core contents of the right to adequate housing. The Committee could also consider adopting a general comment on forced evictions.

194. The Committee on the Elimination of Racial Discrimination should consider adopting a general recommendation on the right to adequate housing as enshrined in article 5 (iii) (e) of the International Convention on the Elimination of All Forms of Racial Discrimination with a view to clarifying the obligations of States parties to the Convention in this respect.

195. The Committee on the Elimination of Discrimination against Women should consider adopting a general recommendation on women and housing rights as this relates to the provisions of article 14.2 of the Convention on the Elimination of All Forms of Discrimination against Women, with a view to clarifying the obligations of States parties to the Convention in this respect.

196. The Committee on the Rights of the Child should, in the light of resolution 1994/8 on children and housing rights of the Subcommission on Prevention of Discrimination and Protection of Minorities and Commission on Human Settlements resolution 15/14 (1995) on concrete measures towards the full realization of children's housing rights, look into the housing rights aspects of the Convention on the Rights of the Child in its examination of reports submitted by States parties and in its interpretive work on the Convention on the Rights of the Child.

197. The Human Rights Committee should, in view of the indivisibility and interdependence of all human rights, consider enhancing its attention to the rights enshrined in the International Covenant on Civil and Political Rights which have a direct bearing upon the enjoyment of the human right to adequate housing, both in the context of examining States reports and with regard to complaints received pursuant to the Optional Protocol to the Covenant.

5. Regional human rights organs

198. The regional human rights organs, in particular the European Court of Human Rights, the European Committee of Independent Experts, the African Commission on Human and People's Rights and the Inter-American Commission and Court of Human Rights should consider adopting interpretive documents elaborating the content and implications of housing rights norms relevant to the organ in question, as established in the legal texts these organs are responsible for overseeing. While considering complaints on issues relating to housing rights these organs should take into account legal developments on those rights as reflected in the relevant instruments of international human rights law.

6. The United Nations specialized and other agencies

199. Many, if not most, of the United Nations specialized and other agencies can play a constructive role in the pursuit of the human right to adequate housing. Indeed, the International Covenant on Economic, Social and Cultural Rights clearly foresees a role for four specialized agencies in the implementation of the Covenant. All relevant United Nations agencies should seek to establish, in accordance with their specific areas of competence and expertise, measures clearly designed to promote the human right to adequate housing.

200. The Special Rapporteur would encourage all United Nations agencies, when in possession of information relevant to the enjoyment or non-enjoyment of the human right to adequate housing, to submit such information to the appropriate United Nations human rights mechanism, in particular the Committee on Economic, Social and Cultural Rights, and to the High Commissioner for Human Rights.

201. The International Labour Organization (ILO) should give consideration to revising ILO Recommendation No. 115 on worker's housing in order to bring relevant

ILO standards on housing into line with the current content and interpretation of the human right to adequate housing as established under international law.

202. The United Nations Educational, Scientific and Cultural Organization (UNESCO) should study comprehensively the cultural aspects of the human right to adequate housing and the role played by economic and development policies at national and international levels that have an impact on the skills and identities of people. UNESCO could also initiate a study on the state of national policies and programmes concerned with the survival of diversity in the housing field and the retention of local technology and conservation strategies for meeting energy needs necessary for the protection of housing rights.

203. The World Health Organization (WHO) should continue to expand its attention to the interrelationships between housing and health and develop relevant indicators on the right to health and the right to housing. The WHO Health Principles of Housing are a useful starting point for this initiative.

204. The Food and Agriculture Organization (FAO) should, in keeping with its Constitution, and the provisions of the International Covenant on Economic, Social and Cultural Rights, take effective measures to promote the reform of agrarian systems and of access to land, including the gaining of land rights by smallholders and marginal farmers, with a special focus on the rights of women in these groups. In the pursuit of more equitable land distribution and genuine land reform efforts, FAO should seek to ensure the provision of sustained security of tenure for all landless peasants and farm workers. FAO should consider generating international conventions along these lines, following the example set by ILO regarding people's livelihood opportunities.

205. The United Nations Centre for Human Settlements (UNCHS) (Habitat) should vigorously pursue the full implementation of the UNCHS housing rights strategy (HS/C/15/INF.7), recognizing the importance of generating United Nations-wide support and assistance towards this end. In this respect, the United Nations Centre for Human Settlements should develop expertise relating to the human right to adequate housing, with particular attention being devoted to pursuing active measures geared towards the implementation and enforcement of this right. With specific regard to the World Summit on Human Settlements (Habitat II), both the Commission on Human Settlements and the United Nations Centre for Human Settlements (Habitat) should conscientiously pursue the reaffirmation and strengthening of existing sources of the human right to adequate housing as contained in, inter alia, the Vancouver Declaration on Human Settlements (1976) and the Global Strategy for Shelter to the Year 2000 (1988) and Commission on Human Settlements resolution 14/6 of 5 May 1993, entitled "The human right to adequate housing."

206. The United Nations Children's Fund (UNICEF) should, in the light of resolution 1994/8 ("Children and housing rights") of the Subcommission on Prevention of Discrimination and Protection of Minorities and resolution 15/14 (1995) ("Concrete measures towards the full realization of children's housing rights") of the Commission on Human Settlements, consider devoting attention to the housing rights of children through

the appointment of one or more officials with exclusive competence in this area. Specific and expanded attention should be paid by UNICEF to the housing rights of street children and other children being forced to live in especially vulnerable conditions.

207. The United Nations Research Institute for Social Development (UNRISD) should seek to expand its intensive research programme to include more extensive analysis on human rights issues, including housing rights, relating to its existing programmes on structural adjustment, participatory democracy, indicators, ethnic conflict and social integration.

208. The Office of the United Nations High Commissioner for Refugees (UNHCR) could consider devoting attention to the fulfillment of housing rights, as this is one of the fundamental social-economic rights to be accorded to refugees and internally displaced persons. Such a step would be in conformity with article 21 of the Convention relating to the Status of Refugees and its 1967 Protocol. UNHCR should explore whether housing rights violations could constitute grounds for obtaining refugee status and whether such violations constitute a basis for well-founded fear of persecution.

209. The United Nations Development Programme (UNDP) should include housing rights matters in its Human Development Index and devote substantially more attention than at present to the housing rights issues relevant to its development mandate. Likewise, UNDP should expand its financial assistance to projects designed to promote the enhanced enjoyment of the human right to adequate housing.

210. The World Bank should ensure that any policy, practice, project or programme it supports is not or will not result in any violation of the human right to adequate housing. Specific attention should be paid in this respect to any projects involving the involuntary resettlement of persons from their homes and/or lands. This institution should not in any instance finance projects involving forced evictions of any size, recognizing its dismal record in such practices since its inception. The World Bank should respect articles 55 and 56 of the Charter of the United Nations, which *inter alia* apply to itself, and ensure that it in no manner compromises, either actively or passively, the human rights obligations of States to which it provides financial assistance. Regarding the World Bank's housing policy, a more concerted effort should be made to apply a housing rights approach to such matters, rather than relying so heavily on the provision of housing by the market.

211. The International Monetary Fund (IMF) should respect articles 55 and 56 of the Charter of the United Nations, which inter alia apply to itself, and ensure that it in no manner compromises, either actively or passively, the human rights obligations of States to which it provides financial assistance. In its pursuit of structural adjustment programmes and social safety nets, IMF should ensure that it does not in any way encourage or assist States to violate their existing human rights obligations under international human rights law.

212. The United Nations Volunteers (UNV) should provide training and volunteer efforts on housing rights issues in the implementation of its mandate.

213. The United Nations Statistical Division should develop indicators on housing rights, as proposed in this report by the Special Rapporteur, and include an assessment of the status of housing rights in its documentation.

214. The United Nations Institute for Training and Research (ITAR) should provide training courses on the human right to adequate housing, with a view to promoting the full realization of this right. Where current programmes exist, and where relevant, housing rights modules could be incorporated.

215. The Committee on Human Settlements of the Economic Commission for Europe (ECE) should examine enjoyment of the human right to adequate housing within member countries of ECE.

216. The Economic and Social Commission for Asia and the Pacific (ESCAP) should develop effective mechanisms to monitor State compliance with existing and future housing rights obligations as enshrined in international law, in view of the current absence of a regional human rights treaty in this region.

7. Other United Nations bodies

217. The Special Committee to Investigate Israeli Practices Affecting the Human Rights of the Palestinian People and Other Arabs of the Occupied Territories should devote substantial attention to ongoing violations of the right to adequate housing, particularly those relating to land confiscation, house demolitions, forced evictions, housing-based discrimination and the illegal establishment of Israeli settlements.

218. The Commission on Sustainable Development should seek to apply faithfully the relevant provisions contained in chapter 7 of Agenda 21 and incorporate a housing rights approach in the cross-sectoral programme on human settlements. Particular attention should be paid to ensuring State compliance with chapters 7.6 and 7.9 (b) that recognize the right to housing and the need for legal provision of people against eviction from their homes or lands.

219. The Commission on the Status of Women should consider expanding its work on the discrimination faced by women in their living environment in urban areas (E/CN.6/1994/3) to rural areas. The Commission could consider adopting as a priority theme the impact on women of evictions and other violations of housing and land rights.

8. Regional organizations

220. The Organization of American States (OAS) should pursue the amendment of the Additional Protocol to the American Convention on Human Rights on Economic, Social and Cultural Rights to include an explicit right to adequate housing, consistent with the fact that most OAS member States have recognized this right in their national Constitutions and considering that the overwhelming majority of OAS member States

have ratified other international human rights treaties containing this right. In the interim period, all OAS member States which have not yet done so, should speedily ratify the Additional Protocol. OAS should also seek to expand substantially its activities on economic, social and cultural rights, with due reference to the human right to adequate housing.

221. The Organization of African Unity (OAU) should develop programmes devoted to the full realization of the human right to adequate housing in OAU member States and consider amending the African Charter on Human and People's Rights to include an explicit right to adequate housing.

222. The Council of Europe should ensure the inclusion of the human right to adequate housing in the to be amended European Social Charter, and, to the extent possible, request the European Commission on Human Rights to include housing matters within its areas of competence.

223. The Organization for Economic Cooperation and Development (OECD) should, in the framework of the Development Assistance Committee, seek to promote the full realization of the human right to adequate housing.

224. The Organization for Security and Cooperation in Europe (OSCE) should devote expanded attention to the housing rights clauses in OSCE texts, recognizing the potential instability which can result from widespread denials of housing rights.

9. World conferences

225. The Fourth World Conference on Women, to be held in Beijing in September 1995 should include the reports of the Special Rapporteur among the documents to be made available to the participants. The Summit should include in its conclusions and recommendations explicit targets relating to the full realization of the right to adequate housing for all women.

226. The United Nations Conference on Human Settlements (Habitat II), to be held in June 1996, should reaffirm the fundamental nature of the basic human right to adequate housing, in conformity with Commission on Human Settlements resolution 14/6 of 5 May 1993, and designate specific measures geared towards the full implementation, enforcement and enjoyment of the human right to adequate housing before the year 2000.

. . .

Chapter 3
The Relationship Between the Enjoyment of Human Rights, in Particular Economic, Social and Cultural Rights, and Income Distribution (excerpts)

. . .

Introduction

D. Brief review of the previous reports on income distribution and human rights

13. In the preliminary report (E/CN.4/Sub.2/1995/14) to the Sub-Commission, the Special Rapporteur underlined that income distribution, both internationally and nationally, was the principal indicator of social integration and of the fulfilment of minimum requirements in respect of economic, social and cultural rights, enabling human beings to live in society. The object of this first report, presented in August 1995, was to analyse the relationship between economic, social and cultural rights, income distribution, and equality of opportunities. It was argued that it was necessary to rethink economic, social and cultural rights in an increasingly globalized and intercommunicating world. It was asserted that greater communication between societies would bring growing homogenization of accepted and acceptable "standards" and levels of realization of human rights in general and of economic, social and cultural rights in particular. The first report also contained the guidelines for the future work: (a) analysis of the various forms of economic, political, social and cultural discrimination; (b) analysis of the causes of the gap between rich and poor countries in relation to income distribution; (c) the development of indicators enabling a more detailed analysis of income distribution at the national level; and (d) the search for means of determining how most effectively to strengthen activities in respect of the realization of economic, social and cultural rights. In addition to these elements, the Special Rapporteur

Final report prepared by Mr José Bengoa, Special Rapporteur to the Sub-Commission on Prevention of Discrimination and Protection of Minorities, E/CN.4/Sub.2/1997/9.

willingly endorsed the request of the Sub-Commission to devote special attention to matters related to extreme poverty, the right to development and the right to education.

14. At the forty-eighth session of the Sub-Commission in 1996, the Special Rapporteur presented a progress report (E/CN.4/Sub.2/1996/14) which was divided into five parts. In the Introduction, the report stated that income distribution was an appropriate indicator of the degree of equity or lack of it in a society and of the presence or absence of opportunities within a sector of the population or a geographical area. It was a tool for monitoring the fulfilment of human rights. Part one of the report analysed the issues of income distribution at the international level, and international cooperation and the gap between rich and poor countries. Part two elaborated the issue of income distribution at the national level and included some comparative analysis. Part three investigated the relationship between education, discrimination and income distribution. In this second report, presented in August 1996, an attempt was made to operationalize the concepts of income distribution by presenting data and elaborating an indicator to permit fuller and more complex understanding of the phenomenon. The main objective was to establish different types of income distribution in different types of countries and conditions of development and to relate the question of income distribution, both theoretically and statistically, to poverty. This second report gave an important empirical basis for realization of the analysis in the third report.

15. In the conclusion, the report expanded upon the concept of "equal opportunities" which permits a practical understanding of the relationship between the phenomenon of discrimination and the rights of individuals. In this connection, the Special Rapporteur stated that:

". . . The absence of equal opportunities leads to manifest discrimination and a violation of the rights of individuals. Negative income distribution is one of the forms taken by the lack of equal opportunities, both internationally and nationally" (para. 34).

". . . An equal opportunities policy should involve adequate and additional measures to ensure that the group or sector suffering from discrimination enjoys conditions similar to those of the rest of the population . . . This duty lies with the State, and this is fully stipulated in international instruments" (para. 36).

". . . In the sphere of international cooperation, there is a need for the clearer application of the concept of 'equal opportunities.' In many cases international cooperation has been paternalistic in nature, aims at solving a small or large passing problem, but does not tackle the underlying causes . . ." (para. 38).

16. The object of this third report is to relate the process of globalization of the economy and societies that is occurring at the end of the XX century with the concomitant phenomena of inequity in the distribution of wealth and sharp increases in the phenomenon of poverty. The final objective of the report is to signal the challenges to the human rights system posed by the process of globalization, especially in the field of economic, social and cultural rights.

E. Definitions and perspectives of the report

17. The distribution of wealth in societies can be understood in many modes and manners. The form of distribution of land ownership, for example of agricultural land, was for a long time one of the main criteria for understanding equity or inequity in a given society. Income distribution in agrarian or traditional societies should be analysed principally by the way in which ownership is distributed, and, consequently, by the use of systems of personal services. In modern societies, especially at the end of the last century, it was considered that "ownership of the means of production" was the principal phenomenon and that it affected all aspects of social life and culture. Today it is not uncommonly considered that the most important factor is the way in which cultural goods, knowledge and information are distributed, and the informal networks of relationships between people. Obviously these discussions are absolutely beyond the practical scope of a study on income distribution and human rights. It is for this reason that a definition permitting a much more neutral and operational understanding of the concept has been adopted. By income distribution at the international level we mean the way in which the overall product (the sum of physical production, services and trade) is distributed between the countries of a region or a group of selected countries. Income distribution at the national level in a given society would consist in the way in which the overall product produced by the national economy within a year is distributed between the households that comprise and compose that society. Accumulated capital, properties and knowledge acquired are only taken into account in this operational definition in so far as they represent actual income for the families or households that constitute the unit of analysis.

18. The method of understanding distribution and income at the international level consists simply in comparing a country's annual product with the global product of the region or group of countries in question. At the national level household incomes will determine how the national product is distributed internally. This operational method, used by consensus to measure income distribution, obviously has many limitations in that it does not account for a large number of production, trading and service activities that are not included in the "national accounts" or "household accounts." Semilegal, clandestine or simply illegal and criminal lucrative activities remain outside these accounting systems and in some cases represent substantial shares of the income of both countries and individuals. Some maintain that household income accounting is simpler at the lowest income levels, while at the higher levels it is more difficult because of the complexity and tax avoidance. Thus there are many methodologists who maintain that all income distribution figures are thereby devalued and should be still more concentrated.

19. This operational manner of conceptualizing distribution enables it to be understood whether income is more or less concentrated in a society. The population, the indicator most often used, is divided for this purpose into five quintiles (20% of the population) and various comparisons are made between them. The most common is comparison of the top quintile with the bottom quintile. Because of its neutral and relatively objective nature, most specialists regard this as "a good indicator of equity" and it is currently the one most widely used. Because of its non-value and neutral character,

it is a "relative indicator" valid only for comparative analyses. This indicator is best used with historical series in the same country. Hence it is not possible to say what is the "ideal income distribution," since this will depend on the type of society, the nature of its historical development, and a very complex series of factors.

20. While it is not possible to determine "ideal" income distribution, it is possible to signal when situations are occurring where the high concentration of wealth in a few hands is producing devastating social effects with consequences so serious as to threaten the "social integration" of the society in question, or at the international level, the balance of a given region. "Intolerable levels of income inequality" would arise if there were systematic growth of inequity in a society (or at the international level) with a crude concentration of product in the hands of one group or sector of society. From a human rights perspective, it is generally felt that this would entail violation of the economic, social and cultural rights of the population, incurring permanent discrimination and violation of the fundamental rights of individuals.

21. The overall body of codified documents on human rights is thus the best criterion by which to determine when an economic situation becomes a situation of permanent and persistent violation of the rights of individuals, of their economic, social and cultural rights. Both in theory and in practice, it is possible to establish a distinction between economic behaviour and its evaluation in the perspective of human rights. A particular economy could show positive macroeconomic indicators, for example, growth, inflation, national accounts, exports, etc., notwithstanding the existence within it of "intolerable levels of income inequality," very high degrees of discrimination, social exclusion, and poverty. The rights of individuals established in codified human rights documents thus constitute the only general criterion for the establishment of minimum acceptable or unacceptable standards in economic and social matters at the national and international levels.

22. Income distribution in a society is directly related to existing levels of poverty. This question was analysed in detail in the second report. There are societies in which poverty is generalized and indicators of income distribution, as is logical, show figures of low concentration. In these societies of an agrarian nature, the income indicator is not sufficiently appropriate to cover the concentration of agricultural ownership, and inequality in matters not directly connected with the distribution of product through systems of monetary income. In the industrialized and industrializing societies, however, income concentration always brings relative poverty in the lower group or groups. It has been shown statistically that when there are very sharp increases in income concentration and inequality, immediate outbreaks of poverty occur. This is what has happened in many of the developed countries in the last decade as a consequence of adjustment processes and cutbacks in social programmes. Income concentration leaves one sector of society in a relatively defenceless situation and thus in growing conditions of poverty. Very often these are the same people as the groups subject to most discrimination in societies, either by reason of their sex (women heads of households), age (old people and children), ethnic group (migrants, indigenous peoples and minorities), race or other derived forms of discrimination such as education. Poverty and

destitution are understood in this report as phenomena related and in some cases concomitant with poor international and national income distribution.

I. Globalization and Income Distribution

23. Economic, social and cultural rights should be discussed against the background of the processes of globalization that have been occurring in the world in the last ten years. This is both a theoretical and political challenge as these rights were formulated in a context that was totally different economically and above all politically: the post-war period, the cold war, the existence of a socialist bloc and of competitive capitalism based on strong nation states. Present-day trends in economics and society worldwide are entirely different and require a rethinking of economic, social and cultural rights. As well as postulating their juridical validity and applicability, we therefore signal the need to relocate these rights in the current processes of change.

. . .

IV. Conclusions and Recommendations

A. Conclusions and suggestions

81. Income distribution, in conclusion, has shown itself to be a good indicator of the degree of equity or inequity of a given economy and society at the international and at the national levels. Poor income distribution constitutes a specific type of discrimination that very often aggregates with other discrimination, such as ethnic, gender, race, or minorities who experience discrimination for diverse reasons of language, religion or customs, and has as a consequence the new forms of poverty that are the scourge of the world today. When they attain persistent and permanent levels, poor income distribution and poverty are a violation of the rights of persons, and of their capacity to realize and enjoy the rights established by the international community.

82. The "justiciability" of human rights, and especially of economic, social and cultural rights, is the greatest challenge to the juridical system for the protection of persons at both national and international levels. There has been much advance in the last few years. By "justiciability" we mean the process whereby the rights established in the International Covenants on Human Rights and other instruments may effectively be claimed in courts of justice and public bodies and justice may be administered as in the case of any other right that has been violated. This is an evolving process of the utmost importance. The rights established in the Covenants and international instruments that have been adopted constitute the basic framework to make possible a humanely balanced economic globalization and prevent tendencies to "perverse" globalization from imposing themselves.

83. For economic, social and cultural rights to be adequately exercised the first step consists in ratification of the Covenants and treaties on the rights of workers, and other

instruments of protection. The Special Rapporteur appeals to those countries which have not yet ratified the International Covenant on Economic, Social and Cultural Rights (134 ratifications as at 31 December 1996) to do so. Global ratification and acceptance of the Covenant is fundamental for the improvement of the human condition.

84. The Special Rapporteur would also like to recall that, as stated Part I, paragraph 5, of the Vienna Declaration and Programme of Action, "all human rights are universal, indivisible and interdependent and interrelated. The international community must treat human rights globally in a fair and equal manner, on the same footing, and with the same emphasis" [. . .]. With regard to the contents of this report, special attention should be devoted to the implementation of article 7 on the right of everyone to the enjoyment of just and favourable conditions of work and, *inter alia*, fair wages and equal remuneration for work of equal value. Likewise, the right of everyone to an adequate standard of living, including adequate food, clothing and housing, and to the continuous improvement of living conditions, as set out in article 11 of the Covenant, can be considered as another basic element of a more just society. Article 13 on the right to education and article 15 on, *inter alia*, the right of everyone to enjoy the benefits of scientific progress and its applications bring other important contributions to the debate.

85. Sustainable human development must become the first priority of the international community. The so-called "globalization" of the market risks being an empty word if the benefits of globalization are not shared among all sectors of the population, at the national and the international level. A part of the benefits deriving from economic growth should systematically be reinvested, both nationally and internationally, in human beings. This operation is not a charitable exercise: it is the first step toward the re-establishment of the human being, and not the market, as the first priority. Needless to say, this re-investment in the human being will certainly be beneficial to trade and economic exchanges in general, because it will revive moribund economic activities and will permit more human being-friendly new business to be explored.

86. The report concludes with the need to review and increase the level of international cooperation. The Special Rapporteur appeals to governments, international agencies and nongovernmental organizations to press for free trade agreements and treaties, and multilateral, bilateral, regional and other agreements making for greater globalization of economic relations to include a chapter or special protocol on international cooperation.

87. A strong, almost visionary political will would allow the implementation of article 2 of the Covenant, wherein each State Party undertakes "to take steps, individually and through international assistance and cooperation, especially economic and technical, to the maximum of its available resources, with a view to achieving progressively the full realization of the rights recognized in the Covenant" . . . As it will have been observed in this final report, States are not putting the "maximum available resources" into achieving greater balance in the distribution of income at the international level, and are not always doing so at the national level.

88. The implementation of universally recognized human rights is one of the basic elements of a new way of perceiving international relations, and is linked to the achievement of a more just world. International cooperation must be rebuilt on a new basis: the colonialist, often paternalistic approach must be replaced by a new attitude based on equal partnership wherein all actors are on an equal footing and have the same rights and the same responsibilities. The Special Rapporteur appeals for an increase in international cooperation, in self-sustaining development programmes, training and education of local management capacities.

89. The Special Rapporteur addresses an appeal to the collective and decision-making bodies of the United Nations, governments and specialized agencies, to generate dialogue between countries so that the developed countries (and, some say, the developing countries) attain the target of devoting 0.7 percent of their GDP to international cooperation.

90. Efforts have to be made to ensure that workers in developing countries receive fair remunerations, related to those paid in developed countries, and are not exploited for the mere economic benefit of transnational corporations. Similarly, States should ensure that enterprises operating abroad are not involved in commercial relations based on human rights violations such as bonded labour, child labour and debt bondage. The Special Rapporteur appeals to countries to step up their labour regulation controls to prevent the appearance of new covert forms of slavery. He also appeals to governments that have not ratified the labour conventions of the International Labour Organisation to do so. He appeals to workers' organizations to make use of the machinery of the United Nations system for the protection of human rights, so as not to allow the processes of globalization to be accompanied by a widespread increase in the exploitation of workers and their families.

91. The final report shows that the concepts of "equal opportunities" and "sustainable human development" are closely linked. The concept of "equal opportunities" means giving all human beings a chance to improve their conditions: it does not ensure that everyone's lot will improve, but it should make sure that the destiny of an individual is not predetermined because of his/her social background. There will be no large-scale human development if "equal opportunities" are not guaranteed. Basic human indicators such as life expectancy, adult illiteracy, infant mortality and equality between the sexes must be taken into account in the drafting of economic policies. An effective struggle in favour of the right to education and against extreme poverty will make a substantial contribution to the creation of a system of "equal opportunities." Moreover, societies that are increasingly divided into two blocs, the rich and the poor, could not fully enjoy the benefits of their accomplishments because they will constantly be threatened by social strife and internal turmoil, a situation not conducive to the promotion and observance of human rights.

Chapter 4

The Question of the Impunity of Perpetrators of Human Rights Violations (excerpts)

. . .

I. Preliminary Considerations

18. Article 22 of the Universal Declaration of Human Rights specifies that "Everyone . . . is entitled to realization, through national effort and international cooperation . . . of the economic, social and cultural rights indispensable for his dignity and the free development of his personality." Further to the reference to international cooperation, the International Covenant on Economic, Social and Cultural Rights provides in Article 2, paragraph 1, that "Each State Party to the present Covenant undertakes to take steps, individually and through international assistance and cooperation, especially economic and technical, to the maximum of its available resources, with a view to achieving progressively the full realization of the rights recognized in the present Covenant."

19. The commitment thus made is a guarantee for the legal protection of these rights. While it is true that many studies have been made of economic, social and cultural rights and of collective rights such as the right to development and the right to a healthy environment from the point of view of their history, legal basis, regulation or scope, there have been very few on ways of combating violations of them. Any serious study of the kind will be concerned with giving these rights a definite legal value, the basis for which exists in the numerous relevant international human rights instruments.

20. Before listing some of these instruments and in response to requests by some representatives of States or non-governmental organizations, it is important to outline a definition of the impunity which is the subject of this report. Impunity can be understood as the absence or inadequacy of penalties and/or compensation for massive and

Report submitted by Mr. El Hadji Guissé, Special Rapporteur to the Sub-Commission on the Prevention of Discrimination and Protection of Minorities, E/CN.4/Sub.2/1997/8.

grave violations of the human rights of individuals or groups of individuals. This definition is applicable to civil and political rights, as well as economic, social and cultural rights, and also to collective or communal rights.

21. To be complete and effective, the campaign against impunity must be preceded by a serious and thorough investigation to bring to light the factual sources of the violations and identify the perpetrators and the victims so that the former can be punished and the damage done to the latter can be appropriately remedied.

22. The campaign against impunity should focus on the absence of penalties or compensation and the inadequacy of penalties or compensation already in existence or contemplated. The obligation to protect and promote all human rights includes that to punish and compensate the harm and damage which result from their violation.

23. Numerous international legal instruments incorporate the principle of combating impunity with regard to the violations of economic, social and cultural rights and the right to development. Although the legal framework for the right to a healthy environment is still lacking, that does not prevent it from being included in the existing legal framework. The most important instruments enshrining this principle include the Charter of the United Nations and the Universal Declaration of Human Rights:

(a) The Charter of the United Nations: its Preamble states that the peoples of the United Nations are determined "to reaffirm faith in fundamental human rights" and "to promote social progress and better standards of life in larger freedom." Article 1, paragraph 3, stipulates that one of the Purposes of the United Nations is "to achieve international cooperation in solving international problems of an economic, social, cultural, or humanitarian character, and in promoting and encouraging respect for human rights and for fundamental freedoms for all without distinction as to race, sex, language, or religion." Article 55 adds: "With a view to the creation of conditions of stability and well-being which are necessary for peaceful and friendly relations among nations based on respect for the principle of equal rights and self-determination of peoples, the United Nations shall promote . . . universal respect for, and observance of, human rights and fundamental freedoms for all without distinction as to race, sex, language, or religion";

(b) The Universal Declaration of Human Rights: according to Article 22, everyone "is entitled to realization, through national effort and international cooperation . . . , of the economic, social and cultural rights indispensable for his dignity and the free development of his personality."

24. This principle has been taken up and developed by other international instruments adopted by the United Nations and by the specialized agencies affiliated to it, including:

(a) The International Covenant on Economic, Social and Cultural Rights which, in its Article 2, provides that each State Party to the Covenant, shall undertake to take steps, to the maximum of its available resources, with a view to achieving progressively the full realization of the rights recognized in the Covenant. This commitment means that the State must both ensure effective enjoyment of these rights and establish the legal framework rendering it possible to protect them and punish their violation;

(b) The Proclamation of Tehran of 1968, by which the international community reaffirmed its determination to put an end to gross denials of human rights and to intensify efforts and initiatives at the national and international levels in the area of human rights. The International Conference on Human Rights at Tehran had been the opportunity to review the progress made in protecting human rights since the adoption of the Universal Declaration of Human Rights, to assess the effectiveness of the methods and techniques used and to identify the main obstacles encountered in the area;

(c) The Declaration on the Establishment of a New International Economic Order (General Assembly resolution 3201 (S-VI));

(d) The Programme of Action on the Establishment of a New International Economic Order (General Assembly resolution 3202 (S-VI));

(e) The Declaration on Social Progress and Development (General Assembly resolution 2542 (XXIV));

(f) The Declaration of Principles of International Law concerning Friendly Relations and Cooperation among States in accordance with the Charter of the United Nations (General Assembly resolution 2625 (XXV));

(g) The Charter of Economic Rights and Duties of States (General Assembly resolution 3281 (XXIX));

(h) General Assembly resolution 3362 (S-VII) on development and international economic cooperation;

(i) The Philadelphia Declaration of 1944, which is part of the Constitution of the International Labour Organization (ILO);

(j) The Tripartite Declaration of Principles Concerning Multinational Enterprises and Social Policy of 1977, adopted by the Governing Body of the International Labour Organization. Article 4 of the Declaration states that the principles set out in the Declaration are commended to Governments, employers' and workers' organizations and the multinational enterprises themselves. Article 8 stipulates that all the parties concerned by the Declaration should respect the Universal Declaration of Human Rights and the International Covenants;

(k) The Declaration on the Right to Development of 1986 (General Assembly resolution 41/128); and

(l) The Vienna Declaration and Programme of Action of 1993.

25. Regional conventions and declarations take closer account of the special characteristics of the peoples they govern. Consequently, they are in no way opposed to the provisions of the universal instruments but are complementary to them. The two sets

of instruments constitute an important legal machinery for the more effective protection and promotion of all human rights. The following instruments at the regional level may be mentioned:

(a) The African Charter on Human and Peoples' Rights (in particular Articles 20, 21 and 22);

(b) The European Social Charter; and

(c) The Protocol of Amendment to the Charter of the Organization of American States of 1985 and the 1988 Additional Protocol to the American Convention on Human Rights in the area of Economic, Social and Cultural Rights.

26. These instruments and many more unequivocally lay down the obligation of individuals, groups of persons, States and the international community to combat impunity for those who violate economic, social and cultural rights. In certain States, where the promotion and protection of human rights is a Government concern, appropriate legislation has been drafted to punish any human rights violations over and above the incorporation into domestic law of the international legal standards in order to make it possible for national legal, administrative or economic authorities to apply them.

27. This final report is focused on three points:

(a) The first concerns certain practices which give rise to violations of economic, social and cultural rights. While some of these practices now belong to history, they have nevertheless left entire peoples in complete destitution without any reparation. Other more current practices are the cause of serious violations of economic, social and cultural rights;

(b) The second point relates to the consequences of such practices for economic, social and cultural rights and for collective rights; and

(c) The third point concerns the actual campaign against impunity; it will deal with the organization of the campaign in terms first of preventive measures and then of jurisdictional ones.

. . .

IV. The campaign Against Impunity for Perpetrators of Violations of Economic, Social and Cultural Rights

117. Organizing the campaign against impunity for perpetrators of violations of economic, social and cultural rights, if it is to have any effect, requires comprehensive, detailed and objective investigations. To this end, it will be useful to consult the analysis regarding impunity for perpetrators of violations of civil and political rights. As far as the violations of economic, social and cultural rights discussed in this report are concerned, there appear to be two types of action worth considering:

(a) Preventive action, including all political, economic, legislative and administrative measures aimed at eliminating all practices and all procedures conducive to violations of economic, social and cultural rights; and

(b) Repressive and/or remedial action, aimed at penalizing violations which have already been committed. Sanctions could take the form of a series of practical measures, such as restitution, indemnification, compensation, cancellation, reparation, reinstatement, etc.

118. Clearly, where economic, social and cultural rights are concerned, remedial sanctions are by far the most important and the most significant, which does not mean to say that the importance of repressive sanctions should be overlooked. Both types of sanctions respond to the need for justice required to satisfy public opinion and to achieve national reconciliation, where appropriate.

A. Prevention of violations of economic, social and cultural rights

119. The experience of several decades of efforts to realize economic, social and cultural rights has brought to light many difficulties related to the very nature of the rights concerned and to the specific character of the peoples and regions of the world which are their beneficiaries. While it is true that every people or region has its own specific character, the necessary interdependence between the different human rights must not be overlooked. Preventing the violation of these rights is a task which must be jointly undertaken by the States and the international community. It should also be remembered that each State is responsible for drafting appropriate legislation and regulations and for implementing an economic and social policy allowing individuals and peoples to enjoy their economic, social and cultural rights.

120. The preventive measures being considered here are important and go some way towards offsetting the vagueness surrounding economic offences and the related sanctions. One doubt, as regards international law in particular, concerns the empirical means deployed. In this respect, there should be close cooperation among States and between them and the international community.

Successful prevention of violations of economic, social, cultural, or of any other rights, is undoubtedly the ideal solution, though also the most difficult to achieve. It requires an effort to inform and re-educate public opinion and a more courageous political attitude on the part of the Governments of the States on whose territories violations of human rights are committed.

121. From an international point of view, it is worth recalling the now classic suggestion that a more coercive and more coherent legal framework should be set up to induce States to accept and carry out their obligations under international law, which now clearly provides for State responsibility. This recognition of State responsibility was further strengthened by the Brussels Convention of 25 May 1962 on the liability of operators of nuclear ships, the International Convention of 29 November 1969 on civil liability for oil pollution damage and the Vienna Convention of 29 November 1971 on the international liability for damage caused by space objects.

122. Recommendations on international cooperation for crime prevention and criminal justice in the context of development were adopted at the Eighth United Nations Congress on the Prevention of Crime and the Treatment of Offenders held at Havana in August and September 1990. In those recommendations, Governments were urged to promulgate laws to combat transnational crime and illegal international transactions. It was mentioned that, since even legitimate enterprises, organizations and associations were sometimes involved in transnational criminal activities affecting national economies, Governments should adopt measures to control such activities. They should also collect information from various sources so as to have a solid basis for the detection and punishment of enterprises and organizations, their officials, or both, if they were involved in such activities. It was suggested that States should devise effective criminal legislation to combat the corrupt activities of public officials, which could hinder development and damage individuals or the entire nation.

123. In other words, in domestic law, all mechanisms and practices leading to violations of economic, social and cultural rights should be identified as punishable offences, giving entitlement to compensation. In its General Comment No. 3 (1990), the Committee on Economic, Social and Cultural Rights discussed the nature of States parties' obligations under Article 2, paragraph 1, of the International Covenant on Economic, Social and Cultural Rights and stated, inter alia, that the adoption of legislative measures was by no means exhaustive of the obligations of the States parties and that the phrase "by all appropriate means" should be given its full and natural meaning; such measures should include the provision of judicial remedies with respect to those rights. That means, incidentally that States should avoid any deliberately retrogressive measures in that regard.

124. At the international level, measures to prevent violations of economic, social and cultural rights are of many different kinds. Some of them could be drawn up by the United Nations in cooperation with the Member States, while others would be prepared by States in the framework of regional organizations. They could also result from an action by the specialized agencies of the United Nations system. Measures which could be taken by the United Nations include the preparation and adoption of an optional protocol to the International Covenant on Economic, Social and Cultural Rights, like the one already existing with regard to civil and political rights. It would be supported by the obligation on the part of States to report to the Committee on Economic, Social and Cultural Rights concerning measures taken for the effective enjoyment of these rights and the penalties applied to the perpetration of violations thereof. Although applying the procedures of an optional protocol would not give the Committee any jurisdictional authority, it would provide an opportunity through regular reports and individual communications to submit useful recommendations to the States parties and would make a major contribution to the campaign against impunity for violations of economic, social and cultural rights. Pending the establishment and functioning of such a procedure, it would be worthwhile encouraging the Committee on the Elimination of Racial Discrimination, the Human Rights Committee and the

Working Group on Communications (1503 Procedure) to examine periodic reports by States and individual communications submitted to those United Nations bodies.

125. The international community should endeavour to rectify current deviations from the missions of the international financial institutions. In 1944, the Bretton Woods Conference agreed to set up two international financial institutions: the International Monetary Fund (IMF) and the World Bank. Article 1 of the IMF Articles of Agreement establishes six purposes for the Fund, one of them being to facilitate the expansion and balanced growth of international trade and thereby to contribute to the promotion and maintenance of high levels of employment and real income and to the development of productive resources. The international community must attempt to bring these institutions back to their initial purposes.

126. In the preparation of preventive measures against violations of economic, social and cultural rights, the non-governmental organizations could, within the framework of their information and popularization activities, help the campaign considerably by denouncing such violations and suggesting solutions. With regard more specifically to cultural wealth, it would be important and essential to prepare and have the States adopt a convention protecting the cultural wealth of peoples, to declare any traffic involving such wealth to be a crime against humanity and to ask States to elaborate domestic legislation protecting it.

B. Jurisdictional measures against impunity

127. Violations of economic, social and cultural rights give entitlement to a remedy for the damage they have caused. From the point of view of domestic legislation, such violations are offences and subject to two types of sanction, repressive and compensatory. Under its guarantee obligation, the State has to provide the necessary legal framework to safeguard the enjoyment of economic, social and cultural rights. States in general, as well as all other subjects of law, must cease to accord only a programmatic value to economic, social and cultural rights. The best way of achieving this is to incorporate the international legal standards into domestic law, so that they can be invoked before the domestic authorities and courts.

128. If violations extend beyond domestic boundaries and affect several countries, the international responsibility of their perpetrators, whether individuals, human groups, companies, States or regional or international organizations, becomes engaged. There are thus two types of responsibility, national and international. It should be pointed out that these are not cumulative; they are complementary or supplementary. Thus, the international responsibility of a subject of law can be invoked only when no domestic remedy is available or if domestic remedies have been exhausted or are inadequate. The point here is to lay the foundations of the juridical status and justiciability of economic, social and cultural rights. A serious study of these two notions must be undertaken, for without them the legal reality of economic, social and cultural rights is utopian.

129. While, under domestic law, criminal law offences are dealt with under enforceable legislation, the same is not true in international law, where States freely decide their conduct. Thus, an international offence, as determined by international legal standards, is the result of an act or of conduct that is morally and legally imputable to a subject of international law. Punishment of an economic crime and remedying the damage it causes raise three questions: (a) Who is responsible for the offence or violation which is the source of the damage?; (b) Who is the victim of the resultant damage?; and (c) What forms of remedy are possible?

1. Who is responsible?

130. In many cases, those responsible for violations of economic, social and cultural rights and of the collective rights with an economic content such as the right to development or the right to a healthy environment, are sometimes international entities applying policies which constitute veritable sources of large-scale and serious violations of collective and individual rights in the countries with weak economies. At this level, the responsibility is collective. The most typical example is the case of debt management by the international financial institutions. Another example is the case of structural adjustment programmes whose consequences are disastrous for the economies of the developing countries. The responsibility of the international community is great with regard to these economic policies favouring the developed countries which widen daily the gap between rich and poor countries. The maintenance of the existing economic order with these injustices and its failure to adapt to today's economic realities, rectification of which has been constantly demanded but in vain, is also a responsibility of the international community. In the case of the violations which now form part of history, it is for the international community to undertake the necessary actions to remedy justly the harm done to the victim peoples. It should do so in cooperation with all the actors on the international stage.

131. The violations committed by the transnational corporations in their mainly transboundary activities do not come within the competence of a single State and, to prevent contradictions and inadequacies in the remedies and sanctions decided upon by States individually or as a group, these violations should form the subject of special attention. The States and the international community should combine their efforts so as to contain such activities by the establishment of legal standards capable of achieving that objective. The same is true of the looting of the cultural heritage of the third-world peoples and countries. Until quite recently, only States were subject of international law but individuals and groups of individuals can now take legal action or be summoned before international authorities to answer for their activities. The international community must establish a legal framework which will make it possible to bring actions, with some hope of success, for redress or punishment, a framework that would be supplemented by the principle of universal jurisdiction. To meet this responsibility more effectively, the international community must obtain from the States the commitment to include in their domestic legal systems international standards concerning human rights as a whole, while respecting their international obligations.

132. Under both domestic and international law, an act violating the rights of an individual or a group renders the perpetrator responsible. The juridical acts that give rise to obligations entailing the responsibility of a subject of law (an individual or a State) are specified by law. It is true that State responsibility is indisputable in positive law. It has, in fact, gained recognition, however belatedly, in the domestic sphere, where it had long seemed virtually incompatible with the lopsided relationship between the State and its subjects. The modern State engages in activities, some of which are government acts connected directly with the exercise of sovereignty while others are management activities carried out exactly like private activities subject to the rules of private law. In all cases, the responsibility of the State can be engaged in the event of violation of the rights of an individual or a group. Economic, social and cultural rights are generally connected with an economic activity and it is in this framework that they are most often violated.

133. The responsibility of the State is entire when the violations result from the malfunctioning of the civil service, whatever be the cause. The State cannot invoke either its own legislation or the incompetence or disobedience of its agents to exonerate it from its responsibility, whether the actions in question are government ones or purely managerial. In connection with the behaviour of State agents, abundant case-law from the Nürnberg International Tribunal that neither disobedience to or the execution of a clearly unlawful order reduces in any way the responsibility of the State. An occupying Power is responsible, under the Geneva Conventions, for violations committed in the occupied territory. The implementation of such responsibilities requires a certain amount of cooperation between States and the international community.

134. Violations of economic, social and cultural rights can also be perpetrated by private individuals. In the vast majority of States, such violations are punishable offences or are, at any rate, subject to a procedure of civil compensation. It is for the State to devise an adequate legal framework. It is most reprehensible that certain States should establish legislation which protect the goods or property of certain national companies and give them total impunity for any violations they commit of the economic, social and cultural rights of citizens or private economic groupings. Thus, in some countries, there is no means of obtaining execution on the property of nationalized companies. There can be no attachment of any of their goods although, in more and more cases, they are acting like private companies or individuals.

2. Who is the victim?

135. The victims or passive subjects of violations of economic, social and cultural rights can be groups or individuals. International human rights rules are said to create obligations *erga omnes* by reason of the indivisibility of the thing which is protected. To obtain a clearer idea of the concept of victim, it is worthwhile referring to the Declaration of Basic Principles of Justice for Victims of Crime and Abuse of Power. States are not always interested in protecting human rights in the individual sense. They are more sensitive to the protection of rights which are more fundamental than humanitarian.

They generally undertake to enable individuals to avail themselves of mechanisms which monitor their rights, as is the case for civil and political rights.

136. "Victims," according to the Declaration, means "persons who, individually or collectively, have suffered harm, including physical or mental injury . . . or substantial impairment of their fundamental rights." In this case, the victims are those who have directly and personally suffered the harm arising from the violations. Another, broader, approach is to understand by victim anyone who can prove that he has suffered harm or has an interest in taking action. The injury for which reparation is requested may be material or moral. All national legislations have long accepted compensation for moral injury, both for the direct victim and for his heirs. In the international sphere, this idea would seem to be slowly but surely gaining acceptance. It may be inferred from the current case law of the international legal bodies that the basis for determining the amount and nature of the compensation is not solely the physical or material injury or damage but also the direct or indirect moral injury. In its observations on communication No. 107/1981, the Human Rights Committee stated that the mother of a disappeared person was herself a victim: "The Committee understands the anguish and stress caused to the mother by the disappearance of her daughter and by the continuing uncertainty concerning her fate and whereabouts. . . . In these respects, she too is a victim of the violations of the Covenant suffered by her daughter. . . ." Other international bodies, such as the Committee on the Elimination of Racial Discrimination, the Commission of Inquiry set up by the International Labour Organization and the European Court of Human Rights, have all confirmed the principle of compensation for moral injury. In view of the massive and systematic violations of which the third-world peoples have been victims in the recent past, such as slavery, colonization and cultural looting, it is obvious that there could only be a global remedy, the purpose of which is to re-establish these peoples in their communal rights by returning to them the goods of which they have been unlawfully dispossessed. These collective claims can be managed and successfully concluded only with the cooperation of the international community and the manifestation of the will of every actor on the international stage.

137. The status of victim and the rights attaching thereto are transmissible to the successors. This concept of successor should be understood in a wide sense and comprise, in addition to the direct victim and his heirs and assigns, legal entities whose purpose is to defend the economic rights of individuals or groups whose rights have been violated. This is the case of trade unions and could be that of non-governmental organizations. As regards trade unions, the case-law of the European Court of Human Rights has already enshrined the principle by enabling them to submit to it for consideration a collective labour conflict. In economic matters, the victims are often groups of people since the rights violated are often collective ones that affect large segments of the population. This in no way extenuates individual violations of economic, social and cultural rights. The many different forms of violation require different kinds of penalties, mainly of an economic nature as mentioned above.

3. Possible remedies

138. The State has the obligation to establish the necessary legal framework to punish violations of economic, social and cultural rights in accordance with the provisions of the international instruments mentioned above. This idea is summarized in the decision handed down by the Inter-American Court of Human Rights in the *Velásquez Rodríguez* case:

"The State has a legal duty to take reasonable steps to prevent human rights violations and to use the means at its disposal to carry out a serious investigation of violations committed within its jurisdiction, to identify those responsible, to impose the appropriate punishment and to ensure the victim adequate compensation."

139. The remedies for damage resulting from violations of economic, social and cultural rights will vary according to whether the rights violated are collective or individual. In the case of collective rights, the penalties must be of an essentially reparative nature. Thus, for example, compensation in the form of cancellation of debt and debt-servicing could partly repair the injury caused by slavery and colonization. As already pointed out, there are numerous historical and legal reasons to justify, in a great many cases, cancelling and in others renegotiating debt on more satisfactory terms, periods of repayment, grace periods and rates of interest. The question of debt has consistently been raised by the developing countries. Indeed, cancellation of the debt of formerly colonized countries was raised as long ago as the second session of the United Nations Conference on Trade and Development, held at New Delhi. Mr. Louis Nègre, the then Minister of Finance of Mali, made the following statement:

"Many countries could legitimately have contested the legal validity of debts contracted under the auspices of foreign Powers. Beyond purely legal considerations and rightful claims, we merely wish to ask the creditor countries to show a greater spirit of equity or even justice by proposing, as a test of their goodwill, the cancellation of all debts contracted during the colonial period by interests that were essentially not our own, and for whose servicing our States are unjustly responsible."

140. History has shown that the huge present-day inequalities between developed and poor countries are the result of centuries of plundering and exploitation during which civilizations, social structures and indigenous modes of production were destroyed and during which the ecosystems of Africa, America and Asia were pillaged. The spoliation of many countries and the impoverishment of large segments of the population are continuing in different forms: deterioration of the terms of trade, transfer of resources from the South to the North, capital flight, structural adjustment, etc. As for cultural goods and those illegally acquired during the period of apartheid, the adequate form of remedy is restitution where this is possible. Those who have been illegally dispossessed must be able to retrieve their full property and cultural goods must be given back to the peoples who are their genuine owners.

141. As for the violations of individual rights, the harm they have caused can be remedied

in several ways such as rehiring (in matter of employment), compensation, rehabilitation, ending the violations, etc. These actions presuppose the existence of a useful and effective system of recourse to the national courts and administrative authorities. In the final analysis, it is most important that the victims, whatever the form of remedy sought, should obtain satisfaction in accordance with the legal provisions in force. Recourse proceedings, though not a remedy in themselves, make it possible to achieve a remedy. That is why the State must, in the framework of its legislation, provide the legal regime for these remedies.

V. Suggestions and Recommendations

A. Suggestions

142. At the present stage of efforts to combat impunity for perpetrators of violations of economic, social and cultural rights, the following suggestions may be made:

(a) In view of the massive violations of the economic, social and cultural rights of countries and peoples that were colonized or subjected to slavery, and as compensation for the injury suffered, part of the debt and debt-servicing of the States concerned could be cancelled; where appropriate, the remaining part could then be renegotiated on fairer and more humane terms. This approach would make it possible to eliminate several sources of violations of economic, social and cultural rights;

(b) Violations of economic, social and cultural rights could be declared international crimes that are consequently subject to the principles of universal jurisdiction and imprescriptibility, so that they can be punished at any time and in any place. Reforms of the present domestic and international legal systems could be proposed to States and international institutions in order to lead them to perform the mission of guaranteeing and protecting economic, social and cultural rights;

(c) An optional protocol on economic, social and cultural rights, similar to that for civil and political rights, could be drawn up and adopted by States, which would thus be required to report on the measures taken or to be taken for genuine implementation and improved protection of economic, social and cultural rights;

(d) The international community, international institutions, States and non-governmental organizations should, as a matter of priority, endeavour to ensure that States which have not yet done so ratify the International Labour Organization conventions and recommendations concerning the right to work, the right to social security and the right to secure and stable employment, thereby providing workers and their families with conditions for a decent life. The international community and States should take all the necessary measures to protect the rights of vulnerable segments of the population and give very serious consideration to holding a large-scale discussion on the practice of embargoes and economic sanctions which are imposed on States and have adverse consequences for the realization of the economic, social and cultural rights of the segments concerned;

(e) More elaborate standards could be proposed to States to combat impunity in cases of corruption, misappropriation of public or private funds, abuse of trust by public officials, and tax and customs fraud and, lastly, efforts to combat them could be strengthened and greater consideration given to the harm suffered by the victims, whether States or individuals; and

(f) Machinery for monitoring the management of public affairs could be established and constantly improved by providing material and financial assistance to States requesting it, helping them in particular to identify and study the mechanisms which permit, facilitate or ensure impunity for perpetrators of violations of economic, social and cultural rights.

Chapter 5
The Right to Adequate Food and to be Free from Hunger (excerpts)

I. The Issues and the Mandate

The issues

1. The Commission on Human Rights has repeatedly affirmed that hunger constitutes an outrage and a violation of human dignity. The present update of my previous study on the right to adequate food is based on the conviction that the widespread failure by States and the international community to ensure freedom from hunger and enjoyment by all of the right to food constitutes one of the most serious shortcomings of the human rights agenda. The adoption of urgent measures is required at the national, regional and international levels for the elimination of hunger and the creation of conditions in which all people can enjoy their right to food and nutrition. Unless this is done, the credibility of the human rights edifice is in serious doubt.

2. There is no disagreement that the right to food and nutrition is a core human right. On the occasion of the 1998 World Food Day (16 October) the President of the United States, Bill Clinton, referred to the right to food as the most basic human right. Freedom from want was one of the four fundamental freedoms referred to by an earlier United States President, Franklin D. Roosevelt, in his famous "four freedoms" address in 1941, which sparked the preparation of the Charter of the United Nations and later the Universal Declaration of Human Rights. The States parties to the International Covenant on Economic, Social and Cultural Rights have recognized that freedom from hunger is a fundamental human right, and have undertaken to take the necessary steps, to the maximum of their available resources, to eliminate hunger.

3. And yet more than 800 million people do not have food to meet their basic nutritional needs. This is a frighteningly high number, and hard to reconcile with the expressed commitment by States to ensure the enjoyment of human rights by everyone. There is a vast task to be completed before everyone can enjoy this fundamental human right. It is necessary, therefore, to examine the existing gap between the human rights commitments and the reality of today.

Report submitted by Mr. Asbjørn Eide, Special Rapporteur to the Sub-Commission on Prevention of Discrimination and Protection of Minorities, 1998. E/CN.4/Sub. 2/1998/9.

. . .

The outline

6. Chapter II of the present report describes the scope and consequences of malnutrition and hunger. The major purpose of that chapter is to create awareness of the seriousness of the situation. Recent scientific studies have led to the conclusion that the long-range consequences of malnutrition are much more serious than previously known.

7. Chapter III points out that the human rights issues are now taken seriously. Significant commitments were made at the World Food Summit in 1996, and special attention is given to the objectives set out its Plan of Action which calls for clarification of the right to food and the preparation of a coordinated strategy for its implementation. The follow-up is described, leading up to the adoption on 12 May 1999 of General Comment No. 12 by the Committee on Economic, Social and Cultural Rights (annex). Chapter IV explores the interpretation of relevant human rights provisions with particular attention to Article 11 of the International Covenant on Economic, Social and Cultural Rights, drawing on General Comment No. 12.

8. Chapter V discusses the steps to be taken by States in order to ensure freedom from hunger and to implement the right to food. It also gives two examples of country situations where efforts to develop a human rights strategy to food have been started.

9. Chapter VI examines the treatment of the right to food and nutrition in relevant treaty bodies, while chapter VII reviews the treatment of the right by the Commission on Human Rights and its special rapporteurs on country situations.

10. Chapter VIII examines the evolving roles of the specialized agencies and other bodies in regard to the right, and shows that there has been a great increase in support for a human rights approach to food and nutrition issues.

11. Chapter IX briefly examines the right to food in the context of ongoing processes of globalization, and points out that these processes have created new challenges and dangers as well as new opportunities; corrective action has to be taken in order to prevent avoidable negative consequences.

12. Chapter X contains the conclusions and the recommendations. Some of these are addressed to States with regard to their implementation of the right to food and nutrition within their jurisdiction; others are addressed to States with regard to their international obligations towards other States and to the population living in other States. Still others are addressed to the High Commissioner for Human Rights, to the treaty bodies, and to United Nations bodies and the specialized agencies.

II. Malnutrition and Hunger—Dimensions, Consequences and Emerging Issues

13. The scope of malnutrition and hunger is appalling in its magnitude and an outrage to the conscience of humankind. My 1998 progress report on the update contains

statistics regarding malnutrition and provides a general overview of the nature and magnitude of nutrition-related diseases. In the year that has passed since then some figures have been reconsidered and adapted, such as in the case of malnutrition assessed by underweight of children: I reported last year that around 170 million children under 5 years of age were considered underweight, while the most recent authoritative figure is put at "more than 200 million".

14. The Director-General of the World Health Organization recently gave the following examples of the impact of malnutrition on disease: 208 million people are stunted and 49 million are wasted; more than 900 million people suffer from goitre, 16 million are severely retarded and another 50 million suffer other forms of brain damage due to a deficiency of iodine; 3 million children are at increased risk of infection, blindness and death because they are vitamin A-deficient; anaemia and iron deficiency affect more than 2,000 million people the world over; and some 22 million children and more than 200 million adults are obese, and thus at significant risk from a range of serious non-communicable diseases and other threats to health.

15. One can hardly say that the overall problem has improved much although there are some positive signs and trends in some parts of the world (see the 1998 progress report), and there are single-country experiences that may give hope to other States wishing to address the problem in a sustained manner.

16. This final report highlights some of the most significant major new concerns and ways of understanding the causes of malnutrition as they have emerged since my study was submitted in 1987. Scientific evidence and practical experience over the last decade have converged on a much more integrated picture than we were able to draw in 1987. Only by understanding the nature and complexity of the problems stemming from the non-fulfilment of the right to adequate food, can we interpret this right more fully and identify the corresponding national and international obligations of States.

17. Inadequate access to food and suboptimal nutritional status may have multiple interacting causes, some of them deeply rooted in malfunctioning of the society. The previously widespread but erroneous notion that insufficient global and even national food production was the cause of hunger has now generally been discarded. There is greater recognition of the need for systemic and integrated analyses and approaches towards solutions. The translation from theoretical principles to practical action requires transcending the borders of single sectors and organizations with their often firmly established agendas and portfolios.

18. Three areas need particular attention: firstly, the new emphasis on the so-called "life-cycle approach" to understanding and addressing malnutrition; secondly, the revitalized associated understanding of the critical role of women and young girls as mediators of both societal and biological processes leading to and perpetuating malnutrition between generations; thirdly, the rapidly changing distribution of the "global burden of disease" between the developing and the industrialized world as well as within the developing world. In addressing all of these concerns human rights ought to come into play, enforcing consideration of the "right to adequate food" in a very broad economic, social and human development perspective.

The "life-cycle approach" to understanding malnutrition

19. The pernicious impact of malnutrition can affect the whole life-span of human beings. This has now become obvious and makes it even more urgent to take wide-ranging corrective measures. We know that poverty is a vicious circle and malnutrition may greatly affect work capacity in adults, thus contributing to the perpetuation of poverty. The tremendous impact of malnutrition on human, family and societal development is indisputable.

20. Until recently the effects of hunger and various forms of malnutrition were normally related to susceptibility at various age-levels and remedies were considered in terms of the need to attack the problem at that stage through food supplementation or other forms of rehabilitation. Although there was always a discussion of the consequences of infant and young child malnutrition in terms of small, but otherwise healthy adults, as well as a certain undocumented fear of permanent brain damage from foetal undernutrition, it was only in the 1990s that new theories and evidence from long-term studies led to the idea that early-life malnutrition also affected susceptibility to disease in later life.

21. Findings and theories put forward during the present decade suggest that foetal and young-infant malnutrition may in fact "programme" an individual for susceptibility to nutrition-related chronic diseases in later life, such as heart diseases, obesity and diabetes. It is ironic that these diseases, which were thought to be caused by "over-eating" in the industrialized world, are now sweeping the poor world with unprecedented speed. They imply disability, disease and death much earlier than expected for people who survived the critical years of childhood in poor societies. Furthermore, the risk factors which add to the biological programming effects are themselves frequently related to poverty, for example, certain fat and sugary foods are known to produce "cheap energy".

22. The scope and gravity of this life-cycle malnutrition is closely related to adverse social and biological factors which may combine to influence the nutrition and reproductive performance of women in ways that may critically affect their offspring while still in the womb and have consequences for the life-cycle of the next generation. The ACC/SCN report summarizes the seriousness of the complex interrelationships at work as follows:

"The acceptance by the international community that poorly fed adults are economically less effective now needs to be linked to new findings of up to 1 billion adults who are malnourished, with a reduced work capacity and an enhanced susceptibility to infections. The remarkably high rates of anaemia in children, men and women in many parts of the globe not only impair work capacity but permanently damage the normal brain development of infants. Now, however, it is also clear that the commonest form of 'childhood' malnutrition, involving stunted growth, is also closely linked to impaired mental as well as physical development. Thus, the capacity of societies to develop economically is being handicapped for decades by our current failure to eliminate malnutrition and anaemia in both children and adults. The impact of poor nutrition is therefore now seen as affecting the whole life-cycle. Malnourished mothers, particularly in Asia, are producing low-birth-weight babies who are not only immediately at risk but also become stunted as young children, with a double handicap of physical and mental limitations. In some societies this affects half of the population, with new evidence that in Asia poorly growing girls grow into malnourished adults who then in pregnancy pass on the long-term impact of their own poor development during foetal life to the next generation. To break this intergenerational cycle is exceptionally important—not only a fundamental ethical issue but also a priority for any Government concerned for the future intellectual and economic capacity of its people."

The particular role of women and young girls as both victims and "mediators" in the generation of malnutrition

23. Women who are socially disadvantaged in ways that can affect their reproductive functions can contribute to a vicious circle: young girls are often underfed and mothers-to-be may start their early pregnancies in a nutritionally suboptimal state, giving birth to low-birth-weight children who may also have had suboptimal nourishment in the womb. Added to such a bad start in life may be inadequate feeding patterns and repeated infectious diseases in infancy and as a young child. These adverse factors may combine to affect vital human development processes, including brain development, in the most critical formative years.

24. Underfed and under-cared-for mothers are thus affected socially and biologically, demonstrating the need for a continuing gender-role analysis in all undertakings aimed at improving food and nutrition. This must in turn be seen in the context of responsibilities and rights of women, including those of young girls. We are faced with both an ethical imperative vis-à-vis women themselves, and an imperative to safeguard future generations from being exposed to the same mutually reinforcing risks and thereby further perpetuating the situation. The vicious circle must be broken.

25. The problem has been that women's chores—giving birth and nurturing the new generation, as well as seeing to household food and economic security overall, have too often been considered as belonging to the domestic sphere and therefore outside State responsibility. We have begun to understand better to what extent these chores are at the very heart of problems that, because they are often defined in aggregate terms, tend to be missed when identifying crucial points for intervention. Renewed consideration of the linkages between women's rights and the right to adequate food and feeding is warranted, in the context of the consideration of the systemic linkages between the processes that create poverty and the manifestation of poverty itself, and cultural factors resulting in discrimination against women.

26. A special case in point is women's opportunities for breastfeeding their children, thereby providing them with the most appropriate food for infants at least up to 6 months of age—human milk. The State has an obligation to respect women's right to provide this food and to protect and facilitate the necessary conditions for them to do so, at least for six months. This may require legislative and supportive measures protecting

mothers from being forced to stop nursing or to shift to alternative food, including mothers' milk substitutes, before their infants' physiology has matured to a stage when they can tolerate and utilize food other than human milk.

The distribution of the burden of nutrition-related disease

27. It is also clear from what has been said about the life-cycle approach that the picture we used to have of hunger, malnutrition and ill-health being caused by inadequate food intake—undernutrition in developing countries and "overnutrition" in the rich countries—has changed, and dramatically so. We find all the major nutrition-related diseases in most countries, and spread among social classes at that. This has led to the expression "the double burden of disease" to describe what poor societies now are experiencing. The typical diseases found in developing societies—above all infectious diseases which in combination with undernutrition lead to high mortality, especially among children—continue to take their toll and drain poor health budgets; in addition, the new diseases add to the drain in terms of early disability or loss of breadwinners.

28. Especially intriguing is the finding of differential rates of malnutrition among women and young children in different developing societies. The most outstanding example is provided by a comparison of trends in South Asia and in sub-Saharan Africa. Women and young children in South Asia appear to be significantly worse off than in Africa. Several theories have been put forward to try to explain this without any firm conclusions having been reached. The lesson to be drawn, however, in assessing the nutritional status of populations is that the underlying causality is often much more complex than a single-factor explanation such as overall lack of food. And yet, adverse nutritional trends are all too often used to "demonstrate" the need for increased food production as the remedy. The "right to adequate food" may be as much a question of the full realization of the rights of women as of ensuring a bundle of nutrients handed over through food supplementation schemes.

29. To combat malnutrition is required not only from a human rights perspective; the case for nutrition is a strong one also in economic terms. James Lovelace, Director of the Health, Nutrition and Population Network of the World Bank, argues that development thinkers, planners and practitioners have for too long failed to recognize how, and how deeply, malnutrition is implicated in the genesis and persistence of poverty. "The pervasive malnutrition of children, and also of women and men, has surreptitiously undermined and frustrated development efforts in many fields. Nutrition should become the new frontier, attacking stunted development and compromised growth of people, especially the young." He also argued that we know how to solve the problem of malnutrition: "Carefully selected interventions and approaches are not only a human rights imperative but make eminent economic sense as well. States and the international community cannot afford not to do so, because malnutrition is very expensive for society."

30. Human rights arguments and economic arguments in favour of improved food and

nutrition are thus both important and can live side-by-side, not being opposed to one another. The point is that the rationale for human beings to be well fed should not be perceived and advocated in economic terms alone—the dignity of men, women and children must be superimposed on any mere utilitarian argument. Human rights pays off economically, and successful economic interventions will enhance the realization of human rights: these are two sides of the same coin and both can be promoted.

. . .

IV. Clarifying the Right to Food and Nutrition and the Corresponding State Obligations

44. The right to food forms part of the broader right to an adequate standard of living. The right to an adequate standard of living—or to livelihood—sums up the main concern underlying all economic and social rights, which is to integrate everyone into a humane society. The ultimate purpose of promoting the right to adequate food is to achieve nutritional well-being for the individual child, woman and man. Human nutritional status is determined by at least three major clusters of conditions which interact in a dynamic fashion, relating to food, health and care, and with education as a cross-cutting dimension. Food alone is not sufficient to ensure good nutrition for the individual. The right to adequate food is a necessary, but not alone sufficient component of the right to adequate nutrition. The full realization of the latter depends also on parallel achievements in the fields of health, care for the vulnerable, and education. Later instruments, especially the Convention on the Rights of the Child, recognize this broader right to nutrition as well as its cross-cutting nature relative to many other rights, including civil and political rights.

45. Article 11 of the ICESCR focuses on the food dimensions of the broader concept. The call by the World Food Summit for a better definition of the right to food as contained in Article 11 has now in broad outline been met through the process described in chapter III and culminated with the adoption by the Committee on Economic, Social and Cultural Rights of General Comment No. 12. This is a most significant step in the process towards clarification of the content of the right to food and the steps that should be taken for its realization. Given its origin as the official interpretation by the treaty body responsible for monitoring States parties' implementation of the right to adequate food, this general comment will in the time ahead stand as the most authoritative document formulated to date regarding the right to food.

46. The full text of the general comment on the right to adequate food should be studied as an integral part of this update. The author fully endorses the content of the general comment. Below follow some observations regarding the structure and the main highlights of its contents: the dignity, adequacy and sustainability of availability and access to food.

47. The foundation principle of the human rights system is that everyone is "born free and equal in dignity and rights and should act towards each other in a spirit of fraternity" (UDHR, art. 1). The Committee affirms in its general comment (para. 4)

that "the right to adequate food is indivisibly linked to the inherent dignity of the human person and is indispensable for the fulfilment of other human rights enshrined in the International Bill of Human Rights. It is also inseparable from social justice, requiring the adoption of appropriate economic, environmental and social policies, at both the national and international levels, oriented to the eradication of poverty and the fulfilment of all human rights for all."

48. The general comment expresses the core content of the right to adequate food as follows (para. 8):

- The availability of food in a quantity and quality sufficient to satisfy the dietary needs of individuals, free from adverse substances, and acceptable within a given culture;

- The accessibility of such food in ways that are sustainable and that do not interfere with the enjoyment of other human rights.

49. The content of "adequacy" is to some extent determined by prevailing social, economic, cultural, climatic, ecological and other conditions, but there are some core elements which are applicable under all circumstances and are spelled out in greater detail by the Committee. "Sustainability" incorporates the notion of long-term availability and accessibility and is intrinsically linked to the notion of adequate food or food security, implying food being accessible for both present and future generations.

50. In clarifying the content of the term adequate, the general comment (paras. 7–11) lays out in some detail the meaning of the sub-concepts of dietary needs, absence of adverse substances, and cultural or consumer acceptability. The concept of sustainability is explained in terms of availability and accessibility—both physical and economic—for different groups of people (paras. 12–13). This level of detail is very useful as it offers an opportunity for more nuanced reporting by States parties on the realization of the right to adequate food, which only attains full meaning when "food" also reflects the enjoyment of other rights which will ultimately determine accessibility and constitutes a true carrier of nutritional health.

On State obligations, nationally and internationally

51. In very general terms, the legal obligations of States parties to the ICESCR which are set out in Article 2 of the Covenant have been spelled out in earlier general comments and are now spelled out in paragraphs 14–16 of the general comment, to which I refer.

52. My 1987 study was intended as a contribution to the clarification of the nature and levels of State obligations under economic and social rights. Drawing on my earlier work, I introduced an analytical framework under which State obligations can be assessed on three levels: the obligation to respect, the obligation to protect, and the obligation to assist and fulfil human rights. The framework proved very useful, and has since been taken widely into use. In my progress report in 1998 I explained my previously elaborated framework in greater detail, as follows: (para. 9).

(a) Since State obligations must be seen in the light of the assumption that human beings, families or wider groups seek to find their own solutions to their needs, States should, at the primary level, respect the resources owned by the individual, her or his freedom to find a job of preference, to make optimal use of her/his own knowledge and the freedom to take the necessary actions and use the necessary resources—alone or in association with others—to satisfy his or her own needs. The State cannot, however, passively leave it at that. Third parties are likely to interfere negatively with the possibilities that individuals or groups otherwise might have had to solve their own needs;

(b) At a secondary level, therefore, State obligations require active protection against other, more assertive or aggressive subjects—more powerful economic interests, such as protection against fraud, against unethical behaviour in trade and contractual relations, against the marketing and dumping of hazardous or dangerous products. This protective function of the State is widely used and is the most important aspect of State obligations with regard to economic, social and cultural rights, similar to the role of the State as protector of civil and political rights;

(c) At the tertiary level, the State has the obligation to facilitate opportunities by which the rights listed can be enjoyed. It takes many forms, some of which are spelled out in the relevant instruments. For example, with regard to the right to food, the State shall, under the International Covenant (art. 11 (2)), take steps to "improve measures of production, conservation and distribution of food by making full use of technical and scientific knowledge and by developing or reforming agrarian systems".

(d) At the fourth and final level, the State has the obligation to fulfil the rights of those who otherwise cannot enjoy their economic, social and cultural rights. This fourth level obligation increases in importance with increasing rates of urbanization and the decline of group or family responsibilities. Obligations towards the elderly and disabled, which in traditional agricultural society were taken care of by the family, must increasingly be borne by the State and thus by the national society as a whole.

53. The Committee has now generally endorsed this approach in its general comment 12 (para. 15). It will be noted that the Committee has decided to use the three levels of obligations, as originally suggested by me, but has subdivided the third level into the obligation to facilitate and to provide (fulfil), as I have suggested in my later work.

54. Economic and social rights, like all other human rights, are often violated, but there has been some controversy over what constitute a violation of such rights, including the right to food. This is dealt with in the general comment (paras. 17–20). Violations of the Covenant occur when a State fails to ensure the satisfaction of, at the very least, the minimum essential level required to be free from hunger. Resource constraints do not free the Government from responsibility; it still has to show that every effort has been made to use all the resources at its disposal in an effort to satisfy, as a matter of priority, those minimum obligations. Any discrimination in access to food, as well as to means and entitlements for its procurement, constitutes a violation of the Covenant. Violations can occur through the direct action of States or other entities insufficiently regulated by States. Non-State actors also have responsibilities, and the

State should provide an environment that facilitates implementation of these responsibilities. In regard to the private business sector, whether national or transnational, a code of conduct should be agreed upon and made use of.

55. While Article 11 of the ICESCR is the key provision in regard to the right to food, it should be kept in mind that issues relating to food and nutrition are dealt with in numerous other international instruments. Of particular importance are Article 24 of the Convention on the Rights of the Child and Articles 12 and 14 of the Convention on the Elimination of All Forms of Discrimination against Women, both of which deal with the right to adequate nutrition.

56. Important provisions are also found in international humanitarian law as laid down principally in the four Geneva Conventions of 1949 and the two Additional Protocols of 1977. It prohibits the starvation of civilian populations, as well as the destruction of objects indispensable to their survival, such as foodstuffs, agricultural areas, crops, livestock, drinking water installations and irrigation works. It also prohibits methods or means of warfare likely to cause widespread, long-term damage to the environment, thereby jeopardizing the health or survival of the population. It contains provisions concerning humanitarian assistance and relief operations, including the free passage of such essentials as food, medicines and other goods of primary necessity.

57. Much of international humanitarian law was designed for an environment of armed conflict which has undergone significant changes in recent years, notably since the end of the cold war. There has been a shift from conflicts between States—the traditional focus of humanitarian law—to armed conflicts within States, and a rise in intra-State tensions and disturbances short of outright armed conflict. Human rights, including freedom from hunger, continue generally to apply also during armed conflict. The allocation of responsibility between the different actors involved in the conflict, as well as the rights, obligations and roles of international agencies, are matters of controversy in great need of clarification.

V. Ensuring Freedom from Hunger and Implementing the Right to Adequate Food at the National Level

58. Conditions differ widely between countries and the most appropriate ways and means to ensure freedom from hunger and to implement the right to adequate food therefore also varies considerably. Each State party to the ICESCR and the Convention on the Rights of the Child must nevertheless take the measures required under the particular conditions prevailing in its country to ensure that everyone is free from hunger, and thereupon move as quickly as possible to a situation where everyone can enjoy their right to adequate food. In so doing, the different levels of State obligations outlined in the general comment and discussed above in chapter IV should be applied, using the particular combination of measures warranted by the national situation.

59. Every country should therefore develop a national strategy to implement the right to food, or if such a national strategy is already in place, it should be revised in light of

the observations made in general comment 12. The first step in any such strategy should be to map the situation for the different groups and the different regions within the country, taking into account the differences that might exist on the basis of gender, ethnicity or race, and between rural and urban areas. Such mapping is necessary to identify those who are food insecure and to develop appropriate responses to food insecurity.

60. Food security is currently defined as access by all people at all times to the food needed for a healthy and active life. Achieving food security means ensuring that sufficient food is available, that supplies are relatively stable and that those in need of food can obtain it. National food security would therefore mean that everyone has effective entitlements to adequate food or resources for food and that there is in principle enough food to go around. Achieving food security at household level means ensuring that sufficient food is available throughout the territory, that supplies are relatively stable and that everyone within that territory in need of food has the capacity to obtain it for a healthy and productive life. Food insecurity is understood as the reverse: where some people at some or all times do not have access to adequate food and therefore cannot lead a healthy and active life.

61. Food security can therefore be seen as the corollary of the right to food: the State must take the necessary measures to ensure food security for everyone under its jurisdiction. In their national efforts to identify the groups which are food insecure, States should review—periodically and/or when special circumstances cause significant changes, including serious economic depressions—who is likely to be affected and how different groups may be affected differently on the basis of chronic or transitory vulnerability.

62. Having identified the groups which are food insecure, the national strategy should recreate food security for those groups and the population as a whole, formulate policies required for this purpose and identify the resources available, including human resources which, through self-help, can contribute to meet the goals set. When new and severe resource constraints emerge, caused by a process of economic adjustment, economic recession, climatic conditions or other factors, measures should be undertaken to ensure as a minimum that vulnerable population groups and individuals do not face hunger. This should be achieved through social programmes, safety nets and international assistance.

63. The right to food can only be fully achieved if it is linked to the realization of all other human rights. In the elaboration and implementation of the national strategy for the right to food, people's informed participation is essential. Appropriate decentralization is required to ensure that the particular conditions in the different regions of the country are taken into account, but the central Government remains at all times ultimately responsible for ensuring the enjoyment of this and other human rights.

64. Care must be taken to ensure sustainable management of natural and other resources required for access to food, including the management of land, water and fishery resources. Furthermore, attention must be given to all aspects of the food chain,

from production to consumption. Attention must further be given to the processing of food in order to ensure food safety, to the physical distribution of food in order to enable access for all, and to improving markets, *inter alia* in order to prevent misleading and potentially harmful influences. At the level of the consumer, adequate information is required on the composition of healthy diets. Sanitary conditions and clean water are essential in ensuring that the food actually consumed is safe.

65. The strategy should give particular attention to the need to prevent discrimination in access to food or resources for food. It should keep in mind the need to give particular attention to vulnerable groups and to the gender situation. Indigenous peoples and some minorities often suffer from more serious malnutrition than the average population, and we have seen that women in many societies face far greater difficulties than men. The strategy should therefore include, *inter alia*: guarantees of full and equal access, particularly for women, to economic resources, including the right to inheritance and ownership of land and other property, credit, natural resources and appropriate technology; measures to respect and protect self-employment and work which provides a remuneration ensuring a decent living for wage earners and their families (as stipulated in Article 7 (a) (ii) of the Covenant); maintaining registries on land rights (including forests) and fishing resources important for food production or other means of livelihood in rural areas; special legislation to protect the land rights of indigenous peoples and prevent forced evictions from their land; measures to protect or secure entitlements to land or other sources of livelihood among vulnerable smallholders, landless peasants and urban poor without discrimination as to race or ethnicity.

. . .

X. Conclusions and Recommendations

Conclusions

126. Three major points emerge from this update of the study on the right to adequate food:

• Firstly, that since 1987 there has been a much better and more widely shared understanding of the impact of hunger and malnutrition, and a more general awareness that their consequences are far worse than was previously recognized;

• Secondly, that there is a much broader recognition of the right to be free from hunger and to adequate food as human rights. The adoption by the World Food Summit in 1996 of its Plan of Action was a major watershed in attitudes towards this issue. The adoption by the Committee on Economic, Social and Cultural Rights in May 1999 of general comment 12 has contributed significantly to the clarification of the content of the right and the corresponding State obligations. The consultations conducted by the High Commissioner for Human Rights and the symposium organized by the ACC/SCN have deepened and broadened that recognition;

• Thirdly, that international institutions now broadly endorse the human rights approach to food and nutrition issues and have pledged themselves to act, separately and collectively, to contribute to the realization of these rights. The information given in chapter VIII about the commitments by UNICEF, FAO, WHO, WFP, IFAD and UNHCR, and the involvement of bodies such as the ACC/SCN, show that there is a new and potentially powerful momentum to act in a concerted way to eliminate the scourge of hunger from humanity.

127. The two main questions which remain are these: Will States, in light of the urgency of the matter, take all possible steps within their available resources to bring hunger to an end and to move towards full realization of the right to food? Secondly: Are other States, and thereby the international community, prepared to shoulder what is at least their moral obligation to respect and protect food and nutrition security in other countries and contribute as necessary, individually and collectively, to facilitating and fulfilling such security in countries in need?

128. The next few years will show whether States are prepared to move from rhetoric to realization of these rights which, if done in a concerted way, is fully within the power of the international community. Without energetic implementation both at the national and the international level, however, the insight gained will not lead to the aims set; at a minimum this includes the reduction of the number of undernourished people to half their 1996 level by 2015.

Recommendations

129. Many of the recommendations which follow have their origins in the consultations convened by the High Commissioner and the ACC/SCN symposium held on 12 and 13 April 1999.

130. Recommendations concerning national implementation by States:

(a) States should elaborate a strategy for the realization for everyone within their territory of freedom from hunger and the right to adequate food. The strategy should include the elaboration of framework legislation as proposed in general comment 12, setting out its purpose; the targets or goals to be achieved and the time-frame to be set for the achievement of those targets; the means by which the purpose could be achieved described in broad terms, in particular the intended collaboration with civil society and the private sector and with international organizations; institutional responsibility for the process; and the national mechanisms for its monitoring;

(b) As part of the strategy, States should develop or expand national indicators on food insecurity in line with the FIVIMS initiative coordinated by FAO (see chapter VIII). This system is intended to absorb data from various bases within other United Nations agencies including the comprehensive nutrition-related data set compiled by UNICEF in some regions;

(c) Other essential parts of the strategy are (i) to develop and maintain mechanisms to monitor progress towards the realization of the right to adequate food for all, and it should for this purpose establish appropriate mechanisms for handling the technical food and nutrition dimensions of domestic and international reporting; (ii) to identify the factors and difficulties affecting the degree of implementation of their obligations; and (iii) to facilitate the adoption of corrective legislative and administrative measures. This is important also where the country concerned has demonstrable resource constraints and where international assistance is therefore required to supplement exhausted domestic resources;

(d) As recommended by the ACC/SCN Commission on Nutrition Challenges for the 21st Century, national nutrition councils should be established in all countries; as part of their agenda they should expand the constituency of analysts and practitioners who can help advance the nutrition message and mission through the perspective of human rights and strengthen national nutrition monitoring and surveillance systems, improve methods of analysis and expand this analysis to include issues of accountability, contribute to improved national reporting on the nutrition situation, promote national endorsement of the draft international code of conduct on the right to adequate food, and promote dialogue between the nutrition and human rights communities so as to strengthen both communities and help provide the knowledge-based and operational skills needed to advance the human right to food and nutrition.

131. Recommendations to States regarding international cooperation and prevention of deprivation:

(a) States should recognize the essential role of international cooperation and comply with their commitment to take joint and separate action to achieve the full realization of the right to adequate food;

(b) States should respect the enjoyment of the right to food in other countries; among other things this means that they should at all times refrain from using food as a weapon. States participating in international sanctions should ensure that they do not lead to the deprivation of necessary food for the population;

(c) States should protect the right to food in other countries which, *inter alia*, requires that they should monitor the impact of their external aid and trade, as well as the impact of transnational corporations under their jurisdiction, on the enjoyment of the right to food in other countries and take corrective measures where a negative impact can be shown;

(d) States should facilitate access to food in countries other than their own, and provide the necessary aid when required. This does not necessarily or only mean food aid, but various categories of aid which enable the local population concerned to develop sustainable and effective entitlements to food either by its own production or by income generation. Donor States should increase their awareness of the importance of the effective enjoyment of the right to food, and make it a major concern in their development assistance;

(e) Creditor countries should adopt substantial debt relief measures in ways which facilitate the realization of the right to food and other economic and social rights for vulnerable groups in developing countries;

(f) States parties to international agreements, whenever relevant, should ensure that the right to adequate food is given due attention and consider the development of further international legal instruments to that end.

Chapter 6
Violence Against Women (excerpts)

. . .

III. International Legal Standards

A. Protection from violence

79. Women have been invisible in the development and growth of modern international law. Though law is assumed to be gender-neutral, the norms and standards of international law are generally unconcerned with the "women's" question. In recent times this approach has changed, especially in the field of international human rights law. The problems associated with gender inequality and violence against women have gained increasing recognition by the international community. There is a concerted effort to eradicate violence against women as part of a worldwide campaign on women's human rights.

80. Many international legal instruments dealing with human rights include the protection of women from violence in their provisions. The Universal Declaration of Human Rights, in Article 1, states that "all human beings are born free and equal in dignity and rights." Article 2 provides that "everyone is entitled to all the rights and freedoms set forth in this Declaration, without distinction of any kind, such as race, colour, sex, language, religion, political or other opinion, national or social origin, property, birth or other status." Article 3 of the Universal Declaration provides that "everyone has the right to life, liberty and security of person." Article 5 provides that "no one shall be subjected to torture or to cruel, inhuman or degrading treatment or punishment." The non-discrimination clause, taken together with Articles 3 and 5, means that any form of violence against women which can be construed as a threat to her life, liberty or security of person or which constitutes torture or cruel, inhuman or degrading treatment is not in keeping with the Universal Declaration and is therefore a violation of the international obligations of Member States.

Preliminary report submitted by the Special Rapporteur on violence against women, its causes and consequences, Ms. Radhika Coomaraswamy, in accordance with Commission on Human Rights resolution 1994/45, E/CN.4/1995/42. Original footnote omitted.

81. Other instruments, such as the International Covenant on Civil and Political Rights and the International Covenant on Economic, Social and Cultural Rights, likewise prohibit violence against women. Article 2 of the International Covenant on Civil and Political Rights contains a non-discrimination clause similar to that contained in Article 2 of the Universal Declaration. In addition, Article 26 of the Covenant argues:

"All persons are equal before the law and are entitled without any discrimination to the equal protection of the law. In this respect, the law shall prohibit any discrimination and guarantee to all persons equal and effective protection against discrimination on any ground such as . . . sex."

This, taken in conjunction with Article 6.1 of the Covenant, which protects the right to life, Article 7, which protects everyone from torture or cruel, inhuman or degrading treatment or punishment, and Article 9.1, which protects the right to liberty and security of person, means that the Covenant may be construed as covering the issue of gender-based violence.

82. Article 3 of the International Covenant on Economic, Social, and Cultural Rights guarantees the equal right of men and women to the enjoyment of all rights set forth in that Covenant and many of the substantive rights set out in the Covenant cannot be enjoyed by women if gender-based violence is widespread. For example, Article 7 of the International Covenant on Economic and Social Rights ensures the right of everyone to the enjoyment of just and favourable conditions of work. This, by implication, entails that women must be free of violence and harassment at the workplace.

83. In times of war, the Convention relative to the Protection of Civilian Persons in Time of War, of 12 August 1949 (the Fourth Geneva Convention), states clearly in its Article 27 that "Women shall be especially protected against any attack on their honour in particular against rape, enforced prostitution or any form of indecent assault." This section is echoed in common Article 3 of the Geneva Conventions and in Protocol II to the Geneva Conventions.

84. The most extensive instrument dealing exclusively with the rights of women, however, is the Convention on the Elimination of All Forms of Discrimination against Women, which came into force in September 1981. Although this instrument does not explicitly deal with violence against women, except in the areas of trafficking and prostitution (art. 6), many of the anti-discrimination clauses contained in it provide for the protection of women from violence. Additionally, many of the recent recommendations of the monitoring body of the Convention, the Committee for the Elimination of Discrimination Against Women (CEDAW), especially General recommendation No. 19, have addressed the issue of gender-based violence and provide the sole source of legally binding material at the international level dealing expressly with violence against women.

85. The Convention on the Elimination of All Forms of Discrimination against Women is perhaps best described as an international bill of rights for women as it sets out in detail both what is to be regarded as discrimination against women and the measures that have to be taken in order to eliminate this discrimination. Women's rights are conceptualized as human rights and a "non-discrimination" model is adopted, so that

women's rights are seen to be violated if women are denied the same rights as men. Article 1 of the Convention defines discrimination against women as

"any distinction, exclusion or restriction made on the basis of sex which has the effect or purpose of impairing or nullifying the recognition, enjoyment or exercise by women, irrespective of their marital status, on a basis of equality of men and women, of human rights and fundamental freedoms in the political, economic, social, cultural, civil or any other field."

Violence is not expressly mentioned but a proper interpretation of the definition allows it to be included by implication.

86. Furthermore, CEDAW has on various occasions recommended that the issue of violence against women be included in the reports submitted to it by the State Parties. In General recommendation 12, adopted in 1989, the Committee requested that States include in their reports information about violence against women and the measures taken to eliminate such violence.

87. General recommendation No. 19, formulated in 1992, deals entirely with violence against women and explicitly states that gender-based violence is a form of discrimination which seriously inhibits a woman's ability to enjoy rights and freedoms on a basis of equality with men and asks that State parties have regard to this when reviewing their laws and policies. The recommendation further states that when reporting under the Convention States parties should take this into consideration. It also argues that the definition of "discrimination" in Article 1 of the Convention includes gender-based violence, which is in turn defined in recommendation 19 as "violence directed against a woman because she is a woman or which affects women disproportionately. It includes physical, mental, or sexual harm or suffering, threats of such acts, coercion and other deprivations of liberty."

88. General recommendation 19 also deals with specific articles of the Convention and how they relate to violence against women. The specific areas discussed are (i) traditional attitudes, customs and practices (arts. 2 (f), 5 and 10 (c)), (ii) all forms of traffic and exploitation of prostitution of women (art. 6), (iii) violence and equality in employment (art. 11), (iv) violence and health (art. 12), (v) rural women (art. 14) and (vi) family violence (art. 16).

89. General recommendation 19 argues that certain traditions and customs and practices whereby women are regarded as subordinate or as having stereotyped roles perpetuate various practices, including violence and coercion, and that such prejudices and beliefs may be used to justify gender-based violence as a form of protection or control of women, as a result of which women are deprived of the equal enjoyment of their human rights and fundamental freedoms.

90. With regard to prostitution, and traditional as well as new forms of trafficking, the recommendation states that these activities put women at special risk of violence and abuse. States parties are directed to take special preventative and punitive steps against such violence.

91. On the question of employment, General recommendation 19 states that gender-specific violence such as sexual harassment in the workplace can seriously impair equality in employment. With regard to health issues, States are directed to provide a support service for all victims of gender-based violence, including refuge, specially trained health workers, rehabilitation and counselling services.

92. The General recommendation also recognizes that rural women are at special risk of violence because of the persistence of traditional attitudes in many rural communities and it imposes an obligation on States to ensure that services for victims of violence are accessible to rural women. Where necessary, special services should be provided for isolated communities.

93. Violence in the family is seen to be widespread and present in every part of the world and measures necessary to eradicate family violence are listed.

94. General recommendation 19 also directs State parties, in their reports, to describe the extent of each problem in their countries, the measures taken to prevent and punish the occurrence of such problems, and the effectiveness of such measures.

95. The Declaration on the Elimination of Violence against Women deals exclusively with violence against women. The document is a comprehensive statement of international standards with regard to the protection of women from violence. Although the Declaration is not legally binding, it sets out international norms which States have recognized as being fundamental in the struggle to eliminate all forms of violence against women.

96. This Declaration is the first real set of international standards to deal specifically with the problem of violence against women. For the purposes of the Declaration, violence against women is defined in Article 1 as

"any act of gender-based violence that results in, or is likely to result in, physical, sexual, or psychological harm or suffering to women, including threats of such acts, coercion or arbitrary deprivation of liberty, whether occurring in public or private life."

97. The Preamble to the Declaration clearly locates the roots of gender-based violence in "historically unequal power relations between men and women, which have led to domination over and discrimination against women by men and to the prevention of the full advancement of women," recognizing that "violence against women is one of the crucial social mechanisms by which women are forced into a subordinate position compared with men." The Preamble also identifies groups of women who are especially vulnerable to violence. These include women belonging to minority groups, refugee women, migrant women, women living in rural or remote communities, destitute women, women in detention, female children, women with disabilities, elderly women and women in situations of armed conflict. Vulnerability and historicity are thus seen as the dual principles which are responsible for violence against women.

98. Violence against women is defined in the Declaration as including, but not being limited to, physical, sexual and psychological violence that occurs in the family. Such

violence includes battering, sexual abuse of female children in the household, dowry related violence, marital rape, female genital mutilation and other traditional practices harmful to women, non-spousal violence and violence related to exploitation. The Declaration also points to the prevalence of violence in the general community, including rape, sexual abuse, sexual harassment and intimidation at work, in educational institutes and elsewhere, trafficking in women and forced prostitution. Finally it recognizes violence which is either perpetrated or condoned by the State. The definition of violence contained in the Declaration appears, therefore, to be a broad one whereby violence is not strictly construed as meaning only the actual use of physical force, but implies the right to inquire against all forms of action which disempower women because of the fear of violence, whether the fear is instilled by the State, actors in the community or members of the family.

. . .

101. The earlier sections of this chapter clearly show that women's rights have become an integral part of international human rights law and that violence against women is a violation of human rights for which States are accountable. States therefore have an international obligation with regard to the protection of these rights as part of the general regime of international human rights law.

102. Except for categories such as "pirates" and "international war criminals," private individuals and agencies are not generally bound by international human rights law. But States may be responsible for their failure to meet international obligations even when violations originate in the conduct of private individuals. State responsibility for the violation of women's human rights by private actors is anticipated by customary international law. States are held legally responsible for acts or omissions of private persons in the following instances:

(a) The person is an agent of the state;

(b) Private acts are covered by provisions of a treaty obligation;

(c) There is State complicity in the wrongs perpetrated by private actors;

(d) State failure to exercise due diligence in the control of private actors.

103. The "due diligence" standard has been generally accepted as a measure of evaluating a State's responsibility for violation of human rights by private actors.

104. The standards developed by customary international law have been expanded by international and regional human rights conventions and recent judicial decisions. For example, in the 1988 *Valesquez* case, the Inter-American Court of Human Rights imposed liability on Honduras for its lack of due diligence in preventing unexplained "disappearances," whether by the State or private actors. States were also held responsible for the organization of the government apparatus and structures of public power in order to make them capable of juridically ensuring free and full enjoyment of human rights.

105. Besides complying with the "due diligence" standard for the protection of human rights, States are required by international human rights instruments to ensure equal protection of the law for their citizens. If data collected provides evidence of systematic, discriminatory, non-prosecution by the State of crimes of violence against women, then, it is argued, States have violated their responsibility under international human rights law. Research does suggest that the investigation, prosecution and sentencing of, for example, crimes of domestic violence occur with much less frequency than of other similar crimes. Wife murderers receive greatly reduced sentences, domestic battery is rarely investigated and rape frequently goes unpunished. These examples stand in direct contrast to the treatment of violent crimes against male victims. The pervasiveness of domestic violence and its frequent non-prosecution by Governments, as well as the new emphasis on equal protection of the law as a central human rights concern, have made it possible to conceptualize crimes such as domestic violence as a human rights issue and to hold Governments accountable for this discrimination.

106. This emerging trend towards holding States responsible for actions of certain private actors is reflected both in the Convention on the Elimination of All Forms of Discrimination against Women and the Declaration on the Elimination of Violence Against Women. Discrimination under the Convention is not restricted to actions by or on behalf of the State; this is expressly acknowledged, in regard to violence, in General Recommendation 19. Article 2 (e) of the Convention states that States parties are required "to take all appropriate measures to eliminate discrimination against women by any person, organization or enterprise." This provision expressly covers State responsibility for violations by private actors. Article 16 explicitly refers to discrimination in the family and Recommendation 19 clearly includes family violence within its purview.

107. The Declaration sums up the current standards in operation as they relate specifically to the question of violence against women. Article 4 (c) proclaims that States should "exercise due diligence to prevent, investigate and, in accordance with national legislation, punish acts of violence against women, whether those acts are perpetrated by the State or by private persons." All States are not only responsible for their own conduct or the conduct of their agents, but are now also responsible for their failure to take necessary steps to prosecute private citizens for their behaviour, in compliance with international standards. This emergence of State responsibility for violence in society plays an absolutely crucial role in efforts to eradicate gender-based violence and is perhaps one of the most important contributions of the women's movement to the issue of human rights.

C. Obligations of the State

108. The obligations of the State with regard to the elimination of violence against women are comprehensively spelt out in Article 4 of the Declaration on the Elimination of Violence against Women. The State is obliged to condemn violence against women and is expected not to invoke custom, tradition, or religion to avoid the obligation; the State is expected to pursue all "appropriate means," "without delay" in

adopting a policy of eliminating violence against women. Among other obligations of the State outlined in Article 4 are:

(a) Ratification of the Convention on the Elimination of All Forms of Violence against Women (art. 4 (a));

(b) Specific directives with regard to the development of legal and administrative mechanisms to ensure effective justice for victims of violence (art. 4 (d));

(c) To ensure that there is specialized assistance in terms of support and rehabilitation for women victims of violence (art. 4 (g));

(d) Training of judicial and police officials (art. 4 (i));

(e) Reform of educational curricula (art. 4 (j));

(f) Promotion of research (art. 4 (k));

(g) Full reporting of the problem of violence against women to international human rights mechanisms (art. 4 (m)).

109. A basic premise of both the Convention and the Declaration appears to be that the law and legal institutions have an important role to play in realizing the gender equality and elimination of violence envisaged in these instruments. It is possible to perceive the emphasis given, in these international instruments, to law as a tool that can be used in combination with other mechanisms to deliver justice and equity to women. However, both documents refrain from placing an undue reliance on strictly legal mechanisms at the expense of other methods. They make provision for the use of non-legal mechanisms, such as rehabilitation and education of the judiciary and other officials to make them sensitive to issues of gender, as necessary complements to the law in efforts to eliminating gender-based violence.

110. The Convention was the first international instrument to target tradition and culture as influential forces in shaping gender roles and family values. The Declaration followed in its footsteps in this regard. Among the obligations of the State set out in the Declaration is the obligation to "adopt all appropriate measures, especially in the field of education, to modify the social and cultural patterns of conduct of men and women and to eliminate prejudices, customary practices and all other practices based on the idea of the inferiority or superiority of either of the sexes and on stereotyped roles for men and women" (art. 4). This is a landmark in the battle against gender-based violence, as such prejudices are most prominent in the areas of culture, community and family, which are precisely the spheres of most importance to many women. If, therefore, the State were able to bring about fundamental changes in the patterns of socialization which tend to disempower women and create an atmosphere in which violence against them appears more legitimate, it would be a significant step towards the elimination of gender-based violence.

111. In this regard, it should be mentioned that some of the States that have ratified the Convention have entered reservations indicating that they will accept it only in so

far as it does not conflict with certain national customs, practices, or laws. This has caused much disagreement as it is widely felt that many of these reservations are incompatible with the basic obligations of the Convention. States should, therefore, be requested to be more circumspect about entering reservations, and consider whether the contemplated reservation is compatible with the spirit of the Convention.

112. Another of the obligations imposed on States by these international instruments should help to alleviate a major problem with regard to the elimination of violence against women, which is the lack of statistics available on the issue. Both the Convention and the Declaration impose an obligation on States to encourage research and the compilation of statistics on the subject of gender-based violence. Article 4 (k) of the Declaration directs States to

"Promote research, collect data and compile statistics, especially concerning domestic violence, relating to the prevalence of different forms of violence against women and encourage research on the causes, nature, seriousness and consequences of violence against women and on the effectiveness of measures implemented to prevent and redress violence against women; those statistics and findings of the research will be made public."

Such statistics and research should help both by providing the basic material with which those working in the field of gender-based violence can make their programmes more effective, and by making the problem of violence more visible to the general public and the international community at large.

. . .

215. Several international instruments address the issue of prostitution directly. States should be actively encouraged to accede to the International Covenant on Civil and Political Rights and the Convention on the Elimination of All Forms of Discrimination Against Women. Article 6 of this Convention, in particular, obligates States parties to take all appropriate measures to "suppress all forms of traffic in women and exploitation of prostitution of women." Such measures could involve enacting legislation to prosecute all those involved in the exploitative organizations surrounding prostitution and trafficking, including brothel owners, pimps, airlines; increasing the statutory age for rape to 18, and actively prosecuting clients who violate this law; and establishing commissions of inquiry to investigate allegations of abuse and complicity by government agents.

. . .

2. Violence against women in situations of armed conflict

(a) General

261. Rape of women and girls in situations of armed conflict, whether civil or international, constitutes by definition a grave breach of international human rights and

humanitarian law. The Fourth Geneva Convention of 1949 states that "Women shall be especially protected against any attack on their honour, in particular against rape, enforced prostitution, or any form of indecent assault" (art. 27). Article 147 includes in the list of acts constituting grave breaches of the Convention "wilfully causing great suffering or serious injury to body or health." The International Committee of the Red Cross has interpreted this to include rape. In addition, acts of sexual assault against women are outlawed by international humanitarian law through normative provisions prohibiting violence against the physical integrity, dignity and security of the person. They include common Article 3 of the Geneva Conventions, in so far as it prohibits "violence to life and person," "cruel treatment," "torture" or "outrages upon personal dignity," and Protocol II Additional to the Geneva Conventions, relating to the protection of non-international armed conflicts, which expressly forbids "outrages upon personal dignity, in particular humiliating and degrading treatment, rape, enforced prostitution and any form of indecent assault" (art. 4.2 (e)).

262. The Vienna Declaration and Programme of Action, adopted by the World Conference on Human Rights in June 1993, states:

"Violations of the human rights of women in situations of armed conflict are violations of the fundamental principles of international human rights and humanitarian law. All violations of this kind, including in particular murder, systematic rape, sexual slavery, and forced pregnancy, require a particularly effective response" (Part II, para. 38).

263. Yet, although rape is one of the most widely used types of violence against women and girls, it remains the least condemned war crime; throughout history, the rape of hundreds of thousands of women and children in all regions of the world has been a bitter reality.

264. At the international level, with regard to the prosecution of war crimes, there seems to be a newly emerging trend, namely the setting up of international expert commissions and tribunals. The international community has adopted a more institutionalized response to the atrocities committed in the territories of the former Yugoslavia and in Rwanda in particular. The precursors to such tribunals were the International Military Tribunal at Nuremberg and the International Military Tribunal for the Far East (Tokyo Tribunal). Although rape as a war crime was not an issue before these early tribunals, they set the precedent for international prosecution of alleged war crimes.

. . .

(c) Legal standards

305. Both international law and the national law of asylum countries govern the protection of refugee women. The basic international instrument for the protection of refugees is the 1951 Convention relating to the Status of Refugees and its 1967 Protocol. The United Nations High Commissioner for Refugees is charged with providing

international protection to refugees and with seeking durable solutions to their problems. The Convention defines a refugee as a person who has a well-founded fear of persecution arising from nationality, race, religion, membership of a particular social group, or political opinion. The European Parliament in 1984 determined that women facing cruel or inhuman treatment as a result of seeming to have transgressed social mores should be considered a particular social group for purposes of determining refugee status.

306. The Executive Committee of UNHCR has acknowledged that gender can be a factor in persecution on the basis of one of the five listed categories, and moreover, that women can in certain circumstances be considered to constitute a "particular social group." The Executive Committee of the High Commissioner's Programme, in Conclusion No. 39 on Refugee Women and International Protection (1985), recognized that States, in the exercise of their sovereignty, are free to adopt the interpretation that women asylum seekers who face harsh or inhumane treatment due to having transgressed the social mores of the society in which they live may be considered a "particular social group."

307. In addition to the 1951 Convention, women refugees are also protected by all international human rights instruments and mechanisms, and in particular the Convention on the Elimination of All Forms of Discrimination against Women, the Declaration on the Protection of Women and Children in Emergency and Armed Conflict, the International Covenants on Civil and Political Rights and on Economic, Social and Cultural Rights and, more generally, by the Universal Declaration of Human Rights. The Convention on the Rights of the Child also provides international protection for the human rights of girls.

308. National laws and policies in part determine what legal status an individual receives once she arrives in the country of asylum, where she will live and what assistance will be provided to her. It has been pointed out that assistance and protection is afforded to refugees presumptively in many developing countries, whereas extensive evidentiary hurdles need to be overcome in most industrialized countries.

309. Criminal acts of violence against refugee women are punishable under national laws. In part because of extensive international organization and non-governmental organization involvement in refugee situations, however, Governments have tended either to abdicate responsibility or to act in nominal and ineffective ways.

Policies and Practices That Impact Women's Reproductive Rights and Contribute to, Cause or Constitute Violence Against Women

Introduction

1. The present report examines policies and practices that impact women's reproductive rights and contribute to, cause or constitute violence against women. Many forms of violence against women result in violations of women's reproductive rights because

such violence often imperils their reproductive capacities and/or prevents them from exercising reproductive and sexual choices. Similarly, many reproductive rights violations constitute violence against women per se, defined as "any act of gender-based violence that results in, or is likely to result in, physical, sexual or psychological harm or suffering to women, including threats of such acts, coercion or arbitrary deprivation of liberty, whether occurring in public or in private life." Inadequate levels of knowledge about human sexuality and inappropriate or inadequate reproductive health information and services, culturally imbedded discrimination against women and girls, and limits on women's control over their own sexual and reproductive lives all contribute to violations of women's reproductive health.

. . .

2. Violations resulting from State failure to meet minimum core obligations

66. Just as direct State action can result in violence against women, a State's inaction or failure to meet minimum core obligations can result in further violence against women. Government failure to take positive measures to ensure access to appropriate health-care services that enable women to safely deliver their infants as well as to safely abort unwanted pregnancies may constitute a violation of a woman's right to life, in addition to the violation of her reproductive rights. Along the same lines, government failure to provide conditions that enable women to control their fertility and childbearing, as well as to bring voluntary pregnancies to term, constitutes a violation of a woman's right to security of the person.

(a) Failure to provide comprehensive health services

(i) Government funding for research into women's reproductive health issues

67. The key to the development of effective policies addressing a minimum core of obligations is a showing by the State that it has based its reproductive policies on reliable data regarding the incidence and severity of diseases and conditions hazardous to women's reproductive health, and on the availability and cost effectiveness of preventive and curative measures. As underscored in the Beijing Platform for Action (para. 109 (h)),

"[Governments should] (h) Provide financial and institutional support for research on safe, effective, affordable and acceptable methods and technologies for the reproductive and sexual health of women and men, including more safe, effective, affordable and acceptable methods for the regulation of fertility, including natural family planning for both sexes, methods to protect against HIV/AIDS and other sexually transmitted diseases and simple and inexpensive methods of diagnosing such diseases, among others . . . ."

68. All too often, State policies derive from the perceived moral requirements of the community, or even the needs and priorities of the health profession, rather than a

careful epidemiological and social assessment of women's health needs. As a result institutions dedicated to promoting women's reproductive health lack adequate access to scientific resources to contribute to the understanding of factors relating to reproductive health and to expand reproductive choice. Research into the prevention, detection and treatment of mammary, cervical and uterine tumors would significantly improve women's morbidity and mortality rates, as these three diseases account for almost half the deaths caused by malignant tumors in women aged between 15 and 64.

(ii) Maternal mortality

69. Government failure to prevent maternal mortality compromises a woman's right to life and her right to security of person. In spite of information from the international Safe Motherhood initiative demonstrating the preventability of pregnancy-related deaths, many States fail to take the necessary steps to reduce maternal mortality.

70. Maternal deaths are deaths among women who are pregnant or who have been pregnant during the previous 42 days. The risks and complications related to pregnancy and childbirth are among the leading causes of maternal deaths. Most maternal deaths are preventable. While some countries have taken steps to reduce maternal mortality, it is estimated that over 585,000 deaths occur among women of reproductive age due to preventable complications in pregnancy, childbirth, or unsafe abortions. These are not mere misfortunes or unavoidable natural disadvantages of pregnancy but rather preventable injustices that Governments are obliged to remedy through their political, health and legal systems. Ninety-nine per cent of these deaths happen in developing countries. Of these, South Asian countries contribute the highest number of maternal deaths, followed by African countries and Latin American countries. One in every 10,000 women dies in Northern Europe compared to 1 in 21 women in Africa. A woman's lifetime risk of dying from pregnancy-related complications or during childbirth is 1 in 48 in the developing world, versus 1 in 1,800 in the developed world.

71. Both the ICPD Programme of Action (para. 8.21) and the Beijing Platform for Action (para. 106(i)) urge Governments to reduce maternal mortality by one half of their 1990 levels by the year 2000, and to cut the levels by an additional one half between the years 2000 and 2015. However, as the target date nears, maternal deaths remain a common occurrence. The most common causes for the great number of maternal deaths are the woman's age, spacing of pregnancies, and the desirability of the pregnancy. The woman's health, dietary needs, financial resources and her unequal status in society, and the resulting poor schooling and early marriage of girls, are also relevant factors, as is the lack of adequate training for health care workers in the areas of prenatal care, delivery and post-partum care. Moreover, cultural and religious beliefs may serve to mask the incidence of maternal deaths that could be prevented by inexpensive and available interventions.

72. Broad-ranging social and economic reforms have had an adverse effect on maternal mortality. In the Latin American and Caribbean region, structural adjustment policies during the 1980s and early 1990s and health care reform resulted in a shift from

the Government as a key provider of health services to a promoter of either private or public general health insurance. This has had an adverse impact on the ability of low-income groups–especially rural and indigenous people–to gain access to health care services. As a result, rural and urban clinics do not have the facilities to perform Caesarean operations or to treat other complicated births. The staff lack training in family planning methods, and the nurse-to-patient and doctor-to-patient ratios are very high. Even where adequate medical facilities exist, the cost of these services can be prohibitive. With respect to the Asian region, the recent economic crisis has had an impact on maternal care.

(iii) Non-provision of contraceptive information

73. A failure of Governments and service providers to recognize a woman's right to control her fertility may translate into a failure to provide accurate and objective information regarding the full range of contraceptive methods. Non-provision of contraception and contraceptive advice may also result from discrimination in the delivery of health services. In some societies, contraceptive advice is not given to unmarried persons or adolescents. Even where a woman is married, in the absence of authorization by her husband or male partner, she may be denied access to reproductive health services and health services more generally.

74. Because husbands often take little or no responsibility for contraception and vasectomy is rarely mentioned or considered as a contraceptive measure, women must act to control their fertility in order to preserve their own health. Most women have some idea about contraceptive methods, be they traditional ways or modern methods. However, misinformation and fears of the ill effects of contraceptive methods on the health and the ability to bear children often deter women from using them.

75. The unmet need for family-planning services is substantial. It is estimated that 350 million out of 747 million married women of reproductive age are not using contraceptives. One hundred million would prefer to space their next birth or not have any more children. Twenty-five per cent would prefer to delay or avoid pregnancy. In China contraceptive use is prevalent (91 per cent), but knowledge of how contraceptive methods work and are used is limited. The story of a newlywed Chinese girl who was not using contraception even though she did not want a child provides a telling account. When asked why she did not use contraception, she replied,

"I read in a journal that recently married couples would not get pregnant because the successful meeting of mature sperm and egg takes over 48 hours. We are newly married and have sexual intercourse almost every night. I thought that with old and new sperm eating each other, none of them would survive more than 48 hours. Therefore, I thought no pregnancy would happen."

76. In order to provide full recognition of a woman's right to reproductive autonomy, reproductive health care must provide complete and impartial information regarding the full range of contraceptive methods and reproductive health issues generally.

(b) Failure to address physical and psychological violence perpetrated by health care providers

77. In some countries, physical and psychological violence against women of low socio-economic status occurs in public health facilities. These violations are often ignored or inadequately addressed by administrative and judicial authorities. A recent report documents numerous cases in Peru of physical and psychological violence against women who use public reproductive health services, including rape, assault, and numerous forms of verbal abuse. For example, María testified that:

"the doctor made me enter and didn't let my sister or my father come in and told the nurse to stay outside. Then he told me to take off my clothes, my pants and blouse, and to lay down on the table. There I was without clothes. Then the doctor told me: 'So you are pregnant? Who could you have been with?' I felt him put his fingers in my private parts. He was hurting me a lot, and then I realized that both his hands were on my waist and he was thrusting himself into me and hurting me. He was abusing me. I was scared and he told me that 'that is how it is.' Then I pushed him away and started to cry, he told me that I had nothing wrong with me and to put on my clothes."

78. Even in the relatively few cases in which women were willing to file formal complaints, health officials and the judicial system failed to provide adequate remedies to the victims. Such violations are clearly extreme examples of government failure to meet core obligations to provide comprehensive and quality reproductive health care services to all women, regardless of their social and economic status in their societies.

III. Recommendations

79. States should ratify all international human rights instruments. States should withdraw any reservations to these instruments, particularly those regarding the human rights of women.

80. States must ensure that the foremost concern in the formulation and implementation of reproductive health and family planning programmes is respect for the individual rights of women.

81. States should create and promote a process of cross-sectoral and interdisciplinary collaboration, focusing on training and capacity-building for treaty bodies, agencies and non-governmental organizations on the issue of women's reproductive and sexual health.

82. States must exercise due diligence to prevent violence against women in order to protect their human rights, including, among others, specific laws to combat rape, domestic violence, trafficking and forced prostitution, female genital mutilation, sex-selective abortions and female infanticide.

83. States should pass and enforce a minimum legal age limit for marriages. States must undertake training programmes to sensitize health workers providing reproductive

health services–including those who work in antenatal clinics, maternity services and family planning services–to the possibility of gender violence among their clients.

84. States should take all measures necessary to eradicate discrimination and violence against women who use public health care services, and to guarantee institutional settings in which women's human rights are respected.

85. States should provide increased education to health workers and ensure easy availability of information about the human rights implications of reproductive health, including State obligations under international law.

86. States should provide training to health workers in women's reproductive rights, including training with respect to how to identify violations during physical examinations, as well as how to provide appropriate intervention information.

87. States should implement training programmes to provide those who work in minority communities with linguistic and cultural training sensitive to the differences of their clientele.

88. States must take appropriate measures to monitor reproductive health services and ensure that these services are offered without any form of discrimination, coercion or violence, and that information disseminated by health workers is comprehensive and objective.

89. States should provide financial and institutional support for the creation of support groups, shelters, crisis centres with counselling and legal assistance, and women-only police stations with trained workers and 24-hour hotlines.

90. States should provide financial and institutional support for research on safe and effective methods for the regulation of fertility, protection against sexually transmitted diseases, including HIV/AIDS, and confidential testing and diagnosis of STDs.

91. States should provide financial and institutional support for research into the prevention, detection and treatment of illnesses associated with women's reproductive health, particularly those with the highest indicators of maternal mortality and morbidity.

92. States should engage in systematic research and collection of data with respect to the incidence of violations of women's reproductive and sexual health, and use such data to inform future State policies that impact women's rights to reproductive and sexual health.

93. States should provide financial and technical support for organizations and institutions dedicated to promoting women's reproductive and sexual health, and engage in collaborative relationships with such institutions and organizations in the formulation of government reproductive health policies.

Chapter 7
The Right to Education (excerpts)

. . .

III. Realization and Legal Enforcement of the Right to Education

30. As the Special Rapporteur noted in her preliminary report, the general question of whether economic, social and cultural rights are justiciable does not apply to the right to education, which is litigated both domestically and internationally. Owing to space constraints, the Special Rapporteur has included in this report only a couple of references to pertinent court cases through which various dimensions of the right to education have been enforced.

31. The adoption of the Optional Protocol to the Convention on the Elimination of All Forms of Discrimination against Women promises to increase international remedies for gender discrimination. It has also reinforced the conceptual universality of human rights because remedies will be provided for civil and political, as well as economic, social and cultural rights. On the domestic level, Norway has set a commendable precedent, having incorporated in its domestic law both the International Covenant on Civil and Political Rights and the International Covenant on Economic, Social and Cultural Rights. Such developments promise to broaden and strengthen the work of domestic courts which have mapped out the nature and scope of the right to education.

A. Availability

32. As the Special Rapporteur has emphasized in all her previous reports, the obligation of the State to make schooling available constitutes one pillar of the individual right to education, and the failure of the State to sustain available schooling constitutes an apparent violation of the right to education. The African Commission on Human and Peoples' Rights found that a two-year-long closure of universities and secondary schools in Zaire (as it was at the time) constituted a violation of article 17 of the African Charter on Human and Peoples' Rights, which guarantees the right to education.

Progress Report of the Special Rapporteur on the right to education, Ms. Katarina Tomasevski, E/CN.4/2000/6.

33. States' practice with regard to ensuring that schools are available for all school-age children reveals a variety of models: the State can fund diverse schools but not operate any, or operate a network of State schools without funding any non-State schools. The extremes of a State's monopoly over education or its complete dissociation from education, neither of which would be consistent with international human rights law, are rare. Between these two extremes, the existing jurisprudence has laid down general principles for the interpretation and application of international human rights law.

1. Public funds and private schools

34. Much international jurisprudence has originated from demands upon States to finance education developed as an alternative to uniform public schooling. A variety of models developed in Western Europe, in part due to the "principle of subsidiarity according to which the State filled the gaps left by private sector provision (private and church schools)." The emergence of the State as the funder and/or provider of education is fairly recent in the history of education. The inherited mosaic of pre-State provision of education has greatly influenced this variety of models. Free education is generally conceptualized in terms of access to public schools, with States' practice varying with regard to subsidies for non-public schools. The distinction between free (State school) or fee-paying (private) schooling has been widely recognized worldwide.

35. The jurisprudence focusing on public funding to facilitate the exercise of freedom to establish and operate schools guaranteed under international human rights law has overcome a boundary between civil and political rights, which are often perceived as being costless, and economic, social and cultural rights, viewed as costly. In the Special Rapporteur's view, it has thereby reaffirmed the indivisibility of human rights in general, as well as within education.

36. The Human Rights Committee found that a State "cannot be deemed to act in a discriminatory fashion if it does not provide the same level of subsidy for the two [public and private] types of establishment, when the private system is not subject to State supervision." In a similar case, which dealt with the provision of free textbooks and school meals to children in public but not in private schools, the Committee affirmed its previous view, adding that "the preferential treatment given to public sector schooling is reasonable and based on objective criteria" This affirmation of the priority of public over private schools goes beyond funding: the role of education in the socialization of children prioritizes inclusiveness over segregation. In the well-known words of the Supreme Court of the United States, "separate educational facilities are inherently unequal."

37. The European Commission on Human Rights has during its previous existence affirmed that the State has no obligation to subsidize private schools while it has a right to subject such schools to regulation and supervision because it is responsible for ensuring that all education complies with prescribed standards. Domestic courts have been dealing with this subject-matter in different countries and have followed the thrust of international human rights law. The Supreme Court of Canada, having examined a

complaint against a denial of public funding to private religious schools, has affirmed that the purpose of public schools is provision of education for all members of the community. The exercise of parents' freedom to educate their children in accordance with their religious beliefs in separate schools (or at home) prevents their children from taking advantage of public schools and creates costs for the parents; such exercise of parental freedom does not entail an entitlement to public funding, however.

38. Moreover, the existing jurisprudence probes into issues which lie at the boundary between political and legal processes. Resource allocation is generally seen as a political decision and unelected courts cannot usurp the prerogatives of elected parliamentarians. Court cases which have halted the allocation of State funds to private schools or required Governments to strengthen public schools have imposed human rights correctives upon resource allocation, however. Such court cases have often been a response to the recent trends of privatization and commoditization of education, and especially to international endorsements of school vouchers.

39. Through the voucher schemes, Governments enable individual learners to make payments to the school of their choice, or make payment directly to the chosen school. The amount of payments usually corresponds to the admission and/or tuition costs. The rationale for school vouchers is enhancement of consumer (in this case parental) choice and an assumed enlargement of this choice through competition amongst schools. An additional, albeit implicit reason, has been a wish to subject public schools to competition, their being seen as having monopolized schooling. The distinction between public and private, State and non-State, fee-charging and free schools—and the diversity which they embody—is likely to be eroded if proposals for introduction of vouchers gain ground; only schools able to attract learners and/or funding will be left. The rationale behind vouchers perceives States as merely providing some funding to learners or schools to the detriment of the full range of the States' human rights obligations, namely to ensure that schooling is available, accessible, acceptable and adaptable.

40. The ongoing debate about school vouchers started within the realm of economics, focusing on consumer choice and competitiveness while excluding the notion of education as a public good. Court cases have brought the issue into the realm of the rule of law. The voucher scheme introduced in 1993 in Puerto Rico was declared unconstitutional in the part which accorded to selected pupils a financial grant of $1,500 for transfer from public to private school. The constitutional prohibition on diverting public funds to private schools reached back to the separation between church and State and was upheld, although the voucher scheme did not revolve around secular or religious schools. Rather, it was aimed at financially stimulating transfer from public to private schools (thus also transferring tax revenue to private schools) with the aim of increasing choice, contrary to the constitutional requirement that public funds be used solely for public schools.

41. Controversies relating to vouchers routinely revolve around economic arguments, thus departing from the meaning and purpose of the right to education. Amongst the existing jurisprudence, the Supreme Court of Colombia has ably clarified why education should not be governed by economic arguments alone:

". . . although the Constitution protects economic activities, private initiative and competition as well as recognizing the right of private entities to establish schools, these liberties cannot negate nor can they diminish the nature of education as public service and its social function; education is also and above all else a fundamental right.

" . . . education—even if private—has to be provided in the conditions which guarantee equality of opportunity in access to education, and all forms of discrimination and 'elitism' are thus repugnant to its nature of public service with profound social contents; these, by virtue of excessive economic demands, automatically deny access to intellectually able persons solely because [of] their levels of income."

2. The status of teachers

42. Although it is possible to imagine schooling taking place without schools but not without teachers, the attention to schools and textbooks in international education strategies is immense while they are relatively silent about teachers. Teaching is a labour-intensive profession and the Special Rapporteur is not convinced that recent ideas about replacing humans by technological devices will ever materialize, nor that they would be beneficial if they do materialize. For schooling that takes place without a school, water, sanitation, desks and chairs, books, blackboards, pens and paper, a teacher makes all the difference and the absence of a teacher prevents schooling from taking place. For teenagers in OECD countries who have replaced socialization by surfing the web, the Special Rapporteur has not seen a single piece of evidence claiming benefits for their social skills, tolerance or even basic literacy.

43. The advantage of teaching being labour-intensive is that employment of large numbers of people is possible—even necessary—to educate the millions of children and young people in the world. Since teachers are locally trained, hired and paid, there is the additional advantage that there is no need for foreign exchange, unlike for schools or schoolbooks that may be provided through loans which have to be repaid, or which may have to be imported. It seems, however, that instead of being seen as actors indispensable for schooling, teachers are often perceived as enemies of their own vocation. One reason for this view of teachers as a burden rather than an asset is the sheer size of the teaching profession and the proportion of education budgets allocated to teachers' salaries. In a country where school-age children represent one third of the population, a ratio of one teacher to every 50 children makes teachers 0.6 per cent of the population. As there is little besides teachers in the schooling process in many poor countries, teachers' salaries necessarily form the bulk of the education budget. The consecutive crises through which education has passed in recent decades has triggered a constant search for ways of cutting education budgets. Because teachers' salaries constitute the bulk of education budgets, they were the obvious first target for budgetary cuts.

44. The protection of the human rights of teachers sometimes slips into oblivion if teachers are considered as "a production factor" rather than as people. The applicable international human rights standards are many because the problems teachers encounter are complex and multi-layered. They range from discrimination on the internationally

prohibited grounds to teachers' recruitment and deployment, to the protection of professional and academic freedom, or to the role of teachers in human rights education. Problems in their enforcement have included teachers' status as civil and/or public servants leading to the denial of their trade union freedoms, or the definition of teaching as an essential service leading to the denial of their right to strike.

B. Accessibility: school fees

45. Where schools and teachers are available, access to schooling can be impeded by a variety of obstacles. As announced in her preliminary report, the Special Rapporteur is focusing in the present report on school fees. Much concern followed their introduction in the 1980s for previously free primary education, resulting in decreased enrolments and reduced access to primary schooling. International mobilization for "adjustment with a human face," as UNICEF aptly put it, led to a general acceptance of the need to protect primary education from budgetary cuts, but the Special Rapporteur feels that insufficient attention has been paid to ensuring that school fees are indeed abolished as international human rights law requires.

46. The explicit wording of international human rights treaties requires primary education to be compulsory and free of charge. The assumption that compulsory schooling equals primary education in length is, however, no longer valid. It bears repeating that the Special Rapporteur's mandate is oriented towards progressive implementation of compulsory education free of charge. Table 3 highlights correspondence between the length of primary and compulsory schooling, as well as differences between the two. In the majority of countries for which data are available (96), compulsory schooling has been lengthened far beyond primary schooling. The trend of lengthening compulsory schooling follows a double rationale: on the one hand, the raising of the school-leaving age prevents children from venturing into adulthood too early (be it in employment or marriage), on the other hand, it provides all children with a common core education, in the inclusive ideal in the same school and classroom also. Countries in which the two remain equal in length (60) have become a minority; in more than 40 countries education is compulsory for six years or less, while just under 40 countries have lengthened compulsory education to 10 years or more. The Special Rapporteur deems that these data merit emphasizing because the emerging international consensus on securing basic education for all, free of charge, could have two effects: it could confine guaranteed schooling to the 6–11 age group if the prevalent statistical definition is applied, or it could prolong it beyond primary to lower secondary education if the desirable definition of basic education (up to 15 years of age) prevails, keeping children in school till they reach the minimum age for employment.

47. Table 3 reflects to a large extent the economic capacity of individual countries to provide their young generation with schooling. Countries in which compulsory schooling is the shortest (such as Bangladesh, the Lao People's Democratic Republic, Nepal or Viet Nam) share financial obstacles to lengthening education, while the tendency in Western Europe to extend compulsory education beyond 10 years (in Belgium, Germany

and the Netherlands, for example) reflects the necessary merger of willingness and ability to do so. This issue has obtained increasing importance at the turn of the millennium with the switch towards knowledge-based economy, society or development in general, and is revisited in section IV below.

48. Considerations of affordability pervade any analysis of free-of-charge education and many questions have been raised in the past few decades about compatibility between fiscal and educational policy, that is, between fiscal targets defined in terms of reducing public expenditure and the funding necessary to ensure universal primary education free of charge. The global consensus on the need to make and keep primary education free of charge was ruptured in the early 1980s. Most analysts attribute the advocacy for school fees to the World Bank's research and policy-making for Africa and a great deal of critique followed the linkage between school fees and structural adjustment programmes. This is well known and can be omitted. Rather, the Special Rapporteur would like to note that the critique of school fees has had the unanticipated effect of subsequently diminishing the availability of information about them.

49. While international law requires primary education to be free of charge, education cannot be free of cost in theory or in practice. For Governments, it is one of the major items in their budgets and public investment in education represents between 80 and 90 per cent of the total. Parents finance their children's education through general taxation, sometimes also paying additional charges but always funding the cost of education beyond the Government's contribution. What is recorded as governmental investment (often called expenditure) is supplemented by parents, who bear the cost of books, transportation and school meals, uniforms, pens and pencils, or sports equipment.

50. As the Special Rapporteur noted in her preliminary report, the requirement upon Governments to make primary education free implies that Governments should eliminate financial obstacles in order to enable all children—no matter how poor—to complete primary schooling. The link between primary education being free and compulsory is emphasized in all three pertinent human rights instruments. Imposing a requirement upon children to attend school whose cost their parents cannot afford would make compulsory education illusory.

51. The reservations to the two global human rights treaties with regard to making primary education free and compulsory indicate the general acceptance of this postulate. As noted above, the mosaic of diverse pre-State schools such as existed in Western Europe at the time when the provision on the right to education was drafted (1950–52) influenced the approach to the role of the State under the European Convention on Human Rights, and reservations thereto have affirmed States' reluctance to finance diverse schools that tend to emerge from the exercise of parental freedom of choice. The fact that most States have committed themselves to ensuring free primary education affirms the explicit wording of global human rights treaties, and one can thus look further into what the meaning of "free" is in the practice of States.

52. In the Special Rapporteur's view, school fees represent a form of regressive taxation.

TABLE 3. Correspondence and difference between primary and compulsory schooling

Countries with equal length of compulsory and primary schooling

Albania (8), Bangladesh (5), Benin (6), Bolivia (8), Brazil (8), Burundi (6), Cameroon (6), Cape Verde (6), Central African Republic (6), Chad (6), Chile (8), Colombia (5), Côte d'Ivoire (6), Djibouti (6), El Salvador (9), Equatorial Guinea (5), Ethiopia (6), FYR of Macedonia (8), Guatemala (6), Guinea (6), Guinea-Bissau (6), Haiti (6), Honduras (6), Iran (5), Iraq (6), Jamaica (6), Kenya (8), Lao PDR (5), Lesotho (7), Libya (9), Malawi (8), Mauritania (6), Mexico (6), Morocco (6), Myanmar (5), Nepal (5), Nicaragua (6), Nigeria (6), Panama (6), Paraguay (6), Philippines (6), Peru (6), Poland (8), Samoa (8), Sao Tome and Principe (4), Senegal (6), Sudan (8), Suriname (6), Swaziland (7), Syria (6), Tanzania (7), Thailand (6), Togo (6), Trinidad and Tobago (7), United Arab Emirates (6), Uruguay (6), Vanuatu (6), Viet Nam (5), Yemen (9), Zambia (7)

Countries where compulsory schooling is longer than primary schooling

Antigua and Barbuda (10–7), Algeria (9–6), Argentina (10–7), Armenia (11–4), Australia (10–7), Austria (9–4), Azerbaijan (11–4), Bahamas (9–6), Bahrain (9–6), Barbados (11–7), Belarus (9–4), Belgium (12–6), Belize (10–8), Brunei Darussalam (12–6), Bulgaria (8–4), Burkina Faso (7–6), Canada (10–6), China (9–5), Comoros (9–6), Congo (10–6), Costa Rica (10–6), Croatia (8–4), Cuba (9–6), Cyprus (9–6), Czech Republic (9–4), Denmark (9–6), Dominica (11–7), Dominican Republic (10–8), Ecuador (10–6), Egypt (8–5), Eritrea (7–5), Estonia (9–6), Fiji (8–6), Finland (9–6), France (10–5), Gabon (10–6), Germany (12–4), Georgia (9–4), Ghana (8–6), Greece (9–6), Grenada (11–7), Guyana (8–6), Hungary (10–4), Iceland (10–7), India (8–5), Indonesia (9–6), Ireland (9–6), Israel (11–6), Italy (8–5), Japan (9–6), Kazakhstan (11–4), Kiribati (9–7), Kuwait (8–4), Kyrgyzstan (10–4), Lebanon (9–5), Liberia (10–6), Lithuania (9–4), Luxembourg (9–6), Madagascar (6–5), Mali (9–6), Malta (11–2), Mauritius (7–6), Moldova (11–4), Monaco (10–5), Mongolia (8–4), Mozambique (7–5), Namibia (10–7), Netherlands (13–6), New Zealand (10–6), Niger (8–6), Norway (9–6), Portugal (9–6), Republic of Korea (9–6), Romania (8–4), Russia (9–3), Seychelles (10–6), Slovakia (9–4), Slovenia (8–4), South Africa (9–7), Spain (8–6), Sri Lanka (9–5), St Kitts and Nevis (12–7), St. Lucia (10–7), St. Vincent and the Grenadines (10–7), Sweden (9–6), Switzerland (9–6), Tajikistan (9–4), Tonga (8–6), Tunisia (9–6), Turkey (8–5), Ukraine (9–4), United Kingdom (11–6), United States (10–6), Venezuela (10–9), Zimbabwe (8–7), Yugoslavia (8–4)

Source: UNESCO, *World Education Report 2000*, table 4, pp. 134–137.

Note: This table reproduces data on the length of compulsory and primary schooling, available from UNESCO, which originate from ministries of education and thus do not necessarily match those reported by the same countries under the human rights treaties. The first number in parentheses after the country names refers to the length of compulsory schooling in years and the second to the length of primary schooling. The only countries where primary schooling seems to be longer than compulsory schooling are Jordan (9–10), Rwanda (6–7) and Tuvalu (7–8).

Their justification routinely points to the inability (or unwillingness) of a Government to generate sufficient revenue through general taxation. Payment for primary schooling ruptures the key principle of taxation whereby people who cannot contribute to public services that are meant for all are not required to do so. School fees are most often charged for enrolment, tuition and examinations. Where tuition is free, charges can be levied for the use of educational facilities and materials (such as laboratories, computers or sports equipment), or for extracurricular activities (such as excursions or sports events), or generally for educational development or school maintenance. Such fees can sometimes seem minuscule (for example, $4 per year) from the viewpoint of people whose annual income is expressed in six or more digits, but they represent a considerable burden for parents whose annual income is written in three digits or less, particularly because these charges are added to all the other costs of their children's education which they have to bear. There is little information available about the financial costs of the administration and collection of such school fees in small and remote primary schools. Whether the imposition of such fees has proved too costly in every sense of this term remains an open question.

53. School fees at the primary school level are charged in a number of countries and this practice is reflected in the documentation generated by the reporting procedures under human rights treaties. The Special Rapporteur has opted for this source of information because it is authoritative, although not comprehensive in coverage. Only those countries which included information about school fees in their reports or in responses to queries from treaty bodies have been included, if their reports were available at the time of writing. The information in cited documents applied at the time the reports were submitted or discussed and the situation may have changed in the meantime. The coverage is illustrative rather than comprehensive and the Special Rapporteur will be grateful for all corrections and additions.

54. For some countries, an explicit reference to the charging of some form of school fees could be found in the documentation, for others it is unclear what type of fees, levies or contributions are being charged and whether financial contributions by parents that are described as voluntary can be made or withheld without having any effect on their children's schooling. Besides school fees, levies or contributions in their different guises, direct costs of education include textbooks (which are provided free of charge in some countries, while they are subsidized in many), supplies and equipment (notebooks, sketchbooks, pens and pencils), transportation (provided free of charge in few countries), meals (also provided free of charge in some countries, sometimes as an inducement to parents to send their children to school) and school uniforms where these are required for school attendance. These costs can be prohibitively high, as has been noted quite a few times in the context of the reporting procedures of the human rights treaty bodies and they have broadened the question of the meaning of free education beyond school fees; financial barriers to access to primary education result in the lack of access to school for poor children and thus retrogression rather than progressive realization of the right to education.

55. States' practice also includes examples of the elimination of financial barriers to access to education, in the form of subsidies to poor families to enable them to send

their children to school. Such subsidies are intended to eliminate all direct and indirect costs of primary education, compensating families for the opportunity cost of schooling children. The general idea that costs of education should be borne in proportion to financial ability thus found expression in subsidies to the poorest so as to redress their inability to dispense with the children's contribution to the survival of the family. This issue is revisited below in section III.D on working children.

C. Acceptability: pregnancy as a disciplinary offence

56. The Special Rapporteur has noted in all her previous reports the constantly increasing attention to girls' access to school and their persistence in schooling and will review recent developments in her next report. She deems it necessary to move beyond availability and accessibility, and has chosen pregnancy as a disciplinary offence because it points to questioning the acceptability of school discipline, as well as the general orientation of education.

57. The Commission on Human Rights has emphasized the role of education in enhancing the ability of women to make informed choices. The practice of defining pregnancy as a disciplinary offence routinely leads to the expulsion of the pregnant girl from school, sometimes precluding her from continuing education. The lack of access to information that would have enabled the girl to make any choice, least of all an informed one, is usually the background to this practice. The frequent clash between societal norms which pressurize girls into early pregnancy and legal norms which aim to keep them in school makes this phenomenon difficult to tackle. Moreover, the practice of expelling pregnant teachers from school forms part of not too distant history and points to the heritage of precluding the exposure of schoolchildren to pregnancy. If the expulsion of pregnant schoolteachers seems to have become history, this is not so if teachers are not married.

58. Information about the definition of pregnancy as a disciplinary offence leading to expulsion from school is regretfully fragmentary. As far as the Special Rapporteur could ascertain for Africa (although the available information is scarce and outdated), pregnant girls are expelled from primary and secondary schools in Liberia, Mali, Nigeria, Swaziland, Tanzania, Togo, Uganda and Zambia, while change has been introduced in Bolivia, Botswana, Chile, Côte d'Ivoire, Guinea, Kenya and Malawi. Such information is usually collected as the first step towards affirming the girls' right to education. The coming into force in November 1999 of the Charter on the Rights and Welfare of the African Child, which includes an explicit requirement that States ensure that pregnant girls have an opportunity to continue with their education, is likely to increase the momentum for change.

59. Change does not come easily. The views of parents, teachers and community leaders tend to support the expulsion of pregnant girls from school, rationalizing this punitive choice by the need to uphold a moral norm which prohibits teenage sex—pregnancy being considered as irrefutable proof that this norm was breached and as

entailing punishment. Punitiveness sometimes also encompasses schoolboys who father children, but never adult men who seem responsible for most teenage pregnancies, more than 70 per cent in Botswana. Societal norms are not automatically changed through the adoption of international or domestic guarantees of the equal right to education for girls nor are they usually altered through democratic decision-making, in which girls routinely do not have a voice. Law thus provides a good starting point for the process of change.

60. The Supreme Court of Colombia has established an important precedent by demanding that school regulations, which envisaged penalization of pregnancy by suspending pregnant girls from schooling and rerouting them into tutorials, should be altered and the pregnant girls to whom they were applied returned to normal schooling. The opinion of the Court is worth quoting because of its importance for the interpretation of the nature and scope of the pregnant girls' right to education:

". . . although a suspension from school attendance does not imply a definitive loss of the right to education, it does imply the provision of instruction to the pregnant schoolgirl in conditions which are stigmatizing and discriminatory in comparison with other pupils in her ability to benefit from [the right to education]. Surely, the stigmatization and discrimination implied in the suspension from school attendance have converted this method of instruction into a disproportionate burden which the pupil has to bear solely because she is pregnant, which, in the opinion of the Court, amounts to punishment.

The conversion of pregnancy—through school regulations—into a ground for punishment violates fundamental rights to equality, privacy, free development of personality, and to education."

D. Adaptability: education for working children

61. The Special Rapporteur has closely observed recent developments with regard to the elimination of child labour, especially linkages which are being forged between schooling and working. These span a negative dimension (enforcement of the prohibition of exploitative child labour), as well as a positive one (provision of schooling to working children). The adoption of ILO Convention No. 182 reinforced the definition of a child as a person up to the age of 18 with respect to safeguards against intolerable forms of child labour, re-emphasized States' obligations to ensure access to free basic education for all children, and mandated vocational training for children removed from labouring.

62. The International Labour Organization has reinforced its early link between the age for completion of compulsory education and the minimum age for employment, and the Special Rapporteur has exerted a great deal of effort to attain acceptance of this link in international education strategies. As she has pointed out many times, the shift to "basic" from primary and/or compulsory education has had the detrimental

side effect of lowering the school-leaving age and thus leaving children in limbo until they reach the minimum age of employment.

63. ILO-IPEC aims to set in motion "a process geared to reform and change in social attitudes and in public and corporate policies that will lead to sustainable prevention and abolition of child labour from within a country." Both prevention and abolition of child labour have posed additional challenges to education. Prevention of child labour necessitates a conceptual shift in the orientation of education towards the acknowledgement of one simple fact: "the unavoidable labour reality is very much local," and any global or foreign models require adaptation to that local reality. The dominant trend in human rights towards conceiving work as access to employment in the formal sector rather than self-employment in the informal sector (whether subsistence or entrepreneurship) does not provide a promising background for responding to this challenge nor does the heritage of designing primary education so as to lead pupils to secondary and higher education. Adaptability is often hampered by school curricula "developed centrally by groups of 'experts' who design them to prepare children for the next level of education, to which many children will be unable to proceed."

64. Opportunities for working children to "learn and earn" have been grounded in the necessity for poor people—including children—to work so as to be able to survive. Full-time education then appears to be a luxury rather than a basic right of the child, and changing that cruel reality requires a great deal of political and financial commitment. The Supreme Court of India has accepted this "learn and earn" approach for non-hazardous employment of children below 14 years of age, mandating a reduction of daily working hours to six, coupled with at least two hours of education at the expense of the employer. For hazardous work, the Court has recalled that child labour could not be eliminated without tackling underlying poverty and suggested ensuring work for an adult member of the family in lieu of the child or, if this is impossible within the limits of the economic capacity of the State, the provision of a minimum income to the family in order to enable them to send the child to school payable as long as the child is attending school.

65. Adaptation of education to local circumstances requires protection against the institutionalization of disadvantage which can result in "educational ghettos." A shift away from denigrating vocational education as inferior to academic education is necessary, as is the acceptance of resource requirements for in-school vocational education and training. The increasing shortage of public sector jobs worldwide is likely to facilitate altering the inherited hierarchy within education, which prioritized general at the expense of vocational education.

IV. The Changing Legal Status of Education and the Need to Mainstream Human Rights

66. The definition of education as a human right does not guide many international or domestic education strategies; the recent emergence of a focus on education as a

means for creating human capital and the prospect of education being purchased and sold as service create a great challenge for reaffirming education as a human right and as a public good. Contemporary changes can be illustrated by the usage of the term "rights" to denote shareholders' or creditors' rights, rather than in the sense attributed to this term in international human rights law. The Special Rapporteur welcomes the initiative of the Sub-Commission on the Promotion and Protection of Human Rights in placing globalization and trade liberalization on the human rights agenda with a view to "fully integrating human rights in the processes of economic policy formulation" as well as ensuring that "human rights principles and obligations are fully integrated in future negotiations in the World Trade Organization."

. . .

Chapter 8

Effects of Structural Adjustment Policies on the Full Enjoyment of Human Rights (excerpts)

. . .

II. Links Between Structural Adjustment and the Realization of Economic, Social and Cultural Rights

. . .

58. In many countries currently engulfed by war and internal conflict, adjustment-induced social unrest provided the initial impetus for ethnic, tribal, religious fundamentalist and nationalist frenzy which eventually led to armed conflict. This reassessment of the nature of policy reforms is particularly striking because adjustment programmes are meant, according to their designers, to shift resources towards the poor. But while increases in food prices and cutbacks in government expenditures and employment have taken place as planned, overall economic growth—which was expected to counteract these developments—has not. The negative consequences of "orthodox" adjustment policies are evident in the following areas.

1. Increased unemployment

59. During the years 1978–1995, of the 43 countries on which the ILO has published statistics, 31 countries, or 72 percent, suffered a rise in unemployment during the years of IMF funding. Similarly, the Inter-American Development Bank reports that half of the 20 Latin American countries for which it has official data experienced rising unemployment in the 1980s and 1990s, during which time these countries received considerable and ongoing IMF lending. The increase in the rate of unemployment is not confined to low-performing adjustment countries alone. The growth in countries that

Report submitted by the Independent Expert, Mr. Fantu Cheru, to the Commission on Human Rights, E/CN.4/1999/50.

are touted by the IMF and the World Bank as "model adjustment countries" with high GNP growth, such as Chile, Uganda and Ghana, has largely been "jobless growth."

60. The *World Employment Report 1998–99* says that unemployment in Latin America increased between 1991 and 1996, reaching 7.4 percent in 1997. These figures probably underestimate the magnitude of the problem. In Asia, the financial crisis was responsible for 10 million people in the region being unemployed overnight. In Indonesia alone, unemployment in 1998 is estimated to reach between 9 and 12 percent of the labour force, compared with about 4 percent in 1996. The situation in East Asia, Latin America and the Russian Federation is likely to get worse before it gets better since many emerging markets in the three regions are caught in a global pullback by investors, which could push unemployment and underemployment up sharply.

2. Dramatic increase in the poverty rate

61. Although accurate statistics are hard to come by, the UNDP *Human Development Report* and reports from the United Nations regional economic commissions provide startling information on both the persistence of poverty in many developing countries despite adherence to structural adjustment programmes for well over a decade. Among the 4.4 billion people who live in developing countries, three fifths have no access to basic sanitation; almost one third are without safe drinking water; one quarter lack adequate housing; one fifth live beyond the reach of modern health services; one fifth of the children do not get as far as grade five in school and one fifth are undernourished.

62. Rural poverty, a dominant feature of life in all regions of the world, affects the lives of close to 1 billion people. While urban poverty is also a growing phenomenon, the rural poor still account for over 80 percent of the total number of poor people in more than 110 developing countries. The proportion of the rural population whose income and consumption fall below nationally defined poverty lines is estimated at 31 percent in Asia (46 percent if China and India are excluded), 60 percent in sub-Saharan Africa, 61 percent in Latin America and the Caribbean, and 26 percent in the Near East and North Africa. In the 42 least developed countries, as much as 69 percent of the total rural population lives in poverty. In the two regions with the highest incidence of income poverty—sub-Saharan Africa and South Asia—poverty is increasing in both absolute and real terms, according to the *Human Development Report, 1997*, and the majority of countries in these regions have been under IMF/World Bank surveillance. While those segments of society that are fully engaged in export activities—the primary focus of adjustment programmes—have benefited enormously and have consequently consolidated their economic power, the vast majority of the population have seen their living standards fall drastically.

3. Fall in real wages

63. Poverty is further accentuated by the downward pressure on wages and by the dramatic loss of purchasing power of the poor. In an attempt to contain inflation, wage

restraint is advocated by SAP. The problem is further accentuated by the deliberate decision to keep wages low in order to attract foreign direct investment. According to ILO, real wages in most African countries, for example, have fallen 50 and 60 percent since the early 1980s. In the Russian Federation, for example, rising economic turmoil has been accompanied by negative growth in real wages, now, at least, 60 percent of their 1989 level. In a growing number of cases, enterprises cannot pay any wages at all to their employees for months at a time.

64. The ILO *World Employment Report 1998–99* says that the majority of new jobs in developing countries are being created in the informal sector, which employs about 500 million workers. Yet, SAPs ignore the importance of informal sector activity. Despite lip-service, no concrete proposals have been offered by the IMF and the World Bank to capture the dynamism of the informal sector and to redirect adjustment funds to assist entrepreneurs to upgrade their skills, technology, or to enable them to have access to substantial amounts of capital necessary for expansion.

4. Decrease in budgetary allocations to social services

65. Because debtor nations must service their debt in order to receive further international assistance, many of these countries are forced to divert a large portion of their resources from investment in the productive and social sectors. The cuts mandated by structural adjustment have been indiscriminate, thereby affecting basic services which are essential for long-term development and the realization of the economic, social and cultural rights of citizens. The magnitude of the social and economic crisis in the transition economies of Central and Eastern Europe is underscored by a significant deterioration of health and education indicators. Specifically, indiscriminate application of structural adjustment programmes have jeopardized the following rights:

(a) The right to food. SAPs have put the right to food in jeopardy. There is convincing evidence that shows nutritional levels decrease among poorer segments of the population as a result of removal of food subsidies. Growing unemployment has a similar result. The switching of agricultural policies, primarily from food production for local consumption to production of coffee, tobacco or cotton to generate foreign exchange, has also resulted in drastic decline in food production and in reduced nutritional levels and malnutrition;

(b) The right to education. Article 26 of the Universal Declaration of Human Rights declared that everyone has the right to education. The Convention on the Rights of the Child has also established the right to early development and education. Thanks to extraordinary efforts during the 1960s and 1970s, the percentage of children completing at least four years of primary education had reached 50 percent or more in almost all developing countries. But since the 1980s, increasing debt and consequent implementation of structural adjustment programmes led many Governments to freeze or cut educational spending. As UNESCO has noted, primary schooling often suffered disproportionately, and there was significant slippage in sub-Saharan Africa. The percentage of 6 to 11-year-olds enrolled in school dropped from a high of 55 percent in 1979 to 45 percent in 1995. At risk here can be one of the areas in which sub-Saharan Africa has fared well—the reduction of inequalities between boys and girls in school enrolments. Girl's enrolments grew from 36 percent in 1960 to 63 percent in 1980. But in the face of increased fees, families may keep their daughters away from school when forced to choose which children to educate. Given the critical correlation between child welfare and the level of mothers' education, this could have important implications for infant and child health in the long term;

(c) The right to shelter. When wages are low or when they decrease, or when wage earners are unemployed as a result of structural adjustment programmes—as is more often the case—workers do not have enough resources to meet their basic needs, particularly housing. Furthermore, high interest rates ultimately kill the dream to own a home, and the devaluation of currency also increases the cost of construction materials. With the withdrawal of the State from direct provision of housing or housing subsidies to the poor and the deregulation of the rental market, the poor are exploited by private property owners, often paying over half of their meagre income on rent. Forced evictions are widespread as land values skyrocket due to pressure to build expensive dwellings for high-income groups. The property boom could also increase the cost of basic construction inputs, such as lumber, bricks and cement, also consumed by low-end consumers.

(d) The right to health. Article 25 of the Universal Declaration of Human Rights encourages the right to a standard of living adequate for health and well-being. The goal of "Health for all by the year 2000" agreed upon in the Almaty Declaration has been severely undermined by cutbacks in government health budgets as social and development objectives have been superseded by financial imperatives. The failure of the IMF and World Bank to protect health, nutrition and education budgets from general fiscal retrenchment in the design of structural adjustment programmes is a grave policy error. Drastic cuts inevitably have adverse consequences for social welfare and these in turn impinge on the economic productivity of human resources, generating resentment against Government by marginalized citizens. According to one authoritative source, the drug trade in Peru, Colombia and Bolivia is closely related to the significant social erosion in those countries as a result of the debt crisis and the accompanying policy of structural adjustment.

5. High incidence of labour repression

66. There are certain labour standards which have been almost universally accepted as fundamental human rights as set out in various United Nations treaties. These include: the elimination of child labour exploitation, prohibition of forced labour, freedom of association, the right to organize and bargain collectively, and non-discrimination in employment. Despite the almost universal recognition that certain workers' rights are basic human rights, there is countless evidence that these rights are continually repressed in many parts of the world. The exploitation of child labour is particularly appalling and remains a serious problem.

67. As indebted countries compete among themselves to offer cheaper labour to attract foreign direct investment (FDI), their labour standards are declining drastically. Many Governments rescind or modify national labour and social legislation to establish export processing zones (EPZs). The glue that links developing countries to the process of global integration is the policy of structural adjustment, with its emphasis on liberalization and free trade. The free-trade zones, where much of the overseas assembly work takes place, are havens for United States investment, complete with Government-subsidized electricity and other infrastructure. The zones mean more freedom for business and less freedom for people. The use of child labour and women in export processing zones has become extensive, bordering on a modern-day version of "slavery."

III. Adjustment with Transformation

A. Changing course: proposal for an alternative strategy

110. Poverty, marginalization and widespread alienation remain the most significant and pervasive problems facing many indebted countries in the third world and East European countries. These problems cannot be adequately addressed until the current approach to structural adjustment is fundamentally altered.

111. Macroeconomic reforms such as devaluation, pricing policy, and budget and tax reforms are necessary components of a balanced and integrated national development strategy. But implementation of these policies will have little impact on long-term sustainable development, sound management of natural resources, or on the reduction of poverty and inequality unless accompanied by fundamental transformation of unjust economic and political structures both at national and global levels. In short, a realignment of economic structures is as much a matter of realignment of power structures which, more often than not, will be resisted by powerful social and political groups within a given country or powerful forces in the global economy.

112. Some third world leaders and Western donors insist that restoring growth and repaying the debt will resolve the larger development problem in the shortest time possible. But that will merely maintain the ties of dependency on the market system, and growth is restored at great cost to the majority of poor people. It may get things back to "normal," but "normal" is exploitative and immoral when the laws of the market prevail unregulated and in the absence of support programmes for those in need. Almost 20 years of futile experiment with structural adjustment programmes has eroded the social welfare of millions of poor people across the third world and denied their economic, social and cultural rights.

B. Adjustment with transformation: underlying principles

113. An alternative "adjustment with transformation" should emphasize sustainable economic growth combined with social justice. This would entail adjusting economies to meet human needs and not vice versa. The Copenhagen Declaration on Social Development (para. 91), for example, called on Governments to ensure that, in structural

adjustment programmes, social development goals are included; basic social programmes and expenditures are protected from budget reduction; and the impact of structural adjustment programmes should be reviewed and altered to reduce their negative effects and improve their positive impacts. Furthermore, adjustment with transformation should have the following elements:

1. Promoting human development and gender equality

114. "Adjustment with transformation" should be geared to start the broad process of human development and empowerment. Empowerment is the very essence of human development, not just a means to an end. Political and economic reforms in the third world must seek to empower ordinary men and women to take charge of their lives, to make communities more responsible for their own development, and to make Governments listen to their people. The process of empowerment involves transforming the economic, social, psychological, political and legal circumstances of the currently powerless. It involves the development of autonomous and coherent popular organizations, and the defence of, and education about, the legal rights of the popular sector. It also involves a form of socio-economic and political restructuring which will remove the locus of power from the current custodians of State power, enable disadvantaged men and women to meet their basic needs and to fully participate in decision-making, and provide opportunities to challenge internal and external exploiters.

2. According priority to meeting basic human needs

115. "Adjustment with transformation" must place emphasis on alleviating poverty and meeting the basic needs of the people, who are the principal resources to build on. The provision of health care, basic nutrition and education are the basic building blocks of a human-centred transformation strategy. Malnourished people unable to receive health and educational services are in no position to improve their own well-being or indeed contribute productively to the nation. Nutritional imbalances are as crucial as trade imbalances, and high infant mortality rates require the same immediate action as high rates of inflation. Therefore, how countries incorporate human concerns should be an integral part of their adjustment programmes. This implies a critical look at existing models—primarily export-led growth—currently promoted by international financial institutions. Export-led growth has carried as a corollary the erosion of basic human needs. The cooperation of third world Governments with local and international private interests in a triple alliance has meant that none of the three is beholden to or likely to serve the needs of the poor. Encouraging developing countries to become self-reliant in food production is a key component needed to ensure that countries can weather balance-of-payments storms with their people's welfare intact.

3. Ensuring democratic representation and decision-making

116. "Adjustment with transformation" must ensure that the people have a significant

voice in shaping how development policies in general are formulated and implemented. There is rarely commitment by the people to any policy which is imposed from above or from outside by those who assert that they have the knowledge and arrogate to themselves the authority to decide for others. Participation is a human right. People should be enabled to reflect on their own problems and to articulate their own ideas of solutions to such problems. Only if this is done can development be seen as a liberating process, one which creates conditions for people and societies, particularly those presently oppressed and marginalized, to identify their own needs, mobilize their own resources and shape their future. Adjustment programmes must, therefore, inspire, mobilize and engage the initiative and resourcefulness of the poor for productive efforts. This approach demands their democratic participation in decisions concerning their lives and their future.

117. At the international level, democratization and social reform in the third world are contingent upon the degree of internal change in the core countries and their institutions. International financial institutions, so long dominated by the G-7 countries, need to be democratized. Currently, representation and voting in the Bretton Woods institutions are based on economic power: "one dollar, one vote." Thus the G-7 exercise dominant influence over these institutions' decisions, while the vast majority of poorer countries have no real power at all. As a result, these institutions continue to enforce their own definitions of development around the world with little regard for the consequences of their policies on the majority of poor people in developing countries. Ideally, institutions like the IMF and informal forums like the Paris Club should be reshaped to ensure that non-governmental organizations of debtor countries—such as peasant and workers' unions—have input into fashioning their countries' adjustment programmes. Until large numbers of informed citizens demand these changes, it will be very difficult to affect decision-making in the multilateral institutions.

4. Guaranteeing fair reward for labour

118. This principle is relevant to all institutions governing the world economic order, whether they govern finance, trade or development. At the level of national economies, the world economic system should guarantee fair and remunerative prices to developing country producers of raw materials, and institutions governing world trade should be reformed or built anew to further this principle. For the debtors of our era, just as in the 1930s, it is catch-22. Countries struggling to export their way out of the debt crisis ought at least to earn a fair price for their wares, and be able to sell them without undue encumbrance. Neither condition holds true today. Raw material prices have fallen drastically. The IMF's own data prove this. Prices for the 34 commodities expressed in Special Drawing Rights, the Fund's composite currency that avoids the distortions of an oscillating dollar, dropped by 13 percent in 1990 alone.

119. At the level of the individual labourer, decisions by the multilateral institutions should not undermine labour rights. Currently, IMF programmes often seek to reduce real wages and reinforce government repression of workers seeking better wages or working conditions.

5. Equitable sharing of the debt burden

120. Democratic treatment and accountability implies greater equity in sharing the burden of adjustment both at the local and international level. The costs of the $1.5 trillion third world debt will be paid by someone. They must, however, be lifted from the poorer majorities who have had the least role in creating the crisis. The burden must be shared more equitably among countries as well as social groups and the world's transnational bank lenders. This requires an end to disguising the problem, to maintaining the fiction that the bulk of these loans are still "performing" in any meaningful way.

121. It is on the foundation of these principles that the range of proposed solutions to the social and economic crisis are assessed, and that new proposals for advancing human-centred development are offered.

IV. Recommendations

A. Actions to be taken at the international level

1. Debt cancellation for the heavily indebted poor countries

122. Significant debt reduction is necessary for the recovery and resumption of growth in many poor indebted countries. Priority should be given to: (i) countries emerging out of years of devastating civil war (so-called post-conflict countries); and (ii) countries that have been devastated by natural disasters. Even for countries not classified as severely indebted, the debt overhang poses tremendous constraints to growth. However, any debt-cancellation programme must have broad-based citizen support and be consonant with a national economic plan that is formulated with broad consultation with all the relevant national actors, particularly civil society organizations. This is a proposal currently being pushed by the Global Jubilee 2000 campaign on debt reduction.

123. Western Governments can take a lesson from a proposal under consideration by the United States House of Representatives. The United States branch of the Jubilee Campaign has introduced legislation to the 106th Congress which contains the following:

(a) The legislation provides for the cancellation of bilateral debt owed by poor countries to the United States Government for concessional loans or credits given through United States foreign assistance or agricultural development programmes;

(b) The legislation also authorizes at least a 90 percent reduction of debts owed the United States by poor countries as a result of non-concessional (market rate) loans, guarantees, or credits provided through United States foreign assistance, arms sales, commodity programmes or export promotion underwriting;

(c) The legislation gives priority to countries which have demonstrated a sustained commitment to poverty alleviation or have recently suffered a major natural disaster, but it excludes countries with excessive military spending, gross violations of human rights, blatant drug trafficking or ethnic conflicts;

(d) The legislation requires countries to establish, through transparent and participatory process, a Human Development Trust Fund whose resources will be dedicated to reducing the number of persons living in poverty, expanding access of the poorest members of society to basic social services, including education, health, clean water and sanitation, and preventing the degradation of the environment.

2. Instituting human rights conditionality in future lending

124. While "conditionality" is a contentious issue as it is considered to be undermining the sovereignty of nations, it is desirable as long as it is based on "human development" and "human rights" criteria, and on broad consultation with civil society organizations and national Governments. This requires greater transparency and accountability by lenders, particularly the World Bank and the IMF. The secrecy surrounding adjustment programmes should be eliminated. Specifically, all letters of intent to the IMF should spell out the projected impact of economic adjustment policies on jobs, wealth distribution and basic needs.

125. Conditionality ensures that debt relief provided is used effectively and not squandered on corruption, military expenditure and grandiose projects with little if any benefit in terms of sustainable growth or poverty reduction. Each country should establish a monitoring unit composed of representatives of Government, donors and civil society to monitor compliance by Governments.

3. Establishing international mechanisms to retrieve money stolen by corrupt leaders

126. The pressure of debt on some poor countries can be eased if an international effort is mounted to retrieve large sums of money taken away illegally by many corrupt third world leaders. This will require the same level of attention, if not more, by Western countries as they give to the tracking of money laundered through commercial banks by drug traffickers. The recent decision by the Swiss Government to compensate survivors of the Nazi holocaust for stolen gold and money deposited in Swiss banks could be used as a precedent for doing the same with large sums of money taken away by third world elites.

4. Reform of the international economic, financial and trade systems

127. Long-term development in indebted countries is impossible without a basic restructuring of world financial, monetary and trade systems. Much more effort by the international community will be required to establish a more propitious trading and financial climate within which debtor nations can hope to increase their exports and attract various forms of financing needed to achieve a positive momentum in their economic development. Measures to end recession, to stimulate trade and ease financial constraints should be considerably more important than aid transfers. Specifically,

ensuring fair prices for commodities and market access for these products are of dominant importance. This requires structural changes in the field of primary commodity trade, by giving the least developed better access to Northern markets, encouraging more processing of their commodities before export, and extending the preferential treatment now accorded them.

5. Natural resource preservation

128. Future lending should be made conditional on assessing its impact on the environment and the resource base the poor depend on. The financing of large dams that would result in displacement of large numbers of people and ruin the ecosystem should be discouraged if possible. Projects of that magnitude should not be contemplated without proper consultation with the affected communities.

Chapter 9

Human Rights and Extreme Poverty (excerpts)

. . .

III. Action at the National Level

82. All Governments shall formulate integrated poverty eradication strategies and policies and implement national poverty eradication plans or programmes in a participatory manner, to address the structural causes of poverty, encompassing action at local, national, subregional, regional and international levels. Those plans should establish, within each national context, strategies and affordable time-bound goals and targets for the substantial reduction of overall poverty and the eradication of absolute poverty.

83. The United Nations Consultative Committee on Programme and Operational Questions (CCPOQ) adopted in September 1998 a matrix entitled "Freedom from Poverty: Actions and Partnerships" for inclusion in its Operational Activities Reference Manual. The matrix provides a common United Nations approach to poverty eradication and people-centred sustainable development. In particular, the following action areas are suggested:

(a) Creating a broad enabling environment to combat poverty and promote pro-poor economic growth (through both internal and external measures);

(b) Investing in and maintaining needed physical infrastructure, including infrastructure targeted for low-income communities;

(c) Promoting access to basic social services for all, including health, reproductive health and family planing services, education and sanitation, adopting special measures to reach women and children;

(d) Securing sustainable livelihoods for the poor, including access to productive assets such as credit;

Report submitted by Ms. A.-M. Lizin, independent expert, Commission on Human Rights, E/CN.4/1999/48.

(e) Advancing gender equality and equity, including the economic, legal and political empowerment of women;

(f) Ensuring sustainable food security in low-income households and the right to food;

(g) Regenerating the natural resource base on which the poor depend;

(h) Good governance and political empowerment of the poor; and

(i) Providing social protection for vulnerable people, including indigenous peoples.

84. The United Nations Development Assistance Framework (UNDAF) has developed a list of indicators to facilitate the United Nations system's assessments at the country level. Account has been taken of the World Summit for Children, the International Conference on Population and Development, the World Summit for Social Development and the Convention on the Rights of the Child. All United Nations Funds and Programmes conducting development activities in a country shall join together, under the leadership of the resident coordinator, to prepare UNDAF, in full consultation with the Government concerned as well as with civil society, local NGOs and international donors. Entities such as the specialized agencies and the Bretton Woods institutions are encouraged to join in the preparation of UNDAF, in order to maximize the United Nations system's collaboration in support of country priorities.

85. Some of these indicators are particularly relevant for the eradication of extreme poverty, among them the estimated population size by age and sex, urban-rural population distribution, life expectancy at birth, and mortality and fertility indicators such as infant mortality rate by sex, under-five mortality rate by sex, maternal mortality rate, total fertility rate and current population growth rate. Regarding health conditions, UNDAF indicators suggested were: proportion of the population with access to health services; proportion of under-five children underweight by sex; proportion of births attended by appropriately trained health personnel; contraceptive prevalence rate, by method and age; and HIV adult prevalence rate.

86. In addition, the World Social Summit set four immediate health and nutrition related goals: that by the year 2000, life expectancy should be not less than 60 years in any country; mortality rates of infants and children under five years should be reduced by one third of the 1990 level or 50 to 70 per 1,000 live births, whichever is less; reduction in maternal mortality by one half of the 1990 level; and attainment by all peoples of the world of a level of health that will permit them to lead a socially and economically productive life and, to this end, ensuring primary health care for all.

87. As regards education, UNDAF used indicators reflecting the basic educational status of the population, with emphasis on basic education. They are: adult literacy rate by sex; net primary enrolment ratio by sex; percent reaching grade 5; and net secondary enrolment ratio by sex.

88. Since universal primary education is central in the fight against poverty, the World Social Summit set a target of universal access to basic education and completion of primary education by at least 80 percent of primary school-age children by the year 2000.

Enrolment in secondary education still remains unsatisfactory despite progress. Developing countries as a whole increased gross enrolment ratios from 42 percent in 1990 to 46 percent in 1993. In comparison, there is 95 percent enrolment in the industrialized countries and in countries with economies in transition.

89. As regards the gender gap, in a majority of countries the illiteracy rate among women is significantly higher than for men. According to the *World Education Report 1995* published by the United Nations Educational, Scientific and Cultural Organization, in 65 countries the gap between the male and female adult literacy rates is estimated to be higher than 10 percent; in another 40 countries, it is estimated to be higher than 20 percent. Adult illiteracy is still increasing in sub-Saharan Africa, Arab States and southern Asia, with women forming a substantial majority in each case.

90. UNDAF income and employment indicators are focused on how they affect people's well-being in terms of income levels, employment and poverty: GNP per capita and average annual growth rate for the last 10-year period (in constant US dollars); percentage of population below the poverty line by sex (and for those younger than 18 years old), calculated according to monetary value of the minimum food basket and food expenditures as a percentage of total expenditures; percentage of labour force engaged in agriculture, industry and services by sex and by status (employer, self-employer, employee and unpaid family worker); and percentage of children aged 10–14 who are working.

91. The World Social Summit set the goal of achieving food security for all. In the developing world, the absolute number and the proportion of undernourished people fell between 1990 and 1992, but in 30 countries the percentage increased. All in all, about 840 million people in the developing world were undernourished in the early 1990s. The situation was worse in sub-Saharan Africa, where the number of undernourished people doubled, affecting 43 percent of the total population in 1990–1992. The World Food Summit in 1996 adopted as a target the reduction in the number of undernourished people to half the 1996 level by 2015. A mid-term review is to be held to ascertain whether it is possible to achieve that target by 2010.

92. UNDAF Habitat (housing conditions and people's access to supportive infrastructure) indicators shall include: percentage of population with access to adequate sanitation, safe drinking water and electricity; and number of people per room (excluding bathroom).

93. UNDAF environmental indicators shall include as: arable land per capita; percentage change in total square kilometres of forest land in the last 10 years; and percentage of the population that relies on traditional fuels for energy use.

94. Human security and social justice shall be checked against indicators showing whether social conditions provide personal security, such as freedom from violence and equitable opportunities for human development. Indicators shall refer to: number of victims of violence per 1,000 people by sex and age; and number of persons in prison per 100,000 people. Indicators of gender inequality and any other inequalities, such as those by age and by ethnic origin, shall also be included.

95. Finally, United Nations Funds, Programmes and agencies should promote a policy of mainstreaming a gender perspective and use gender analysis as a tool for the integration of a gender dimension into the planning and implementation of policies, strategies and programmes on poverty eradication.

. . .

VI. Women In Extreme Poverty

111. Poverty hits women especially hard and leads to serious violations of their rights. Extreme poverty can be linked with prostitution and with the exploitation, both sexual and physical (forced labour), of young girls from very poor backgrounds (prostitution and slavery rings). Unemployment and illiteracy are also particular problems for women. Women prisoners' conditions are in general an affront to their dignity. Local traditions sometimes make birth control impossible or are demeaning to women (no access to employment, forced marriage, very low age of marriage, no civil status for girls, etc.).

112. In practical terms, it would be useful to set up a women's affairs section in each police department, since women account for a large percentage of the extremely poor and, once they begin to be criminalized, they are more likely than men to fall victim to abuse of every kind. Similarly, police training should include a special component on respect for women's rights.

113. The most shocking situation is without doubt that of women prisoners, particularly those who are extremely poor. Those in prison for debt never have the money to pay their debts or fines. One possible way of dealing with this would be to set up reception centres run by trained staff.

114. The exponential increase in prostitution is a reflection of the spread of poverty. Prostitution is a cancer that must be excised from the activities on which trafficking, Mafia operations and corruption are based. The ultimate goal is a complete ban on prostitution, for its very existence is an affront to women's dignity.

VII. Conclusions

115. Extreme poverty means denying the enjoyment of all human rights to 1.3 billion people in the world, a majority of them women, thus violating their human dignity. Poverty is therefore the most massive cause of human rights violations in the world. Human dignity and the international community cannot accept this situation any longer, because eradicating poverty is an ethical, social, political and economic imperative.

116. Extreme poverty is thus a violation of all human rights, striking as it does at the two main human rights principles: the equal dignity of all human beings and the principle of non-discrimination. The poverty trap in which the poorest of the poor find themselves shows how human rights are indivisible and interdependent: the right to an adequate standard of living, to housing, to education, to work, to good health, to

employment, to the protection of the family, to respect for privacy, to legal status and registration as a citizen, to life and physical integrity, to justice and participation in political, social and cultural life.

117. Society must also alter the way it looks at the poorest of the poor: the sense of dignity that inspires the very poor is no different from the human dignity of any other person. The socially excluded do not feel that their dignity is recognized or respected, since the most common response they receive from society is a policy of welfare rather than human rights for all.

118. Deep poverty can exclude people from society, placing them in an illegal situation in their own country. Such people perceive social service or police intervention as actions they cannot appeal, since justice is by and large out of their reach. Society should see the poor as people who are capable of thinking, reflecting and having something to say about poverty, the world and human rights. A better understanding of poverty and better policies to eradicate it can be developed only by understanding the poor themselves and therefore by working in partnership with them.

119. Human rights must be the basis for any policy to combat social exclusion and poverty, for they are a powerful tool for creating social cohesion and genuine democracy. Social exclusion should therefore be looked at from the standpoint of the indivisibility of human rights; social policy should be tolerant of cultural diversity; a voice should be given to those who have no voice; and violations of the human rights of the most deprived should be outlawed in the same way as torture.

120. Bodies responsible for curbing poverty should therefore collaborate more closely with NGOs working with very poor groups in the field. The contribution of those living in extreme poverty could be of decisive importance in current thinking on "sustainable human development" and the right to development, especially since the concept of development is no longer viewed only from an economic standpoint, but also in social and cultural terms.

121. The ideas of the poorest of the poor are therefore perfectly in order in the debates taking place in various international organizations (UNDP, the World Bank, IMF, UNHCHR, UNCTAD, WTO). Efforts to increase cooperation among various bodies should also be increased and continued, not only within the United Nations system, but also with other international and regional bodies and with and among NGOs.

122. Poverty eradication must therefore be consolidated as an absolute priority throughout the United Nations system, in the context of the first United Nations Decade for the Eradication of Poverty (1997–2006), to be carried out at both international and national levels. Development strategies must take fully into account the realization of human rights, the indicators provided for, and the full participation of the poorest people, in particular women, in drawing up and implementing appropriate national plans of action.

123. Combating poverty is feasible, but it costs about $80 billion a year, which implies important transfers of resources through international cooperation. Donor countries

should urgently reverse the decline in their official development assistance to developing countries, which amounted to just 0.25 percent of GDP in 1996. The General Assembly call upon developed countries to commit themselves to the agreed target of 0.7 percent of GNP for overall development assistance should be emphasized, as well as the Assembly's call upon both developed and developing countries to allocate 20 percent of their official development assistance and 20 percent of their national budget, respectively, to basic social programmes. The 20/20 Initiative should include basic education, primary health care, including reproductive health and population programmes, nutrition programmes and safe drinking water and sanitation, as well as the institutional capacity for delivering those services.

124. At the national level, it is the Government's political will that is the key to success. Implementation of the human rights of the very poor is not necessarily expensive. The poor may be found in every country; even rich countries have two categories, namely, poor indigenous populations and poor migrants from developing countries—asylum seekers, undocumented (illegal) migrants, and refugees, political or otherwise. In every case, the right to civil status extends the right to life to thousands of children (girls in particular) who live in extreme poverty. This simple right saves their life, for it keeps them away from those who traffic in human beings.

125. Combating extreme poverty and implementing the rights of the poorest of the poor involves designing and funding a range of basic social services which reach out to the very poor, and ensuring respect for human rights, in particular within the judicial system and by the police.

126. Our age is characterized by globalization, and the technical revolution underway must comprise democratic and social aspects. The implementation of human rights and the eradication of extreme poverty will mark the first steps towards global progress. Economic globalization must be conceived as a balance between the free market and the role of the State, in particular as regards the provision of essential social services.

127. One of the most important aspects of poverty is individual mobility: every two years, one third of poor people climb out of poverty but their place is taken by others. Poverty is thus a process rather than a condition. In addition, the poorest of the poor are frequently the forgotten groups in countries where there is no rule of law; the fight against corruption and for the rule of law is thus a fight for respect for the very poor.

VIII. Recommendations

A. Universal ratification of relevant instruments

128. The 54 States—with a total population of 2.5 billion—that have not yet ratified the International Covenant on Economic, Social and Cultural Rights, are urged to do so. Similarly, all States should be encouraged to ratify the International Convention on the Elimination of All Forms of Racial Discrimination and the Convention on the

Elimination of All Forms of Discrimination against Women. States should, on request, be able to receive any technical cooperation they may need from the Office of the United Nations High Commissioner for Human Rights.

129. Moreover, the draft optional protocols to the International Covenant on Economic, Social and Cultural Rights and the Convention on the Elimination of All Forms of Discrimination against Women, making it possible for their monitoring bodies to receive individual communications, are of great importance.

130. The protection of economic, social and cultural rights would be reinforced by the ratification of regional instruments, such as the European Social Charter (Revised), and the "Protocol of San Salvador" on economic, social and cultural rights.

B. Minimum guaranteed income

131. All domestic legislation should guarantee the right of every person to whom it applies to a guaranteed minimum income by making the necessary budgetary appropriations. This right would facilitate access to the individual rights that are the basis of essential social services: social and medical welfare, food, housing, employment, training, schooling, education and culture. Extreme poverty should under no circumstances be a justification for the violation of human rights. As regards health, the State should implement programmes covering primary health-care charges, hygiene questions and specific diseases connected with extreme poverty.

C. Resources

132. The international community should express its solidarity with third-world States by aiming to devote 0.7 percent of the national budget to official development assistance. It should also encourage the 20/20 Initiative and a transfer of resources—international as well as domestic—from the military sector to the social sector.

133. The world economic situation would be more equitable if capital flows were regulated and the unsustainable external debt of the highly indebted poor countries cancelled, and if a start was made on the democratic reform of international financial and trade institutions.

134. The adoption of framework legislation on microfinance, acceptable to domestic banking systems and prioritizing women's needs should make it easier for microenterprises to embark on new projects and thereby create work and reduce poverty.

D. Local social welfare bodies

135. Local authorities, through their UNDP-based network of towns against poverty, are well placed to develop local social welfare facilities by providing them with the resources and the powers necessary to identify poverty and distribute welfare effectively. The role of local authorities in maintaining civil registers is also important.

136. Local institutions should also give citizens, including the poorest among them, opportunities to become involved and participate in decision-making processes by promoting more equitable, transparent and accountable institutions.

E. Occupational reintegration programmes

137. Job-creation programmes should set aside a number of jobs for the extremely poor. Domestic legislation should also promote policies to assist entry or re-entry to the labour market by prioritizing specific action on behalf of the poorest segments of the population: women, single mothers, children, migrants, members of minorities and indigenous populations, the disabled, internally displaced persons, older people and the homeless.

F. Human rights information and education for the poorest of the poor

138. Special human rights education techniques must be developed in order to reach persons living in extreme poverty, many of whom are illiterate. Information should be transmitted in a simple fashion, using national media and outreach techniques, by the local authorities in the areas where such groups live. This information should be supplemented by simple manuals and strip cartoons showing what services are available.

139. In addition, the human rights education components developed by UNHCHR for the United Nations Decade for Human Rights Education should be supplemented by materials suitable for extremely poor groups. Emphasis should be placed on the right to reject socially exclusive or racist behaviour on the right to food, to housing, to education and to health, and women's right to reject violence.

G. The poorest of the poor in prisons

140. Extreme poverty causes many persons to fall foul of the law, and it is they who constitute the vast majority of the prison population. After having served their term in prison, the poorest remain there because they are unable to pay their fines. Judicial procedure should therefore be adjusted to take account of this situation, alternatives to prison should be found and court officials given special training.

H. Access to justice

141. Each State should find specific ways of ensuring that legal aid and legal counsel is available free of charge to all persons living in extreme poverty. Appropriate training should be given to the experts concerned.

142. Alternatives to judicial proceedings, such as mediation, should also be encouraged provided they are free choices. Mediation must, however, be conditional on full respect for human rights and not become a substitute for judicial remedies; it could be used in both individual and group disputes, as well as to prevent disputes.

I. Social workers

143. Social workers have always been the main point of contact for the socially excluded, many of whom regard them as wielding enormous power and whose decisions can rarely be discussed or appealed. They should therefore be trained to assume a role as human rights agents and as experts on the lives of the poorest and most marginalized.

J. Technical assistance

144. A technical assistance programme to ensure respect for the rights of the poorest of the poor should be available to any Government on request. Special training programmes should be developed for social workers and court officials, as well as for members of the police force, since people living in extreme poverty regularly come into contact with the police in their daily life (through begging, stealing to live, or being homeless in the streets). Criminalization can be a very rapid process unless police officers have had suitable training. Relations between the police and welfare bodies should be the responsibility of a special police department.

K. Combating corruption

145. Corruption undermines democracy and disrupts the process of collecting taxes and redistributing them among those living in extreme poverty. Social democratization polices should be adopted to ensure respect for human rights in countries affected by corruption.

L. The impact of armed conflicts

146. Refugees and internally displaced persons—often the poorest of the poor—should be given priority in State social policy. Programmes to regularize the situation of undocumented migrants should be adopted by host countries. Access to education is the key factor in integrating migrants, and contact with migrants' countries of origin also constitutes a promising approach.

147. International economic sanctions, particularly when imposed by the Security Council, should be conceived in such a way as to avoid aggravating conditions of extreme poverty in the countries concerned. In particular, they should be compatible with the effective exercise of human rights—and especially economic, social and cultural rights—by civilians.

M. Draft declaration

148. A meeting with the independent expert should be organized in 1999 in order to draw up for the international community the basic elements of a preliminary draft declaration on human rights and extreme poverty. The draft should use as its starting

point the preamble common to the two international Covenants of 1966, as well as other relevant instruments which recognize that the ideal of the free individual, delivered from fear and poverty, cannot be achieved without the creation of conditions allowing each person to enjoy all human rights.

149. The draft should call on States to base their anti-poverty policy on human rights that aim at the eradication, rather than the reduction, of poverty. It should also provide guarantees for the future after poverty has been eradicated. State strategies, devised in partnership with the populations involved and their representative organizations, should aim at enabling the poorest of the poor to exercise the full range of rights and freedoms granted to citizens in their country.

Section Two Regional Instruments and Resources

Chapter 1
European Social Charter

Preamble

The governments signatory hereto, being members of the Council of Europe,

Considering that the aim of the Council of Europe is the achievement of greater unity between its members for the purpose of safeguarding and realising the ideals and principles which are their common heritage and of facilitating their economic and social progress, in particular by the maintenance and further realisation of human rights and fundamental freedoms;

Considering that in the Convention for the Protection of Human Rights and Fundamental Freedoms signed at Rome on 4 November 1950, and the Protocols thereto, the member States of the Council of Europe agreed to secure to their populations the civil and political rights and freedoms therein specified;

Considering that in the European Social Charter opened for signature in Turin on 18 October 1961 and the Protocols thereto, the member States of the Council of Europe agreed to secure to their populations the social rights specified therein in order to improve their standard of living and their social well-being;

Recalling that the Ministerial Conference on Human Rights held in Rome on 5 November 1990 stressed the need, on the one hand, to preserve the indivisible nature of all human rights, be they civil, political, economic, social or cultural and, on the other hand, to give the European Social Charter fresh impetus;

Resolved, as was decided during the Ministerial Conference held in Turin on 21 and 22 October 1991, to update and adapt the substantive contents of the Charter in order to take account in particular of the fundamental social changes which have occurred since the text was adopted;

Recognising the advantage of embodying in a Revised Charter, designed progressively to take the place of the European Social Charter, the rights guaranteed by the Charter as amended, the rights guaranteed by the Additional Protocol of 1988 and to add new rights,

529 U.N.T.S. 89, *entry into force* 26 February 1965.

Have agreed as follows:

Part I

The Parties accept as the aim of their policy, to be pursued by all appropriate means both national and international in character, the attainment of conditions in which the following rights and principles may be effectively realised:

Everyone shall have the opportunity to earn his living in an occupation freely entered upon.

All workers have the right to just conditions of work.

All workers have the right to safe and healthy working conditions.

All workers have the right to a fair remuneration sufficient for a decent standard of living for themselves and their families.

All workers and employers have the right to freedom of association in national or international organisations for the protection of their economic and social interests.

All workers and employers have the right to bargain collectively.

Children and young persons have the right to a special protection against the physical and moral hazards to which they are exposed.

Employed women, in case of maternity, have the right to a special protection.

Everyone has the right to appropriate facilities for vocational guidance with a view to helping him choose an occupation suited to his personal aptitude and interests.

Everyone has the right to appropriate facilities for vocational training.

Everyone has the right to benefit from any measures enabling him to enjoy the highest possible standard of health attainable.

All workers and their dependents have the right to social security.

Anyone without adequate resources has the right to social and medical assistance.

Everyone has the right to benefit from social welfare services.

Disabled persons have the right to independence, social integration and participation in the life of the community.

The family as a fundamental unit of society has the right to appropriate social, legal and economic protection to ensure its full development.

Children and young persons have the right to appropriate social, legal and economic protection.

The nationals of any one of the Parties have the right to engage in any gainful occupation in the territory of any one of the others on a footing of equality with the nationals of the latter, subject to restrictions based on cogent economic or social reasons.

Migrant workers who are nationals of a Party and their families have the right to protection and assistance in the territory of any other Party.

All workers have the right to equal opportunities and equal treatment in matters of employment and occupation without discrimination on the grounds of sex.

Workers have the right to be informed and to be consulted within the undertaking.

Workers have the right to take part in the determination and improvement of the working conditions and working environment in the undertaking.

Every elderly person has the right to social protection.

All workers have the right to protection in cases of termination of employment.

All workers have the right to protection of their claims in the event of the insolvency of their employer.

All workers have the right to dignity at work.

All persons with family responsibilities and who are engaged or wish to engage in employment have a right to do so without being subject to discrimination and as far as possible without conflict between their employment and family responsibilities.

Workers' representatives in undertakings have the right to protection against acts prejudicial to them and should be afforded appropriate facilities to carry out their functions.

All workers have the right to be informed and consulted in collective redundancy procedures.

Everyone has the right to protection against poverty and social exclusion.

Everyone has the right to housing.

Part II

The Parties undertake, as provided for in Part III, to consider themselves bound by the obligations laid down in the following articles and paragraphs.

Article 1. The right to work

With a view to ensuring the effective exercise of the right to work, the Parties undertake:

to accept as one of their primary aims and responsibilities the achievement and maintenance of as high and stable a level of employment as possible, with a view to the attainment of full employment;

to protect effectively the right of the worker to earn his living in an occupation freely entered upon;

to establish or maintain free employment services for all workers;

to provide or promote appropriate vocational guidance, training and rehabilitation.

Article 2. The right to just conditions of work

With a view to ensuring the effective exercise of the right to just conditions of work, the Parties undertake:

to provide for reasonable daily and weekly working hours, the working week to be progressively reduced to the extent that the increase of productivity and other relevant factors permit;

to provide for public holidays with pay;

to provide for a minimum of four weeks' annual holiday with pay;

to eliminate risks in inherently dangerous or unhealthy occupations, and where it has not yet been possible to eliminate or reduce sufficiently these risks, to provide for either a reduction of working hours or additional paid holidays for workers engaged in such occupations;

to ensure a weekly rest period which shall, as far as possible, coincide with the day recognised by tradition or custom in the country or region concerned as a day of rest;

to ensure that workers are informed in written form, as soon as possible, and in any event not later than two months after the date of commencing their employment, of the essential aspects of the contract or employment relationship;

to ensure that workers performing night work benefit from measures which take account of the special nature of the work.

Article 3. The right to safe and healthy working conditions

With a view to ensuring the effective exercise of the right to safe and healthy working conditions, the Parties undertake, in consultation with employers' and workers' organisations:

to formulate, implement and periodically review a coherent national policy on occupational safety, occupational health and the working environment. The primary aim of this policy shall be to improve occupational safety and health and to prevent accidents and injury to health arising out of, linked with or occurring in the course of work, particularly by minimising the causes of hazards inherent in the working environment;

to issue safety and health regulations;

to provide for the enforcement of such regulations by measures of supervision;

to promote the progressive development of occupational health services for all workers with essentially preventive and advisory functions.

Article 4. The right to a fair remuneration

With a view to ensuring the effective exercise of the right to a fair remuneration, the Parties undertake:

to recognise the right of workers to a remuneration such as will give them and their families a decent standard of living;

to recognise the right of workers to an increased rate of remuneration for overtime work, subject to exceptions in particular cases;

to recognise the right of men and women workers to equal pay for work of equal value;

to recognise the right of all workers to a reasonable period of notice for termination of employment;

to permit deductions from wages only under conditions and to the extent prescribed by national laws or regulations or fixed by collective agreements or arbitration awards.

The exercise of these rights shall be achieved by freely concluded collective agreements, by statutory wage-fixing machinery, or by other means appropriate to national conditions.

Article 5. The right to organize

With a view to ensuring or promoting the freedom of workers and employers to form local, national or international organisations for the protection of their economic and social interests and to join those organisations, the Parties undertake that national law shall not be such as to impair, nor shall it be so applied as to impair, this freedom. The extent to which the guarantees provided for in this article shall apply to the police shall be determined by national laws or regulations. The principle governing the application to the members of the armed forces of these guarantees and the extent to which they shall apply to persons in this category shall equally be determined by national laws or regulations.

Article 6. The right to bargain collectively

With a view to ensuring the effective exercise of the right to bargain collectively, the Parties undertake:

to promote joint consultation between workers and employers;

to promote, where necessary and appropriate, machinery for voluntary negotiations between employers or employers' organisations and workers' organisations, with a view to the regulation of terms and conditions of employment by means of collective agreements;

to promote the establishment and use of appropriate machinery for conciliation and voluntary arbitration for the settlement of labour disputes;

and recognise:

the right of workers and employers to collective action in cases of conflicts of interest, including the right to strike, subject to obligations that might arise out of collective agreements previously entered into.

Article 7. The right of children and young persons to protection

With a view to ensuring the effective exercise of the right of children and young persons to protection, the Parties undertake:

to provide that the minimum age of admission to employment shall be 15 years, subject to exceptions for children employed in prescribed light work without harm to their health, morals or education;

to provide that the minimum age of admission to employment shall be 18 years with respect to prescribed occupations regarded as dangerous or unhealthy;

to provide that persons who are still subject to compulsory education shall not be employed in such work as would deprive them of the full benefit of their education;

to provide that the working hours of persons under 18 years of age shall be limited in accordance with the needs of their development, and particularly with their need for vocational training;

to recognise the right of young workers and apprentices to a fair wage or other appropriate allowances;

to provide that the time spent by young persons in vocational training during the normal working hours with the consent of the employer shall be treated as forming part of the working day;

to provide that employed persons of under 18 years of age shall be entitled to a minimum of four weeks' annual holiday with pay;

to provide that persons under 18 years of age shall not be employed in night work with the exception of certain occupations provided for by national laws or regulations;

to provide that persons under 18 years of age employed in occupations prescribed by national laws or regulations shall be subject to regular medical control;

to ensure special protection against physical and moral dangers to which children and young persons are exposed, and particularly against those resulting directly or indirectly from their work.

Article 8. The right of employed women to protection of maternity

With a view to ensuring the effective exercise of the right of employed women to the protection of maternity, the Parties undertake:

to provide either by paid leave, by adequate social security benefits or by benefits from public funds for employed women to take leave before and after childbirth up to a total of at least fourteen weeks;

to consider it as unlawful for an employer to give a woman notice of dismissal during the period from the time she notifies her employer that she is pregnant until the end of her maternity leave, or to give her notice of dismissal at such a time that the notice would expire during such a period;

to provide that mothers who are nursing their infants shall be entitled to sufficient time off for this purpose;

to regulate the employment in night work of pregnant women, women who have recently given birth and women nursing their infants;

to prohibit the employment of pregnant women, women who have recently given birth or who are nursing their infants in underground mining and all other work which is unsuitable by reason of its dangerous, unhealthy or arduous nature and to take appropriate measures to protect the employment rights of these women.

Article 9. The right to vocational guidance

With a view to ensuring the effective exercise of the right to vocational guidance, the Parties undertake to provide or promote, as necessary, a service which will assist all persons, including the handicapped, to solve problems related to occupational choice and progress, with due regard to the individual's characteristics and their relation to occupational opportunity: this assistance should be available free of charge, both to young persons, including schoolchildren, and to adults.

Article 10. The right to vocational training

With a view to ensuring the effective exercise of the right to vocational training, the Parties undertake:

to provide or promote, as necessary, the technical and vocational training of all persons, including the handicapped, in consultation with employers' and workers' organisations, and to grant facilities for access to higher technical and university education, based solely on individual aptitude;

to provide or promote a system of apprenticeship and other systematic arrangements for training young boys and girls in their various employments;

to provide or promote, as necessary:

adequate and readily available training facilities for adult workers;

special facilities for the retraining of adult workers needed as a result of technological development or new trends in employment;

to provide or promote, as necessary, special measures for the retraining and reintegration of the long-term unemployed;

to encourage the full utilisation of the facilities provided by appropriate measures such as:

reducing or abolishing any fees or charges;

granting financial assistance in appropriate cases;

including in the normal working hours time spent on supplementary training taken by the worker, at the request of his employer, during employment;

ensuring, through adequate supervision, in consultation with the employers' and workers' organisations, the efficiency of apprenticeship and other training arrangements for young workers, and the adequate protection of young workers generally.

Article 11. The right to protection of health

With a view to ensuring the effective exercise of the right to protection of health, the Parties undertake, either directly or in cooperation with public or private organisations, to take appropriate measures designed *inter alia*:

to remove as far as possible the causes of ill-health;

to provide advisory and educational facilities for the promotion of health and the encouragement of individual responsibility in matters of health;

to prevent as far as possible epidemic, endemic and other diseases, as well as accidents.

Article 12. The right to social security

With a view to ensuring the effective exercise of the right to social security, the Parties undertake:

to establish or maintain a system of social security;

to maintain the social security system at a satisfactory level at least equal to that necessary for the ratification of the European Code of Social Security;

to endeavour to raise progressively the system of social security to a higher level;

to take steps, by the conclusion of appropriate bilateral and multilateral agreements or by other means, and subject to the conditions laid down in such agreements, in order to ensure:

equal treatment with their own nationals of the nationals of other Parties in respect of social security rights, including the retention of benefits arising out of social security legislation, whatever movements the persons protected may undertake between the territories of the Parties;

the granting, maintenance and resumption of social security rights by such means as the accumulation of insurance or employment periods completed under the legislation of each of the Parties.

Article 13. The right to social and medical assistance

With a view to ensuring the effective exercise of the right to social and medical assistance, the Parties undertake:

to ensure that any person who is without adequate resources and who is unable to secure such resources either by his own efforts or from other sources, in particular by benefits under a social security scheme, be granted adequate assistance, and, in case of sickness, the care necessitated by his condition;

to ensure that persons receiving such assistance shall not, for that reason, suffer from a diminution of their political or social rights;

to provide that everyone may receive by appropriate public or private services such advice and personal help as may be required to prevent, to remove, or to alleviate personal or family want;

to apply the provisions referred to in paragraphs 1, 2 and 3 of this article on an equal footing with their nationals to nationals of other Parties lawfully within their territories, in accordance with their obligations under the European Convention on Social and Medical Assistance, signed at Paris on 11 December 1953.

Article 14. The right to benefit from social welfare services

With a view to ensuring the effective exercise of the right to benefit from social welfare services, the Parties undertake:

to promote or provide services which, by using methods of social work, would contribute to the welfare and development of both individuals and groups in the community, and to their adjustment to the social environment;

to encourage the participation of individuals and voluntary or other organisations in the establishment and maintenance of such services.

Article 15. The right of persons with disabilities to independence, social integration and participation in the life of the community

With a view to ensuring to persons with disabilities, irrespective of age and the nature and origin of their disabilities, the effective exercise of the right to independence, social integration and participation in the life of the community, the Parties undertake, in particular:

to take the necessary measures to provide persons with disabilities with guidance, education and vocational training in the framework of general schemes wherever possible or, where this is not possible, through specialised bodies, public or private;

to promote their access to employment through all measures tending to encourage employers to hire and keep in employment persons with disabilities in the ordinary working environment and to adjust the working conditions to the needs of the disabled or, where this is not possible by reason of the disability, by arranging for or creating sheltered employment according to the level of disability. In certain cases, such measures may require recourse to specialised placement and support services;

to promote their full social integration and participation in the life of the community in particular through measures, including technical aids, aiming to overcome barriers to communication and mobility and enabling access to transport, housing, cultural activities and leisure.

Article 16. The right of the family to social, legal and economic protection

With a view to ensuring the necessary conditions for the full development of the family, which is a fundamental unit of society, the Parties undertake to promote the economic, legal and social protection of family life by such means as social and family benefits, fiscal arrangements, provision of family housing, benefits for the newly married and other appropriate means.

Article 17. The right of children and young persons to social, legal and economic protection

With a view to ensuring the effective exercise of the right of children and young persons to grow up in an environment which encourages the full development of their personality and of their physical and mental capacities, the Parties undertake, either directly or in co-operation with public and private organisations, to take all appropriate and necessary measures designed:

to ensure that children and young persons, taking account of the rights and duties of their parents, have the care, the assistance, the education and the training they need, in particular by providing for the establishment or maintenance of institutions and services sufficient and adequate for this purpose;

to protect children and young persons against negligence, violence or exploitation;

to provide protection and special aid from the state for children and young persons temporarily or definitively deprived of their family's support;

to provide to children and young persons a free primary and secondary education as well as to encourage regular attendance at schools.

Article 18. The right to engage in a gainful occupation in the territory of other Parties

With a view to ensuring the effective exercise of the right to engage in a gainful occupation in the territory of any other Party, the Parties undertake:

to apply existing regulations in a spirit of liberality;

to simplify existing formalities and to reduce or abolish chancery dues and other charges payable by foreign workers or their employers;

to liberalise, individually or collectively, regulations governing the employment of foreign workers;

and recognise:

the right of their nationals to leave the country to engage in a gainful occupation in the territories of the other Parties.

Article 19. The right of migrant workers and their families to protection and assistance

With a view to ensuring the effective exercise of the right of migrant workers and their families to protection and assistance in the territory of any other Party, the Parties undertake:

to maintain or to satisfy themselves that there are maintained adequate and free services to assist such workers, particularly in obtaining accurate information, and to take all appropriate steps, so far as national laws and regulations permit, against misleading propaganda relating to emigration and immigration;

to adopt appropriate measures within their own jurisdiction to facilitate the departure, journey and reception of such workers and their families, and to provide, within their own jurisdiction, appropriate services for health, medical attention and good hygienic conditions during the journey;

to promote co-operation, as appropriate, between social services, public and private, in emigration and immigration countries;

to secure for such workers lawfully within their territories, insofar as such matters are regulated by law or regulations or are subject to the control of administrative authorities, treatment not less favourable than that of their own nationals in respect of the following matters:

remuneration and other employment and working conditions;

membership of trade unions and enjoyment of the benefits of collective bargaining;

accommodation;

to secure for such workers lawfully within their territories treatment not less favourable than that of their own nationals with regard to employment taxes, dues or contributions payable in respect of employed persons;

to facilitate as far as possible the reunion of the family of a foreign worker permitted to establish himself in the territory;

to secure for such workers lawfully within their territories treatment not less favourable than that of their own nationals in respect of legal proceedings relating to matters referred to in this article;

to secure that such workers lawfully residing within their territories are not expelled unless they endanger national security or offend against public interest or morality;

to permit, within legal limits, the transfer of such parts of the earnings and savings of such workers as they may desire;

to extend the protection and assistance provided for in this article to self-employed migrants insofar as such measures apply;

to promote and facilitate the teaching of the national language of the receiving state or, if there are several, one of these languages, to migrant workers and members of their families;

to promote and facilitate, as far as practicable, the teaching of the migrant worker's mother tongue to the children of the migrant worker.

Article 20. The right to equal opportunities and equal treatment in matters of employment and occupation without discrimination on the grounds of sex

With a view to ensuring the effective exercise of the right to equal opportunities and equal treatment in matters of employment and occupation without discrimination on the grounds of sex, the Parties undertake to recognise that right and to take appropriate measures to ensure or promote its application in the following fields:

access to employment, protection against dismissal and occupational reintegration;

vocational guidance, training, retraining and rehabilitation;

terms of employment and working conditions, including remuneration;

career development, including promotion.

Article 21. The right to information and consultation

With a view to ensuring the effective exercise of the right of workers to be informed and consulted within the undertaking, the Parties undertake to adopt or encourage measures enabling workers or their representatives, in accordance with national legislation and practice:

a) to be informed regularly or at the appropriate time and in a comprehensible way about the economic and financial situation of the undertaking employing them, on the understanding that the disclosure of certain information which could be prejudicial to the undertaking may be refused or subject to confidentiality; and

b) to be consulted in good time on proposed decisions which could substantially affect the interests of workers, particularly on those decisions which could have an important impact on the employment situation in the undertaking.

Article 22. The right to take part in the determination and improvement of the working conditions and working environment

With a view to ensuring the effective exercise of the right of workers to take part in the determination and improvement of the working conditions and working environment in the undertaking, the Parties undertake to adopt or encourage measures enabling workers or their representatives, in accordance with national legislation and practice, to contribute:

to the determination and the improvement of the working conditions, work organisation and working environment;

to the protection of health and safety within the undertaking;

to the organisation of social and socio-cultural services and facilities within the undertaking;

to the supervision of the observance of regulations on these matters.

Article 23. The right of elderly persons to social protection

With a view to ensuring the effective exercise of the right of elderly persons to social protection, the Parties undertake to adopt or encourage, either directly or in co-operation with public or private organisations, appropriate measures designed in particular:

to enable elderly persons to remain full members of society for as long as possible, by means of:

adequate resources enabling them to lead a decent life and play an active part in public, social and cultural life;

provision of information about services and facilities available for elderly persons and their opportunities to make use of them;

to enable elderly persons to choose their life-style freely and to lead independent lives in their familiar surroundings for as long as they wish and are able, by means of:

provision of housing suited to their needs and their state of health or of adequate support for adapting their housing;

the health care and the services necessitated by their state;

to guarantee elderly persons living in institutions appropriate support, while respecting their privacy, and participation in decisions concerning living conditions in the institution.

Article 24. The right to protection in cases of termination of employment

With a view to ensuring the effective exercise of the right of workers to protection in cases of termination of employment, the Parties undertake to recognise:

the right of all workers not to have their employment terminated without valid reasons for such termination connected with their capacity or conduct or based on the operational requirements of the undertaking, establishment or service;

the right of workers whose employment is terminated without a valid reason to adequate compensation or other appropriate relief.

To this end the Parties undertake to ensure that a worker who considers that his employment has been terminated without a valid reason shall have the right to appeal to an impartial body.

Article 25. The right of workers to the protection of their claims in the event of the insolvency of their employer

With a view to ensuring the effective exercise of the right of workers to the protection of their claims in the event of the insolvency of their employer, the Parties undertake to provide that workers' claims arising from contracts of employment or employment relationships be guaranteed by a guarantee institution or by any other effective form of protection.

Article 26. The right to dignity at work

With a view to ensuring the effective exercise of the right of all workers to protection of their dignity at work, the Parties undertake, in consultation with employers' and workers' organisations:

to promote awareness, information and prevention of sexual harassment in the workplace or in relation to work and to take all appropriate measures to protect workers from such conduct;

to promote awareness, information and prevention of recurrent reprehensible or distinctly negative and offensive actions directed against individual workers in the workplace or in relation to work and to take all appropriate measures to protect workers from such conduct.

Article 27. The right of workers with family responsibilities to equal opportunities and equal treatment

With a view to ensuring the exercise of the right to equality of opportunity and treatment for men and women workers with family responsibilities and between such workers and other workers, the Parties undertake:

to take appropriate measures:

to enable workers with family responsibilities to enter and remain in employment, as well as to reenter employment after an absence due to those responsibilities, including measures in the field of vocational guidance and training;

to take account of their needs in terms of conditions of employment and social security;

to develop or promote services, public or private, in particular child daycare services and other childcare arrangements;

to provide a possibility for either parent to obtain, during a period after maternity leave, parental leave to take care of a child, the duration and conditions of which should be determined by national legislation, collective agreements or practice;

to ensure that family responsibilities shall not, as such, constitute a valid reason for termination of employment.

Article 28. The right of workers' representatives to protection in the undertaking and facilities to be accorded to them

With a view to ensuring the effective exercise of the right of workers' representatives to carry out their functions, the Parties undertake to ensure that in the undertaking:

they enjoy effective protection against acts prejudicial to them, including dismissal, based on their status or activities as workers' representatives within the undertaking;

they are afforded such facilities as may be appropriate in order to enable them to carry out their functions promptly and efficiently, account being taken of the industrial relations system of the country and the needs, size and capabilities of the undertaking concerned.

Article 29. The right to information and consultation in collective redundancy procedures

With a view to ensuring the effective exercise of the right of workers to be informed and consulted in situations of collective redundancies, the Parties undertake to ensure that employers shall inform and consult workers' representatives, in good time prior to such collective redundancies, on ways and means of avoiding collective redundancies or limiting their occurrence and mitigating their consequences, for example by recourse to accompanying social measures aimed, in particular, at aid for the redeployment or retraining of the workers concerned.

Article 30. The right to protection against poverty and social exclusion

With a view to ensuring the effective exercise of the right to protection against poverty and social exclusion, the Parties undertake:

to take measures within the framework of an overall and co-ordinated approach to promote the effective access of persons who live or risk living in a situation of social exclusion or poverty, as well as their families, to, in particular, employment, housing, training, education, culture and social and medical assistance;

to review these measures with a view to their adaptation if necessary.

Article 31. The right to housing

With a view to ensuring the effective exercise of the right to housing, the Parties undertake to take measures designed:

to promote access to housing of an adequate standard;

to prevent and reduce homelessness with a view to its gradual elimination;

to make the price of housing accessible to those without adequate resources.

Part III

Article A. Undertakings

Subject to the provisions of Article B below, each of the Parties undertakes:

to consider Part I of this Charter as a declaration of the aims which it will pursue by all appropriate means, as stated in the introductory paragraph of that part;

to consider itself bound by at least six of the following nine articles of Part II of this Charter: Articles 1, 5, 6, 7, 12, 13, 16, 19 and 20;

to consider itself bound by an additional number of articles or numbered paragraphs of Part II of the Charter which it may select, provided that the total number of articles or numbered paragraphs by which it is bound is not less than sixteen articles or sixty-three numbered paragraphs.

The articles or paragraphs selected in accordance with sub-paragraphs b and c of paragraph 1 of this article shall be notified to the Secretary General of the Council of Europe at the time when the instrument of ratification, acceptance or approval is deposited.

Any Party may, at a later date, declare by notification addressed to the Secretary General that it considers itself bound by any articles or any numbered paragraphs of Part II of the Charter which it has not already accepted under the terms of paragraph 1 of this article. Such undertakings subsequently given shall be deemed to be an integral part of the ratification, acceptance or approval and shall have the same effect as from the first day of the month following the expiration of a period of one month after the date of the notification.

Each Party shall maintain a system of labour inspection appropriate to national conditions.

Article B. Links with the European Social Charter and the 1988 Additional Protocol

No Contracting Party to the European Social Charter or Party to the Additional Protocol of 5 May 1988 may ratify, accept or approve this Charter without considering itself bound by at least the provisions corresponding to the provisions of the European Social Charter and, where appropriate, of the Additional Protocol, to which it was bound.

Acceptance of the obligations of any provision of this Charter shall, from the date of entry into force of those obligations for the Party concerned, result in the corresponding provision of the European Social Charter and, where appropriate, of its Additional Protocol of 1988 ceasing to apply to the Party concerned in the event of that Party being bound by the first of those instruments or by both instruments.

Part IV

Article C. Supervision of the implementation of the undertakings contained in this Charter

The implementation of the legal obligations contained in this Charter shall be submitted to the same supervision as the European Social Charter.

Article D. Collective complaints

The provisions of the Additional Protocol to the European Social Charter providing for a system of collective complaints shall apply to the undertakings given in this Charter for the States which have ratified the said Protocol.

Any State which is not bound by the Additional Protocol to the European Social Charter providing for a system of collective complaints may when depositing its instrument of ratification, acceptance or approval of this Charter or at any time thereafter, declare by notification addressed to the Secretary General of the Council of Europe, that it accepts the supervision of its obligations under this Charter following the procedure provided for in the said Protocol.

Part V

Article E. Non-discrimination

The enjoyment of the rights set forth in this Charter shall be secured without discrimination on any ground such as race, colour, sex, language, religion, political or other opinion, national extraction or social origin, health, association with a national minority, birth or other status.

Article F. Derogations in time of war or public emergency

In time of war or other public emergency threatening the life of the nation any Party may take measures derogating from its obligations under this Charter to the extent strictly required by the exigencies of the situation, provided that such measures are not inconsistent with its other obligations under international law.

Any Party which has availed itself of this right of derogation shall, within a reasonable lapse of time, keep the Secretary General of the Council of Europe fully informed of the measures taken and of the reasons therefor. It shall likewise inform the Secretary General when such measures have ceased to operate and the provisions of the Charter which it has accepted are again being fully executed.

Article G. Restrictions

The rights and principles set forth in Part I when effectively realised, and their effective exercise as provided for in Part II, shall not be subject to any restrictions or limitations not specified in those parts, except such as are prescribed by law and are necessary in a democratic society for the protection of the rights and freedoms of others or for the protection of public interest, national security, public health, or morals.

The restrictions permitted under this Charter to the rights and obligations set forth herein shall not be applied for any purpose other than that for which they have been prescribed.

Article H. Relations between the Charter and domestic law or international agreements

The provisions of this Charter shall not prejudice the provisions of domestic law or of any bilateral or multilateral treaties, conventions or agreements which are already in force, or may come into force, under which more favourable treatment would be accorded to the persons protected.

Article I. Implementation of the undertakings given

Without prejudice to the methods of implementation foreseen in these articles the relevant provisions of Articles 1 to 31 of Part II of this Charter shall be implemented by:

laws or regulations;

agreements between employers or employers' organisations and workers' organisations;

a combination of those two methods;

other appropriate means.

Compliance with the undertakings deriving from the provisions of paragraphs 1, 2, 3, 4, 5 and 7 of Article 2, paragraphs 4, 6 and 7 of Article 7, paragraphs 1, 2, 3 and 5 of Article 10 and Articles 21 and 22 of Part II of this Charter shall be regarded as effective if the provisions are applied, in accordance with paragraph 1 of this Article, to the great majority of the workers concerned.

Article J. Amendments

Any amendment to Parts I and II of this Charter with the purpose of extending the rights guaranteed in this Charter as well as any amendment to Parts III to VI, proposed by a Party or by the Governmental Committee, shall be communicated to the Secretary General of the Council of Europe and forwarded by the Secretary General to the Parties to this Charter.

Any amendment proposed in accordance with the provisions of the preceding paragraph shall be examined by the Governmental Committee which shall submit the text adopted to the Committee of Ministers for approval after consultation with the Parliamentary Assembly. After its approval by the Committee of Ministers this text shall be forwarded to the Parties for acceptance.

Any amendment to Part I and to Part II of this Charter shall enter into force, in respect of those Parties which have accepted it, on the first day of the month following the expiration of a period of one month after the date on which three Parties have informed the Secretary General that they have accepted it.

In respect of any Party which subsequently accepts it, the amendment shall enter into force on the first day of the month following the expiration of a period of one month after the date on which that Party has informed the Secretary General of its acceptance.

Any amendment to Parts III to VI of this Charter shall enter into force on the first day of the month following the expiration of a period of one month after the date on which all Parties have informed the Secretary General that they have accepted it.

Part VI

Article K. Signature, ratification and entry into force

This Charter shall be open for signature by the member States of the Council of Europe. It shall be subject to ratification, acceptance or approval. Instruments of ratification, acceptance or approval shall be deposited with the Secretary General of the Council of Europe.

This Charter shall enter into force on the first day of the month following the expiration of a period of one month after the date on which three member States of the Council of Europe have expressed their consent to be bound by this Charter in accordance with the preceding paragraph.

In respect of any member State which subsequently expresses its consent to be bound by this Charter, it shall enter into force on the first day of the month following the expiration of a period of one month after the date of the deposit of the instrument of ratification, acceptance or approval.

Article L. Territorial application

This Charter shall apply to the metropolitan territory of each Party. Each signatory may, at the time of signature or of the deposit of its instrument of ratification, acceptance or approval, specify, by declaration addressed to the Secretary General of the Council of Europe, the territory which shall be considered to be its metropolitan territory for this purpose.

Any signatory may, at the time of signature or of the deposit of its instrument of ratification, acceptance or approval, or at any time thereafter, declare by notification addressed to the Secretary General of the Council of Europe, that the Charter shall extend in whole or in part to a non-metropolitan territory or territories specified in the said declaration for whose international relations it is responsible or for which it assumes international responsibility. It shall specify in the declaration the articles or paragraphs of Part II of the Charter which it accepts as binding in respect of the territories named in the declaration.

The Charter shall extend its application to the territory or territories named in the aforesaid declaration as from the first day of the month following the expiration of a period of one month after the date of receipt of the notification of such declaration by the Secretary General.

Any Party may declare at a later date by notification addressed to the Secretary General of the Council of Europe that, in respect of one or more of the territories to which the Charter has been applied in accordance with paragraph 2 of this Article, it accepts as binding any articles or any numbered paragraphs which it has not already accepted in respect of that territory or territories. Such undertakings subsequently given shall be deemed to be an integral part of the original declaration in respect of the territory concerned, and shall have the same effect as from the first day of the month following the expiration of a period of one month after the date of receipt of such notification by the Secretary General.

Article M. Denunciation

Any Party may denounce this Charter only at the end of a period of five years from the date on which the Charter entered into force for it, or at the end of any subsequent period of two years, and in either case after giving six months' notice to the Secretary General of the Council of Europe who shall inform the other Parties accordingly.

Any Party may, in accordance with the provisions set out in the preceding paragraph, denounce any article or paragraph of Part II of the Charter accepted by it provided that the number of articles or paragraphs by which this Party is bound shall never be less than sixteen in the former case and sixty-three in the latter and that this number of articles or paragraphs shall continue to include the articles selected by the Party among those to which special reference is made in Article A, paragraph 1, subparagraph b.

Any Party may denounce the present Charter or any of the articles or paragraphs of Part II of the Charter under the conditions specified in paragraph 1 of this article in respect of any territory to which the said Charter is applicable, by virtue of a declaration made in accordance with paragraph 2 of Article L.

Article N. Appendix

The appendix to this Charter shall form an integral part of it.

Article O. Notifications

The Secretary General of the Council of Europe shall notify the member States of the Council and the Director General of the International Labour Office of:

any signature;

the deposit of any instrument of ratification, acceptance or approval;

any date of entry into force of this Charter in accordance with Article K;

any declaration made in application of Articles A, paragraphs 2 and 3, D, paragraphs 1 and 2, F, paragraph 2, L, paragraphs 1, 2, 3 and 4;

any amendment in accordance with Article J;

any denunciation in accordance with Article M;

any other act, notification or communication relating to this Charter.

In witness whereof, the undersigned, being duly authorised thereto, have signed this revised Charter.

Done at Strasbourg, this 3rd day of May 1996, in English and French, both texts being equally authentic, in a single copy which shall be deposited in the archives of the Council of Europe. The Secretary General of the Council of Europe shall transmit certified copies to each member State of the Council of Europe and to the Director General of the International Labour Office.

Appendix to the Revised European Social Charter

Scope of the Revised European Social Charter in terms of persons protected

Without prejudice to Article 12, paragraph 4, and Article 13, paragraph 4, the persons covered by Articles 1 to 17 and 20 to 31 include foreigners only in so far as they are nationals of other Parties lawfully resident or working regularly within the territory of the Party concerned, subject to the understanding that these articles are to be interpreted in the light of the provisions of Articles 18 and 19.

This interpretation would not prejudice the extension of similar facilities to other persons by any of the Parties.

Each Party will grant to refugees as defined in the Convention relating to the Status of Refugees, signed in Geneva on 28 July 1951 and in the Protocol of 31 January 1967, and lawfully staying in its territory, treatment as favourable as possible, and in any case not less favourable than under the obligations accepted by the Party under the said convention and under any other existing international instruments applicable to those refugees.

Each Party will grant to stateless persons as defined in the Convention on the Status of Stateless Persons done in New York on 28 September 1954 and lawfully staying in its territory, treatment as favourable as possible and in any case not less favourable than under the obligations accepted by the Party under the said instrument and under any other existing international instruments applicable to those stateless persons.

Part I, paragraph 18, and Part II, Article 18, paragraph 1

It is understood that these provisions are not concerned with the question of entry into the territories of the Parties and do not prejudice the provisions of the European Convention on Establishment, signed in Paris on 13 December 1955.

Part II

Article 1, paragraph 2

This provision shall not be interpreted as prohibiting or authorising any union security clause or practice.

Article 2, paragraph 6

Parties may provide that this provision shall not apply:

to workers having a contract or employment relationship with a total duration not exceeding one month and/or with a working week not exceeding eight hours;

where the contract or employment relationship is of a casual and/or specific nature, provided, in these cases, that its non-application is justified by objective considerations.

Article 3, paragraph 4

It is understood that for the purposes of this provision the functions, organisation and conditions of operation of these services shall be determined by national laws or regulations, collective agreements or other means appropriate to national conditions.

Article 4, paragraph 4

This provision shall be so understood as not to prohibit immediate dismissal for any serious offence.

Article 4, paragraph 5

It is understood that a Party may give the undertaking required in this paragraph if the great majority of workers are not permitted to suffer deductions from wages either by law or through collective agreements or arbitration awards, the exceptions being those persons not so covered.

Article 6, paragraph 4

It is understood that each Party may, insofar as it is concerned, regulate the exercise of the right to strike by law, provided that any further restriction that this might place on the right can be justified under the terms of Article G.

Article 7, paragraph 2

This provision does not prevent Parties from providing in their legislation that young persons not having reached the minimum age laid down may perform work in so far as it is absolutely necessary for their vocational training where such work is carried out in accordance with conditions prescribed by the competent authority and measures are taken to protect the health and safety of these young persons.

Article 7, paragraph 8

It is understood that a Party may give the undertaking required in this paragraph if it fulfills the spirit of the undertaking by providing by law that the great majority of persons under eighteen years of age shall not be employed in night work.

Article 8, paragraph 2

This provision shall not be interpreted as laying down an absolute prohibition. Exceptions could be made, for instance, in the following cases:

if an employed woman has been guilty of misconduct which justifies breaking off the employment relationship;

if the undertaking concerned ceases to operate;

if the period prescribed in the employment contract has expired.

Article 12, paragraph 4

The words "and subject to the conditions laid down in such agreements" in the introduction to this paragraph are taken to imply inter alia that with regard to benefits which are available independently of any insurance contribution, a Party may require the completion of a prescribed period of residence before granting such benefits to nationals of other Parties.

Article 13, paragraph 4

Governments not Parties to the European Convention on Social and Medical Assistance may ratify the Charter in respect of this paragraph provided that they grant to nationals of other Parties a treatment which is in conformity with the provisions of the said convention.

Article 16

It is understood that the protection afforded in this provision covers single-parent families.

Article 17

It is understood that this provision covers all persons below the age of 18 years, unless under the law applicable to the child majority is attained earlier, without prejudice to the other specific provisions provided by the Charter, particularly Article 7.

This does not imply an obligation to provide compulsory education up to the abovementioned age.

Article 19, paragraph 6

For the purpose of applying this provision, the term "family of a foreign worker" is understood to mean at least the worker's spouse and unmarried children, as long as the latter are considered to be minors by the receiving State and are dependent on the migrant worker.

Article 20

It is understood that social security matters, as well as other provisions relating to unemployment benefit, old age benefit and survivor's benefit, may be excluded from the scope of this article.

Provisions concerning the protection of women, particularly as regards pregnancy, confinement and the post-natal period, shall not be deemed to be discrimination as referred to in this article.

This article shall not prevent the adoption of specific measures aimed at removing de facto inequalities.

Occupational activities which, by reason of their nature or the context in which they are carried out, can be entrusted only to persons of a particular sex may be excluded from the scope of this article or some of its provisions. This provision is not to be interpreted as requiring the Parties to embody in laws or regulations a list of occupations which, by reason of their nature or the context in which they are carried out, may be reserved to persons of a particular sex.

Articles 21 and 22

For the purpose of the application of these articles, the term "workers' representatives" means persons who are recognised as such under national legislation or practice.

The terms "national legislation and practice" embrace as the case may be, in addition to laws and regulations, collective agreements, other agreements between employers and workers' representatives, customs as well as relevant case law.

For the purpose of the application of these articles, the term "undertaking" is understood as referring to a set of tangible and intangible components, with or without legal personality, formed to produce goods or provide services for financial gain and with power to determine its own market policy.

It is understood that religious communities and their institutions may be excluded from the application of these articles, even if these institutions are "undertakings" within the meaning of paragraph 3. Establishments pursuing activities which are inspired by certain ideals or guided by certain moral concepts, ideals and concepts which are protected by national legislation, may be excluded from the application of these articles to such an extent as is necessary to protect the orientation of the undertaking.

It is understood that where in a state the rights set out in these articles are exercised in the various establishments of the undertaking, the Party concerned is to be considered as fulfilling the obligations deriving from these provisions.

The Parties may exclude from the field of application of these articles, those undertakings employing less than a certain number of workers, to be determined by national legislation or practice.

Article 22

This provision affects neither the powers and obligations of states as regards the adoption of health and safety regulations for workplaces, nor the powers and responsibilities of the bodies in charge of monitoring their application.

The terms "social and socio-cultural services and facilities" are understood as referring to the social and/or cultural facilities for workers provided by some undertakings such as welfare assistance, sports fields, rooms for nursing mothers, libraries, children's holiday camps, etc.

Article 23, paragraph 1

For the purpose of the application of this paragraph, the term "for as long as possible" refers to the elderly person's physical, psychological and intellectual capacities.

Article 24

It is understood that for the purposes of this article the terms "termination of employment" and "terminated" mean termination of employment at the initiative of the employer.

It is understood that this article covers all workers but that a Party may exclude from some or all of its protection the following categories of employed persons:

workers engaged under a contract of employment for a specified period of time or a specified task;

workers undergoing a period of probation or a qualifying period of employment, provided that this is determined in advance and is of a reasonable duration;

workers engaged on a casual basis for a short period.

For the purpose of this article the following, in particular, shall not constitute valid reasons for termination of employment:

trade union membership or participation in union activities outside working hours, or, with the consent of the employer, within working hours;

seeking office as, acting or having acted in the capacity of a workers' representative;

the filing of a complaint or the participation in proceedings against an employer involving alleged violation of laws or regulations or recourse to competent administrative authorities;

race, colour, sex, marital status, family responsibilities, pregnancy, religion, political opinion, national extraction or social origin;

maternity or parental leave;

temporary absence from work due to illness or injury.

It is understood that compensation or other appropriate relief in case of termination of employment without valid reasons shall be determined by national laws or regulations, collective agreements or other means appropriate to national conditions.

Article 25

It is understood that the competent national authority may, by way of exemption and after consulting organisations of employers and workers, exclude certain categories of workers from the protection provided in this provision by reason of the special nature of their employment relationship.

It is understood that the definition of the term "insolvency" must be determined by national law and practice.

The workers' claims covered by this provision shall include at least:

the workers' claims for wages relating to a prescribed period, which shall not be less than three months under a privilege system and eight weeks under a guarantee system, prior to the insolvency or to the termination of employment;

the workers' claims for holiday pay due as a result of work performed during the year in which the insolvency or the termination of employment occurred;

the workers' claims for amounts due in respect of other types of paid absence relating to a prescribed period, which shall not be less than three months under a privilege system and eight weeks under a guarantee system, prior to the insolvency or the termination of the employment.

National laws or regulations may limit the protection of workers' claims to a prescribed amount, which shall be of a socially acceptable level.

Article 26

It is understood that this article does not require that legislation be enacted by the Parties.

It is understood that paragraph 2 does not cover sexual harassment.

Article 27

It is understood that this article applies to men and women workers with family responsibilities in relation to their dependent children as well as in relation to other members of their immediate family who clearly need their care or support where such responsibilities restrict their possibilities of preparing for, entering, participating in or advancing in economic activity. The terms "dependent children" and "other members of their immediate family who clearly need their care and support" mean persons defined as such by the national legislation of the Party concerned.

Articles 28 and 29

For the purpose of the application of this article, the term "workers' representatives" means persons who are recognised as such under national legislation or practice.

Part III

It is understood that the Charter contains legal obligations of an international character, the application of which is submitted solely to the supervision provided for in Part IV thereof.

Article A, paragraph 1

It is understood that the numbered paragraphs may include articles consisting of only one paragraph.

Article B, paragraph 2

For the purpose of paragraph 2 of Article B, the provisions of the revised Charter correspond to the provisions of the Charter with the same article or paragraph number with the exception of:

Article 3, paragraph 2, of the revised Charter which corresponds to Article 3, paragraphs 1 and 3, of the Charter;

Article 3, paragraph 3, of the revised Charter which corresponds to Article 3, paragraphs 2 and 3, of the Charter;

Article 10, paragraph 5, of the revised Charter which corresponds to Article 10, paragraph 4, of the Charter;

Article 17, paragraph 1, of the revised Charter which corresponds to Article 17 of the Charter.

Part V

Article E

A differential treatment based on an objective and reasonable justification shall not be deemed discriminatory.

Article F

The terms "in time of war or other public emergency" shall be so understood as to cover also the threat of war.

Article I

It is understood that workers excluded in accordance with the appendix to Articles 21 and 22 are not taken into account in establishing the number of workers concerned.

Article J

The term "amendment" shall be extended so as to cover also the addition of new articles to the Charter.

Chapter 2
European Social Charter Collective Complaints Procedure

Preamble

The member States of the Council of Europe, signatories to this Protocol to the European Social Charter, opened for signature in Turin on 18 October 1961 (hereinafter referred to as "the Charter"),

Resolved to take new measures to improve the effective enforcement of the social rights guaranteed by the Charter;

Considering that this aim could be achieved in particular by the establishment of a collective complaints procedure, which, inter alia, would strengthen the participation of management and labour and of non-governmental organisations,

Have agreed as follows:

Article 1

The Contracting Parties to this Protocol recognise the right of the following organisations to submit complaints alleging unsatisfactory application of the Charter:

a. international organisations of employers and trade unions referred to in paragraph 2 of Article 27 of the Charter;

b. other international non-governmental organisations which have consultative status with the Council of Europe and have been put on a list established for this purpose by the Governmental Committee;

c. representative national organisations of employers and trade unions within the jurisdiction of the Contracting Party against which they have lodged a complaint.

Article 2

1. Any Contracting State may also, when it expresses its consent to be bound by this Protocol, in accordance with the provisions of Article 13, or at any moment thereafter,

Additional Protocol to the European Social Charter Providing for a System of Collective Complaints, 1995. E.T.S. 158, *entry into force* 7 January 1998.

declare that it recognises the right of any other representative national non-governmental organisation within its jurisdiction which has particular competence in the matters governed by the Charter, to lodge complaints against it.

2. Such declarations may be made for a specific period.

3. The declarations shall be deposited with the Secretary General of the Council of Europe who shall transmit copies thereof to the Contracting Parties and publish them.

Article 3

The international non-governmental organisations and the national non-governmental organisations referred to in Article 1.b and Article 2 respectively may submit complaints in accordance with the procedure prescribed by the aforesaid provisions only in respect of those matters regarding which they have been recognised as having particular competence.

Article 4

The complaint shall be lodged in writing, relate to a provision of the Charter accepted by the Contracting Party concerned and indicate in what respect the latter has not ensured the satisfactory application of this provision.

Article 5

Any complaint shall be addressed to the Secretary General who shall acknowledge receipt of it, notify it to the Contracting Party concerned and immediately transmit it to the Committee of Independent Experts.

Article 6

The Committee of Independent Experts may request the Contracting Party concerned and the organisation which lodged the complaint to submit written information and observations on the admissibility of the complaint within such time-limit as it shall prescribe.

Article 7

If it decides that a complaint is admissible, the Committee of Independent Experts shall notify the Contracting Parties to the Charter through the Secretary General. It shall request the Contracting Party concerned and the organisation which lodged the complaint to submit, within such time-limit as it shall prescribe, all relevant written explanations or information, and the other Contracting Parties to this Protocol, the comments they wish to submit, within the same time-limit.

If the complaint has been lodged by a national organisation of employers or a national trade union or by another national or international non-governmental organisation, the Committee of Independent Experts shall notify the international organisations of employers or trade unions referred to in paragraph 2 of Article 27 of the Charter, through the Secretary General, and invite them to submit observations within such time limit as it shall prescribe.

On the basis of the explanations, information or observations submitted under paragraphs 1 and 2 above, the Contracting Party concerned and the organisation which lodged the complaint may submit any additional written information or observations within such time limit as the Committee of Independent Experts shall prescribe.

In the course of the examination of the complaint, the Committee of Independent Experts may organise a hearing with the representatives of the parties.

Article 8

The Committee of Independent Experts shall draw up a report in which it shall describe the steps taken by it to examine the complaint and present its conclusions as to whether or not the Contracting Party concerned has ensured the satisfactory application of the provision of the Charter referred to in the complaint.

The report shall be transmitted to the Committee of Ministers. It shall also be transmitted to the organisation that lodged the complaint and to the Contracting Parties to the Charter, which shall not be at liberty to publish it. It shall be transmitted to the Parliamentary Assembly and made public at the same time as the resolution referred to in Article 9 or no later than four months after it has been transmitted to the Committee of Ministers.

Article 9

On the basis of the report of the Committee of Independent Experts, the Committee of Ministers shall adopt a resolution by a majority of those voting. If the Committee of Independent Experts finds that the Charter has not been applied in a satisfactory manner, the Committee of Ministers shall adopt, by a majority of two-thirds of those voting, a recommendation addressed to the Contracting Party concerned. In both cases, entitlement to voting shall be limited to the Contracting Parties to the Charter.

At the request of the Contracting Party concerned, the Committee of Ministers may decide, where the report of the Committee of Independent Experts raises new issues, by a two-thirds majority of the Contracting Parties to the Charter, to consult the Governmental Committee.

Article 10

The Contracting Party concerned shall provide information on the measures it has taken to give effect to the Committee of Ministers' recommendation, in the next report which it submits to the Secretary General under Article 21 of the Charter.

Article 11

Articles 1 to 10 of this Protocol shall apply also to the articles of Part II of the first Additional Protocol to the Charter in respect of the States Parties to that Protocol, to the extent that these articles have been accepted.

Article 12

The States Parties to this Protocol consider that the first paragraph of the appendix to the Charter, relating to Part III, reads as follows:

"It is understood that the Charter contains legal obligations of an international character, the application of which is submitted solely to the supervision provided for in Part IV thereof and in the provisions of this Protocol."

Article 13

This Protocol shall be open for signature by member States of the Council of Europe signatories to the Charter, which may express their consent to be bound by:

signature without reservation as to ratification, acceptance or approval; or

signature subject to ratification, acceptance or approval, followed by ratification, acceptance or approval.

A member State of the Council of Europe may not express its consent to be bound by this Protocol without previously or simultaneously ratifying the Charter.

Instruments of ratification, acceptance or approval shall be deposited with the Secretary General of the Council of Europe.

Article 14

This Protocol shall enter into force on the first day of the month following the expiration of a period of one month after the date on which five member States of the Council of Europe have expressed their consent to be bound by the Protocol in accordance with the provisions of Article 13.

In respect of any member State which subsequently expresses its consent to be bound by it, the Protocol shall enter into force on the first day of the month following the expiration of a period of one month after the date of the deposit of the instrument of ratification, acceptance or approval.

Article 15

Any Party may at any time denounce this Protocol by means of a notification addressed to the Secretary General of the Council of Europe.

Such denunciation shall become effective on the first day of the month following the expiration of a period of twelve months after the date of receipt of such notification by the Secretary General.

Article 16

The Secretary General of the Council of Europe shall notify all the member States of the Council of:

any signature;

the deposit of any instrument of ratification, acceptance or approval;

the date of entry into force of this Protocol in accordance with Article 14;

any other act, notification or declaration relating to this Protocol.

In witness whereof the undersigned, being duly authorised thereto, have signed this Protocol.

Done at Strasbourg, this 9th day of November 1995, in English and French, both texts being equally authentic, in a single copy which shall be deposited in the archives of the Council of Europe. The Secretary General of the Council of Europe shall transmit certified copies to each member State of the Council of Europe.

Chapter 3
European Convention on Human Rights and Fundamental Freedoms—Protocol One

The Governments signatory hereto, being Members of the Council of Europe,

Being resolved to take steps to ensure the collective enforcement of certain rights and freedoms other than those already included in Section I of the Convention for the Protection of Human Rights and Fundamental Freedoms signed at Rome on 4th November, 1950 (hereinafter referred to as 'the Convention'),

Have agreed as follows:

Article 1

Every natural or legal person is entitled to the peaceful enjoyment of his possessions. No one shall be deprived of his possessions except in the public interest and subject to the conditions provided for by law and by the general principles of international law.

The preceding provisions shall not, however, in any way impair the right of a State to enforce such laws as it deems necessary to control the use of property in accordance with the general interest or to secure the payment of taxes or other contributions or penalties.

Article 2

No person shall be denied the right to education. In the exercise of any functions which it assumes in relation to education and to teaching, the State shall respect the right of parents to ensure such education and teaching in conformity with their own religious and philosophical convictions.

Article 3

The High Contracting Parties undertake to hold free elections at reasonable intervals by secret ballot, under conditions which will ensure the free expression of the opinion of the people in the choice of the legislature.

213 U.N.T.S. 262, *entry into force* 18 May, 1954.

Article 4

Any High Contracting Party may at the time of signature or ratification or at any time thereafter communicate to the Secretary-General of the Council of Europe a declaration stating the extent to which it undertakes that the provisions of the present Protocol shall apply to such of the territories for the international relations of which it is responsible as are named therein.

Any High Contracting Party which has communicated a declaration in virtue of the preceding paragraph may from time to time communicate a further declaration modifying the terms of any former declaration or terminating the application of the provisions of this Protocol in respect of any territory.

A declaration made in accordance with this article shall be deemed to have been made in accordance with paragraph 1 of Article 63 of the Convention.

Article 5

As between the High Contracting Parties the provisions of Articles 1, 2, 3 and 4 of this Protocol shall be regarded as additional articles to the convention and all the provisions of the Convention shall apply accordingly.

Article 6

This Protocol shall be open for signature by the Members of the Council of Europe, who are the signatories of the Convention; it shall be ratified at the same time as or after the ratification of the Convention. It shall enter into force after the deposit of ten instruments of ratification. As regards any signatory ratifying subsequently, the Protocol shall enter into force at the date of the deposit of its instrument of ratification.

The instruments of ratification shall be deposited with the Secretary-General of the Council of Europe, who will notify all the Members of the names of those who have ratified.

Done at Paris on the 20th day of March 1952, In English and French, both text being equally authentic, in a single copy which shall remain deposited in the archives of the Council of Europe. The Secretary-General shall transmit certified copies to each of the signatory Governments.

Chapter 4
European Convention on the Legal Status of Migrant Workers (excerpts)

. . .

Chapter I

Article 1. Definition

For the purpose of this Convention, the term "migrant worker" shall mean a national of a Contracting Party who has been authorised by another Contracting Party to reside in its territory in order to take up paid employment.

This Convention shall not apply to:

a. frontier workers;

b. artists, other entertainers and sportsmen engaged for a short period and members of a liberal profession;

c. seamen;

d. persons undergoing training;

e. seasonal workers; seasonal migrant workers are those who, being nationals of a Contracting Party, are employed on the territory of another Contracting Party in an activity dependent on the rhythm of the seasons, on the basis of a contract for a specified period or for specified employment;

f. workers, who are nationals of a Contracting Party, carrying out specific work in the territory of another Contracting Party on behalf of an undertaking having its registered office outside the territory of that Contracting Party.

E.T.S. 093, *entry into force* 1 May 1983.

Chapter II

Article 2. Forms of recruitment

The recruitment of prospective migrant workers may be carried out either by named or by unnamed request and in the latter case shall be effected through the intermediary of the official authority in the State of origin if such an authority exists and, where appropriate, through the intermediary of the official authority of the receiving State.

The administrative costs of recruitment, introduction and placing, when these operations are carried out by an official authority, shall not be borne by the prospective migrant worker.

Article 3. Medical examinations and vocational test

Recruitment of prospective migrant workers may be preceded by a medical examination and a vocational test.

The medical examination and the vocational test are intended to establish whether the prospective migrant worker is physically and mentally fit and technically qualified for the job offered to him and to make certain that his state of health does not endanger public health.

Arrangements for the reimbursement of expenses connected with medical examination and vocational test shall be laid down when appropriate by bilateral agreements, so as to ensure that such expenses do not fall upon the prospective migrant worker.

A migrant worker to whom an individual offer of employment is made shall not be required, otherwise than on grounds of fraud, to undergo a vocational test except at the employer's request.

Article 4. Right of exit—right to admission—administrative formalities

Each Contracting Party shall guarantee the following rights to migrant workers:

- the right to leave the territory of the Contracting Party of which they are nationals;
- the right to admission to the territory of a Contracting Party in order to take up paid employment after being authorised to do so and obtaining the necessary papers.

These rights shall be subject to such limitations as are prescribed by legislation and are necessary for the protection of national security, public order, public health or morals.

The papers required of the migrant worker for emigration and immigration shall be issued as expeditiously as possible free of charge or on payment of an amount not exceeding their administrative cost.

Article 5. Formalities and procedure relating to the work contract

Every migrant worker accepted for employment shall be provided prior to departure for the receiving State with a contract of employment or a

definite offer of employment, either of which may be drawn up in one or more of the languages in use in the State of origin and in one or more of the languages in use in the receiving State. The use of at least one language of the State of origin and one language of the receiving State shall be compulsory in the case of recruitment by an official authority or an officially recognised employment bureau.

Article 6. Information

The Contracting Parties shall exchange and provide for prospective migrants appropriate information on their residence, conditions of and opportunities for family reunion, the nature of the job, the possibility of a new work contract being concluded after the first has lapsed, the qualifications required, working and living conditions (including the cost of living), remuneration, social security, housing, food, the transfer of savings, travel, and on deductions made from wages in respect of contributions for social protection and social security, taxes and other charges. Information may also be provided on the cultural and religious conditions in the receiving State.

In the case of recruitment through an official authority of the receiving State, such information shall be provided, before his departure, in a language which the prospective migrant worker can understand, to enable him to take a decision in full knowledge of the facts. The translation, where necessary, of such information into a language that the prospective migrant worker can understand shall be provided as a general rule by the State of origin.

Each Contracting Party undertakes to adopt the appropriate steps to prevent misleading propaganda relating to emigration and immigration.

Article 7. Travel

Each Contracting Pary undertakes to ensure, in the case of official collective recruitment, that the cost of travel to the receiving State shall never be borne by the migrant worker. The arrangements for payment shall be determined under bilateral agreements, which may also extend these measures to families and to workers recruited individually.

In the case of migrant workers and their families in transit through the territory of one Contracting Party en route to the receiving State, or on their return journey to the State of origin, all steps shall be taken by the competent authorities of the transit State to expedite their journey and prevent administrative delays and difficulties.

Each Contracting Party shall exempt from import duties and taxes at the time of entry into the receiving State and of the final return to the State of origin and in transit:

a. the personal effects and movable property of migrant workers and members of their family belonging to their household;

b. a reasonable quantity of hand-tools and portable equipment necessary for the occupation to be engaged in.

The exemptions referred to above shall be granted in accordance with the laws or regulations in force in the States concerned.

Chapter III

Article 8. Work permit

Each Contracting Party which allows a migrant worker to enter its territory to take up paid employment shall issue or renew a work permit for him (unless he is exempt from this requirement), subject to the conditions laid down in its legislation.

However, a work permit issued for the first time may not as a rule bind the worker to the same employer or the same locality for a period longer than one year.

In case of renewal of the migrant worker's work permit, this should as a general rule be for a period of at least one year, in so far as the current state and development of the employment situation permits.

Article 9. Residence permit

Where required by national legislation, each Contracting Party shall issue residence permits to migrant workers who have been authorised to take up paid employment on their territory under conditions laid down in this Convention.

The residence permit shall in accordance with the provisions of national legislation be issued and, if necessary, renewed for a period as a general rule at least as long as that of the work permit. When the work permit is valid indefinitely, the residence permit shall as a general rule be issued and, if necessary, renewed for a period of at least one year. It shall be issued and renewed free of charge or for a sum covering administrative costs only.

The provisions of this Article shall also apply to members of the migrant worker's family who are authorised to join him in accordance with Article 12 of this Convention.

If a migrant worker is no longer in employment, either because he is temporarily incapable of work as a result of illness or accident or because he is involuntarily unemployed, this being duly confirmed by the competent authorities, he shall be allowed for the purpose of the application of Article 25 of this Convention to remain on the territory of the receiving State for a period which should not be less than five months. Nevertheless, no Contracting Party shall be bound, in the case provided for in the above sub-paragraph, to allow a migrant worker to remain for a period exceeding the period of payment of the unemployment allowance.

The residence permit, issued in accordance with the provisions of paragraphs 1 to 3 of this Article, may be withdrawn:

a. for reasons of national security, public policy or morals;

b. if the holder refuses, after having been duly informed of the consequences of such refusal, to comply with the measures prescribed for him by an official medical authority with a view to the protection of public health;

c. if a condition essential to its issue or validity is not fulfilled.

Each Contracting Party nevertheless undertakes to grant to migrant workers whose residence permits have been withdrawn, an effective right to appeal, in accordance with the procedure for which provision is made in its legislation, to a judicial or administrative authority.

Article 10. Reception

After arrival in the receiving State, migrant workers and members of their families shall be given all appropriate information and advice as well as all necessary assistance for their settlement and adaption.

For this purpose, migrant workers and members of their families shall be entitled to help and assistance from the social services of the receiving State or from bodies working in the public interest in the receiving State and to help from the consular authorities of their State or origin. Moreover, migrant workers shall be entitled, on the same basis as national workers, to help and assistance from the employment services. However, each Contracting Party shall endeavour to ensure that special social services are available, whenever the situation so demands, to facilitate or co-ordinate the reception of migrant workers and their families.

Each Contracting Party undertakes to ensure that migrant workers and members of their families can worship freely, in accordance with their faith; each Contracting Party shall facilitate such worship, within the limit of available means.

Article 11. Recovery of sums due in respect of maintenance

The status of migrant workers must not interfere with the recovery of sums due in respect of maintenance to persons in the State of origin to whom they have maintenance obligations arising from a family relationship, parentage, marriage or affinity, including a maintenance obligation in respect of a child who is not legitimate.

Each Contracting Party shall take the steps necessary to ensure the recovery of sums due in respect of such maintenance, making use as far as possible of the form adopted by the Committee of Ministers of the Council of Europe.

As far as possible, each Contracting Party shall take steps to appoint a single national or regional authority to receive and dispatch applications for sums due in respect of maintenance provided for in paragraph 1 above.

This Article shall not affect existing or future bilateral or multilateral agreements.

Article 12. Family reunion

The spouse of a migrant worker who is lawfully employed in the territory of a Contracting Party and the unmarried children thereof, as long as they are considered to be minors by the relevant law of the receiving State, who are dependent on the migrant worker, are authorised on conditions analogous to those which this Convention applies to the admission of migrant workers and according to the admission procedure prescribed by such law or by international agreements to join the migrant worker in the territory of a Contracting Party, provided that the latter has available for the family housing considered as normal for national workers in the region where the migrant worker is employed. Each Contracting Party may make the giving of authorisation conditional upon a waiting period which shall not exceed twelve months.

Any State may, at any time, by declaration addressed to the Secretary-General of the Council of Europe, which shall take effect one month after the date of receipt, make the family reunion referred to in paragraph 1 above further conditional upon the migrant worker having steady resources sufficient to meet the needs of his family.

Any State may, at any time, by declaration addressed to the Secretary-General of the Council of Europe, which shall take effect one month after the date of its receipt, derogate temporarily from the obligation to give the authorisation provided for in paragraph 1 above, for one or more parts of its territory which it shall designate in its declaration, on the condition that these measures do not conflict with obligations under other international instruments. The declarations shall state the special reasons justifying the derogation with regard to receiving capacity.

Any State availing itself of this possibility of derogation shall keep the Secretary-General of the Council of Europe fully informed of the measures which it has taken and shall ensure that these measures are published as soon as possible. It shall also inform the Secretary-General of the Council of Europe when such measures cease to operate and the provisions of the Convention are again being fully executed.

The derogation shall not, as a general rule, affect requests for family reunion submitted to the competent authorities, before the declaration is addressed to the Secretary-General, by migrant workers already established in the part of the territory concerned.

Article 13. Housing

Each Contracting Party shall accord to migrant workers, with regard to acess to housing and rents, treatment not less favourable than that accorded to its own nationals, insofar as this matter is covered by domestic laws and regulations.

Each Contracting Party shall ensure that the competent national authorities carry out inspections in appropriate cases in collaboration with the respective consular authorities, acting within their competence, to ensure that standards of fitness of accommodation are kept up for migrant workers as for its own nationals.

Each Contracting Party undertakes to protect migrant workers against exploitation in respect of rents, in accordance with its laws and regulations on the matter.

Each Contracting Party shall ensure, by the means available to the competent national authorities, that the housing of the migrant worker shall be suitable.

Article 14. Pretraining—schooling—linguistic training—vocational training and retraining

Migrant workers and members of their families officially admitted to the territory of a Contracting Party shall be entitled, on the same basis and under the same conditions as national workers, to general education and vocation training and retraining and shall be granted access to higher education according to the general regulations governing admission to respective institutions in the receiving State.

To promote access to general and vocational schools and to vocational training centres, the reciving State shall facilitate the teaching of its language or, if there are several, one of its languages to migrant workers and members of their families.

For the purpose of the application of paragraphs 1 and 2 above, the granting of scholarships shall be left to the discretion of each Contracting Party which shall make efforts to grant the children of migrant workers living with their families in the receiving State—in accordance with the provisions of Article 12 of this Convention—the same facilities in this respect as the receiving State's nationals.

The workers' previous attainments, as well as diplomas and vocational qualifications aquired in the State of origin, shall be recognised by each Contracting Party in accordance with arrangements laid down in bilateral and multilateral agreements.

The Contracting Parties concerned, acting in close co-operation shall endeavor to ensure that the vocational training and retraining schemes, within the meaning of this Article, cater as far as possible for the needs of migrant workers with a view to their return to their State of origin.

Article 15. Teaching of the migrant worker's mother tongue

The Contracting Parties concerned shall take actions by common accord to arrange, so far as practicable, for the migrant worker's children, special courses for the teaching of the migrant worker's mother tongue, to facilitate, inter alia, their return to their State of origin.

Article 16. Conditions of work

In the matter of conditions of work, migrant workers authorised to take up employment shall enjoy treatment not less favourable than that which applies to national workers by virtue of legislative or administrative provisions, collective labour agreement or custom.

It shall not be possible to derogate by individual contract from the principle of equal treatment referred to in the foregoing paragraph.

Article 17. Transfer of savings

Each Contracting Party shall permit, according to the agreements laid down by its legislation, the transfer of all or such parts of the earnings and savings of migrant workers as the latter may wish to transfer.

This provision shall apply also to the transfer of sums due by migrant workers in respect of maintenance. The transfer of sums due by migrant workers in respect of maintenance shall on no account be hindered or prevented.

Each Contracting Party shall permit, under bilateral agreements or by other means, the transfer of such sums as remain due to migrant workers when they leave the territory of the receiving State.

Article 18. Social security

Each Contracting Party undertakes to grant within its territory, to migrant workers and members of their families, equality of treatment with its own nationals, in the matter of social security, subject to conditions required by national legislation and by bilateral or multilateral agreements already concluded or to be concluded between the Contracting Parties concerned.

The Contracting Parties shall moreover endeavour to secure to migrant workers and members of their families the conservation of rights in course of acquisition and aquired rights, as well as provision of benefits abroad, through bilateral and multilateral agreements.

Article 19. Social and medical assistance

Each Contracting Party undertakes to grant within its territory, to migrant workers and members of their families who are lawfully present in its territory, social and medical assistance on the same basis as nationals in accordance with the obligations it has assumed by virtue of other international agreements and in particular of the European Convention on Social and Medical Assistance of 1953.

Article 20. Industrial accidents and occupational diseases—industrial hygiene

With regard to the prevention of industrial accidents and occupational diseases and to industrial hygiene, migrant workers shall enjoy the same rights and protection as national workers, in application of the laws of a Contracting Party and collective agreements and having regard to their particular situation.

A migrant worker who is victim of an industrial accident or who has contracted an occupational disease in the territory of the receiving State shall benefit from occupational rehabilitation on the same basis as national workers.

Article 21. Inspection of working conditions

Each Contracting Party shall inspect or provide for inspection of the conditions of work of migrant workers in the same manner as for national workers. Such inspection shall be carried out by the competent bodies or institutions of the receiving State and by any other authority authorised by the receiving State.

Article 22. Death

Each Contracting Party shall take care, within the framework of its laws and, if need be, within the framework of bilateral agreements, that steps are taken to provide all help and assistance necessary for the transport to the State of origin of the bodies of migrant workers deceased as the result of an industrial accident.

Article 23. Taxation on earnings

In the matter of earnings and without prejudice to the provisions on double taxation contained in agreements already concluded or which may in future be concluded between Contracting Parties, migrant workers shall not be liable, in the territory of a Contracting Party, to duties, charges, taxes or contributions of any description whatsoever either higher or more burdensome than those imposed on nationals in similar circumstances. In particular, they shall be entitled to deductions or exemptions from taxes or charges and to all allowances, including allowance for dependants.

The Contracting Parties shall decide between themselves, by bilateral or multilateral agreements on double taxation, what measures might be taken to avoid double taxation on the earnings of migrant workers.

Article 24. Expiry of contract and discharge

On the expiry of a work contract concluded for a special period at the end of the period agreed on and on the case of anticipated cancellation of such a contract or cancellation of a work contract for an unspecified period, migrant workers shall be accorded treatment not less favourable than that accorded to national workers under the provisions of national legislation or collective labour agreements.

In the event of individual or collective dismissal, migrant workers shall receive the treatment applicable to national workers under national legislation or collective labour agreements, as regards the form and period of notice, the compensation provided for in legislation or agreements or such as may be due in cases of unwarranted cancellation of their work contracts.

Article 25. Re-employment

If a migrant worker loses his job for reasons beyond his control, such as redundancy or prolonged illness, the competent authority of the receiving State shall facilitate his re-employment in accordance with the laws and regulations of that State.

To this end the receiving State shall promote the measures necessary to ensure, as far as possible, the vocational retraining and occupational rehabilitation of the migrant worker in question, provided that he intends to continue in employment in the State concerned afterwards.

Article 26. Right of access to the courts and administrative authorities in the receiving State

Each Contracting Party shall secure to migrant workers treatment not less favourable than that of its own nationals in respect of legal proceedings. Migrant workers shall be entitled, under the same conditions as nationals, to full legal and judicial protection of their persons property and their right and interests; in particular, they shall have, in the same manner as nationals, the right of access to the competent courts and administrative authorities, in accordance with the law of the receiving State, and the right to obtain the assistance of any person of their choice who is qualified by the law of that State, for instance in disputes with employers, members of their families or third parties. The rules of private international law of the receiving State shall not be affected by this Article.

Each Contracting Party shall provide migrant workers with legal assistance on the same conditions as for their own nationals and, in the case of civil or criminal proceedings, the possibility of obtaining the assistance of an interpreter where they cannot understand or speak the language used in court.

Article 27. Use of employment services

Each Contracting Party recognises the right of migrant workers and of the members of their families officially admitted to its territory to make use of employment services under the same conditions as national workers subject to the legal provisions and regulations and administrative practice, including conditions of access, in force in that State.

Article 28. Exercise of the right to organise

Each Contracting Party shall allow to migrant workers the right to organise for the protection of their economic and social interests on the conditions provided for by national legislation for its own nationals.

Article 29. Participation in the affairs of the undertaking

Each Contracting Party shall facilitate as far as possible the participation of migrant workers in the affairs of the undertaking on the same conditions as national workers.

Chapter IV

Article 30. Return home

Each Contracting Pary shall, as far as possible, take appropriate measures to assist migrant workers and their families on the occasion of their final return to their State of origin, and in particular the steps referred to in paragraphs 2 and 3 of Article 7 of this Convention. The provision of financial assistance shall be left to the discretion of each Contracting Party.

To enable migrant workers to know, before they set out on their return journey, the conditions on which they will be able to resettle in their State of origin, this State shall communicate to the receiving State, which shall keep available for those who request it, information regarding in particular:

possibilities and conditions of employment in the State of origin;

financial aid granted for economic reintegration;

the maintenance of social security rights aquired abroad;

steps to be taken to facilitate the finding of accomodation;

equivalence accorded to occupational qualifications obtained abroad and any tests to be passed to secure their official recognition;

equivalence accorded to educational qualification, so that migrant workers' children can be admitted to schools without down-grading.

Chapter V

Article 31. Conservation of acquired rights

No provision of this Convention may be interpreted as justifying less favourable treatment than that enjoyed by migrant workers under the national legislation of the receiving State or under bilateral and multilateral agreements to which that State is a Contracting Party.

Article 32. Relations between this Convention and the laws of the Contracting Parties or international agreements

The provisions of this Convention shall not prejudice the provisions of the laws of the Contracting Parties or of any bilateral or multilateral treaties, conventions, agreements or arrangements, as well as the steps taken to implement them, which are already in force, or may come into force, and under which more favourable treatment has been, or would be, accorded to the persons protected by the Convention.

. . .

Chapter 5
European Community Charter of Fundamental Social Rights for Workers (excerpts)

Title I: Fundamental Social Rights of Workers—Freedom of Movement

1. Every worker of the European Community shall have the right to freedom of movement throughout the territory of the Community, subject to restrictions justified on grounds of public order, public safety or public health.

2. The right to freedom of movement shall enable any worker to engage in any occupation or profession in the Community in accordance with the principles of equal treatment as regards access to employment, working conditions and social protection in the host country.

3. The right to freedom of movement shall also imply:

i) harmonization of conditions of residence in all Member States, particularly those concerning family reunification;

ii) elimination of obstacles arising from the non-recognition of diplomas or equivalent occupational qualifications;

iii) improvement of the living and working conditions of frontier workers.

In the Commission's Programme

Revision of the regulation on the right of workers to remain in a member country after having been employed there.

Extension, to cover all insured persons, of the measures which enable workers to continue to avail themselves of social security benefits when they move from one member country to another.

Study of the problems involved in the transfer from one member country to another of

Adopted at Strasburg, 9 December 1989.

rights acquired under supplementary social security schemes; opening of a debate on this subject.

Proposal on the working conditions of workers from one Member State who are engaged in the provision of services (subcontracting, etc.) in another. Also a proposal to include in public contracts a labour clause to ensure equal treatment for workers detached by a firm from another member country.

Examination of the living and working conditions of Community citizens living in frontier regions and of frontier workers in particular.

Employment and remuneration

4. Every individual shall be free to choose and engage in an occupation according to the regulations governing each occupation.

5. All employment shall be fairly remunerated. To this end, in accordance with arrangements applying in each country:

(i) workers shall be assured of an equitable wage, i.e., a wage sufficient to enable them to have a decent standards of living;

(ii) workers subject to terms of employment other than an open-ended full-time contract shall benefit from an equitable reference wage;

(iii) wages may be withheld, seized or transferred only in accordance with national law; such provisions should entail measures enabling the worker concerned to continue to enjoy the necessary means of subsistence for him or herself and his family.

6. Every individual must be able to have access to public placement services free of charge.

In the Commission's Programme

Publication of an annual report on employment in Europe.

Creation of an "employment observatory" for the Community, to forecast trends in labour supply and demand.

Development of the research and action programmes already launched on job creation for specific groups (long-term unemployed, young people, local initiatives, etc.).

Improvement of systems for internation exchange of vacancies and applications for employment which have not been satisfied at national level.

Evaluation of the effectiveness of the European Social Fund's activities in helping to find jobs for young people and for the long-term unemployed.

Opinion on the measures taken by the Member States to guarantee the right to an equitable wage.

Proposal for a directive setting minimum requirements for contracts and employment relationships other than full-time open-ended contracts (part-time working, fixed-term working, casual work, etc.).

Improvement of living and working conditions

7. The completion of the internal market must lead to an improvement in the living and working conditions of workers in the European Community. This process must result from an approximation of these conditions while the improvement is being maintained, as regards in particular the duration and organization of working time and forms of employment other than open-ended contracts, such as fixed-term contracts, part-time working, temporary work and seasonal work.

The improvement must cover, where necessary, the development of certain aspects of employment regulations such as procedures for collective redundancies and those regarding bankruptcies.

8. Every worker of the European Community shall have a right to a weekly rest period and to annual paid leave, the duration of which must be progressively haromonized in accordance with national practices.

9. The conditions of employment of every worker of the European Community shall be stipulated in laws, a collective agreement or a contract of employment, according to arrangements applying in each country.

In the Commission's Programme

Proposal for a directive on the adaption of working time and of essential working conditions, particularly in regard to the well-being and health of workers.

Proposal for a directive to establish on a general basis a form of written proof of an employment contract and of its principal conditions.

Revision of the directive setting out procedures for information and consultation prior to collective redundancies, in particular so that it applies in cases of transfrontier restructuring.

Drawing up a memorandum on the social integration of migrants from countries outside the Community (education, housing, etc.).

Social protection

According to the arrangements applying in each country:

10. Every worker of the European Community shall have a right to adequate social protection and shall, whatever his status and whatever the size of the undertaking in which he is employed, enjoy an adequate level of social security benefits.

Persons who have been unable to either enter or re-enter the labour market and have no means of subsistence must be able to receive sufficient resources and social assistance in keeping with their particular situation.

In the Commission's Programme

Recommendation on convergence of Member States' objectives in regard to social protection.

Recommendation setting out common criteria for the guarantee given by Member States of sufficient resources and social assistance for the least advantaged citizens.

Freedom of association and collective bargaining

11. Employers and workers of the European Community shall have the right of association in order to constitute professional organizations or trade unions of their choice for the defence of their economic and social interests.

Every employer and every worker shall have the freedom to join or not to join such organizations without any personal or occupational damage being thereby suffered by him.

12. Employers or employers' organizations, on the one hand, and workers' organizations, on the other, shall have the right to negotiate and conclude collective agreements under the conditions laid down by national legislation and practice.

The dialogue between the two sides of industry at European level which must be developed, may, if the parties deem it desirable, result in contractual relations in particular at inter-occupational and sectoral level.

13. The right to resort to collective action in the event of a conflict of interests shall include the right to strike, subject to the obligations arising under national regulations and collective agreements.

In order to facilitate the settlement of industrial disputes the establishment and utilization at the appropriate levels of conciliation, mediation and arbitration procedures should be encouraged in accordance with national practice.

14. The internal legal order of the Member States shall determine under which conditions and to what extent the rights provided for Articles 11 and 13 apply to the armed forces, the police and civil service.

In the Commission's Programme

Continuation and development of dialogue with the social partners and a communication on their role in collective bargaining, including collective agreements at the European level.

Vocational training

15. Every worker of the European Community must be able to have access to vocational training and to benefit therefrom throughout his working life. In conditions governing access to such training there may be no discrimination on grounds of nationality.

The competent public authorities, undertakings or the two sides of industry, each within their own sphere of competence, should set up continuing and permanent training systems enabling every person to undergo retraining, more especially through leave for training purposes, to improve his skills or to acquire new skills, particularly in the light of technical development.

In the Commission's Programme

Proposal for measures to improve access to training for all workers throughout their working lives.

Revision of the general principals for vocational training originally established at the Community level in 1983.

Rationalization and better coordination of Community programmes in the field of initial and continued vocational training.

Development and rationalization of Community programmes for youth exchanges and exchange of young workers.

Continuation of work on comparability of vocational training qualifications between the member countries.

Equal treatment for men and women

16. Equal treatment for men and women must be assured. Equal opportunities for men and women must be developed.

To this end, action should be intensified to ensure the implementation of the principle of equality between men and women as regards in particular access to employment, remuneration, working conditions, social protection, education, vocational training and career development.

Measures should also be developed enabling men and women to reconcile their occupational and family obligations.

In the Commission's Programme

Preparation of a third action programme on equal opportunities for women.

Proposal for a directive on the protection of pregnant women at work.

Recommendation on methods of child care.

Recommendation setting out a code of good conduct on the protection of working women in pregnancy and maternity.

Information, Consultation and Participation of Workers

17. Information, consultation and participation of workers must be developed along appropriate lines, taking account of the practices in force in the various Member States.

This shall apply especially in companies or groups of companies having establishments or companies in two or more Member States of the European Community.

18. Such information, consultation and participation must be implemented in due time, particularly in the following cases:

i) when technological changes which, from the point of view of working conditions and work organization, have major implications for the work force, are introduced into undertakings;

ii) in connection with restructuring operations in undertakings or in cases of mergers having an impact on the employment of workers;

iii) in cases of collective redundancy procedures;

iv) when transfrontier workers in particular are affected by employment policies pursued by the undertaking where they are employed.

In the Commission's Programme

Proposal on the information, consultation and participation of workers in undertakings of European or transnational scale.

Proposal on equity sharing and financial participation by workers.

Health protection and safety at the workplace

19. Every worker must enjoy satisfactory health and safety conditions in his working environment. Appropriate measures must be taken in order to achieve further harmonization of conditions in this area while maintaining the improvements made.

These measures shall take account, in particular, of the need for the training, information, consultation and balanced participation of workers as regards the risks incurred and the steps to eliminate or reduce them.

The provisions regarding implementation of the internal market shall help to ensure such protection.

In the Commission's Programme

Proposals for directives on minimum health and safety requirements in a range of sectors: transport, shipping and fisheries, temporary or mobile work sites, the drilling industries, quarrying and open-cast mining.

Proposal for a directive on minimum requirements in regard to exposure of workers to certain physical agents (vibration, electromagnetic radiation, etc.).

Revision of the directive on exposure to asbestos at work.

Proposal for a directive on safety and health signs at the workplace.

Proposal for a directive on specific information for workers exposed to certain dangerous substances and industrial agents.

Revision of the European schedule of industrial diseases and recommendation on its adoption by the Member States.

Proposal to create a special European agency to provide scientific and technical support in the fields of safety, hygiene and health in the workplace.

Protection of children and adolescents

20. Without prejudice to such rules as may be more favourable to young people, in particular those ensuring their preparation for work through vocational training, and subject to derogations limited to certain light work, the minimum employment age must not be lower than the minimum school-leaving age and, in any case, not lower than 15 years.

21. Young people who are in gainful employment must receive equitable remuneration in accordance with national practice.

22. Appropriate measures must be taken to adjust labour regulations applicable to young workers so that their specific development and vocational training and access to employment are met.

The duration of work must, in particular, be limited—without it being possible to circumvent this limitation through recourse to overtime—and night work prohibited in the case of workers of under 18 years of age, save in the case of certain jobs laid down in national legislation or regulations.

23. Following the end of compulsory education, young people must be entitled to receive initial vocational training of a sufficient duration to enable them to adapt to the requirement of their future working life; for young workers, such training should take place during working hours.

In the Commission's Programme

Proposal for a directive approximating the laws of the Member States on the protection of young people in regard to employment (minimum age, working hours, etc.).

Elderly persons

According to the arrangements applying in each country:

24. Every worker of the European Community must, at the time of retirement, be able to enjoy resources affording him or her a decent standard of living.

25. Every person who has reached retirement age but who is not entitled to a pension or who does not have other means of subsistence must be entitled to sufficient resources and to medical and social assistance specifically suited to his needs.

In the Commission's Programme

Communication and proposal for an action programme to support pilot projects, exchanges of information, etc.

Proposal to organize a "Year of the Elderly" in 1993.

Disabled persons

26. All disabled persons, whatever the origin and nature of their disablement, must be entitled to additional concrete measures aimed at improving their social and professional integration.

These measures must concern, in particular, according to capacities of the beneficiaries, vocational training, ergonomics, accessibility, mobility, means of transport and housing.

In the Commission's Programme

Preparation of a third Community action programme on integration and equality of opportunity for the disabled.

Proposal for a directive to promote better travel possiblities for workers with motor disabilities.

Title II: Implementation of the Charter

27. It is more particularly the responsibility of the Member States in accordance with national practices, notably through legislative measures or collective agreements, to guarantee the fundamental social rights in this Charter and to implement the social measures indispensable to the smooth operation of the internal market as part of strategy of economic and social cohesion.

28. The European Council invites the Commission to submit as soon as possible initiatives which fall within its powers, as provided for in the Treaties, with a view to the adoption of legal instruments for the effective implementation, as and when the internal market is completed, of those rights which come within the Community's area of competence.

29. The Commission shall establish each year, during the last three months, a report on the application of the Charter by the Member States and by the European Community.

30. The report of the Commission shall be forwarded to the European Council, the European Parliament and the Economic and Social Committee.

Chapter 6
Treaty Establishing the European Community (excerpts)

Preamble

Resolved to ensure the economic and social progress of their countries by common action to eliminate the barriers which divide Europe,

Affirming as the essential objective of their efforts the constant improvement of the living and working conditions of their peoples,

Part One: Principles

Article 2

The Community shall have as its task, by establishing a common market and an economic and monetary union and by implementing the common policies or activities referred to in Articles 3 and 3a, to promote throughout the Community a harmonious and balanced development of economic activities, sustainable and non-inflationary growth respecting the environment, a high degree of convergence of economic performance, a high level of employment and of social protection, the raising of the standard of living and quality of life, and economic and social cohesion and solidarity among Member States.

Article 3

For the purposes set out in Article 2, the activities of the Community shall include, as provided by this Treaty and in accordance with the timetable set out therein:

(i) a policy in the social sphere comprising a European Social Fund;

(o) a contribution to the attainment of a high level of health protection;

(p) a contribution to education and training of quality and to the flowering of the cultures of the Member States;

Adopted at Rome, 25 March 1957, *entry into force* 1 January 1958.

. . .

Title VIII. Social Policy, Education, Vocational Training and Youth

Chapter 1. Social Provisions

Article 117

Member States agree upon the need to promote improved working conditions and an improved standard of living for workers, so as to make possible their harmonisation while the improvement is being maintained.

They believe that such a development will ensue not only from the functioning of the common market, which will favour the harmonisation of social systems, but also from the procedures provided for in this Treaty and from the approximation of provisions laid down by law, regulation or administrative action.

Article 118

Without prejudice to the other provisions of this Treaty and in conformnity with its general objectives, the Commission shall have the task of promoting close co-operation between Member States in the social field, particularly in matters relating to:

• employment;

• labour law and working conditions;

• basic and advanced vocational training;

• social security;

• prevention of occupational accidents and diseases;

• occupational hygiene; the right of association, and collective bargaining between employers and workers.

To this end, the Commission shall act in close contact with Member States by making studies, delivering opinions and arranging consultations both on problems arising at national level and on those of concern to international organisations.

Before delivering the opinions provided for in this Article, the Commission shall consult the Economic and Social Committee.

Article 118a

1. Member States shall pay particular attention to encouraging improvements, especially in the working environment, as regards the health and safety of workers, and shall set as their objective the harmonisation of conditions in this area, while maintaining the improvements made.

2. In order to help achieve the objective laid down in the first paragraph, the Council, acting in accordance with the procedure referred to in Article 189c and after consulting the Economic and Social Committee, shall adopt, by means of directives, minimum requirements for gradual implementation, having regard to the conditions and technical rules obtaining in each of the Member States.

Such directives shall avoid imposing administrative, financial and legal constraints in a way which would hold back the creation and development of small and medium-sized undertakings.

3. The provisions adopted pursuant to this Article shall not prevent any Member State from maintaining or introducing more stringent measures for the protection of working conditions compatible with this Treaty.

Article 118b

The Commission shall endeavour to develop the dialogue between management and labour at European level which could, if the two sides consider it desirable, lead to relations based on agreement.

Article 119

Each Member State shall during the first stage ensure and subsequently maintain the application of the principle that men and women should receive equal pay for equal work.

For the purpose of this Article, "pay" means the ordinary basic or minimum wage or salary and any other consideration, whether in cash or in kind, which the worker receives, directly or indirectly, in respect of his employment from his employer.

Equal pay without discrimination based on sex means:

(a) that pay for the same work at piece rates shall be calculated on the basis of the same unit of measurement;

(b) that pay for work at time rates shall be the same for the same job.

Article 120

Member States shall endeavour to maintain the existing equivalence between paid holiday schemes.

Article 121

The Council may, acting unanimously and after consulting the Economic and Social Committee, assign to the Commission tasks in connection with the implementation of common measures, particularly as regards social security for the migrant workers referred to in Arts. 48 to 51.

Article 122

The Commission shall include a separate chapter on social developments within the Community in its annual report to the European Parliament.

The European Parliament may invite the Commission to draw up reports on any particular problems concerning social conditions.

Chapter 2. The European Social Fund

Article 123

In order to improve employment opportunities for workers in the internal market and to contribute thereby to raising the standard of living, a European Social Fund is hereby established in accordance with the provisions set out below: it shall aim to render the employment of workers easier and to increase their geographical and occupational mobility within the Community, and to facilitate their adaptation to industrial changes and to changes in production systems, in particular through vocational training and retraining.

Article 124

The Fund shall be administered by the Commission.

The Commission shall be assisted in this task by a Committee presided over by a member of the Commission and composed of representatives of Governments, trade unions and employers' organisations.

Article 125

The Council, acting in accordance with the procedure referred to in Article 189c and after consulting the Economic and Social Committee, shall adopt implementing decisions relating to the European Social Fund.

Chapter 3. Education, Vocational Training and Youth

Article 126

1. The Community shall contribute to the development of quality education by encouraging co-operation between Member States and, if necessary, by supporting and supplementing their action, while fully respecting the responsibility of the Member States for the content of teaching and the organization of education systems and their cultural and linguistic diversity.

2. Community action shall be aimed at:

• developing the European dimension in education, particularly through the teaching and dissemination of the languages of the Member States;

• encouraging mobility of students and teachers, inter alia, by encouraging the academic recognition of diplomas and periods of study;

• promoting cooperation between educational establishments;

• developing exchanges of information and experience on issues common to the education systems of the Member States;

• encouraging the development of youth exchanges and of exchanges of socio-educational instructors;

• encouraging the development of distance education.

3. The Community and the Member States shall foster co-operation with third countries and the competent international organizations in the sphere of education, in particular the Council of Europe.

4. In order to contribute to the achievement of the objectives referred to in this Article, the Council:

• acting in accordance with the procedure referred to in Article 189b, after consulting the Economic and Social Committee and the Committee of the Regions, shall adopt incentive measures, excluding any harmonization of the laws and regulations of the Member States;

• acting by qualified majority on a proposal from the Commission, shall adopt recommendations.

Article 127

1. The Community shall implement a vocational training policy which shall support and supplement the action of the Member States, while fully respecting the responsibility of the Member States for the content and organization of vocational training.

2. Community action shall aim to:

• facilitate adaptation to industrial changes, in particular through vocational training and retraining;

• improve initial and continuing vocational training in order to facilitate vocational integration and reintegration into the labour market;

• facilitate access to vocational training and encourage mobility of instructors and trainees and particularly young people;

• stimulate co-operation on training between educational or training establishments and firms;

• develop exchanges of information and experience on issues common to the training systems of the Member States.

3. The Community and the Member States shall foster co-operation with third countries and the competent international organizations in the sphere of vocational training.

4. The Council, acting in accordance with the procedure referred to in Article 189c and after consulting the Economic and Social Committee, shall adopt measures to contribute to the achievement of the objectives referred to in this Article, excluding any harmonization of the laws and regulations of the Member States.

Title IX. Culture

Article 128

1. The Community shall contribute to the flowering of the cultures of the Member States, while respecting their national and regional diversity and at the same time bringing the common cultural heritage to the fore.

2. Action by the Community shall be aimed at encouraging cooperation between Member States and, if necessary, supporting and supplementing their action in the following areas:

• improvement of the knowledge and dissemination of the culture and history of the European peoples;

• conservation and safeguarding of cultural heritage of European significance;

• non-commercial cultural exchanges;

• artistic and literary creation, including in the audiovisual sector.

3. The Community and the Member States shall foster cooperation with third countries and the competent international organizations in the sphere of culture, in particular the Council of Europe.

4. The Community shall take cultural aspects into account in its action under other provisions of this Treaty.

5. In order to contribute to the achievement of the objectives referred to in this Article, the Council:

• acting in accordance with the procedure referred to in Article 189b and after consulting the Committee of the Regions, shall adopt incentive measures, excluding any harmonization of the laws and regulations of the Member States. The Council shall act unanimously throughout the procedures referred to in Article 189b;

• acting unanimously on a proposal from the Commission, shall adopt recommendations.

Title X. Public Health

Article 129

1. The Community shall contribute towards ensuring a high level of human health protection by encouraging cooperation between the Member States and, if necessary, lending support to their action.

Community action shall be directed towards the prevention of diseases, in particular the major health scourges, including drug dependence, by promoting research into their causes and their transmission, as well as health information and education.

Health protection requirements shall form a constituent part of the Community's other policies.

2. Member States shall, in liaison with the Commission, coordinate among themselves their policies and programmes in the areas referred to in paragraph 1. The Commission may, in close contact with the Member States, take any useful initiative to promote such coordination.

3. The Community and the Member States shall foster co-operation with third countries and the competent international organizations in the sphere of public health.

4. In order to contribute to the achievement of the objectives referred to in this Article, the Council:

• acting in accordance with the procedure referred to in Article 189b, after consulting the Economic and Social Committee and the Committee of the Regions, shall adopt incentive measures, excluding any harmonization of the laws and regulations of the Member States;

• acting by a qualified majority on a proposal from the Commission, shall adopt recommendations.

Title XI. Consumer Protection

Article 129a

1. The Community shall contribute to the attainment of a high level of consumer protection through:

(a) measures adopted pursuant to Article 100a in the context of the completion of the internal market;

(b) specific action which supports and supplements the policy pursued by the Member States to protect the health, safety and economic interests of consumers and to provide adequate information to consumers.

2. The Council, acting in accordance with the procedure referred to in Article 189b and after consulting the Economic and Social Committee, shall adopt the specific action referred to in paragraph 1(b).

3. Action adopted pursuant to paragraph 2 shall not prevent any Member State from maintaining or introducing more stringent protective measures. Such measures must be compatible with this Treaty. The Commission shall be notified of them.

. . .

Chapter 7
American Declaration of the Rights and Duties of Man

Whereas:

The American peoples have acknowledged the dignity of the individual, and their national constitutions recognize that juridical and political institutions, which regulate life in human society, have as their principal aim the protection of the essential rights of man and the creation of circumstances that will permit him to achieve spiritual and material progress and attain happiness;

The American States have on repeated occasions recognized that the essential rights of man are not derived from the fact that he is a national of a certain state, but are based upon attributes of his human personality;

The international protection of the rights of man should be the principal guide of an evolving American law;

The affirmation of essential human rights by the American States together with the guarantees given by the internal regimes of the states establish the initial system of protection considered by the American States as being suited to the present social and juridical conditions, not without a recognition on their part that they should increasingly strengthen that system in the international field as conditions become more favorable,

The Ninth International Conference of American States

Agrees:

To adopt the following

American Declaration of the Rights and Duties of Man

Preamble

All men are born free and equal, in dignity and in rights, and, being endowed by

Adopted by the Ninth International Conference of American States, Bogotá, Colombia, 2 May 1948.

nature with reason and conscience, they should conduct themselves as brothers one to another.

The fulfillment of duty by each individual is a prerequisite to the rights of all. Rights and duties are interrelated in every social and political activity of man. While rights exalt individual liberty, duties express the dignity of that liberty.

Duties of a juridical nature presuppose others of a moral nature which support them in principle and constitute their basis.

Inasmuch as spiritual development is the supreme end of human existence and the highest expression thereof, it is the duty of man to serve that end with all his strength and resources.

Since culture is the highest social and historical expression of that spiritual development, it is the duty of man to preserve, practice and foster culture by every means within his power.

And, since moral conduct constitutes the noblest flowering of culture, it is the duty of every man always to hold it in high respect.

Chapter One: Rights

Article I

Every human being has the right to life, liberty and the security of his person.

Article II

All persons are equal before the law and have the rights and duties established in this Declaration, without distinction as to race, sex, language, creed or any other factor.

Article III

Every person has the right freely to profess a religious faith, and to manifest and practice it both in public and in private.

Article IV

Every person has the right to freedom of investigation, of opinion, and of the expression and dissemination of ideas, by any medium whatsoever.

Article V

Every person has the right to the protection of the law against abusive attacks upon his honor, his reputation, and his private and family life.

Article VI

Every person has the right to establish a family, the basic element of society, and to receive protection therefor.

Article VII

All women, during pregnancy and the nursing period, and all children have the right to special protection, care and aid.

Article VIII

Every person has the right to fix his residence within the territory of the state of which he is a national, to move about freely within such territory, and not to leave it except by his own will.

Article IX

Every person has the right to the inviolability of his home.

Article X

Every person has the right to the inviolability and transmission of his correspondence.

Article XI

Every person has the right to the preservation of his health through sanitary and social measures relating to food, clothing, housing and medical care, to the extent permitted by public and community resources.

Article XII

Every person has the right to an education, which should be based on the principles of liberty, morality and human solidarity.

Likewise every person has the right to an education that will prepare him to attain a decent life, to raise his standard of living, and to be a useful member of society.

The right to an education includes the right to equality of opportunity in every case, in accordance with natural talents, merit and the desire to utilize the resources that the state or the community is in a position to provide.

Every person has the right to receive, free, at least a primary education.

Article XIII

Every person has the right to take part in the cultural life of the community, to enjoy the arts, and to participate in the benefits that result from intellectual progress, especially scientific discoveries.

He likewise has the right to the protection of his moral and material interests as regards his inventions or any literary, scientific or artistic works of which he is the author.

Article XIV

Every person has the right to work, under proper conditions, and to follow his vocation freely, insofar as existing conditions of employment permit.

Every person who works has the right to receive such remuneration as will, in proportion to his capacity and skill, assure him a standard of living suitable for himself and for his family.

Article XV

Every person has the right to leisure time, to wholesome recreation, and to the opportunity for advantageous use of his free time to his spiritual, cultural and physical benefit.

Article XVI

Every person has the right to social security which will protect him from the consequences of unemployment, old age, and any disabilities arising from causes beyond his control that make it physically or mentally impossible for him to earn a living.

Article XVII

Every person has the right to be recognized everywhere as a person having rights and obligations, and to enjoy the basic civil rights.

Article XVIII

Every person may resort to the courts to ensure respect for his legal rights. There should likewise be available to him a simple, brief procedure whereby the courts will protect him from acts of authority that, to his prejudice, violate any fundamental constitutional rights.

Article XIX

Every person has the right to the nationality to which he is entitled by law and to change it, if he so wishes, for the nationality of any other country that is willing to grant it to him.

Article XX

Every person having legal capacity is entitled to participate in the government of his country, directly or through his representatives, and to take part in popular elections, which shall be by secret ballot, and shall be honest, periodic and free.

Article XXI

Every person has the right to assemble peaceably with others in a formal public meeting or an informal gathering, in connection with matters of common interest of any nature.

Article XXII

Every person has the right to associate with others to promote, exercise and protect his legitimate interests of a political, economic, religious, social, cultural, professional, labor union or other nature.

Article XXIII

Every person has a right to own such private property as meets the essential needs of decent living and helps to maintain the dignity of the individual and of the home.

Article XXIV

Every person has the right to submit respectful petitions to any competent authority, for reasons of either general or private interest, and the right to obtain a prompt decision thereon.

Article XXV

No person may be deprived of his liberty except in the cases and according to the procedures established by pre-existing law.

No person may be deprived of liberty for non-fulfillment of obligations of a purely civil character.

Every individual who has been deprived of his liberty has the right to have the legality of his detention ascertained without delay by a court, and the right to be tried without undue delay or, otherwise, to be released. He also has the right to humane treatment during the time he is in custody.

Article XXVI

Every accused person is presumed to be innocent until proved guilty.

Every person accused of an offense has the right to be given an impartial and public hearing, and to be tried by courts previously established in accordance with pre-existing laws, and not to receive cruel, infamous or unusual punishment.

Article XXVII

Every person has the right, in case of pursuit not resulting from ordinary crimes, to seek and receive asylum in foreign territory, in accordance with the laws of each country and with international agreements.

Article XXVIII

The rights of man are limited by the rights of others, by the security of all, and by the just demands of the general welfare and the advancement of democracy.

Chapter Two: Duties

Article XXIX

It is the duty of the individual so to conduct himself in relation to others that each and every one may fully form and develop his personality.

Article XXX

It is the duty of every person to aid, support, educate and protect his minor children, and it is the duty of children to honor their parents always and to aid, support and protect them when they need it.

Article XXXI

It is the duty of every person to acquire at least an elementary education.

Article XXXII

It is the duty of every person to vote in the popular elections of the country of which he is a national, when he is legally capable of doing so.

Article XXXIII

It is the duty of every person to obey the law and other legitimate commands of the authorities of his country and those of the country in which he may be.

Article XXXIV

It is the duty of every able-bodied person to render whatever civil and military service his country may require for its defense and preservation, and, in case of public disaster, to render such services as may be in his power.

It is likewise his duty to hold any public office to which he may be elected by popular vote in the state of which he is a national.

Article XXXV

It is the duty of every person to co-operate with the state and the community with respect to social security and welfare, in accordance with his ability and with existing circumstances.

Article XXXVI

It is the duty of every person to pay the taxes established by law for the support of public services.

Article XXXVII

It is the duty of every person to work, as far as his capacity and possibilities permit, in order to obtain the means of livelihood or to benefit his community.

Article XXXVIII

It is the duty of every person to refrain from taking part in political activities that, according to law, are reserved exclusively to the citizens of the state in which he is an alien.

Chapter 8
American Convention on Human Rights

Preamble

The American states signatory to the present Convention,

Reaffirming their intention to consolidate in this hemisphere, within the framework of democratic institutions, a system of personal liberty and social justice based on respect for the essential rights of man;

Recognizing that the essential rights of man are not derived from one's being a national of a certain state, but are based upon attributes of the human personality, and that they therefore justify international protection in the form of a convention reinforcing or complementing the protection provided by the domestic law of the American states;

Considering that these principles have been set forth in the Charter of the Organization of American States, in the American Declaration of the Rights and Duties of Man, and in the Universal Declaration of Human Rights, and that they have been reaffirmed and refined in other international instruments, worldwide as well as regional in scope;

Reiterating that, in accordance with the Universal Declaration of Human Rights, the ideal of free men enjoying freedom from fear and want can be achieved only if conditions are created whereby everyone may enjoy his economic, social, and cultural rights, as well as his civil and political rights; and

Considering that the Third Special Inter-American Conference (Buenos Aires, 1967) approved the incorporation into the Charter of the Organization itself of broader standards with respect to economic, social, and educational rights and resolved that an inter-American convention on human rights should determine the structure, competence, and procedure of the organs responsible for these matters,

Have agreed upon the following:

Adopted at San José, Costa Rica 22 November 1969, *entry into force* 18 July 1978.

Part I—State Obligations and rights protected

Chapter I—General Obligations

Article 1. Obligation to respect rights

1. The States Parties to this Convention undertake to respect the rights and freedoms recognized herein and to ensure to all persons subject to their jurisdiction the free and full exercise of those rights and freedoms, without any discrimination for reasons of race, color, sex, language, religion, political or other opinion, national or social origin, economic status, birth, or any other social condition.

2. For the purposes of this Convention, "person" means every human being.

Article 2. Domestic legal effects

Where the exercise of any of the rights or freedoms referred to in Article 1 is not already ensured by legislative or other provisions, the States Parties undertake to adopt, in accordance with their constitutional processes and the provisions of this Convention, such legislative or other measures as may be necessary to give effect to those rights or freedoms.

Chapter II—Civil and political rights

Article 3. Right to juridical personality

Every person has the right to recognition as a person before the law.

Article 4. Right to life

1. Every person has the right to have his life respected. This right shall be protected by law and, in general, from the moment of conception. No one shall be arbitrarily deprived of his life.

2. In countries that have not abolished the death penalty, it may be imposed only for the most serious crimes and pursuant to a final judgment rendered by a competent court and in accordance with a law establishing such punishment, enacted prior to the commission of the crime. The application of such punishment shall not be extended to crimes to which it does not presently apply.

3. The death penalty shall not be reestablished in states that have abolished it.

4. In no case shall capital punishment be inflicted for political offenses or related common crimes.

5. Capital punishment shall not be imposed upon persons who, at the time the crime was committed, were under 18 years of age or over 70 years of age; nor shall it be applied to pregnant women.

6. Every person condemned to death shall have the right to apply for amnesty, pardon, or commutation of sentence, which may be granted in all cases. Capital punishment shall not be imposed while such a petition is pending decision by the competent authority.

Article 5. Right to humane treatment

1. Every person has the right to have his physical, mental, and moral integrity respected.

2. No one shall be subjected to torture or to cruel, inhuman, or degrading punishment or treatment. All persons deprived of their liberty shall be treated with respect for the inherent dignity of the human person.

3. Punishment shall not be extended to any person other than the criminal.

4. Accused persons shall, save in exceptional circumstances, be segregated from convicted persons, and shall be subject to separate treatment appropriate to their status as unconvicted persons.

5. Minors while subject to criminal proceedings shall be separated from adults and brought before specialized tribunals, as speedily as possible, so that they may be treated in accordance with their status as minors.

6. Punishments consisting of deprivation of liberty shall have as an essential aim the reform and social readaptation of the prisoners.

Article 6. Freedom from slavery

1. No one shall be subject to slavery or to involuntary servitude, which are prohibited in all their forms, as are the slave trade and traffic in women.

2. No one shall be required to perform forced or compulsory labor. This provision shall not be interpreted to mean that, in those countries in which the penalty established for certain crimes is deprivation of liberty at forced labor, the carrying out of such a sentence imposed by a competent court is prohibited. Forced labor shall not adversely affect the dignity or the physical or intellectual capacity of the prisoner.

3. For the purposes of this article, the following do not constitute forced or compulsory labor:

a. work or service normally required of a person imprisoned in execution of a sentence or formal decision passed by the competent judicial authority. Such work or service shall be carried out under the supervision and control of public authorities, and any persons performing such work or service shall not be placed at the disposal of any private party, company, or juridical person;

b. military service and, in countries in which conscientious objectors are recognized, national service that the law may provide for in lieu of military service;

c. service exacted in time of danger or calamity that threatens the existence or the well-being of the community; or

d. work or service that forms part of normal civic obligations.

Article 7. Right to personal liberty

1. Every person has the right to personal liberty and security.

2. No one shall be deprived of his physical liberty except for the reasons and under the conditions established beforehand by the constitution of the State Party concerned or by a law established pursuant thereto.

3. No one shall be subject to arbitrary arrest or imprisonment.

4. Anyone who is detained shall be informed of the reasons for his detention and shall be promptly notified of the charge or charges against him.

5. Any person detained shall be brought promptly before a judge or other officer authorized by law to exercise judicial power and shall be entitled to trial within a reasonable time or to be released without prejudice to the continuation of the proceedings. His release may be subject to guarantees to assure his appearance for trial.

6. Anyone who is deprived of his liberty shall be entitled to recourse to a competent court, in order that the court may decide without delay on the lawfulness of his arrest or detention and order his release if the arrest or detention is unlawful. In States Parties whose laws provide that anyone who believes himself to be threatened with deprivation of his liberty is entitled to recourse to a competent court in order that it may decide on the lawfulness of such threat, this remedy may not be restricted or abolished. The interested party or another person in his behalf is entitled to seek these remedies.

7. No one shall be detained for debt. This principle shall not limit the orders of a competent judicial authority issued for nonfulfillment of duties of support.

Article 8. Right to a fair trial

1. Every person has the right to a hearing, with due guarantees and within a reasonable time, by a competent, independent, and impartial tribunal, previously established by law, in the substantiation of any accusation of a criminal nature made against him or for the determination of his rights and obligations of a civil, labor, fiscal, or any other nature.

2. Every person accused of a criminal offense has the right to be presumed innocent so long as his guilt has not been proven according to law. During the proceedings, every person is entitled, with full equality, to the following minimum guarantees:

a. the right of the accused to be assisted without charge by a translator or interpreter, if he does not understand or does not speak the language of the tribunal or court;

b. prior notification in detail to the accused of the charges against him;

c. adequate time and means for the preparation of his defense;

d. the right of the accused to defend himself personally or to be assisted by legal counsel of his own choosing, and to communicate freely and privately with his counsel;

e. the inalienable right to be assisted by counsel provided by the state, paid or not as the domestic law provides, if the accused does not defend himself personally or engage his own counsel within the time period established by law;

f. the right of the defense to examine witnesses present in the court and to obtain the appearance, as witnesses, of experts or other persons who may throw light on the facts;

g. the right not to be compelled to be a witness against himself or to plead guilty; and

h. the right to appeal the judgment to a higher court.

3. A confession of guilt by the accused shall be valid only if it is made without coercion of any kind.

4. An accused person acquitted by a nonappealable judgment shall not be subjected to a new trial for the same cause.

5. Criminal proceedings shall be public, except insofar as may be necessary to protect the interests of justice.

Article 9. Freedom from ex post facto laws

No one shall be convicted of any act or omission that did not constitute a criminal offense, under the applicable law, at the time it was committed. A heavier penalty shall not be imposed than the one that was applicable at the time the criminal offense was committed. If subsequent to the commission of the offense the law provides for the imposition of a lighter punishment, the guilty person shall benefit therefrom.

Article 10. Right to compensation

Every person has the right to be compensated in accordance with the law in the event he has been sentenced by a final judgment through a miscarriage of justice.

Article 11. Right to privacy

1. Everyone has the right to have his honor respected and his dignity recognized.

2. No one may be the object of arbitrary or abusive interference with his private life, his family, his home, or his correspondence, or of unlawful attacks on his honor or reputation.

3. Everyone has the right to the protection of the law against such interference or attacks.

Article 12. Freedom of conscience and religion

1. Everyone has the right to freedom of conscience and of religion. This right includes freedom to maintain or to change one's religion or beliefs, and freedom to profess or disseminate one's religion or beliefs, either individually or together with others, in public or in private.

2. No one shall be subject to restrictions that might impair his freedom to maintain or to change his religion or beliefs.

3. Freedom to manifest one's religion and beliefs may be subject only to the limitations prescribed by law that are necessary to protect public safety, order, health, or morals, or the rights or freedoms of others.

4. Parents or guardians, as the case may be, have the right to provide for the religious and moral education of their children or wards that is in accord with their own convictions.

Article 13. Freedom of thought and expression

1. Everyone has the right to freedom of thought and expression. This right includes freedom to seek, receive, and impart information and ideas of all kinds, regardless of frontiers, either orally, in writing, in print, in the form of art, or through any other medium of one's choice.

2. The exercise of the right provided for in the foregoing paragraph shall not be subject to prior censorship but shall be subject to subsequent imposition of liability, which shall be expressly established by law to the extent necessary to ensure:

a. respect for the rights or reputations of others; or

b. the protection of national security, public order, or public health or morals.

3. The right of expression may not be restricted by indirect methods or means, such as the abuse of government or private controls over newsprint, radio broadcasting frequencies, or equipment used in the dissemination of information, or by any other means tending to impede the communication and circulation of ideas and opinions.

4. Notwithstanding the provisions of paragraph 2 above, public entertainments may be subject by law to prior censorship for the sole purpose of regulating access to them for the moral protection of childhood and adolescence.

5. Any propaganda for war and any advocacy of national, racial, or religious hatred that constitute incitements to lawless violence or to any other similar action against any person or group of persons on any grounds including those of race, color, religion, language, or national origin shall be considered an offense punishable by law.

Article 14. Right of reply

1. Anyone injured by inaccurate or offensive statements or ideas disseminated to the public in general by a legally regulated medium of communication has the right to

reply or to make a correction using the same communications outlet, under such conditions as the law may establish.

2. The correction or reply shall not in any case remit other legal liabilities that may have been incurred.

3. For the effective protection of honor and reputation, every publisher, and every newspaper, motion picture, radio, and television company, shall have a person responsible who is not protected by immunities or special privileges.

Article 15. Right of assembly

The right of peaceful assembly, without arms, is recognized. No restrictions may be placed on the exercise of this right other than those imposed in conformity with the law and necessary in a democratic society in the interest of national security, public safety or public order, or to protect public health or morals or the rights or freedom of others.

Article 16. Freedom of association

1. Everyone has the right to associate freely for ideological, religious, political, economic, labor, social, cultural, sports, or other purposes.

2. The exercise of this right shall be subject only to such restrictions established by law as may be necessary in a democratic society, in the interest of national security, public safety or public order, or to protect public health or morals or the rights and freedoms of others.

3. The provisions of this article do not bar the imposition of legal restrictions, including even deprivation of the exercise of the right of association, on members of the armed forces and the police.

Article 17. Rights of the family

1. The family is the natural and fundamental group unit of society and is entitled to protection by society and the state.

2. The right of men and women of marriageable age to marry and to raise a family shall be recognized, if they meet the conditions required by domestic laws, insofar as such conditions do not affect the principle of nondiscrimination established in this Convention.

3. No marriage shall be entered into without the free and full consent of the intending spouses.

4. The States Parties shall take appropriate steps to ensure the equality of rights and the adequate balancing of responsibilities of the spouses as to marriage, during marriage, and in the event of its dissolution. In case of dissolution, provision shall be made for the necessary protection of any children solely on the basis of their own best interests.

5. The law shall recognize equal rights for children born out of wedlock and those born in wedlock.

Article 18. Right to a name

Every person has the right to a given name and to the surnames of his parents or that of one of them. The law shall regulate the manner in which this right shall be ensured for all, by the use of assumed names if necessary.

Article 19. Rights of the child

Every minor child has the right to the measures of protection required by his condition as a minor on the part of his family, society, and the state.

Article 20. Right to nationality

1. Every person has the right to a nationality.

2. Every person has the right to the nationality of the state in whose territory he was born if he does not have the right to any other nationality.

3. No one shall be arbitrarily deprived of his nationality or of the right to change it.

Article 21. Right to property

1. Everyone has the right to the use and enjoyment of his property. The law may subordinate such use and enjoyment to the interest of society.

2. No one shall be deprived of his property except upon payment of just compensation, for reasons of public utility or social interest, and in the cases and according to the forms established by law.

3. Usury and any other form of exploitation of man by man shall be prohibited by law.

Article 22. Freedom of movement and residence

1. Every person lawfully in the territory of a State Party has the right to move about in it, and to reside in it subject to the provisions of the law.

2. Every person has the right lo leave any country freely, including his own.

3. The exercise of the foregoing rights may be restricted only pursuant to a law to the extent necessary in a democratic society to prevent crime or to protect national security, public safety, public order, public morals, public health, or the rights or freedoms of others.

4. The exercise of the rights recognized in paragraph 1 may also be restricted by law in designated zones for reasons of public interest.

5. No one can be expelled from the territory of the state of which he is a national or be deprived of the right to enter it.

6. An alien lawfully in the territory of a State Party to this Convention may be expelled from it only pursuant to a decision reached in accordance with law.

7. Every person has the right to seek and be granted asylum in a foreign territory, in accordance with the legislation of the state and international conventions, in the event he is being pursued for political offenses or related common crimes.

8. In no case may an alien be deported or returned to a country, regardless of whether or not it is his country of origin, if in that country his right to life or personal freedom is in danger of being violated because of his race, nationality, religion, social status, or political opinions.

9. The collective expulsion of aliens is prohibited.

Article 23. Right to participate in government

1. Every citizen shall enjoy the following rights and opportunities:

a. to take part in the conduct of public affairs, directly or through freely chosen representatives;

b. to vote and to be elected in genuine periodic elections, which shall be by universal and equal suffrage and by secret ballot that guarantees the free expression of the will of the voters; and

c. to have access, under general conditions of equality, to the public service of his country.

2. The law may regulate the exercise of the rights and opportunities referred to in the preceding paragraph only on the basis of age, nationality, residence, language, education, civil and mental capacity, or sentencing by a competent court in criminal proceedings.

Article 24. Right to equal protection

All persons are equal before the law. Consequently, they are entitled, without discrimination, to equal protection of the law.

Article 25. Right to judicial protection

1. Everyone has the right to simple and prompt recourse, or any other effective recourse, to a competent court or tribunal for protection against acts that violate his fundamental rights recognized by the constitution or laws of the state concerned or by this

Convention, even though such violation may have been committed by persons acting in the course of their official duties.

2. The States Parties undertake:

a. to ensure that any person claiming such remedy shall have his rights determined by the competent authority provided for by the legal system of the state;

b. to develop the possibilities of judicial remedy; and

c. to ensure that the competent authorities shall enforce such remedies when granted.

Chapter III—Economic, Social and Cultural Rights

Article 26. Progressive development

The States Parties undertake to adopt measures, both internally and through international co-operation, especially those of an economic and technical nature, with a view to achieving progressively, by legislation or other appropriate means, the full realization of the rights implicit in the economic, social, educational, scientific, and cultural standards set forth in the Charter of the Organization of American States as amended by the Protocol of Buenos Aires.

Chapter IV—Suspension of Guarantees, Interpretation, and Application

Article 27. Suspension of guarantees

1. In time of war, public danger, or other emergency that threatens the independence or security of a State Party, it may take measures derogating from its obligations under the present Convention to the extent and for the period of time strictly required by the exigencies of the situation, provided that such measures are not inconsistent with its other obligations under international law and do not involve discrimination on the ground of race, color, sex, language, religion, or social origin.

2. The foregoing provision does not authorize any suspension of the following articles: Article 3 (Right to Juridical Personality), Article 4 (Right to Life), Article 5 (Right to Humane Treatment), Article 6 (Freedom from Slavery), Article 9 (Freedom from Ex Post Facto Laws), Article 12 (Freedom of Conscience and Religion), Article 17 (Rights of the Family), Article 18 (Right to a Name), Article 19 (Rights of the Child), Article 20 (Right to Nationality), and Article 23 (Right to Participate in Government), or of the judicial guarantees essential for the protection of such rights.

3. Any State Party availing itself of the right of suspension shall immediately inform the other States Parties, through the Secretary-General of the Organization of American States, of the provisions the application of which it has suspended, the reasons that gave rise to the suspension, and the date set for the termination of such suspension.

Article 28. Federal clause

1. Where a State Party is constituted as a federal state, the national government of such State Party shall implement all the provisions of the Convention over whose subject matter it exercises legislative and judicial jurisdiction.

2. With respect to the provisions over whose subject matter the constituent units of the federal state have jurisdiction, the national government shall immediately take suitable measures, in accordance with its constitution and its laws, to the end that the competent authorities of the constituent units may adopt appropriate provisions for the fulfillment of this Convention.

3. Whenever two or more States Parties agree to form a federation or other type of association, they shall take care that the resulting federal or other compact contains the provisions necessary for continuing and rendering effective the standards of this Convention in the new state that is organized.

Article 29. Restrictions regarding interpretation

No provision of this Convention shall be interpreted as:

a. permitting any State Party, group, or person to suppress the enjoyment or exercise of the rights and freedoms recognized in this Convention or to restrict them to a greater extent than is provided for herein;

b. restricting the enjoyment or exercise of any right or freedom recognized by virtue of the laws of any State Party or by virtue of another convention to which one of the said states is a party;

c. precluding other rights or guarantees that are inherent in the human personality or derived from representative democracy as a form of government; or

d. excluding or limiting the effect that the American Declaration of the Rights and Duties of Man and other international acts of the same nature may have.

Article 30. Scope of restrictions

The restrictions that, pursuant to this Convention, may be placed on the enjoyment or exercise of the rights or freedoms recognized herein may not be applied except in accordance with laws enacted for reasons of general interest and in accordance with the purpose for which such restrictions have been established.

Article 31. Recognition of other rights

Other rights and freedoms recognized in accordance with the procedures established in Articles 76 and 77 may be included in the system of protection of this Convention.

Chapter V—Personal Responsibilities

Article 32. Relationship between duties and rights

1. Every person has responsibilities to his family, his community, and mankind.

2. The rights of each person are limited by the rights of others, by the security of all, and by the just demands of the general welfare, in a democratic society.

Chapter 9
Additional Protocol to the American Convention on Human Rights in the Area of Economic, Social and Cultural Rights ("Protocol of San Salvador")

Preamble

The States Parties to the American Convention on Human Rights "Pact San José, Costa Rica,"

Reaffirming their intention to consolidate in this hemisphere, within the framework of democratic institutions, a system of personal liberty and social justice based on respect for the essential rights of man;

Recognizing that the essential rights of man are not derived from one's being a national of a certain State, but are based upon attributes of the human person, for which reason they merit international protection in the form of a convention reinforcing or complementing the protection provided by the domestic law of the American States;

Considering the close relationship that exists between economic, social and cultural rights, and civil and political rights, in that the different categories of rights constitute an indivisible whole based on the recognition of the dignity of the human person, for which reason both require permanent protection and promotion if they are to be fully realized, and the violation of some rights in favor of the realization of others can never be justified;

Recognizing the benefits that stem from the promotion and development of cooperation among States and international relations;

Recalling that, in accordance with the Universal Declaration of Human Rights and the American Convention on Human Rights, the ideal of free human beings enjoying freedom from fear and want can only be achieved if conditions are created whereby everyone may enjoy his economic, social and cultural rights as well as his civil and political rights;

Adopted at San Salvador, El Salvador, 17 November 1988, *entry into force* 16 November 1999.

Bearing in mind that, although fundamental economic, social and cultural rights have been recognized in earlier international instruments of both world and regional scope, it is essential that those rights be reaffirmed, developed, perfected and protected in order to consolidate in America, on the basis of full respect for the rights of the individual, the democratic representative form of government as well as the right of its peoples to development, self-determination, and the free disposal of their wealth and natural resources; and

Considering that the American Convention on Human Rights provides that draft additional protocols to that Convention may be submitted for consideration to the States Parties, meeting together on the occasion of the General Assembly of the Organization of American States, for the purpose of gradually incorporating other rights and freedoms into the protective system thereof, have agreed upon the following Additional Protocol to the American Convention on Human Rights "Protocol of San Salvador:"

Article 1. Obligation to adopt measures

The States Parties to this Additional Protocol to the American Convention on Human Rights undertake to adopt the necessary measures, both domestically and through international co-operation, especially economic and technical, to the extent allowed by their available resources, and taking into account their degree of development, for the purpose of achieving progressively and pursuant to their internal legislations, the full observance of the rights recognized in this Protocol.

Article 2. Obligation to enact domestic legislation

If the exercise of the rights set forth in this Protocol is not already guaranteed by legislative or other provisions, the States Parties undertake to adopt, in accordance with their constitutional processes and the provisions of this Protocol, such legislative or other measures as may be necessary for making those rights a reality.

Article 3. Obligation of nondiscrimination

The State Parties to this Protocol undertake to guarantee the exercise of the rights set forth herein without discrimination of any kind for reasons related to race, color, sex, language, religion, political or other opinions, national or social origin, economic status, birth or any other social condition.

Article 4. Inadmissibility of restrictions

A right which is recognized or in effect in a State by virtue of its internal legislation or international conventions may not be restricted or curtailed on the pretext that this Protocol does not recognize the right or recognizes it to a lesser degree.

Article 5. Scope of restrictions and limitations

The State Parties may establish restrictions and limitations on the enjoyment and exercise of the rights established herein by means of laws promulgated for the purpose of preserving the general welfare in a democratic society only to the extent that they are not incompatible with the purpose and reason underlying those rights.

Article 6. Right to work

1. Everyone has the right to work, which includes the opportunity to secure the means for living a dignified and decent existence by performing a freely elected or accepted lawful activity.

2. The State Parties undertake to adopt measures that will make the right to work fully effective, especially with regard to the achievement of full employment, vocational guidance, and the development of technical and vocational training projects, in particular those directed to the disabled. The States Parties also undertake to implement and strengthen programs that help to ensure suitable family care, so that women may enjoy a real opportunity to exercise the right to work.

Article 7. Just, equitable, and satisfactory conditions of work

The States Parties to this Protocol recognize that the right to work to which the foregoing article refers presupposes that everyone shall enjoy that right under just, equitable, and satisfactory conditions, which the States Parties undertake to guarantee in their internal legislation, particularly with respect to:

a. Remuneration which guarantees, as a minimum, to all workers dignified and decent living conditions for them and their families and fair and equal wages for equal work, without distinction;

b. The right of every worker to follow his vocation and to devote himself to the activity that best fulfills his expectations and to change employment in accordance with the pertinent national regulations;

c. The right of every worker to promotion or upward mobility in his employment, for which purpose account shall be taken of his qualifications, competence, integrity and seniority;

d. Stability of employment, subject to the nature of each industry and occupation and the causes for just separation. In cases of unjustified dismissal, the worker shall have the right to indemnity or to reinstatement on the job or any other benefits provided by domestic legislation;

e. Safety and hygiene at work;

f. The prohibition of night work or unhealthy or dangerous working conditions and, in general, of all work which jeopardizes health, safety, or morals, for persons under

18 years of age. As regards minors under the age of 16, the work day shall be subordinated to the provisions regarding compulsory education and in no case shall work constitute an impediment to school attendance or a limitation on benefiting from education received;

g. A reasonable limitation of working hours, both daily and weekly. The days shall be shorter in the case of dangerous or unhealthy work or of night work;

h. Rest, leisure and paid vacations as well as remuneration for national holidays.

Article 8: Trade union rights

1. The States Parties shall ensure:

a. The right of workers to organize trade unions and to join the union of their choice for the purpose of protecting and promoting their interests. As an extension of that right, the States Parties shall permit trade unions to establish national federations or confederations, or to affiliate with those that already exist, as well as to form international trade union organizations and to affiliate with that of their choice. The States Parties shall also permit trade unions, federations and confederations to function freely;

b. The right to strike.

2. The exercise of the rights set forth above may be subject only to restrictions established by law, provided that such restrictions are characteristic of a democratic society and necessary for safeguarding public order or for protecting public health or morals or the rights and freedoms of others. Members of the armed forces and the police and of other essential public services shall be subject to limitations and restrictions established by law.

3. No one may be compelled to belong to a trade union.

Article 9: Right to social security

1. Everyone shall have the right to social security protecting him from the consequences of old age and of disability which prevents him, physically or mentally, from securing the means for a dignified and decent existence. In the event of the death of a beneficiary, social security benefits shall be applied to his dependents.

2. In the case of persons who are employed, the right to social security shall cover at least medical care and an allowance or retirement benefit in the case of work accidents or occupational disease and, in the case of women, paid maternity leave before and after childbirth.

Article 10: Right to health

1. Everyone shall have the right to health, understood to mean the enjoyment of the highest level of physical, mental and social well-being.

2. In order to ensure the exercise of the right to health, the States Parties agree to recognize health as a public good and, particularly, to adopt the following measures to ensure that right:

a. Primary health care, that is, essential health care made available to all individuals and families in the community;

b. Extension of the benefits of health services to all individuals subject to the State's jurisdiction;

c. Universal immunization against the principal infectious diseases;

d. Prevention and treatment of endemic, occupational and other diseases;

e. Education of the population on the prevention and treatment of health problems, and

f. Satisfaction of the health needs of the highest risk groups and of those whose poverty makes them the most vulnerable.

Article 11: Right to a healthy environment

1. Everyone shall have the right to live in a healthy environment and to have access to basic public services.

2. The States Parties shall promote the protection, preservation, and improvement of the environment.

Article 12: Right to food

1. Everyone has the right to adequate nutrition which guarantees the possibility of enjoying the highest level of physical, emotional and intellectual development.

2. In order to promote the exercise of this right and eradicate malnutrition, the States Parties undertake to improve methods of production, supply and distribution of food, and to this end, agree to promote greater international co-operation in support of the relevant national policies.

Article 13: Right to education

1. Everyone has the right to education.

2. The States Parties to this Protocol agree that education should be directed towards the full development of the human personality and human dignity and should strengthen respect for human rights, ideological pluralism, fundamental freedoms, justice and peace. They further agree that education ought to enable everyone to participate effectively in a democratic and pluralistic society and achieve a decent existence and should foster understanding, tolerance and friendship among all nations and all racial, ethnic or religious groups and promote activities for the maintenance of peace.

3. The States Parties to this Protocol recognize that in order to achieve the full exercise of the right to education:

a. Primary education should be compulsory and accessible to all without cost;

b. Secondary education in its different forms, including technical and vocational secondary education, should be made generally available and accessible to all by every appropriate means, and in particular, by the progressive introduction of free education;

c. Higher education should be made equally accessible to all, on the basis of individual capacity, by every appropriate means, and in particular, by the progressive introduction of free education;

d. Basic education should be encouraged or intensified as far as possible for those persons who have not received or completed the whole cycle of primary instruction;

e. Programs of special education should be established for the handicapped, so as to provide special instruction and training to persons with physical disabilities or mental deficiencies.

4. In conformity with the domestic legislation of the States Parties, parents should have the right to select the type of education to be given to their children, provided that it conforms to the principles set forth above.

5. Nothing in this Protocol shall be interpreted as a restriction of the freedom of individuals and entities to establish and direct educational institutions in accordance with the domestic legislation of the States Parties.

Article 14: Right to the benefits of culture

1. The States Parties to this Protocol recognize the right of everyone:

a. To take part in the cultural and artistic life of the community;

b. To enjoy the benefits of scientific and technological progress;

c. To benefit from the protection of moral and material interests deriving from any scientific, literary or artistic production of which he is the author.

2. The steps to be taken by the States Parties to this Protocol to ensure the full exercise of this right shall include those necessary for the conservation, development and dissemination of science, culture and art.

3. The States Parties to this Protocol undertake to respect the freedom indispensable for scientific research and creative activity.

4. The States Parties to this Protocol recognize the benefits to be derived from the encouragement and development of international cooperation and relations in the fields of science, arts and culture, and accordingly agree to foster greater international co-operation in these fields.

Article 15. Right to the formation and the protection of families

1. The family is the natural and fundamental element of society and ought to be protected by the State, which should see to the improvement of its spiritual and material conditions.

2. Everyone has the right to form a family, which shall be exercised in accordance with the provisions of the pertinent domestic legislation.

3. The States Parties hereby undertake to accord adequate protection to the family unit and in particular:

a. To provide special care and assistance to mothers during a reasonable period before and after childbirth;

b. To guarantee adequate nutrition for children at the nursing stage and during school attendance years;

c. To adopt special measures for the protection of adolescents in order to ensure the full development of their physical, intellectual and moral capacities;

d. To undertake special programs of family training so as to help create a stable and positive environment in which children will receive and develop the values of understanding, solidarity, respect and responsibility.

Article 16. Rights of children

Every child, whatever his parentage, has the right to the protection that his status as a minor requires from his family, society and the State. Every child has the right to grow under the protection and responsibility of his parents; save in exceptional, judicially-recognized circumstances, a child of young age ought not to be separated from his mother. Every child has the right to free and compulsory education, at least in the elementary phase, and to continue his training at higher levels of the educational system.

Article 17. Protection of the elderly

Everyone has the right to special protection in old age. With this in view the States Parties agree to take progressively the necessary steps to make this right a reality and, particularly, to:

a. Provide suitable facilities, as well as food and specialized medical care, for elderly individuals who lack them and are unable to provide them for themselves;

b. Undertake work programs specifically designed to give the elderly the opportunity to engage in a productive activity suited to their abilities and consistent with their vocations or desires;

c. Foster the establishment of social organizations aimed at improving the quality of life for the elderly.

Article 18. Protection of the handicapped

Everyone affected by a diminution of his physical or mental capacities is entitled to receive special attention designed to help him achieve the greatest possible development of his personality. The States Parties agree to adopt such measures as may be necessary for this purpose and, especially, to:

a. Undertake programs specifically aimed at providing the handicapped with the resources and environment needed for attaining this goal, including work programs consistent with their possibilities and freely accepted by them or their legal representatives, as the case may be;

b. Provide special training to the families of the handicapped in order to help them solve the problems of coexistence and convert them into active agents in the physical, mental and emotional development of the latter;

c. Include the consideration of solutions to specific requirements arising from needs of this group as a priority component of their urban development plans;

d. Encourage the establishment of social groups in which the handicapped can be helped to enjoy a fuller life.

Article 19. Means of protection

1. Pursuant to the provisions of this article and the corresponding rules to be formulated for this purpose by the General Assembly of the Organization of American States, the States Parties to this Protocol undertake to submit periodic reports on the progressive measures they have taken to ensure due respect for the rights set forth in this Protocol.

2. All reports shall be submitted to the Secretary General of the OAS, who shall transmit them to the Inter-American Economic and Social Council and the Inter-American Council for Education, Science and Culture so that they may examine them in accordance with the provisions of this article. The Secretary General shall send a copy of such reports to the Inter-American Commission on Human Rights.

3. The Secretary General of the Organization of American States shall also transmit to the specialized organizations of the inter-American system of which the States Parties to the present Protocol are members, copies or pertinent portions of the reports submitted, insofar as they relate to matters within the purview of those organizations, as established by their constituent instruments.

4. The specialized organizations of the inter-American system may submit reports to the Inter-American Economic and Social Council and the Inter-American Council for Education, Science and Culture relative to compliance with the provisions of the present Protocol in their fields of activity.

5. The annual reports submitted to the General Assembly by the Inter-American Economic and Social Council and the Inter-American Council for Education, Science and

Culture shall contain a summary of the information received from the States Parties to the present Protocol and the specialized organizations concerning the progressive measures adopted in order to ensure respect for the rights acknowledged in the Protocol itself and the general recommendations they consider to be appropriate in this respect.

6. Any instance in which the rights established in paragraph a) of Article 8 and in Article 13 are violated by action directly attributable to a State Party to this Protocol may give rise, through participation of the Inter-American Commission on Human Rights and, when applicable, of the Inter-American Court of Human Rights, to application of the system of individual petitions governed by Articles 44 through 51 and 61 through 69 of the American Convention on Human Rights.

7. Without prejudice to the provisions of the preceding paragraph, the Inter-American Commission on Human Rights may formulate such observations and recommendations as it deems pertinent concerning the status of the economic, social and cultural rights established in the present Protocol in all or some of the States Parties, which it may include in its Annual Report to the General Assembly or in a special report, whichever it considers more appropriate.

8. The Councils and the Inter-American Commission on Human Rights, in discharging the functions conferred upon them in this article, shall take into account the progressive nature of the observance of the rights subject to protection by this Protocol.

Article 20. Reservations

The States Parties may, at the time of approval, signature, ratification or accession, make reservations to one or more specific provisions of this Protocol, provided that such reservations are not incompatible with the object and purpose of the Protocol.

Article 21. Signature, ratification or accession

Entry into Effect

1. This Protocol shall remain open to signature and ratification or accession by any State Party to the American Convention on Human Rights.

2. Ratification of or accession to this Protocol shall be effected by depositing an instrument of ratification or accession with the General Secretariat of the Organization of American States.

3. The Protocol shall enter into effect when eleven States have deposited their respective instruments of ratification or accession.

4. The Secretary General shall notify all the member states of the Organization of American States of the entry of the Protocol into effect.

Article 22. Inclusion of other rights and expansion of those recognized

1. Any State Party and the Inter-American Commission on Human Rights may submit for the consideration of the States Parties meeting on the occasion of the General Assembly proposed amendments to include the recognition of other rights or freedoms or to extend or expand rights or freedoms recognized in this Protocol.

2. Such amendments shall enter into effect for the States that ratify them on the date of deposit of the instrument of ratification corresponding to the number representing two thirds of the States Parties to this Protocol. For all other States Parties they shall enter into effect on the date on which they deposit their respective instrument of ratification.

Chapter 10

Inter-American Convention on the Prevention, Punishment and Eradication of Violence Against Women (excerpts)

The State Parties to this Covention,

Recognizing that full respect for human rights has been enshrined in the American Declaration of the Rights and Duties of Man and the Universal Declaration of Human Rights, and reaffirmed in other international and regional instruments;

Affirming that violence against women constitutes a violation of their human rights and fundamental freedoms, and impairs or nullifies the observance, enjoyment and exercise of such rights and freedoms;

Concerned that violence against women is an offense against human dignity and a manifestation of the historically unequal power relations between women and men;

Recalling the Declaration on the Elimination of Violence against Women, adopted by the Twenty-Fifth Assembly of Delegates of the Inter-American Commission of Women, and affirming that violence against women pervades every sector of society regardless of class, race or ethnic group, income, culture, level of education, age or religion and strikes at its very foundations:

Convinced that the elimination of violence against women is essential for their individual and social development and their full and equal participation in all walks of life; and

Convinced that the adoption of a convention on the prevention, punishment and eradication of all forms of violence against women within the framework of the Organization of American States is a positive contribution to protecting the rights of women and eliminating violence against them,

Have agreed to the following:

. . .

Adopted at Belem do Para, Brazil, 9 June 1994, *entry into force* 5 March 1995.

Article 5

Every woman is entitled to the free and full exercise of her civil, political, economic, social and cultural rights, and may rely on the full protection of those rights as embodied in regional and international instruments on human rights. The States Parties recognize that violence against women prevents and nullifies the exercise of these rights.

Chapter 11
African [Banjul] Charter on Human and Peoples' Rights

Preamble

The African States members of the Organization of African Unity, parties to the present convention entitled "African Charter on Human and Peoples' Rights",

Recalling Decision 115 (XVI) of the Assembly of Heads of State and Government at its Sixteenth Ordinary Session held in Monrovia, Liberia, from 17 to 20 July 1979 on the preparation of a "preliminary draft on an African Charter on Human and Peoples' Rights providing inter alia for the establishment of bodies to promote and protect human and peoples' rights";

Considering the Charter of the Organization of African Unity, which stipulates that "freedom, equality, justice and dignity are essential objectives for the achievement of the legitimate aspirations of the African peoples";

Reaffirming the pledge they solemnly made in Article 2 of the said Charter to eradicate all forms of colonialism from Africa, to coordinate and intensify their cooperation and efforts to achieve a better life for the peoples of Africa and to promote international cooperation having due regard to the Charter of the United Nations. and the Universal Declaration of Human Rights;

Taking into consideration the virtues of their historical tradition and the values of African civilization which should inspire and characterize their reflection on the concept of human and peoples' rights;

Recognizing on the one hand, that fundamental human rights stem from the attributes of human beings which justifies their national and international protection and on the other hand that the reality and respect of peoples rights should necessarily guarantee human rights;

Considering that the enjoyment of rights and freedoms also implies the performance of duties on the part of everyone;

OAU Doc. CAB/LEG/67/3 rev. 5, 21 I.L.M. 58 (1982), adopted June 27, 1981, *entery into force* 21 October 1986.

Convinced that it is henceforth essential to pay a particular attention to the right to development and that civil and political rights cannot be dissociated from economic, social and cultural rights in their conception as well as universality and that the satisfaction of economic, social and cultural rights ia a guarantee for the enjoyment of civil and political rights;

Conscious of their duty to achieve the total liberation of Africa, the peoples of which are still struggling for their dignity and genuine independence, and undertaking to eliminate colonialism, neo-colonialism, apartheid, zionism and to dismantle aggressive foreign military bases and all forms of discrimination, particularly those based on race, ethnic group, color, sex. language, religion or political opinions;

Reaffirming their adherence to the principles of human and peoples' rights and freedoms contained in the declarations, conventions and other instrument adopted by the Organization of African Unity, the Movement of Non-Aligned Countries and the United Nations;

Firmly convinced of their duty to promote and protect human and peoples' rights and freedoms taking into account the importance traditionally attached to these rights and freedoms in Africa;

Have agreed as follows:

Part I: Rights and Duties

Chapter I: Human and Peoples' Rights

Article 1

The Member States of the Organization of African Unity parties to the present Charter shall recognize the rights, duties and freedoms enshrined in this Chapter and shall undertake to adopt legislative or other measures to give effect to them.

Article 2

Every individual shall be entitled to the enjoyment of the rights and freedoms recognized and guaranteed in the present Charter without distinction of any kind such as race, ethnic group, color, sex, language, religion, political or any other opinion, national and social origin, fortune, birth or other status.

Article 3

1. Every individual shall be equal before the law.
2. Every individual shall be entitled to equal protection of the law.

Article 4

Human beings are inviolable. Every human being shall be entitled to respect for his life and the integrity of his person. No one may be arbitrarily deprived of this right.

Article 5

Every individual shall have the right to the respect of the dignity inherent in a human being and to the recognition of his legal status. All forms of exploitation and degradation of man particularly slavery, slave trade, torture, cruel, inhuman or degrading punishment and treatment shall be prohibited.

Article 6

Every individual shall have the right to liberty and to the security of his person. No one may be deprived of his freedom except for reasons and conditions previously laid down by law. In particular, no one may be arbitrarily arrested or detained.

Article 7

1. Every individual shall have the right to have his cause heard. This comprises: (a) the right to an appeal to competent national organs against acts of violating his fundamental rights as recognized and guaranteed by conventions, laws, regulations and customs in force; (b) the right to be presumed innocent until proved guilty by a competent court or tribunal; (c) the right to defence, including the right to be defended by counsel of his choice; (d) the right to be tried within a reasonable time by an impartial court or tribunal.

2. No one may be condemned for an act or omission which did not constitute a legally punishable offence at the time it was committed. No penalty may be inflicted for an offence for which no provision was made at the time it was committed. Punishment is personal and can be imposed only on the offender.

Article 8

Freedom of conscience, the profession and free practice of religion shall be guaranteed. No one may, subject to law and order, be submitted to measures restricting the exercise of these freedoms.

Article 9

1. Every individual shall have the right to receive information.

2. Every individual shall have the right to express and disseminate his opinions within the law.

Article 10

1. Every individual shall have the right to free association provided that he abides by the law.

2. Subject to the obligation of solidarity provided for in 29 no one may be compelled to join an association.

Article 11

Every individual shall have the right to assemble freely with others. The exercise of this right shall be subject only to necessary restrictions provided for by law in particular those enacted in the interest of national security, the safety, health, ethics and rights and freedoms of others.

Article 12

1. Every individual shall have the right to freedom of movement and residence within the borders of a State provided he abides by the law.

2. Every individual shall have the right to leave any country including his own, and to return to his country. This right may only be subject to restrictions, provided for by law for the protection of national security, law and order, public health or morality.

3. Every individual shall have the right, when persecuted, to seek and obtain asylum in other countries in accordance with laws of those countries and international conventions.

4. A non-national legally admitted in a territory of a State Party to the present Charter, may only be expelled from it by virtue of a decision taken in accordance with the law.

5. The mass expulsion of non-nationals shall be prohibited. Mass expulsion shall be that which is aimed at national, racial, ethnic or religious groups.

Article 13

1. Every citizen shall have the right to participate freely in the government of his country, either directly or through freely chosen representatives in accordance with the provisions of the law.

2. Every citizen shall have the right of equal access to the public service of his country.

3. Every individual shall have the right of access to public property and services in strict equality of all persons before the law.

Article 14

The right to property shall be guaranteed. It may only be encroached upon in the interest of public need or in the general interest of the community and in accordance with the provisions of appropriate laws.

Article 15

Every individual shall have the right to work under equitable and satisfactory conditions, and shall receive equal pay for equal work.

Article 16

1. Every individual shall have the right to enjoy the best attainable state of physical and mental health.

2. States parties to the present Charter shall take the necessary measures to protect the health of their people and to ensure that they receive medical attention when they are sick.

Article 17

1. Every individual shall have the right to education.

2. Every individual may freely, take part in the cultural life of his community.

3. The promotion and protection of morals and traditional values recognized by the community shall be the duty of the State.

Article 18

1. The family shall be the natural unit and basis of society. It shall be protected by the State which shall take care of its physical health and moral.

2. The State shall have the duty to assist the family which is the custodian or morals and traditional values recognized by the community.

3. The State shall ensure the elimination of every discrimination against women and also ensure the protection of the rights of the woman and the child as stipulated in international declarations and conventions.

4. The aged and the disabled shall also have the right to special measures of protection in keeping with their physical or moral needs.

Article 19

All peoples shall be equal; they shall enjoy the same respect and shall have the same rights. Nothing shall justify the domination of a people by another.

Article 20

1. All peoples shall have the right to existence. They shall have the unquestionable and inalienable right to self-determination. They shall freely determine their political status and shall pursue their economic and social development according to the policy they have freely chosen.

2. Colonized or oppressed peoples shall have the right to free themselves from the bonds of domination by resorting to any means recognized by the international community.

3. All peoples shall have the right to the assistance of the States parties to the present Charter in their liberation struggle against foreign domination, be it political, economic or cultural.

Article 21

1. All peoples shall freely dispose of their wealth and natural resources. This right shall be exercised in the exclusive interest of the people. In no case shall a people be deprived of it.

2. In case of spoliation the dispossessed people shall have the right to the lawful recovery of its property as well as to an adequate compensation.

3. The free disposal of wealth and natural resources shall be exercised without prejudice to the obligation of promoting international economic co-operation based on mutual respect, equitable exchange and the principles of international law.

4. States parties to the present Charter shall individually and collectively exercise the right to free disposal of their wealth and natural resources with a view to strengthening African unity and solidarity.

5. States parties to the present Charter shall undertake to eliminate all forms of foreign economic exploitation particularly that practiced by international monopolies so as to enable their peoples to fully benefit from the advantages derived from their national resources.

Article 22

1. All peoples shall have the right to their economic, social and cultural development with due regard to their freedom and identity and in the equal enjoyment of the common heritage of mankind.

2. States shall have the duty, individually or collectively, to ensure the exercise of the right to development.

Article 23

1. All peoples shall have the right to national and international peace and security. The principles of solidarity and friendly relations implicitly affirmed by the Charter of the United Nations and reaffirmed by that of the Organization of African Unity shall govern relations between States.

2. For the purpose of strengthening peace, solidarity and friendly relations, States parties to the present Charter shall ensure that: (a) any individual enjoying the right of asylum under 12 of the present Charter shall not engage in subversive activities against his country of origin or any other State party to the present Charter; (b) their territories

shall not be used as bases for subversive or terrorist activities against the people of any other State party to the present Charter.

Article 24

All peoples shall have the right to a general satisfactory environment favorable to their development.

Article 25

States parties to the present Charter shall have the duty to promote and ensure through teaching, education and publication, the respect of the rights and freedoms contained in the present Charter and to see to it that these freedoms and rights as well as corresponding obligations and duties are understood.

Article 26

States parties to the present Charter shall have the duty to guarantee the independence of the Courts and shall allow the establishment and improvement of appropriate national institutions entrusted with the promotion and protection of the rights and freedoms guaranteed by the present Charter.

Chapter 12
African Charter on the Rights and Welfare of the Child (excerpts)

Preamble

The African Member States of the Organization of African Unity, Parties to the present Charter entitled "African Charter on the Rights and Welfare of the Child,"

Considering that the Charter of the Organization of African Unity recognizes the paramountcy of Human Rights and the African Charter on Human and Peoples' Rights proclaimed and agreed that everyone is entitled to all the rights and freedoms recognized and guaranteed therein, without distinction of any kind such as race, ethnic group, colour. sex, language, religion, political or any other opinion, national and social origin, fortune, birth or other status,

Recalling the Declaration on the Rights and Welfare of the African Child (AHG/ST.4 Rev.l) adopted by the Assembly of Heads of State and Government of the Organization of African Unity, at its Sixteenth Ordinary Session in Monrovia, Liberia, from 17 to 20 July 1979, recognized the need to take appropriate measures to promote and protect the rights and welfare of the African Child,

Noting with concern that the situation of most African children, remains critical due to the unique factors of their socio-economic, cultural, traditional and developmental circumstances, natural disasters, armed conflicts, exploitation and hunger, and on account of the child's physical and mental immaturity he/she needs special safeguards and care,

Recognizing that the child occupies a unique and privileged position in the African society and that for the full and harmonious development of his personality. The child should grow up in a family environment in an atmosphere of happiness, love and understanding,

Recognizing that the child, due to the needs of his physical and mental development requires particular care with regard to health, physical, mental, moral and social development. and requires legal protection in conditions of freedom, dignity and security,

Adopted at Addis Ababa, 11 July 1990, *entry into force* 29 November 1999.

Taking into consideration the virtues of their cultural heritage, historical background and the values of the African civilization which should inspire and characterize their reflection on the concept of the rights and welfare of the child,

Considering that the promotion and protection of the rights and welfare of the child also implies the performance of duties on the part of everyone,

Reaffirming adherence to the principles of the rights and welfare of the child contained in the declaration, conventions and other instruments of the Organization of African Unity and in the United Nations and in particular the United Nations Convention on the Rights of the Child; and the OAU Heads of State and Government's Declaration on the Rights and Welfare of the African Child.

Have agreed as follows:

Part I: Rights and Duties

Chapter One: Rights and Welfare of the Child

Article 1. Obligation of States Parties

1. Member States of the Organization of African Unity Parties to the present Charter shall recognize the rights, freedoms and duties enshrined in this Charter and shall undertake to the necessary steps, in accordance with their Constitutional processes and with the provisions of the present Charter, to adopt such legislative or other measures as may be necessary to give effect to the provisions of this Charter.

2. Nothing in this Charter shall affect any provisions that are more conductive to the realization of the rights and welfare of the child contained in the law of a State Party or in any other international Convention or agreement in force in that State.

3. Any custom, tradition, cultural or religious practice that is inconsistent with the rights, duties and obligations contained in the present Charter shall to the extent of such inconsistency be discouraged.

Article 2. Definition of a child

For the purposes of this Charter, a child means every human being below the age of 18 years.

Article 3. Non-discrimination

Every child shall be entitled to the enjoyment of the rights and freedoms recognized and guaranteed in this Charter irrespective of the child's or his/her parents' or legal guardians' race, ethnic group, colour, sex, language, religion, political or other opinion, national and social origin, fortune, birth or other status.

Article 4. Best interests of the child

1. In all actions concerning the child undertaken by any person or authority the best interests of the child shall be the primary consideration.

2. In all judicial or administrative proceedings affecting a child who is capable of communicating his/her own views, and opportunity shall be provided for the views of the child to be heard either directly or through an impartial representative as a party to the proceedings and those views shall be taken into consideration by the relevant authority in accordance with the provisions of appropriate law.

Article 5. Survival and development

1. Every child has an inherent right to life. This right shall be protected by law.

2. States Parties to the present Charter shall ensure, to the maximum extent possible, the survival, protection and development of the child.

3. Death sentence shall not be pronounced for crimes committed by children.

Article 6. Name and nationality

1. Every child shall have the right from his birth to a name.

2. Every child shall be registered immediately after birth.

3. Every child has the right to acquire a nationality.

4. States Parties to the present Charter shall undertake to ensure that their Constitutional legislation recognize the principles according to which a child shall acquire the nationality of the State in the territory of which he has been born if, at the time of the child's birth, he is not granted nationality by any other State in accordance with its laws.

Article 7. Freedom of expression

Every child who is capable of communicating his or her own views shall be assured the rights to express his opinions freely in all matters and to disseminate his opinions subject to such restrictions as are prescribed by laws.

Article 8. Freedom of association

Every child shall have the right to free association and freedom of peaceful assembly in conformity with the law.

Article 9. Freedom of thought, conscience and religion

1. Every child shall have the right to freedom of thought, conscience and religion.

2. Parents and where applicable, legal guardians shall have a duty to provide guidance and direction in the exercise of these rights having regard to the evolving capacities, and best interests of the child.

3. States Parties shall respect the duty of parents and where applicable, legal guardians to provide guidance and direction in the enjoyment of these rights subject to the national laws and policies.

Article 10. Protection of privacy

No child shall be subject to arbitrary or unlawful interference with his privacy, family home or correspondence, or to the attacks upon his honour or reputation, provided that parents or legal guardians shall have the right to exercise reasonable supervision over the conduct of their children. The child has the right to the protection of the law against such interference or attacks.

Article 11. Education

1. Every child shall have the right to an education.

2. The education of the child shall be directed to:

(a) the promotion and development of the child's personality, talents and mental and physical abilities to their fullest potential;

(b) fostering respect for human rights and fundamental freedoms with particular reference to those set out in the provisions of various African instruments on human and peoples' rights and international human rights declarations and conventions;

(c) the preservation and strengthening of positive African morals, traditional values and cultures;

(d) the preparation of the child for responsible life in a free society, in the spirit of understanding tolerance, dialogue, mutual respect and friendship among all peoples ethnic, tribal and religious groups;

(e) the preservation of national independence and territorial integrity;

(f) the promotion and achievements of African Unity and Solidarity;

(g) the development of respect for the environment and natural resources;

(h) the promotion of the child's understanding of primary health care.

3. States Parties to the present Charter shall take all appropriate measures with a view to achieving the full realization of this right and shall in particular:

(a) provide free and compulsory basic education:

(b) encourage the development of secondary education in its different forms and to progressively make it free and accessible to all;

(c) make the higher education accessible to all on the basis of capacity and ability by every appropriate means;

(d) take measures to encourage regular attendance at schools and the reduction of drop-out rates;

(e) take special measures in respect of female, gifted and disadvantaged children, to ensure equal access to education for all sections of the community.

4. States Parties to the present Charter shall respect the rights and duties of parents, and where applicable, of legal guardians to choose for their children's schools, other than those established by public authorities, which conform to such minimum standards may be approved by the State, to ensure the religious and moral education of the child in a manner with the evolving capacities of the child.

5. States Parties to the present Charter shall take all appropriate measures to ensure that a child who is subjected to schools or parental discipline shall be treated with humanity and with respect for the inherent dignity of the child and in conformity with the present Charter.

6. States Parties to the present Charter shall have all appropriate measures to ensure that children who become pregnant before completing their education shall have an opportunity to continue with their education on the basis of their individual ability.

7. No part of this Article shall be construed as to interfere with the liberty of individuals and bodies to establish and direct educational institutions subject to the observance of the principles set out in paragraph I of this Article and the requirement teal the education given in such institutions shall conform to such minimum standards as may be laid down by the States.

Article 12. Leisure, recreation and cultural activities

1. States Parties recognize the right of the child to rest and leisure, to engage in play and recreational activities appropriate to the age of the child and to participate freely in cultural life and the arts.

2. States Parties shall respect and promote the right of the child to fully participate in cultural and artistic life and shall encourage the provision of appropriate and equal opportunities for cultural, artistic, recreational and leisure activity.

Article 13. Handicapped children

1. Every child who is mentally or physically disabled shall have the right to special measures of protection in keeping with his physical and moral needs and under conditions which ensure his dignity, promote his self-reliance and active participation in the community.

2. States Parties to the present Charter shall ensure, subject to available resources, to a disabled child and to those responsible for his care, of assistance for which application

is made and which is appropriate to the child's condition and in particular shall ensure that the disabled child has effective access to training, preparation for employment and recreation opportunities in a manner conducive to the child achieving the fullest possible social integration, individual development and his cultural and moral development.

3. The States Parties to the present Charter shall use their available resources with a view to achieving progressively the full convenience of the mentally and physically disabled person to movement and access to public highway buildings and other places to which the disabled may legitimately want to have access to.

Article 14. Health and health services

1. Every child shall have the right to enjoy the best attainable state of physical, mental and spiritual health.

2. States Parties to the present Charter shall undertake to pursue the full implementation of this right and in particular shall take measures:

(a) to reduce infant and child morality rate;

(b) to ensure the provision of necessary medical assistance and health care to all children with emphasis on the development of primary health care;

(c) to ensure the provision of adequate nutrition and safe drinking water;

(d) to combat disease and malnutrition within the framework of primary health care through the application of appropriate technology;

(e) to ensure appropriate health care for expectant and nursing mothers;

(f) to develop preventive health care and family life education and provision of service;

(g) to integrate basic health service programmes in national development plans;

(h) to ensure that all sectors of the society, in particular, parents, children, community leaders and community workers are informed and supported in the use of basic knowledge of child health and nutrition, the advantages of breastfeeding, hygiene and environmental sanitation and the prevention of domestic and other accidents;

(i) to ensure the meaningful participation of non-governmental organizations, local communities and the beneficiary population in the planning and management of a basic service programme for children;

(j) to support through technical and financial means, the mobilization of local community resources in the development of primary health care for children.

Article 15. Child labour

1. Every child shall be protected from all forms of economic exploitation and from performing any work that is likely to be hazardous or to interfere with the child's physical, mental, spiritual, moral, or social development.

2. States Parties to the present Charter take all appropriate legislative and administrative measures to ensure the full implementation of this Article which covers both the formal and informal sectors of employment and having regard to the relevant provisions of the International Labour Organization's instruments relating to children, States Parties shall in particular:

(a) provide through legislation, minimum wages for admission to every employment;

(b) provide for appropriate regulation of hours and conditions of employment;

(c) provide for appropriate penalties or other sanctions to ensure the effective enforcement of this Article;

(d) promote the dissemination of information on the hazards of child labour to all sectors of the community.

Article 16. Protection against child abuse and torture

1. States Parties to the present Charter shall take specific legislative, administrative, social and educational measures to protect the child from all forms of torture, inhuman or degrading treatment and especially physical or mental injury or abuse, neglect or maltreatment including sexual abuse, while in the care of the child.

2. Protective measures under this Article shall include effective procedures for the establishment of special monitoring units to provide necessary support for the child and for those who have the care of the child, as well as other forms of prevention and for identification, reporting referral investigation, treatment, and follow-up of instances of child abuse and neglect.

Article 17. Administration of juvenile justice

1. Every child accused or found guilty of having infringed penal law shall have the right to special treatment in a manner consistent with the child's sense of dignity and worth and which reinforces the child's respect for human rights and fundamental freedoms of others.

2. States Parties to the present Charter shall in particular:

(a) ensure that no child who is detained or imprisoned or otherwise deprived of his/her liberty is subjected to torture, inhuman or degrading treatment or punishment;

(b) ensure that children are separated from adults in their place of detention or imprisonment;

(c) ensure that every child accused in infringing the penal law:

(i) shall be presumed innocent until duly recognized guilty;

(ii) shall be informed promptly in a language that he understands and in detail of the charge against him, and shall be entitled to the assistance of an interpreter if he or she cannot understand the language used;

(iii) shall be afforded legal and other appropriate assistance in the preparation and presentation of his defence;

(iv) shall have the matter determined as speedily as possible by an impartial tribunal and if found guilty, be entitled to an appeal by a higher tribunal;

(d) prohibit the press and the public from trial.

3. The essential aim of treatment of every child during the trial and also if found guilty of infringing the penal law shall be his or her reformation, re-integration into his or her family and social rehabilitation.

4. There shall be a minimum age below which children shall be presumed not to have the capacity to infringe the penal law.

Article 18. Protection of the family

1. The family shall be the natural unit and basis of society. it shall enjoy the protection and support of the State for its establishment and development.

2. States Parties to the present Charter shall take appropriate steps to ensure equality of rights and responsibilities of spouses with regard to children during marriage and in the even of its dissolution. In case of the dissolution, provision shall be made for the necessary protection of the child.

3. No child shall be deprived of maintenance by reference to the parents' marital status.

Article 19. Parent care and protection

1. Every child shall be entitled to the enjoyment of parental care and protection and shall, whenever possible, have the right to reside with his or her parents. No child shall be separated from his parents against his will, except when a judicial authority determines in accordance with the appropriate law, that such separation is in the best interest of the child.

2. Every child who is separated from one or both parents shall have the right to maintain personal relations and direct contact with both parents on a regular basis.

3. Where separation results from the action of a State Party, the State Party shall provide the child, or if appropriate, another member of the family with essential information concerning the whereabouts of the absent member or members of the family. States Parties shall also ensure that the submission of such a request shall not entail any adverse consequences for the person or persons in whose respect it is made.

4. Where a child is apprehended by a State Party, his parents or guardians shall, as soon as possible, be notified of such apprehension by that State Party.

Article 20. Parental responsibilities

1. Parents or other persons responsible for the child shall have the primary responsibility of the upbringing and development the child and shall have the duty:

(a) to ensure that the best interests of the child are their basic concern at all times;

(b) to secure, within their abilities and financial capacities, conditions of living necessary to the child's development; and

(c) to ensure that domestic discipline is administered with humanity and in a manner consistent with the inherent dignity of the child.

2. States Parties to the present Charter shall in accordance with their means and national conditions the all appropriate measures;

(a) to assist parents and other persons responsible for the child and in case of need provide material assistance and support programmes particularly with regard to nutrition, health, education, clothing and housing;

(b) to assist parents and others responsible for the child in the performance of child-rearing and ensure the development of institutions responsible for providing care of children; and

(c) to ensure that the children of working parents are provided with care services and facilities.

Article 21. Protection against harmful social and cultural practices

1. States Parties to the present Charter shall take all appropriate measures to eliminate harmful social and cultural practices affecting the welfare, dignity, normal growth and development of the child and in particular:

(a) those customs and practices prejudicial to the health or life of the child; and

(b) those customs and practices discriminatory to the child on the grounds of sex or other status.

2. Child marriage and the betrothal of girls and boys shall be prohibited and effective action, including legislation, shall be taken to specify the minimum age of marriage to be 18 years and make registration of all marriages in an official registry compulsory.

Article 22. Armed conflicts

1. States Parties to this Charter shall undertake to respect and ensure respect for rules of international humanitarian law applicable in armed conflicts which affect the child.

2. States Parties to the present Charter shall take all necessary measures to ensure that no child shall take a direct part in hostilities and refrain in particular, from recruiting any child.

3. States Parties to the present Charter shall, in accordance with their obligations under international humanitarian law, protect the civilian population in armed conflicts and shall take all feasible measures to ensure the protection and care of children who are affected by armed conflicts. Such rules shall also apply to children in situations of internal armed conflicts, tension and strife.

Article 23. Refugee children

1. States Parties to the present Charter shall take all appropriate measures to ensure that a child who is seeking refugee status or who is considered a refugee in accordance with applicable international or domestic law shall, whether unaccompanied or accompanied by parents, legal guardians or close relatives, receive appropriate protection and humanitarian assistance in the enjoyment of the rights set out in this Charter and other international human rights and humanitarian instruments to which the States are Parties.

2. States Parties shall undertake to cooperate with existing international organizations which protect and assist refugees in their efforts to protect and assist such a child and to trace the parents or other close relatives or an unaccompanied refugee child in order to obtain information necessary for reunification with the family.

3. Where no parents, legal guardians or close relatives can be found, the child shall be accorded the same protection as any other child permanently or temporarily deprived of his family environment for any reason.

4. The provisions of this Article apply mutatis mutandis to internally displaced children whether through natural disaster, internal armed conflicts, civil strife, breakdown of economic and social order or howsoever caused.

Article 24. Adoption

States Parties which recognize the system of adoption shall ensure that the best interest of the child shall be the paramount consideration and they shall:

(a) establish competent authorities to determine matters of adoption and ensure that the adoption is carried out in conformity with applicable laws and procedures and on the basis of all relevant and reliable information, that the adoption is permissible in view of the child's status concerning parents, relatives and guardians and that, if necessary, the appropriate persons concerned have given their informed consent to the adoption on the basis of appropriate counselling;

(b) recognize that inter-country adoption in those States who have ratified or adhered to the International Convention on the Rights of the Child or this Charter, may, as the last resort, be considered as an alternative means of a child's care, if the child cannot be placed in a foster or an adoptive family or cannot in any suitable manner be cared for in the child's country of origin;

(c) ensure that the child affected by inter-country adoption enjoys safeguards and standards equivalent to those existing in the case of national adoption;

(d) take all appropriate measures to ensure that in inter-country adoption, the placement does not result in trafficking or improper financial gain for those who try to adopt a child;

(e) promote, where appropriate, the objectives of this Article by concluding bilateral or multilateral arrangements or agreements, and endeavour, within this framework to ensure that the placement of the child in another country is carried out by competent authorities or organs;

(f) establish a machinery to monitor the well-being of the adopted child.

Article 25. Separation from parents

1. Any child who is permanently or temporarily deprived of his family environment for any reason shall be entitled to special protection and assistance;

2. States Parties to the present Charter:

(a) shall ensure that a child who is parentless, or who is temporarily or permanently deprived of his or her family environment, or who in his or her best interest cannot be brought up or allowed to remain in that environment shall be provided with alternative family care, which could include, among others, foster placement, or placement in suitable institutions for the care of children;

(b) shall take all necessary measures to trace and re-unite children with parents or relatives where separation is caused by internal and external displacement arising from armed conflicts or natural disasters.

3. When considering alternative family care of the child and the best interests of the child, due regard shall be paid to the desirability of continuity in a child's up-bringing and to the child's ethnic, religious or linguistic background.

Article 26. Protection against apartheid and discrimination

1. States Parties to the present Charter shall individually and collectively undertake to accord the highest priority to the special needs of children living under Apartheid and in States subject to military destabilization by the Apartheid regime.

2. States Parties to the present Charter shall individually and collectively undertake to accord the highest priority to the special needs of children living under regimes practising racial, ethnic, religious or other forms of discrimination as well as in States subject to military destabilization.

3. States Parties shall undertake to provide whenever possible, material assistance to such children and to direct their efforts towards the elimination of all forms of discrimination and apartheid on the African Continent.

Article 27. Sexual exploitation

1. States Parties to the present Charter shall undertake to protect the child from all forms of sexual exploitation and sexual abuse and shall in particular take measures to prevent:

(a) the inducement, coercion or encouragement of a child to engage in any sexual activity;

(b) the use of children in prostitution or other sexual practices;

(c) the use of children in pornographic activities, performances and materials.

Article 28. Drug abuse

States Parties to the present Charter shall take all appropriate measures to protect the child from the use of narcotics and illicit use of psychotropic substances as defined in the relevant international treaties, and to prevent the use of children in the production and trafficking of such substances.

Article 29. Sale, trafficking and abduction

States Parties to the present Charter shall take appropriate measures to prevent:

(a) the abduction, the sale of, or traffick in children for any purpose or in any form, by any person including parents or legal guardians of the child;

(b) the use of children in all forms of begging.

Article 30. Children of imprisoned mothers

1. States Parties to the present Charter shall undertake to provide special treatment to expectant mothers and to mothers of infants and young children who have been accused or found guilty of infringing the penal law and shall in particular:

(a) ensure that a non-custodial sentence will always be first considered when sentencing such mothers;

(b) establish and promote measures alternative to institutional confinement for the treatment of such mothers;

(c) establish special alternative institutions for holding such mothers;

(d) ensure that a mother shall not be imprisoned with her child;

(e) ensure that a death sentence shall not be imposed on such mothers;

(f) the essential aim of the penitentiary system will be the reformation, the integration of the mother to the family and social rehabilitation.

Article 31. Responsibilities of the child

Every child shall have responsibilities towards his family and society, the State and other legally recognized communities and the international community. The child, subject to his age and ability, and such limitations as may be contained in the present Charter, shall have the duty;

(a) to work for the cohesion of the family, to respect his parents, superiors and elders at all times and to assist them in case of need;

(b) to serve his national community by placing his physical and intellectual abilities at its service;

(c) to preserve and strengthen social and national solidarity;

(d) to preserve and strengthen African cultural values in his relations with other members of the society, in the spirit of tolerance, dialogue and consultation and to contribute to the moral well-being of society;

(e) to preserve and strengthen the independence and the integrity of his country;

(f) to contribute to the best of his abilities, at all times and at all levels, to the promotion and achievement of African Unity.

Index

Note: "ESCR" is used in this index as an abbreviation for "economic, social, and cultural rights"